MW01442395

Patrick White Centenary:
The Legacy of a Prodigal Son

PATRICK WHITE CENTENARY:
THE LEGACY OF A PRODIGAL SON

Edited by

Cynthia vanden Driesen
Bill Ashcroft

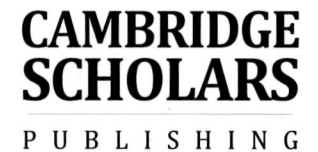

CAMBRIDGE SCHOLARS
PUBLISHING

Patrick White Centenary: The Legacy of a Prodigal Son
Edited by Cynthia vanden Driesen and Bill Ashcroft

This book first published 2014

Cambridge Scholars Publishing

12 Back Chapman Street, Newcastle upon Tyne, NE6 2XX, UK

British Library Cataloguing in Publication Data
A catalogue record for this book is available from the British Library

Copyright © 2014 by Cynthia vanden Driesen, Bill Ashcroft and contributors

All rights for this book reserved. No part of this book may be reproduced, stored in a retrieval system, or transmitted, in any form or by any means, electronic, mechanical, photocopying, recording or otherwise, without the prior permission of the copyright owner.

ISBN (10): 1-4438-6040-9, ISBN (13): 978-1-4438-6040-6

TABLE OF CONTENTS

List of Abbreviations x

Acknowledgements xi

Introduction xiii
Cynthia vanden Driesen

Part I: Revaluations

Chapter One 2
Australia's Prodigal Son
John Barnes

Chapter Two 22
Horizons of Hope
Bill Ashcroft

Chapter Three 43
"Splintering and Coalescing": Language and the Sacred
in Patrick White's Novels
Lyn McCredden

Chapter Four 63
Incorporating the Physical Corporeality, Abjection and the Role
of Laura Trevelyan in *Voss*
Bridget Grogan

Chapter Five 82
Patrick White: Crossing the Boundaries
John McLaren

Chapter Six 98
The Myth of Patrick White's Anti-Suburbanism
Nathanael O'Reilly

Chapter Seven..110
Patrick White: The Quest of the Artist
Satendra Nandan

Chapter Eight..125
Patrick White and Australia: Perspective of an Outsider
Pavithra Narayanan

Chapter Nine...141
Inscribing Landscapes in Patrick White's Novels
Jessica White

Part II: Genre

Chapter Ten..152
"A Glorious, Terrible Life": The Dual Image in Patrick White's
Dramatic Language
May-Brit Akerholt

Chapter Eleven..164
Looking at Patrick White Looking: Portraits in Paint and on Film
Greg Battye

Chapter Twelve...181
Patrick White-Lite: Fred Schepisi's Filmic Adaptation
of *The Eye of the Storm*
Sissy Helff

Chapter Thirteen...196
The Novelist as Occasional Poet: Patrick White and Katharine
Susannah Prichard
Glen Phillips

Part III: Individual Novels

Chapter Fourteen..210
In the Shadow of Patrick White
Meira Chand

Chapter Fifteen 222
The Spirit of the Creative Word in Patrick White's *Voss*
Antonella Riem

Chapter Sixteen 241
"Violent" Aboriginals and "Benign" White Men: White's
Alternative Representation of the Encounter in *Voss*
Harish Mehta

Chapter Seventeen 257
White's Tribe: Patrick White's Representation of the Australian
Aborigine in *A Fringe of Leaves*
Jeanine Leane

Chapter Eighteen 269
Patrick White's Children: Juvenile Portraits in *Happy Valley*
and *The Hanging Garden*
Elizabeth Webby and Margaret Harris

Chapter Nineteen 280
The Hanging Garden
Alastair Niven

Chapter Twenty 291
Patrick White: Twyborn Moments of Grace
Brian Kiernan

Part IV: Comparative Studies

Chapter Twenty-One 302
The Shift from Commonwealth to Postcolonial Literatures:
Patrick White's "The Twitching Colonel" and Manuka Wijesinghe's
Theravada Man
Isabel Alonso-Breto

Chapter Twenty-Two 319
The Unity of Being-Synergies Between White's Mystic Vision
and the Indian Religio- Spiritual Tradition
Gursharan Aurora

Chapter Twenty-Three 339
Es tablishing a Connection: Resonances in *Gurugranth Sahib*
and Works of Patrick White
Ishmeet Kaur

Chapter Twenty-Four 354
Patrick White and James K. Baxter: Public Intellectuals
or Suburban Jeremiahs?
Mark Williams

Chapter Twenty-Five 368
Smelly Martyrs: Patrick White's Dubbo Ushers in Roy's Velutha
and Malouf's Gemmy
Julie Mehta

Part V: Socio-Political Issues

Chapter Twenty-Six 384
Australia and its First Peoples
Fred Chaney

Chapter Twenty-Seven 400
Aboriginal Progress in the Native Title Era: Truth and Substantive
Equality in *Terra Australis*
Anne de Soyza

Chapter Twenty-Eight 413
Rewriting Australia's Foundation Narrative: White, Scott
and the *Mabo Case*
Kieran Dolin

Chapter Twenty-Nine 429
Patrick White, "Belltrees" and the 'Station Complex':
Some Reflections
Vicki Grieves

Chapter Thirty 443
Mabo – Twenty Years On: An Indigenous Perspective
Keith Truscott

Chapter Thirty-One 458
"This Poem is a Sea Anchor": Robert Sullivan's Anchor
Jane Stafford

Chapter Thirty-Two 470
Flaws in the Glass: Why Australia did not Become a Republic ...
after Patrick White
Stephen Alomes

Chapter Thirty-Three 486
Negotiating "Otherness": The Muslim Community in Australia
Ameer Ali

Contributors 496

Index 507

LIST OF ABBREVIATIONS

Novels

Happy Valley - HV
The Aunt's Story - AS
The Tree of Man - TM
Voss - V
The Solid Mandala - SM
Riders in the Chariot - RC
The Vivisector – VIV
The Eye of the Storm - ES
The Twyborn Affair - TA
The Hanging Garden - HG

Plays

"The Ham Funeral" - HF
"Night on Bald Mountain" - NBM
"Season at Sarsaparilla" - SS
"Big Toys" – BT

Short Stories

"The Twitching Colonel" - TC
"The Night the Prowler" – NP
"The Cockatoos" - COC

ACKNOWLEDGEMENTS

We thank the contributors to this publication for their patience and co-operation. Their efforts will undoubtedly help take interest in White's oeuvre to new heights. We are grateful to the numerous referees who assisted with expert views on papers submitted for comment, kindly giving further help when requested.

Sincere thanks are extended to Greg Battye (University of Canberra) vice-president of the Association for the Study of Australia in Asia (ASAA) for collegial help and expert assistance not only with numerous editorial tasks but also with gaining access to William Yang's impressive photograph of White for the book cover. Without Greg's unfailing assistance, completing this project would have been so much more difficult. Other friends of ASAA Stephen Alomes (Royal Melbourne Institute of Technology) and Kate Jones helped with reading of exceptionally challenging work; Glen Phillips' (Centre for Landscape and Language, Perth,) suggestions for the book cover were much appreciated. Satendra Nandan (University of Canberra) was a constant source of encouragement Kieran Dolin (University of Western Australia) was endlessly helpful with information relating to documenting evidence concerning legal research, and a range of other issues. Elizabeth Webby (University of Sydney) was always generous when appeals were made to her wisdom and long experience of the Australian literary scene.

Professor Mohan Ramanan Dean of the Faculty of Humanities, University of Hyderabad and the ASAA Conference teams worked tirelessly to ensure the success of the conference which provided the basis for this book. We thank the Australia India Council for the provision of strategic funding through the years. We must duly acknowledge also the support of the University of Western Australia and the University of New South Wales.

Ms Reshma Fernandes (UWA) assisted patiently with the initial preparation of the manuscript. Rohan vanden Driesen's technological wizardry was, as with so many ASAA projects, wholly indispensable.

INTRODUCTION

CYNTHIA VANDEN DRIESEN
UNIVERSITY OF WESTERN AUSTRALIA

White is known to have speculated, at times, as to whether his works would be read after his death. That his reputation is in no danger of fading is surely attested by this birth centenary publication – the outcome of a conference held in India in December, 2012. It was attended by some of the best-known of White scholars as well as some excellent new contributors from all over the world; the latter being a promising augury for the future. White had an awareness of Indian culture, though it was his wide acquaintance with European culture that saturated his work, along with his deep roots in his native Australia. Perhaps it needs to be stated here that the epigraph to White's earliest novel, *Happy Valley* (1939) was a quotation from Gandhi; and his earliest published short story, "The Twitching Colonel" (1937) records the experience of a retired British colonel who is literally consumed, it would appear, by what he has experienced in India.

This particular volume emerged out of the 6th ASAA conference (2012) – which had necessitated a special re-alignment of the normal tri-ennial conference schedules so that we could accommodate this birth centenary. (We had just completed our scheduled fifth conference, which had been held only in the previous year – also in Hyderabad but at Osmania University). While most of the chapters in this collection are contributions from the conference there are a small number of invited contributions designed to supplement perceived gaps in the collection; all of these, of course, from recognised authorities in the field of White studies. Conference attendees were allowed ample space and time to expand the initial conference presentations into complete research papers. It is a matter worthy of comment that so many conference participants/contributors to this book had also been active participants at the first national conference on Patrick White (held at Flinders University in Adelaide, 1978): Bill Ashcroft, May-Brit Akerholt, John Barnes, Kirpal Singh, and Cynthia vanden Driesen - testifying to decades of interest and accumulated expertise on the subject of White's work.(Shepherd and Singh, 1978).It was fortunate that Kirpal Singh, a co-organiser of that early conference and now an eminent figure on the international literary and cultural scene most particularly in Singapore and Australasia, attended the Indian conference and delivered a lively and provocative plenary presentation on the occasion. Unfortunately due to pressing time constraints, he was unable to despatch his completed paper for inclusion in this publication. His valued participation in the event is duly acknowledged here.

The divisions in the presentation of the Contents of this volume have been designed, with some difficulty, to work along some discernibly unifying thematic motifs. Within each group though, there is a great deal of interesting variety, as there is between the different parts of the volume. This complexity necessitates a somewhat lengthy introduction for which the patience of the reader is invoked.

Revaluations

The essays begin with a section entitled "Revaluations" which appropriately emphasises the achievement of this particular celebratory publication marking the centenary of White's birth. John Barnes, in looking over the entire trajectory of White's long career notes the several transitions in critical estimates of the writer and his reputation in a mode that seems somewhat reflective of a personal odyssey of his own. Expressing, at the first national conference, some reservations regarding Patrick White's ability to convince re the mystical experience at the centre of his work, he comments; "It is a disturbing judgment but one that cannot be ignored, raising as it does the central question of the "reality" of White's vision." (Shepherd and Singh 1978, 2) At this conference his evaluation was much less equivocal:

There can hardly be any doubt that his [White's] fiction has had an influence on Australian literature and culture for which there is no parallel. It would certainly seem that judged from the vantage point of over six decades, this 'prodigal son's' return to Australia in 1948 has had a significance that neither he nor anyone else could have foreseen.

All of the plenary speakers at the centenary conference focused on broad and evolving perceptions of White's work ranging from his earliest works to the latest. Perhaps all were seeking to convey that sense of a general revaluation, which seemed so appropriate to the celebratory nature of the Indian conference and this publication. Two contradictory trends through decades of earlier White criticism appear finally to achieve a kind of resolution: one - that White's efforts to convey a meaningful notion of the transcendental truths he probed were ultimately foiled by the limitations of language; the other - that White's great achievement was to project an unique sense of the gritty concreteness of the everyday world; it was not possible that the twain could ever meet. Ashcroft, Barnes and McCredden all establish their most recent views that in White's work the two worlds are in fact indubitably integrated and that the perceptions projected through the one are crucial to a grasp of the other. Whatever the variations in the modalities through which they worked through, the synergies in the final conclusions are striking. It can be expected that for a long while these chapters will offer conclusive pronouncements on White's achievement.

Most of these critics are eminent professional observers of the Australian literary scene. Ashcroft is indeed an internationally acclaimed theorist in cultural studies; and John Barnes is still an iconic figure in the field of Australian studies. Lyn McCredden, a more recent contributor to White criticism provides an impressive discussion of the inter-relationship of these aspects of White's works:

> The powerful inner lives of Patrick White's characters move out restlessly, hopefully, eschewing authoritative knowing, seeking artistic possibilities in what this essay has been arguing is a sacred struggle. The sacred, in the works of Patrick White, is the impossible, constant longing to make meaning: an honouring of

"all that I have ever lived, splintering and coalescing", a bowing to what is beyond human language and knowing.

Bridget Grogan, a gifted young White scholar from South Africa with a doctoral thesis on his work (her geographic location indicates the continuing spread of White studies globally) is fascinated with the capacity of the White text to focus on the spiritual and the transcendental while never losing focus on the physicality, the sheer fleshly existence of the protagonists. John McLaren, a long-time White observer and editor of a collection of essays on White, celebrates in eulogistic mode the writer's characteristic ability to move beyond conventional limits in his exploration of human experience.

Even chapters, which seem to deal with recurrent themes in White's texts, introduce a new note, a divergence from the established patterns of discourse on the particular topic. For instance, Nat O'Reilly makes the point that the general assumption of White's rejection of suburbia has been too easily made:

> His narrative technique makes it impossible to identify any one position as White's. *Riders in the Chariot* presents an ambivalent attitude toward suburbia, containing both celebration and condemnation, and previous assertions by critics that White and his fiction are anti-suburban have failed to take into account the nuances and complexity of White's representations of suburbia.

Jessica White, Patrick White's grand- niece, and herself a writer, explores the familial connection with the land. Jessica works around the intriguing notion, beginning with her own childhood close to the land and notes how it marked her own skin with freckles and other signs which imprinted on her body the lived experience of contact with the land. She notes how several of White's protagonist like Mary Hare and others carry this imprint and works through to an impassioned appeal to readers to read this writer for the rewards the effort would bring. It is worth quoting her description of White's prose for its evocative appeal:

> Readers, I think, need to take a leaf from the page of the receptive Mary Hare and to burrow through the vegetation of White's

writing. Some might be frustrated by what they perceive as overwriting, but to me his language is like the Australian bush: on first glance a swathe of muted greys and greens that, as you walk slowly through it, reveals itself to be hundreds of beautiful, tiny leaves, strips of bark and minute blossoms.

Himself a creative writer, Satendra Nandan is preoccupied with establishing the importance of the artist in White's work. He traces the emergence of White's vision of the artist through a focus on three works: *Voss*, *Riders in the Chariot* and *The Vivisector*. Through a sustained concentration particularly on *The Vivisector*, where the artist figure is placed in the central position of protagonist Nandan shows that White's artist is perennially engaged in a search for the Infinite.

Pavithra Narayan's discussion is particularly significant for this celebratory collection. She highlights the status White has now achieved in the Australian context stating that the birth centenary year provides an opportunity to revisit White, the 'political writer. Her view is that we need to re-examine our world against the backdrop of his critical essays and public speeches. White's role here accords with what Edward Said has indicated is the particular importance of the writer in the contemporary world - of "speaking the truth to power, being a witness to persecution and suffering." (Said 2001)

Genre

May-Brit Akerholt's discussion of White's drama is marked with the sensitivity and insights to which her long professional involvement with the theatre gives her ease of access. This practical expertise combined with her academic research (she has published a book on White's drama) confers a particular distinction on her contribution.

Greg Battye's chapter contests the opinion of Didier Maleuvre that photography "cannot yield a portrait." Battye, himself a photographer of repute, brings his professional expertise to bear in contesting Didier's claim His careful research shows how William Yang's black and white photos were used by artist Whitely to round out his famous painting of White and establishes his (Greg's) view that "photographs can capture not just the moment but also the life." This chapter presents a fine, perceptive and scholarly analysis in which the technicalities are handled with a finesse that enhances the intrinsic interest of the chapter. It is a truly innovative contribution to White studies. Helff's examination of the filmic version of White's *The Eye of the Storm* shows how new technologies can generate ancillary works of art which enhance the potential for further growth of possibilities in the appreciation of White's texts. Along with Battye, Helff also indicates some fascinating new directions in which White studies can grow in showing how White's oeuvre can intersect with other media, such as photography and film.

White's poetry has not received much critical attention. This is hardly surprising, since apart from his earliest, mostly undergraduate, forays into the genre White's main work has been in the genre of the novel. Glen Phillips' discussion of this early poetry of White's, (in tandem with a comparison with the work of Katharine Susannah Prichard and showing some synergies between them) highlights its links with the English poetry of the period and reveals an unexpectedly intimate grounding in his British context – despite his avowals of feeling alienated from it. It might be argued however that White's best poetry is to be found in the novels – their creative use of language, their concentrated imaginative power, and the powerful insights afforded into human experience.

Individual Novels

Few of the chapters concentrate entirely on a single novel but each provides new interest in what might appear like well-trodden terrain. Meira Chand's "In the Shadow of Patrick White," recounts an early, and unusual, introduction to White's work in a bookshop in Japan and the lasting attraction established. She assesses her writing of a particular novel of her own in tandem with a consideration of *A Fringe of Leaves*, a novel in which she detects synergies with her own project. The chapter is appealing in the insights afforded into how a writer from a completely different cultural context can become attracted to the genius of White.

It may be thought that there is an undue concentration on the single novel *Voss*. (White himself wondered at his readers' perennial fascination with this novel, as John Barnes records in the preamble to his Chapter). Nevertheless, each of these discussions offers a fresh insight. Antonella Riem's study of how White's language works in this novel is underpinned by a wholly unique theoretical view on how language operates in a colonial context. Harish Mehta's innovative study of the 'diplomatic' encounter between the Aborigines and the white explorers in this text offers considerable food for thought. Jeanine Leane's work presents a first-ever achievement in White criticism in that it offers an appraisal by an Indigenous critic of his representation of the black/white encounter in Australia from an Indigenous perspective.

Elizabeth Webby and Margaret Harris, at present collaborating in a major research project on the archive of White papers held at the National Library in Canberra, elucidate a delicate theme that has hardly drawn commentary from White critics before - White's empathetic and sensitive portrayal of children in his novels. An additional interest derives from their drawing on their privileged access to unpublished material. Interesting links are traced between White's first novel *Happy Valley* (1939) and his last (posthumously published) *A Hanging Garden* (2012). This chapter is usefully juxtaposed beside Alastair Niven's challenging speculation, proffered at the end of his incisive discussion of the novel. He suggests that this last work of White's should not be regarded as a fragment abandoned by a writer in his declining years but is, in fact, the product of a confident artist still writing at the height of his powers.

Brian Kiernan's discussion of *The Twyborn Affair* was an invited contribution designed to fill a notable gap in the consideration of this most important work in which White explores the complications of his own familial and personal heritage but which has not attracted sufficient critical study. Himself the author of an early book on White's work (still quoted even in this publication) Kiernan's chapter (a reprint from an earlier work) displays sensitivity to the multiplicity of readings which this literary work invites and keeps a complex of ideas in play in a manner which ensures no foreclosure on the varied possibilities of interpretation.

To some who may think that several of White's novels have not been afforded sufficient discussion, a quick check would show that every work of White's has been cited and considered in one way or another especially in the longer general discussions. The strong impression left by this collection of essays would be that White's influence in the Australian context is not only already massive, it is also poised to grow still further as the essays which follow in the next sections should establish.

Comparative Studies

White's earliest published short story, "The Twitching Colonel" (1937) is given a startling new postcolonial interpretation by European scholar Isabel Alonso-Breto whose comparison of this work to that of a Sri Lankan writer juxtaposes the postcolonial rebellion of the retired British colonel and that of the seemingly obediently colonised schoolteacher. The daringly experimental nature of this contribution underlines the celebratory aspect of this collection and indicates the chameleon-like possibilities of the White text, its continuing capacity for growth and its openness to varied possibilities of interpretation.

Some contributors have chosen to explore recurring themes or motifs in White's oeuvre with the focus moving beyond the confines of a single novel to trace recurrent thematic patterns. Perhaps the most significant of these would be the motif of religion. Indian scholars who have traced in some detail the affiliations between White's work and several aspects of Indian belief systems have made important contributions Both Gursharan Aurora and Amrit Kaur show an admirable familiarity with White's work as well as with the Indian religious texts and concepts they have selected for comment. They draw impressive and convincing parallels between White's works and their Indian sources with an ease and aplomb which might well explain White's continuing popularity on the sub-continent.

New Zealand scholar Mark Williams, well-known for his scholarly book on White (1993) draws also on his specialist knowledge of the New Zealand context to present a carefully researched and stimulating comparison between White and the eminent New Zealand poet James Baxter. This is an important contribution to this particular collection of essays on White, highlighting as it does, what is emerging as a new focus in approaches to White: "What does it mean to describe White as 'a public intellectual?'" Williams sees here a need to focus on the religious dimension in White's work, in comparing him to "James K. Baxter, a writer both deeply religious and vehemently critical of his nation's moral life and political history." The final chapter in this section takes the international comparisons to White still further with Julie Mehta's fascinating discussion of the postcolonial implications of the concept of abjection exemplified in the fate of the outcast and drawing on parallels between White's Aboriginal fringe-dweller and victim Dubbo in *Riders in the Chariot*, Arundhati Roy's persecuted and murdered outcast Velutha in *The God of Small Things* and Gemmy the rejected black/white man in David Malouf's *Remembering Babylon*. The discussion, prosecuted with Mehta's characteristic energy, mediates a vision of the body of the outcast as an eloquent accusation against the abuse of power, in seemingly civilised societies, and suggests White's continuing influence in the dissemination of these ideas amongst writers and readers alike, well beyond Australia.

Socio-Political Issues

Exploration of these issues was planned from the outset as an integral part of the conference, not only in order to cater to the interests of the Association's multi-disciplinary membership but also to show the impact of White as a public intellectual in the Australian context. In his creative works as well as in his public pronouncements, particularly later in life, White gave frequent and passionate expression to his deep awareness of the injustices done to the Aboriginal people of Australia. His Bi-Centenary speech is perhaps the most impressive of these:

> Aborigines may not be shot and poisoned as they were in the early days of colonisation, but there are subtler ways of disposing of them … They can be induced to take their own lives by the psychic

torment they undergo in police cells ... (Brennan and Flynn 1989,184).

All of the contributors in this section are recognised experts in their field and each records an awareness of significant progress and developments in this area of Australian life with regard to which White felt so deeply and had expressed considerable concern. Each has alluded to White's views in the preambles to their papers. The fact that, perhaps for the first time in Australia, in this publication, Indigenous Australian academics and writers have contributed to a celebratory collection on a white Australian writer is itself a factor of some significance.

Fred Chaney's personal involvement in several of the issues he discusses and his practical contributions at the very highest administrative level in advancing Indigenous causes; (he was, at one time, Chair of Reconciliation, Australia), confers a particular distinction and authority on his contribution. Anne De Soyza is another author who has been a player, in a practical sense, in the field in which she writes about. In this discussion she outlines an example of forward thinking on the perennial problem of assisting Indigenous progress by confronting the established idea that this could only be achieved by retaining an overarching allegiance to traditional ways and showing the need for a radical re-thinking of this policy.

Kieran Dolin, a qualified lawyer as well as a literary researcher, combines his specialist knowledge of the law with his literary expertise to assess the impact of the revolutionary *Mabo* land rights decision on Australian writing. Dolin investigates how the founding myths of Australia are being re-written since the *Mabo* case, which represents a watershed in the advancement of Indigenous rights. Keith Truscott offers a rare Indigenous perspective on the key development of the *Mabo* decision in the Aboriginal story in Australia. He encapsulates in it an innovative new interpretation of the term 'Indigenous' which is reflective of the celebratory mood released in the Aboriginal psyche by the revolutionary legislation which restored a people's self-respect.

Vicki Grieves has researched widely on the shadowed relationship between white station owners and Aboriginal workers in the pastoral industry. In her presentation at the conference she discussed an investigation regarding a family possibly connected with White's family home but continuing difficulties in obtaining permission from the family resulted in her abandoning this project. Nevertheless the chapter still evokes interest in this little-known aspect of black/white encounters and indicates the opening up of this area to scholarly investigation.

New Zealand has a special partnership role in the Association and New Zealand scholars have always made a distinctive contribution to ASAA conferences and publications. In this book, Mark Williams has submitted an impressive comparison of White with New Zealand writer James Baxter as public intellectuals in their different contexts; while Jane Stafford's detailed and sensitive commentary on a New Zealand writer also helps reinforce the cultural links that exist between the two countries. White himself acknowledged the awareness of a bond with these 'neighbours' in an address in Auckland:

> Dear Neighbours … It comforts me – and many others of like mind in my country – that you are here across the Tasman – and that we can rely on you to support us in our ideals for the South Pacific …

In the same speech he relates the story of his childhood devotion to a Solomon Islander a gardener on the family property with whom he had shared a deep bond of understanding and affection. (Brennan and Flynn 1989:167)

The two last essays deal with other public issues outside those of Indigenous concerns which were also areas of concern to White. Stephen Alomes proffers, with considerable empathy, even passion, an astute analysis of why an Australian republic could not be achieved through the last public referendum held on this issue. He goes to considerable lengths to show his awareness of the implications for Australian sovereignty; concerns which he notes were shared by White. Ameer Ali's discussion, like those of all the writers in this section, is stamped with the distinctiveness of firsthand knowledge of the public issues involved. Beginning with a highly apposite quote from a speech by White, Ameer grasps the opportunity here of stimulating discussion at an international level on an issue which is of considerable importance not just within the Australian context but worldwide.

In these, as in the other essays that centre on public issues it should be noted that contributors shows an awareness of White's own thinking on the topic being discussed and align their own discussions accordingly. The broadening of focus resulted in an enrichment of the intellectual encounters at the conference itself and has contributed to the general interest of this book. Moreover, it has served to reinforce White's status as public intellectual - contributing most strikingly to the impression that his work has achieved and will continue to achieve even more impressively in the future, of what he set out as the original ambition of his writing career. This had been the motive dictating his decision to return to his native Australia rather than settle in London, the cultural Mecca for so many other Australian artists of his time - his wish to help people this country with "a race possessed of understanding." (White 1958, 40)

Works Cited

Barnes, John.1978, *Patrick White A Critical Symposium,* ed. Ron Shepherd and Kirpal Singh: Adelaide: Centre for Research into New Literatures in English: 1-4.

Said, Edward. 2001, "The Public Role of Writers and Intellectuals," 17 September. http://www.thenation.com/doc/20010917/essay. Accessed 20 Jan.2014.

White, Patrick. "A Prodigal Son," 1958, *Australian Letters* 1, 3: 37 – 40.

Part I

Revaluations

CHAPTER ONE

AUSTRALIA'S PRODIGAL SON

JOHN BARNES
La Trobe University

Preamble: Meeting Patrick White, July 1988

In his later years Patrick White, with his black beret and walking stick, became a familiar, easily recognisable public figure. I did not need anyone to explain who he was when I met him on the grounds of La Trobe University one afternoon in July, 1988. He had come to the Bundoora campus to give, what proved to be, his last public speech. It was his second visit to the university: in 1984 he had given a very successful lunchtime talk supporting the newly formed Nuclear Disarmament Party. This time he was speaking in the evening, giving the final talk in a series named after Ben Meredith, the first Master of Menzies College. I had been invited to chair his talk and to join the small group who were to dine with him at the college beforehand.

Patrick White was now obviously very frail – just how frail I did not realise until I read David Marr's *Life* and his *Patrick White Letters* years later. Shrunken and hollow-cheeked, looking older than he was, he hardly seemed to be the same man who had visited us only four years earlier. The conversation over dinner, which was hosted by the Vice-Chancellor and his wife, was polite, restrained and inconsequential, probably because everyone, including Patrick, was on their best behaviour. There was an awkward silence, though, when he asked if any of us knew about rap-dancing. A group of middle-aged academics, we had not researched that topic! When the subject of his own writing came up, as it was bound to do, he complained that university teachers were interested only in *Voss*.

"No-one teaches *The Aunt's Story*," he asserted, sounding like a man who had suffered a personal injury. *The Aunt's Story* is my favourite White novel, and I was that year teaching it in the Australian Literature course; but the dinner did not seem to be the place to challenge what sounded like an often-voiced prejudice against university teachers, so I let the unfair criticism pass.

An excited crowd, mostly students, and a television cameraman greeted Patrick at the university theatre where he was to speak. There was a sense in the air that this was a special occasion. By the time we were settled on the stage, all seats had been taken, the doors had been closed, and there was uproar outside, as those who had been shut out banged on the doors and shouted to be admitted. The theatre had 499 seats, one short of the 500 for which safety regulations require the attendance of a fire officer. As the protests grew louder, the Vice-Chancellor, who was seated in the audience, rose and advised the attendants that he would take full responsibility for breaking the rules. After the doors were opened, the aisles were completely filled and the doorways were crowded.

This was my first experience of an Australian writer being treated as a celebrity. When I mentioned in my introduction that he was the first and only Australian winner of the Nobel Prize for Literature I was interrupted by applause. And when Patrick came to the microphone there was prolonged applause. "Very kind of you", he said; "Hope we shall still be friends at the end." He need not have worried.

It was the year of the Bicentenary, which he called in his talk "the year of the great Australian lie." His theme was "a sense of integrity – particularly our own," and the audience enthusiastically responded to his account of what was wrong with Australians, a large proportion of whom he characterised as "children at heart – kidults". His talk was more a recital of what he disliked than an argument about contemporary society. There were two entertaining moments when one got a glimpse of the actor in White. Having complained that the Bicentenary celebrations would leave us "all but broke," and dismissing "babbling about the Games" (Sydney hosted the Olympic Games 12 years later), he promoted, "as shamelessly as an ABC radio ad" a cheese – Gippsland Blue was the "best in the world. Not a racehorse or a boxer, but a humble, civilising cheese." Then, turning to politics, he uttered a *cri de coeur* to then Foreign Minister Bill Hayden who, it was rumoured, would soon become Governor-General. (He did.) "DON'T DO IT, BILL," shouted Patrick, to the delight of the audience."

After this theatrical flourish, he offered what amounted to a *credo*. Acknowledging that he was seen as "a bitter, angry old man," he said that he was 'angry' because "the earth is angry" (an indirect reference to his concern about the effect of nuclear testing on the environment), and he went on to voice his conviction that "we must all, in the years to come, work towards a civilisation based on humanity". Underlying his mocking portrait of what he had called "a kidult society" was his belief that "most people hunger after spirituality." Patrick White always rejected the claim that he was a moralist who preached sermons in his novels, but in what he thought would be his last public performance, he took on the role of a preacher, telling his flock: "Follow the path of humility and humanity, and Australia might develop a civilisation worthy of the name."

The audience responded with a perfect storm of applause. After the closing civilities – the Master of Menzies College thanked Patrick for a talk that "offered comfort to the afflicted and afflicted the comfortable" – several students came on stage and asked me if he would sign copies of his books. I doubted that he would as he looked exhausted, but he immediately came back to the lectern – which caused more people to come up with their books to be signed. Although he grumbled, "Why is it always *Voss*, *Voss*?" he did not refuse to sign any of the copies, mostly well-worn paperbacks and mostly *Voss*, which were thrust at him. It was an appropriate ending to a memorable evening.

[The text of the talk is available in Brennan and Flynn 1989,189 - 195].

The Prodigal Son

In 1948, two talented expatriate Australian novelists returned to Australia with the intention of settling back permanently into their original homeland: Patrick White in Sydney and Martin Boyd in Melbourne. Both men's work had found recognition in Australia;

Boyd was awarded the Gold Medal of the Australian Literature Society for his first major novel, *The Montforts* (1928), and White was given the same award for his first published novel, *Happy Valley* (1939). However, within three years Boyd left Australia, never to return; he had not written anything during his stay. White spent the rest of his life in Australia writing novels, stories and plays, which earned him a greater international reputation than any other Australian writer. He became a major influence upon Australian writing.

White's return to his homeland and his decision to remain despite his increasing disappointment, even anger, at the direction that Australian society was taking, set him apart from the three other prominent expatriate Australian novelists in the twentieth century: Henry Handel Richardson (1870-1946), Martin Boyd (1893-1972), and Christina Stead (1902-83). All of these writers produced their best work while living away from Australia and it would seem, preferred to remain expatriate, though Stead returned late in life, to die in Australia. For each of them, personal relationships that they had formed early in life resulted in their spending their most productive years abroad: for White a personal relationship resulted in his return. Richardson was born in Australia and was aged 17 when her widowed mother took her to Europe. She married in Europe and returned later only for a six-week visit. The two novels on which her Australian reputation rests are autobiographical – *The Getting of Wisdom*, a fictional version of her school years, and the trilogy, *The Fortunes of Richard Mahony*, a version of the life of her Irish-born father, who had died during her Australian childhood. Stead's literary career began after she left Australia in 1928 at the age of 26 and was completed by the time she re-settled in Australia in 1974, nine years before her death in 1983. She lived in several countries and wrote novels with settings in those different countries, notably England, France and America, as well as Australia. Her first novel was set in Sydney, where she had grown up, and a later novel, *For Love Alone,* was based on her own early experience as a young woman, who chose to travel abroad to widen her experience of life and love. Her experience of childhood in Sydney was the subject matter of her masterpiece, *The Man Who Loved Children* (1940), but she transposed the setting to the United States, where she was then living. It wasn't until 1965, that she was 'discovered' in Australia.

Boyd's privileged class and personal circumstances most closely resembled those of White. He was actually born in Switzerland, where his well-to-do parents were travelling, returned at the age of six months to Melbourne and was educated there. At the time of the First World War he went to England to join the British army. After the war he came back to Australia but did not settle; he returned instead to England where he started writing fiction, and remained there for 27 years. When he returned to Australia in 1948, he sought to recover what he had known in the past by restoring his mother's childhood home, the Grange, at Yarra Glen, outside Melbourne, intending to live there permanently. For him Australia meant his family – noted for its artistic talent – and its social eminence. As a writer he described himself fairly accurately as "recording the existence of a vanishing social group" (1972, 232). He was drawn back to England, initially with the idea of making a prolonged visit, with friends there, but eventually abandoned the idea of settling in Australia. The most important thing that happened to him as a writer during the three years in Australia was the discovery, during renovations at the Grange, of his grandmother's diary, which he took back to England with him. This was to prove the mainspring for his best-known work, *The Langton Quartet*, (1988) directly based on the family experience.

"Nostalgia for scenes of childhood" was a powerful element In White's decision to return, but the personal issues he was dealing with, including his feelings about Australia and England, were far more complex than those motivating Boyd. Like Boyd, he had been born abroad – in London, where his parents were travelling – and brought back to Australia at the age of six months. At thirteen he was taken back to England and "dumped" at a private school, Cheltenham College, where "there was never a day when I was not called 'a bloody colonial' or a 'bloody cockney'" (qtd. in Marr 1994, 273). Released from his "expensive prison" after four years and back in Australia, he felt himself to be "a stranger in my own country, even in my own family "(White 1981, 46). Both his parents were from landed families (they were, in fact, second cousins) and initially, he went along with their expectation that he become a jackeroo for a couple of years and work on the land before going to Sydney to prepare for university studies. These were the years, during which he wrote "three rambling, immature novels, fortunately never published" before going back to England (White 1981, 46).

At Cambridge he read modern languages (French and German) and spent his vacations in France and Germany. When he completed the Tripos he chose to stay in England, and with parental financial support set out to make his way as a writer in London. The publication in Sydney of *The Ploughman and Other Poems* (1935), which his parents financed, could be regarded as marking the beginning of his literary career.

In 1939, with the publication of *Happy Valley* – a novel drawing upon his experience of the jackerooing years, but not autobiographical – White could regard himself as an established writer. That novel, published in both Britain and America, was well received by reviewers in Australia, but with reservations. H. M. Green, the Librarian at the University of Sydney noted "the current literary influences, in particular that of Joyce," which he thought had not been thoroughly assimilated. While he thought the novel "outstanding" he found it "cosmopolitan rather than Australian" (1941, 20). Novelist, Seaforth Mackenzie, White's contemporary, was much more receptive, asserting an author's right to handle his material in whichever way he chooses. He praised White's insight and honesty, remarking: "It is the first time such a work has been written by an Australian about Australia" (1941, 4). These were straws in the wind: a modernist writer such as White could expect to find some sympathetic critical responses among creative writers of his own generation, but would almost certainly encounter some resistance from older, established writers and critics, especially from those who were confident that they could recognise what was 'Australian.'

White's next two novels received little critical attention in Australia. *The Living and the Dead* (1941) was, after all, set in London; but *The Aunt's Story* (1948) was set partly in Australia, with a central character who was an Australian, and so the novel could not be ignored entirely by the guardians of the national literature. Green thought it "a clever, rather too obviously clever and elaborately artificial psychological study of a spinster aunt"

(1949, 137) but the editor of *Southerly*, R. G. Howarth, praised the writing as new and exciting. Howarth saw White as challenging Mackenzie "as the most expert Australian stylist in the novel," and found it "gratifying" that White had returned to Australia. He concluded his review with the prophetic words: "What he will give us next will be worth waiting for" (1950, 210). One swallow doesn't make a summer, and White's subsequent comments suggest that he was discouraged by the reception of this novel. In his Nobel Prize speech of (1973) he stated that after *The Aunt's Story* he had wondered if he would "ever write another word" (Brennan and Flynn 1981, 43)

Why, then, did Patrick White decide to settle in Australia where he felt himself to be a stranger, and where he could expect so little stimulus to continue with his literary career? In the post-Cambridge years he had lived in London, and long afterwards he was to confess "at heart I am a Londoner" (qtd.in Marr, 1985, 419). He had travelled in America; and while working with the RAF Intelligence during the Second World War had been stationed for a year in Greece, in 1941. This was the homeland of Manoly Lascaris a man with whom he formed, an intense and lifelong relationship. At the end of the war White was convinced that Greece was the place where he wanted to spend the rest of his life. "Greece was his chief obsession", writes David Marr, [where] "he could live the life of pure being, pure spirit", (1991, 233). His love for Manoly had stimulated a passionate feeling for Greece that had been sustained during the time he lived there during the war. To quote Marr again: "Greece helped White shed the imaginative constraints of his own background, and his life with Manoly Lascaris, who had this history [of the Byzantine past] in his bones, enriched and freed him" (214). He looked forward to a life with Lascaris after the war, and he thought that it would be in Greece.

From Athens in 1945 White, still a serving officer in the RAF, went so far as to write to the Australian Prime Minister, identifying himself with his father's well-known pastoral family and requested that Australia send a small experimental flock of Merinos to help revive Greek agriculture, but the request was unsuccessful. (Marr, 1994, 61) He started to think about the practical realities of the sort of existence that he and Lascaris would have in Greece, and considered buying an agency to import goods into Greece from Australia: Lascaris would manage the business, leaving him free to settle down to write "all the things I have been prevented from writing during the War", he wrote in a letter to Spud Johnson an intimate friend of earlier years in 1945 (Marr 1994, 63). The plan of settling in Greece was eventually abandoned, partly because White began to see himself becoming "the beachcomber all foreigners become when they settle in Greece – tolerated, but never much more than a joke" (1981, 123]. What appears to have been decisive was the attitude of Lascaris, who insisted on their going to Australia: "It was his illusion. I suppose I sensed it was better than mine" (1981, 123).

Finally, as with the other expatriates, it was a personal relationship that determined where he would settle. White paid frequent tributes to Manoly Lascaris, who was for almost half a century his closest companion. Their relationship was sometimes turbulent, but there can hardly be any doubt that Lascaris was, as White said in his Nobel Prize speech, the "mainstay' of his life and work." In Australia Lascaris was mostly in the background, regarding it as his 'fate' to enable White to fulfil his destiny as a writer. After White's death, he was to say: "Living so long under the wings of a great writer is a bitter privilege. Sometimes you don't know if you really exist or have a self, or even if you *are* yourself" (Karalis 1908, 13).

Reading his conversation with the Greek academic Vrasidas Karalis, one is led to wonder at times whether Lascaris is echoing something White wrote or whether what White wrote had echoed something that Lascaris had said. White had as his partner a complex, highly literate man, who was a strong personality, for all his willingness to take second place. It is something of a shock to learn that he was offended by the Australian habit of calling him by his first name, and that he took so seriously the imperial history of his family. Here is an extract from his comments to Karalis, sometime after White's death, translated from the Greek:

> Some days ago, I had a visit, a count from Poland. He talked with such arrogance: 'We belong to the landed gentry. Before the War, we had our own county'. 'I beg your pardon, sir', I replied. 'My

family produced the emperors of Byzantium! We were the true heirs of the senatorial families of Rome – not barbarian upstarts!' These people must be taught their proper place, especially here in the colonies ... (Karalis 2008, 21).

The episode took place in the 1990s. Lascaris's outlook had clearly not been affected by living for half a century in a democratic society.

When White and Lascaris settled in Australia they both felt they were very much outsiders: White says in the Nobel Prize speech that he "had never felt such a foreigner" and in his autobiographical portrait says that they heard that in the neighbourhood Lascaris was thought to be "some sort of black prince" (White 1981, 131). At one stage a homesick Lascaris returned to Greece, uncertain whether he wanted to continue his life with White; but in retrospect he was able to say that he had received more than he had hoped for in Australia. "Listen, young man", he said to Karalis, "to me Australia means one thing: salvation." And he went on to explain: "Australia saved me from ghosts and demons, liberated me from paternal protocols of obedience, gave a new rhythm to my quest for meaning" (Karalis 2008, 137).

For both men their six-acre property at Castle Hill outside Sydney meant not only a shared life but a new beginning, a transformation. David Marr writes: "They worked their acres like peasants, beginning at sunrise and returning to the house after nightfall, stamping the mud off their boots." (1991, 261) The author was now a small farmer. It was a complete break with the life of a boulevardier that he had known in Europe before the War. In Sydney he seems to have made no effort to exploit family contacts, and he also stayed away from the Fellowship of Australian Writers. Part of the attraction of Sydney was the work of painters like Dobell, with whom he did make contact. For the most part, though, he and Lascaris kept to themselves and only gradually became part of the community at Castle Hill

In his conversations after White's death Lascaris was at pains to stress that it was not their homosexuality that caused them to live so privately, but the impact of the war in which they had been involved. He observed to his fellow-Greek, Karalis, "Those who haven't lived through the ravages of War are unable to understand what it means to live an uneventful life in the suburbs or the provinces ... it means bliss and transfiguration, fighting ghosts and creating myths and confronting memories, through mopping cooking, washing, dining in silence" (Karalis 2008, 132) He summed it up in a comment that seems particularly relevant to *The Tree of Man*:"Our chosen solitude was the only way to purify our existence from the stains of experience." (Karalis 2008, 133-4)

There are reflections of White's war experience in his fiction. He gives a few details in *Flaws in the Glass*, but they do not form the basis of any of his novels. He had been in London during the Blitz, and as an Intelligence Officer in North Africa had the task on the battlefield of searching the bodies of the enemy dead for papers. Years afterwards, with characteristic black humour, he wrote to Angela Dawson (in 1970) that "when anything particularly awful was happening during the War, like the Blitz in London, or when one was being shot up or bombed in the Western desert, or escaping into Tobruk in the dark," he used to cheer himself up by thinking that it wasn't as bad as his school years at Cheltenham, "because the enemy is only trying to destroy one's body, not the part that matters." (Marr 1994, 231). His memories of the awful wartime happenings that he witnessed lie behind his vehement support for nuclear disarmament. He made a powerful speech (1984) about the threat of nuclear war recalling a horrifying personal experience recounted to him by a woman he knew:

> During the Blitz in London I came across a Cockney charwoman who had worked for me in the days of peace. Now she was looking pale and exhausted. After a particularly gruelling night in the suburb where she lived, she had gone in search of a friend whose street had become a stretch of rubble along which a search was in progress – when the warden in charge of operations suddenly held up a head, and asked 'Anyone know the body that belonged to this?' '*And*', my Mrs Collins told in her dusty Cockney, 'it was my friend's'.

> Only a vignette – Mrs Collins and her friend's severed head in a London slum – or a charred tank in the Libyan desert, a crew member caught by the ankle as he vainly tried to escape from its

burning hulk, – or a Cretan woman gunned almost in two by allied soldiers who claimed she had given one of their mates VD – all minor details illustrating the gratuitous brutality an individual can be subject to, inside the pattern of a war vast enough to include European Jewry slaughtered in their ghettos or carted off to the gas chambers, the wrecking of noble cities like Coventry and Dresden, and of course the apocalyptic ending to World War II with the disappearance of Hiroshima and Nagasaki in fire, ashes and agony such as mankind probably never experienced before. (Brennan and Flynn 1989, 146-7)

Living at Castle Hill, growing flowers and vegetables, milking two cows and breeding goats and dogs, White and Lascaris were far removed from the 'graveyard' of Europe's wartime suffering. Their new life was a form of retreat from what they had known; and for White it was, at first, a retreat from his literary ambitions. It was three years before he began to write again and in the interim he had undergone a crisis of spiritual belief.

The epigraph to *The Solid Mandala* identifies a central concern of White's fiction: "There is another world, but it is in this one." He was fascinated by the reality of the known world but equally fascinated by the possibility of something beyond the known; 'superhuman realities' that could only be intuited. Unlike some of the commentators on his work but like Flaubert – a novelist whom he admired – he knew that literature does not provide 'answers', but in his novels – much more than in his plays – he sought to express his intuition of a 'core of reality'. In 1937 he had told his Spanish lover that Australia was "a country of frustrations" (qtd. in Marr 1991: 161), a comment more indicative of his personal condition than a considered judgment on the society he was born into. There is a strong sense of frustration and a desire to escape the more mundane realities of existence running through *Happy Valley*, and also *The Living and the Dead*. In *The Aunt's Story* the central character, who has been unable to accept the compromises and limitations of 'normal' life, is released by the death of her mother to explore the prospect of freedom. Although she leaves Australia to travel in Europe and America, she finds there is no 'other' place in which she will be fulfilled, and her odyssey ends in an American asylum. The writing of this sensitive, witty, and brilliantly imaginative study marked the end of White's phase as an expatriate writer. When he came to write his next novel, his personal relationship to Australia had changed and he had himself undergone a significant psychological change: "I don't know when I began to have faith, but it is only a short time since I admitted it," he wrote to his cousin Peggy Garland in 1953, when still working on the first draft of *The Tree of Man* (qtd in Marr 1994, 90).

In his well-known essay, wryly entitled "The Prodigal Son" first written in 1958 (Brennan and Flynn 1989, 13-17), White speaks of how he came to write this novel. The relevant passage, which has been quoted many times and accepted as a literary manifesto, is worth examining, not only for what he is saying here but how he is saying it. He begins with an image that an early explorer or settler from Europe might have used: "the Great Australian Emptiness," and describes himself as taking on the public responsibility of filling a void, an immense void, because he believed in the possibility of helping "to people a barely inhabited country with a race possessed of understanding" as his potential reward (Brennan and Flynn 1989, 13). This sounds like the reaction of a newcomer, a migrant perhaps, who regards himself as the agent of beneficial change, a sort of benefactor and creator of a new society. He draws no creative strength from the existing literature, no inspiration from the people or the place, but is stirred (or even compelled) to take up writing fiction again because of the "Emptiness" that confronted him.

Logically, that would seem to lead to social satire, a form of criticism that would open his readers' eyes to the 'emptiness' of their lives. Satire came readily to White; but although there is satire of social attitudes in *The Tree of Man* that is not the major focus of the novel. In a formulation that would have found ready acceptance among local writers and critics, White declares his intention as wanting "to suggest in this book every possible aspect of life, through the lives of an ordinary man and woman." (Brennan and Flynn, 1989, 15) However, while local writers and critics might have taken this huge claim as a formula for 'The Great Australian Novel' – a notion that came, I think, from a literary competition earlier in the century – they would have found it hard to enter into the frame of mind in which he began to write *The Tree of Man*, which he described as panic at "the exaltation of the "average." In the novel, though he had committed himself to depicting the 'ordinary', he wanted "to discover the extraordinary behind the ordinary, the mystery and the poetry which alone could make bearable the lives of such people, and incidentally, my own life since my return." (Brennan and Flynn 1989, 15)

In other words, the lives of ordinary people would be unbearable if there were nothing more to them than what makes them 'ordinary'. Most important of all, *his* life since his return would have been 'unbearable' without the possibility of 'mystery and poetry'. One can understand why he originally called the work, *A Life Sentence on Earth*. In creating Stan and Amy Parker he was taking on the disguise of "an ordinary man and woman", drawing upon his experience of farming at Castle Hill but the symbolic scenes by which he sought to show the characters' inner lives came from his own Unconscious. In none of his other books did he attempt to create in - depth characters so unlike his conscious self. The book had a significance for him that is only hinted at in his article. In a private letter he wrote to his cousin Peggy Garland, he was more explicit: "When we came to live here, I felt life was, on the surface, so dreary, ugly, monotonous, there must be a poetry hidden in it to give it a purpose, and so I set out to discover that secret core, and *The Tree of Man* emerged." (Marr 1991, 118). While he saw much to mock in the lives around him, he believed that, whether they were conscious of it or not, there were 'ordinary' people who hungered, as he did, after spirituality.

The years that White spent writing this novel were, for him, years of trial and error as he sought to find spiritual direction. After what he later represented as an epiphany, when he fell in the mud at Castle Hill, he persuaded Lascaris to join him in attending Anglican services, "an exercise in organised humility" (White 1981, 144) that, unsurprisingly, did not last long; but the conviction remained that others shared his "hunger after spirituality", and he repeated it in his last public speech (Brennan and Flynn 1989, 195).

One can only speculate on the influence of Manoly Lascaris, who seems to have been a steadier, far less troubled personality than his partner. He belonged to the Greek Orthodox Church and later in White's house in Centennial Park had a collection of icons that formed a shrine. White writes, "My inklings of God's presence are interwoven with my love of the one human being who never fails me." (1981, 145) On one occasion Karalis, struck by Lascaris's reflections on religion, asks him whether he was an influence on White's 'religiosity'. That draws a derisory response: "How can you find sources for your life in the belief of others?" In these conversations with Karalis years after White's death, Lascaris shows an impressive grasp of theological complexities. Speaking of God, "the name that names its absence", he recalls a tense discussion with Patrick out there in Castle Hill and goes on to remark enigmatically that "his death transformed our discussion." (Karalis 2008, 89)

The Tree of Man emerged from White's deeply personal struggles to find meaning in human existence but the narrative is outwardly a simple family chronicle, yet another saga of settling on the land, a topic familiar to Australian readers. Though the focus is on the symbolism through which White tries to express the "mystery and poetry" within, the novel is impressive in its sense of daily life, of time passing and the changing relationships of the characters, especially the married couple, Stan and Amy Parker at the heart of the narrative. To readers outside Australia it could seem an epic of pioneering, and to readers inside Australia an attempt to write the Great Australian Novel.

The acclaim that greeted *The Tree of Man* in America was known in Australia before copies of the book arrived, and helped its reception locally. James Stern, who had welcomed *The Aunt's Story*, led the praise in a front-page article of *The New York Times Book Review* (August 1955, 5), hailing the book as "a timeless work of art". The review was titled, "The Quiet People of the Homestead", with a sub-heading "A Novel That Views Man's Life in the Wilds of Australia with Grandeur and Simplicity." It was illustrated by a Drysdale painting, "Feeding the Dogs" that features in the background, an almost empty, barren landscape. By contrast, one of the best Australian reviews, in the Melbourne *Age*, was headed "A Poet at Loose on Cow Cockies." The Australian reviewers, more familiar with the subject matter than those overseas, were generally welcoming, though criticism of some elements of White's style has fuelled a belief that they were hostile.

A. D. Hope's review in *The Sydney Morning Herald* gets a mention from almost everyone who writes about White's reception at the time: "pretentious and illiterate verbal sludge". On the face of it, the returned expatriate had been savaged by one of the country's most influential critics; but that isn't quite what happened. The phrase which has stuck in people's minds came in the last sentence of the review: "When so few Australian novelists can write prose at all, it is a great pity to see Mr White, who shows on every page some touch of the born writer, deliberately choose as his medium this pretentious and illiterate verbal sludge." (Hope 1956, 15) Compare this comment on White's prose by Douglas Stewart, the equally influential literary editor of the Sydney *Bulletin:* "Mr White writes his bad prose so painstakingly, and with such hints of possible excellence, that one has no doubt that he could write well if he chose" (1956, 58). In the Melbourne *Age* Geoffrey Dutton remarked on "memorable pieces drifting around in this huge novel, dialogues, descriptions and sudden revelations of concealed feelings," but judged that there were times "when the writing seems pretentious and forced" (1956, 209 -210). One more example: H. J. Oliver, writing in *Southerly*, could not "think of any living Australian novelist who could equal Patrick White's achievement in creating the basic rhythms of life" but was critical of the prose, quoting examples of what he regarded as bathos, and going so far as to say that there were whole paragraphs that "read exactly like a three-star extract from *Cold Comfort Farm*" (1956, 170). These critics all alike acknowledged White's great ability but found fault with the kind of prose that he produced in *The Tree of Man*. Hope's critique is singled out because he shows in it, like White, his mastery of the memorable stinging phrase. Hope's words particularly hurt White deeply.

The situation is rich in irony. Hope was as critical as White of the 'emptiness' of Australian society, and he greatly admired Boyd's affirmation of civilised values in his writing. His review of *The Tree of Man* did recognise that, though the novel had "all the earmarks that traditionally distinguish The Great Australian Novel", White was not writing about pioneering; Hope praised the work for having "one essential of the great novelist: the ability to create real people and a real world for them to live in." However, with his extremely conservative view of literary forms, Hope could only deplore that White "tries to write a novel as though he were writing poetry." Hope was opposing what he saw as a trend of modern literature: "It is one of the delusions of our time that novels can be written this way'. Yet in spite of his dislike of poetic prose, Hope acknowledged White's creativity – as did the other Australian reviewers

Writing *The Tree of Man* had been, for White, a "struggle to create completely fresh forms out of the rocks and sticks of words." He discovered meaning in the "boredom and frustration, the ugliness, the bags and iron of Australian life", those very aspects that threatened to make his life unbearable and that seemed so unpromising for art. From the perspective of Australian readers – and writers – this novel demonstrated a different way of handling familiar material. Geoffrey Dutton thought that *The Tree of Man* was the Great Australian Novel. It was "completely unlike any other Australian novel I can recall." He said that White had "abandoned the highroad of Australian fiction with its careful signposts showing how far he is from Sydney or Melbourne, how far from the Boer War or the great depression," and he was "forgetful of the football scores, the local pub and the local idiom."

White had written about ordinary people in what was, in Australian terms, an unfamiliar and idiosyncratic way that did not correspond to conventional expectations. In his essay, "The Democratic Theme," which appeared at the very time that White was writing *The Tree of Man*, A. A. Phillips identified in contemporary Australian novelists a "belief in the importance of the Common Man," and the ability "to present him without condescension or awkwardness" by which Phillips meant a 'square-jawed dinkum' determination to do without the fripperies, the modes – and sometimes the graces – of aesthetic practice.' He summed up the attitude of these novelists as an "unembarrassed preference for revealing the simple verities rather than the sophistications of human nature" (1958, 56). That is a somewhat idiosyncratic description of the so-called 'democratic-realist tradition', which was generally accepted as the *Australian* tradition. It was this conception of what was distinctively Australian that was implicitly challenged by White's performance in, first, *The Tree of Man* and, then, *Voss*.

Faced with White's novels, Left-wing writers and critics were defensive. Labour historian, Ian Turner, thought White's style "a parodist's pushover," and asserted that "Australians are brought up to prefer the plain weaves of their own writers to the Gothic embroidery that is characteristic of Voss." He argued that White "has not succeeded for Australians – because he is exploring, in an Australian environment, a way of thinking that is foreign territory to most Australians" (1962, 36-7). Jack Beasley, a Communist critic, took an even more extreme position. After *Riders in the Chariot* appeared in 1961, he was alarmed by "the adulatory chorus" of reviewers, and urged that "those who cherish our traditions must be prepared to defend them unceasingly" (1962). These however, were minority responses; and within a few years even an avowedly Left-wing journal like *Overland* was keen to publish Patrick White's work. As early as 1958, R. F. Brissenden could conclude a Commonwealth Literary Fund lecture by saying of White: "As Laura Trevelyan says of Voss, the country is his "by right of vision."'. A string of literary prizes followed in quick succession: the ALS Gold Medal for *The Tree of Man* in 1956; the Miles Franklin Award for *Voss* in 1958, and for *Riders in the Chariot* in 1961; established White's dominance of the Australian literary scene beyond doubt, and a flood of academic articles, lectures and theses soon followed.

By 1963 White was being described as "unquestionably the best known and most discussed novelist of the day." That was the opinion of the critic whose review of *The Tree of Man* had hurt White. And though A. D. Hope still thought White guilty of 'over-writing 'he now suggested that his success "is indicative of a break with the naturalistic tradition which has dominated Australian fiction since the turn of the century, and may well be a portent of a more imaginative and a more intellectual sort of fiction." (1963, 12) In a radio review about the time of *The Tree of Man* Hope had referred to Australian literature as 'second-rate', by which he meant that it was provincial, with writers thinking that they had to be consciously Australian.

> The writer's chief task, the expression of an individual vision, has been complicated and distorted by a task which is strictly

irrelevant, the task of not being himself, but of being in some way typically Australian. (1974, 5-6)

Hope's formulation defines very clearly what made White's *The Tree of Man* and the novels which followed so significant for Australian writing: in recognising only 'the task of being himself', White did more than any other writer to change the expectations of Australian readers and to liberate local writers from the 'irrelevant' task of conforming to a notion of 'Australianness'.

Before the advent of Patrick White, one could say that the prevailing view was that the national literature should interpret the making of the Australian nation. In the background of the earlier fiction were the central themes of the European history of Australia, the exploration and settlement of the continent. White's first two novels after his return to Australia were clearly not historical fictions, but at first they tended to be read in the context of these large-scale historical events. Paradoxically, it was because these two novels seemed to situate White's work within the grand narrative of Australian history, and so to confirm his credentials as an Australian writer, that they had had such an immediate and powerful impact. In its subject matter *The Tree of Man* is less characteristic of White than any of his other work, and because it could be read in terms of the pioneering myth, which had such a powerful hold on Australian imagination, for most local readers it was more accessible – despite the difficulties that so many readers had with the style of the two earlier novels.

Part of the appeal of *Voss* for some Australian readers lay in the relationship of the fiction to the history of exploration. In creating the central character White had drawn upon the historical personage, Ludwig Leichhardt; and Douglas Stewart, reviewing the novel, found it fascinating because he was so interested in Leichardt, and described the 'story' as "simply a fictional, freely-imagined account of Leichardt's last journey" (1958, 2). However, with *Riders in the Chariot* and the later novels the full measure of White's challenge to the accepted orthodoxy about how Australian life could be represented in fiction was apparent. In a way that no other Australian writer had done, he made both readers and writers aware of new possibilities for Australian fiction.

The story of Australia's 'Prodigal Son' is full of paradoxes. No one killed the fatted calf on his return, but he became a literary hero, albeit an imperfect and imperfectly understood hero, and finally a celebrity; fiercely protective of his privacy, he lived his last years in a glare of publicity; a member of an established family, he became a 'stirrer', championing radical causes and attacking the Establishment, which responded by courting him; an Australian who thought Australia a 'hateful place', he was acclaimed as a national writer, the country's only winner of the Nobel Prize for Literature. The whirligig of time had brought him his revenges.

It is not unusual for interest in a writer's work to decline for a generation or so after his death. 'Only after a hundred years shall we know whether I am worth writing about', White told David Tacey who had written a book about him (qtd. in Marr 1982: 573). Despite the controversies, there can hardly be any doubt that his fiction has had an influence on Australian literature and culture for which there is no parallel. It would certainly seem that, judged from the vantage point of over six decades, this prodigal son's return to Australia in 1948 has had a significance that neither he nor anyone else could have foreseen.

Works Cited

Beasley, Jack. 1962. "The Great Hatred," *Realist Writer* September: 17-22.

Brissenden, R.F. 1958. *Patrick White*. (Commonwealth Literary Fund Lecture).

Brennan, Paul and Christine Flynn. 1989. Ed.*Patrick White Speaks,* Sydney: Primavera Press.

Dutton, Geoffrey. 1956. "A Poet at Loose on Cow Cockies," *Age* May 12. (Melbourne): 209-10.

Green, H. M. 1941. "Australian Literature 1939-40," *Southerly* 2.1: 17-22.

—. 1949. "Australian Literature 1948," *Southerly* 10.3: 133-39.

Hope, A. D. 1974. "A Second-rate Literature," *Native Companions: Essays and Comments on Australian Literature 1936-1966*, Sydney: Angus and Robertson: 73-75.

—. 1963. *Australian Literature 1950-1962*, Melbourne: Melbourne University Press.
—. 1956. "The Bunyip Stages a Comeback," *Sydney Morning Herald,* June 15: 16.
Howarth, R. G. 1950. "The Imago," [review of *The Aunt's Story*], *Southerly* 1.4: 209-10.
Karalis, Vrasidas. 2008. *Recollections of Mr Manoly Lascaris*. Blackheath, NSW: Brandl & Schlesinger.
Mackenzie, Seaforth. 1939. "Happy and Unhappy," *Desiderata* (Adelaide) May: 19-20.
Marr, David. 1991. *Patrick White: A Life*. Sydney: Random House.
—. Ed. 1994. *Patrick White Letters*. Sydney: Random House.
Oliver, H. J. 1956. "The Expanding Novel," *Southerly* 17.3: 168-70.
Phillips, A. A. 1955. "The Democratic Theme" *Overland,* no. 5; reprinted in *The Australian Tradition: Studies in a Colonial Culture*, Melbourne: F. W. Cheshire 1958.
Stern, James. 1955. "The Quiet People of the Homestead," *New York Times Book Review*, 14 August: 5, 13.
Stewart, Douglas. 1956. "*The Tree of Man,*" *The Bulletin*: 2, 58.
Turner, Ian. 1958. 12, June "The Parable of *Voss*," *Overland* June 12: 36-7.
White, Patrick. 1981. *Flaws in the Glass*. London: Jonathan Cape.

CHAPTER TWO

HORIZONS OF HOPE

BILL ASHCROFT
UNIVERSITY OF NEW SOUTH WALES

There is no clearer demonstration of the fact that reading is a social and historical act than the reception of Patrick White. The relationship between reader and writer, or reader and text, is never innocent, but reflects the social concerns of the time. With literature and literary analysis, it also reflects the concerns dominating the institutions of literary criticism. White's work entered Australian literary culture at a time when the country was experiencing a post-war nationalist resurgence, leading up to the establishment of a chair of Australian literature at Sydney University – the first such chair, and the belated recognition that Australia *did* have a literature, and, indeed, was experiencing a birth into respectability – just as hunger for an Australia literature of world stature was growing.

This was the cultural milieu of White's emergence, and there is still no Australian writer of greater stature, although by the late 1980s, certainly after his death, interest in White appeared to have waned considerably. He was too modernist, perhaps too literary, too transcendental, simply too *hard*, and if not actively rejected for the prominence of his interest in the sacred, this added to his plummeting popularity. White has always been a political writer, concerned with the marginal, the poor, the weird, the outsider, but this has hardly ever been the way in which he has been read because his literary aesthetic is so powerful. Yet his postcolonial reading of Australian culture and society has always been, for me, his most exciting feature. Re-reading White now, I am struck by the prominence and the insistence of his project to discover the possibilities of an Australia freed from the overwhelming demands of imperial culture. How this coincided with the trajectory of his search for a re-placed, renewed Australian sacred is one of the most intriguing mysteries of his work.

White's vision of Australia must be understood in terms of *arrival* and the sense of expectation propelling a renewed vision of the scenes of childhood. While the country of his childhood promised so much, he saw it as constantly undermined by the pettiness, superficiality, inauthenticity and imperial deference of a society unsure of itself. His sense of the superficiality of Australian life is tracked down to Sarsaparilla, to the poverty of spirit, the mendacity and inauthenticity of the individuals who inhabit and characterise the un-freedom of suburban life. The resentful claim, in mis-readings such as Simon During's (1996), that this is just an elitist and irascible criticism of a society he didn't understand, completely misses the point that his work is deeply imbued with a hope for what that society, a postcolonial new world society, could become.

White's novels continually repel attempts to attach them to the curmudgeonly biographical author. No matter how redolent of his life and belief, his novels always take us out to the very edges of belief, to the vista of the possible, to the horizon of the spirit. Books such as *Flaws in the Glass* (1981) and *Memoirs of Many in One* (1986) are not just biographical records, but demonstrations of the feature of the writing that reaches into the future. The famous moment of epiphany recorded in *Flaws in the Glass*, where he slips and falls over in the mud, functions almost allegorically as a context and a beginning for his work.

> Half blinded by rain ... cursing through watery lips a God in whom I did not believe. I began laughing finally at my own helplessness and hopelessness ... it was the turning point. My disbelief appeared as farcical as my fall. (1981, 144)

The most striking word here is not so much 'God' or 'belief' as 'hopelessness.' The direction of White's work can only be understood fully if we see in it the sense of hope emerging from this turning point, the vision of a different world from the world he had left behind in England, the hope for a society freed of its colonial baggage. This is significant because the dimension nobody attaches to White's work is *hope*. For all the criticisms of his supposed modernism and aestheticism, the moment of epiphany is one that unites spirituality and social justice. The search for God is also at the same time a search for a place for the outsider, a demand for the acceptance of difference. Because of the enormous aesthetic edifice of his work, and his famously misanthropic personality, we are apt to forget the fact that from the moment in the mud White's own sense of social and political justice was finely tuned and actively public.

White understood intimately the ambiguities of a settler colonial society: the colonial pretensions and cultural cringe; the fact that it is both coloniser and colonised; that its potential for carving something new in the Antipodes is constantly compromised by the imperial vision on which it was founded – the vision of an Anglo-Saxon revival in the South Seas. The problem with utopia is that it is the imperial vision that often predominates. Voss puts this succinctly when he says: "Your future is what you will make it. Future," said Voss, "is will." (V 68) Voss's will is immersed in the project of self-deification but this is itself an intensely realised summation of the kind of imperial pretension that sees the new land as a *tabula rasa*.

Despite the ideal Australia he visualised during his exiles – "a landscape without figures," (White 1981, 49) the utopian dimension of White's work refuses to resolve itself into a picture of utopia. Greece is the closest he comes to it, but it is a self consciously nostalgic utopia, as we see in *The Twyborn Affair* (1979) in Angelo's illusion of perfection in his sainted wife Anna and the Smyrna to which he can never return. (TA 36) Rather the utopian reveals itself in the insistence of 'becoming' over 'being,' indeed, the insistence that becoming is the prime dimension of being, even if it shows itself in various forms of self-laceration. This is why sexual ambivalence can be a powerful trope for the human condition - self is only realised in the process of discovery: "the real E has not yet been discovered," (TA 79) says Eudoxia at the beginning of her/his journey through multiple selves. White recognised in his own sexuality in *Flaws in the Glass* "the freedom being conferred on me to range through every variation of the human mind, to play so many roles in so many contradictory envelopes of flesh." (1981, 35) White's genius lies in his capacity to evoke intensely experienced human becoming in its social possibilities

Australia as heterotopia

If White has no picture of Australia as utopia and every reference to the remembered paradise such as Angelo's Smyrna is seen as nostalgic, how does future thinking display itself in his work? I think it does this by imagining Australia as a heterotopia rather than a utopia. Heterotopias are spaces in which Foucault locates a state of permanent disturbance and disruption:

> *Utopias* afford consolation: although they have no real locality there is nevertheless a fantastic, untroubled region in which they are able to unfold; ... *Heterotopias* are disturbing, probably because they secretly undermine language ... (1970, xviii)

In his essay "Of Other Spaces" (1967) Foucault suggests that unlike utopias, heterotopias are real sites. Society designates sites for work, for recreation, for rest, for education, for transportation, and so on. But Foucault is interested in 'counter-sites,' places positioned on the outside of cultural space, irrelevant to the practical functioning of everyday life: cemeteries, gardens, brothels, ships, holiday camps, or colonies. These are real places but absolutely different from other sites and from each other: not utopias but 'heterotopias,' displacements from normal social spaces. Heterotopias disrupt the order of things as they erupt in various kinds of disjunction, transition, even oxymoron and tautology. Colonial spaces are such counter sites, and they are real places that both disturb the literary imagination while allowing its utopian function free rein, because the various forms of dislocation, disjunction and transition they display ensure that they are deeply inflected with uncertain but luminous possibilities. In an obvious way a colonial heterotopia offers the opportunity to think about the future differently by releasing the connection with the 'normal social space' of the past. It is interesting to see how this persists in White's writing. The garden of *The Hanging Garden* is a heterotopic space, which seems to belong to nobody, exists outside normal social space, and lacks the function even of gardening, but it is a space in which Gil can detect the possibilities of the future in simple objects, which become objects of wonder, and signs of his own unfolding future.

If we can accept Foucault's assertion that utopias – placeless places – are imbued with the idea of the sacred, then heterotopias are characterised by a partial de-sanctification. The relationship between utopia, with its sacred imaginary, and heterotopia, with its sacred trace, is comprehensively embodied in the metaphor of the mirror:

> The mirror is, after all, a utopia, since it is a placeless place. In the mirror, I see myself there where I am not, in an unreal, virtual space that opens up behind the surface; ... But it is also a heterotopia in so far as the mirror does exist in reality, where it exerts a sort of counteraction on the position that I occupy ... The mirror functions as a heterotopia in this respect: it makes this place that I occupy at the moment when I look at myself in the glass at once absolutely real, connected with all the space that surrounds it, and absolutely unreal, since in order to be perceived it has to pass through this virtual point which is over there. (1967, 24)

This captures the metonymic relation Foucault is striving for in the apparent contrast between the 'placeless place' of the utopian, and the real, yet only partially desacralised, reflection of that utopia in the heterotopia. This partially desacralised space is perfect for the author's task of chasing down a postcolonial earthed sacred. It also captures the capacity of the author to see a place at once both absolutely real, connected with all the space that surrounds it, yet absolutely unreal in the sense that it occupies a space of pure potentiality. The particular efficacy of the mirror when thinking about the writer's engagement with colonial space is that heterotopia operates dialectically between the real and the unreal, the proximate and the possible, the uncanny and the *Heimlich*. The 'flaws' in the glass are a function of the continuous interaction of past and future – they are both there and not there, both appearance and prophecy. The postcolonial reading of Australia hinges on this dialectic, constantly engaging what we can understand as the consequences of colonisation. Reaching into the future the work first identifies the displacement, the unhousedness of Australian life but balances it with a sense of the possibility of home. The heterotopia is a space in which the utopian impulse can operate with impunity and continuity because its moral disturbances and social and spiritual disruptions will never finally allow the consolation of utopia.

Uncanniness: The *unheimlich*

There are many ways in which the colonial experience can be described as uncanny. But the colonial encounter with Australian space was almost fated to be an experience of the sublime, given the influence of eighteenth century philosophy and aesthetics on the representation of 'wild' places, and the experience of the uncanny that characterised much Australian cultural life. This was a different kind of sublime, a horizonal sublime that confirmed the colonial subject's out-of-placeness or *unheimlichkeit*. As Tom Radclyffe says in *Voss*: "Everyone is still afraid, or most of us, of this country, and will not say it. We are not yet possessed of understanding." (31)

There is a moment at the beginning of *The Tree of Man,* when Stan Parker begins to clear some land, which encapsulates completely the ambivalence of a settler society occupying this uncanny space.

> Then the man took the axe and struck at the side of a hairy tree, more to hear the sound than for any other reason. And the sound was cold and loud. The man struck at the tree, and struck, till several white chips had fallen. He looked at the scar in the side of the tree. The silence was immense. It was the first time anything like this had happened in this part of the bush. (TM 3)

This is an iconic moment. It sets the tone of the novel as an *opus* of Australian settlement. The moment is one of sound and destruction. Nothing like this had ever happened in the bush before. The novel goes on to engage the great myths of Australian existence: fire, flood, drought, struggle, settlement, the fencing of land as property and the subsequent identification of place as property. The silence of the bush is the sound of the uncanny, of Stan Parker's feeling of *unheimlichkeit* – not-at-homeness. It is a postcolonial moment in which the tension between the spirit of place and displacement become starkly revealed.

This attempt to reinvent Europe in colonial space has more ludicrous examples, such as Norbert Hare's attempt in the novel, *Riders in the Chariot* (1961) to reconstruct Xanadu in the Australian bush. Norbert's attempt to build his pleasure dome is an allegory of settlement, which makes his daughter Mary's ability to evade it all the more poignant.

> What he required, and did, in fact acquire, was an exquisite setting for his humours: the park of exotic, deciduous trees, the rose garden which his senses craved, pasture for the pedigree Jersey cows which would fill his silver jugs with cream, and stables for the horses which he drove himself with virtuosity. (RC 21)

Xanadu is an imperial folly, an attempt to impress on the unyielding landscape the civilised dignity of money, power and cultivation. In this respect it is an allegory of colonial settlement, one that is soon overthrown by the bush it attempts to subdue.

Stan Parker's land clearing and Norbert Hare's Xanadu are consequences of a vigorous 19th century racial discourse that saw the mission of Empire as the spread of the British race. In contrast, White the political historian captures the *unheimlich* nature of the enterprise by peopling his landscapes with its Indigenous inhabitants, while White the novelist captures it with an abundant imagery of displacement, in isolated houses, bleak suburbs, and dislocated people. One of the commonly recurring images is that of that supremely English flower, the rose. In *The Aunt's Story* a rose garden is planted on the South side of the wall because Mrs Goodman wanted one (20). But very soon Theodora walks in a garden of dead roses (26) a sign of the decay of the old and the unfortunate fact of the sun coming from the North. Hurtle Duffield brings Nance a bunch of roses that seem to intensify the pathos of their relationship: "The rosebuds drooping from her hands had the heads of strangled birds. 'They've died.' He forced his hoarse voice: 'Too much sun. They couldn't stand the heat.'" (VIV 240)

When Himmelfarb visits the Jewish family the Rosenbaums who have become the Rosetrees in Australia: "Had he been blind, he could have walked by holding on to ropes of roses." (RC 382) Roses emphasise the fact that Rosenbaums have, for all their protestations of being Australian, become English, a kind of double cultural cringe.

Indeed this doomed project to impress Europe on the Australian landscape is accompanied by a cultural cringe of people of a certain class trying to be English that occurs too often in the novels to enumerate. "I feel I am in *Europe,*" gushes Fanny Goodman when she moves into Audley. (AS 97) Whether it is Hurtle Duffield's parents' timidity in England, "apologising to the servants, which they never bothered to do at home," (VIV 135) or Olivia Davenport when inviting Hurtle to a *soiree*, pronouncing 'Europe' as though "tasting her own party for a flavour she feared it might lack" (VIV 309) the desire and timidity of the upper classes is patent. But the poverty of spirit of Sarsaparilla is also best explained by its inability to impress itself on the Australian earth. Suburbs dumped on the bush, the roads petering out "first in dust, then in paddock, with dollops of cow manure ... and the brittle spires of seeded thistles" (SM 83) seem to inject into their inhabitants the anxiety of their heterotopic displacement, the superficiality and inauthenticity of their presence on the land. But they are also morally and spiritually enclosed spaces in which difference is a scandal.

But for all this English pretension and suburban bleakness, which White seems to have understood very well, his most resonant example of imperial arrogance reasserting itself on the *tabula rasa* of Australian soil is a German explorer. Voss is a complex, arrogant, self-possessed and unlovable character that represents an overweening European pretension, a belief that the surfaces of the earth exist for the purpose of personal fulfilment, even transcendence. As well as a symbol of imperial arrogance and dominance, he is a symbol of the vast unmapped territory of human pride. "The map?" repeated the German, "I will first make it ..." (V 26) But, Le Mesurier observes:

In this disturbing country ... it is possible more easily to discard the inessential and to attempt the infinite. You will burn up most likely, you will have the flesh torn from your bones, you will be tortured probably in many horrible and primitive ways, but you will realize that genius of which you sometimes suspect you are possessed (V 38-9)

For Voss, Australia remains the vast abstraction of its landscape, the canvas for his story of failed self-deification, the horizonal sublime of early settlement and exploration: "If he were to leave that name on the land ... it would be rather on some desert place, a perfect abstraction that would arouse no feeling of tenderness in posterity." (V 45)

Heimat

Voss signifies the uncanny in the sense that not only is he not-at-home in this landscape but he also has no intention of making it home. The utopian impulse in White begins by recognising the uncanniness, but conceiving colonial space as promising something beyond the uncanny, for it is absolutely real in its resistance to settlement, but unreal in the potential it offers – its horizon of possibility. This promises something even beyond a mundane sense of belonging – a radical sense of the possibility of home that Ernst Bloch calls *Heimat*.

For Bloch, art and literature have a significant utopian function because their *raison d'être* is the imaging of a different world – what he calls its "anticipatory illumination." The anticipatory illumination is the revelation of the "possibilities for rearranging social and political relations to produce *Heimat*, Bloch's word for the *home* that we have all sensed but have never experienced or known "It is *Heimat* as utopia ... that determines the truth content of a work of art." (Zipes 1989, xxxiii) *Heimat* becomes the promise in post-colonial writing that replaces the promise of nation. It may lie in the *future* but the promise of *heimat* transforms the present. But *Heimat* is a very contentious term cunningly and ironically deployed by Bloch. *The Principle of Hope* was written between 1938 and 1947 during the time when the Nazis were deploying the term to identify Germany as an Aryan homeland. *Heimat* is a term dense with historical controversy and cultural baggage, a fact of which the Jewish Marxist philosopher, Ernst Bloch, was certainly aware.

Nothing could better describe White's relationship with the Australia conceived in his writing than the clash between the experience of Sarsaparilla and the idea of "the home we have sensed but never experienced or known." White's home was in his writing. He was as ambivalent about Australia as any of the restless characters in the work of Henry Handel Richardson or of Martin Boyd. But the *heimat* conceived as a constant potentiality is intimated in the writing through two constantly interwoven trajectories: movement and proximity, becoming and being, the play of different selves and the luminosity of objects. For it is absolutely real in its resistance to settlement, but unreal in the potential it offers – its horizon of possibility. This promises something even beyond a mundane sense of belonging – a radical sense of the possibility of home that Ernst Bloch calls *Heimat*.

Becoming

Continual movement, continual becoming is itself the discovery of self in the many selves.

> The ultimate spiritual union is probably as impossible to achieve as the perfect work of art or the unflawed human relationship. In matters of faith, art, and love I have had to reconcile myself to starting again where I began. (White 1981, 74)

To matters of art, faith and love we might add the matter of finding a spiritual home. Australia, which had been the subject of idealisation and disdain, is finally the place of much 'starting again' in the movement towards the home that had never been experienced. The movement of becoming may not always be an arc of growth and fulfilment. Theodora Goodman, after ruining a potential engagement by displaying greater skills in marksmanship than her suitor Frank, grieves over the little hawk she had so deliberately shot; "I was wrong, she said, but I shall continue to destroy myself right down to the last of my several lives." (AS 73-4) But in the main the priority of 'becoming' over 'being' is a movement towards *heimat,* which is confirmed in one of the most quoted passages in White's work, Le Mesurier's epiphany:

> In the beginning I used to imagine that if I were to succeed in describing with accuracy something this little cone of light with the blurry edges, for instance, or this common pannikin, then I would be expressing all truth. But I could not. My whole life had been a failure, lived at a most humiliating level, always purposeless, frequently degrading. Until I became aware of my power. The mystery of life is not solved by success, which is an end in itself, but in failure, in perpetual struggle, in becoming. (V 289)

In the *horizonality* of the simplest objects, like a cone of light, and the implications of that horizonality for human life, the need for continual becoming is manifest. The writer engages with the journey towards *heimat,* over and over again, for it is in the writing that the utopian potentiality of the imagination is most fully realised. But writing also reveals that the journey towards potentiality can never be finally completed, any more than Le Mesurier's desire to describe at least one part of the world. It is the rough Brendan Boyle of Jildra who comes out with a surprisingly astute and even visionary perception about the processes of self-discovery:

> 'To peel down to the last layer,' he yawned. 'There is always another, and yet another, of more exquisite subtlety. Of course every man has his own obsession. Yours would be, it seems, to overcome distance, but in much the same way, of deeper layers, of irresistible disaster ... (V 179-80)

> There is possibly no better description of the relationship between utopianism, the constant peeling, and utopia, the elusive and non-existent essence.

The Proximate: The luminosity of tangible things

In a curious way, the insistence on becoming, while by definition offering a trajectory into the future, is something that constantly celebrates the Now, particularly if we see it as peeling down to the last layer, and in this way *Heimat* is the home that is constantly anticipated in the ordinary, the promise of the future embedded in the present. But more than this, such potentiality is embedded in ordinary objects, because the presence of such objects offers a form of knowledge beyond interpretation:

> As all oblivious objects become known, and with the same nostalgia, the tin cup, for instance, standing in the unswept crumbs on the surface of your own table. Nothing is more desirable than this simplicity. (TM 17)

The proximate, earthed, tangible, objectified 'Now,' and particularly the familiar mundane objects of everyday life, are imbued with the future, and this explains White's celebration of the indefinable in mundane objects, and why he invests in them the capacity to take us beyond the past and beyond the uncanny.

White here anticipates some contemporary theories of utopia. For Jean Luc Nancy, who wants to move away from some of the transcendental aspects of utopian theory, utopia needs now to be thought as an 'evidence of finitude.

> Utopia is, in and of itself, an evidence of finitude: but not finitude understood as simple limitation; on the contrary, of finitude insofar as the finite being exists precisely at its own limit; where it opens itself to the unlimited. (2012, 7)

By this he means that utopia exists where the plural, worldly and embodied existence of beings, existing at their limits, is exposed to the unlimited, to a (material or actual) infinite or to an irreducible excess over being. Nancy is talking about conscious beings but for the novelist this is where the Presence of mundane objects becomes so important. Utopia is this excess over world, thought, sense and meaning. By existing so patently at their own limits mundane objects touch an untranslatable excess, excess that for White may best be captured by art or music. This is where being meets becoming: the finite representation of utopia is always deferred, always impossible and it is by virtue of this impossibility that utopia – experienced as becoming rather than finitude – takes shape. *Heimat* is constantly anticipated in the ordinary, in the horizonality of the present. This utopian dimension is, however, despite its apparently transcendental nature, constantly set in a social and political perception of an ambivalent and paradoxical society growing towards its future. What makes it amenable to a postcolonial reading is the absolute focus on the promise of the here and now.

The utopian horizonality of objects is directly related to the human, and by implication, the social world, in the trajectory of becoming, which White depicts as a location at the centre of expanding circles of reality. This location elaborates the mysterious relationship between the movement of becoming and the stasis of the proximate. In the spring where Judd washes the lamb's blood off his hands, "Circles expanding on the precious water made it seem possible that this was the centre of the earth." (V 159) It is people's place at the centre of this circle, the position of their ambiguous and unperceived bodies that enables them to see the infinitely extending horizon of meaning around perceived objects. Stan Parker's realisation that he is sitting at the heart of this infinity allows him to see the transcendence of objects: "All was circumference to the centre and beyond that the Worlds of other circles." (TM 494) But he is "the centre of it," and sees the ultimate circle, that of God Himself, as intimated in the gob of spittle. When Elizabeth Hunter looks in her mirror she sees her *Doppelganger*, "aged, dishevelled, ravaged, eyes strained by staring inward, in the direction of a horizon which still had to be revealed." (ES 205) The mirror shows her body as the pivot of the world, while during the storm she is "the flaw at the centre of a jewel of light," (ES 424) and for the same reasons Arthur sees that the "flaw," the "knot" at the centre of his marble, is the "whole point." The mandala shows that we are "surrounded" by perfection in the sense that it remains the ultimate horizon of our existence, and while wholeness is unenclosable by consciousness, we "obtain" infinity when we become aware of its intimation in ordinary experience.

Tables and Chairs

This intimation of ordinary experience, the promise of the here and now, is nowhere more often repeated than in tables and chairs. Glimpses are given to even the most unlikely people, like the gormless Willie Pringle in *Voss* for whom "all truths were locked. So he would look at the heartbreaking beauty and simplicity of a common table or kitchen chair, and realise that in some most important sense their entities would continue to elude him unless he could escape from the prison of his own skull." (V 64)

Indeed, where roses symbolise the uncanny and out of place, tables and chairs come to symbolise access to *heimat* in its infinite, sacred potential. White's sense of the presence of the sacred in material things is symbolized in Himmelfarb's statement to his wife in *Riders in the Chariot* when she asks what ordinary people like her can hold in their minds to receive revelation:

> This table, he replied, touching it gently.
> 'Oh, Mordecai' she whispered, "I am afraid. Tables and chairs will not stand up and save us.'
> God will,' he answered. 'God is in this table.' (RC 141-2)

One of the reasons tables and chairs will save us is their absolute irreducibility. Irreducibility is not essence, neither is it form – many forms of table exist. Rather it is the irreducibility of everyday simplicity, its perfect marriage of form and function that offers certainty – the certainty of the proximate. It is not just 'tableness' to which he is referring, but *this* table. This is the key to what we might call the search for the earthed sacred in White. But such objects are also the key to the utopian in White because they are so powerfully horizonal.

Like Himmelfarb, Hurtle Duffield comes to see the most resonant access to the infinite in the most clearly finite. Thinking of his work later in life he thinks that "he had conceived in paint no more than fragments of the whole … all these and more fused into one – not to be avoided – vision of GOD" but "Mightn't the Whole have been formally contained from the beginning in this square-legged, scrubbed-down, honest-to-God, but lacerated table?" (VIV

385) Talking with Mothersole on the ferry after Hero's death, Hurtle chooses to unburden himself to a complete stranger:

> What could be more honest? I'm not talking about the gimcrack: there's dishonest furniture, just as there are dishonest human beings. But take an honest-to-God kitchen table, a kitchen chair. What could be more real? I've had immense difficulty reaching the core of reality, in I don't know how many attempts, but I think I might have done it at last. (VIV 420)

At the Retrospective of his life's work held at the gallery Hurtle overhears some pretentious snob parroting glib clichés of the numinous dimension of his paintings: "'Numen' is the word I've been trying to remember all the evenin. Not apropos. I'll probably die a sceptic." (605) His thoughts run wild:

> O numinous occasion sighted in distorting mirrors of variable treachery! Now that the trap was closing in on him what he longed for was a room of reasonable proportions furnished with a table and chair ... yet the tables and chairs now appeared the most honest works he had ever conceived, and probably for that reason, the most nearly numinous. (VIV 605)

In this way, utopia becomes an 'outside' place that operates at the heart of the real, it is a non-place of meaning, ground, or of time and place that always opens within, and always has the potential to interrupt, any and all experience of a situated, historical world. Here I think is the key to White's celebration of the luminous possibility of objects. They intimate that Presence from which the non-place of utopia is constantly projected.

Mere Words: The Prison House of language

So the horizon that touches all things at their limit, a horizon most obvious in the luminosity of objects, brings together a number of concerns in the writing: the insistence on becoming; the always present utopian potential of life; the sacredness of that potential; and the cultural implications of that potential. But paradoxically the novelist is adamant that this horizonality is resistant to language. When Norbert Hare goads Mary about being one of the *illuminati* she claims not to understand such things: "But the truth is what I understand. Not in words. I have not the gift for words. But know." (RC 39) The question of belief posed by Mrs Jolley brings Mary closest to an expression of that sacred:

> 'I believe. I cannot tell what I believe in, any more than what I am. It is too much. I have no proper gift. Of words, I mean. Oh yes I believe! I believe in what I see, and what I cannot see. I believe in a thunderstorm, and wet grass, and patches of light, and stillness. There is such a variety of good.

"Words," thinks Judd, "were not the servants of life, but life, rather was the slave of words." (V 203) The inadequacy of words is one of the most persistent and most paradoxical aspects of White's writing. Pinning his faith on music and art as the access to the ineffable, the novelist nevertheless continues to reveal in words the aspiration and the journey of his characters towards that experience of the sacred illuminated in the ordinary. Roland Barthes speaks of the utopia of the text: for him all text is drawing and his choice to write in fragments is an attempt to break out of the prison house of language. This suggests something of White's ambivalence about words, and the way in which his work is punctuated by bursts of visual and musical revelation. But it also explains something of the extraordinarily evocative nature of his literary language.

Mrs Godbold's love is revealed in action rather than words, and her epiphany occurs in music, when, listening to organ music in the deserted church

> The organ lashed together the bars of music until there was a whole shimmering scaffold of sound. And always the golden ladders rose, extended and extended, as if to reach the window of a fire. But there was no fire, only bliss, surging and rising, as she herself climbed upon the heavenly scaffolding and placed still other ladders, to reach higher ... (RC 236)

Alf Dubbo comes closest to revealing what words cannot express – the presence of the sacred captured in pure colour: "His secret self was singing at last in great bursts ... in his innermost mind his hands continued to praise with the colours of which he was capable. (RC 397)

When Arthur finds in the encyclopaedia that "The Mandala is the symbol of totality" (SM 238) and realises the symbolic power of his marble, he asks his father about the meaning of 'totality.' At his father's clumsy attempts to explain, "Arthur realised that Dad would never know, any more than Waldo. It was himself, who was, and would remain, the keeper of mandalas, who must guess their final secret through touch and light." (SM 240) And for Arthur it is the dance he dances for Mrs Poulter rather than any words that reveals him as the agent of redemption:

> Till in the centre of their mandala he danced the passion of all their lives, the blood running out of the backs of his hands, water out of the hole in his ribs. His mouth was a silent hole, because no sound was needed to explain. (SM 267)

White's apparently paradoxical lack of faith in words is perhaps not as strange as it seems. How often have we heard the statement, in everyday encounters: 'I *know* what I mean but I can't find the words'? What kind of knowledge could this be? What kind of experience is that 'intention' to mean something which can only be recognised as 'what I intended to say' *after* the words have been found? This is precisely the relationship between language and the possible for which White is striving, and he has a number of respectable philosophical antecedents in this. For Merleau Ponty: "Language bears the meaning of thought as a footprint signifies the effort and movement of a body." (1964, 41) For Gadamer, language 'has something speculative about it'

> as the realisation of meaning, as the event of speech, of communication, of understanding. Such a realisation is speculative, in that the finite possibilities of the word are oriented towards the sense intended, as towards the infinite. (1975, 426)

But in addition to this, in the colonial context, language is more than speculative; it is inherited baggage loaded with a history. Indeed Ellen Gluyas is colonised by language and writing, once she is educated and obliged to keep a journal. (FL 47) "Books held more for Austin Roxburgh than the life around him." (FL 54) The colonising language comes with a cultural genealogy that continually defers *Heimat* when approached in language for which it is inadequate. This helps us to understand that despite his professed distrust for words White's own language engages a postcolonial process of transformation as he wrestles with its uncanniness and its cultural baggage. This uncanny inadequacy of language and the capacity of other forms of art to apprehend the horizonality of objects, is, I would suggest, both utopian and in the sense of pushing into an unknown future, a postcolonial reverence for the here-and-now over the past.

In fact all simple tangible objects point somewhere just beyond reach. The idea of Mallebranch that "prayer is absolute, unmixed attention" captures perfectly the capacity of objects to intimate the sacred. Yet even at his most apparently transcendental White is most committed to the material. For while ordinary things are mystical in their promise, they confirm, in their here-and-now-ness the possibility of throwing off the shackles of cultural inheritance.

The power White sees in material things, and indeed in the *painting* of such objects is reminiscent of Heidegger in *Poetry, Language, Thought* (1971) when he talks about Van Gogh's painting of peasant shoes. Van Gogh's shoes are not 'mere' shoes but a manifestation 'of the peasant world which permeates the soul of their visibility'. They also reveal the mode of unhiddenness, the way in which 'truth' embodies itself in things, (1971, 33-7) although the shoes in the painting have nothing around them to which they might belong, not even clods of soil to give a hint to their use. They are provided with no specific context, only undefined space. And yet, as Heidegger states, "from the dark opening of the worn insides of the shoes the toilsome tread of the worker stares forth. " For all their apparent isolation, the shoes, rather than 'embodying' an essence of meaning, suggest the horizon, suggest the contexts in which they have meaning. The 'accumulated tenacity of the wearer's slow trudge through the fields swept by a raw wind' constitutes the meaning of the shoes. For in the shoes vibrates the silent call of the earth, its quiet gift of the ripening grain and its unexplained self-refusal in the fallow desolation of the wintry field … the wordless joy of having once more withstood want, the trembling before the impending childbed and shivering at the surrounding menace of death. (1971, 34)

Heidegger's apprehension of the meaning of the shoes, brings to sight that which is yet concealed. His poetic response to the painting is a reaching out beyond the object to its world, a widening of the access to meaning that is provided by the object itself. For Heidegger as for White the painting of such simple objects invests them with a Presence that is horizontal and limitless, but which can be simply known. Like Mary Hare, who "hasn't the gift of words, but knows". As does Amy Parker when she sees Mr Gage's painting of a 'blasphemous' Christ, in the form of a fettler killed beside railway tracks. She "looked at the picture of Christ, and *knew* about It (TM 289) As Philip Rothko famously said, 'The subject of the painting is the painting', or as Hurtle Duffield says when asked what his paintings mean: 'If you could put it in words, I wouldn't want to paint' (VIV 204) which is a direct quote from Matisse.

When Alf Dubbo reveals the painting of the furnace, with the Angel of the Lord,

> He could at least admire the feathery texture of the angel's wings as a problem overcome, while forgetting that a little boy on a molten morning had held a live cockatoo in his hands, and opened its feathers to look at their roots, and become involved in a mystery of down. Later perhaps, falling asleep, or waking, it might occur to the man how he had understood to render the essence of divinity. (RC 404)

The angel's wings and the cockatoo feathers are of the same order of mystery, yet the one is utterly material, utterly present. And he realises that the very material mystery of the cockatoo's feathers is the *essence* of divinity. Nothing could be more located, more corporeal, yet nothing more elusive than this moment. The utopian excess of the tangible, material feathers is the same order of mystery as Le Mesurier's candle flame. This utopian excess of ordinary things comes to us from the future, which is why the trajectory of continual becoming is intimately involved with the luminosity of that material presence.

Art is deeply utopian for White because it is suffused with a sense of the sacred. In fact for him it embodies the sacred because it is unmatched in providing the experience of Presence, which is a constant movement towards the meaning that never arrives, an apprehension beyond meaning. As the Nicholson epigraph to *The Vivisector* has it: "As I see it painting and religious experience are the same thing, and what we are all searching for is the understanding and realisation of infinity." Art touches the sacred not only because it touches the infinite, but because the created text itself *comes to us from the future*. It comes from the future and keeps coming because its final meaning never arrives. Interpretation attempts to lock meaning into the present but for White it was the new and the ordinary that offers Presence, as the epigraph to *The Solid Mandala* suggests, "There is another world, but it is in this one". The capacity to simply *know* without saying explains the young Hurtle Duffield's relationship with the chandelier, "which he can touch but which receives him as into another world of silence and beauty." (VIV 32) Experiencing wonder in the presence of this object stimulates his vocation as an artist.

Ernst Bloch's belief that art and literature are perfectly poised to anticipate a utopian future appears to be shared deeply by Patrick White. Despite the lower place he gives to words his writing and his wrestling with language manages to intimate that which he sees most powerfully in art and music: the fact that the infinite touches the tangible at the very limit, the very insistence of its finitude. This is why his journey away from the uncanny displacement of a settler culture towards *heimat* – the home we have sensed but not yet experienced – is a constant dialogue between becoming and being, horizon and proximity. This is why the future is a presence offered in the very luminosity of objects. Ultimately the complex fabric of his work reveals the heterotopic space of Australia hovering on the edge of a future that lies at the very heart of the real.

Works Cited

Bloch, Ernst. 1988. *The Utopian Function of Art and Literature: Selected Essays.*Trans. Jack Zipes and Frank Mecklenburg. Minneapolis: University of Minnesota Press.
During, Simon. 1996. *Patrick White.* Melbourne: Oxford University Press.
Foucault, Michel. 1967. "Of Other Spaces," *Diacritics* 16 (Spring 1986): 22-27.
—. 1970. *The Order of Things: an Archeology of the Human Sciences.* London: Tavistock.
Gadamer, Hans Georg. 1975. *Truth and Method.* Ed. Garrett Barden and John Cumming. New York: Seabury Press.
Heidegger, Martin. 1971. *Poetry, Language, Thought.* Trans. Albert Hofstadter. New York: Harper & Row.
Merleau-Ponty, Maurice. 1964. *Signs.* Trans. (and introd).Richard McCleary. Evanston: Northwestern University Press.
Nancy, Jean Luc. 2012. "In Place of Utopia," Patricia Vieira and Michael Marder ed. *Existential Utopia: New Perspectives on Utopian Thought.* New York: Continuum: 3-11.
White, Patrick. 1948. *The Aunt's Story.* London: Eyre and Spottiswoode.
—. 1956. *The Tree of Man.* London: Eyre and Spottiswoode.
—. 1957. *Voss,* London: Eyre and Spottiswoode.
—. 1961. *Riders in the Chariot.* London: Eyre and Spottiswoode.
—. 1966. *The Solid Mandala.* London: Eyre and Spottiswoode.
—. 1970. *The Vivisector.* London: Jonathan Cape.
—. 1973. *The Eye of the Storm.* London: Jonathan Cape.
—. 1976. *A Fringe of Leaves.* London: Jonathan Cape.
—. 1979. *The Twyborn Affair.* London: Jonathan Cape.
—. 1981. *Flaws in the Glass.* London: Jonathan Cape.
—. 2012. *The Hanging Garden.* Sydney: Knopf.
Zipes, Jack. 1988. "Introduction: Toward a Realization of Anticipatory Illumination," *The Utopian Function of Art and Literature: Selected Essays*, Ernst Bloch, trans. Jack Zipes and Frank Mecklenburg. Minneapolis: University of Minnesota Press.

Chapter Three

"Splintering and Coalescing": Language and the Sacred in Patrick White's Novels

Lyn McCredden
Deakin University

In the years directly after World War Two, novelist Patrick White confronted a series of thresholds. Each one would take him further into his vocation as a writer of astounding, dense, haunting novels. The young Patrick White did not, of course, know this at the time. He first needed to cross the world, returning from his beloved London to become an Australian again. He had to begin writing about Australia, about being Australian, but not just this. He began to seek ways of writing about how meaning is made, in Australia and beyond; and how meaning is made alone, and in community. This struggle to make and unmake meaning, it will be argued, is a languaged, sacred struggle.

Critic James Clements historicises this quest for meaning in sacred terms, in *Mysticism and the Mid-Century Novel*. Clements' work places White in international and historical contexts, offering detailed readings of White alongside other mid-twentieth century novelists: Iris Murdoch, Saul Bellow and William Golding. Clements describes these authors, as "mystical" in diverse ways, and as drawing on

> Kataphasis … or … 'up-speaking': a technique of pushing language to its breaking point, utilizing its inherent ambiguity and aporia as a generator of unresolving meaning. Kataphatic techniques include the use of over- determined symbols, an emphasis on the

non-signifying elements of language (musicality, prosody, ontology) the adoption of cabbalistic and anagogic interpretive techniques ... the possibility of endless interpretation. (Clements 2011, 22-3)

This essay will ask: are Patrick White's novels constantly alert to the *limits of language*, to its failure, finally, to capture the sacred, the infinite, or the other? In this, White would be aligned to the negative theological tradition. At stake in Clements' definition of mysticism is the nature and status of language and especially of literary language. We can also approach the question of language and what it can achieve a little differently, asking whether literary language in White's novels can be more positively *generative*, pointing to, but potentially also embodying the power of the sacred, in its refusal to settle for the known, the fixed, or the received and constructing new and restless processes of meaning-making which point to existence beyond signification? This essay will argue that we don't have to choose between these different approaches to language, because White practises both the negative and the generative. In fact, Patrick White's life-long search to find ways to imagine meaning through and beyond the written word is indeed a sacred journey where no single mode of using language, no single understanding will be sufficient. It will be argued that the restless glimpses, the trials of language, make up White's corpus of "unresolving meaning."(Clements 2011, 22)

For Clements, the novelists as well as the theologians, the critics and the philosophers of the mid-twentieth century who inform White's work each considers

> the process of destabilizing forms of knowledge in order to accommodate the Other (seeing this approach as being) at the root of *ethical* engagement, and, for some, the very foundation of the literary. It is at the limits of language – where words necessarily exist but are pushed to breaking point – where we can encounter (without encompassing) the Other as other, without reducing or destroying it through its appropriation within common language. (2011, 24)

The distinction between literary and common language is a deeply suspect one arguably, especially in White's work. To see how White seeks to comprehend the other, or the Other, it will be necessary to understand just how earthed, earthy, ordinary, but also evanescent are his verbal intimations of sacredness.

Clements focuses on the conjunctions between the ethical, the literary and what he calls mystical – what this essay will call sacred discourses. Drawing on Levinas, he enlarges the scope of his argument, preparing for his category of "mysticism" by claiming that it is:

> … that which eludes our finite understanding, that provides our desire to engage in the world; if our lives were comprised only of understandable things, we would have few qualms in tucking it away, a puzzle solved. A work of literature, therefore, can contain – or, better, radiate – things that transcend its finite content, as there are forms of knowing that will never sit as still as 'knowledge.' (2011, 19)

From a certain angle, these words drop like balm into political and lived environments whose catch cries are shaped increasingly by economics, use value, employability and solely utilitarian knowledge. The argument this essay will pursue is that knowledge is destabilising in Patrick White's fictions not because it sets up such polarisations as sacred and material, or such categories as stable and unstable knowledge, but because such polarisations are challenged and sometimes, momentarily, dissolved in White's ongoing, languaged *struggle,* his wrestling with the sacred enmeshed in palpable, earthed ordinariness. White wrote of his career as a writer: "I do think composers and musicians come closer to God, also some painters; it is the writer who deals in stubborn, colourless words who is always stumbling and falling." (Qtd. in Marr 1994, 410) Here is the struggle with and of language which we witness in White: his struggle for meaning, a grappling which seeks to comprehend and even *equate* the most common, material, fleshed, earthed, embodied, languaged and abject experiences with the struggle for the sacred.

Clements reminds us of both Jewish and Christian concepts which relate the material and the spiritual: "… the Torah is not only the word, but the flesh of God, just as Christians held that Jesus, the physical manifestation of God, was also the Word of God." (2011, 114) The Christian notion of the Incarnation deeply informs, for example, White's sacred fools – Mary Hare, Mrs Godbold, Arthur Brown and even Eadith Twyborn. In very different ways it also informs his ego-driven, flawed, sometimes monstrous, but always magnificent characters – Hurtle Duffield, Voss, and Elizabeth Hunter. Incarnation – the simultaneity of being earthed and beyond, of being in language and hailed from beyond it - informs White's sense of material, and often abject being. White's struggle to represent or reach an *earthed sacred* might be examined specifically through the following four aspects, each of which has a long discursive history in relation to discourses of the sacred: abjection, violence, egoism, and the ecstatic.

However, it is important to establish from the outset that in so many of the novels there is a *compounding or interlacing* of these four aspects; sometimes one or the other is emphasised, but at his most startling and original, White conjoins them as his characters and his readers are driven through the rigours of his language, to grasp – even if only momentarily and awkwardly – the processes of sacred meaning-making and value. This stands as the first definition or proposition about the sacred: that the pursuit of the sacred is a recurrent human desire for meaning and value, a searching that is never finally satisfied. While some critics might attribute such a desire to White's *modernist* metaphysics, to reduce his writing in this way is to be blind to similar kinds of desires for sacred meaning, which have operated across history and across diverse cultures.

"All Outcasts, Goats and Aboriginals": Abjection and the Sacred

In *Riders in the Chariot* (1961) we encounter abjection as the place of the sacred. Abjection encompasses the boy Alf Dubbo as he flees the sexual abuse of his religious minder, wandering by the "lifestream of all outcasts, goats and aboriginals." (351) Alf fossicks through the rubbish-dump, where "true selves" (378) might be found. In searching, he finds "metho love" and the "livid jags" of sex as he and the whores "danced together on the squeaky bed." (361) The discourses of the sacred, the abject, and the violent interpenetrate here, often comically, as in White's aural pun "metho", reminding us of Mrs. Rosetree's "metho" religion, as she desperately hides her Jewish origins, clinging to the promises of her new, respectable Methodism in the Australian suburbs.

The abject underbelly of the suburbs is, of course, White's characteristic scene. Felicity, in *The Night the Prowler* tunnels through the veneers and proprieties of suburban life, free falling ferociously until at the end of the story she reaches the derelict house from which the fetid smell of mould emanated:

> she looked inside (and what she saw) took her breath away at first. Other smells began to reach her, from rags, sacking, finally, she realized, as she grappled with the tortoiseshell gloom, aged human flesh. It might have been wiser to have resisted looking deeper; but she had to look.
>
> 'What are you doing there?' she asked as soon as she could stop herself feeling disgusted.
>
> 'Living. Or at any rate this is where I what they call live."
>
> She was so horrified that she went inside the house. (White 1974, 151)

Felicity's fall beyond the norms of suburbia brings her to a place of disgust and repulsion, figured as "aged human flesh", so often a symbol for the abject in White's novels. Driven inwardly to embrace the putridness of flesh and death, Felicity, holding the old man's hand as he dies, finally leaves the house with a dizzying realisation and acceptance of the journey of becoming she is on.

In *Flaws in the Glass*, White writes of a threshold moment he had himself experienced in December 1951:

> During what seemed like months of rain I was carrying a tray load of food to a wormy litter of pups down at the kennels when I slipped and fell on my back, dog dishes shooting in all directions I lay where I had fallen, half-blinded by rain, under a pale sky, cursing through watery lips a God in whom I did not believe. I

began laughing finally, at my own helplessness and hopelessness, in the mud and the stench from my filthy old oilskin.

It was the turning point. My disbelief appeared as farcical as my fall. At that moment I was truly humbled. (1981, 144)

This well-known narrative of an earthy, even abject episode in his life is revelatory in a number of ways. Not for White a choir of white-clad angels, nor a transcendent God. No Romanticising. Rather, a cursable God with a quirky sense of humour, his victim wallowing in the farmyard mud and the dog slops; revealing his or her existence in a moment of farce, and "an inkling" of presence. White puts the same intimation of the divine more brutally in the section called "Journeys" in *Flaws in the Glass*, narrating his travels, with Manoly Lascaris in Greece and their trip to the holy mountain, Olympus: "Any true Grecophile will understand when I say that the unsinkable condom and the smell of shit which precede the moment of illumination make it more rewarding when it happens." (157) Excrement, the abject body, and illumination are never far from each other in White's imagination.

It could be argued that White's novel *The Solid Mandala* (1966) is a hymn to the abject world. We first meet the Brown brothers as the two old ladies view them from the bus window:

'Look!' Mrs. Poulter almost shouted.

Mrs Dun was so shaken her upper plate was prised from her jaw and lay for a moment with its mate.

'What?' she protested …

'What we was talking about!' cried Mrs Poulter. 'The two men! The retired brothers!'

Then Mrs. Dun did resentfully notice the two old men, stumping, trudging, you couldn't have said tottering – or if so, it was only caused by their age and infirmities – along what passed for pavement between Barranugli and Sarsaparilla. The strange part was the old gentlemen rose up … she could almost smell those old men. The one in the stiff oil-skin, the other in yellowed herringbone, in each case almost to the ankle … she sensed the scabs, the cracks which wet towels had opened in their old men's skin. (SM. 19)

This is the introductory portrait of Arthur and Waldo Brown. Arthur was modeled as White tells us on his cousin Philip Garland, whose "childish wisdom" did not blossom in the way Arthur's did, but led to life in an asylum. Arthur Brown has a very different, vivid inner life constructed for him by White. He is given two names, and becomes an Australian, abject, "everyday purposes" Aaron; who is identified in Jewish scriptures as a High Priest of the Israelites and the brother of Moses. White uses the symbolic name Aaron, who is described in the book of Malachi 2:6 in this way: "True instruction was in his mouth and nothing false was found on his lips. He walked with me in peace and uprightness, and turned many from sin." and in Psalms 133: 2-3

> It is like precious oil poured on the head,
> running down on the beard,
> running down on Aaron's beard,
> down on the collar of his robe.
>
> It is as if the dew of Hermon
> were falling on Mount Zion
> For there the Lord bestows his blessing,
> even life forevermore.

This is spoken by the Shikhinah, the presence of the divine. The shikhinah that surrounds Arthur is manifested as *humility,* or utter lack of egotism. Arthur – the slow one, the shop assistant, the blurter and blunderer – turns out to be the compassionate visionary, while his Brother Waldo is frighteningly a version of White: the irritable writer, the arrogant scourge of suburbia, the cross-dresser; "… myself at my coldest and worst", White tells us. (1981, 147) But Waldo, unlike White, apprehends very little, and sinks into the deeper edges of abjection, including physical and spiritual self-loathing, and loathing of others, never achieving anything in language.

In what ways is abjection a condition, of sacredness? Arthur is acquainted with the abject, and through him a compassionate wisdom flows. His friends Dulcie and Leonard Saporta recognise him fleetingly as Aaron, the high priest, naming their child after him. In one of the closing scenes of the novel, the volatile, processual and restless nature of sacred longing is depicted in terms, which foreshadow those used by Julia Kristeva in *The Feminine and The Sacred*. Kristeva describes the sacred spatially, as "the borderline between nature and culture, the animalistic and the verbal, the sensible and the nameable." (Qtd. in Hansen 2012, 170) For Kristeva the sacred and the abject are deeply related. The sacred, she writes, "resides in that transition, in that passage and not in [the abject's] edges, lower (filth: pubic hair) or upper (the strict prohibition that veils or cuts off heads: the horror of monotheistic fundamentalism)." (Hansen 2012, 171.) "Neither the abject nor the Law in themselves, the sacred is the passage as a possibility of life with meaning." (Hansen 2012, 172)

This sense of the sacred permeates *The Solid Mandala*. In a poignant late scene in the novel, the now aged and derelict Arthur, once honoured as "High Priest" by Dulcie, stumbles on the Jewish Sabbath towards the Saporta's house in the park, after Waldo's death:

> Then, on a street corner, he found himself standing crying, for what, he had forgotten. Unless because it was getting dark too soon.
>
> That night he took the bus out to Dulcie's place, hoping he might find he had been invited.
>
> The house on the edge of the park increased in possibilities at night … Manoeuvring through the outer wall of shrubs, avoiding the webs of light both hung and spread to catch any such intruder, he succeeded in reaching a window, and in clinging to a rope of creepers …
>
> There he hung a while … The Saportas were preparing to dine, amongst their children and their children's children. Several shabbier relatives … were assisting at the ceremony. Only her beauty still aglow inside her revealed Dulcie in the old woman of fuzzy sideburns and locked joints … Leonard Saporta's skin was draped in greyish-yellow folds, though age had not lessened his conviction when he spoke.

'She stretcheth out her hand to the poor; yea, she putteth forth her hands to the needy.'

Arthur longed for Dulcie to put out her hand to him, while knowing she would not, she could not. (SM 308)

Where does sacredness reside here? It resides in the beauty, order and propriety of the Jewish household fulfilling its Sabbath rituals and also in the generosity of the family as they include their "shabbier relatives" at the table. But in taking Kristeva's lead, it is surely *in the gap or passage* or borderline between the solid institutions of family and religion, on the one hand, and the fact of the derelict and needy old man outside the window, to which White is pointing as the site or provocation of the sacred: Arthur as the sacrifice, the abject outsider, the forgotten one, the dirty old man outside the circle of light. Without family, without formal religion, but with extraordinary love and longing, Arthur is represented by White as a sacred figure. Or rather, it is not so much that the figure is sacred in itself, but it is in the longing he lives by, stumblingly, that meaning is sought. Rather than a sacred object, or figure, it is the motion, the restlessness and hope and innocence of Arthur's love - "hoping he might find he had been invited" – which provokes readers' considerations, their acknowledgement of incommensurability, and the need for compassion, here.

Heterogeneous Energies: Violence and the Sacred

There is also *violence* in Arthur's exclusion, and a critique of the institutions that so warmly include, even as they exclude, even as they require a scapegoat or sacrifice. For Georges Bataille in the aftermath of the violence of World War Two, and the glamour and horror of fascism, sacrifice and the sacred are ambivalently bound together. In an essay entitled "Violence and the Sacred: Archaic Connections, Contemporary Aporias, Profane Thresholds", philosopher Mara Magaroni writes of Bataille's work in ways which illuminate White's Arthur:

… Sacrifice in Bataille is a rift in the skin of the law, a bleeding wound exposing the raw violence underneath it. Unfolding, as it does, in that liminal zone where horror climaxes into uncontrollable joy and the painful loss of the self opens up a space for the self's ecstatic fusion with others, sacrifice takes on an ambivalent character, unleashing (within both the subject and the community) the force of heterogeneous energies that always threaten to burst through the frameworks set to contain them." (Margaroni 2012, 122)

White can be read alongside Bataille as equally ambivalent about the workings of institutional religion, *and* more broadly of the sacred and its "heterogeneous energies" (that which is inassimilable, incommensurable). When we read White's prose in *The Solid Mandala,* isn't this what we are seeing, this *passage* between abjection and the law as a highly ambivalent site, one which is so dependent upon readers for acknowledgement, for interpretation? As readers, we are being asked to inhabit the ground between, the passage where what is of moral and ontological value is glimpsed, or dismissed. This space – of violent taboo, *and* of understanding - is also embodied in the figure of Ellen Roxburgh in *A Fringe of Leaves* (1976), as she, the abject outsider, scrabbles to gobble the scraps of human flesh in the dying embers of the camp fire. White's rewriting of Christian communion, in the eating of the flesh that sustains Ellen, is certainly pushing kataphatic boundaries, with its use of over-determined symbols, and hunger for interpretation.

Violence and the sacred can be examined in two parts: the blood-letting sacrifice and martyrdom at the heart of so many religions and societies; and the question of morality – in opposing injustice, the courage to counter violence and scapegoating. Clements writes:

> Both Levinas and Merleau-Ponty understand the other as that which cannot be held still in the mind or in the eye of the perceiver. White's characters never gain absolute knowledge, except, perhaps, in death. The experienced world can never be fully known, but we can approach a perpetual knowing, or, more properly, an infinite and endless attention, made with the whole of our being, to obscurity and otherness. 'Motion,' as White wrote in *Riders in the Chariot,* 'became an expression of truth, the only true permanence.' (2011, 144)

In considering the relationship of violence and sacredness we are also in the realm of the Vivisector-God, where the questions explored in the late 1930s and 40s by Bataille and the *Collège de Sociologie* circle around violence, sacrifice and bloodletting, and are focused on rampant ego, and megalomania, for obvious and immediate historical reasons. We are also reminded of *Voss* (1957) with his violent, sacrificial and visionary ending; as well as the colonial violence of the Australian frontier in *A Fringe of Leaves* (1977) and the transformations of Ellen Roxburgh. The four Riders in the Chariot (1967) are also figures of sacrifice and violent exclusion. Margaroni writes that there are:

> … three works that continue to be seminal for our understanding of the function of the sacred; namely, Marcel Mauss and Henri Hubert's Sacrifice: Its Nature and Functions (1899), Emile Durkheim's The Elementary Forms of Religious Life (1912) and Sigmund Freud's Totem and Taboo (1913). [Are each informed by] … the assumption that the sacred and the social are inseparable. As Durkheim argues the sacred lies at the foundations of secular and non-secular societies alike. Even though the sacred origins of conventions, customs or practices (such as holidays, feasts, commemorations, etc.) may have become oblique in secular modernity, their role for the preservation and strengthening of the identity of distinct societies (their conscious projection of themselves as "communities") remains important. (2012, 115)

So, a central function informing the sacred has long been related to the expressed human need for *sacrifice or scapegoating*. We've already seen the possibility of reading the figure of Arthur, peering into the warmly lit dining room of the Jewish family, as an excluded, sacrificial figure. The ambivalence of sacred processes is captured further by René Girard, who wrote: "Having brought community into existence, the sacred brings about its own expulsion and withdraws from the scene, thereby releasing the community from its direct contact." (Qtd.in Margaroni 2012, 118) Girard also writes: "If the community comes too near the sacred it risks being devoured by it; if, on the other hand, the community drifts too far away, out of range of the sacred's therapeutic threats and warnings, the effects of its fecund presence are lost." (1972,

118) These Girardian concepts of sacred terror capture in a different way Kristeva's processual understanding of sacredness: "the sacred is the passage as a possibility of life with meaning." (Hansen 2012, 171) White's fiction attests to the vision that, opposed to passage and possibility, the fixities of religions, individuals as authorities, the norms, rules and habits of complacent societies all fail to understand the drive of this continual mobility.

Again and again in White's fiction it is the mobile, uneasy figure of the artist who is embraced and afflicted by the sacred – not as holy or authoritative without question – but as a pivotal, restless, flawed figure in this movement or passage of the sacred. In *Riders in the Chariot*, Alf Dubbo's abject "jewellery of wounds" is described as flowing from both blood and paint. (487). Hurtle Duffield in all his egotism, struggles in his quest for God through his paintings on his canvas. Both writing in the aftermath of World War Two, White and Bataille shared an understanding of the spiritual hunger of a bankrupt Western world. For philosopher Georges Bataille, "the spiritual and affective emptiness of liberal democracies … founded themselves on … the principle of homogeneity … the privileging of production, labor, utility, exchange, individuality, calculation, commensurability. (Qtd. Margaroni 2012, 122) White was often attuned to this attitude, especially when he returned after the war to live in Australia, arguably projecting so much of the emptiness and trauma of European society onto the Australia to which he had to re-accommodate himself. For Bataille, and I think very similarly for White, in the mid-twentieth century, the impetus towards the sacred had been lost; older forms of 'community' had been transformed by fascism into the glamour of exclusionary tribes. What had been sullied, for Bataille, in counterpoint to the fascist "principles of homogeneity" were: "… the principle of loss as excessive giving without return, non-productive expenditure, ecstatic fusion with another or others, the intimate experience of death, the communal ritual of sacrifice." (Sanderson 2002, 114)

White often locates these principles of "loss as excessive giving without return" in the eccentric, marginal, individual figures of his novels: Mary Hare, Mrs. Godbold, Arthur Brown. For this reason, amongst others, some critics have found White's work conservative, arguing that it addresses the individual only, and not the political and communal. It is true that the individual ego is what White focuses on in his fiction; but it is his treatment of the individual ego and his relentless questioning of it as the source of truth or knowing, which removes White from the merely individualistic.

"My Own Brash Godhead": The Ego and its Limits

> "For many years I felt no need for a faith either dialectical or mystical, believing as I did in my own brash godhead." (White 1981, 68)

When it comes to ego and its humbling, there are so many characters in White's oeuvre who are made to endure this trajectory: Voss in *Voss,* Hurtle Duffield in *The Vivisector,* Elizabeth Hunter in *The Eye of the Storm,* and even arguably Eudoxia in *The Twyborn Affair,* and the untransformed, contorted Mordecai in *Riders in the Chariot.* We meet again and again arrogant and self-willed characters who undergo transformations, as they are led towards an understanding beyond the self. As Voss early in his journey declares: "I detest humility … Is man so ignoble that he must lie in the dust, like worms?" (V 151) and he later writes to Laura, "I do not intend to stop short of the Throne for the pleasure of grovelling on lacerated knees." (217) But for Voss there is Laura Trevelyan who is impelled to counter his arrogance: "When man is truly humbled, when he has learnt that he is not God, then he is nearest to becoming so" (386) yet while she bandies these strange words with him, she is herself personally losing her faith.

There are also those White characters who embody a more purely humble, lowly, and sacred understanding: Stan in *The Tree of Man,* the "speckled and dappled" Mary Hare in *Riders in the Chariot,* and Mrs. Godbold's humble, suffering servitude. For critic Harris Williams:

> Mrs. Godbold and her ironing "in long, sad, steamy sweeps, singing as she did" [are] her own mode of worship (257). Her "skill in passing the iron over the long strips of fresh, fuming, glistening sheets" echoes the Chariot-language of strips of gleaming light and circling repetitive movement. This is the way she fulfils her

personal mission, which was set in motion after she failed to save her brother as a child being crushed by the wheels of the haywain ... realising that she cannot of her own will "hold off the weight of the entire world." (2009, 56-7)

In stark contrast to Mrs. Godbold's renunciation of will, perhaps the pre-eminent egotist of White's pantheon is the lean, focused Voss. His towering, self-confident will, his "knowing so much", is presented to us through the eyes of Laura and the men whom Voss commands. Nevertheless, he is also much more than this: a figure of pity, an outsider, an *Übermensch manqué*, and finally a man who bows to transformation. White – and many of his readers – is fascinated by this driven figure, even as we critique his angularity, his awkwardness, and his superiority. White presents a curiously ambivalent portrait of the explorer early in the novel. After Voss has paid his first visit to his patron, and has met Laura, he lies weary on a patch of grass back in town:

> An old, grey-headed fellow who happened to approach, in fustian and battered beaver, chewing slowly from a small, stale loaf, looked at the stranger, and held out a handful of bread.
>
> 'Here,' invited the oldish man, himself chewing and quite contented, 'stick this inside of you; then you will feel better.'
>
> 'But I have eaten,' said the German, turning on the man his interrupted eyes. 'Only recently I have eaten.'
>
> At once the German, beneath his tree, was racked by the fresh mortification to which he had submitted himself. ... Unseeing people walked the sandy earth, eating bread, or sat at meat in their houses of frail stone foundations, while the lean man, beneath his twisted tree, became familiar with each blade of withered grass at which he stared, event the joints in the body of the ant.
>
> Knowing so much, I shall know everything, he assured himself, (V 27)

Simultaneously, Voss is *Übermensch*, taking possession "by implicit right"; he is the figure of Christ beneath "his twisted tree" a martyr submitting to mortification; a hungry-looking recipient of charity; a phenomenologist; and sleeping child "breathing the sultry air of the new country." Both possessor – self-contained, in no need of charity and the leader – also possessed; knowing so much and yet still to have so much revealed to him.

White is by no means simply condemning this German figure of authority. Speaking German, and having travelled and lived in Germany for considerable periods before the war, White loved the country and the language. But he had also experienced Hitler and the consequences of megalomania. The ego of Voss is challenged and scattered, as his journey of exploration transforms him into more than he could ever know or dream. Whether we go so far as Laura and declare "He is there still, it is said, in the country, and always will be", the drama of Voss's journey is a sacred one, a learning of the limits of human knowing, a dismantling of his own "brash godhead".

"Skeins of Golden Honey": Ecstatic Fusion

The final aspect of the sacred to be considered is the ecstatic. The springs of the ecstatic in White's characters are seen to be both carnal and sacred: they are captured in the anguished love between Voss and Laura; in Arthur's dance, his giving away of his solid mandalas; in Mrs. Godbold's humble art of living, in Alf Dubbo's learning to paint the chariot, described in this way:

> From certain angles the canvas presented a reversal of the relationship between permanence and motion, as though the banks of a river were to begin to flow alongside its stationary waters. The effect pleased the painter, who had achieved more or less by accident what he had discovered years before while lying in the gutter. So he encouraged an illusion, which was also a truth. (RC 458)

Here again is that sense of the sacred as passage, as motion, through accident but also through art and discipline; through relationship but also through isolation. As has been argued in this essay, White's is a particular, earthed sacred, as vision, otherness, and material reality are bound together and unbound, in continuous motion. Clements amply illustrates that phenomenologist Merleau-

Ponty's and White's worldviews have much in common. Indeed, White's eclectic, experiential, earthed theology and Merleau-Ponty's phenomenological insistence that vision binds the 'sensing and the sensed' (Merleau-Ponty 1964, 162) are analogous systems, but operating, arguably, from different starting points. 'Truth,' Merleau-Ponty wrote, "does not 'inhabit' only the 'inner man,' or more accurately, there is no inner man, man is in the world, and only in the world does he know himself." (Qtd in Clements 2011, 133) It is not possible to think that for White there was "no inner man" (or woman). But for both philosopher and writer, the self and the world are in dynamic, restless, interpenetrative relation. Those characters that most powerfully seek out the sacredness of this relationship, often beyond the norms and values of society, are considered abject, or mad, or different in ways that threaten their identity, and their being. They are God's fools. But they are also the ones who experience ecstasy.

The Solid Mandala's Arthur Brown is White's pre-eminent fool, even his other self, declaring, "Words are not what make you see." (57) He is consequently described by others as 'mad' (208) and 'not all that bright' (16), as he intrudes with his vision and truth-telling into the assorted lives of his family and neighbours. Carrying around his little solid mandalas, in order to give them away, Arthur openly, innocently draws together his inner and outer worlds, following, in Bataille's words, "… the principle of loss as excessive giving without return, non-productive expenditure, ecstatic fusion with another or others, the intimate experience of death, the communal ritual of sacrifice."

So the young Arthur and his neighbour Mrs. Poulter go on their walks, and Arthur dances for his friend, for all those he loves, and for himself:

> Arthur Brown danced, beginning at the fourth corner, from which he would proceed by stages to the fourth, and beyond. He who was so large, so shambly, found movement coming to him on the hillside in the bay of blackberries … In Mrs. Poulter's corner he danced the rite of ripening pears, and little rootling suckling pigs. Skeins of golden honey were swinging and glittering from the child …

Till in the centre of their mandala he danced the passion of all their lives, the blood running out the backs of his hands, water out of the hole in his ribs. His mouth was a silent hole, ... His head hung. Facing her. (White 1966, 265-267)

This dance, with all its intricate movements, instinctual and precise, presents Arthur as a big, shambly buffoon of a Christ figure – embarrassing and clumsily open – but also, wise and giving without any hope of return and hopeful, in the presence of Mrs. Poulter, of giving her his gift. And she accepts it.

Again we see Kristeva's sense of the sacred as residing in transition, in the passage, in movement, in seeming incommensurabilities, in relationship. But in perhaps in more generative mode, Kristeva claims in *The Severed Head: Capital Visions* that artistic experience shows us that there "is a beyond [au-delà] of death ... there exists a resurrection." This is no other "than the life of the trace, the elegance of deed, the grace or brutality of colors, when they dare to display the threshold of the human psyche." (Kristeva 2012, 81)

White's characters are in constant transition – seen in the restless, continually remaking work of the writers, the artists, the bisexuals; as well as the homeless, displaced, exploring figures – strung between flesh and the consumption of the flesh. But equally, the individual ecstasy of Arthur, and many of White's characters, is summoned up as they are obedient to a form of attentiveness which reveals the gulf between self and other, but also their ways of a reaching out in empathy and a bringing together. This is what Arthur enacts pre-eminently in his dance. In a similar way, the novelist Patrick White brings incommensurate and awkward characters together, as with the characters in *Riders in the Chariot*. In the "... creative tension of their conjunction ... they have communicative power, the backbreaking power to suspend disbelief and pull the reader up the hill." (Harris Williams 2009, 65)

Hence, White's is anything but an atomised, solipsistic vision of inner lives. It is the greatness of his fiction that he shows us both the hunger of the individual and the possibilities for constructing sacred community. The work of the artist, for Kristeva and for White, offers a provisional structure ... within which [the reader] can take the jump over the void, confront death and its fear of death, rise above the violence of its affects and drives, awaken to the traps of the sacred, face the challenges of our post-terror age and, more importantly, laugh in recognition of its limits and the "crumbness" of its existence - with distanced pathos; in tender irony; out of pure, life-loving joy. (Margaroni 2012, 130)

The concluding passage of *Flaws in the Glass* exemplifies White's art; his attempts in language to "jump over the void", or at least to imagine it. The passage is indeed Romantic, but wryly, theatrically so, as White offers a "staging" of the narrative of his life, and more particularly his imagined death, in his early morning garden. It is a preview of his final moment as it might occur:

> If I were to stage the end I would set it on the upper terrace, not the one moment of any morning, but all that I have ever lived, splintering and coalescing, the washed pane of a false dawn, steamy draperies of Sydney summers, blaring hibiscus trumpets as well as their exhausted phalluses, ground mist tugging at the dry grass of the Centennial steppes, brass bands practicing against the heat, horses cantering in circles to an accompaniment of shouted commands, liquid calls of hidden birds, a flirt of finches, skittering of wrens, bulbuls plopping round the stone bath carved by Manoly in the early days at Castle Hill, as though in preparation for the Twyborn moment of grace. (1981, 256-7)

Along with the Romanticism of his early morning vision, White maintains a camp, stylish, theatrical eye, with his scene-setting on the upper terrace, sound effects, and alliterative "steamy draperies of Sydney summers". The passage is steeped in the wit and gracefulness of a creative mind which can experience the individual day in all its loved minutiae, but which also reaches out in verbal symbolic power, gathering up all those individual days – "all that I have ever lived" - capturing them in the alliterative, comic perfection of flirting finches, and in the synaesthetics of sight and sound. There is human love for the other who shared his life most intimately and there is also a turning to that final word: "grace". This word captures both the palpable world of colour and style and beauty, even as it hopes – shyly but firmly – to approach a further, final threshold, that "Twyborn moment of grace", an incarnational figuring of the sacred.

The powerful inner lives of Patrick White's characters move out restlessly, hopefully, eschewing authoritative knowing, seeking artistic possibilities in what this essay has been arguing is a sacred struggle. The sacred, in the works of Patrick White, is the impossible, constant longing to make meaning: an honouring of "all that I have ever lived, splintering and coalescing", a bowing to what is beyond human language and knowing.

Works Cited

Biblegateway, New International Version. http://www.biblegateway.com/ Accessed Jan. 25, 2013.

Clément, Catherine and Julia Kristeva. 2001. *The Feminine and the Sacred*. New York: Columbia University Press.

Clements, James. 2011. *Mysticism and the Mid-Century Novel*. London: Palgrave.

Girard, René. 1988. *Violence and the Sacred*. Trans. Patrick Gregory London: The Athlone Press.

Hansen, Sarah Kathryn, "Agamben, Kristeva and the Language of the Sacred," *Philosophy Today* 56.2 (May): 164-174.

Harris Williams, Meg. 2009. "The Evolution of Artistic Faith in Patrick White's *Riders in the Chariot*," *Ariel* 40.4: 47-68.

Kristeva, Julia. 2012. *The Severed Head: Capital Visions,* e-book, Accessed 28 January 2013.

Magaroni, Maria. 2012. "Violence and the Sacred: Archaic Connections, Contemporary Aporias, Profane Thresholds," *Philosophy Today* 56.2 (May): 134.

Marr, David. Ed. 1994. *Patrick White Letters*. Sydney: Random House.

Merleau-Ponty, Maurice. 1964. "Eye and Mind," The *Primacy of Perception,* ed. James Edie. trans. Carleton Dallery, Evanston: Northwestern University Press: 159-190.

Sanderson, Matthew. 2002. "Georges Bataille and Sacred Literature," *Kinesis* 29 (Fall): 114-121.

White, Patrick. 1957. *Voss.* Sydney: Eyre & Spottiswoode.

—. 1961. Riders in the Chariot. Ringwood, Vic.: Penguin.

—. 1966. *The Solid Mandala*. North Sydney: Random House.
—. 1970. *The Vivisector*. London: Jonathan Cape.
—. 1974. "The Night the Prowler," *The Cockatoos*, London: Jonathan Cape.
—. 1977. *A Fringe of Leaves*. Harmondsworth: Penguin.
—. 1979. *The Twyborn Affair.* London: Jonathan Cape.
—. 1981. *Flaws in the Glass: a Self-Portrait*. London: Vintage.

Chapter Four

Incorporating the Physical
Corporeality, Abjection and the Role
of Laura Trevelyan in *Voss*

Bridget Grogan
University of Johannesburg

This essay argues that corporeality forms the focus of a close narrative attention and is ultimately granted a redemptive significance in Patrick White's fiction. The argument therefore opposes the opinions of critics who, at the height of critical interest in White's writing during the 1970s and 1980s, identified White's attention to the body as a sign of radical disgust and thus of a defining dualism that posits the 'purity' of the disembodied spirit in relation to the 'pollution' of the material world. Brian Kiernan, for example, read White's writing as presenting "the soul imprisoned in the corrupting flesh." (1976, 462) For Ron Shepherd, White's novels suggested that the "physical world and bodily existence" is a "facade which must be pierced by the deeper mind in order to arrive at a better understanding." (1978, 29) A.P. Riemer claimed that White's writing is "dedicated to the notion that the body, the flesh and the senses are utterly worthless." (1980, 26)

A number of critics, however, have attested to the importance of the body in White's fiction. David Coad has contended that "[t]he body, the physical, the actual sphere, the taking on of flesh is an essential part of White's double vision of man – a vision based on the idea of the incarnation." (1993, 512) John Colmer would agree: "White's vision, like that of traditional Christianity, turns on the paradox that the spirit is incarnate in the flesh." (1978, 73) Cynthia vanden Driesen has regarded White's treatment of the body as successful in establishing "a sense of the deep relevance and value of the actual physical world to the truly religious spirit." (1978, 85) More recently, Lyn McCredden has identified White's "incarnational understanding", which involves the "sacred and material in constant exchange." (2010, 110) Bill Ashcroft, too, acknowledges the importance of the physical world to White, arguing that the "'unpresentability' of the sublime" is evident in the "reality of material things and the persistent inability of language to fully apprehend it." (2010, 96)

These observations may be read in conjunction with Andrew McCann's important reading, which explores White's "obsession with abjection" as informing an "ethical radicality" running throughout his fiction. (1997, 145) McCann, whose writing attests to the vitality that new theoretical approaches may bring to the interpretation of White's writing, focuses predominantly on White's derogation of normative society and his attention to the abject individuals that it casts aside. However, the interest in abjection McCann identifies is predominantly evident in White's treatment of subjectivity and the body.

White's writing questions the construction and maintenance of subjectivity according to the psychically defensive repudiation of the body that Julia Kristeva, has named 'abjection.' According to Kristeva, disgust or abjection ensures that aspects of the self, particularly corporeality and bodily products, are rejected during the consolidation of subjectivity and maintained as 'other'. Abjection, then, is a condition of horror in response to physicality, which, rendered abject, is defined as "radically separate [and] loathsome" (Kristeva 1982, 2), not because it is necessarily unclean but because it threatens the constructed borders maintaining a neat and foreclosed subjectivity. Physicality, however, is always a part of the self, and abjection exposes the subject's control over the disorderly elements of corporeality as provisional and threatened. The horrifying confrontation with what has been jettisoned in order to consolidate a stable sense of self within the symbolic order therefore involves confronting an aspect of the self which paradoxically threatens to undo the very notion of 'self'. Abject corporeality is, as Elizabeth Grosz maintains, the "unspoken of a stable speaking position, an abyss at the very borders of the subject's identity, a hole into which the subject may fall." (1990, 87)

White's writing consistently explores the construction of rational subjectivity according to the abjection of corporeality. His characters often "recoil" from the "helpless and unreliable body" (TM 114), imagining that they can "dispense with flesh." (V, 34) Quotations such as these explain why White has so often been read as a radical dualist, yet it is my contention that his fiction emphasises dualism in order to subvert it; it foregrounds the theme of abjection to promote the necessity of accepting the flesh. It is via the process of abjection that incorporeal concepts such as 'spirit' or 'mind' have arisen historically. White presents such disembodied notions of subjectivity as symptomatic of a damagingly narcissistic and inwardly orientated ontology that rejects the "flesh of relationships." (TM 124; V112)

Moreover, his writing promotes the conceptual rejection of the material world as a consequence of modernity. It therefore seeks to undermine the distinction between mind and body that has developed into the concept of the self-enclosed, superior 'mind' fundamental to post-Enlightenment thought. Although White's fiction acknowledges the necessary repudiation of corporeality in the consolidation of modern subjectivity, it strives for fleeting moments of redemptive unification in which 'disembodied' reason is subverted and subjectivity dissolves as it comes into accepting contact with its abjects.

Such moments are significant in White's fiction: his characters are defined by a "prolonged waiting for some moment of revelation or fulfilment" (COC 10); some "ultimate in experience" (FL 21) is eventually granted to them in the acknowledgement of corporeality. Submission to the flesh promotes the sought-after "state of pure living bliss" (ES 24) experienced in the dissolution of subjectivity. Thus, in *The Eye of the Storm*, Elizabeth Hunter's aged body is revered by her nurses and is the site of her own revelatory experiences. Ellen Roxburgh in *A Fringe of Leaves* literally re-incorporates the body when she ingests human flesh after stumbling upon an Aboriginal rite. And Stan Parker, at the conclusion of *The Tree of Man*, expresses his final celebration of corporeality when in the last moments of his life, he points to a gobbet of his saliva and pronounces it "God." (TM 495) The body does not remain as 'other' in White's fiction, but is constantly depicted as a necessary and even at times redemptive aspect of the self.

The theme of the necessary acceptance of corporeality is arguably most explicit in *Voss*. Loosely based on the expedition of Ludwig Leichardt, who embarked on two expeditions of of exploration from east to west across the Australian continent, before finally disappearing during the second in 1848, *Voss* charts the physical, psychological and metaphysical journey of the fictional explorer Johann Ulrich Voss, as he and his party venture from the fertile outskirts of the Australian continent into its inhospitable desert interior. The journey is hazardous and physically debilitating, but it is Voss's irrepressible egoism within conditions necessitating the acceptance of corporeal weakness that will harm him the most. In its development of the explorer's monstrous notion of the supreme and disembodied Self, *Voss* depicts the moral failings of European Enlightenment consciousness. Voss is Prussian; his origins recall the identity of the Prussian Enlightenment philosopher, Immanuel Kant. Kant's *Critique of Pure Reason* argues for an *a priori* knowledge called the 'transcendental ego': the self-enclosed consciousness bringing the physical world into being for the perceiver through rational concepts that categorise, order it, and thus construct it. Voss embodies this consciousness, "sufficient in himself" (V 15) and distrusting everything "external to himself." (21)

In Kantian terms, a "concept formed from notions and transcending ... experience is an *idea* or concept of reason" (Kant 1965, 314), and, for Voss, the "Idea, its granite monolith untouched" (44) is all-important. Voss therefore subordinates physical reality to *a priori* rational concepts, attempting to transcend experience in favour of reason. Yet the physical world, dictating his experience and impinging on his consciousness, asserts its indomitability and ultimately destroys his hermetic subjectivity. Voss is incorrect in his assumption that it is "not possible" to "damage the Idea." (44) Reason, the novel suggests, does not precede experience and must yield to the exigencies of the flesh and the physical demands upon it, thereby subverting Voss's Enlightenment assumptions.

Voss situates its protagonist's presumptuously disembodied consciousness within the newly colonised world, associating colonial expansion with Enlightenment notions of the self. Enlightenment consciousness consists of an *a priori* knowledge, Voss, driven by the rationalist will-to-power that defines Enlightenment thought and the colonial project, attempts to subjugate the continent to his reason. Through its depiction of this endeavour, the novel problematises the notion of the explorer-hero: Voss's project is dangerously hubristic. Moreover, Voss's endeavours symbolise the fascism hierarchising 'rational Europeans' over their colonial and racial 'others', the ideological basis of the exploitation of the colonies and the rise and terror of Adolf Hitler, a possible pre-figuring of Voss. This is suggested in his essay entitled "The Prodigal Son" (1958) and its brief allusion to his wartime experiences. Calling for the acknowledgement of corporeality and the compassion that attends this within the post-Enlightenment, twentieth-century context of its reception, *Voss* suggests the ethical and political implications of the refusal to do so.

As Keith Garebian observes, *Voss* is defined by the "radical theme of metaphysical completeness" (1976, 557): it confronts the abject in the attempt to diminish the rationalist concern with repudiation and othering, defence mechanisms that secure subjectivity but that split the self from its constitutive aspects.Peter Beatson reads this splitting in gendered terms, arguing that Voss's subjectivity is "aggressively, self-assertively masculine, it holds itself aloof from any involvement with the world of the senses, the pluralistic world of flux." (1970, 114) For Veronica Brady, this aloofness "generates the monstrous alter ego which condemns [Voss] to a state of division between an arrogant and aggressive outer personality and a secret self within longing for communion with others." (1979, 183) Because of the profound splitting emphasised within the novel, Voss's hubris is presented as inherently fragile. This however, is an aspect of subjectivity premised upon abjection. Julia Kristeva observes that, "abjection is a *precondition of narcissism*. It is coexistent with it and causes it to be permanently brittle." (1982, 13, original emphasis) *Voss* explores, primarily through the characters of Voss and Laura, the masculinist, narcissistic 'self' and the abject feminine from which it protects (and fails to protect) itself.

John Coates argues that White's spiritual view is dependent upon his "emphasis on the spiritual androgyny of man [sic]." (1979, 120) Aggressive masculinity, according to the novel's thematic patterning, requires the incorporation of a complementary, modifying femininity to produce an integrated self- premised upon the reclaiming of its abjects. Accordingly, *Voss* comprises two intersecting narrative strands. Alternating with the narrative concerning Voss and his expedition is the story of Laura Trevelyan, Voss's love interest and spiritual counterpart. The two meet only briefly in person on three occasions at the beginning of the novel and after Voss departs on his expedition. Laura remains within the domestic setting of Sydney. She is, however, linked to Voss by the strength of a relationship, which, despite limited initial interaction, develops into an intuitive, mythic and seemingly mystical understanding transcending distance. Laura is an aspect of Voss that he finds compelling yet for the most part repudiates. She is increasingly associated with corporeality over the course of the narrative and appears to Voss in his hallucinatory moments of suffering in the desert.

Initially, however, Laura is also defined by a defensive abjection as Voss.is. This similarity is important because her eventual acceptance of corporeality allows Laura to become Voss's mystical preceptor and proffers his self-enclosed character the possibility of a redemptive openness to others and otherness. At the beginning of the novel, however, they are depicted as mirror images of each other: they are of "equal stature," (69) share "some guilty secret of personality," (70) and go on to threaten each other "with the flashing weapons of abstract reasoning." (190) Significantly, both are consumed by their loathing for corporeality: Voss has studied toward becoming a surgeon before finding himself "suddenly revolted by the palpitating bodies of men" (13) and Laura, with disgust and priggish class consciousness, rationalises the initial chasm between herself and Rose Portion as rooted in the "bodies of these servants." (53) Besides alerting the reader to the novel's interest in narcissism, this initial mirroring sets the characters up not only as counterparts but as one and the same. Laura, as Voss's reflection, *is* Voss and over the course of the narrative will come to represent those parts of him that he repudiates.

Laura herself, however, observes her inverse mirror reflection in the Bonners' servant, Rose Portion. As an orphan, Laura has been adopted by the Bonners – her aunt and uncle – during her childhood. Their house-servant, Rose, is central to the novel's metaphysics, symbolising physicality and sexuality, aspects (or a "portion") of existence that Laura initially repudiates. The opening sentences, famous for their stylistic oddity, literally give Rose the first word and indicate physicality as the immediate and paramount focus of the text:

> 'There is a man here, miss, asking for your uncle,' said Rose.
> And stood breathing. (7)

The truncated second sentence, beginning in *medias res* and comprising an entire paragraph, foregrounds Rose's audible respiration and depicts her as distastefully corporeal within Laura's apparently focalising perspective. Her heavy breathing pervades the text, emphasised by the opening conjunction, and her body is a disconcerting presence causing the observer to avert his or her gaze:

> Something had made this woman monotonous. Her big breasts moved dully as she spoke, or she would stand, and the weight of her silences impressed itself on strangers. If the more sensitive amongst those she served or addressed failed to look at Rose, it was because her manner seemed to accuse the conscience, or it could have been, more simply, that they were embarrassed by her harelip. (7)

The unusual narration, refusing to commit to any certainty, presents two possible interpretations of Rose and her relationship with Laura: Laura "fail[s] to look at Rose" either because the sight of the servant arouses her guilt or because Rose's facial deformity appals her. During the first half of the novel, then, Laura hovers between two positions – the maintenance of subjectivity (in this case, one of genteel femininity) via abjection and the possibility of submitting to a compassion dependent upon the acceptance of corporeality. Laura's disgust accuses her conscience, and so it would seem that she aspires to a position of acceptance. Either way, Rose's introduction presents her as a disruptive body that Laura must either repudiate or with which she must come to terms.

Laura will eventually incorporate Rose's associations. At the beginning of the novel, however, in contrast to Rose with her harelip and "squat body," (8) she is "flawless," (7) a perception of herself that is in fact deeply flawed. Her character, moreover, exemplifying "White's technique of chiaroscuro portraiture," (Garebian 1976, 559) is not fleshed out in any specific physical detail. While Rose is presented as heavily embodied, Laura's body remains obscured, firstly by the dimness of the room, secondly by the description of her clothing, which is itself barely visible in the gloom, and thirdly by the perpetually ambivalent narrative treatment that contributes to her mysterious nature. Attention is diverted away from the centre of her body toward her extremities – her wrists and enigmatic face:

> Her dress, of that very deep blue, was almost swallowed up, all but a smoulder, and where the neat cuffs divided it from her wrists, and at the collar, which gave freedom to her handsome throat. Her face, it had been said, was long-shaped. Whether she was beautiful it was not at first possible to tell, although she should, and could have been. (9)

Daniel Punday argues that "every narrative implicitly or explicitly defines a certain range of body types" and that "by sorting bodies into types a narrative defines the contrasts that underlie thematic, symbolic, and psychological patterns" (2003, 61). The opening of *Voss* indeed suggests that meaning comes to the fore in the comparison of bodies. In contrast to the presentation of Rose, no real sense of Laura's physicality is proffered. Moreover, she is described as "marble" (7): she is initially one of White's statue-figures, ignoring the corporeal in favour of a frozen and rigidly defended incorporeal identity comprising a combination of Enlightenment rationality and nineteenth-century femininity. In addition to the body, Laura refuses the "fuzz of faith" (9): she has stayed home on a Sunday while the Bonners attend church, thereby refusing religion and inadvertently making herself available for a meeting with Voss. Laura therefore initially resists both body and faith, her refusal implicitly suggesting that the novel associates corporeality and the sacred. Her association with rational control and the repression of a troubling animality is referred to later in the novel when she sits "sculpturally upon her mastered horse, of which the complicated veins were throbbing with blood and frustration." (109)

As this description suggests, the body is not so easily dismissed or suppressed. Laura must overcome her aversion to her inherent animality in order to accept her love for Voss and to submit to the "fuzz of faith", an overcoming symbolised in her increasing affection for Rose. Voss too will find that physical aversion precludes the experience of love. He is to some extent aware that his rejection of the physical is to his own detriment, and although he perversely continues to repudiate it, he longs for the human companionship that he associates with materiality. This leads him to think occasionally of the "material world which his egoism had made him reject. In that world men and women sat at a round table and broke bread together. At times, he admitted, his hunger was almost unbearable." (36) The disgust that physicality nevertheless evokes in Voss arises from the hubris that defines him. For Voss, flesh is soft, yielding and weak. So too is the selfless emotion of love, of which "he did not expect much … for all that is soft and yielding is easily hurt." (41)

Flesh becomes a metaphor for mutuality, and Voss shies from the "flesh of human relationships, a dreadful, cloying tyranny" (112) that threatens the supremacy of the self. Voss, in his obsession with transcendental supremacy and therefore in his rivalry with God, believes that he can "dispense with flesh." (34)

Voss's journey toward the acceptance of corporeality cannot be severed from Laura's, and the latter is unable to "dispense with flesh" (34) in its embodiment as Rose Portion. Although she tries to be kind to Rose, Laura initially shies from the slightest physical communication that elicits a response from the woman. Their interaction is thus greatly inhibited, and Laura is incapable of expressing compassion. It is only with "special effort" that she is able to smile at Rose, because Rose's response is immediate and repellent: "Kindness made her whole body express her gratitude, but it was her body that repelled." (52)

Laura therefore finds herself in a bind, unable to escape her feelings of revulsion. This is a central tension for the character, whose responses are, as we have seen, contradictory: "Laura Trevelyan had continued to feel repelled. It was the source of great unhappiness, because frequently she was also touched." (53) Ambiguity here is again important to an understanding of Laura's transformation from egoist rationalist to humble, corporeal visionary: as the former, she is repulsed and unhappy because Rose brushes her hair and therefore literally "touches" her; as the latter, her disgust is the source of unhappiness because Rose's predicament "touches" her, that is, it evokes her compassion. Touch is significant in a novel that places emphasis upon corporeality and its relation to the affect of compassion. Laura realises that physicality is her fundamental stumbling-block, explaining the issue central to her initial unhappiness: "It is the bodies of these servants, she [tells] herself in some hopelessness and disgust." (53)

At the novel's opening, Rose the housemaid introduces and attends to Voss and Laura and as the novel unfolds it becomes evident that she is a symbolic intermediary in their relationship. On a symbolic level, Voss and Laura are drawn to each other *because* of their corporeality and sexuality, which Rose represents. Physical attraction will remain for the most part unacknowledged, until Laura eventually absorbs Rose's associations, but a strong seam of barely repressed sexual energy defines their relationship from the start. Laura denies and projects her yearnings, simultaneously elevating her class status, with the consequence that the bodies of servants are discomfortingly sexual. The loitering presence and languid sexuality of Jack Slipper, the father of Rose's child, is deeply disturbing to Laura until his departure from the Bonners' property, prompted by his arrest for drunkenness. Jack, however, leaves behind him the pregnant Rose, her "breasts moving in her brown dress," (53) a body continuing to disturb and repel because it awakens Laura's attention to sexuality and becomes associated with her disgust for her own incipient attraction to Voss.

Accordingly, Laura is beset by the image of Rose during the Pringles' picnic, when her affinity to Voss becomes increasingly clear. As Voss stands behind her, it is "by no means disagreeable" and she notices the "little dark hairs" upon his wrists, (70) that telling sign of sexual attraction in White's fiction. But Mrs Bonner's voice, discussing Rose's fainting spell (the first indication of her pregnancy) intrudes upon Laura's euphoria, and suddenly Rose is tangibly present to Laura, "standing in her brown dress, her knuckles pressed tight together. The harelip was fearful." (70) This disruption of Laura's happiness, the first of the novel's many imaginary apparitions of abject femininity, prompts her to refuse Voss's offer of food and to remove herself from his proximity. Watching him, she recalls unwittingly stumbling upon Jack Slipper in the bamboo thicket on the Bonners' property, a dark, secretive, humid setting for illicit sexual encounter:

> Ah, miss, said Jack Slipper, you have come out for a breather, well, the breeze has got up, can you hear it in the leaves? Whatever the source of the friction of the bamboos, it usually sounded cooler in their thicket. But in summer there were also the murmurous voices of insects, and often of men and women, which could create a breathlessness in that corner of the garden. Full moonlight failed to illuminate its secrets. There was a hot, black smell of rotting. The silver flags, breaking and flying on high, almost escaping from their lacquered masts, were brought back continually by the mysterious ganglion of dark roots. (71)

Amidst "murmurous" voices, the "breathlessness" of "men and women" and the secret "hot, black smell of rotting", Laura is drawn toward sexuality and death and the compulsion of mystery associated with both. The "mysterious ganglion of dark roots" (preventing the transcendence of "silver flags") is an image that will recur throughout the novel, foreshadowing Laura's dark hair sodden with sweat during her hallucinatory illness that contributes to the crisis and climax of the novel and that, as a consequence of her delirium combined with Voss's, allows the boundary between the desert and Sydney settings to disintegrate. Thus, from the beginning of *Voss*, the "bodies of these servants", so greatly distressing to Laura, are tied to her experience of her own physicality and her fear of acknowledging it. Laura, in short, rejects her own embodiment.

Rose's sexuality and corporeality extend to the image of the rose itself as symbolic association typically in White's fiction expands via word association and metaphor across the fabric of the text. The progress of Laura's and Voss's relationship is tracked by the transformation roses undergo in the Bonners' garden. During the Bonners' party in the early stages of the novel, for example, when Voss and Laura meet in the garden and cement their mystical and erotic connection, the "… no longer perfect roses were bursting with scent and sticky stamens," (85) an image suggesting the poetic consummation of their relationship and the gradual disintegration of Laura's "flawless" 'incorporeality.' The "flesh of rosy light" (179) links the symbol of the rose to the body and the "flesh of human relationships." (112)

Rose, the character, supported by the imagery of roses, is the abject maternal, the subject-deforming matrix that Voss accesses through the intermediary figure of Laura, who herself comes to accept the body through her eventual acceptance of Rose. As Rose's pregnancy progresses, Laura becomes more attuned to the body. She begins to accept her companion, as the imagery of roses suggests:

> Laura herself had not yet grasped the full sense of that season, only that it was fuller than ever before, and that the flesh of roses was becoming personal, as she cut the long, pointed buds, or heavy blooms that would fall by evening. She had to take it all, even the big, blowing ones.
>
> 'Those will make a mess, miss,' Rose Portion did protest once … '
> All over the tables and carpets. A mess of rose petals. (158-59)

Laura, who must "take it all," must accept corporeality in all its forms. Rose's observation foreshadows the "mess" she herself will make in giving birth, bringing into the novel the disorder of corporeality and sexuality that Mrs Bonner finds so disturbing. This disorder is already at work within Laura, however. In the garden, she is "dazed by roses" and their fertility: "She continued to cut the big heads, in which bees were rummaging. She bent to reach others, till roselight was flooding her face, and she was forced to lower her eyes against the glare of roses." (159) Laura, then, is eventually dazzled by the novel's symbol of corporeality as White's writing, in its poetic quality, emphasises its own materiality. From this point onward, Laura's "faith in reason [is] less" (160) and she begins to merge with the corporeal Rose. She walks in the "overflowing garden, of big, intemperate roses, with the pregnant woman at her side" (160):

> At such times, the two shadows were joined upon the ground. Heavy with the weight of golden sun, the girl could feel the woman's pulse ticking in her own body, and was, in consequence, calmer than she had ever been, quietly joyful, and resigned. As she strolled towards the house, holding her parasol against the glare, though devoured by the tigerish sun, she trusted in their common flesh. The body, she was finally convinced, must sense the only true solution. (160)

Sense, here, overcomes reason, and a "true solution" is not a rational answer so much as a solution of component parts, a merging of characters. Laura's joyful and compassionate acceptance of Rose is a moment of *jouissance* – Lacan describes this as "the sense in which the body experiences itself" (in Braunstein 2003, 103) – in which the borders of the self disintegrate and she blissfully recognises that they are unified in their "common flesh". Pronouns are imprecise: "the girl could feel the woman's pulse ticking in her own body" refers to Laura's merging with Rose, but also to Laura's awakening to her own sexuality. Moreover, "*their* common flesh" may refer to Laura and Rose's shared corporeality but also to that of Laura and Voss. In this interpretation, the shadows "joined on the ground", while again ostensibly referring to those of Laura and Rose, also allude to Laura and Voss's shadow selves – their previously abjected corporeality, compassion and sexuality. As the body "sense[s] the only true solution", rationality dissolves – is "devoured" – along with the distinction between self and other and therefore between discrete characters.

As Wilson Harris observes, "Rose's grotesque attachment [is] a compulsive nightmare for Laura." (1974, 6) Yet there is freedom in confronting this nightmare. To allow attraction to the abject to prevail, and hence to be drawn over the boundary separating the provisional categories of 'self' and 'other', where meaning and order erode, can be of value in the liberation that it offers from socialised identity. Kristeva herself invokes the imagery of nightmare (in a description strangely appropriate to Voss's exploratory mission, which at its most hallucinatory, follows the apparition of Laura). As she describes it, one who submits to the abject is "on a journey, during the night, the end of which keeps receding. He has a sense of the danger, of the loss that the pseudo-object [the abject] represents for him, but he cannot help taking the risk at the very moment he sets himself apart. And the more he strays, the more he is saved." (8)

Laura embraces the body both literally and figuratively: "the girl who in the past had barely suffered her maid to touch her, on account of a physical aversion such contact invariably caused, suddenly reached out and put her arms round the waist of the swelling woman, and buried her face in the apron" (164). In hugging Rose, Laura embraces corporeality just as she draws another human being toward her. Compassion in White's fiction involves the acceptance of others' physicality and the acknowledgement of the shared experience of embodiment and mortality. When Laura feels Rose's pulse ticking in her own body, for example, or begins to experience Rose's pregnancy as her own, what she undergoes is the dissolution of the self allowed by corporeal empathy. Laura's symbolic pregnancy, via the figure of Rose, is therefore not merely the dream manifestation of her love for Voss, as it is commonly understood by critics, of whom David Tacey is one example:

> Conveniently, the entire sexual issue is parcelled out to Laura's maid, whose profane coupling with Jack Slipper leads to the timely birth of the unwanted child. Even more conveniently, the mother dies soon after the birth, leaving Laura to cherish her very own spiritual child. The whole episode involving Mercy is an ugly and unnecessary literalization of the 'fruit' of the Voss/Laura marriage, but more to the point it serves to highlight the tremendous gulf between sexuality and love in White's world. (1988, 75)

Tacey ignores the accumulation of imagery that presents Rose as a fundamental aspect of Laura's character – her corporeality – that she gradually reincorporates. If Voss and Laura's relationship is disembodied, it is not because of a "gulf between sexuality and love". On the contrary, White emphasises dualism in order to undermine it. Voss's love is dependent upon his acknowledgement of corporeality and therefore sexuality. Hence Mercy as the symbolic manifestation of Voss and Laura's 'spiritual' love cannot be adequately comprehended without due consideration to Laura's overcoming of her aversion to corporeality and otherness via her relationship with Rose. The necessity of surmounting the enclosure of aversion similarly dominates Voss's metaphysical journey.

In reclaiming her corporeality, and in her unbidden and seemingly mystical appearances to Voss in the desert, reminding him of the importance of compassion and of acknowledging the flesh, Laura, like Rose before her, becomes tinged with the abject. The "lovely colours of putrescence" (388) gain numerous associations as the narrative unfolds: "green and brown, of mud, and slime, and uncontrolled faeces, and the bottomless stomach of nausea" (270) contribute to the novel's indexes of abjection. Rose wears a dress of "brown stuff" (8) and when she collapses "in her brown gown" at the Bonners' table, the first sign of her pregnancy, she "look[s] a full sack, except that she was stirring and moaning, even retching" (50). Peter Beatson observes, moreover, that "there is a close link established between Rose and the country: they are both 'brown', 'monotonous', and from both are averted the genteel eyes of those who do not like to see the stark ugliness of their appearance" (1970: 120). Both corporeality and the indigenous landscape are constructed as abject in relation to "genteel", colonial, 'European' identity. Laura's acceptance of Rose is therefore her acceptance of the Indigenous landscape and her first movement toward the white indigeneity that White's fiction conceptualises as a possibility.

Laura herself is frequently described as clad in "sombre green" (59) and her moments of happiness are indicated in her "green laughter." (158) Wearing the green associated with the body, abjection, indigenous Australia and the poetic dimension of the novel, she enters Voss's experience as the corporeality, irrationality and feminised indigenous landscape against which he defends himself. A breeze blows through the "shiny indigenous leaves" (198):

All the immediate world was soon swimming in the same liquid green. She was clothed in it. Green shadows almost disguised her face, where she walked among the men, to whom, it appeared, she was known, as others were always known to one another, from childhood, or by instinct. ... Then [Voss] noticed how her greenish flesh was spotted with blood ... (198-99)

Walking among the men, marked with the sign of the body (the 'other' known to the self "from childhood, or by instinct"), Laura takes on Rose's associations. Her green proliferates in the novel as an index of decay and abjection: pot-holes in the desert fester with "green scum" (23); "green water and rotting fruit" (32) pervade the text; "dead green" (69) is a *memento mori*, as are "green skeleton ferns." (148) As physical suffering overwhelms the expedition, the men become tinged with green: "Greenish-yellow teeth were rattling in the skulls, from which men looked out, luminous, but deceived." (268) Eventually, when Voss comes to terms with abject corporeality, he will experience the mystical possibilities of "green flesh, watered by the dew ... shooting nightly in celestial crops." (359) As the novel insists, "divine powers [are] not disguised by the earth-colours." (281)

Perhaps Laura's association with the body is best exemplified in the illness that marks the crisis of her mystically-shared experience with Voss: the "brain fever", a psychosomatic upheaval of the mind confounding all reason and leaving the Bonners shaken and perplexed. Laura's illness is prefigured by her feigned headache at the beginning of the novel, her excuse for not attending church and therefore associated with her decision to "become what, she suspected, might be called a rationalist." (9) This begins the novel's interest in imagery of the head, with its attendant associations of rationality and the subversion thereof. Laura's hair, in her sickness, unfurls like the fronds of unreason and fever. She appears to Voss in his moment of shared suffering, their communion indicated by the image of hair:

> His mouth was filled with the greenish-black tips of hair, and a most exquisite bitterness.
>
> 'You are not in possession of your faculties,' he said to her at last.

'What are my faculties,' she asked.

> Then they were drifting together. They were sharing the same hell, in their common flesh, which he had attempted so often to repudiate. ...

'Do you see now?' she asked. 'Man is God decapitated. That is why you are bleeding. (363-64)

The "greenish-black tips of hair" are associated not only with unreason, but also with physical decay. Laura has in one of Voss's earlier hallucinations "bathe[d] her hair in all flesh, whether of imperial lilies, or the black, putrefying, human kind." (188) As Voss "drifts together" with Laura in a dream of "common flesh", a term also used in the description of Laura's merging with Rose in the garden (363; 160), he is infiltrated by the flux of her hair with its associations of flesh, death and decay. Irrationality is emphasised as Laura loses her faculties to the extent that she has no knowledge of what they are, her loss of rationality prompting her "drifting together" with Voss.

Her closing aphorism is a claim for the 'Godliness' of irrationality that occurs with the acceptance of corporeality: "Man is God decapitated", she argues, her words recalling the decapitated Christ of whom Palfreyman has dreamt and foreshadowing Voss's eventual decapitation. Laura suggests that "Man" is an imperfect "God", but, more importantly, that when humanity relinquishes its obsession with reason, when this is severed from the body by the "decapitation" involved in accepting one's abjects, then illumination may result. Kristeva would agree: "The mystic's familiarity with abjection is a fount of infinite *jouissance* ... where the subject is reabsorbed ... into communication with the Other and with others." (1982: 127)

In conclusion, a significant process of corporeal acceptance through relations with others shapes the treatment of the body in *Voss*. Rose Portion symbolises animality, corporeality and sexuality, aspects of existence repudiated but eventually embraced by Laura Trevelyan who thereafter becomes associated with the abject herself, arising in Voss's visions to test his self-sufficiency and to threaten the borders of his subjectivity. Laura's appearances to Voss suggest that he should embrace humility in the face of the inconceivable alterity beyond the limits of his consciousness, an alterity seemingly incorporating the physical world, corporeality, notions of the feminine, unknowable regions of the self, and, linked to all of the above, an overwhelming sense of the unrepresentable sacred.

Works Cited

Ashcroft, Bill. 2010. "The Presence of the Sacred in Patrick White," *Remembering Patrick White: Contemporary Critical Essays,* ed. Elizabeth McMahon and Brigitta Olubas. Amsterdam: Rodopi: 95-108.

Beatson, Peter. 1970. "The Three Stages: Mysticism in Patrick White's *Voss,*" *Southerly* 30: 111-121.

Brady, Veronica. 1979. "The Novelist and the New World: Patrick White's *Voss,*" *Texas Studies in Literature and Language* 21.2: 169-185.

Braunstein, Nestor. 2003. "Desire and Jouissance in the Teachings of Lacan," *The Cambridge Companion to Lacan*, ed. Jean-Michel Rabate. Cambridge: Cambridge University Press: 102-115.

Coad, David. 1993. "Patrick White: Prophet in the Wilderness," *World Literature Today,* 67.3: 510-14.

Coates, John. 1979. "*Voss* and Jacob Boehme: A Note on the Spirituality of Patrick White," *Australian Literary Studies* 9: 119-22.

Colmer, John. 1978. "Duality in Patrick White," *Patrick White: A Critical Symposium*, eds. Ron Shepherd and Kirpal Singh. Adelaide: Centre for Research in the New Literatures in English: 70-76.

Garebian, Keith. 1976. "The Desert and the Garden: The Theme of Completeness in *Voss*," *Modern Fiction Studies* 22.4: 557-569.

Grosz, Elizabeth. 1990. "The Body of Signification," *Abjection, Melancholia and Love: The Work of Julia Kristeva,* ed. John Fletcher and Andrew Benjamin.London: Routledge: 80-103.

Harris, Wilson. 1974. *Fossil and Psyche*. Austin: African and Afro-American Studies and Research Centre, University of Texas.

Kant, Immanuel. 1965. *The Critique of Pure Reason*. New York: St Martin's Press.
Kiernan, Brian. 1976. "The Novels of Patrick White," *The Literature of Australia*, ed. Geoffrey Dutton. Harmondsworth: Penguin: 461-484.
Kristeva, Julia. 1982. *Powers of Horror: An Essay on Abjection*. Trans. Leon S. Roudiez. New York: Columbia University Press.
McCann, Andrew. 1997. "The Ethics of Abjection: Patrick White's *Riders in the Chariot*." *Australian Literary Studies* 18.2: 145-155.
McCredden, Lyn. 2010. "Voss: Earthed and Transformative Sacredness," *Remembering Patrick White: Contemporary Critical Essays,* ed. Elizabeth McMahon and Brigitta Olubas. Amsterdam: Rodopi: 109-123.
Punday, Daniel. 2003. *Narrative Bodies: Toward a Corporeal Narratology*. New York: Palgrave Macmillan.
Riemer, A.P. 1980. "Eddie and the Bogomils – Some Observations on *The Twyborn Affair*," *Southerly* 40: 112-29.
Shepherd, Ron. 1978. "An Indian Story: 'The Twitching Colonel'," *Patrick White: A Critical Symposium*, ed. Ron Shepherd and Kirpal Singh. Adelaide: Centre for Research in the New Literatures in English: 117-122.
Tacey, David. 1988. *Patrick White: Fiction and the Unconscious*. Melbourne: Oxford University Press.
vanden Driesen, Cynthia. 1978. "Patrick White and the 'Unprofessed Factor': The Challenge before the Contemporary Religious Novelist," *Patrick White: A Critical Symposium*, ed.Ron Shepherd and Kirpal Singh. Adelaide: Centre for Research in the New Literatures in English: 77-85.
White, Patrick. 1958. "The Prodigal Son," *Australian Letters* 1, 3: 37-40.
—. 1974. *The Cockatoos*. Harmondsworth: Penguin.
—. 1973. *The Eye of the Storm*. London: Penguin.
—. 1955. *The Tree of Man*. London: Eyre & Spottiwoode.
—. 1957. *Voss*. London: Vintage.
—. 1976. *A Fringe of Leaves*. London: Vintage.

CHAPTER FIVE

PATRICK WHITE:
CROSSING THE BOUNDARIES

JOHN MCLAREN
VICTORIA UNIVERSITY OF TECHNOLOGY

Australian history is a history of division. Lacking territorial borders to be defended against hostile peoples, we have made our own inner borders of class, gender and ethnicity. Without barriers of place, we have constructed divisions between city and country, Sydney and the bush, male and female, foreigners and native born, workers and masters. We have ruthlessly dispossessed the first peoples of this land and then attempted to confine them within the walls of reservations consigning them also to cultural and material deprivation. Besides these divisions there has been a further perceived division between the land and its European settlers. A constant theme in Australian fiction has been the attempt to find national narratives that will resolve these divisions. Henry Handel Richardson's *The Fortunes of Richard Mahony* (1930) is a tragedy of border-crossings that leaves its central protagonist alienated both from old country and new.

Richardson projects onto the future possible reconciliation between the questing spirit of the migrant and the implacable nature of the land. Since then perhaps many new generations of Australians have learned to love the country that alienated their forebears. Novels by Xavier Herbert (1938) and Brian Penton (1934) or more recently Roger McDonald (1994) and Kate Grenville (2005) show just how difficult this task of learning is.

Patrick White's fiction has generally been discussed in the context of building an Australian identity, or of challenging the realist tradition by insisting on a mystical or transcendental dimension to human life. Cynthia vanden Driesen has traced the development of some of these critical approaches, and has herself situated White's work in the context of post-colonial settler society, and the challenge White offers to its ignorance or denigration of Indigenous culture. (2009) White's fiction consistently shows individuals striking out for freedom in a series of attempts to escape the social, cultural, racial and geographic boundaries imposed on them.

Like many of his contemporaries, White found himself an exile at home in Australia and left to find civilisation abroad, in England and Europe. Then he reversed the pattern by returning to his homeland in his maturity. He still found himself an exile. With his partner, Manoly Lascaris, he followed the example of his forebears, albeit on a smaller scale, by carving out a rural estate that would implant European culture in a new land. His family may have felt affiliated with the gentry but he worked in an attempted replicating the lifestyle of the peasantry. Nevertheless, within the few acres he owned, he established through his writing an elect of the mind, and of the spirit, which supplied the principal subject of his fiction. Like Richardson, White in his own life as well as in his writing crossed many borders. Born in England, he was brought up in Australia but sent to an English public school. He returned to England for his University education, retuned to spend a short time in Australia before embarking on his writing career in England. After the War and observing the decimation it created in Europe at first hand, he decided to return finally to Australia.

He also moved in his writing, between sex and gender, class and nationality, country and suburbia. Besides, a division or border between the enlightened and the philistine runs throughout his work. In his first novel, *Happy Valley* (1939) the characters find themselves trapped within the borders of a country town that precludes any chance of enlightenment. They lack words to express the anger and hatred and love they feel, and are condemned to live in, "the religion of the world, of Happy Valley with its eyes closed to the possibilities of truth." (HV 218) Yet, on the last pages of the novel, Oliver, fleeing the town with Alys in what appears to be a desperate attempt to rebuild their relationship decides to remain. He seems to find a kind of reconciliation through acceptance of the flux of life:

> A flux of moving things fused, and Alys Browne, he felt, is a part of me for all time, this is not altogether lost, it is altogether an intimate relationship ... This is a part of man, to withstand his relationships the ebb and flow of the seasons, the sullen hostility of rock, the anaesthesia of snow ... he is immune from all but the ultimate destruction of the inessential outer shell. (325)

This epiphany anticipates the closing scene of *The Tree of Man*, where the continuing life of the boy carving his initials into the tree after the death of his grandfather Stan transcends all the conflicts and doubts that Stan has endured throughout his life.

In the later works, the protagonists seek freedom through a quest for enlightenment, not by recourse to reason, but by opening themselves to intimations of a spirit beyond their everyday existence. In *The Living and the Dead* (1942) this distinction is, as the title suggests, is schematic; in *The Aunt's Story* (1948), Theodora as a child has intimations of the spirit, but her escape from the mundane is also a descent into madness, The elect, those who are shown to attain to spiritual wholeness in White's later works seem to have finally to accept separation from others. Stan Parker is separated from his wife; Arthur the dreamer from his rationalist brother Waldo; the chariot Riders from the common folk around them; the explorer Voss from the merchants who sponsor him. Yet, as Bridget Grogan reminds us, the spiritual wisdom of his *iluminati* is firmly grounded in their corporeality. They achieve transcendence by accepting the body (Grogan 2010).

Stan Parker, in *The Tree of Man* (1956) achieves enlightenment only through a life-time of seeking through the mundane routines of his hard work on his farm. He is a person to whom things happen, rather than one who makes them happen. Stan has a moment of epiphany among the cabbages but then joins with others in combating the ravages of the flood. The child comes from the floods, and disappears again. Stan goes to war, and returns apparently unchanged. Eventually, he is able to perceive God in a gob of spit. His life would appear to contain nothing eventful, yet, as his grandchild perhaps recognises, through him the tree of man has lived and grown stronger.

The Tree of Man adopts one of the two archetypal patters of Australian, or colonial, settlement. The famous first sentences say it all:

> A cart drove between two big stringybarks and stopped. The horse, shaggy and stolid as the tree, sighed and took root ... The man who sat in the cart got down ...
>
> Then the man took an axe and struck the side of the hairy tree. (3)

Although we learn that the man has travelled less than a day's journey from a township and the settled lands around it, this has is presented as the initial act of taking possession of a new land. The setting is the bush of Australian legend, ballad and painting. Even the trees are identified, not as generalised trees that might be noticed by a stranger, but as the specific species that provided fuel for bush stoves and the building materials of the first huts. The man's first act is to commence the destruction of this bush to turn the land to his purposes. The horse that has brought him, and will enable him to complete his act of possession by hauling his plough "takes root," making the country instantly their own. Man, horse and cart, symbols of agency, action and instrumentality, fill what is presented as empty bush. Throughout the novel, the obstacles to the man's settlement will be the land itself, and a few other newcomers who compete with him for its space. There is no suggestion that this new community has displaced any earlier people.

The Tree of Man follows the familiar pattern of the family saga of settlement. Jennifer Rutherford, however, has shown how White also undermines the pattern of the saga even as he enacts it. She points out that the opening sentences of *The Tree of Man* "run aground in a generalized lassitude." Rather than reducing a wilderness, he shows his protagonist character "retreating, collapsing in acedia, sloth, torpor ..." (Rutherford 2010, 60-61) Rather than filling a *terra nullius*, she argues that the man, Stan Parker, is a *homo nullius*. Nowhere in the novel is he able to find words to communicate to another whatever meaning he has made in his life. His words, "never reach their destination." (TM 62) Yet, in

White's world, not reaching a destination may be the equivalent of finding it, by being open to the present.

White's next novel, *Voss* (1957) belongs with the literature of exploration. It is a quest narrative, in which the eponymous protagonist turns his back on civilisation in order to seek a spiritual truth in the wilderness. Unlike the opening of the previous novel with the man bringing settlement to the empty bush, this work starts in a comfortable bourgeois home in Sydney, then follows a journey away from civilisation into an interior that, far from being empty, is populated with members of an older race who possess a kind of spirituality that appears alien to the newcomers. Unlike *The Tree of Man*, its characters are free with words to express their inner state. In the earlier parts of the novel, these words fail to lodge with their hearers, who disregard or reject them. But as Voss pursues his quest beyond the boundaries of settled society, and his words fail to reach any physical hearer, they lodge in the unconscious of Laura, his spiritual wife who, while she remains physically in Sydney still shares his spiritual quest.

Voss even contains glimpses of the utopian ideal that prompted the establishment of Botany Bay as a place of reform where hardened criminal would see the error of their ways and find redemption through hard work on the land. Sanderson's estate Rhine Towers is a transplanted model of European culture. In Rhine Towers, Sanderson extends the highest social values of care and compassion. Voss' initial determination to set up camp for his party, refusing Sanderson's offer of accommodation in the house, reflects a determination not to be led aside from his quest. As he explains, it is not for him "to build a solid house and live in it the kind of life that is lived in such houses. ... Honest people can destroy most effectually such foundations as some of us have." (141) Through such observations Voss turns his journey from a practical quest for worldly wealth and knowledge into a spiritual one where enlightenment will overcome human weakness. To do otherwise would return him to the shallows of the society he had left behind him in Sydney. Judd, the practical man attempts to turn back from this quest, and is consigned to a life as a demented figure haunting the wilderness where Voss had found his truth.

From this perspective, Rhine Towers is not a place of refuge, but the last border Voss must cross on his search. It is from Rhine Towers that Voss writes the letter to Laura that both declares his love and explains that he expects for no material gains from his expedition, but hopes he will find in Laura "a companion of strength and judgement" as he "must stumble almost daily over the savage rocks of circumstance." (164) Laura is the only person who, although physically absent, can accompany him fully over these rocks, where his actual companions will fall away. Laura, continuing to live within the confines of Sydney, will, through some kind of mystical communion with Voss, achieve an insight that allows her to transcend these boundaries.

Voss takes with him Judd, the practical man, who could easily have been the hero of the novel, but instead he is the traitor whose name suggests Judas. The narrative gives no reasonable grounds for this rejection except that Judd remains attached to the practical world of material things. Judd sacrifices his own comforts initially to go with Voss, and remains loyal to him until the practical futility of the expedition becomes apparent. Even then, he acts with dignity and courage in confronting Voss.

> "I will not! I will not!" he cried at last, shaking his emaciated body.
>
> Since his own fat paddocks, not the deserts of mysticism, nor the transfiguration of Christ, are the fate of the common man, he was yearning for the big breasts of his wife that would smell of fresh baked bread even after she had taken off her shift.
>
> ... That evening ... he approached their leader and said
>
> "Mr Voss, sir, I do not think we are intended to go any further. I have thought it over, and am turning back." (167-68)

Voss will not turn back; he cleaves to the wilderness. He loses his followers one by one, through exhaustion or by death at the hands of the Aborigines. His own death comes through a combination of these, but it is presented as the death of the god, who has first been brought into sacramental union with nature and then ritually sacrificed.

His death in turn changes the Aborigines. At first they had been his guides but later, agents of their own fate as they, like the whites, choose to aid or leave him. When they cut him down, however, they become agents of the country itself. Once the Europeans cross the borders of settlement they lose the ability to control or direct their own actions. Voss's only connection with a wider society, and his only link to the future, is through his mystical bond with Laura. Their lives run parallel despite the distance. This can be metaphorical, as when the exploring party "rode down the terrible steps of the Bonners' deserted house, and onwards." (382) This sentence both completes a scene in Laura' sickroom and introduces a stage in Voss's disintegration. Laura shares the enlightenment he achieves by giving himself to the country. Voss's letters are scattered in the desert, but somehow his experience becomes hers. As he dies, she passes through the crisis of a fever, exclaiming at its climax "Dear Christ, now at last I understand your suffering." (410) It appears that this understanding has passed into Laura who, unlike Voss, once past the crisis of her illness is enabled to bring up the child, Mercy, and to take up the threads of life again as headmistress of a successful girls' school.

After several novels in which the important borders are social or spiritual, White returns, to borders that are primarily physical and territorial in *A Fringe of Leaves* (1976*)*. Austin Roxburgh travels to the colonies in search of knowledge his brother Garnett in search of wealth. In the course of the novel, its chief protagonist, Ellen Roxburgh, born Ellen Gluyas, crosses the borders between Cornwall and England and also between the servant class and the gentry when she leaves her home on the farm to marry Austin Roxburgh. Roxburgh is a man who, wherever he travels, never crosses the borders imposed by society. A dedicated reader of the classics, he uses them to hold experience at bay. As the narrator remarks when they are caught in a shipwreck, Austin "would do his best till the end to impose some sort of logic on unreason." (FL 169)

Ellen however crosses borders as she comes to them. She crosses a border from England and living in an English country home into a rough convict society when she and Austin travel to Van Diemen's Land, still savage beneath its outer veneer of civilisation. Her brief liaison with Austin's brother, Garnet, takes her across a border to purely fleshly experience. The shipwreck off the coast of the yet-to-be-named Fraser Island on their return voyage takes her over her furthest borders. The wreck precipitates them from the order of civilisation, represented by the ship, to a disorder in which they have no control over their fate. With Austin, Ellen crosses first from the safety of the ship to the desolation of the coast, then through the trees that fringe it, and then into Aboriginal society, where she wears a personal fringe of leaves in her new state of enslavement. The leaves that had hidden the savagery of the land become a screen for her remaining modesty, or self-belief. Finally, she crosses another border to join her fortunes to those of her rescuer, the convict, Jack Chance. She is able after a time in the wilderness to return again to the polite society of the colony, where she is able to take her place again.

The novel is set in the early nineteenth century, when Austin Roxburgh travels to the colonies in search of knowledge: his brother Garnet has travelled there earlier in search of wealth. Austin is enfeebled by intellect; Garnett limited by his carnality. Neither, therefore, can achieve unity. This is reserved for the main protagonist, Ellen Roxburgh.

In the course of the novel, she crosses the borders between Cornwall and England and between the servant class and the gentry. Austin is a man who, wherever he travels, never crosses the borders imposed by society. Reader of the classics, he uses them to hold experience at bay. Ellen however crosses borders as she comes to them. She crosses the border into a rough convict society when they travel to Van Diemen's Land, still savage beneath its veneer of civilisation. Her brief liaison with Garnet, takes her across a border from marital fidelity into purely fleshly experience. The shipwreck off the coast of the yet-to-be-named Fraser Island on their return voyage takes her over her furthest borders. She crosses from the wrecked ship to the boat and thence to the desolation of the coast. Next through the trees that surround it, she enters the Aboriginal world. She is stripped of her Western dress and wears a fringe of leaves in her new state of enslavement and nakedness. She crosses another border to join her fortunes with those of her rescuer, the convict, Jack Chance as she traverses the wilderness with him.

Finally she crawls back into the white settlement to be restored to the polite society of the colony, where she is able to take her place, but she is now permanently changed within and recognises her capacity for belonging to more than one world.

The novel offers both a critique of monocultural Australia and an alternative vision of what it may entail for the settler to attain full humanity on this continent. Like the visionaries in his earlier works, Ellen becomes fully human by experiencing cruelty, degradation and scorn. These experiences set those who survive them apart from their fellows. Ellen learns to accept others and to surrender to the land, rather than join the polite society of the settlers of Hobart Town or Moreton Bay in their attempts to tame it and impose a 'civilisation' which produces only barbarity. She has crossed the final border to a state that does not require borders in order to be itself. This state, like that of the Aborigines, is both intensely local and universal. But this vision cannot be generalised. In Christian terms, those who share it constitute a redeemed, not a redeeming, elect. They are set apart and contained by the new borders of their vision.

The novel in which a White protagonist crosses the furthest boundaries is *The Twyborn Affair.* This novel crosses borders between Europe and England and between these places and Australia; between city and bush, male and female, mistress and servitor. The title itself, suggesting thrice-born, takes the book away from the works that had preceded it, which all have at their centre a chronicle, however tortured, of one lifetime: birth, life and death. This novel does not even present us with a single protagonist, but the title he used for a later memoir, referring to a person who is both the one in three and the three in one which could have describe the situation in this work. (*Memoirs of the Many in One*) Following this fissiparous character, White takes the reader across the borders of nation and place, and of individual, social and sexual identity. These crossings take the characters into areas of experience and situations through which the characters yearn to complete themselves, yet finally their hopes for completion fail, as each anticipated epiphany disappoints.

The border crossing begins on the first two pages, where we encounter Mrs Golson in the south of France. She is being chauffeured through smelly saltpans and ragged pines in the hope of escaping the "sewerish" atmosphere around the hotel where she is staying. We learn that she has already crossed several borders – from Joan Sewell of the Sweat-free Hats to Joan Golson of Golson's Emporium, and from Sydney to the English society of Lady Tewkes, whose "unflinching eyelids, the non-committal smiles of the English with what is regrettably colonial …" effortlessly make Joan feel a colonial. (13) When in France, finding herself unquestionably foreign comes as a relief. Yet France also brings her to up against the final barrier of her friend Eadie Twyborn's child, who crosses all boundaries.

White does not deal as savagely with Mrs Golson as he does with some of her counterparts in earlier novels, but acknowledges her awareness of a void in her life which she will never succeed in filling. Eadie Twyborn has taught her "the poetry of rebellion", and her dreams of fulfilment take concrete form when she sights the exotic couple, Angelos and Eudoxia, and fantasises on the possibility of a voluptuous affair. Her pursuit of her dream takes place against a background of uncertainty as the people around her face the prospect of a war that will invade both their physical and mental borders. Even her stolid husband feels threatened as he watches through his window the "same anonymous bourgeois figures … advancing and retreating," generating a suspicion that "the world of menace held him in its sights." (TA 91)

The three parts of the novel are virtually separate novellas, linked through the single figure of Eudoxia/Eddie. The first part poises the Australians Joan Golson and her husband 'Curly' against the exotic Eudoxia and her Greek partner Angelos Vatatzes. Joan's first sight of them as they play a piano together is to her a vision of a transcendent world where she maybe united with them in a single world of "music and a sensual embrace." (21) Yet this unity eludes her throughout their brief acquaintance. Angelos, who is described as "an aged revenant', (95) has known only one satisfying human relationship – with his wet-nurse, and he now appears to be lost outside the boundaries of time and space as a reincarnation of Nicaean-Byzantine Emperors. (32) Eudoxia similarly is incomplete, even with Angelos. She feels life has withheld things from her, when she wants to experience everything. (26) Her relationship with Angelos had promised a love that would transcend time and place, but it has proved to be merely a sensual coupling with aged flesh. To Joan she is strangely disturbing, stirring memories of her childhood friend Eadie Twyborn. For Eudoxia, Joan arouses in her a memory of her own mother chalking on a cork moustache before going with Eadie to attend a respectable adult party. (38, 45) Joan both attracts and repels Eudoxia.

Brought together by an accident, the Australian couple spend a disastrous musical afternoon with the exotic couple. Later, Eudoxia and Angelos flee along the coast to Nice, where he dies. His last words to her, "I've had from you, dear boy, the only happiness I've ever known," (126) contradict his earlier denial, but also opens the question of gender, only implied up to this point. The letter Joan finally writes to her friend Eadie acts not only as a kind of eulogy for Eudoxia, who does not again appear under that name in the novel, but also as a confession of the unfulfilled love she had felt for her, of her wish to "lie with this divine creature, breast to breast, mouth to mouth," in such love as she had never hoped to experience, but which would have destroyed her. (128)

In the second part Eddie/Eudoxia has retreated across the gender border. He returns to his male identity as he travels back from a Europe that has moved from decadence to war. A decorated war hero, he throws his medals down a London grating before he takes ship to Australia: Fremantle, Sydney and his family home, and eventually to the Monaro, where he becomes a jackeroo. The setting reflects White's own earlier life, but also recalls his first novel, *Happy Valley*. In both novels a coarse bushman, marked by red body hair, represents the force of nature the protagonists try to avoid. (HV, 144, 209; TA, 176) In the earlier novel the doctor, Oliver Halliday, seeks escape from the boundaries of the country town. In *The Twyborn Affair*, Eddie at first finds only disorder in the Australia he returns to. In Fremantle, paint is gloomy, houses dilapidated, people intrusive and, like the shipboard socialites, empty-headed. The Greek café he visits serves greasy fish.

He finds the same disharmony when he arrives at his family home in Sydney. Although its furnishings are still lavish, if showing some signs of decay, its childhood memories and the people within it threaten him. His mother menaces him with attempts at intimacy, his father by withholding it. He maintains his spirits with recollections of his parents breaking boundaries: his mother with a corked moustache, spangled gown and pomegranate shawl, and his father the Judge in high-heels and black silk stockings. (153)

His escape to jackerooing in the country is a relief to all. Travelling around the world, fighting a war, changing genders, taking an exotic lover, he has found no borders that he can cross permit a unity of flesh and spirit, self and offers an escape from all of this. He hopes that his journey beyond the boundaries of the city and across the boundary of class to the ambiguous position of jackeroo will return him to nature and the uncomplicated feelings of childhood. He does on several occasions find himself at peace with the place, but his feelings are complicated by lusts that he finds both compulsive and disgusting. He finds his person invaded by erotic or amorous approaches from the station owner's wife, Marcia Lushington, as well as from the property manager, Doug Prowse. His successive seductions, or near rapes, cross the borders of class, but remain restricted to lust, rather than leading to the universal love he envisages. His attempt to return briefly to the identity of Eudoxia is thwarted by the return of Marcia's husband, who he knows could not comprehend this transformation. (282-3) Yet the husband, like the other people he meets on the farm or his own family, is not presented as an enemy of enlightenment like the outsiders in the other novels White wrote after *Happy Valley*. Rather, they share his predicament as people who are unable to break the restraints of the everyday to fill a void they feel in their lives.

The benevolence Marcia generates in Eddie comes from a voice "wooing him back into childhood, the pervasive warmth of a no longer sexual, but protective body, cajoling him into morning embraces ... reviving memories of toast, chilblains, rising bread" and all else his life has lost." (222) Yet Marcia herself, with his mother and Joan Golson, constitute a fearful feminine trio who threaten him by driving him to "assert his own masculine identity". Only Eudoxia enables him to avoid this confinement. (222-3) When the Golsons visit the station, Eddie avoids meeting them, not because he rejects Joan, but because she represents this threat to his freedom. Instead, he dreams of a universal benediction, when

> Finally he saw he was sitting beside Helen of the Harelip. They were seated on the brink of a rock pool, its water so clear and motionless they dared not breathe for fear they might ruffle its surface into some ugly and disturbing patterns. Whether the emotions they shared were joyful, it was difficult if not impossible to tell, only that they were united by an understanding as remote from sexuality as the crystal water in the rock basin below. (273)

The malformed innocent is a familiar figure in Patrick White. Helen's importance in this case is that she stands apart from humanity even as Eddie identifies her with nature. It is no easy or romantic absorption, flying as it does almost in the face of the actual resistant nature of the countryside. Only as he yields to the property, does he find that his "loss of faith in himself" has been replaced by an affinity with the landscape surrounding him:

> It happened very gradually, in spite of a sadistic wind, the sour grass, deformed trees, rocks crouching like great animals deformed by time. A black wagtail swivelling on a grey-green fence-post might have been confusing an intruder had he not been directing one who knew the password. The red road winding through the lucerne flat into the scurfy interior seemed to originate in memory, along with the wood-carving, boy-scout knots, and plasticine castle. For all the contingent's knowledgeable remarks on wool, scours, fluke and bluestone ... the scene's subtler depths were reserved for the outcast-initiate. (194)

The other people of the Monaro appear indifferent to landscape, "except as a source of economic returns and a fate they must accept." (248) Eddie has the password to understanding because as outsider he can see the country for what it is, but as insider he can understand the direction it is offering to his life. This acceptance of the land engenders a general goodwill which becomes extended to all its people. He enjoys the company of his work-mates, of the rabbiter and butcher, and of the women:

> It was the landscape he had loved, peopled with those magic-lantern projects without their knowing, like Greg Lushington the Crypto-poet, Mr Justice Twyborn the Bumbling Father, Peggy

Tyrrell of the Football Team. Even, perhaps, Don Prowse the Brute Male. (TA. 294)

But his contentment is transient, "as capricious as a Monaro spring." (249) Marcia Lushington, who becomes his mistress in the affair that constitutes the greater part of the action in this part of the novel, is excluded. She demands sex, but wants to call it love. Eddie deliberately upsets her by referring to it as 'fucking.' The word offends her, destroying her romantic illusions, but it also indicates Eddie's inability to reconcile his sexual desires with his integration with the land. (281)

In the first section of the novel, Eddie had tried to become the kept woman, escaping gender but caught in the power exchange with her husband. Eudoxia is the trophy woman of a lost imperial society living on in Angelo's fantasy. In the second part, White has constructed a pre-capitalist society which unites its entire people in the common endeavour of running the station. Within their allotted roles, they are each free to live as they choose, and the society gives each a due of respect and, where necessary, support. The dim-witted are employed, the wayward girl is fixed with a partner, labourers and housekeepers have secure places and authority. This society lives in rough harmony with the land. But even as Eddie discovers this harmony he finds it no longer satisfies him. The land allows no place for carnal desires, which, at least for those of his class, lead only to sterility. The station is haunted by the dead children of its owner.

The third part of the novel takes us back to a London in the aftermath of the Great War and the Depression. Eddie, now Eadith, has become the Madam of a brothel. This change constitutes his ultimate attempt to escape from restrictions and the boundaries society has placed on him. Neither trophy nor producer, he/she is now both the ultimate consumer and the supplier of commodities for a fragmented swarm of displaced aristocrats. The brothel is both an unacknowledgeable institution outside the boundaries of society, and a microcosm of a society that satisfies desire but has lost its productive functions. It is a fantasy of an Abbey, with Eadie as Abbess, and her girls, the whores, as nuns. They are sold as commodities to satisfy the fantasies of their clients, and, when not servicing these needs, they become consumers of food, drink and cosmetics. Beyond this haven, as the gloom of war descends, the streets of London fill with lost and bewildered children being hurriedly evacuated to the supposed safety of the countryside

The centre of this third part of the novel is Eadith's relationship to her patron, Lord Gravenor. Unlike Greg Lushington, Gravenor, has no productive role, even as a landowner. When Eadith finally visits his country residence, it is a mere folly, not the centre of a thriving estate. London is filled with the hangers-on of society, and affluent Australians visiting 'Home.' Among these, Eadith sees Joan Golson, and her own mother Eadie, both now widowed.

Outside the brothel, the world, on the brink of another war, seems purposeless. Eadie attempts to establish various relationships, with the housekeeper, some of the girls, Gravenor's sister, but they all fall short of fulfilment. Between her and Gravenor, however, there is a genuine love. They desire each other, and he wishes to marry her, but this would require Eadith to become Eddie again. Eddie may not be her true self, but neither is Eadith. She knows that Gravenor, trapped in his own masculine identity, could never accept Eadith as a man. This is the reverse of the situation she found herself in on the Monaro, where desire could never bloom into love. In London, love blooms, but the boundary of gender prevents it from achieving the carnal expression that would be its fulfilment. Eadith's search for love is thwarted, until eventually, just before her extermination by a bomb, she recovers her mother. At last they know each other. Their communication, inscribed in a notebook, sums up Eddie/Eudoxia/Eadith's life: "Are you my son Eddie?" "No, but I am your daughter Eadith." (422) after this, they are able to converse with each other until the blitz swallows them. This is the closest either will come to fulfilment.

This is probably the least hopeful ending of any of White's novels. His characters may have escaped social and geographic boundaries, but they are finally foiled by gender. Although the novel ends at the beginning of a war that many saw as a struggle between civilisation and barbarism, this belongs only in the background of White's novel, and he does not show his characters choosing sides or playing effective roles. Eddie had already made this choice in the First World War; he had disowned it when he discarded his medals. The Second World War is present only in the mindless destructiveness of the Blitz and the confusion of the children. Neither Eddie nor Eadith's yearnings for the love that is their deepest need is fulfilled even at the final moment when they make their crossing of the final border to death.

Works Cited

Grogan, Bridget. 2010. 'Resuscitating the Body: Corporeality in the Fiction of Patrick White, JASAL 12.3. http://www.nla.gov.au/openpublish/index.php/jasal/issue/view/235/showToc. Accessed Jan. 25, 2013.

Rutherford, Jennifer. 2010. 'Homo Nullius: the politics of pessimism',

Remembering Patrick White: contemporary critical essays, ed. Elizabeth McMahon and Brigitta Olubas. Amsterdam: Rodopi: 109 -123.

vanden Driesen, Cynthia. 2009. *Writing the Nation: Patrick White and the Indigene.* Amsterdam & New York: Rodopi.

White, Patrick, 1939. *Happy Valley: a novel*. London/Toronto/Sydney: Harrap.

—. 1941. *The Living and the Dead*. London: Eyre and Spottiswoode.

—. 1948. *The Aunt's Story*. London: Eyre & Spottiswoode.

—. 1956. *The Tree of Man*. London: Eyre & Spottiswoode.

—. 1957. *Voss*. London: Eyre & Spottiswoode.

—. 1976. *A Fringe of Leaves*. London: Jonathan Cape.

—. 1979. *The Twyborn Affair*. London: Jonathan Cape.

—. 1987. *Memoirs of the Many in One* Sydney: Penguin.

CHAPTER SIX

THE MYTH OF PATRICK WHITE'S
ANTI-SUBURBANISM

NATHANAEL O'REILLY
TEXAS CHRISTIAN UNIVERSITY

Any detailed examination of suburbia in the Australian novel must address the work of White, who published two novels in the 1960s that are widely considered classic examples of anti-suburbanism in Australian literature: *Riders in the Chariot* (1961) and *The Solid Mandala* (1966). This essay is based broadly on my research for my recent book regarding Patrick White's engagement with suburbia: *Exploring Suburbia:The Suburbs in the Contemporary Australian Novel* (2012). However, where the book focuses on *The Solid Mandala*, in this chapter, the focus is solely on *Riders in the Chariot*. The invitation to present this segment at the Conference enabled me to test my research directly on an international group of specialists in White studies through this discussion. (The book itself was also launched in India, at the Centenary conference in Hyderabad in November 2012).

The body of work that I term "Australian suburban fiction" begins with White's novels; indeed, White was the first prominent Australian novelist to use a suburban setting. White has often been labelled "anti-suburban," and *Riders in the Chariot* and *The Solid Mandala*, both set in fictional suburbs of Sydney, have been considered the primary evidence of White's alleged disdain for suburbia and its inhabitants. To cite a number of examples: Joseph Dewey argues that White "caustically satirized ... [Australia's] suburban culture" (2004, 752); the authors of *The Oxford Companion to Australian Literature* claim that White's fictional suburb Sarsaparilla "represents the materialism, ugliness and 'exaltation of the average' that he deplores" (Wilde et al 1991, 72; 608); Andrew McCann argues that White sometimes demonstrates a "paranoid fear of suburbia" and is "often vehemently anti-suburban" (1997, 145; 1998, 59); Dianne Powell concludes that White's suburban novels "confirm rather than question the images of the suburbs as places of boredom, prejudice and vulgarity" (1993, 127-28); Elizabeth Webby argues that *Riders in the Chariot* and *The Solid Mandala* "are particularly critical of the closed minds and averted eyes of those living respectably in suburbia" (2000, 11-12); Robin Gerster insists that White displays "sniggering contempt for suburban (usually female) philistinism" (1990, 567); Garry Kinnane labels White "anti-suburban" and groups him with other anti-suburban artists (1998, 41-42); and Simon During states unequivocally, "White hated the suburbs." (1996, 16)

Moreover, critics often repeat other scholars' claims that White is anti-suburban, seemingly without questioning the accuracy of such claims. However, Veronica Brady points out that although "White has usually been seen as a ferocious critic of Australian suburban life," (2005, 172) two of Andrew McCann's articles question the veracity of the dominant interpretation of White's work as anti-suburban. However, McCann is a rare exception to the critical orthodoxy regarding White's portrayal of suburbia. For far too long, critics have erroneously labelled both White and his work "anti-suburban." In an article published in *Antipodes* in 2006, I made the same mistake, describing White as anti-suburban simply because I had repeatedly read that claim in the work of other critics. After conducting a thorough examination of White's suburban novels, I realized that I was mistaken to accept the claims of the numerous critics who have labelled White anti-suburban. In the following discussion I provide a new interpretation of White's relationship with suburbia and demonstrate that *Riders in the Chariot* presents a much more ambivalent and nuanced representation of suburbia than critics have previously acknowledged.

In 1958, White published an essay entitled "The Prodigal Son" which became his most famous work of non-fiction prose. White's biographer David Marr claims the essay contains White's "most devastating attack ... against Australia. He wrote nothing like it again, and nothing he has written is so often quoted." (1958, 328) In the essay, White explains his reasons for returning to Australia from abroad and provides criticisms of Australian society that have been used as evidence by critics who argue that White is elitist, anti-suburban and anti-Australian. The oft-quoted passage from "The Prodigal Son" follows:

> In all directions stretched the Great Australian Emptiness, in which the mind is the least of possessions, in which the rich man is the important man, in which the schoolmaster and the journalist rule what intellectual roost there is, in which beautiful youths and girls stare at life through blind blue eyes, in which human teeth fall like autumn leaves, the buttocks of cars grow hourly glassier, food means cake and steak, muscles prevail, and the march of material ugliness does not raise a quiver from the average nerves. (White 1958, 38-39)

White does not mention suburbia at all, and the phrase "in all directions" implies that the "Great Australian Emptiness" exists in all parts of Australian society, whether urban, rural or suburban. Moreover, White specifically refers to a mindset rather than a physical location. While White sees consumer goods and architecture that he does not find aesthetically pleasing as symptoms of widespread anti-intellectualism, it takes a leap of logic to read the passage as proof of the author's anti-suburbanism.

Moreover, White refers to the state of Australian society as he perceived it upon his return to Australia, not at the time he wrote the article, more than a decade later. Interestingly, White presented a contrary perspective in 1947 while corresponding with his American publisher:

> "The people are beginning to develop, and take an interest in books, and painting, and music, to an extent that surprises me, knowing them fourteen years ago. One gets the impression that a great deal is about to happen." (Qtd. Ackland 2002, 405)

In the same year, White wrote to another friend, "Even the uglier aspects of the place have their significance and rightness, to me." (Qtd. Marr 1992, 245) These brief examples reveal that White's attitudes towards Australian culture were more complex than "The

Prodigal Son" suggests. The frequent quotation of the above passage from "The Prodigal Son" has created a distorted view of White's attitudes towards Australian society.

In "The Prodigal Son," White points out that in the ten years between his purchase of "Dogwoods" at Castle Hill, and the time of writing the essay, he had "hardly stirred" from his outer-suburban home. (1958, 37) White lived at Castle Hill for another eight years after composing "The Prodigal Son," bringing his residence in the suburb to a total of eighteen years. (White 1981, 138) If White really hated suburbia, he probably would not have voluntarily dwelt there for almost two decades. Moreover, the fact that White based his fictional suburbs of Sarsaparilla, Barranugli and Paradise East on Castle Hill and used them as the settings for two novels, a novella, two plays and several short stories, indicates a fascination with suburban life and a desire to explore it thoroughly.

In "The Prodigal Son," White declares that what he perceived to be "the exaltation of the 'average'" in Australian society was what made him "panic most" upon his return to Australia. (1958, 39) However, rather than find other subject matter, White chose to focus on the average, writing *The Tree of Man*, in which he sought "to discover the extraordinary behind the ordinary, the mystery and the poetry which alone could make bearable the lives of ... [average] people." (1958, 39) In another frequently quoted passage from "The Prodigal Son," White declares, "Above all I was determined to prove that the Australian novel is not necessarily the dreary, dun-coloured offspring of journalistic realism." (1958, 39) Thus, not only did White seek to push the Australian novel in new directions through Modernist experimentation, he chose to do so using suburbia as his setting.

White admits that after several years at Castle Hill he "began to see things for the first time. Even the boredom and frustration presented avenues for endless exploration; even the ugliness, the bags and iron of Australian life, acquired a meaning." (1958, 39) Hence, rather than being a site unworthy of the artist's attention, suburbia is for White a locale in which experimentation, insight and discovery are both a possibility and a reality.

Although White's home at Castle Hill was not typically a suburban dwelling, being a six-acre farm rather than a quarter-acre block, it became so as Sydney expanded. A map in Marr's biography shows Dogwoods close to a police station, banks, a cinema, and the post office. Marr describes Dogwoods as "not really a country house but a bungalow," while White described it as "'a bit of Strathfield in a paddock,'" (Marr 1992, 262) referring to a more central suburb of Sydney. In 1955, White planned to move to a more typically suburban setting. Due to ill health, he decided to sell Dogwoods and find "a modern house in an acre of garden bush"; however, he received no offers and was unable to sell the property at the time. (Marr 1992, 302-303) In 1959, White wrote, "My so-called farm has now been swallowed up by suburbia," and Marr states that by that time Castle Hill "had grown into a suburban shopping centre." (Marr 1992, 350)

Most of the narrative of *Riders in the Chariot* is set in Sarsaparilla, the fictional suburb White based on Castle Hill. Like British novelists H.G. Wells and George Orwell before him, White proved with *Riders in the Chariot* that a serious work of art can draw on suburbia and its inhabitants for both its subject matter and inspiration. White uses the suburban setting to explore a multiplicity of themes, including immigration, the legacy of colonialism, spirituality, religion, the role of the artist in society, the relationship between humans and nature, family relationships, class, consumerism, racism, intolerance, bigotry, suffering and redemption. *Riders in the Chariot* focuses on the spiritual journeys of four characters: Miss Hare, an elderly spinster and only child of a once-wealthy family; Mrs. Godbold, a poor English immigrant who makes a livelihood by taking in laundry; Mordecai Himmelfarb, a Jewish Holocaust-survivor refugee immigrant; and Alf Dubbo, an Aboriginal man afflicted with tuberculosis. Other characters who play important roles are Mrs. Jolley and Mrs. Flack, both representatives of middle-class suburban values. It is apparent from just a brief description of White's cast of characters that *Riders in the Chariot* reveals the richness, complexity and variety of life in suburbia. Close readings of White's characters and themes demonstrate White's subtle exploration of suburbia, revealing that White was not an anti-suburban writer and that his representations of suburbia are in fact complex and ambivalent.

Miss Hare's rejection of conventional behaviour can be interpreted as a criticism of suburban values; conversely, she can be viewed as evidence that suburbia contains a variety of people following diverse lifestyles, and that suburbia is not homogeneous, nor is it necessarily "plastic" and in conflict with nature. Although Miss Hare prefers to be alone, her ill health requires her to employ a housekeeper, Mrs. Jolley, a widow from suburban Melbourne. (22) White establishes the women as opposites from the outset and sets up the conflict that inevitably ensues. When Miss Hare later expresses her fear that Mrs. Jolley is unhappy at Xanadu, Mrs. Jolley replies, "a lady does expect something different," specifying "a home, and a Hoover, and kiddies' voices." (67) Here White aligns Mrs. Jolley with stereotypical suburban values, such as domesticity, cleanliness, motherhood and consumerism.

White uses the contentious relationship between Miss Hare and Mrs. Jolley to explore spirituality and religion, subjects rarely associated with Australian suburbia. When Mrs. Jolley inquires if Miss Hare is a Christian, Miss Hare replies, "'It would not be for me to say, even if I understood exactly what that means'" (73-74). Mrs. Jolley, in contrast, boldly declares, "'I attended the C. of E. [Church of England] ever since I was a kiddy.'" (74) Mrs. Jolley, with her certainty and adherence to mainstream Christian views, is juxtaposed to Miss Hare, who admits, upon being pressed, "'I believe. I cannot tell you what I believe in, any more than what I am ... Oh, yes, I believe! I believe in what I see, and what I cannot see." (74) Mrs. Jolley is both unable to understand or accept a spiritual position different from her own, so much so that she is enraged.

Thus, while Miss Hare represents a spirituality and communion with nature unrestricted by either religion or structures built by humans, Mrs. Jolley takes refuge in a religion with clear boundaries and a suburban ethos that is similarly defined and solid. Miss Hare dreads conversations with Mrs. Jolley, which the narrator describes as "the piles of brick that Mrs Jolley built to house her family in, the red brick boxes increasing and encroaching" (77). Although White's narrator employs images of suburbia in a negative manner in this passage, it would be a mistake to read it as an attack on suburbia by White or evidence of his alleged anti-suburbanism, since such a reading relies on a conflation of White and his narrator. Even if White conveys some of his own attitudes and prejudices, either through his narrator or his characters, his narrative technique employs numerous points of view and his characters present a variety of attitudes, making it impossible to identify any one position as White's.

White's characterisation of Mrs. Godbold allows him to deal with issues common in suburban fiction, such as domestic violence and immigration. While the domestic violence can be read as a negative depiction of suburbia (or simply a realistic, neutral depiction), Mrs. Godbold is unlike the other immigrants in the novel in that she is not discriminated against or pressured to assimilate, undoubtedly because she is English. White thus demonstrates that immigrants are ill-treated due to racism and xenophobia, rather than because they are not Australian-born. Mrs. Godbold also serves as evidence that suburbia is not solely populated by evil suburban housewives like Mrs. Jolley and Mrs. Flack, but also by morally upright women who are more concerned with helping others than acquiring the latest consumer products and gossiping about their neighbours.

Near the end of the novel, after the deaths of Himmelfarb and Dubbo and the disappearance of Miss Hare, Xanadu (Miss Hare's crumbling mansion) is demolished. The residents of Sarsaparilla, including Mrs. Jolley and Mrs. Flack, gather to watch the destruction, which they find entertaining. (605; 611-13) Not only is the house razed, but the native bush that Miss Hare loved is also destroyed. In a passage similar to those found in many suburban novels, White describes the destruction of the natural environment by suburban development: "the bulldozers went into the scrub at Xanadu. The steel caterpillars mounted the rise, to say nothing of any sapling, or scrubby growth that stood in their way, and down went resistance." (624) After Xanadu is demolished, the site is "shaved right down to a bald, red, rudimentary hill" on which the developers erect pre-fabricated homes. (624) In the novel's clearest anti-suburban passage, which David Malouf describes as "one of … [White's] most savage sermons on the ugly, characterless fibro homes that have replaced the grand folly of Xanadu" (2002, ix-x), White depicts the lives of the residents of the new development as fragile, conformist, lacking in meaning and boring. The new homes cling to

> bare earth, where ... the wafer-walls of the new homes ... rub together at night, and sleepers might have been encouraged to enter into one another's dreams, if these had not been similar. Sometimes the rats of anxiety could be heard gnawing already at Bakelite or plastic ... So that, in the circumstances, it was not unusual for people to run outside and jump into their cars. All of Sunday they would visit, or be visited ... Then, on finding nothing at the end, they would drive around, and around. They would drive and look for something to look at. (636)

However, the unmistakably anti-suburban sentiments of the passage are countered five pages later. Several years after the construction of the new homes, Mrs. Godbold visits the site where Xanadu once stood Upon arriving at the new development, "Mrs. Godbold could not help admiring the houses for their signs of life: for the children coming home from school, for a row of young cauliflowers, for a convalescent woman, who had stepped outside in a dressing gown to gather a late rose." (640) Unlike White's narrator, Mrs. Godbold sees the suburban development as full of vitality, rather than conformity, boredom and meaningless, empty lives. Mrs. Godbold begins visiting the new development frequently, "where the new homes rocked and shouted with life." (641)

Malouf describes the passage as a "beautiful coda to the book," claiming, "Only the greatest masters can stand aside and allow themselves to be admonished by one of their creations whose vision, by some miracle of autonomy, is larger than their own." (2002, ix-x) However, Malouf's suggestion that White is being admonished by Mrs. Godbold rests on the assumption that the anti-suburbanism in the aforementioned passage represents White's own attitude towards suburbia. In fact, White's inclusion of an opposing viewpoint (Mrs. Godbold's) is evidence that he is not necessarily anti-suburban. One must not assume that the narrator, or a certain character, speaks for the author. White presents a number of conflicting attitudes towards suburbia – all, some or none of which may represent the author's personal views.

Riders in the Chariot undoubtedly contains some anti-suburban material; however, claims that the novel and its author are anti-suburban need to be made with caution. Such claims rely on a reductive interpretation of the novel that conflates White and his narrator and ignores material that either celebrates suburbia or fails to fit into a pro-suburban/anti-suburban binary. Simon During argues that White was part of a modernist literary movement "that can only be understood in terms of its critique of contemporary culture," and claims that White made his reputation through novels "profoundly critical ... of contemporary Australian ways of life, such as suburbia, middle-class affluence and love of sport." (1996, 36, 11) However, being critical of contemporary culture does not make one anti-suburban, since, as the second quotation from During acknowledges, suburbia is only one facet of Australian society.

Robin Gerster acknowledges that White depicts suburbia as a location in which artistic creation occurs, even while arguing that White hates the suburbs and views them as aesthetically barren and ugly (1990, 573); he claims White turns suburbia "into a geographic hell ruled by female demons." (1990, 567) Even if Gerster's depiction of White's characterisation of Mrs. Jolley, Mrs. Flack and Shirl Rosetree were accurate, an author's contempt for the behaviour of a group of characters by no means equates to contempt or hatred for suburbia. Gerster goes on to accuse White of possessing a "waspish preoccupation" with "suburban materialism" and posits that he "employs the Shirl Rosetrees of this world as the most common denominators against which the few spiritually rich suburbanites are celebrated for their difference." (1990, 567) Again, even if one accepts Gerster's assessment of White's attitude towards suburbia and its residents, the fact remains that White celebrates residents of suburbia, and that, as Gerster himself phrases it, suburbanites can be "spiritually rich." (1990, 567)

Regarding the 'Riders,' often viewed by critics as outsiders in suburbia, Jacqueline Banerjee argues,

> Surely the point is that *no* society can admit such people. The herd instinct, the instinct for survival – call it what you will – self-interest under some guise or another will close the ranks against

those who are born, or made, too sensitive to life's sufferings; too earnest in their search for truth through them" (1979, 111).

Thus, Banerjee views White's depiction of the rejection of the 'Riders' by the citizens of Sarsaparilla as a criticism of the 'herd instinct' or mob mentality, rather than a criticism of suburbia. Indeed, the mock-crucifixion of Himmelfarb could have occurred anywhere, not just in suburbia, as White has argued. Kerryn Goldsworthy argues that rather than criticising a specific community, such as the suburban community of Sarsaparilla, the target of White's critique is "an *absence* of any coherent sense of community in ordinary Australian life." (2000: 128) Carolyn Bliss acknowledges that *Riders in the Chariot* "ends by celebrating more than it questions or condemns. Even the virulent satire ... is tempered by Mrs. Godbold's final awareness that life in any form is precious." (1986, 98) Even *if* White does convey some of his own attitudes and prejudices through his narrator and characters, his narrative technique makes it impossible to identify any one position as White's. *Riders in the Chariot* presents an ambivalent attitude toward suburbia, containing both celebration and condemnation, and previous assertions by critics that White and his fiction are anti-suburban have failed to take into account the nuances and complexity of White's representations of suburbia. Thus, the notion that White is an anti-suburban writer must be seen for what it truly is: pure myth.

Works Cited

Ackland, Michael. 2002. "Patrick White," *Dictionary of Literary Biography 260. Australian Writers, 1915-1950*, ed. Selina Samuels. Detroit: Thomson Gale: 400-415.

Bannerjee, Jacqueline. 1979. "A Reassessment of Patrick White's *Riders in the Chariot*," *The Literary Half-Yearly* 20.2: 91-113.

Bliss, Carolyn. 1986. *Patrick White's Fiction: The Paradox of Fortunate Failure*. New York: St. Martin's.

Brady, Veronica. 2005. "God, History, and Patrick White," *The Sacred in Australian Literature*, ed. Bill Ashcroft, Frances

Devlin-Glass and Lyn McCredden, Special Issue of *Antipodes* 19.2 (Dec.): 172-176.

Dewey, Joseph. 2004. "Patrick White (1912-1990)," *World Writers in English, Volume II: R. K. Narayan to Patrick White*, ed. Jay Parini. New York: Scribner's: 747- 65.

During, Simon. 1996. *Patrick White.* Melbourne: Oxford University Press.

Gerster, Robin. 1990. "Gerrymander: The Place of Suburbia in Australian Fiction," *Meanjin* 49.3: 565-575.

Goldsworthy, Kerryn. 2000. "Fiction from 1900 to 1970," *The Cambridge Companion to Australian Literature,* ed. Elizabeth Webby.Cambridge: Cambridge University Press: 105-133.

Kinnane, Garry. 1998. "Shopping at Last! History, Fiction and the Anti-Suburban Tradition, *Writing the Everyday: Australian Literature and the Limits of Suburbia,* ed. Andrew McCann. Special Issue of *Australian Literary Studies* 18.4 :41-55.

Malouf, David. 1961. "Introduction.*Riders in the Chariot,"* New York Review of Books 2002: v-x.

Marr, David. 1992. *Patrick White: A Life.* New York: Knopf.

McCann, Andrew. 1998. "Decomposing Suburbia: Patrick White's Perversity," *Writing the Everyday: Australian Literature and the Limits of Suburbia,*ed. Andrew McCann. Special Issue of *Australian Literary Studies* 18.4: 56-71.

—. 1997 "The Ethics of Abjection: Patrick White's *Riders in the Chariot,*" *Australian Literary Studies* 18.2 (October): 145-155.

O'Reilly, Nathanael. 2006. "Rejecting and Perpetuating the Anti-Suburban Tradition: Representations of the Suburbs in *The Tax Inspector, Johnno* and *Cloudstreet*," *Antipodes* 20.1 (June): 20-25.

—. 2012. *Exploring Suburbia: The Suburbs in the Contemporary Australian Novel*. Amherst, NY: Teneo Press.

Powell, Diane. 1993. *Out West: Perceptions of Sydney's Western Suburbs.* St. Leonards, New South Wales: Allen & Unwin.

Webby, Elizabeth. 2000."Introduction", *The Cambridge Companion to Australian Literature,* ed. Elizabeth Webby, Cambridge: Cambridge University Press: 1-18.

White, Patrick. 1981. *Flaws in the Glass: A Self-Portrait*. London: Penguin.

—. 1958. "The Prodigal Son." *Australian Letters* 1.3: 37-40.
—. 1961. *Riders in the Chariot.* London: Eyre & Spottiswoode.
—. 1966. *The Solid Mandala.* London: Eyre & Spottiswoode.
Wilde, William H. et.al. 1991. *The Oxford Companion to Australian Literature*. Melbourne: Oxford University Press.

CHAPTER SEVEN

PATRICK WHITE:
THE QUEST OF THE ARTIST

SATENDRA NANDAN
UNIVERSITY OF CANBERRA

One of the epigraphs to *The Vivisector* is a quotation from the English painter Ben Nicholson. It expresses a major theme in White's fiction for it expresses the idea that both the artist and the mystic are searching for "the understanding and realisation of infinity." Several of White's characters attempt to reach or reveal the Infinite in their lived lives or artistic creations. Even in his first published short story, "The Twitching Colonel", there are suggestions of a yearning for a self beyond the conscious self. The Colonel longs to transcend the ephemeral: "I shall strip myself of the onion-folds of prejudice, till standing naked though conscious I see myself complete or else be consumed like the Hindu conjurer who is translated into space." (TC. 602-609) Theodora Goodman in *The Aunt's Story* reaches a heightened awareness where "light and silence ate into the hard, resisting barriers of reason, hinting at some ultimate moment of clear vision" (VIV. 290). Stan Parker's lifetime search in *The Tree of Man* ends with a vision "that One, and no other figure, is the answer to all sums." (TM. 497) Voss believes that in this "disturbing country" ... it is possible more easily to discard the inessential and to attempt the infinite." (V. 38)

The search for the Infinite occurs in many novels where an artist figure appearsand is integral to the character's existence. Through his art, the artist strives towards an understanding of the unknown and the unseen. The quest for this ultimate revelation sometimes becomes so obsessive that the act of creation itself acquires associations of a sacred ritual. The artist is regarded as a creator akin to God; Nature is looked upon as the art of God, the original artist. Edgar Allan Poe, as Beebe shows, illuminates this in his work. (Beebe 1964, 114-117)

> The whole visible universe is but a storehouse of images and signs to which the imagination will give a relative place and value; it is a sort of pasture which the imagination must digest and transform. (Beebe 1964, 131-32)

The artist endeavours through his art not to supersede God but to imitate Him. This attempt at imitation becomes a ceaseless search for the infinite, a quest which is basic to White's work. As Kiernan has observed, "Fundamental to each of White's novels is a creative tension between being and essence, an ambivalence between the compulsion to identify the self with the fluctuant natural world and the urge to transcend it, to escape from the processes of time and Nature into pure being that the permanent forms inherent in Nature proclaim." (1971, 46)

In contemporary literature, the artist figure has become a compelling metaphor of man's complex existence. For example, Thomas Mann uses an old myth in *Dr.Faustus* to unravel the moral and creative contradictions of a society, through Adrian Leverkühn, the diseased genius, so gifted and accursed. In the works of Yeats and Eliot the images of the artist are presented as being engaged in seeking, through human experience, an ultimate apprehension of reality. There is perhaps a deeper affinity of sensibilities between Eliot and White than has been realised. Eliot as an American and White as an Australian are each able to endow the fragmented modern experience with a composite vision. White, like Eliot, is preoccupied with what F. O. Matthiessen defined as the central realisation of the contemporary artist:

> ... a realisation [that] can lead either to chaos or to a sense of the potential unity of life ... The problem for the artist is to discover some unified pattern in this variety; and yet, if he believes as Eliot does that poetry should embody a man's reaction to his whole experience, also to present the full sense of its complexity. (1972, 35)

Few contemporary novelists have attempted to project a vision of this bewildering variety of experience with more poetic intensity than White. This develops into the artist's quest for the Infinite because below the flux of time and life, he is aware of a common and continuing principle underlying all manifestations of existence. It is an attempt to grasp the essential nature and spiritual unity of the essence of life through the artist's imagination. White lays bare an experience that is profoundly religious in its final apprehension and aesthetic in its expression. The aesthetic acts of creation acquire the resonances of worship.

White has described Alf Dubbo's efforts at painting as "worshipful acts" and explores this further through the more sophisticated character of Hurtle Duffield. White spoke of his own exploration of the religious experience through Duffield:

> I do it through Duffield whose "celebration of the world in painting" is of course "a mode of worship". I think Duffield realised this from the beginning, though only unconsciously. Finally it emerges as I try to show. Only at the end will he admit it. I believe that most people if they are honest with themselves, have in them the germ of religious faith, but they are either too lazy or too frightened, or too ashamed intellectually to accept the fact. (Wilkes and Herring 1973, 142)

Several critics have paid particular attention to this aspect of White's *oeuvre* (Morley 1972; Green 1973; Beatson1976). I shall explore through three novels: *Voss* (1957), *Riders in the Chariot* (1961) and *The Vivisector* (1970) this cardinal strand in White's *ouevre*. In the first, the poet and the explorer discover their strength and weakness in the devastating wilderness of a vast desert, away from human society. In the second novel the artist is an unknown Aboriginal man who creates the intimations of immortality through the sterility, and cruelty endured in the suburb of Sarsparilla. In the last novel, the artist is a famous painter with a great reputation who attempts in his final paintings to unravel the mystery of Infinity through the spaces of his own imagination. It may be impossible to achieve the final revelation or to communicate it, but to attempt to do so is necessary. Integral to this search are the themes of suffering and loving kindness, evil and the possibility of redemption, arrogance and humility, mystery and simplicity; all of these are an inevitable part of the striving for ultimate knowledge. White may have been influenced by the concept of *malheur* as defined by Simone Weil. (Weil in Cabaud 1964, 209: Weil 1951, 63-42)

With *Voss,* "The Great Australian Emptiness" itself becomes a powerful metaphor for the desert within man. Voss's adventure across unexplored Australia leads him to turn inwards into the nature of his own self and being. The multiple significances of Voss's quest are well summed up by R.F.Brissenden:

> *Voss* is ... a parable in which Patrick White tries to illuminate in religious terms, the struggle in man's heart between pride and humility, faith in oneself and faith in God, and in which he tries also to analyse and lay bare the nature of Australian life, to cut through to the spiritual centre of Australian society. (1969, 25-26)

This is most illuminatingly and enigmatically explored in the relationship between the artist, Frank Le Mesurier, and the explorer, Johann Ulrich Voss. A great deal has been written about Voss and Laura's telepathic relationship but the other major theme - the theme that reinforces Laura's commitment to Voss - has rarely been explicated. G.A. Wilkes has commented on this:

> The critical flurry caused by the "telepathic" episodes, however, has obscured some more essential processes at work in the book, and has hindered inquiry into such questions as why the perception of a transfigured world should lead Voss to the discovery that "each visible object has been created for purposes of love." (Wilkes 1973, 134)

Much of this awareness is brought about in Voss by the gradually developing nexus between the artist and the explorer until both, in their journey, reach the same point of self-apprehension and through that the apprehension of a composite reality Laura has sensed the spiritual depths within Voss. She sees him "possessed by an understanding" (31) which others don't even aspire to. It is, however, in his confrontation with the poet Le Mesurier that he begins to see the flickerings of other realities. The poet is introduced early in the novel:

> He was somewhat moody. He would be looking at a spider, or into the grain of the balusters ... Frank Le Mesurier could not look too much, though what he did with what he saw was not always evident. He did not communicate at once. (36)

There is an element of quiet pride in the poet and it is he who challenges the German on the ship, asking him about his motives for coming to Australia. And it is to him that Voss reveals his honest answer: "'Yes', answered Voss, without hesitation, 'I will cross the continent from one end to the other. I have every intention to know it with my heart.'" (36) What Voss does not realise is that both the poet and the country will bring to him a greater knowledge of the human heart. A sense of kinship develops between the two "for the dark, young, rather exquisite, but insolent fellow did not cling like Harry Robarts." (37)

In their meeting amongst the scrub and rocks of the Domain, their real natures are further dissected and displayed. To Voss's deliberately provocative question about his purpose in life, the poet gives an enigmatic but prophetic reply: "'I rather suspect," he added, " it is something I shall not discover till I am at my last gasp'" (38). They become aware of an affinity of souls and when Voss invites him to join the expedition, his frank answer is, "'I am not sure that I want to cut my throat just yet.'" Voss's equally prophetic reply, "To make yourself, it is necessary to destroy yourself," establishes between them an essential honesty.

Thus the physical expedition turns out eventually to be a spiritual quest. Voss's party is carefully selected to offer the leader his severest challenges in human relationships: Palfreyman is a scientist, Harry Robarts, an idiot, Turner, a drunkard, Angus, a landowner, Judd, a convict, Le Mesurier, a poet, and the Aboriginals, old Dugald and young Jackie. The most powerful impact on Voss's personality is made by the poet. As the expedition makes its tortuous progress, Voss receives the confidences of the members of his party: "Voss received these confidences, and locked them up quickly" (151) to be used at some future occasion but Le Mesurier is the one, "who would not tell." (151)

Voss suspects him of some subterranean strength. It appears that the poet derives his strength from the physical world in which he sees resonances of his own creativity. For example, when they arrive at Rhine Towers Le Mesurier's response is a physical as well as spiritual:

> Already the evening of his arrival, upon scenes of splendour such as he had known to exist but never met, Frank Le Mesurier had begun to change. The sun's sinking had dissolved all hardnesses. ... (152)

This golden splendour grows into a creative inspiration as he reaches out to the created world:

> All that this man had not lived began to be written down. His failures took shape, but in flowers, and mountains, and in words of love. When his poem was written, it was burning on the paper. At last, he had done this. (152)

But what Le Mesurier is "hiding" is his growing awareness as an artist of the humanity which Voss is continually denying - something Laura had sensed in their brief meetings. In one of her letters she writes: "For I do respect some odd streak of humanity that *will* appear in you in spite of all your efforts after reading poetry, for instance, or listening to music, while your eyes are still closed." (199) Voss writes to Laura of Le Mesurier and his strength: "So, we have our visions. Frank Le Mesurier has experienced something of importance that he is keeping hidden from me." (231) Voss tests him through sending him alone into a terrible storm where he becomes one with the elements:

> he was dissolved, he was running into crannies, and
> sucked into the mouths of the earth, and disputed,
> and distributed but again, and again, for some purpose,
> was made one by the strength of a will not his own. (266)

He composes a poem where "the silky seed that fell in milky rain from the Moon was raised up by the Sun's laying his hands upon it. ... it was seen that the world of fire and the world of ice were the same." (266)

For Voss, a crucial act of humility comes when he tends Le Mesurier in his illess and sees "the true colours of hell." (288) Le

Mesurier tells Voss that the roots of his poetry go down to the soil of perpetual struggle and failure: When the poet adds "of course, we are both failures," (290) Voss's admission of this truth unites them "at last." (290) Having known and understood each other's secrets, they sleep.

Le Mesurier's understanding sharpens into so intense an empathy, that he begins to see Laura in his imagination and is filled with "love and poetry, as is only right, between the spasms of suffering" (304). Voss is frightened by the poet's self-knowledge. When he finally looks into Le Mesurier's book of poems, he responds "from the deepest part of him, from the beginning of his life" (317). Le Mesurier's *Conclusion* becomes, at the end, Voss's own heartfelt prayer:

> O God, my God, I pray that you will take my spirit out of this my body's remains, and after you have scattered it, grant that it shall be everywhere, and in the rocks, and in the empty water holes, and in true love of all men, and in you O God at last. (317)

In *Voss* the explorer and the artist, the man and the woman, attain "the communion of souls" (448) while exploring the spiritual experience in the desert of rationality and arrogance, away from ordinary society In *Riders in the Chariot*, it is amidst the complex life of a suburb, that the quest for the Infinite continues through the life-experience of the four central characters: Mary Hare, the mad woman from Xanadu, Mordecai Himmelfarb, the Jew from Germany, Ruth Godbold, the simple English washerwoman and Alf Dubbo, the half-caste Aboriginal artist. In the opening conversation between Himmelfarb and Miss Hare, all the important motifs of the novel are hinted at: the evil that corrodes and destroys: the capacity for resurrection; the ever present phenomenal world; and the timeless image of the Chariot, suggesting man's innate and perennial hunger for the Infinite.

In the portrayal of the artist and his creative acts the artist Dubbo is given insights into the lives of Miss Hare, Himmelfarb, and Mrs Godbold. Only by apprehending the nature of their realities, does Dubbo finally compose a comprehensive artistic view of the Infinite in the physical world and the creatures who dwell in its crevices with whom the mad woman, Miss Hare finds her sense of identification: "But the earth is wonderful ... It has brought me back when, otherwise I shall have died." (RC 172) It is her father's cryptic remark, "Who are the riders in the Chariot, eh, Mary?" that leads her "to expect of life some ultimate revelation." (26)

This mystery, this revelation, she finally glimpses in the fellowship of the other three illuminates. When she encounters Dubbo, "their souls had stroked each other with reassuring feather but very briefly, for each had suddenly taken fright. (68) With the arrival of Himmelfarb in Sarsaparilla events move to climactic revelation. To emphasise the Jew's final trial and suffering, and to relate it to a universal context, the novelist portrays his life vividly in Germany. The Jewish faith, a way of life with his parents and community, becomes to him "like a winter overcoat oppressive and superfluous." (112) After his miraculous escape from Friedendorf, Himmelfarb arrives in Australia and, at Harry Rosetree's factory, meets Dubbo and develops a wordless but deeply empathetic relationship with him. If Miss Hare is aware of the Infinite through instinct, and Himmelfarb through a renunciation of the intellect, Mrs God bold, the third illuminate, walks the same path with faith and love.

Mrs. Godbold experiences moments of both mystical joy and of profound sorrow. Her first experience of great music in the cathedral makes her float "in the cloud of indecision, soothed by the infinitely kind fingers." (265) When she encounters the Aborigine Dubbo in the squalid surrounding of the brothel to which she has gone on the chance of 'saving' her husband, she meets the artist who makes her recall the music in "the cathedral of her home town" (318). Immediately they establish an inner rapport (319) in the chaos at Mrs Khalil's. Mrs. Godbold's simple, compassionate act of wiping the blood from the abo's mouth becomes "her work of art, her act of devotion." (320)

It is in the artist's creative crucible that the colours of life will have to be mixed before they acquire significance beyond individual experience. Himmelfarb's crucifixion becomes the catalyst that brings the illuminates together and stirs the artist's imagination to create a comprehensive, composite whole out of life's disparate experiences. Thus set against a world dominated by "social and economic faith on which stone mansions are built," (335) the faith of the illuminates is challenged.

Having established the spiritual affinity between the two outcasts, the novelist delineates the making of Dubbo's comprehensive imagination – an imagination that will give final meaning, coherence and definition to the disjointed but kindred experience of all the illuminates. White connects Dubbo's imagination to the river on the banks of which he is reared. The boy grows up in Numburra convinced of "some potentiality" (355) in the creative act which time and life will reveal. Adopted by Rev Timothy Calderon and his sister Mrs. Pask, he gains knowledge of his vocation and destiny as a painter. He sees a painting of the Chariot by a French painter and is given a book on painting which ignites his imagination:

When the rector reads the Gospel of St John "of spiritual love and beauty," (361) the boy fails to see the face of Jesus. It takes him a whole life-time to discover the true face of Jesus. Dubbo intuitively feels that he will have to go throughout the terrors of the flesh before he will be able to grasp the Infinite. Gradually the efforts at painting acquire the semblance of acts of worship and the experience of suffering becomes the essential factor in Dubbo's artistic growth. Abused by his protector and subsequently by all the other human beings he encounters, it is his arrival in Sarsaparilla and meeting with the other three initiates that prepares him for his final act of worship rendered through his paintings.

Dubbo's final phase begins with his encounter with Himmelfarb and a state of trust is established by a subtler than human means. On the actual day of Himmelfarb's torture, Dubbo has the artist's premonition that something will happen to Himmelfarb for "while standing on the flat floor, Alf Dubbo was stationed as if upon an eminence, watching what he alone was gifted or fated enough to see. Neither the actor, nor the spectator, he was that most miserable of human beings, the artist." (RC. 457) Towards the end of the novel each illuminate experiences a vision of truth but it is only the artist Alf Dubbo who is able to confer on their shared experience a truly coherent character and unity. In Mrs Godbold's shack he has finally seen the expression of love that has escaped him all his life. The vision of the women caring for the dying Himmelfarb is transfused into a vision of Christ's Deposition. He leaves convinced that at last he has an understanding of the Infinite, which his art must now embody and express.

The painting of the Four Living Creatures expresses the artist's final understanding the essence of their individual experiences:

> One figure might have been done in marble, massive, white, inviolable. A second was conceived in wire, with a star inside the cage, and a crown of barbed wire. The wind was ruffling the harsh, fox coloured coat of the third ... The fourth was constructed of bleeding twigs and spattered leaves, but the head could have been a whirling spectrum. (514-15)

In composing his last work of art, Dubbo integrates his lifes's manifold experiences into a single, protean vision. The quest of the artist is to give that vision coherence and permanence and a meaning beyond. If the inherent evil in a society is portrayed with frightening reality, the possibility of redemption, of faith, of continuity of life is asserted with considerable imaginative power.

In *The Vivisector* the artist-figure moves centre-stage; he is the protagonist of the novel, whose life becomes an integrating, ever-expanding metaphor for the same quest, and the profound attempt at the "realisation of Infinity" which has characterised the struggles of the artist figures in the two previous novels coincides with the moment of death. His final vision is perhaps most evocatively presented in the last moments of Hurtle Duffield.

This discussion will concentrate mainly on the last section of this novel and the focus it develops at that stage to highlight this aspect of the artist's quest. The search for a supreme reality is reinforced and enfolded in his relationship with his hunchback sister, Rhoda, and his love for another artist, Kathy Volkov. Kathy takes his artistic spirit into the future. It is, however, only when Duffield is able to relate to the others "stroked by God" – Cec Cutbush, the grocer, Mrs. Volkov, Kathy's mother – that he is able finally to cross the last and the longest spiritual desert and attain the final vision of the infinite in the "vertiginous blue." (White 1970, 641)

The meeting of Rhoda and Duffield in the last phase of their lives is carefully orchestrated by the novelist. It is accidental but fateful. Their reunion is deeply spiritual. Hurtle discovers that

Rhoda already knows he is living in Flint Street. Beneath her unemotional exterior he can feel her spirit reaching out, to embrace his. When Rhoda declines to go with him, for the first time Duffield, the artist, appeals to human feelings. The moving scene where the brother and sister pull the go-cart towards the artist's house reveals not only the human aspect of both, but also the burden of solitude both will have to bear together. When they reach his house, the paintings – the "raison d'etre of his existence" – are "shimmering." (458) Rhoda refuses to acknowledge their beauty, implying perhaps, that these works of art pale before the true understanding of life which he has still to acquire. Rhoda tells him that she has been staying with a friend who is rich in Christian charity and has not been destroyed by suffering, nor has the "compulsion to plumb the depths." (461) The thematic significance of this friend, Christina Mcbeath, becomes clear only towards the end of the novel when through her letter she inspires Duffield to attempt his last painting.

He persuades Rhoda to stay with him ostensibly "to tie the end of my life to the beginning" (467) but really so that by "his sister's presence Kathy Volkov would be protected from debauch and himself from destruction. (468) What Rhoda's affliction and hunchback have made patently obvious to her, the artist's ego has prevented him from seeing. Nevertheless, his paintings remain his one source of strength and solace. Kathy's departure, in pursuit of her art, is a further blow to his egotism.

His sickness is more than pneumonia: it is a spiritual malaise. About this time Rhoda informs him that Mrs. Volkov has suffered a "mild stroke." (510) Duffield hasn't met Mrs. Volkov but a secret relationship develops between them something akin to the relationship between Dubbo and Himmelfarb. He is able to relate himself to Mrs Volkov with intense empathy:

> It was the sudden thought of a blighted hand which paralysed him as he floundered into bed. So he lay wondering whether he believed in God the Merciful as well as God the Vivisector; he wondered whether he believed in God as he lay massaging his right hand. (510)

This capacity to suffer vicariously for others gradually brings about in the artist the disintegration of the shell of his ego. It is only when he achieves this that the reach for the infinite begins. He is also able to understand a deeper disillusionment with Kathy in the light of his past and realises that:

> He had sympathised with the passionate illusions of several women, and could hardly be held responsible for their impulse to destroy themselves through what they misunderstood as love; until finally: he had himself been destroyed by a little egotistical girl whom he valued above his vocation. (528)

With this comes the realisation: "Rhoda, the reality, not Katherine Volkov, the figment, was what he had been given to love." (529) Thus while Kathy remains in his imagination as a "flawed masterpiece" compared to other women in his life and one "in which the artist most nearly conveyed his desires and faith" it is Rhoda who is an inner "growth which he had learnt to live with." (536) During this period he creates some of his greatest paintings.

As he walks carrying a sheep's heart for Rhoda's infernal cats, through Shitter Lane, he has his first stroke in front of Cec Cutbush's shop. Only for a brief moment he glimpses the deep secret relationship between the artist and the "vertiginous blue": "The colours vibrating. Too vivid. The extra indigo sky above casseta houses the drab human drabs." Hang on to the last and first secret the indigo." (571) After this first fall comes the awareness that hitherto "he had functioned intermittently by painful vibrations followed by illumination. But now he vibrated all the time, the light wouldn't switch on." (573) Don Lethbridge, whom Rhoda employs to help Hurtle recover physically, becomes a bridge between his physical and imaginative being. In a sense it is Cutbush, the grocer, who opens the door of his final perception. He tells him that the artist's house is "a place of pilgrimage … It was like as if, after attending regular service for years in a not very eyesthetical church, the same surrounding was illuminated by a – religion!" (582) There follows, what is a new awakening in Duffield thanks to Cutbush.

In these inner struggles to attain ultimate knowledge the artist tries to "master the razor-edge where simplicity unites with subtlety" (592). Later as he sits "teetering on the edge of the bed, dreading the desert he had to cross", he realises that "experience never lessened the prospect of tortures, the possibility of failures, even death if the spirit refused to accompany him … (625) But Duffield is too great an artist to deny the sheer physicality of existence. Indeed, he must finally grasp the infinite through this world, not by rejecting it. With this truth throbbing in him, on the "significant morning" he makes "his way from object to object opening and closing drawers, he was trying to relate what he saw with what he knew." (628) Finally the "wrestling match" starts as he is "beginning again" and with a heightened and new awareness of the Infinite, he climbs the" scaffold" and attempts to compress his new found truth into a painting which by its "compression, would convey the whole." (629) Lethbridge sees this work as the "whole of life." (631) Only the artist knows that some indefinable, indispensable element is missing from the painting. The core of the elusive, unattainable Infinite is still absent from this creative act.

So in winter he sits with Rhoda, who reads newspapers, especially the death notices. Then he receives, through Rhoda, a letter from Mrs. Volkov. Mrs Volkov's experience, narrated in the letter, acts as a catalyst to his imagination and throws him his last creative challenge: "I dreamed of God's Love and an understanding of His Purposes." From her own experience she gives the incident of the moment among pine trees when she was stung by a wasp as her "hand was put" in the wasp's hanging nest. After momentary pain, she sees "only sea and sky as one, and herself like a rinsed plate." It is that momentary vision of the oneness of creation that has prevented her from being "struck to the ground, even in the cruellest moments." (637)

With this confession from almost a stranger, the artist understands the meaning of suffering, which leads to the conquest of the ego so that one can be part of a larger Self. Mr. Cutbush's remark – "stroked by God" – illuminates his own fate as the Great Invalid and Mrs. Volkov reaffirms it, "I believe the afflicted to be united in the same purpose" and hopes that the artist, the most afflicted, sees farther than the "mere human diseased." (638) In his last painting the vivisector is finally vivisected: "the direction in which he had to go was already pricked out in him [and] somewhere in the lowest depths of mind or board, he had a sudden irrelevant, half formed vision of a tucked-up mongrel dog, beggarly tail scraping the ground between its legs" (638). The image will not be blotted out and it recurs "clamped to the operating table" (638). The great artist will not plead for mercy especially when he is about to enter a "hinterland of infinite prospects." (638)

Hurtle Duffield, the artist, works for a week on "what he no longer considered a painting"; rather he is "being worked on … all his life he had been reaching towards this vertiginous blue without truly visualising, till lying on the pavement he was dazzled not so much by a colour as a longstanding secret relationship" (641). With that knowledge, the artist makes his last efforts to capture in art "the otherwise unnameable I-N-D-I-G-O. Only reach higher. Could. And will." (641) Attaining this incalculable height – the last inch of the summit – is both impossible incommunicable even for the artist: and that finally explains the truth of the three stages in the consciousness of the artist as embodied in the graffiti which he had inscribed prophetically on the wall of his sunlit dunny:

God the Vivisector
God the Artist
God
(412)

In Duffield's ultimate efforts language breaks down: the human mediums of communication – language and art – reveal their inadequacies, only the artist glimpses in the heart of light, an ineffable reality. Thus the quest for the Infinite again ends in death – death suggesting possibly an opening to a final inexpressible revelation. The final struggle of the great artist, "towards the summit of his life" (611) is achieved through the path of suffering and affliction or what Weil has termed *malheur*. As Jacques Cabaud points out, there is a supernatural interpretation of *malheur*: "The infinity of time and space separates us from God. *Malheur* defeats the creative act and, by a supernatural mechanism as inevitable as that of nature, brings us back to God, yet only if we so wish." (Cabaud 1964, 210)

Affliction, then, is that "marvel of divine technique." a simple and ingenious device enabling the immensity of a 'blind, brutal and cold' force to enter into the depths of the soul of a finite creature. The weight of necessity falling from the creature directs all its quickening force upon a single point, the centre of the soul, and pierces it so that "By the rent eternity enters." That is possibly the last act of human creativity. The artist's quest costs nothing less than life and through the suffering involved, the artist – the most egotistical of beings – is pared to that level of existence in which he recognises, acknowledges and affirms in his paintings the presence of a power greater than himself.He has finally attained the vision of Infinity for which he has sought all his life.

Works Cited

Beatson, Peter. 1976. *The Eye in the Mandala*. London: Paul Elek.
Beebe, Maurice. 1964. *Ivory Towers and Sacred Founts*. New York: New York UniversityPress.
Cabaud, Jacques.1964. *Simone Weil*. London: Harvill Press.
Green, Dorothy. 1973. "The Edge of Error," *Quadrant* (December): 36-47.
Kiernan, Brian. 1971. *Images of Society and Nature*. Melbourne: Oxford University Press.
Morley, Patricia. 1972. *The Mystery of Unity*. Brisbane: University of Queensland Press.
White, Patrick. 1937. "The Twitching Colonel," *London Mercury* 35.210, (April): 602-9.
—. 1939. *Happy Valley*. London: George Harrap.
—. 1948. *The Aunt's Story*. London: Eyre & Spottiswoode.
—. 1956. *The Tree of Man*. London: Eyre & Spottiswoode.
—. 1957. *Voss*. London: Eyre & Spottiswoode.
—. 1961. *Riders in the Chariot*. London: Eyre and Spottiswoode.
—. 1970. *The Vivisector*. London: Jonathan Cape.
—. 1989. [1958] "The Prodigal Son," Paul Brennan and Christine Flynn, ed. *Patrick White Speaks*. Sydney: Primavera Press.
Wilkes, G. A. and Thelma Herring. Ed. 1970. *Ten Essays on Patrick White*. Sydney: Angus & Robertson.

Chapter Eight

Patrick White and Australia: Perspective of an Outsider

Pavithra Narayanan
Washington State University, Vancouver

> Unfortunately we live in black times with less and less that may be called good, and I suppose I must reflect the blackness of those times. I tried to write a book about saints, but saints are few and far between. If I were a saint myself I could project my saintliness, perhaps, endlessly in what I write. But I am a sensual and irritable human being. Certainly the longer I live, the less I see to like in the human beings of whom I am one. (Qtd. in Marr 1991, 453)

Reflecting, however briefly, on the state of the world in this year of Patrick White's birth centenary (2012), his view that, "we live in black times," rings more true than ever. There is not a single country unaffected by neoliberal economic globalisation and imperialism. Some regions of the world seem to live in a state of perpetual war. If technological advancements and economic mobility have enabled greater international and global interactions, they have also intensified parochial nationalisms and gross inequities between nations and between people within a single nation. Immigration is a contentious issue, the gap between the rich and the poor continues to widen, governments are openly influenced by corporations, there is increasing gloom about rising costs, unemployment, and lack of housing and healthcare even in the more prosperous nations of the western world.

I admire Patrick White for not writing about saints; sanctity seems of less relevance than the sheer capacity to survive amidst the challenges of modern-day life. There are people who survive and a great many more who keep on struggling to survive. What is also admirable about White is that his writings disturb his readers just enough so that the writer, like his protagonists, is far from idolised. Australia has never been quite sure of its relationship with its Nobel Prize laureate who helped to place Australian literature on the international literary map and at the same time was one of his country's most scathing critics. The country seemed to find it easier to label the writer as a bitter man, a pessimist, a cynic, or an outcast, rather than probe the question, as White did, as to "why we have become what we are today" (White 1981, 104). White's birth centenary year gives us an opportunity to revisit White, not just to examine his literary prowess, but to revisit White, the political writer, and to examine or re-examine our world against the backdrop of White's critical essays and later, the public speeches in his later years as passionate political activist.

Born on May 28, 1912 in England, the Australian novelist, short-story writer, playwright, essayist, and public speaker the multi-talented Patrick White, remains a central figure in the Australian cultural context. In the span of five decades, White produced twelve novels, three short story collections, eleven plays, one screenplay, and one autobiography. His thirteenth novel, *The Hanging Garden*, an unfinished manuscript, was published posthumously in 2012. White's essays, public speeches, and personal letters have also been compiled into two edited collections. His audiences mostly know him through his impressive and substantial novels. White's fictional narratives delineate the subtle inner journeys of the mind; they reflect the influence of writers such as Pavel, Chekov, James Joyce, D. H. Lawrence, Marcel Proust, and Gustave Flaubert. Each of his novels appear to trace a process of self-destruction, but it is an annihilation which is shown to be necessary, as Voss declares the protagonist is obliged "to make or find oneself." (V 1957, 31), the process is not cathartic? Suffering and self-negation, in White's fiction, illuminate the predicament of individuals who reject, and are rejected by, a society that is dedicated to materialism. His literary characters, White remarked, are representations of himself (1981, 23), and the themes of alienation and otherness which pervade his novels are grounded in the author's personal experiences of hostility he encountered as an Australian artist and citizen.)

White's first essay, "The Prodigal Son" (1958), written as a reply to Alistair Kershaw's defence of his decision to leave Australia again and to return finally to his life as an expatriate writer in London. (Dutton 1995, 213) This essay focuses on the politics of identity of both the author and Australia. It is about an artist who sees himself as expatriate, who is seen as both an outsider and an insider in Australia, who is forced to answer questions about life choices, and who finds that the place he has finally decided to call home is not an idyllic place to live. The essay is also about Australian materialism, or, as White described it, "the Great Australian Emptiness" which values wealth, exalts the average, and has little room for intellectual endeavours. (Brennan and Flynn, 15) Australia is central in White's work, but his perceptions about "the ugliness, the bags and iron of Australian life" (Brennan and Flynn, 17) were not informed by his experiences as an exile. His writings are not about a homeland that he left, but about one to which he had returned. White, therefore, is not an expatriate; he is not even a "prodigal son" because Australia was never a benevolent parent to him. The title of the essay and the rationale offered for returning and staying in Australia suggests that White felt that his choice to live outside Australia for twenty years might have been a mistake, at least as far as his literary career was concerned.

In letters to friends and family, White spoke of finding his roots and his conviction that he had made the right decision to settle in Australia. (1996, 72) His letter to his cousin, Peggy Garland, further indicates that he saw himself as an Australian writer: "Oddly enough, I feel I am intended to stay in Australia and write about it. I am vain enough to think I can write about it in a way that the others can't – and anyway, I can't write about anything else." (1996, 97) However, following mixed reviews his early novels received from Australian critics, White's re-discovery of his "home country," which he described as an "interesting experience" in 1946, turned into a painful one within a decade. (1996, 68)

Commenting on critiques of *Voss* and the notion of the "great Australian novel" White wrote:

> How sick I am of the bloody word AUSTRALIA. What a pity, I am part of it; if I were not, I would get out to-morrow. As it is, they will have me with them till my bitter end, and there are about six more of my un-Australian Australian novels to fling in their faces …" (1996, 130)

Voss (1957) received Australia's first Miles Franklin award and three years later, the award was given to his next novel, *Riders in the Chariot* (1961). This appreciation for White developed slowly, but, as David Marr notes, "Australia's critics were never really forgiven this tepid welcome home. (1996, 74)

White's novels often received acclaim overseas, however, within Australia, literary opinion of the author was, and is still, divided. (Dutton 1971, 6) Australian critics and writers seem to either passionately defend or to loathe the writer. Geoffrey Dutton speculates that Australia's mixed reactions to White might be a result of "critics not having any familiar cubby-hole for this strange Antipodean," but this did not stop them from comparing White "to almost every famous modern author, tossing in Tolstoy for good measure." (1971, 5) Samuel Beckett, Vladimir Nabokov, William Faulkner, Halldór Laxness, Thomas Mann, Janet Frame, Wole Soyinka, and Wilson Harris, are some of the writers with whom White has been positioned.

Despite his literary reputation, the enormous scholarly attention his writings receive, and his contributions to literary culture, many critics point out that White's "name seems temporarily and inexplicably lost" in Australia (Shakespeare 2012). Writer and journalist Barnaby Smith surmises that White is "either unknown or written off by the majority of Australians" because the author "never came across with softness or amiability" and also because of "the perceived formidableness of his work." (2012) Observations about White's temperament, in addition to debates about his Australianness, dominate many assessments of White. In a review of *The Twyborn Affair*, Rosemary Dinnage writes that White, the "turgid, crotchety, tortuous, racked, oblique writer," was "entirely committed to being an Australian writer and all his books are concerned, tenderly or savagely, with his homeland." However, she concludes that he is an "outsider" since "he was educated in

England and only went back to Australia to live in 1948." (1980, 25)

White's lineage, literary influences, large themes, and the perception that his novels are *unrepresentative* of Australia or its literary tradition are some of the other reasons scholars cite for the trouble they have in perceiving White as an Australian writer. (Budurlean 2009, 20-21) The underlying questioning of White's identity derives from the notion that critics imagine that they have the right to, provide a frame of reference for defining national/individual identity

For White, being an Australian imposed on him an unending endeavour of "self-searching," (Brennan and Flynn 1989, 47) of seeking and facing the truth about himself and his homeland. Despite moments of despair about the state of affairs in Australia and occasional urges to leave the country, it was in Australia, White hoped "to continue living, and while I still have the strength, to people the Australian emptiness in the only way I am able." ((Brennan and Flynn,1989, 44) This was White's promise to his fellow citizens - a promise to stay, to not run away at the "onset of philistinism," "to see things out," and to do whatever he could, because, as White said, on the same occasion, Australia, "after all, is my country." Until his death, White remained a politically engaged artist and citizen who was committed towards building an Australia that was "based on humility and humanity." (Brennan and Flynn 1989, 194) But there was no escape from queries about his decision to make Australia his home. Even after living in the country for twenty-five years, in an interview following his Nobel Prize award in1973, the writer was asked, "Would you ever think of going back overseas again?" A 61-year old White replied, "Not by now because I'm too old." (Charlton 1973)

It is not uncommon for scholars, critics, and interviewers to lay the burden of proof on authors to explain their writing, their choice of language, and their reasons for, or for not, migrating. Whatever the merits of such queries may be, in White's case, this line of inquiry offered his readers their first glimpse of White in his role as a public intellectual, or, as Dorothy Green describes it, "the voice of … [his] country's conscience." (1991, 1) His letters, essays and speeches became a space for the visionary artist to take a moral and ethical stance against injustice and power and White actively engaged with issues concerning Indigenous rights, environmentalism, war, nuclear disarmament, materialism, and nationalism. In part, it is this "political activism," in addition to "efforts by academics in our universities to break the canon in the name of greater inclusiveness and democracy," Geordie Williamson laments in a recent review of *The Hanging Garden* that "damaged" White's reputation (2012). The ways through which literary texts and figures acquire and sustain popular or canonical value are complex and complicated, but the critics' coupling of the author's activism and scholars' pursuit of canon reforms could explain Australia's neglect of White. However, to advocate greater attention to White's fiction is a myopic argument that reflects long-standing debates about functions and roles of scholars and writers.

Readers love a novelist who explores truth through fictional narratives, but a writer who speaks "truth to power" through political essays, public speeches and media outlets disrupts imaginary boundaries that define literary and aesthetic practices. The genre of non-fiction also removes the comfortable distance provided by fiction from where a reader can participate in discussions about suffering, alienation, and truth. Furthermore, the author makes it impossible to divide the categories "writer" and "activist" when he steps into the public sphere and engages with political and social issues of the day. It is in this position as a public intellectual that White becomes an outsider, or what Edward Said has called a metaphorical exile, who is restless, "never … fully adjusted, always feeling outside the chatty, familiar world inhabited by natives … constantly being unsettled, and unsettling others." (1994, 39)

There is no doubt that White's intellectual and public engagements with Australian politics, policies and practices, disrupted, disturbed, and unsettled his audiences. He knew that his political speeches would position him, yet again, as "an outsider" in Australia, a status that he had to come to terms with for most of his life. His homosexuality, his "un-Australian Australian novels," and his expatriate years had marked him over and over again as an outsider, but this positioning only strengthened his conviction that he had a moral responsibility to actively speak out against injustice, discrimination, war, "hypocrisy, side-stepping, and arrogant disregard for truth." (Brennan and Flynn 1989, 86) If by sticking his neck out and expressing his beliefs publicly he became even more of "an outsider," White said, it "won't be any great hardship as I've been that as far back as I can remember - something strange and unacceptable in the eyes of those who believe they see straight" (Brennan and Flynn 1989, 116). White's outsider hood had shaped his creativity and activism and also empowered him with "courage of a kind" that he wanted "every Australian to acquire." Civic responsibility, according to White, outweighed costs that individuals might pay for speaking the truth, for challenging institutions of power, or for attempting to change society. It was imperative, the author maintained, that "each of us search for the good faith in us which may help save the world, even if we risk turning ourselves into outsiders in this materialistic, muscular Australian society." (Brennan and Flynn 1989, 117)

White's work as a public intellectual won him both admirers and critics. David Marr, Dorothy Green, Brigid Rooney, Brian Kiernan, Geoffrey Dutton, Alma Budurlean, and R. F. Brissenden are some of the scholars who appreciate and acknowledge the significance of White's activism. Rooney points out that White played a leading and influential role in the 1960s when "a new cultural intelligentsia arose ... as the bearers of a progressive ... vision of nation." (2009, xvi) But the image that he had of "his fellow Australians, not only as they were, but as they might be" also provoked strong reactions from the public and his readers. (Green, 1991: 1) While political and intellectual disagreements are to be expected, the personal attacks on White are troubling. Irked that despite White's harsh criticisms of Australia, the author is perceived as a national and literary icon, critics like David Tacey, Philip Adams and Simon During seem to regard White as undeserving of his celebrity and literary status. Their prejudicial references to White as "that queer, largely Australia-hating writer" (During 1996, 100), also the writer who "despised Australians for most of his career ... knocking over cultural values, hitting at established authorities, destroying anything sacred," (Tacey 1990, 62) and one whose "gift for hatred almost exceeded his gift for literature," (Adams 1991, 41) appear to be attempts to confine White's image to that of someone filled with hatred, particularly a hatred for Australia.

Even if White's expressions about his frustrations with Australian society might have provoked such narrowly conceived perceptions of the author, his work, along with his refusal to ignore social injustices, environmental issues, and political corruption, and his ability to imagine and fight for an Australia that is not defined by material excesses, refute the notion that White hated Australia. The author's radical politics challenge his audience to think differently and to break out of their insularity and some of the objections to White seem to stem from a difficulty to de-link the writer from the activist. But, as Said pointed out, such a separation is unnecessary and what we should concentrate on is what the artist and the public intellectual "have in common as they intervene in the public sphere." (2001)

The convergence of the two roles, writer and political activist, was not only "unavoidable" but also not mutually exclusive for White. (Brennan and Flynn 1989, 90) Although he recognised that it might be "bad for artists to become political," being apolitical was not an option. While an emotional longing, a nostalgia for home brought White back to Australia in 1948, he continued living there because he felt that he had "to fight certain elements in the place." (Qtd. in Charlton 1973) The realm of fiction can be a stylistically limiting and secluded space for activism, and White found it necessary to move into the public sphere to voice his political and social concerns. As a writer and citizen, he believed he had a responsibility to society, the kind of responsibility defined by Noam Chomsky as one suggesting that as "moral agent[s]" writers are obliged "to try to bring the truth about matters of human significance to an audience that can do something about them." (Chomsky 1996, 56)

Some of the "matters of human significance" that White addressed in his public speeches included philistinism, suburban development, nationalism, anti-Semitism, and the treatment of immigrants and Australia's Indigenous populations. White understood the risks involved with his political activism, but he refused to trade his morality and his principles for popularity, and he paid a price:

> In some way, White had offended against the unwritten law of Australianism ... In our slap-on-the-back democracy he was obviously anything but average; stringy-bark and green hide may have been the mainstay of Australia, but here was a man insisting that now it was time for imagination and humility to take their place; amongst those who laughed and gave it a fair go he cried out in agony and looked without sentiment at tragedy ... [This] writer whose blood went deep into his country's history, whose whole task was to find out why life was not right in his own country, was firmly told by those in charge that he was neither an artist nor a patriot. (Dutton 1971, 6)

White was unfazed by the "unpatriotic" charges levelled at him and had no tolerance for the flag-waving kind of nationalism that has come to define patriotism. Advocating a civic nationalism, he asked:

> Isn't it more important to join with other concerned groups, regardless of nationality, class, politics, profession or sex, in attempting to control the super powers and their satellites, and to remind our own leaders constantly of their election promises, as the itch to turn uranium into gold, edges them closer to selling out on humanity? (Brennan and Flynn 1989, 142)

White consistently stressed the importance of uniting with others and often reminded his audiences that even "small scale passive resistance can work wonders." (Brennan and Flynn 1989, 108) The author's advocacy for collective action, his call to youth to build a better future (Brennan and Flynn 1989, 189; 110), and his participation in public meetings and rallies not only demonstrated that White was an inveterate campaigner but also that he was not the isolated individual he sometimes presented himself to be. Although he said he preferred to do things alone and did not belong to political parties or unions, "not even the Fellowship of Australian writers." (Brennan and Flynn 1989, 96-7) He was acutely aware that social and political change would happen only if he and other "members of the universal family" united in a common struggle. He believed in the power of collective resistance and called for solidarity:

We, the people of the world, *may* hold the key to the situation if we can only unite – trade unions, families, artists, and intellectuals, and most important in Australia, the Aborigines to whom many of the mining sites belong by tradition. We are in it together, all classes, all colours. We must resist the lust for undue wealth, which is what inspires our politicians, regardless of the effect this lust will have on future generations – if there *is* a future. (Brennan and Flynn 1989, 101)

White's emphasis on the collective and on people banding together in his political speeches and writings is completely different from his fictional narratives, within which the focus is on solitary journeys of self-discovery. This shift from the "I" to the "We" is perhaps one of the most significant transformations in White and marks his transition from artist to public intellectual.

White's political activism and public interventions evolved slowly. It was during the Whitlam years that the writer "became political, first from exhilaration, then through a sense of outrage." (Brennan and Flynn 1989, 90) He gave his first public speech in Centennial Park on June 18, 1972 at a rally protesting the building of an Olympic sports complex. Confronted with the brutal reality of being displaced and evicted from his home, a sixty-year old White told his audience that as a "reckless anti-civilisation gathers momentum," it was important to protect parks "from the pressure of political concrete." (Brennan and Flynn 1989, 28) The same day, he led a protest at the Sydney Town Hall and addressed the idea of progress: "What, I wonder, constitutes this progress that we are urged to believe in?" the writer asked (Brennan and Flynn 1989, 31).

Over the years, White continued to voice his concerns about the huge investments in sports, capitalist developments, and the alliances between capitalists and politicians. White did not claim to either be an expert on the political and social issues he talked about or to have all the answers. What he, a privileged individual, knew for certain was "that what is regarded as success in a rational materialistic society … amounts to nothing and will not help us rout the destructive forces threatening us today." (Brennan and Flynn 1989, 114-15) He viewed money as "one of the curses of life from century to century, breeding war, despair in the poor, dishonesty in the ambitious, while the hungry are encouraged to believe they will eat if they go along with what is planned for them." (Brennan and Flynn 1989, 141) Firmly rejecting the neo-liberal narrative of progress, White argued that "civilisation is not a matter of money and concrete." (Brennan and Flynn 1989, 35) The enormous costs of capitalist expansions that White reiterated in his speeches are all too familiar today. Large-scale evictions have become one of the cornerstones of the pattern of industrial development and in Australia and many other countries, the endless scramble for land and minerals, innumerable mining and development projects, public policies that favour corporations, and the continual betrayals of peoples by governments have affected millions of communities. In the face of such destruction and exploitation, how can producing works of fiction "seem anything but trivial?" the writer asked. (Brennan and Flynn 1989, 99) For White, taking on the role as a public intellectual was a conscientious and a necessary decision.

White used the public exposure he received as a Nobel Laureate (1973) and Australian of the Year (1974) to fight for justice for the Aborigines, and to call attention to Hiroshima, the threat of nuclear weaponry, uranium policies, as well as Australia's hypocrisy, its intellectual and moral vacuity, and its subservience to Britain, the United States, and Japan. His celebrity status attracted more than a thousand people to the launch of the People for Nuclear Disarmament, which he co-sponsored with Judith Wright in Melbourne on October 21, 1981. (Brennan and Flynn 1989, 98) It was here that White gave his first public speech on nuclear energy, which he regarded to be a global issue that Australians could not ignore: "The implications of nuclear warfare are so immense that it's tempting to turn our backs – to persuade ourselves it can't concern Australia. Until, if we're honest, we have to admit that beside this global issue nothing else matters." (Brennan and Flynn 1989, 99)

White actively campaigned against the development of nuclear facilities, linking the mining of uranium for nuclear energy to the injustice done to the Aborigines, to whom the land belongs. Taking a cue from Gandhi, he preached non-violence in the hope that "all those who face the contingency of nuclear or any kind of war ... will not ... [be] so callous that they ignore the greatest opportunity for unity." (Brennan and Flynn 1989, 125) Unfortunately, Australia's history, similar to the histories of other countries, is marked with numerous instances of missed opportunities.

In 1982, if there was reason to be concerned that Australia was selling uranium to "Finland, West Germany, Sweden and France" (Brennan and Flynn 1989, 106) in 2012, there is now, cause for even greater concern with Australia's promise to sell uranium to India, despite the fact that India is yet to sign the nuclear non-proliferation treaty, and despite Australia's deplorable "history of uranium mining ... and its impact on Aboriginal people" (Hudson 2012). White rightly said that, "Facing the uranium issue honestly is what may save Australia and set an example to the rest of the world." (Brennan and Flynn 1989, 158) White's plea in 1984 "to terminate immediately all mining and export of Australian uranium, and to repudiate all commitments to previous Australian governments to mining, processing and export of uranium" fell on deaf ears. (Brennan and Flynn 1989, 158) More than two decades later, policy makers are still not listening to those who advise against mining operations and development of nuclear facilities.

Amidst anti-nuclear protests in India and warnings from Australia, in October 2012, the Prime Ministers of India and Australia shook hands, made trade promises, talked about a new beginning of an Indo-Australian relationship, and celebrated this alliance. Neither head of state cared to ask: what do Aboriginal groups who do not want uranium mined from their lands, who do not "want to bequeath a legacy for future generations of a toxic environment" have to celebrate? (Boylan, 2010) What new beginning is in store for the Indian fishing community in Koodankulam, who do not want a nuclear plant near their homes, who do not want their lands to be dumping grounds for uranium waste? The rights of Indigenous and disadvantaged populations have always been secondary to industrial and mining projects and as White pointed out:

> The most innocent victims of the universal swindle are ... the Australian Aborigines who, after the original invasion of their land, are now invaded by uranium miners who drive bulldozers across

their burial grounds and sacred sites and smash or steal their sacred emblems. (Brennan and Flynn 1989: 107)

It was to remind Australia of its violent and invasive history that White refused to publish or produce any work in 1988 the year celebrating the country's 200th anniversary of the arrival of the British in Sydney.

Explaining his boycott in a televised address, White stated, the idea of the Bicentenary troubled him, and that there was too little in Australia's past and present that he could feel proud of. It was the need for justice for the Aborigines that made him oppose the national celebrations. White also rightly observed that today, Indigenous populations do not need to be killed or forcefully removed from their lands as they were in the past but there were subtler ways of destroying them (Brennan and Flynn 1989, 184) White was not alone in his opinion about the Bicentenary. "More than 15,000 aborigines and thousands of white supporters" carried banners with messages that stated "40,000 years Is Not a Bicentennial" and that Australia day represented "200 Years of White Lies" and a "Bicentennial Invasion." (Fineman, 1988) It was through this kind of peaceful demonstration that White believed, that Australia could move in the right direction.

During his lifetime, White was often angry, angry at the way marginalised communities, the environment, and the earth are treated. As he said, "If the earth is angry, the human beings who inhabit it have cause to be angry too." (Brennan and Flynn 1989, 194) White's feelings of anger and outrage never stopped him from believing in his country, he also never stopped believing that his fellow citizens had the potential to change. (Brennan and Flynn 1989, 195). A meaningful celebration, recognition and understanding of White's legacy must include these conversations. If we must "play the game of positioning great writers" (Smith 2012), then let us place Patrick White with other justice- oriented writer-intellectuals, such as Harold Pinter, who also believed that "as citizens, to define the *real* truth of our lives and our societies is a crucial obligation which devolves upon us all. It is in fact mandatory," if we hope to restore "what is so nearly lost to us – the dignity of man." (Pinter 2005)

Works Cited

Adams, Philip. 1991. "Phillip Adams," *Patrick White: A Tribute*, ed. Clayton Joyce. North Ryde: Angus and Robertson: 41-5.
Boylan, Jessie. 2010. "Australia's Aboriginal communities clamor against uranium mining," *The Guardian* (August), http://www.guardian.co.uk/ environment/2010/aug/09/australia-aboriginaluranium-mining. Accessed 12 September 2012.
Brennan, Paul and Christine Flynn. Ed. 1989. *Patrick White Speaks*. Sydney: Primavera Press.
Budurlean, Alma. 2009. *Otherness in the novels of Patrick White*. Frankfurt: Peter Lang.
Charlton, Mike. 1973. "Interview of Nobel laureate Patrick White" for ABC's "Four Corners." *YouTube*. https://www.youtube.com/watch?v=j02E06UFOcg. Accessed 15 May 2012.
Chomsky, Noam. 1996. *Powers and prospects: Reflections on human nature and the social order*." Boston: South End Press.
Craven, Peter. 2012. "Coloured by the literary richness of White," *The Australian* 26 May. http://www.theaustralian.com.au/news/features/coloured-by-the-literary-richness-of-white/story-e6frg6z6-1226367246087. Accessed 8 August 2012.
Dinnage, Rosemary. 1980. "Her life as a man," *The New York Review* (April 17): 25-28.
During, Simon. 1996. *Patrick White*. Melbourne: Oxford University Press.
Dutton, Geoffrey. 1971. *Patrick White*. Melbourne: Oxford University Press.
—. 1994. *Out in the open: An autobiography*. St Lucia: University of Queensland Press.
Fineman, Mark. 1988. "Australia: Bicentennial Celebrated: Penal Colony to Modern Nation: Australians throw a Bicentennial Blowout." *Los Angeles Times* (27 January). http://articles.latimes.com/1988-01-27/news/mn-26047_1_penal-colony. Accessed 15 July 2012.

Green, Dorothy. 1991. "Dorothy Green," in *Patrick White: A Tribute*, ed. Clayton Joyce. North Ryde: Angus and Robertson: 1-7.

Hudson, Phillip. 2012. "Prime Minister Julia Gillard will start negotiations to sell uranium to India." *Herald Sun* 16 October. http://www.theaustralian.com.au/news/prime-minister-julia-gillard-will-start-negotiations-to-sell-uranium-to-india/story-e6frg6n6-1226496590713. Accessed 18 October 2012.

Marr, David. 1991. *Patrick White: A Life*. London: Jonathan Cape.

—. Ed. 1994. *Patrick White Letters*. Chicago: University of Chicago Press.

—. 2003. "The Role of the Writer in John Howard's Australia." The Colin Simpson Lecture, (29 March). http://www.safecom.org.au/david-marr.htm. Accessed 10 October 2012.

Pinter, Harold. 2005. "Nobel Lecture: Art, Truth, and Politics." Nobelprize. http://www.nobelprize.org/nobel_prizes/literature/laureates/2005/pinter-lecture-e.html. Accessed 5 May 2012.

Rooney, Brigid. 2009. *Literary Activists: Writer-Intellectuals and Australian Public Life*. St. Lucia: University of Queensland Press.

Said, Edward. 1994. *Representations of the Intellectual: The 1993 Reith Lectures*. New York: Pantheon Books.

—. 2001. "The Public Role of Writers and Intellectuals." *The Nation* (17 September). http://www.thenation.com/doc/20010917/essay. Accessed 12 May 2012.

Shakespeare, Nicholas. 2012. "Patrick White: Under the Skin." *The Telegraph*: (19 October). http://www.telegraph.co.uk/culture/books/bookreviews/9617484/Patrick-White-Under-the-Skin.html. Accessed 23 October 2012.

Smith, Barnaby. 2012. "Homelands: Patrick White – A Personal Odyssey," *The Quietus* (September 28). http://thequietus.com/articles/10153-patrick-white-voss-anniversary.

Tacey, David. 1990. "The End of Genius (*Memoirs of Many in One*)," *Critical Essays on Patrick White,* ed. Peter Wolfe. Boston: G. K. Hall: 60-65.

Williamson, Geordie. 2012. "Patrick White, the outcast, returns to the fold with *The* Hanging *Garden,*" *The Australian* (31 March). http://www. theaustralian.com.au/arts/review/patrick-white-the-outcast-returns-to-the-fold-with-the-hanging-garden/story-fn9n8gph-1226312389892. Accessed 4 June 2012.

Williams, Mark. 1993. *Macmillan Modern Novelists: Patrick White.* London: Macmillan.

White, Patrick. 1957. *Voss.* London: Vintage.

—. 1981. *Flaws in the Glass: A self-portrait.* London: Jonathan Cape.

CHAPTER NINE

INSCRIBING LANDSCAPES IN PATRICK WHITE'S NOVELS

JESSICA WHITE
INDEPENDENT SCHOLAR

I grew up on a property in northwest New South Wales, which was once owned by Ivy Voss of Hughenden. Ivy married Frederick George White, who was Patrick White's uncle and my great-grandfather. While Patrick was at school, he sometimes stayed with Ivy and George at Mittabah in the NSW Southern Highlands. He didn't like Ivy much, as David Marr writes: "The boy thought she was a monster. Her maiden name was Voss, and he kept the name in mind, waiting for thirty years to revenge himself" (1992, 59) with, the novel *Voss*.

My grandfather Owen took out a loan to buy Ivy's property, but George gave him the money for it instead. Owen and his three sons, one of whom was my father, worked the land, and my weekends were spent exploring creeks with my brother, rounding up sheep for shearing with my cousins during holidays, or, when I was an adolescent, jogging through paddocks for kilometres in an effort to remain slim. After a summer without sunscreen (for this was the 80s), I was extremely tanned and, when the tan faded, I was sprinkled permanently with freckles. The stippling of my skin was testimony to the time I spent outdoors and the attachment to the land I formed during that time. My childhood was literally written on my skin.

It is through a similar process – by marking the skins of white characters such as Voss, Ellen Roxburgh and Mary Hare – that Patrick White attempts to articulate a process of becoming

Australian. In charting these characters' transformations, he also left his mark on the Australian literary and cultural landscape. Some commentators have suggested that such a mark is also due to his prickly persona, and that the loftiness of the man has become conflated with his writing, rendering it inaccessible to many. I would argue that this is a position resorted to by those who are apathetic, or suspicious of innovation, and that it is only by reading White, and by opening ourselves to his texts, allowing ourselves to be imprinted and scored by them, that we can be altered by the originality and beauty of his writing.

A Fringe of Leaves opens with references to hands and their treatment by the Australian climate. Mr and Mrs Merivale, with their friend Miss Scrimshaw, pull away from Circular Quay in a carriage, having visited Ellen Roxburgh and her husband who are docked and waiting for winds to carry them back to England. Mrs Merivale's hands are 'stuffed' (FL 9) into kid gloves, while the skin of her husband's hands, she observes, has been 'altered inexorably by those first years in a hard land into something almost part of it' (10). Mr Merivale's occupation as a surveyor offers him a relationship with the landscape, at the same time seeming to cast him as a creature in it, as suggested by his wife's association of his skin with "a lizard which had once stared at her, through bleached grass, from a scorched earth." (FL 10)

The reference to the effect of the Australian climate on Mr Merivale's skin as he goes about his work is a foreshadowing of the relationship that Ellen Roxburgh, shipwrecked with her husband, begins to form with her Australian surroundings. Cast into a lifeboat for a dreary return to the mainland, Ellen looks at her roughening hands and "noticed she was returning, and not by slow degrees, to nature." (FL 195) This also heralds a return to the Ellen Gluyas of her youth, with her red, chapped hands before she was appropriated by the wealthy Mr Roxburgh and moulded into a lady.

It should not be surprising, given these descriptions of hands and skin, that the etymology of the verb 'to write' comes from the old English word 'wrítan' meaning 'to score' or 'to scratch'. As Constance Classen notes in *The Book of Touch,* 'this makes writing like an inscription on skin (for what do we scratch more frequently?) – an analogy supported by the fact that the parchment once used for writing in Europe was made out of animal skins. (2005, 6) The skins of many of White's characters are marked thus by their travails in the bush or beneath a harsh sun, demonstrating the landscape's inscription on their bodies, and their subsequent metamorphosis into Australian creatures. White articulates this transformation in a description of Ellen's walk through the bush one early morning before the awakening of the Indigenous people who have captured and adopted her:

> She was rewarded at last when the scrub through which she had been struggling was transformed into a mesh of startling if chilly beauty. Where she had been slapped and scratched at first, she was now stroked by the softest of fronds … she felt accepted, rejuvenated. She was the 'Ellen' of her youth … the label of a name was flapping and skirring ahead of her among the trunks of great moss-bound trees, as its less substantial echo unfurled from the past, from amongst fuchsia and geum and candy-tuft, then across the muck-spattered yard, the moor with its fuzz of golden furze and russet bracken. (270-271)

Here, the scratching gives way to stroking, as Ellen's current self calls up her former, younger self, the two blended together through images of flora of two different countries. The transition mirrors her return to a more sensual self that deprived of nourishment, gorges where it can on food and on the startling beauty of the bush. Later, making her escape with the convict Jack Chance, Ellen's skin becomes "almost as rough as bark," (FL. 329) signalling her imbrication within the landscape, as Mr Merivale has been with his leathery skin. She has been reconstituted as a woman who, as she says to Miss Scrimshaw at the novel's close, has been "slashed and gashed too often;" (402):the equanimity in her tone, a sense that her rough handling has grounded her and made her "ineluctably earthbound," (402) and that this is a surprisingly positive thing.

When Ellen Roxburgh and the second mate Mr Pilcher, the only survivors of the wreck, meet in the Commandant's house in Moreton Bay to share their experiences, Mrs Roxburgh comments that she had "learned a great deal, of which I should otherwise remain ignorant," (378) while Mr Pilcher, by contrast, "was so thin as to look transparent in places, and even more deeply lined than before." (375) Why should it be that Ellen Roxburgh has been enlarged by her experiences, while Mr Pilcher has been wounded by them, particularly when he had formerly boasted to Mr Roxburgh that, had he found himself convicted, he'd "find a way to join the bolters ... [and] learn the country by heart, like any of your books, Mr Roxburgh, and find more to it perhaps?" (151) Perhaps Ellen's adoption by the Indigenous people permits her sensual nature to flourish in close connection with the bush.

However, this shift has not been made by the bush alone, but also through the inscriptions – the cutting and battering – by her Aboriginal captors. Ellen is burnt with sticks (263) pushed "with such force and complete disregard for decency that she bumped her head against a tree" (274) and her hair is torn out (251) and reconstituted with wax and feathers. While this is an unsavoury way of depicting the Indigenous people, it might also be a means by which White suggests that, in order for Ellen and his non-Indigenous readers to acknowledge an Indigenous consciousness, a little force may sometimes be necessary. To be scored and scratched, beaten and to be made earthbound, then, is not necessarily something detrimental, but rather occasions openness to one's surroundings.

This exposure to environment, and the subsequent changes it elicits in White's characters, is also evident in *Voss*, where the explorer, on his journey into the interior, is "Blackened and yellowed by the sun, dried in the wind." 169) Cynthia vanden Driesen notes that this process "makes him seem more and more aligned to the landscape and the Indigenous people," (2009, 59) an affinity which is underscored by his interactions with them. Where Ellen Roxburgh is forced into a relationship with her Indigenous captors, Voss' interactions with the Indigenous people reveal his awareness of and respect for their autonomy. On the expedition, the labourer Turner refers to them as "dirty blacks" (V. 340) but Voss, in an encounter where Palfreyman the ornithologist is speared by the Indigenous people, calls to the ex-convict Judd to hold his fire, forbidding him "to make matters worse by shooting at this people." (340)

Given this closeness – at least compared with the characters alongside him – to the land and its Indigenous inhabitants, it is appropriate that Voss is referred to by metaphors of earth. For example, he describes his idea of venturing into the interior as being "like a worm ... butting my head at whatsoever darkness of earth" (44) suggesting a deep engagement with the country before his expedition has even commenced. Once darkened by the sun on his travels, he resembles "some root, of dark and esoteric purpose." (169) Following the trajectory of this earthy imagery, Voss's death results in his absorption into the Australian soil, both literally and figuratively. Once beheaded by the Aboriginal, Jackie, "his blood ran out upon the dry earth, which drank it up immediately," (394) while Judd comments later that Voss "is still there – that is the honest opinion of many of them – he is still there, in the country, and always will be." (443) In this instance, Voss is not only marked by the landscape, but ground down until he is, as he dreamed at his hosts the Sandersons before embarking into the interior, absorbed by the land: "At once the hills were enfolding him. All that he had observed, now survived by touch. So he was touching those same hills and was not surprised at their suave flesh." (139)Through dreams and at the moment of his death, he reaches his knowledge about himself through the landscape's touch upon his skin.

Writing about "skin knowledge," or "the knowledge of the world one acquires through one's skin" David Howe elucidates "a longstanding philosophical tradition of attributing some form of intelligence to the sentient body," which stretches back to antiquity.(2005, 33) Urban Westerners, he continues, don't have much contact with the ground, perceiving it as dirty or contaminating. They walk on it in feet encased in shoes, and assume that the only person who sits on a pavement is one who has "literally reached bottom: the homeless, the intoxicated or the insane." (Howe 2005, 29)

This is the opinion which Norbert Hare, owner of the elaborate property Xanadu in *Riders in the Chariot*, holds of his daughter Mary. Norbert espouses the tradition which builds edifices over the landscape in the name of progress and asserting dominion over the natural world. As such, he is disgusted and alienated when Mary had "thrown herself on the ground and begun to hollow out a nest in the grass with little feverish jerks of her body and foolish grunts, curling round in the shape of a bean or position of a foetus." (24)

Mary's explanation, "Now I know what it feels like to be a dog," (24) indicates an openness to other forms of sentience and ways of knowing, as does the shape of her body. As a bean or foetus, it hints at the possibility of growth, rather than the pruning and control carried out by her father.

Mary Hare's intimacy with the soil suggests that she is already at that place which Voss had reached at his death, and at which Ellen Roxburgh arrived after living with the Aborigines and approaching their worldview. Mary, who is "[s]peckled and dappled, like any wild thing native to the place," (16) has entered into a dialogue with her surroundings, preferring to engage with them than with more conventional societal norms. The expectation that she would rule Xanadu with a husband crumbles with the property after her parents' deaths, and she continues to communicate with the natural world, digging her "blunt, freckled fingers into the receptive earth." (13) The use of the word 'receptive' indicates, again, that she is open to the consciousness of other creatures and environments. This stance is also signalled in the novel's opening on her return from the post office, where her dress is caught on a barbed wire fence:

> 'You could get torn,' Mrs Godbold warned, who had come up to the edge of the road in search of something, whether child, goat, or perhaps just the daily paper.
>
> 'Oh, I could get torn,' Miss Hare answered. 'But what is a little tear?' (7-8)

In her acceptance that she might be cut, and that other ideas might seep in, Mary Hare approaches the role of the artist as described by Veronica Brady in her essay "Towards an Ecology of Australia." (1955) "Essentially we are trapped by a particular view of the world, the imperial view which brought us here in the first place." (1999:147) Mr Bonner's view, which exemplifies this attitude, perceives Australia as "the country of the future," (V. 28) a place from which one can get rich through possession of the land, where achievement is measured by those who are settling it. (29) He believes, as with Mary Hare's father, in stamping Western civilisation onto the earth "through homes and public edifices."

As Laura Trevelyan observes, however, Voss "does not intend to make a fortune out of this country, like other men. He is not all money talk." (V. 28) and the difference between the two men becomes more apparent the further Voss travels. Where Mr Bonner asserts himself with his wealth and belief in monuments and buildings, Voss is attenuated by starvation and exhaustion, ground down until he accepts his fate at the hands of the Aborigines. In doing so, Voss relinquishes his sense of superiority, and acknowledges the failure of the Western consciousness in the heart of the country.

While this acknowledgement comes too late for Voss, at least it does come, demonstrating that it is necessary to adapt, to become freckled or dark-skinned, to attempt to respond to the country as Indigenous people do, in order to survive in Australia. I agree with Veronica Brady when she writes, "It is not possible, nor would it be right, for non-Aboriginal Australians to adopt Aboriginal culture. This would involve a repetition of the original act of appropriation, attempting to take possession of the culture as we took possession of the land." (1999,147) However I do believe that to open ourselves up, to be cut and marked by another environment and culture, leads us to recognise that a Western consciousness, which has degraded the land and decimated its first people, might not necessarily be the best way forward. While these scars and freckles might only be skin-deep, and suggest only a superficial change, their presence on our body does act as a continuing reminder of the necessity for change.

Unfortunately for Patrick White, his significant attempts to render this awareness have been overshadowed by his reputation for scratchiness and prickliness. His reference to "the Great Australian Emptiness, in which the mind is the least of possessions" (1982, 15) in his 1958 article "The Prodigal Son" seems to have caused decades of offence, resurfacing in a panel at the Sydney Writers Festival in 2012. Somewhat absurdly titled 'Is Patrick White un-Australian?' it was chaired by Michael Cathcart of ABC Radio National's *Books and Arts Daily*, who suggested that White's prickliness and self-confessed snobbery were conflated with his writing. All three panellists, Geordie Williamson, Gail Jones and Ivor Indyk – disagreed. As Geordie Williamson put it:

GW: There's always been an ambivalent relationship to this man. I think it's partly because he didn't set out to make himself likeable, he was abrasive in his public utterances, he carried in his DNA certain class prerogatives that I think grated against people.

MC: So do you think people are hearing the voice of the man who was so hard to like in the books?

GW: I don't think they read the books, because if you do read the books, then you hear the other thing, the thing that makes him so magnificent and so admirable. I think he was a man of great integrity, and that integrity obliged him to speak to our better natures.

Williamson then added, "To try and draw White into his social utterances and to judge him by them is to come at him from the wrong angle." His comments are supported by the observation that White's class was conducive rather than detrimental to the creation of his texts, as Brigid Rooney notes in *Literary Activists*, "If White's alienation from the ordinary – his tourist-like observation of 'residents' – was a function of his social privilege and his distance from economic necessity, it was also generative of texts that represented everyday Australian culture with the lucidity of the insider-outsider." (55) In addition, his ill-adjustment to elements of his background may have helped him to sympathise with the less-privileged. In *Flaws in the Glass*, he refers to comments to his boyhood self as a 'changeling,' (5) while his sense of being a 'freak,' (46) of not following the path of his plodding pastoral forbears by marrying and producing heirs and lording over acres, is marked. While he may have been irascible, he did use his literary fame, or, as Rooney puts it, his 'symbolic capital' (31) to agitate and scratch against complacency for issues such as nuclear disarmament and Aboriginal rights, a position which identifies not with the pastoral blue bloods, but the common man.

The argument that because Patrick White's writing is elitist because had a wealthy background and didn't suffer fools, appears to be wheeled out to generate controversy, for there are any number of passionate advocates of White who will jump to his defence, not least Gail Jones, who noted in the panel, "it does dismay me and

distress me that somehow because he was not such a nice bloke that we ought not to bother." I cannot help but wonder, too, if this accusation that White is difficult is used simply to dismiss him because, in our contemporary culture, we find it difficult to make time to sit down with a novel which requires stillness and patience. Tired, working women only have energy to flick through the pages of the flaccid *Fifty Shades of Grey* rather than engage with the refracting surfaces of White's prose. Nor is this a dilemma confined to White's works; novels such as Alexis Wright's *Carpentaria*
(2006) and Kim Scott's *Benang* (1999) also require space in which to be receptive to the lyricism of the writing.

Readers, I think, need to take a leaf from the page of the receptive Mary Hare and to burrow through the vegetation of White's writing. Some might be frustrated by what they perceive as overwriting, but to me his language is like the Australian bush: on first glance a swathe of muted greys and greens that, as you walk slowly through it, reveals itself to be hundreds of beautiful, tiny leaves, strips of bark and minute blossoms. As White himself wrote of his style, "I am interested in detail. I enjoy decoration. By accumulating this mass of detail you throw light on things in a larger sense: in the long run it all adds up. It creates a texture – a background, a period, which makes everything you write more convincing." (1982, 23) In delving into such backgrounds and periods, in being scratched by and exposed to the density of his prose, his readers will, one hopes, recognise and champion his rendering of those who struggle to find, or who are forced into, a mode of being beyond the mainstream.

Works Cited

Brady, Veronica. 1999. "Towards an Ecology of Australia: Land of the Spirit," *Worldviews: Environment, Culture. Religion* 3: 139-155.

Classen, Constance. 2005, "Fingerprints: Writing About Touch," *The Book of Touch*, ed. Constance Classen. Oxford and New York: Berg: 1-9.

Howe, David. 2005, "Skinscapes: Embodiment, Culture, and Environment," in *The Book of Touch*, ed. Constance Classen, Oxford and New York: Berg: 27-39.

"Is Patrick White un-Australian?" Books and Arts Daily. Radio National. http://www.abc.net.au/radionational/programs/booksandartsdaily/is-patrick-white-un-australian3f/4030160. Accessed 14 June 2012.

Marr, David. 1992. *Patrick White: A Life.* North Sydney: Random House.

Rooney, Brigid. 2009. *Literary Activists: Writer-intellectuals and Australian Public Life.* St Lucia: University of Queensland Press.

vanden Driesen, Cynthia. 2009. *Writing the Nation: Patrick White and the Indigene.* Amsterdam: Rodopi.

White, Patrick. 1961. *Riders in the Chariot.* London: Eyre & Spottiswoode.

—. 1974. *Voss.* Harmondsworth: Penguin

—. 1976. *A Fringe of Leaves.* London: Jonathan Cape.

—. 1982. *Flaws in the Glass: A Self-Portrait.* London: Jonathan Cape.

PART II

GENRE

CHAPTER TEN

"A GLORIOUS, TERRIBLE LIFE":
THE DUAL IMAGE IN PATRICK WHITE'S DRAMATIC LANGUAGE

MAY-BRIT AKERHOLT
UNIVERSITY OF SYDNEY

I am very familiar with the plays of Henrik Ibsen, both from my Norwegian upbringing and from a thesis I wrote, some years ago at Macquarie University. I always thought that one of the most innovative (and most misunderstood) aspects of Ibsen's work was the way he juxtaposed opposite forces and forms, creating a co-existence of tragedy and comedy, exploring several levels of action and characterisation simultaneously – and very differently – from a number of writers such as possibly the greatest dramatist of all, Shakespeare. Then I started researching the drama of Patrick White, for yet another thesis. As I was working, I began to realise that White and Ibsen both combine portrayals of the darker side of life but combined this with comedic elements.

One night in the theatre I saw how a director (Jim Sharman) and an actor (Robyn Nevin) made this aspect of one of White's plays, *A Cheery Soul* (1967) come alive onstage. I watched Sharman's production on three occasions, fascinated by the way Nevin exploited the text in order to make something happen through the words, to make a line suddenly reverberate with another level of meaning. From the moment she exploded down the stairs in the auditorium towards the Custances' kitchen, Nevin seemed an apparition from hell and a comic figure; at the same time, she was ominous and she was funny. Sharman said he wanted her right on her entrance to create an instant *rapport* with the audience and at the same time also give them a kind of shock. This would emphasise that Miss Docker is an ambiguous character, simultaneously insufferable and pitiful; her indomitable cheerfulness as destructive as it is well-meaning.

This is dramatised by White and by Sharman in one particular moment: Miss Docker provokes an angry outburst from her hostess Mrs Custance, who believes (with the audience) that her guest has decided to buy a piece of mutton to criticise the lack of meat in the Custance diet. Yet 'the cheery soul' is just as busily engaged in acts of goodness:

> MISS DOCKER. ... By the way, guess what I'm doing tomorrow. I'm going up to the butcher's to buy a couple of mutton shanks.
>
> MRS CUSTANCE (*incensed*) You'll have no need to buy food in *this* house!
>
> MISS DOCKER. It's that Mrs. Apps. Pernicious anaemia! If you ask me she's starved for love. Well, I'm going to make Mrs. Apps a basinful of broth.
>
> MRS CUSTANCE. (*genuinely impressed, though at the same time humouring a child*) I think that's a wonderful idea, Miss Docker.
>
> MISS DOCKER. (*smiling, childlike*) Eh? (*growing serious*) There are so many professing Christians. ... Mind you, I think a lot of things just don't cross their poor minds. (*Her voice rising almost hysterically to a note of desperation*) But you can't leave people to starve. Can you? Now, can you? (CS 198)

On the last line, Nevin turned her head to the audience with a silent, horrible cry of pure anguish etched on her face. And the audience's laughter was replaced with a shocked silence at the recognition of her loneliness and lovelessness. As I watched Nevin transform the character of Miss Docker for a few seconds, I suspect I had one of my first experiences of my mind working dramaturgically. That is, I had seen how a moment in the text gives rise to an action, or *re*-action.

Nevin's performance resonated when I later read an article by Michael Billington about the British family of actors, the

Redgraves, suggesting that part of their various successes was due to an "ability to live in two dimensions at once that has been passed down the Redgrave line ... [an] ability to endow characters with a secret life. You could argue that all good acting is based on contradiction and duality." (Billington 2003, 14) As an example, the article mentions how Vanessa Redgrave transformed a routine historical drama (*Mary Queen of Scots*) by translating herself into a political metaphor for justice. Richard Schechner alludes to a similar ability when he argues that a skilled performer has three halves, and that the centre, the 'I,' "stands outside observing and to some degree controlling both the knower and the feeler." (Schechner 1988, 316)

In "A Cheery Soul" I watched the actress translate herself into a metaphor for loneliness (and injustice). I experienced her 'three halves,' her 'I' simultaneously entering the reality of the theatrical action *and* stepping outside it to watch and comment on it, as if from an ironic distance. White had created a moment in the writing that enabled an actor to transform words on the page into a live, theatrical event. The combination of text and performance created a memorable action; a moment on stage that could happen because the text offered it to the actor. This powerful piece of writing from White was brought to life by a superb actress who knew how to transform writing into performance. Now I had seen 'Brecht's *Gestus*' in action – that famous moment when Helene Weigel's Mother Courage in the original production of "Mother Courage and Her Children" lifts her head back, stretches her mouth wide, and holds this grotesque position in a 'silent scream' when her son is killed, unable to give other, verbal or physical, expression to her sense of complete and utter devastation. I began to see all White's texts in the light of how the *'Gestus'* was brought into play. I began to see the many ways that, because White understood the actor's art and craft, his dramatic writing gives them a dialogue they can work with; that they can manipulate and transform into action.

When I translated Ibsen's play "John Gabriel Borkman" for a production, the rich, eloquent and persuasive dramatic dialogue of Patrick White, as well as the exuberant and expressive voice of Dorothy Hewett, was, not for the first time, inspirations for my translation work. Hewett – one of Australia's boldest and most colourful playwrights and poets – claimed that Australians were afraid of using language, afraid of imagination and suspicious of eloquence. One certainly cannot be afraid of using extremes of language when you translate "John Gabriel Borkman." Emotions run havoc; the language is rich in imagery and expresses obsessive emotions, volatile tempers and burning beliefs. The characters speak lines such as "the wolf is howling again. The sick wolf"or"She is a hard woman. As hard as the iron ore I once dreamt of prising from the bowels of the mountains."

I was reminded of the nature of Miss Quodling's speeches, the goat woman of "The Night on Bald Mountain.". When she arrived on the mountain, "it was just as if I was the first person born in an empty world. It was huge and lonely, and I had to get used to it." And when her illusions shatter as she realises she is neither ruler of her goats nor of the mountain, she can be reborn because she believes in a continuation: "there is no such thing as *nothun*! (*Softer*) The silence will breed again ... in peace ... a world of goats ... perhaps even men!" (356). There is nothing similar in the content of Ibsen's and White's speeches; but there is a comparable passion and power in the language itself. The two writers both give their characters a dramatic dialogue suffused with the kind of poetic quality that elevates the characters who speak it from the mundane world they inhabit.

However, Miss Quodling's lines are not made up of poetry. She speaks a raw – but imaginative – vernacular. Ibsen said in a letter to Edmund Gosse that he sought to depict "human beings, and therefore I would not let them talk 'the language of the gods.'" (Meyer 1974, 398-99)

But just as Ibsen's dramatic dialogue retains much of the poetic quality of his verse, White's language has a sense of poesy which heightens the vigour of his dialogue. He borrowed a little from the 'language of the gods' when he created Miss Quodling, whose rapture and energy of language have the combined force of poetry and verse.

There is always a mixture of colloquial speech and heightened prose in White's dramatic dialogue, often within the same speech, as we see in the goat woman's words. Sometimes it is interspersed with songs or lyric verse, expressive of a character's inner mind, deepest fears and desires, beyond the masks which hide the inner reality. When his plays were first staged, more than one critic complained that "people don't speak like that." No, of course people don't speak the language of drama. The speech of dramatic literature, of all literature, is not 'natural'; characters speak a language made up especially for them, for their situation, their conflict, their environment. As the director Robert Wilson responded, when questioned about naturalism and his formal, ritualistic staging of Brecht's "The Threepenny Opera": "People acting natural onstage is a lie! ... To me, theatre is artificial. The way you speak on stage is not the same way you speak on the street. It's a craft; you have to learn it. If you accept that being on the stage is something artificial, to me that looks more natural." (2013, 8)

The key to good dramatic dialogue is to create a highly artificial language which does not sound like "the way people speak," but like the only way a character *can* speak in that situation, at that time, and, unless a monologue, to that particular character (or characters). "The language must sound natural and the way of expressing it must be characteristic for each person in the play; one person does not express himself the same way as another person." (Beyer 1978, 422) And that is where White's dramatic language excels; in finding languages unique to each character.

It was a rewarding experience to act as the dramaturg on Armfield's production of White's first major play, "The Ham Funeral." The author was present during much of the first week of rehearsals, when we spent every day going through the text in detail. Occasionally he would speak, but mostly he listened to us dissecting every line of his play. At one point Tyler Coppin, who played The Young Man, had problems with a particular line, which caused much debate among us all, and finally Armfield turned to White and said, "Patrick, what does this line mean?" White lifted the book and he read the line, the words ringing out in his inimitable voice; then he lowered the book and said, "That's what the line means." And it was a revelation. The meaning is not in a paraphrase of the words, but in the very quality of the words themselves, in their sound, their placement.

I was brought back to "The Ham Funeral" rehearsal room when I was translating the Norwegian contemporary author Jon Fosse's play "Death Variations" for a co-production by East Coast Theatre Company and B Sharp Belvoir in 2005. At one stage I had problems with a particular passage, and as it turned out, so did the rest of the creative team once we were in the rehearsal room. I approached Fosse. His reply was what almost amounted to an essay, but the gist of it reminded me of White's reaction during the rehearsals of "The Ham Funeral." I single out a few words of dramaturgical wisdom: "All good texts have something in them that resists being understood ... The best dramatic texts accumulate something 'incomprehensible' through the way they are written. ... Let it be meaningless, but try to make it heavy with sound and with rhythm." Yes. Language can be so bursting with an emotion, and attitude, that it explodes as a meaningful language. We wanted to paraphrase the lines, make them ordinary and take away the very reason they work as drama.

White and Fosse were both telling the theatre artists who were working to make their words come alive to trust the text. The responses of both writers revealed something essential about the nature of dramatic language. The meaning lies in the words themselves, in the poetry of the language, the rhythm, the intonation, and the images it evokes. Language is visceral. Trust the language. Trust the images in it. When the actors let the language work for them, and set it free, it becomes drama and action; it releases the character.

In all great theatre, it is "*les mots qui saignent*" – it is the words that bleed, that "imitate the gestures and the state of mind of the characters ... the words that adopt an attitude, not the body; that are woven, not the garments; that sparkle, not the armour; that growl, not the storm; that threaten, not Juno; that laugh, not Cytherea; that bleed, not the wounds." (Foucault 1964, 21-22) It is the words that give birth to a gesture, the words that force the body to adopt an attitude.

No one knew better than White that the rhythm of dialogue is a complex and living organism, it is the heartbeat that gives the language energy, and fuels the actor's imagination. The words need the kind of energy that makes a moment *sing* in the theatre, not just *happen*. The texture of language is almost physical: fat or thin, flowing or staccato, kicking or stroking, it is simultaneously complex and logical (like a brain); its moods vary from sunny to thunderous and everything in between. I learnt from White's drama that we must think of creative language as a form of commitment. It means the courage to be dense, complex, obscure, excessive, poetic, the flair to be sparse, succinct, understated. It means being able to 'see' and 'hear' language, as well as read it.

And that is how I think of the language of Miss Quodling. Her soliloquies combine a poetic quality with a raw, energetic idiom to create a dialogue which reflects the very rhythms of life. It is a language that sets in relief that of the other characters – the sterile prose of the learned Professor Sword and the more naïve pensiveness of the language spoken by the innocent heroine figure of Stella Summerhayes. Brissenden describes the quality of her language thus:

> Miss Quodling, the sibylline goat woman, speaks with a quintessentially Australian accent; her idiom is tough, slangy, humorous, sardonically realistic and amazingly fluent and flexible. It is the range which surprises and delights: in her speeches Patrick White has enlarged the dimensions of the Australian language in a unique and creative way, revealing unsuspected potentialities for poetry and eloquence." (Brissenden 1964, 253)

As Brissenden's quotation suggests, too, the major feat of White's achievement in the opening monologue of "Night on Bald Mountain," is to create a dramatic language which is simple in its directness, rich in its nuances, poetic in its elation. It is a language that emphasises both the vulnerability of the goat woman, her human frailty, and the larger-than-life, awesome quality which makes her ruler of the mountain, one with nature and creation. Miss Quodling's language creates simultaneously the realistic surface of everyday life and the core of her personality, the spiritual quality of her nature. The mixture of the vernacular and the poetic quality Brissenden talks of, conveys the fusion of heightened perception, wry humour and compassion which is the foundation of this character's very nature, as evidenced in this speech:

> MISS QUODLING: Fair-ee! If you put yer foot in the milk again, I'll dong you! ... My Dolores! You're the wisest goat that ever ... You're my darling thing!
>
> And you ... you big bugger in there, you Samson ... want to get at'em, eh? Well, it's not your time. ... You've had'em! Only the visiting ladies now ... if you're lucky ... Nature, it's something, it's ... something ... You be careful, Jessica, with the bellyful you've got. Triplets ... Dolores! You leave Jessica alone! ... if there's anything I hate, it's a goat with horns. ... Wall-eyed, cow-hocked thing! I hate you, bloody Dolores! ... No, I don't. Dolores? You're the best." (NBM 270)

"The Ham Funeral" also exhibits this opposition of an almost visceral, energetic vernacular and the poetry of the 'language of the gods'. Downstairs are the Lustys, Alma and Will, with their locked-up passions and silent withdrawals, yet they are tangible, physical presences; upstairs is the inert Young Man, and his spirit, the Girl-Anima, locked away in the opposite but identical room. The physical rather than cerebral nature of the Lusty relationship is dramatised in Alma's robust language:

> ALMA: Will Lusty found 'is tongue! If a court 'ud asked me was you still there, I wouldn't 'uv known wot to answer. Reminds me of a kid I used to be friendly with ... got me to take a squint at a fart 'e'd caught in a bottle ..." (HF 26)

Like Miss Docker – like most of White's female characters – Alma has an ambiguous nature (and function in the play). She is simultaneously a life-giving source and a death-bringing agent, at once fruitful and barren:

> ALMA: Alma Jagg breathed life into the hedges. The frost melted when I lay beneath 'awthorns. I touched the warm, moist earth with my 'and. ... Afterwards, when the flowers came, I lay back ... and crushed 'em. (HF 65)

Nola Boyle of "The Season at Sarsaparilla" is also a physical representation of lust, like Alma, caught up in the mechanism of her body. They both love *love*, they have a natural urge to give, but they also feast on passion with a voracious appetite. Creativity and destruction reign side by side in both characters; but their creativity is of a different kind. Like Alma, Nola uses her body and her senses to experience the nature around her; or rather, the nature around her feeds her senses:

> NOLA: I could eat the roses! Dawdling in the back yard.... I'd take off me clothes, and sit amongst the falling roses. I've never felt the touch of roses on my body. Green in the shade. Green for shade. Splotchy. You can imagine the petals, trickling, trickling, better than water, because solid. (SS 125)

But Nola's heat is also likened to that of a bitch in season, ruthless, biological; there is a conflict in her passion which makes it destructive:

> NOLA: It's this blasted body! It's put together wrong. If your hips was to work different ... Or there weren't none of those pulses in your throat. (SS 150)

The fertile Alma creates, she makes thing grow with the warmth of her hand, only to kill what she creates, crushing the flowers as they grow. Nola, however, while embodying the same paradox as Alma, lacks the ability to breathe life into nature and inspiration into aspiring poets, as Alma to the Young Man. Nola is, in the final instance, "about as barren as an old boot" (166). But Nola is a Sarsaparillan; she belongs to a social environment, a community, a suburb. She may rebel against conformity and feel this ambiguous affinity with a nature she cannot quite control, but she is also like the "thin, prissy operated women" she despises; also operated on by the men around her. (125) Nola is part of the monolithic rhythm of the other Sarsaparillans, the Girlie Pogsons and the Mavis Knotts:

> THREE WOMEN: (in unison, as they dust or sweep) Laundry's over, thank God! Laundry's Monday. Tuesday for the Cash-and-Carry ... mucking around the shops.
>
> ALL. (sweeping, flicking, rubbing) Mucking around ... mucking around. ... There's the pictures, too, of an afternoon. Warm as velvet on a winter afternoon. (SS 93)

This is an expressive example of another side of White's dramatic dialogue – here it works through use of elliptical language and understatement. In a few words, he builds up images of a whole society and their daily lives. He may express a whole complex theme through a few lines of dialogue as when Mrs. Lillee reflects: "I never thought to ask the glass. ... Nobody human contradicted my face. (CS 217-18) In the same way as the three women's speech dramatises the routines of a suburb, Mrs Lillie's lines express an image of the Sarsaparillan failure to face life, the characters' failure to look into their own actions for the answer to their loneliness, or lovelessness.

With "Big Toys" White moves back to the city – but a very different city environment than that of the Lustys' kitchen. Mag Bosanquet is White's first trendy woman; a city product, she is a perfect blend of rich bitch and soignée socialite, spiced with a risqué naughtiness. The sterility of her life, sexual and otherwise, is quickly established in the image of the burst balloon, "some ugly old wrinkled scrotum" (BT 5) which she fishes for with an elegant toe. The change in this female character from all the previous ones is seen in the nature of the dramatic dialogue. Rhetoric and brittle artificiality of language replace the poetic quality and colourful vitality of the earlier characters, as seen in Mag's retort when Terry, the trade union man, suggests that her useless hands have never scrubbed a floor:

> MAG: My friends warned me that Communists are without a sense of humour.... As a matter of fact, I don't do anything like that. Ritchie wouldn't want me to. We have a Spanish 'treasure'. We get on terribly well. I really think we understand each other. (BT 10)

Ritchie gives Mag a necklace of emeralds, and when Terry asks if they are real, Mag's ironic reply, "Terry, you'll have to learn I'm the greatest sucker for glass," (BT 18) describes the quality of the Bosanquets' city life. The stones reflect the panoramic image of the Sydney skyline of the set (as stipulated by White). I would also suggest that they echo the image of the city's lights in Miss Quodling's speech:

MISS QUODLING: Bit cheap, perhaps. I call them the rhinestones of Sydney. Too much glitter. (Reverie) When I was a young girl at Auntie's, there was a flash young feller used ter come around. Thought 'e could catch me with a rhinestone necklace. Well I wasn't taken in. (Drily) I kept the necklace, though. The whole thing fell apart." (NBM 348)

The necklace in both Mag's and Miss Quodling's speeches is an image suggesting that those characters are simultaneously victims and creators of that of which they are victims. They emphasise both the potential growth and the lack of development of the individuals caught in a sterile society they have themselves helped to create, whether it is on the mountain, the suburb or the city. It is White's way of dramatising the paradox of life embodied by his female characters: that of barren fruitfulness. Their dramatic enigma is that they are often barren and fruitful at the same time. To listen to the vigorous vernacular and the heightened poetic quality of White's dramatic dialogue is to experience how he extends the horizons of a myopic Australian existence and gives it a spiritual life by letting the characters' thoughts and visions and inner imagination take a verbal, living form. He creates a dramatic language which combines economy with imagination, and poetic expression with colloquial speech; a language which is unique in its essential understanding of the characters' individual natures, and essential to the understanding of their actions and behaviour.

A terrible, glorious life indeed.

Works Cited

Akerholt, May-Brit. 1988. *Patrick White*. Australian Playwrights. Amsterdam: Rodopi.
—. 1984. "Female Figures in Dorothy Hewett and Patrick White," *Westerly* 1:69-77.
Beyer, Edvard. 1978. *Henrik Ibsen. Samlede Verker 4* (*Collected Works 4*). Oslo: Gyldendal Norsk Forlag.
Billington, Michael. 2003."Something in the Redgrave Gene", *The Guardian*, reprinted in *The Sydney Morning Herald,* 11.7:14.

Brissenden, R.F. 1964. "The Plays of Patrick White", *Meanjin* 23.3, (September): 243-56.
Foucault, Michel. 1964. "Les mots qui saignent." *L'Express*, 688.29 (August): 21-22.
Meyer, Michael. 1974. *Ibsen*. Harmondsworth: Penguin.
Palmer, Jennifer. 1979. Ed. *Contemporary Australian Playwrights*. Adelaide: Adelaide University Union Press.
Schechner, Richard. 2005. [1977] *Performance Theory*. London and New York: Routledge.
White, Patrick. 1974. [1965].*Four Plays*.Melbourne: Sun Books
—. *Collected Plays Volume II*.Sydney: Currency Press.

CHAPTER ELEVEN

LOOKING AT PATRICK WHITE LOOKING:
PORTRAITS IN PAINT AND ON FILM

GREG BATTYE
UNIVERSITY OF CANBERRA

In a lecture on portraiture given at Australia's National Portrait Gallery and broadcast on ABC Radio National (Maleuvre 2010b), Didier Maleuvre offered the view that photography "cannot yield a portrait" and that "late 20th century portraiture enlisted photography in part to undermine the human face, to depersonalise it." In terms of both art history and mediated representation, Maleuvre knows whereof he speaks: he is Professor of French and Comparative Literature at the University of California Santa Barbara, and affiliated with the University's Centre for Film, Television and New Media – in which capacity we can presume that he is not broadly hostile to photography in general. He is the author of several major books and numerous journal articles on art and art history, including *The Religion of Reality: Inquiry into the Self, Art, and Transcendence* (2006), which "deals with the two forces in modern culture that command the centrality and force of religion: the self, on the one hand, and art, on the other." (Maleuvre 2006, 1) That book is underscored throughout by Maleuvre's concern that "scientific rationalisation has purged the world of mystery and ... flushed the very idea of the mysterious from knowledge and understanding." (Maleuvre 2006, 2) In respect of art at least, it seems that he would like to put some of that mystery back

Maleuvre's talk on ABC Radio National makes it clear that he believes that portraits are at the very core of what painting is about, and that the manner in which the best painted portraits manage to capture the essences of their human subjects is a mystery available only to painters and paintings, never to photographers and photographs. Maleuvre's quintessential portraitist is Rembrandt, and his radio talk certainly helps heighten our sensitivity to Rembrandt's rare gift, but his comparative denigration of photography's capacities for portrayal, in the same talk, rest mostly on simple assertion that what paintings have, photographs cannot. While he provides some evidence for his assertion, that evidence strikes me as incomplete and unconvincing.

The challenge in examining Maleuvre's contention is to find, and compare, painted and photographic portraits of the same person. As it happens, this rare opportunity is afforded us by a small group of portraits of Patrick White. This paper is mostly about that complex relationship between photographed and painted portraits: about the strengths and weaknesses of each, over which the respective proponents often adopt very combative positions. I hope that in making the case for a particular understanding of these portraits of White, the paper also provides some insights into White himself, and his relationship with the world – one that was similarly complex, and often equally combative.

This discussion centres on three pictures: two of William Yang's black and white photographs of Patrick White taken in Yang's Kings Cross studio in 1980, and the large colourful portrait of White by Brett Whiteley, *Patrick White at Centennial Park, 1979-1980*. The first of Yang's images, "*Patrick White #1*" is held by Australia's National Portrait Gallery and can be found on their website (Yang 1980a), while the other photograph in the series referred to in this paper, "*Patrick White #3*," is held by the National Library of Australia in Canberra, but can be seen on the website of the State Library of New South Wales (Yang 1980b). Brett Whiteley's portrait is held by the New South Wales State Parliament but can also be seen on the website of the National Portrait Gallery. (Whiteley 2013) Yang was a friend of White's from 1977 until the end of White's life, and portrayed White's many moods in a range of photographic styles and settings and with varying degrees of formality, even collaborating with White on some semi-jocular images purporting to show the author after his death. An extensive selection of these photographs can be found in

Yang's own book on White (Yang 1995). Whiteley was also a friend of White's, roughly during the decade 1970-1980, but eventually fell foul of the writer's irascible temperament as is briefly described later in this paper.

The dates for the respective painting and photographs, as incorporated in their titles, conceal an important fact about the order in which they were completed, and thus also partly conceal an important aspect of the connection between the photographs and the paintings. The dating of the painted portrait as "*1979-1980*" appears to indicate that the painting pre-dates the photographs, and the commencement of Whiteley's work does indeed pre-date them – but thereby hangs my tale. The actual time sequence for the three works supports the arguments I want to make about photographs and paintings: that photographs should not be so readily dismissed from the lexicon of tools for what Amanda Smith, introducing the recorded version of Maleuvre's talk, calls "not just capturing the moment, but capturing the life" (Maleuvre 2010), and that photographs may sometimes offer insights not obtainable by any other means.

Let me start by indicating the kind of argument Maleuvre uses to favourably distinguish the painted portrait from the photograph. He firstly determines what a portrait is, and what it must do: firstly and most obviously, it must present a likeness of the person portrayed, without which we cannot make a connection between the portrayal and the person. Secondly, the work needs to "convey a sense of what it's like to be this person." (Amanda Smith, in Maleuvre 2010) There are of course complex exceptions to the first requirement: Melbourne graphic designer W. H. Chong, coincidentally in a weblog article about the task of drawing a portrait of Patrick White from photographs for the cover of the Australian Book Review, (Chong 2011) talks of how the self-portrait exhibition at Federation Square in Melbourne earlier in 2012 had been filled with numerous pictures that bore not only no resemblance to the artist portrayed, but little resemblance to any human figure at all. But I digress.

On likeness in portraits, Maleuvre makes the important and appropriate observation that likeness is constructed, both in the making of the work and in the interaction between the work and the viewer. This appears to be a built-in human trait; as he says, "[i]nfants are portrait makers of sorts when they interpret the blur of nose and eye and mouth and cheek as mom's face" (Maleuvre 2010). Likeness thus "belongs to the observer" (Maleuvre 2010); we see a likeness between people, or between a person and a picture of a person, because perceiving that likeness is part of the process of perception itself. Even though we might be able to argue for our view of a likeness, as in for example 'Sir Winston Churchill, his son Sir Randolph Churchill, and the actor Anthony Hopkins, share a likeness because of the shape of their faces and the flesh around the eyes and mouth' (paraphrasing Maleuvre 2010), but our assertion will only likely find favour with somebody who already shares the same perception, not because of the assertion itself.

With this understanding of likeness though, Maleuvre has provided no distinction between painting and photography, even if he believes that one medium is better equipped than the other to undertake the task of making a likeness. The same process of perception, in the viewer of the image, happens with both. It's entirely possible to take a photograph of someone that is not recognizable as a likeness of that person, just as it is possible (even more easily, for most of us) to paint a portrait of someone that nobody will interpret as a likeness of that person. As W. H. Chong says, "[w]hen we don't recognize a photo of someone we know, we think we're at fault. But no, the photo is telling us how malleable likeness can be" (Chong 2011). As almost anyone will attest who has attended an art gallery in the company of another person, and looked at and talked about portraits with that person, this malleability applies equally to painting.

The photo is also probably telling us something about the level of difficulty, and the nature of the task, involved in making a good photographic portrait of somebody. This is where Maleuvre starts, in my humble opinion, to go badly wrong, although the views he expresses are by no means unique to him. A sample:

> Photographic portraiture seeks not participation, but the fly-by capture of an unguarded moment. But a split second is a tiny, tiny quantum and a human being is too big a thing to fit in so small a sliver of time. And the human being, moreover, doesn't see in one five-hundredth of a second. Photography, therefore, shows us what

no-one has ever seen or no-one ever sees: this is why in my view photography cannot yield a portrait. Its nature is primarily forensic or archival. What it cannot do, photography, is describe. And without description, without the labour of seeing your way around the landscape of a face, the photographic portrait is an oxymoron. How long it will seem an oxymoron to future generations depends on our remaining alive to the danger Rembrandt's portraits warn us against: the danger of, let's say, casualness, of everyday blindness, of quick acquaintance. Rembrandt's romance of the face reminds us that we humanly exist by each other's attention, through a moral, creative act of mutual depiction (Maleuvre 2010).

He is not alone in this view, and nor are his views conditioned only by his particular enthusiasm for Rembrandt or for Rembrandt's period. Here is David Hockney, a sometime photographer as well as a contemporary painter, talking about his 'joiners', large composite pictures he assembled from many separate photographs in the 1980s:

> I had wanted to put time into the photograph more obviously than just in the evidence that my hand pressed the shutter, and there it was, it could be done. The big joiners ... took about four hours to do. Consequently there are four hours of layered time locked in there. I've never seen an ordinary photograph with four hours of layered time. That's much longer than you would take to look at it! This is what it's overcome. For me the main problem in photography always came down to that. Any painting or drawing contains time because you know it took time to do. (Joyce 1988, 18)

In the first place then, Maleuvre and Hockney both equate the duration of the photographic exposure with the time taken to make the work; in the second place, they both equate the time taken to make the work with the time that the resulting picture somehow 'contains', and by implication with the depth and intensity of the information the picture can convey. Both these assumptions are, I think, incomplete if not actually inaccurate and poorly conceived as a representation of what happens in making a photograph and a photographic portrait in particular.

The release of the shutter button to make a photographic exposure is of course the culminating, summative event in a sequence, but it is not identical with the act of making the photograph. It is an event that finally, but only partly, determines what that particular exposure will look like. We should remember that photography is 'writing with light,' and it is light – not the camera, or the lens, or the recording medium, or the darkroom, or the computer – that is the photographer's raw material. The arrangement of lighting for a studio portrait, or the arrangement of the subject in relation to existing natural or artificial light sources in the case of an available-light photograph, is an iterative process that takes up far more time than the making of the exposure. Even the notion of exposure time itself merits more careful examination: we conventionally think of exposure times as 'instant,' as effectively durationless, even when the actual duration is a time period that is comprehensible and usable in other contexts – 1/100th of a second, for example, a common photographic exposure duration, is a time period by which the first and second place-getters in a contemporary athletic competition might be separated. The manner in which we understand even extremely short time periods, and what might happen within them, is thus always strongly contextual.

The unavoidable physical and causal links between photographs and the optical, electronic and mechanical instruments and processes necessary for their production have always worked against establishing a clear understanding of what it is that photographers, rather than cameras, do. If we are to attribute appropriate agency to photographers, then we must attend to the events that take place prior to and beyond the time of exposure. The exposure is an event that is initiated by the photographer's actions, but the brevity of exposure times, in general, prevents their encompassing both the initiation and the completion of any intentional human act.

But there are other points to be made about the relativity of the exposure time itself. Although no full cycle of intentional human action can be encompassed within such short intervals, nevertheless in terms of physics, the science for which the measurement of time and the consequences of time are perhaps most critical, even 1/1000 of a second is an interval within which a lot can happen. Well ...

consider, for instance, the origin of the universe. Via traces still visible from platforms such as the Hubble space telescope, science has enabled us to look in detail at what happened in and around the very beginning of the universe, when an incomprehensible 'singularity' of infinite density and temperature suddenly expanded to essentially infinite size. There is an identifiable sequence of 6 distinct 'epochs' in this process, culminating in the Hadron Epoch, by which stage the fundamental forces which act within and between atomic particles had become separate from each other, and the universe occupied something close to the volume of the universe as it exists now, although very different in physical composition. The entire time between zero (the big bang itself) and the end of the Hadron Epoch occupies one second, and the middle of the Hadron Epoch is somewhere between 10^{-4} and 10^{-3} seconds from the big bang – or in photographic fractions, between 1/10,000 of a second and 1/1000 of a second.

By comparison, at the time of writing, the fastest shutter speed generally available in a commercial DSLR camera is 1/8000 of a second, while one second falls comfortably at the low end of a wide range of long exposure times that might be used for low-light photography. The range of exposure times ordinarily used in photography is thus able to encompass the entire duration of the beginning of existence itself; to merely describe it collectively as 'instantaneous' would be to discard everything about the extraordinary changes *within* that time period which make it so interesting. And as we shall see later, although *intentional* actions can't be contained within typical photographic exposure times, changes in the behaviour and appearance of a photographic subject certainly can – in ways that differentially affect painted and photographed portraits.

To move on – Patrick White and the painter Brett Whiteley had known each other for a number of years before Whiteley commenced his portrait of White, *Patrick White at Centennial Park, 1979-1980,* in 1979. A keen and discerning art collector, White had initially been resistant to Whiteley's "lush and beautiful" work (Marr 1992, 519) in the early 70s, being perhaps wary of the wave of fashionable enthusiasm the paintings were attracting, but also feeling the work to be merely derivative of the English painter

Francis Bacon. This was an informed and reasonable view; Whiteley and Bacon had met in London in 1961 and had maintained a friendship that turned into an artistic mentoring of Whiteley by Bacon, and Whiteley continued to use avowedly Baconesque motifs and styles for the rest of his career. White was also well qualified to recognise Bacon's influence when he saw it: the Australian painter Roy de Maistre who was later, briefly, a lover of White's in London (and who remained a friend for life) had 'discovered' Bacon working as a young furniture designer and interior decorator, and had encouraged him to turn to painting. Through this and other connections, White had met Bacon in the 1930s, (Marr 1992, 149, 169) and maintained ongoing knowledge of Bacon's work as well as sporadic contact with Bacon himself, on occasional trips to London.

By 1970, White's view of Whiteley had recovered from his 'resistance,' and he was describing Whiteley's *'Paintings and Assemblages'* exhibition at the Bonython gallery in Sydney as the work of a "great painter." (Marr 1994, 365) The two men connected and became friends; Whiteley visited White's home across from Centennial Park where he dazzled, and sometimes puzzled, the writer with what seemed to be a "new language," and with his stories of how the "acid people" saw things in just the way White did. (Marr 1992, 519) Writing to Whiteley in 1972, White appended a postscript saying: "At one time I thought Francis B. would be your downfall as a painter, but now I see you are making the right use of him." (Marr 1994, 394) Broadly similar agreement on political issues, both local and national, brought them closer: Whiteley passed out on a couch at a dinner party at White's home on the night of the dismissal of the Whitlam government, on November 11 1975. (Adelaide 2011) White bought several Whiteley paintings, including at least one of the gigantic Sydney Harbour views for which the painter had become most widely famous.

In 1978 Whiteley became the first artist to win three of Australia's most significant art prizes in the same year: the Archibald Prize for portraiture, the Wynne Prize for landscape, and the Sulman Prize for genre painting. The die was cast: with his confidence in full bloom under the influence of these successes, in

April 1979 Whiteley mapped out his far-reaching ideas and ambitions for the immediate future:

> the first, to introduce into his body only vegetables, fruit, distilled water and maybe a bit of milk; the second, to travel like a Gypsy, beginning in China; and the third, to remain as he was, and paint four portraits over the coming two years: of Albert Einstein, Howard Hughes, Patrick White and Sir Kenneth Clark. (Engledow 2012)

Whiteley began to sketch White as the author was working on his autobiography *Flaws in the Glass*, in which he wrestled even more intensely than usual with who he was, what to say about who he was, and how to say it. Whiteley's studies and sketches for his painting (see Engledow 2012) reflect the development of quite a broad and deep connection between the two men; White sat obligingly in his study overlooking Martin Road as the layout of the whole picture was planned, and sat for closer, more detailed sketches of his face; they walked together in White's beloved Centennial Park across the road from the house, and talked of fundamental philosophical issues. But there were difficulties.

In *Flaws in the Glass* White was already writing that "double values abound amongst those I used to respect; and as for myself, I have never disguised a belief that, as an artist, my face is many-faceted, my body protean, according to time, climate, and the demands of fiction." (White 1981, 152) White also wrote that "the little that is subtle in the Australian character comes from the masculine principle in its women, the feminine in its men," (White 1981, 154) but there is very little in Whiteley's preliminary facial sketches that show a feminine side to White, or any of White's humour. Sarah Engledow, curator for the White-Whiteley exhibition at the Australian National Portrait Gallery in 2012 commemorating White's birth, and the author of the notes for the exhibition says that they show White "only as irascible, suspicious and supercilious." (Engledow 2012)

Significantly, I think, the preparatory sketches also show White in nearly every case as looking away from the painter. This is hardly unheard of in painted portraits, although certainly there are at least as many cases where portrait subjects do indeed look directly at the painter, and thus directly at the viewer. The time for which a model or subject sits in the same pose for a painting may well make such a direct gaze an uncomfortable, even embarrassing aspect of the process, perhaps even for both parties. Maleuvre (2010) offers an interesting observation about his hero among portrait painters, Rembrandt: that while Rembrandt's male subjects are mostly painted as looking directly at the artist and the viewer, he is apparently embarrassed to look so directly and intensely into a woman's face, and thus his female subjects are inevitably depicted in three-quarter profile or complete profile. This is a clue to another difference in the strengths of painting and photography, in relation to portraits – to which I will return.

Whiteley's portrait needed to achieve the two things already identified as necessary attributes of any portrait: achieving a likeness of the subject, and communicating something about the subject's world. The second of these was achieved straightfowardly enough, although in the process the seeds were sown for the irreparable, and perhaps inevitable, breach between the writer and the painter. Whiteley's painting mixes metaphorical or conceptual representations with literal ones: Centennial Park can be glimpsed through the railings of White's fence just as it would have been in real life, although the house is well above street level, the painting depicts an essentially level plane extending from interior to exterior space. The Sydney Opera House, perhaps symbolising the few aspects of Australian culture that White felt to be to the nation's credit, can be glimpsed to the left of the picture as though seen from the western side of Circular Quay; but White's house in Centennial Park was directly south of Circular Quay and faced east and slightly south, making this view impossible even if it had been – which it is not – close enough to the Opera House to have such a view, and unimpeded by the intervening landscape.

At least one part of White's world was shown absolutely literally: the list of White's loves and hates which had been drawn up at Whiteley's request in order to penetrate beyond White's fiercely guarded privacy, and to know something of his inner life. This list, made (in White's view) for the artist's eyes only and for the interim purpose of assisting with the painting, famously became physically part of the painting for all to see and read, and attention was specifically drawn to it in a 'Column 8' piece in the Sydney Morning Herald in 1980. Although a social connection between the two men seemingly continued at least beyond completion of the portrait, with White – clearly a careful and conservative investor in all domains of his life, whatever his political leanings – purchasing another Whiteley work after the portrait was finished, White later pointed to the inclusion of the list in the portrait as the last straw in what he perceived as the slow decline of their friendship.

He wrote to Whiteley, inter alia, of what he saw as "that vein of dishonesty from which so many of your acts and attitudes stem" and of how he found this perceived dishonesty "distressing in one I wanted to accept as a friend," though still declaring also that "[a]t your best you are a genius." (Marr 1994, 548-549) In fairness, it should be noted that drawing up lists of likes, dislikes, plans, intentions and so forth seems to have been a routine practice of Whiteley's, and as one whose somewhat unconventional personal life was already often on show, Whiteley would undoubtedly have been less concerned about making the same kinds of revelation about his own life. Possibly he expected White, as a fellow artist, to naturally feel the same way; if so, he was certainly mistaken.

The portrait certainly thus included significantly more of White's life than White himself had bargained for, but meanwhile Whiteley had great difficulty with achieving a proper likeness of White's face. I can't help thinking that White's refusal to meet Whiteley's gaze, in the preliminary sketches, is readable as the beginning of White's slow burn of resentment about Whiteley and his "dishonesty." White's repeated lifelong terminations of friends and acquaintances often followed a pattern: sudden angry and powerful reaction to some minor perceived infringement, later traceable to a gradually accumulating, long-standing resentment over a sequence of other issues about which nothing had been said at the time. In the sketches, White does not merely look away at some more temporarily interesting phenomenon; he looks grim, sulking, resentful. This was not the face Whiteley wanted in his picture (even though the final result is still one of melancholy, at best – but truthfully so).

Whiteley turned to the photographer William Yang for assistance, and early in 1980 Yang took several photographs of

White – using which Whiteley, after some intensive further work on the face alone, was able to render its mercurial emotional landscape to his satisfaction. What we see when we compare the painting and the photographs is that, with respect to the face alone – the likeness – it is Yang's photographs, not Whiteley's many sketches, that determine how the face is finally executed.

If all are brought to the same size, a comparison of the head alone, in the painting, with the two photographs, reveals an astonishing level of similarity. White's face in the painting is not a copy of either photograph, but meticulously and inventively combines the two. With "*Patrick White #3*," the painting shares the overall attitude of the head, and the detailed position and shape of the mouth and upper lip, the nose, the furrow in the centre of the brow above the nose bridge, the creases in the forehead, the right ear, and the wisp of hair over the right side of White's brow. With "*Patrick White #1*," the painting shares most particularly what is absent in Whiteley's own preparatory sketches: an almost direct gaze, very slightly downward but almost painful in its open and direct expression of melancholy. With respect to the question of likeness, but not only likeness, surely the photographs provide the gold standard in this case, and it is Whiteley's deployment of them in the painting that confirms such a view. This explicitly contradicts Maleuvre's contention, exemplified most strikingly (in his view) by Rembrandt, that only by painting "the overlapping acts of coming to know the sitter over time," only by "patiently modelling and layering the subject, feeling his way around the face one brush stroke at a time, down the meanders of growing acquaintance that took a minimum of three months," can a portrait be made to truly realise a person's identity (Maleuvre 2010).

This assertion, in turn, takes us back to the question of time once more, and to the alleged inadequacy of photography's 'instant' view of the face. This is the kind of thing that is most often argued either on grounds that can never really provide a resolution – aesthetic opinion, or professional preference either for painting or for photography – or perhaps by reference to the infinite but closed circuits of contemporary cultural theory. But there is other evidence that needs to be brought to bear here. Firstly, cognitive science confirms what philosophical and artistic investigations have always observed: that we live in a permanent state of uncertainty about the degree to which the bodily states and behaviours (including facial expressions) of other people reflect their internal (and thus invisible) states of mind. We attend continuously and closely to the behaviour of others because it is the only indicator we have of their states of mind, and we need to know about the mental states of others in order to behave appropriately towards them. But at the same time, we ensure that we *perform* our own bodies and behaviour as far as possible, precisely to ensure that our behaviour is *not* a constantly reliable and transparent indicator of our internal thinking, and that we are thus not vulnerable to people who might take advantage of knowing what we are thinking. And we know, of course, that everybody else is doing the same thing, and that this renders our observations of their behaviour problematic. And we know that they know that we know ... and so on.

Many cultural representations, particularly narrative-based ones, depend on this constant comedy of errors in mental attribution. In particular they often deal with the rare and brief moments of what Lisa Zunshine calls 'embodied transparency,' when our performative guard is down and our real thoughts or feelings are transparently revealed by behaviour or expression, in a moment of 'perfect readability.' (Zunshine 2008, 76) This, presumably, is just what the able portrait painter seeks. By the lengthy and repeated observation of a sitter's expression from close up, the painter is able to compare expressions and behaviours over time, to correlate those expressions and behaviours with ideas, opinions, thoughts and values expressed in conversation between painter and subject over the same period, and then to render the 'real,' inner person, the subject as transparently revealed.

We do not need to cast any aspersions on Rembrandt's extraordinary abilities, or on his magnificent works, to see that photography might sometimes offer a quite different solution to the quest for embodied transparency. Human reaction times are highly variable between subjects, and extremely task-dependent, but a good visual choice reaction time for a healthy young adult is about 200 milliseconds, or 1/5 of one second. This gives us some idea of the speed with which a photographer might react, by pressing the shutter button, to an expression on a subject's face. But confounding this is the fleetingly changeable nature of many facial expressions. Paul Ekman's work on micro-expressions tells us that:

> Although most facial expressions last more than one second, micro-expressions last well under a second – perhaps 1/5 to 1/25 of a second. Micro-expressions are typically embedded in movement, often in facial movements that are part of talking. And they are typically followed immediately by a masking facial expression (Ekman and Friesen 2003, 151).

It is difficult then, but by no means impossible, for an experienced photographer who takes multiple rapid exposures, knows how to converse with his or her subject on matters likely to be of close interest to them, and is observant enough about changing expressions to be able to try anticipating some shots rather than relying entirely on rapid reactions, to be successful in capturing micro-expressions, especially if also faced with a cooperative subject. It seems that White's expression in the photographs taken by William Yang may well have been brought about partly by the fact that White found the photographer attractive and was, thus, a cooperative subject. Certainly Yang became White's "favourite photographer" (Marr 1994, n.34) and joined White's social circle; other photographs taken by him, and included in his 1995 book, indicate a familiarity and trust with White and his circle that Whiteley, by contrast, never managed to achieve.

Perhaps these photographs are as they are because of William Yang's exceptional abilities as a photographer, as proven many times over by his whole body of work. It's also quite possible that far from masking his thoughts and feelings, White was being – rarely – as open and transparent as he knew how to be, making Yang's task that much easier. Whatever the explanation, it seems to me that William Yang's photographs provide considerably more insight into White as a person than Whiteley's portrait does, and that Whiteley was able to make use of the photographs for his painting because of that insight.

Just as physical knocks or sicknesses can sometimes leave a mark on faces and bodies, so also can unhappiness and exclusion. At his mother's instigation, White and his sister were essentially estranged from his parents almost from birth, living separately from them in an adjoining flat, when in Sydney, with a nanny. (White 1981, 10) At the age of 10 he was sent first to a boarding primary school in Moss Vale in the New South Wales southern highlands, and then to a public school, Cheltenham College, in England.

With each step the distance from his parents was further increased, and by the time he reached Cheltenham he had been sent as far away from them as was physically possible: literally to the opposite end of the earth. One might reasonably expect such a message of rejection to leave its mark. At Cheltenham, his "dangerous, unknowable housemaster, Arthur Bishop, was so threateningly tall that he sometimes smashed light bulbs as he mercilessly caned boys in his "malign obsession to stamp out filth" (Marr 1992, 70). White endured four miserable years there and wrote specifically, later, of how "when the gates of my expensive prison closed I lost confidence in my mother, and never forgave." (1981, 12)

It is most specifically in *"Patrick White #1"* that I believe we can see some of these life experiences, reflected. Of course, we would all like to see what Rembrandt might have done with this face, but I can't help feeling that Didier Maleuvre's final comments about Rembrandt's portraiture also seem to fit Yang's photographs remarkably comfortably:

> Rembrandt's faces are in need of us: this is their simple, poignant confession. Their humanity is the humanity we give them. They tell us that the human face is a sensitive plate. When we stop touching it with the soft beams of recognition, it goes flat, it dulls and it dies. The portrait lives not by internal combustion, but in the same way the human face comes alive, in the precise degree to which it is encountered. Rembrandt took on the duty of building the human conversation and this is a duty he passes on to us now. How we pick up from here, how long we remain alive to the call of these impossibly soulful eyes, tracks the health of our ongoing, fragile humanity. (Maleuvre 2010b)

Works Cited

Adelaide, Debra. 2011. "No one comes to see me now: Manoly Lascaris and Patrick White's ghost," *The Monthly* (December 2011-January 2012, No. 74). Available online from http://www.themonthly.com.au/manoly-lascaris-and-patrick-white-s-ghost-no-one-comes-see-me-now-debra-adelaide-4312.

Chong, W. H. 2013. *How to make a portrait (of Patrick White)* [Weblog]. Crikey/Private Media Pty Ltd 2011. Accessed Feb. 14 2013 http://blogs.crikey.com.au/culture-mulcher/2011/04/14/how-to-make-a-portrait-of-patrick-white/. Accessed Feb. 14 2013.

Ekman, Paul and Wallace V. Friesen. 2003. *Unmasking the Face: A Guide to Recognizing Emotions From Facial Expressions.* Cambridge, MA: Malor Books.

Engledow, Sarah. 2012. *Whiteley: the Portrait of Patrick White by Brett Whiteley.* National Portrait Gallery, Canberra 2012. Accessed February 14 2012
http://www.portrait.gov.au/site/exhibition_subsite_whitewhiteley.php.

Joyce, Paul. 1988. *Hockney on photography: conversations with Paul Joyce.* Ed.W. Brown. London: Jonathan Cape Ltd.

Maleuvre, Didier. 2010a. *The Horizon: A History of our Infinite Longing.* Berkeley, California: University of California Press.

Maleuvre, Didier. 2010b. *Artworks Feature: On Portraiture* [Radio broadcast]. ABC Radio National, Australia 2010
http://www.abc.net.au/radionational/programs/artworks/artworks-feature-on-portraiture/2973930-transcript. Accessed Feb.12 2013.

Marr, David. 1992. *Patrick White: A Life.* Sydney: Random House/ Vintage.

—. Ed. 1994. *Patrick White: Letters.* Sydney: Random House Australia.

White, Patrick. 1981. *Flaws in the Glass: a self-portrait.* London: Jonathan Cape Ltd.

Whiteley, Brett. 2013. *Patrick White at Centennial Park* [Oil painting]. National Portrait Gallery Canberra1980. Accessed February 14 2013. Available from
http://www.portrait.gov.au/site/exhibition_subsite_whitewhiteley.php.

Yang, William. 2013. *Patrick White #1* [Silver gelatin photograph]. National Portrait Gallery, Canberra 1980(a) Accessed February 14 2013.
http://www.portrait.gov.au/site/collection_info.php?searchtype=basic&searchstring=yangwhite&irn=13&acno=1998.13.
Accessed February 14 2013.
—. 2013. *Patrick White #3* [Silver gelatin photograph]. National Library of Australia, Canberra 1980(b) Accessed 14 February 2013.
http://www.sl.nsw.gov.au/events/exhibitions/2012/patrick_white/items/image04.html.
—. 1995. *Patrick White: the late years*. Sydney: Pan Macmillan.
Zunshine, Lisa. 2008. "Theory of Mind and Fictions of Embodied Transparency", *Narrative* 16, 1: 65-92.

Chapter Twelve

Patrick White-Lite: Fred Schepisi's Filmic Adaptation of *The Eye of the Storm*

Sissy Helff
Goethe University Frankfurt, Germany

> "Please don't come back before the storm is over,
> neither of you possess the qualities to survive it" [64:47—64:53]

Fred Schepisi's film, *The Eye of the Storm* is set in the insular cultural landscape of Sydney's suburbs around Centennial Park of the 1970s. Just as in its literary source text, tempests erode textual, visual, temporal and societal facades. The film tells the life-story of the wealthy, but now frail and aged matriarch Elizabeth Hunter (Charlotte Rampling). This mother has asked her two adult children, Basil Hunter (Geoffrey Rush) and 'Princess de Lascabanes' aka Dorothy (Judy Davis) to return from Europe in order to spend time by her bedside in these final days. This reunion highlights salient family tensions and arouses suppressed and unsettling memories.

The motif of the storm (including the calm after the storm) is deeply ingrained in the film's temporal and narrative structure and controls it from its first to its very last sequence. Hence the opening and closing flashbacks present shots that zoom in and out on a much younger Elizabeth. This pictorial refrain introduces and frames the main female character who, when the audience watches Elizabeth appearing on screen, has obviously just survived one such storm.

These framing sequences show Elizabeth, clad in a white, slightly torn and blood-stained, chiffon dress, as she lingers in the shallows meditating on both, her survival and the beauty of life and nature encapsulated in the scene before her. Yet, as the audience will soon learn, it is this very same lady who, cyclone-like, has destroyed all those who had dared to get too near to her in the past. In this light, the Machiavellian matriarch's words from the opening quotation loom large, presenting a perpetual warning for her two grown-up children, Basil and Dorothy.

http://www.rottentomatoes.com/m/the_eye_of_the_storm/pictures/#3

No doubt, the opening and closing scenes thrive on the actress's extraordinary presence. Rampling's refined acting of Elizabeth's joy in having survived the cyclone epitomises the strength of her performance and expresses the core of Patrick White's genuine literary project. Judy Morris adapted Nobel Prize winner Patrick White's novel which presents, as critics agree, classic Schepisi material. (Capp 2011) Schepisi's stellar ensemble and its performance provide an impressive match to White's rich storytelling and style which evokes powerful, even archetypal imagery dealing with existential questions, portraying human flaws, weaknesses, hypocrisies and death. One needs to mention here the availability of the many in-depth analyses of White's literary achievement, from among the earliest like the work of William Walsh (1976) to the more recent publications by vanden Driesen (2009) and McMahon and Olubas. (2010) This paper will explore aspects of how this filmic version of a White text refracts its artistic achievement.

Similar to the position and prestige of the Nobel Prize-winning novelist, Patrick White, the position of the Melbournian film director Fred Schepisi is that of a respected iconic figure within Australia's cultural landscape. And it was in the year of White's great literary success that Fred Schepisi produced his first fiction film, a 30-minute segment for the episodic feature, *Libido* (1973). It would take him another five years to be discovered by international audiences with his filmic adaptation of Thomas Keneally's acclaimed novel *The Chant of Jimmie Blacksmith* (1972). Since then Schepisi continuously demonstrated his mastery of atmosphere and dramatic rhythm in several literary adaptations. *The Eye of the Storm* (2011) presents the latest and probably also, compared to Schepisi's earlier projects, his most complex achievement.

While it may sound somewhat simplistic to compare the lengths of the original novels, it is nevertheless interesting to note that Keneally's *The Chant of Jimmie Blacksmith* comprised approximately 180 pages, whereas White's *The Eye of the Storm* approximates to 600 pages. The aspect of length was also an issue in an interview with Michel Bodey in which Fred Schepisi stressed the fact that it is certainly never easy to translate a 600 page-long *opus magnus* into a 100 page-long film script. (Bodey 2011, 6)

This fact might explain why filmic adaptations of works of such literary weight are often considered problematic. Notwithstanding, Schepisi and his scriptwriter Judy Morris were successful; at least in the eyes of many critics, hence the adaptation was awarded several prizes such as the Jury Prize at Rome International Film Festival in November 2011 and the Special Award 2011 at the Melbourne International Film Festival. Moreover, the film received the FCCA 2012 J. Morris Award for the Best Screenplay and for Best Actress, Supporting Role; the AACTA 2012 Award for Best Costume Design, Judy Davis for Best Lead Actress and also the Award for Best Production Design.

> Some critics, however, are not impressed with Fred Schepisi's film adaptation and claim that his adaptation gives rise to nothing but 'Patrick White-lite.' (Giffin 2011, 113)

Taking Giffin's critical remark as a starting point, this article, in line with recent adaptation studies, seeks to formulate an approach to Schepisi's adaptation that demonstrates how the central *topoi* of the tempest is used in order to artistically challenge and visually erode clearly defined textual and visual domains. This then explains why this chapter goes beyond a comparison between White's novel and Schepisi's film. By doing so it is argued that the Schepisi adaptation and its filmic surplus can only be fully understood if we start taking into account the complexities of new media landscapes and the multimodal ways of perception, since cultural artifacts are differently perceived in times of high modernity. (Appadurai 2005) This claim is particularly true with regard to the genre of literary adaptations. (Elsner et.al.2013, 4)

In this vein, this discussion suggests the need for looking into the methodological tool kit of recent adaptation studies, before seeking to explore the degree to which studies of Australian film incorporate adaptation studies methodologies when discussing major literary adaptations of iconic Australian novels. Finally, my analyses of selected film sequences will demonstrate that Schepisi's 'Eye' does not reduce Patrick White's literary mastery but contributes greatly to a reception of White's work in times of high modernity.

Books and Textual Facades:
Or, What to Make of Literary Adaptations?

While scholars in German-speaking countries prefer utilising the concepts of intertextuality and intermediality in order to describe the medial translation of literary texts into different media, English speaking scholarship regularly chose the concept of adaptation over the two latter. (Krämer 2011, 207) Common to all approaches, however, has been a comparative approach in which the adaptation is only being read in the light of the original text. One result of this approach is the prevailing fidelity criticism (faithful to the source novel) which, as A.R Fulton already emphasised in 1977, frames all debates on adaptation in such a way that most

Discussions of a film based on a novel arrive sooner or later at the comparison of the film with its source. This kind of criticism may have its advantages.but somehow it leads to the mistaken conclusion that the excellence of the film depends on similarity to the novel from which it is adapted. (Giffin 2011, 113-114)

Sarah Cardwell also stresses this point in her study on literary adaptations for television dealing with classics such as Jane Austen's *Pride and Prejudice* (1813) or Evelyn Waugh's *Brideshead Revisited* (1945). While in her study Cardwell opts for introducing a new methodology, she nevertheless foregrounds the idea that it is essential to first explore the manifold dimensions and meanings of adaptations before scholars may convincingly propose alternative non-comparative approaches. (2002, 9) Cardwell hence invests value not so much in interpreting adaptations as interest in "conceptualising adaptations as the cultural form and [the] ontological problem they constitute within theories about adaptation." (Cardwell, 10

The historically dominant fidelity criticism (comparative approach) tends to focus on an investigation of the process of adaptation when exploring the way an adaptation retells the same basic narrative as its source book. Keeping this in mind may also help to explain why Michael Giffin is so dissatisfied with Schepisi's film that he writes:

Of course, the director needs a degree of license; the question is how much. Is it allowed to leave out whole dimensions of the story when cutting it down to a manageable size, rewrite several scenes so they are unrecognizable to those familiar with the story, and include several new scenes that deviate significantly from the story … At what point does the screenplay cease to be faithful when it can't be literally faithful? (Giffin 2011, 114)

At this point it might be interesting to bring in Lucia Krämer's work on adaptation, because she draws our attention to the still influential romantic notion of the genius which, as she argues in line with Rainer Schulze, (2011, 25-49) flares up in the close semantic relation between authenticity and adaptation and the idea of authorship and authority. The authority of the source text's author, she argues, is not only central to the narrative sphere but also important when discussing an adaptation's faithfulness to the original. Krämer explains that authenticity and adaptation, authorship and authority are semantically embedded in a connotation system that stresses the importance of obedience and respect.

It is this particular semantic relation that finally unfolds a double bind, for adaptations are considered less original if they simply reproduce their source texts, yet they are accused of being highly unfaithful if they present free interpretations of, and fresh takes on, their sources. (Krämer 2011, 213) This explains why adaptation studies, having been caught in this methodological dilemma for a long time, were somewhat indiscriminately shifted to and fro between literary and film studies, unable to make a home in either of the two disciplines. Given that one of the dyed-in-the-wool adaptation studies scholars, George Bluestone had published his ground-breaking study *Novels into Film* in the late 1950s, it took the field another fifty years or so, before adaptation studies eventually receive the deserved attention from the humanities.

Visual Facades: Adaptation Studies and Australian Film

In the mid-1990s a paradigmatic change set in which aimed at opening up the field by drawing attention in addition to filmic adaptations to adaptation mediated through other media such as opera, ballet, comics and video games. (Hucheton 2006, 3-4) It is only recently that scholars have started to revise the field in such a way that adaptation studies can be considered an 'independent' research area. The establishment of the Association of *Adaptation Studies* in 2006 and the creation of an international, peer-reviewed journal in 2008 present the first steps of an emerging discipline. The Antipodean branch of adaptation studies became visible through a recent open source project "Adapt: Sharing Adaptation Studies" which can be visited on the website http://www.adapt.edu.au/. The project, which is led by scholars from the University of Tasmania and supported by colleagues from the Universities of Western Australia and Queensland as well as from Monash University, only recently organised an adaptation studies conference in Hobart. All these developments certainly confirm Richard Hand and Katja Krebs's courageous claims of 2008, when they publicly proclaimed the inauguration of a new exciting period which celebrates adaptation studies as a discipline in its own right. (2008, 173-175)

In her article "Fidelity, Simultaneity and the 'Remaking' of Adaptation Studies," the London-based Lindiwe Dovey emphasises the critical potential of adaptation studies since their methodologies help us "to see not the so-called originality and genius of singularly unique works of art, but the contingency of art, and the need to explore the ways in which, and for whom, aesthetic value is created." (2012, 163) The US-based scholar Thomas Leitch follows Rick Altman's line of reasoning (1999) and suggests thinking adaptation against the backdrop of genre conventions. Leitch believes that "there must be textual markers that identify adaptations as such" and which then "invite audiences to recognize them as adaptations." (2008, 108)

Leitch's 'film-immanent' argument was unexpectedly supported by the data of the Australian film industry. In a study on the economic performance of the Australian film industry, Matthew Hancock writes: "The fall [of adaptations released in Australia] is significant because adaptations, both in Australia and in foreign markets like the US, tend to perform well, attracting a higher proportion of box office than their proportion in release." (2010, 3) Implicit in this assumption is the idea that audiences prefer watching adaptations; and although we might not yet know the exact reasons why, Hancock's study demonstrates that

> For titles released in 1999–2008, a comparison of the typical earnings for individual films shows that adaptations perform better in the average than original films ... By comparison, the box office earnings for adaptations are more consistent. Their median box office was almost triple that of original films during the study period ... [thus] a typical adaptation has a good chance of outperforming a typical original film. (2010, 3-4)

Bringing to the fore these economic facts is one way to point to urgency to invite a changed perspective on the Australian film landscape. In many ways Hancock's study also excavates an ignorance, which, to some degree, seems to characterise Australian studies which is marked by a strange absence of adaptation criticism dealing with Australian film.

How can one explain, I wonder, that Felicity Collins and Therese Davis in their recent book on *Australian Cinema after Mabo* (2004) don't even touch upon adaptation and consequently forget to mention the term 'adaptation' altogether in their chapters on Gillian Armstrong's period film *Oscar and Lucinda* (1997) or Phillip Noyce's feature film *Rabbit-Proof Fence* (2002). While a case can be made not to classify the latter film as an adaptation, Armstrong's period film requires to be labelled as one. Collins and Davis' treatment of adaptations is not the exception; rather it presents the norm in Australian cinema studies. Albert Moran and Errol Vieth's *Film in Australia: An Introduction* (2006), a book which certainly has its merits, also manages to circumnavigate adaptations even though the introduction opens with a detailed chapter on "Genre and Australian Film" before the book moves to explore a great many filmic genres. In Moran and Vieth's study, however, the absence of adaptation studies is somewhat annoying, since the authors claim in the preface to their book that

> Recognising and understanding film in terms of particular film classes or types is a necessary first step in their analysis and interpretation. It helps the viewer to grasp not only what a film means but how it means .... It is surely the case that comprehending what is filmic about these films is a necessary first step towards understanding what is Australian about them (2006, xi-xii).

While readers would certainly agree with the authors' last statement, the sheer absence of adaptation studies within *Film in Australia: An Introduction* is somewhat disturbing. By ignoring adaptation as a genre the authors imply the semantic relation between authenticity and adaptation and the idea of authorship and authority. Since the two authors do not clearly position themselves with regard to questions about the role ascribed to the source text's author, Moran and Vieth unnecessarily challenge their own argument. And worse, in this manner, the authors suggest a dialectic relationship between adaptation, authorship and filmic authenticity, which comes alive through a semantic connotation emphasising obedience and respect as central qualities of artwork.

At this point, we need to consider a critical statement by Lindiwe Dovey concerning adaptation studies, in which she highlights the discipline's tremendous potential for contributing to understandings of how notions of high and popular cultural production, or what counts as art and what does not, are produced and sustained rather than intrinsic to texts and objects."

> For, every work that is self-consciously an adaptation [and which is also perceived by critics as such] simultaneously acknowledges the impossibility of the unique artwork and the generic process of remaking that defines [sic] what we experience as art. (2012, 163)

In other words, scholars dealing with Australian studies and film are reminded to pay close attention to the old question of how cultural capital is defined and constructed in the Australian public sphere. Against this backdrop we might then turn to questions dealing with fidelity, yet, in line with Dovey, I believe that the "problem has never been with fidelity *per se*", rather it all boils down to the fact, as Dovey writes, that "fidelity and infidelity with its conditions and contexts have not yet been sufficiently explored." (168) With regard to Australian studies and the Australian visual and cultural landscape we therefore should start raising questions about "when, why, how and for what purpose" individuals, institutions as well as local and global markets demand fidelity to a specific artwork." (168)

Tearing Down Societal Facades: *The Eye of the Storm*

As mentioned earlier, Fred Schepisi's feature film *The Eye of the Storm* (2011) is an adaptation based on Patrick White's novel (1973). While paying homage to its literary source text, Schepisi's film from its very onset presents itself as an independent artifact. Consequently the movie's title *The Eye of the Storm* appears in white lettering against the black screen directly reversing the black ink on white paper symbolism. This visual strategy is accompanied with a sound of rolling waves symbolising the passing of time and the cycle of life. While both motifs are important within the movie itself, they also point beyond the movie's story world addressing the changing perception in general as well as the rapidly altering media landscape. Whilst in humanities and for many bibliophiles, the book remains the central medium, the overall number of readers, representing a formerly vibrant reading culture is decreasing.

At the same time the new media with its portable, mobile and extremely flexible streaming and viewing possibilities greatly influences our perception of the world. We read books on Kindle, view and listen to music videos on our smart phones and watch movies on tablets. All these developments certainly contribute to the fact that the group of moving image lovers (including digital formats such as HD, Blu-ray and 3D) is still growing. Although Schepisi's movie is not a blockbuster, Richard Gray states that the film had a good start when it made "its way into the top 10 on just 18 screens, [and] earned $196,250 for a screen average of $10,903. Technically, this makes it the highest opening weekend screen average for any Australian film [in the year 2011]." (2011)

In any case, as soon as the title's white lettering merges with the pixels of the establishing shot, the heroine Elizabeth Hunter alias Charlotte Rampling moves into the watchers' focus. Elizabeth, a woman in her early fifties, is introduced in a long shot, which takes a bird's eye view. This introductory scene established Elizabeth as the story centre around which all other plotlines rotate, namely the life- stories of her two grown-up children, family friends and servants. As the shot changes, the sound changes, too; thus the rumbling of the sea dissolves into a soft and gentle piano-tune merging with oboe and the sing-song of sea gulls' squawking. While the camera starts zooming in on Elizabeth, her son Basil, the absent narrator whom we only get to know in person somewhat later, starts speaking his mother's story from the off already indicating her dominant perspectives on life: "if it would be written on a page, it would revolve around this day."

From the movie's start, Schepisi is quite clear about the fact that as soon as Elizabeth is present her children leave the scene or remain absent as long as they can. It almost seems as if in anticipation of the next, upcoming catastrophe Basil and Dorothy seek shelter so that the destructive force of the cyclone may drift past without causing too much emotional damage. This idea is visually translated in a sequence of scenes in which Elizabeth is either all alone or with her employees waiting for her children to arrive. Her son Basil, in turn, delays meeting his mother. He even pays the hotel boys so that they misreport his actual arrival in Sydney. Hence it comes as no surprise that his disillusioned account of home allows neither room for homesickness or any other sort of nostalgia.

Dorothy's feelings are much more uncertain … Her ambivalence is vividly illuminated through an awkward combination of sound and images: while the audience watches Dorothy entering her maternal home, Basil, from 'offstage' issues the following reflection: "In faraway lands it is easy to imagine the family maturing gracefully, but one should examine one's reticence to gaze upon the face that so reminds you of your home." And as laid down in Basil's warning, Elizabeth's insults follow swiftly. Yet, there is no denying that at times, the matriarch wishes to reconcile with her children. In the first conversation between mother and her daughter, Elizabeth seeks to approach her daughter in the following way: "Do you think that perhaps we can be of some comfort to each other now, Dorothy? Come, I can't be a threat anymore, can I? [12:00 – 12:12] In this sequence, Dorothy refuses to answer.

The elegant narrative technique again and again combines straightforward shots with ambivalent comments from 'the off.' These storytelling patterns and the radical framing of scenes turn Schepisi's composition into intelligent entertainment. The radical framing is created by presenting the main protagonists in a strict order starting with Elizabeth and her household, then introducing Basil before Dorothy enters the camera light. The same order only in reverse then concludes the film, finally showing a middle-aged Elizabeth knee-deep in the swallows, surrounded by squawking seagulls. The sound of splashing seawater is drowned out by tenderly floating music featuring the classic instruments of oboe, piano and violin. Only then are the credits of the film presented; the director and the scriptwriter are mentioned first, before the original source text of the film is given. In this manner the film presents itself as an independent artifact.

Yet, its literary pedigree is mentioned in most of the movie's reviews. While *The Age* journalist Jake Wilson and the Scoop Media writer Binoy Kampmark open their articles with an immediate reference to Patrick White's literary mastery, *The Sydney Morning Herald* hones in on the family relations of the Schepisi family. The journalist Samantha Selinger-Morris entitles her article "Daddy's girl is all grown up" referring not so much to Elizabeth Hunter's daughter Dorothy but to Fred Schepisi's daughter Alexandra who enacted the "social-climbing" nurse Flora. Flora is an important figure in the film, since she belongs to the small group of working-class characters to be included in the filmic adaptation of the book.

It is an interesting coincidence that Alexandra, when only one year old or so, had also been cast in Schepisi's first international success, the filmic adaptation of Keneally's *The Chant of Jimmie Blacksmith*. It is in this *Sydney Morning Herald* article that a new constellation eventually opens up before our eyes, namely the family tree of the very creative Schepisi clan. Alexandra's open reflection of her uneasiness on acting naked in a movie certainly shifts the viewer's attention away from questions concerning adaptation and source texts. And this focus on the film and the process of filming and acting is further sharpened when reading the parts of Alexandra Schepisi's interview in which she talks about her fears of working with her father. Finally, however, the audience is certainly reminded that it is exactly this nucleus of the family and the question of intimate interaction between family members which has always been at the core of Patrick White's writing in general and in this work, *The Eye of the Storm* in particular.

No doubt, attempting to theorise the complex relationship between extra-filmic worlds and the film's story world is complex and often fraught with problems. An attempt to capture this connection is introduced in Rainer Emig's article on adaptation theory, in which Emig draws our attention once again to the common differentiation between the concepts of 'abrogation' and 'appropriation.' The concepts and their distinction became particularly important in postcolonial theory in the late 1980s (Ashcroft, Griffiths, Tiffin 1989, 37-38) and, as Emig argues, may gain new relevance today. Emig suggests using the two concepts within adaptation theory, for describing "decisions in adaptation processes: the rejection of features or their incorporation and adaptation." (Emig 2012, 19) Thus, he concludes that adapting postcolonial theory may be a promising avenue for theorising adaptations in the future and coming to terms with discourses of authority.

If we ultimately succeed in leaving behind the "implicit discourse of authority" (Emig 2012, 19) we may be equipped for approaching filmic adaptations through a critical lens which focuses on conditions of filmmaking and the rules of a national as well as an international film market that seem significant for controlling visual artifacts as well as all processes of adaptation. In this context, then, questions concerning 'literary' prestige and canonicity may develop new dynamics because the artwork by artists like White and Schepisi present perfect canvasses for negotiating the value of cultural capital in Australia and abroad. It is through filmic adaptations such as Schepisi's *The Eye of the Storm* that we may learn something more about the value of recent feature film in general as well as about the lasting influence of Patrick White's writing on Australian culture and society.

Works Cited

Altman, Rick. 1999. *Film/Genre*. London: BFI.
Appadurai, Arjun. 2005. *Modernity at Large: Cultural Dimensions of Globalization.* Minneapolis Minn: University of Minnesota Press.
Ashcroft, Bill, Helen Tiffin and Gareth Griffiths 1989. *The Empire Writes Back.* London: Routledge.
Armstrong, Gillian (dir.). *Oscar and Lucinda* (1997).
Bluestone, George. 1957. *Novels into Film*. Baltimore, MD: James Hopkins.
Bodey, Michael. 2011. "Let's get Patrick White right, said Fred," *The Australian* (September 10): 6.
Capp, Rose. 2011. "The Eye of the Storm - Movie Review," *The Vine Entertainment* (September 13).
http://www.thevine.com.au/entertainment/movies/the-eye-of-the-storm-movie-review/ Accessed 30.10.2012.

Cardwell, Sarah. 2002. *Adaptation Revisited: Television and the Classic Novel* Manchester: Manchester University Press.
Collins, Felicity and Therese Davis. 2004. *Australian cinema after Mabo*. Cambridge: Cambridge University Press.
Dovey, Lindiwe. 2012. "Fidelity, Simultaneity and the 'Remaking' of Adaptation Studies," *Adaptation and Cultural Appropriation: Literature, Film, and the Arts,* ed. Pascal Nicklas and Oliver Lindner. Berlin/Boston: De Gruyter: 162-185.
Elsner, Daniela.et.al.ed. 2013. *Films, Graphic Novels & Visuals, Developing Multiliteracies in Foreign Language Education - An Interdisciplinary Approach.* Berlin/Münster: Lit Verlag.
Emig, Rainer. 2012. "Adaptation in Theory," *Adaptation and Cultural Appropriation: Literature, Film, and the Arts,* ed. Pascal Nicklas, and Oliver. Berlin/Boston: De Gruyter: 14-24.
Fulton, A.R. 1977. "From Novel to Film," *Film and/as Literature,* ed. John Harrington. Englewood Cliffs, NJ: Prentice-Hall: 151.
Giffin, Michael. 2011. "Adapting Patrick White to the Screen," *Quadrant* (November): 113-114.
Gray, Richard. 2011. "Schepisi's The Eye of the Storm thunders through Australia's weekend box-office," in *The Reel Bits.Com* (September): 19. http://www.thereelbits.com/2011/09/19/schepisi%E2%80%99s-the-eye-of-the-storm-thunders-through-australias-weekend-box-office/. Accessed 30.10.2012.
Hancock, Matthew. 2010. *Mitigating Risk: The Case for More Adaptations in the Australian Film Industry,* Australian Film Television and Radio School, Occasional Paper # 2 (July) http://www.screenaustralia.gov.au/documents/SA_publications/MitigatingRisk.pdf. Accessed. 30.10.2012.
Hand, Richard and Katja Krebs. 2008. "Editorial," *Journal of Adaptation in Film and Performance* 1.3: 173-175.
Hucheton, Linda. 2006. *A Theory of Adaptation*. New York/London: Routledge.
Kampmark, Binoy. 2011. "Filming the Metaphor: Fred Schepisi's The Eye of the Storm," *Scoop Media* 6 November. http://www.scoop.co.nz/stories/HL1111/S00049/filming-the-metaphor-fred-schepisis-the-eye-of-the-storm.htm. Accessed 30.10.2012.

Krämer, Lucia. 2011. "Adaptation als Filmgenre? Die Gattungsdiskussion in den Adaptation Studies unter dem Blickwinkel der Authentizität," *Fictionen von Wirklichkeit: Authentizität zwischen Materialität und Konstruktion* Wolfgang Funk and Lucia Krämer ed. (Bielefeld: transcript): 205-224.
Leitch, Thomas. 2008. "Adaptation, the Genre," *Adaptation* 1.2: 106-120.
Moran, Albert and Errol Vieth. 2006. *Film in Australia: An Introduction* Cambridge: Cambridge University Press.
Noyce, Phillip (dir.). *Rabbit-Proof Fence.* 2002.
Schepisi, Fred (dir.). *Libido.* 1973.
—. *The Chant of Jimmie Blacksmith.* 1978.
—. *The Eye of the Storm.* 2011.
Schulze, Rainer. 2011. "Die Aktualität der Authentizität: Von der Attraktivität des Nicht-Hier und Nicht-Jetzt, der Sprachwissenschaft," *Fictionen von Wirklichkeit: Authentizität zwischen Materialität und Konstruktion* ,Wolfgang Funk and Lucia Krämer ed. (Bielefeld: transcript): 25-49.
Selinger-Morris, Samantha. 2011. "Daddy's girl is all grown up." *The Sydney Morning Herald.* Entertainment. (September 9) http://www. smh.com.au/entertainment/movies/daddys-girl-is-all-grown-up-20110908-1jy84.html#ixzz2AocSmOrE. Accessed 30.10.2012.
White, Patrick. *The Eye of the Storm.* 1973. New York: Viking Press.
Wilson, Jake. 2010 "The Eye of the Storm," *The Age,* Entertainment September 10. http://www.theage.com.au/entertainment/movies/the-eye-of-the-storm-20110909-1k18h.html. Accessed. 30.10.2012.

CHAPTER THIRTEEN

THE NOVELIST AS OCCASIONAL POET:
PATRICK WHITE
AND KATHARINE SUSANNAH PRICHARD

GLEN PHILLIPS
EDITH COWAN UNIVERSITY

Few novelists are appreciated as much for their poetry as for their novels. Perhaps Thomas Hardy and D H Lawrence are among the rare exceptions. Some novelists go so far as to order the destruction of their poetry manuscripts, especially if classifiable as mainly *juvenilia*. I imagine that, as many novelists have done, writing occasional poems in one's youth is a good deal less taxing than the laborious penning of several early novels in draft form. Early 'prentice' works such as these are frequently shredded or burned by novelists when their reputations have been established in the course of their developing careers. In many cases early experimental works are 'raided' by the novelist in later life. Patrick White, when it came to his oeuvre, rarely referred to his early work in poetry; neither indeed have his critics. No such reticence existed on the part of Katharine Susannah Prichard or on the part of the enthusiasts of her work. The more significant of her slim volumes of poems, *The Earth Lover,* was published in 1932 only three years before White's own second small volume, *The Ploughman and Other Poems* (1935).

White's mother Ruth had earlier printed a few of his poems privately, *Thirteen Poems* in 1930 and indeed funded the publication in Sydney of *The Ploughman*, written between the years 1932-1934, while White was an undergraduate at King's College, Cambridge. Prichard, on the other hand had her first book of poetry,

Clovelly Verses, published in London in 1913. This consisted of poems written while spending a holiday on the Cornish coast at the fishing village of Clovelly. This was during her time as an idealistic young journalist in the UK (1912 – 1915). The resultant minor collection of some twenty pages she referred to as "the altogether naïve murmurings of me to myself." That may be a phrase to bear in mind when we are examining the 'occasional verses' of writers who wrote poetry only occasionally and perceived their real vocation to be that of the novelist. This appears to have been the case for herself and her fellow Australian author Patrick White, except that *The Earth Lover* poems appeared some eighteen years later when Prichard's novelistic career was well advanced, while White's collection was published in Sydney only a year after he had finished writing the last of them. Prichard seems to have perceived her early poetry as works of value; White seems to have regarded this early work as essentially 'prentice' efforts.

Prichard's book, on the face of it, seems to show more maturity than White's. Her poems express more developed views on human destiny and her identification with her native land at a time when, in the aftermath of the First World War (the supposed 'war to end all wars'), she had fully embraced Communism as her political creed. In 1931 she was aged 48, whereas White at that time was only a stripling of some 19 years. The next year he departed from Australia to begin his university education in England; his *Ploughman* collection, composed in England, was published in Sydney four years later.

Was White's first real published book then merely a collection also of 'naïve murmurings,' or was it that *The Ploughman and Other Poems* provided some springboard for his ascent into the highest regions of Australian fiction, or was it more nearly simply a diversion, a self-indulgence? Perhaps it was a confirmation that his talents lay firmly outside the undoubted achievements of the contemporary Georgian poets whom he admired, including A. E. Housman (then also living in Cambridge)?

In his exhaustive biography of White, David Marr dismisses this poetry collection as "the laments and love poems of a young homosexual," written in such a well-disguised mode that he could send them back to Australia to his mother without raising the slightest qualms in the family of these being anything but purely literary achievements that would bring honour to the White family. As such they were published. It was of course the accepted way to guardedly express homosexual tendencies in a world still reflecting Queen Victoria's supposed horror of alternative sexual orientations and still shadowed, no doubt, by the infamous trial of Oscar Wilde.

Whereas Marr spends some pages of his biography tracing the links between the poems and White's first series of homosexual romances, White simply airbrushed the poetry phase out of his autobiography *Flaws in the Glass* (1981). On the other hand, his first efforts at novel writing, which began in earnest after his return to Australia after the hated four years at the British public school of Cheltenham, are discussed in some detail. This was the period when he was being prepared hopefully, first as a jackeroo, for a career in the family's wealthy landholdings. Apparently he would spend all day on horseback helping with the station and then 'stay up all night writing' the drafts of some early unsuccessful novels. (Marr 1991, 109)

Pursuing the question of diversionary poetry – writing in the career of a novelist, we might look for emergent poetic instincts during White's higher education phase. When the White family realised he was never going to be a farmer or grazier he was enrolled at Cambridge on the insistence of his mother. And it was during the independent life of an undergraduate that he first discovered that he was not unique in his gender predilections and that indeed, he would go on to find many male lovers in the following years. So it is probably no surprise that what we find recorded in the thirty-three poems published in *The Ploughman* are some of those lovelorn laments

"The Ploughman" as title poem of the volume did draw some praise from Sydney reviewers at the time. Certainly, with respect to imagery, poetic diction and tone, it would not have looked out of place in one of Edward Marsh's popular Georgian anthologies, published by Harold Monroe between 1912 and 1922. But by 1935, when White's poetry collection was printed, the Georgian movement had well and truly declined and the so-called New Country British poets group, led by Auden, Spender, MacNeice and Day-Lewis, was in its ascendancy, while the later surrealist and neo-romantic trends, characterised by the work of George Barker, Dylan Thomas and others, was just discernible over the horizon. White's "Ploughman" begins in Georgian mode:

> I saw a ploughman against the sky
> The wind of the sea in his horses'manes.
> And the share* it was shod with gold;
> Down to the sea, on the curve of the hill,
> A foam of gulls in the furrow,
> The Ploughman walking behind his plough

(*the ploughshare polished by its cutting of the soil.)

In these opening lines we can see and hear the images, the tones of Housman and Hardy (although neither was included in Marsh's anthologies) for they were in different ways the 'spiritual fathers' of Georgian poetry, in its preoccupations with English landscapes. And there are in these lines echoes of most of the Georgian poets, such as Edward Marsh himself, Andrew Young, Edward Thomas, Walter De la Mare and J. C. Squire. White wrote the above poem while taking one of his vacations in Cornwall and also wrote a number of others under influence of the mild Cornish climate and rugged landscape both there and in the Scilly Isles just off that coast. He wrote one poem at Zennor not far from where Lawrence, Mansfield and Middleton Murry had lived two decades previously. Away from the dampness of the fens of Cambridge, perhaps there were reminders of the grandeur of coastal Sydney and the Australian weather of his homeland, for he wrote:

> happy here, happier than
> I thought was possible this side of heaven. ('Lines Written on Leaving the Scilly Islands')

The landscape he paints for us in the title poem "The Ploughman" is, however, profoundly of the English coast: 'Ships/Sailed fleecy into the harbour down below ...' This is no 'new' continent, no New World, for:

> Ploughing, ploughing the bones of the centuries into the earth
> All pain yielded up into the sigh of the gulls.

The relief from pain obviously does not really refer to the break from his university studies, for White was no assiduous scholar; his Second Class Honours was only in the B list. The pain here is perhaps the struggle to come to terms with his sexuality. By his own account he had long felt acutely 'different' from his family and classmates and was oppressed by the relentless homophobia of both British and Australian society at the time. His undergraduate sense of isolation and hopelessness remained painful until he was to encounter, a few years later, the sections of society in Britain, America, Europe and Australia that comprised the closeted yet often brilliant brotherhood of the homosexual community. The limited solace he had found with a few friends at Cambridge was generally brief and anxiety-ridden. In some respects, in this poem, he envies the country ploughman with his simple solitary life and the defined and unchallenged role of rural labourer:

> Only the ploughman remains as he follows
> The plumed and glistening path of his furrow
> Over the field that is strown with gulls.

So ends "The Ploughman" with its temporarily elevated mood, compared with the bulk of the poems in this book, which are more reflective of the painful tossings and turnings of youthful *angst*.

As Reeves has written of the Georgian movement, the poetry White was imitating was then far more popular with British readers than that of the Imagists or of other modernists: 'the celebration of England ... became the principal aim of Georgian poetry,' James Reeves wrote in his introduction to *Georgian Poetry* (1962). In a few others of his *Ploughman* poems White seemed to enjoy the rural charm he seemed to discover in England and so found something to share with a wider public:

> Now that I leave you, islands where I learned
> That simple things can be with beauty shod,
> And that the meaning of the world is burned
> Into the sky and sea ... (Leaving the Scilly Islands')

There is no evidence here of the relentless critical eye that would look at the world and humanity with a searing irony in the Nobel

Prize-winning novels to come. The language of the poetry here is relatively undistinguished, the thoughts rather conventional, and the versification no better than tidy but the last two lines are eloquent with a deeper urgency communicated through the word "burned" and seem to be an augury of a perception of nature that was central to the later novels. This is possibly the best of the poetry in the volume his mother so treasured. The editor of *Georgian Poetry* stated:

> The faults of the Georgian poetry at its most ordinary were technical slackness – the use of imprecise diction and facile rhythm; sentimentality of outlook; trivial and even downright commonplace themes (1962, xvii)

We can notice all these features in the majority of White's poems. For instance, in "Lines Written after an Encounter with Death in a Country Lane," he concludes:

> Like the wild creatures, like this
> That she [death] threw at my feet,
> Blessing or cursing with her kiss,
> I must fly,
> For the year is young and promises bud in the trees;
> I would see the turn of the year
> Before I die. (Polperro, Dec. 1933)

Positive though the poet's resolution to survive may appear here, (White was only in his early twenties at the time) in many of the 33 poems included in the volume there is a brooding melancholic note. In part, it could have been an Australian's reaction against the English and German weather but White himself in the autobiographical *Flaws in the Glass* indicates he was also going through a phase of education or awareness on the brink of manhood, dogged by the sense of being an oddity and no doubt suffering re-activations of the sense of a British prejudice against 'Colonial outsiders', which had been his bitter experience as the only Australian boy enduring British Public School life at Cheltenham College a few years previously. Another understandable cause of White's despondency must have been his severe asthmatic affliction. The English climate made that illness an increasing burden on body and spirit. Marr is more direct in supposing a great deal of the anxiety relates to White's burgeoning homosexual love-life. And it is true that there are plentiful references to the pangs of love in the poems, although perhaps no more than in that of any young poet's early works.

When we examine the poems in *The Ploughman* perhaps it is not surprising that negative words dominate. If we choose 'O Cold, Cold Rain' (Cambridge, November, 1933) the following words set the tone: *cold, tumult, withered, ashy, haggard, cried, squandered, faintly, brittle* – yet this poem finally tells how an image remembered from Spring of a white swan rising from the meadows "tore my heart with the music of her wings." Sadly, a publishing error resulted in the sketch by his artist-collaborator L. Roy Davies, depicting a seagull instead of a swan rising. This engraving actually belongs with the last poem in the book, "To a Gull Blown Inland by a Storm." The image of the swan instead graces the latter poem. I suppose the unconscious irony of the error deflates the poetic intention even more.

Germany was the scene of many youthful vacations. Often he experienced states of depression here, even more than in Britain and a poem he wrote in Heidelberg in July 1933 is as mournful in mood as any written in Britain. In the 25-line poem, "Rain in Summer," for example, a quick scan would pick up the following emotive words: *lost, brooding, weary, barbed, withering, daggers, blood, wrought, grey, heavy, pains, cold, ashes, tongue-tied*. Writing of the atmosphere in the rural landscape outside of the city, White observes: "her [the Air's] claws are barbed with the gold of the sun."But the slight change of mood is far from convincing.

For White's highly successful contemporary, Australian novelist, Katharine Susannah Prichard the 1920s was her decade of greatest success. She had recently (in 1919) married her Victoria Cross-winning soldier hero from Perth, Hugo Throssell; she had played a prominent role in the founding of the Australian Communist Party in 1921 and borne her son, Ric, in the following year. Already with three novels published (one an international prize-winner), the decade yielded her more and more success, including her 1926 Triad Prize-winning play "Brumby Innes," It culminated with

Coonardoo: *The Well in the Shadow* (1929) which won the *Bulletin* novel competition in 1928 and was published in London the following year. Meantime, while she was having great success with her short stories, there were more novels to come, as well as short plays and articles. So her small collection of new poems, *The Earth Lover and Other Verses* (1932), as previously indicated, probably reflected her confidence in her role as an Australian author capable of recognition internationally, rather than in the intrinsic merit of the poetry.

We might remember that her success as a writer was achieved despite the controversies surrounding her political affiliations and her courage to write about forbidden subjects such as the sexual subjection of Aboriginal women to predatory white pastoralists and graziers in the north west of Western Australia. Her brave espousal of causes, particularly the role of women in Australian society, had made most Australian publishers nervous and her play 'Brumby Innes' was never performed in her lifetime.

Bearing in mind that Prichard was a mature woman and a mother by the time this second poetry collection was published, perhaps we can understand why it was the last time she sought a readership for a book of her verse compositions. Was it lack of talent as a poet, a failure to write poetry that would measure up to the modernist trends in poetry of the 1930s or a realisation that her talents lay in narrative fiction? It might well have been that there was little prospect of her earning much from publishing poetry as opposed to prose in Australia. I would argue that although all these factors could explain her lack of success as a poet, the most significant reason would be, as seems the case with Patrick White – she saw the role of the novelist and the opportunity to hold up a mirror to the world of her time and analyse its shortcomings as a greater imperative than pursuing any other literary genre. That is not to say there is no merit in the *Earth Lover* poems, just as it cannot be said there is no merit in White's youthful verses published at much the same time.

To begin with the title poem of Prichard's collection – a reasonably short poem of just twenty-two lines in four verses or stanzas and like White's "Ploughman," in free verse form, abstaining from rhyme or regular metre. She does repeat the phrase "let me lie ..." at the beginning of the first two stanzas and "let me inspire ..." introduces the penultimate stanza. This invocation, presumably to some spirit of the universe (as White was, she too was for the first half of her life an atheist) is more redolent of Georgian poetry or even Victorian than modernist voices of twentieth century poets in her day. As already mentioned, Katharine had written her "Clovelly" poems mainly while holidaying in Cornwall, a coincidental connection with White's early poetry. In "The Earth Lover" she may well have imagined herself back in Cornwall:

> Let me lie in the grass –
> Bathe in its verdure
> As one bathes in the sea –
> Soul-drowned in the herbage,
> The essence of clover,
> Dandelion, camomile, knapweed,
> And centaury.

It seems a little odd that such a devotedly Australian novelist as Prichard, bearing in mind her detailing of the Western Australian karri forests and their wildflowers in *Working Bullocks* (1926), or the raw red semi-desert Pilbara lands in *Coonardoo* (1929) should list in such detail so many English Flowers. She seems to have transferred the settings of her poems to the green fields of England. Perhaps the poetry she knew as a child had come mainly from such a foreign background. In Fiji or later in Australia (and especially in Western Australia) such an array of specifically English herbage would not be a normal experience. Clover is common enough in Australian pastures but what are called dandelions are generally a noxious invader (capeweed) from South Africa. Even the conclusion of the poem has no hint of her adult Australian life on the bush fringe of Perth:

> For I am an earth child,
> An earth lover,
> And I ask no more than to be
> Of the earth, earthy
> And to mingle again with the divine dust.

After Katharine's death in 1969 perhaps it was fitting that her ashes (at her request) were scattered on the rocky slopes of the Darling Ranges where she had lived almost fifty years of her life at her home in Greenmount. Despite her atheist communist principles she seems to invoke some kind of deity, perhaps it might have been an echo of her Celtic (in her case Welsh) origins.

Her love poetry, (she was heterosexual), shows some poetic compatibility with that of White, in its highly personal nature:

> Dear lips
> That to me prove
> My body
> But a chalice, white,
> For your delight,
> My love, my love!
> ('Lips of My Love', 1965: 87)

Perhaps the nearest Prichard came to evoking in her poetry a sense of the Australian context of her life was in the intended poetic dedication to her husband Hugh Throssell for *The Earth Lover* volume. Unfortunately it was accidentally omitted but became in part the title of her son Ric's biography of his mother, *Wild Weeds and Windflowers* (1975):

> To H. V. T. T.
> To you, all these wild weeds
> And wind flowers of my life,
> I bring, my Lord,
> And lay them at your feet;
> They are not frankincense
> Or myrrh,
> But you are Krishna, Christ and Dionysus
> In your beauty, tenderness and strength.
> (*On Strenuous Wings*, 86)

If we make a direct comparison with White's love poetry in another short poem from *The Ploughman*, "Second Life," we may sense that both poets share concepts of the function of poetry as a mode of expressing private feelings of love in public:

> But now the Sun, in risen might,
> Has burned pain deeper in my soul,
> And ecstasy is come to me
> When I sought mere delight.
> For now I must know fear for two,
> And feel joy quicken in my heart
> When joy is yours, such is the price
> I pay for loving you.
> (Cambridge, November 1933)

One important difference requires a brief comment. In Prichard's poetry is the total absence of a sense of potential social disapproval, as the mention of "fear" conjures up in these lines. No matter how sympathetic one is to the circumstances in which White and Prichard penned their published verse, there is no question about the fact that despite the fact that poetry was the genre in which they first tried their artistic talents; it was not a genre to which they remained attached. It was also a genre in which these two writers, so deeply attached to their Australian heritage wrote their most palely derivative work, reflective of their early experience in Britain. Their poetry bears little comparison to their achievement in their prose in short stories and novels. One can only speculate on an explanation for this difference. Neither White nor Prichard showed the slightest interest either in composing narrative poetry that would have provided them with a canvas of larger scope, which was perhaps what both these writers craved to express their more mature experience and vision. Both confined themselves to using poetry as a brief lyrical art form for the expression of transient emotional states. Nevertheless, this early work retains interest as the 'prentice" work beyond which their considerable talents developed to attain to those heights in the genre of the novel which have ensured them a lasting place in Australian literature.

Works Cited

Barnes, J. 1966. "New tracks to travel: the stories of White, Porter and Cowan," *Meanjin Quarterly* 2. (.Winter): 144- 53.
Coonardoo: *The Well in the Shadow*. London: Jonathan Cape.

Giffin, M. 2006. "Four Approaches to Patrick White," *Quadrant* 9.14: 70-75.

Harries, L. 1978. "The Peculiar Gifts of Patrick White," *Contemporary Literature* 19.4: 459-471.

Heseltine, H.P. 1965. "Writer and reader: 'The Burnt Ones,'" *Southerly*, 25.1: 30.

Kippax, H.G. 1964. "Short stories by Patrick White," *The Sydney Morning Herald* (October 24):17.

Marr, David. 1991. *Patrick White: A Life.* Sydney: Random House.

Prichard, S K. 1926. *Working Bullocks.* London: Jonathan Cape.

Prichard, S K. 1932. *The Earth Lover and Other Verses.* Sydney: Sunnybrook Press.

Reeves, James. 1962. Ed. *Georgian Poets.* Harmondsworth: Penguin. Throssell, Ric. 1975. *Wild Weeds and Windflowers.* Sydney: Angus & Robertson.

White, Patrick. 1930. *Thirteen Poems.* Sydney: Privately published.

—. 1935. *The Ploughman and Other Poems.* Sydney: Beacon Books.

—. 1981 *Flaws in the Glass: an Autobiography.* London: Jonathan Cape.

—. 1989. [1958]. "The Prodigal Son," *Patrick White Speaks,* ed. Paul Brennan and Christine Flynn. Sydney: Primavera Press.

PART III

INDIVIDUAL NOVELS

CHAPTER FOURTEEN

IN THE SHADOW OF PATRICK WHITE

MEIRA CHAND
UNIVERSITY OF WESTERN AUSTRALIA

This discussion is not intended to be an academic literary analysis of Patrick White's work; rather, it is more the record of a journey of my own (being also a writer by profession) in the shadow of Patrick White: a series of reflections made in considering aspects of a narrative of my own and observing his handling of a not dissimilar work composed by White.

While working recently on my tenth novel (not yet published) *Brave Sisters,* a historical novel set against the backdrop of colonial India and Singapore I was led to compare the journey of my fictional character an Indian woman Sita, at its centre, with that of Ellen, the woman at the centre of White's novel *A Fringe of Leaves* (1966). Ellen is a fictionalised version of the Englishwoman Eliza Fraser, whose adventures after being shipwrecked on the island (now named Fraser Island) have passed into history. I make no apology for the personal tone of this discussion, for I regard White as a powerful mentor for myself and no doubt for other writers, regardless of ideological positioning or cultural divides. He is in my view 'a writer's writer' and this is a writer's tribute to him.

I must first explain how strongly the shadow of White falls upon my work and for how long his literary influence has influenced my own writing. My first encounter with White's writing was some decades ago, perhaps in 1979 or thereabouts. I had been living in Japan for some years and had just written my first novel, *The Gossamer Fly* (1979). At that time in Japan English books were not easily available, but I came across a paperback copy of *The Aunt's Story* in a bookstore in Kobe and bought it.

From the moment I opened the book, the power of White's language, enthralled me. I then went on to deliberately search for and read other White novels. For me, as a writer, two elements surfaced above all else. The first, was White's unique way with words at once complex, enormously evocative and simultaneously so effective in its precision; he makes language work like a knife, filleting the meat clean off the bone, to reveal deep points of human experience. Take, for example, the moment in *The Aunt's Story* (1948) where Pearl, the pregnant serving girl collapses while helping serve the formal Sunday lunch in the dining room:

> Between the table and the door Pearl Brawne fell, and there was never such a harvest, such a falling gold. Pearl lay on the carpet with the leg of mutton, and gravy on her face. What had happened was immense ... Mother was very calm and straight ...
>
> And her rings flashed. (1948, 32)

With these few words White projects multiple layers of awareness, and effortlessly insinuates whole ranges of emotion. This virtuoso performance, its brilliant economy in orchestrating depths of feeling, social comment and sardonic humour along with a sense of beauty as well as compassion was utterly breathtaking to me as a young writer. The brilliance of White's prose was set in my mind forever, and remains there still, as the measure of what a writer must strive to achieve with the choice and arrangement of words. White's prose is as still and calm as the reflective surface of a lake, beneath which can be glimpsed the lurking dark of unknown depths: here the dire predicament of the pregnant woman, her vulnerability to scorn and dismissal in her inferior servant position is deftly sketched. In spite of the comic detail of the mutton on the floor and the gravy on her face, the innate beauty of Pearl's pregnancy is illuminated by the words "harvest" and "falling gold," a celebration of natural human fertility; a celebration which is also poignantly shadowed by the threat of reprisals. The inevitable price the servant will pay for her transgression is suggested by the "flashing rings" of the mistress whose calmness belies her wrath at the immensity of Pearl's fall from virtue. The passage demonstrates White's conjuring magic with words and his astounding capacity to project significance into seemingly mundane events. The reader immediately grasps why and how, "what had happened was immense ..."

As much as his use of language, and capacity to tease out the complexities of the most mundane events, I have been touched by the themes of transcendence always present in White's work. His characters' perennial yearning to touch the spiritual core of life has affected my own thoughts on building depth into the experiences of my characters. In *The Aunt's Story*, Theodora listens to the music of the cellist, Moraitis:

> Moraitis rose again above the flesh. You were not untouched. There were moments of laceration, which made you dig your nails in your hands. The 'cello's voice was one long barely subjugated cry under the savage lashes of the violins. Moraitis ... wore the expression of ... solitary mirrors. The sun was in his eyes, the sky had passed between his bones. (110)

I take the above quotations from *The Aunt's Story*, rather than *A Fringe of Leaves* which is the main work this paper will refer to, in order to acknowledge more fully my respect for White's powerful writing, a respect first stirred by the influence of that first book upon me. I hold it now in my hands as I read these lines again from pages dry and yellowed, falling apart, patched extensively with adhesive tape. I now have a replacement paperback copy of *The Aunts's Story*, yet it is still this original copy of the White text that I continue to reach for when I begin a new work.

In the writing of each of my own novels this same battered book has rested beside me on my desk. Writers need the friendship and inspiration of other writers; it matters not if they be dead or alive. At times of despair or sterility, the living work of a fellow writer is entered into, as one enters the heart of a friend, for encouragement, for renewal and for inspiration. To me White's work has always been, and still is, just such a source of inspiration.

For the most part I believe what I have derived from his work cannot really be fully and clearly articulated or even demonstrated. My discussion here is a simpler technical exercise – a broad comparison of a historical novel of my own (a work still in progress) with White's *A Fringe of Leaves*. I do not intend to compare my achievement to that of Patrick White, but only to show how some aspects of the process of creating a fictional narrative may be common to all novelists, and to try to assess if possible, how White's influence has worked itself into this particular work even if this exploration must finally remain inconclusive and uncertain.

A novel often takes its rise from a single moment of inspiration. It is commonly acknowledged that for White, the paintings by his friend the famous painter Sydney Nolan of the ordeal of the historic castaway English woman, Eliza Fraser, were the inspiration for his novel, *A Fringe of Leaves*. For me, it was the glimpse of a single, old, black and white photograph taken in 1943 which I came across in a book (Bose and Sinha 1979, 175) that stands as the initiating impulse of my novel, *Brave Sisters*. In that photograph, an Indian woman of obviously humble origins, a new recruit to the Rani of Jhansi Regiment, (then, a newly established all-female unit of the Indian National Army), not as yet in uniform but still wearing her traditional sari, her hair in a long plait, is self-consciously taking a salute for her regiment. Her left arm is lowered, hand out of sight, but I feel it grasps a rifle. The expression on the face of the saluting woman is a mixture of pride and hesitancy as she seems poised to step outside her prescribed life role as meek and obedient female, to assert agency and voice against an inflexible patriarchal tradition.

From that picture my novel *Brave Sisters* took shape, flowing into the invented fictional experiences that allowed my main character to journey through the most testing circumstances of a nationalist war in the 1940s. This was an episode when, in an effort to free India from British rule, Indians overseas banded together under the leadership of the freedom fighter Subhas Chandra Bose. The perspective allowed me to explore how the challenge and the opportunity to accept such a situation could function as a means of achieving major psychological and social change and development within a community of subaltern women.

It was the broad similarity of this patterning of a trajectory of female growth through circumstances of extreme adversity which seems particularly clear and important to me in both *The Aunt's Story* and *A Fringe of Leaves*. Early on in *A Fringe of Leaves*, Miss Scrimshaw says, "Every woman has secret depths with which even she, perhaps, is unacquainted, and which sooner or later must be troubled." (17) It is the exploration of those "secret depths" that White has taught me to attempt in delineating my own fictional characters.

In *A Fringe of Leaves*, Patrick White based his novel on a historical incident, the shipwreck of the *Stirling Castle* in 1836, off the coast of Australia. Eliza Fraser, an Englishwoman, was abducted by Aborigines and, stripped of her clothes and possessions. She lives with them until finally rescued and returned to polite society. In the course of the novel, Ellen meets each new experience head on: enduring, learning, changing, adapting. Even while incarcerated in a totally alien Aboriginal world, Ellen is able to find strange synergies between the European world she has left and the Indigenous world she has entered as a castaway. Ellen becomes aware of a social world that offers curious parallels with, as well as contrasts to, the European world:

> For example, she recalls the labours of her mother-in-law and others who helped her make the transition from farm girl to lady when the women who dress her for her dual role as both slave and goddess in this society work on her appearance "sighing with satisfaction" at the outcome. (vanden Driesen 2009, 90)

A similar passage of transition faces Sita in *Brave Sisters* when, she must cast aside her traditional sari for the first time in exchange for military uniform.

> She had never shown anyone her legs before, not even her husband had seen so much of her naked … her eyes went first to her bare knees and embarrassment curled through her … Although she was dressed she felt naked (96).

Within such invented incidents the vital ingredient of texture conjures up the plausibility required for a reader to enter into the act of "virtual witnessing" (Bender 1997, 7). The beeswax plastered on Ellen's bleeding scalp by the Aboriginal women, like Sita's embarrassment at seeing her own bare limbs, is the texture by which a painful fictional moment is rendered believable, and by which the reader is transported into not only the psychological character of the time and place portrayed, but also the physical reality surrounding the characters, the details that approximate actuality and bring to life an imaginary world.

The multiple experiences and hardships endured by a character are the means by which an age manifests within the lives of the characters and through them history is speaking. We become contemporary with the past, having an inside knowledge of it (Butterfield 2011, 50). The texture of that inside knowledge is powerfully present in White's invention of the starving Ellen's confrontation with ritual cannibalism. Unable to stop herself, she finds herself stooping to pick up a human bone

> There were one or two shreds of half-cooked flesh and goblets of burned fat still adhering to this monstrous object … she had raised the bone and was tearing at it with her teeth … she flung the bone away only after it was cleaned … (244)

Through showing the primal nature of Ellen's character, and the displacements she suffers in life, pitched relentlessly from Cornwall to Cheltenham, to colonial Australian society, to Aboriginal tribe, hemmed in and judged always by the expectations of others, White builds Ellen's character showing by turn her negative and positive complexities, her selfishness and sensuality along with compassion, heroism, and spirituality. Most impressive is that resourcefulness that springs from a basic urgency to liberate and empower herself. It is this force of self-preservation in her nature that sees her through each fraught situation.

Despite her flaws, Ellen is in essence a deeply spiritual woman; even in the most grotesque of moments, the transcendental is never far from the surface in *A Fringe of Leaves*. In the same instant White contrasts Ellen's horror at the grisly discovery and participation in ritual cannibalism with her awe of the "exquisite innocence of the forest morning [that] tempted her to believe that she had partaken of a sacrament." (244)

In *Brave Sisters*, my character, Sita, is incarcerated in the prison of her own gender and her position as a woman in Indian society. This terrible truth is impressed on Sita when she unexpectedly learns of her mother's use of female infanticide as a means of ridding herself of an unwanted daughter. She inadvertently witnesses the murder of a newly- born sister: one moment her mother squats down in the fields to give birth, next, as Sita watches, she goes to the river ostensibly to wash the new baby: "One moment Sita saw the child in her mother's arms, the next she was gone, "Maa!" Sita screamed ... "It is all right. She was just a girl," her mother said softly, turning away." (61)

This experience marks Sita for life, changing her perception of many things, even if at the time she is too young to consciously absorb the full implications of what she has seen, Sita, like all traditional Indian women, would have had the deep spiritual images of *shakti,* handed down from one generation of women to another to draw upon at such times in her life. Her worship of the goddess Durga is pivotal to Sita's life and endows her with inordinate strength.

> Her mother or grandmother had always pointed to the picture of the goddess. Think of the Devi, they said, her *shakti* is great ... Sita had stared up ... at the beatific face of Durga ... a protective presence in the dark wings of her life, silent witness to events ... (Chand, 11)

Ellen's religious sense seems, for the most part of her early life, deeply submerged although there seems some depth of awareness that leads her to submerge herself in the pool at Hyas. Neither has she, as Sita does, a deeply ingrained sense of centuries of a female tradition on which to draw. In a sense she is a lonely figure and her path to vision is a solitary one. Sita is supported by a community of women in early childhood, and even later, while in the army. What Ellen shows is a capacity to use the men she encounters along the way to serve her own purposes although on the surface, she appears a victim of patriarchy. Sita appears more naïve and vulnerable a figure, though her passage to maturity has its own interest.

White's personal search for faith illuminates his fictional themes and is echoed in his character's deepest feelings. In his unflinching observation of the human condition, White seems to me, to fulfill the writer's highest obligation. In each of my novels, as I walk in the Master's shadow, I sense him, a towering figure, on the path ahead. White himself admitted, 'Religion – that's behind all my novels ... the relationship between the blundering human being and God ...' (McGregor 1969, 216) Ellen has a deep yearning for the spiritual but seems uncertain as to how to interpret her many blunders and failures till she attains some understanding in her final vision that "God is *love."*

In *A Fringe of Leaves*, Ellen's journey through displacement also serves to reflect White's rejection of colonialism. Ellen's experience of divergent social and cultural identities leads her to examine and dismantle stereotypes and to ask whether the Indigenous people, living in close harmony with the earth and nature, are not more' civilised' than the colonial society from which the convict, Jack Chance flees to escape torture and rejection. Sita's life similarly projects a critique of colonialism, through her encounter with the Indian freedom fighter, Subhas Chandra Bose, when she hears him speak in Singapore of the excesses of British rule. She is moved to enter the Rani of Jhansi Regiment, a women's military regiment that he establishes. Although far different in time, place and situation, Sita, like Ellen Roxburgh, also faces the disempowerment of her gender and marginal place in society. While White explored the darker aspects of colonial experience through the Eliza Fraser story, Sita's trajectory in *Brave Sisters* also allowed me to examine how the fight against colonialism brought opportunity for growth to my disempowered female character.

According to Rose Tremain, when recreating characters in historical novels, there are two paths the novelist can take. Some writers "look for gaps in what is known about real historical figures and then fill them in with inventions and re-imaginings, thus risking 'biographical unease,' but revelling in the novelist's freedom to narrate the thoughts of real characters." (Tremain 2012) This is the route White takes in *A Fringe of Leaves*. Through his re-shaping of historical material he recasts the original myth of captive English woman tormented by savages to rebirth her as a woman whose emotional and spiritual growth has enabled her capacity to be transformed into "white indigene." (vanden Driesen: 2009) In *Brave Sisters*, I take an alternative path, by "inserting an invented character into a known historical time ... and embarking on a timeless human drama, that of the individual struggling to understand her place in the world." (Tremain 2012)

Although White turned to Australian history for both *Voss* and *A Fringe of Leaves*, historical events by his own admission were not his major concern. He avoided adhering to complete historical veracity because he found "historical reconstructions too limiting … because of the restrictions they place on the imagination." (White 1992, 100) Yet White, like all novelists, has a right to adapt the facts of history to create another version of a story, for history is itself a story. The nexus of history and fiction is an area much debated by historians and novelists. Historians and historical novelists share common ground, often writing out of the same sources. This sharing of territory has occasionally produced friction between the two groups as in the case of the recent debate between Australian historian Inga Clendinnen and novelist Kate Grenville. Clendinnen deplores the free use of factual history by novelists (Clendinnen 2006), while Grenville freely admits that she regards history as a story bank to pillage, a place to do a "smash and grab raid on history … run off with it and turn it into something else." (Clendinnen 2006, 17) This can be viewed as a frank description of the novelist's project but the terminology of accusation needs to be exorcised; no blame should adhere to it. Grenville's rewriting of history in her fiction, like White in *A Fringe of Leaves*, is a legitimate exercise and to state otherwise is to misunderstand the fundamental nature of the historical novel.

Academic inquiry and historical fiction need not necessarily compete or disagree; both can be seen as enriching not competing ways of viewing the past. Fiction offers a way through narrative of accessing past memory, of 'mirroring' our present day selves and understanding the unchanging plight of humanity across time. Nobel Prize winner Toni Morrison regards historical fiction as a form of literary archaeology. She describes the work as journeying to a site "to see what remains were left behind and to reconstruct the world that these remains imply." (Morrison 1987, 112) The writer must rely on the images found in these literary sites; often re-moulding them and even adding to them to yield up a 'new' picture of the past in order to understand it anew and possibly change our relation to it.

The historical novel enters the perspective of time and place to recreate a unique hypothesis of what might have been. The best hypotheses are those that *seem* the most like truth (Bender 1997, 6). Within this imaginary space the novelist establishes an alternative interpretation of a past that may have been distorted or silenced, exploring in multiple and complex contexts sites of possibility and potential. The provisional reality created in the historical novel can be seen as a kind of virtual witnessing that produces an explanatory power not found in ordinary experience.

Whichever path the historical novelist chooses, history is taken hold of and used through the invention of character to examine the lives of ordinary people living through great events. In my position in relation to Sita in *Brave Sisters*, I seem to have considerable freedom and am restrained only broadly in my story by the general socio-historical context. In comparison White, by using a known historical character and a known flow of events would seem to be more constricted, yet what impresses me is the mode in which this character is constructed so as to emerge a totally different character from the original Mrs Fraser. The changes only serve to illuminate and open up further possibilities for interpretation and understanding of that original historic episode. White felt a need to explore the solitary essence of human life. The transcendental themes of suffering as an inevitable condition of that life and a mode of accessing divine grace bring to the character of Ellen Gluyas new depths of spiritual intuition that entirely recast the original source of his inspiration. White's own spiritual quest would seem to direct his rewriting of the Eliza Fraser narrative, turning it into a postmodernist text with a postcolonial perspective. (Ungari 2010) It also acquires the aspect of a narrative with a transcendental significance

In *Brave Sisters* I have chosen to explore the theme of selfhood and women's innate strength and will to survive the most extreme trials against all odds. *Brave Sisters* is the story of Sita's difficult journey towards selfhood, through the brutality of war; she is constantly reaching for something better, rejecting social stereotype, in the throes of her emotional and spiritual growth. By the end of the novel Sita has journeyed like Ellen (and Theodora before her) through experience to a point of transformation. A sense of empowerment and wholeness comes to her at last, she is seen as freed by her sufferings, and emerges, much as Ellen Roxburgh emerges, strengthened and purified and integrated in a way that allows her to take her place in society as well as to understand her role in the larger scheme of things.

My novel, *Brave Sisters*, is finished and I have put back upon the shelf my yellowed, battered copy of *The Aunt's Story*. It is, I am sure, only a temporary residence. A new novel will soon be started, and, as is now my habit, I shall reach for White's inspirational helping hand yet again.

Works Cited

Bose, M. 1982. *The Lost Hero: A Biography of Subash Bose*. London: Quartet Books.
Butterfield, H. 2011. *The Historical Novel*. Cambridge: Cambridge University Press.
Chand, M. 1979. *The Gossamer Fly*. London: John Murray.
—. *Brave Sisters*. (Unpublished.)
Clendinnen, I. 2006. "The history question: Who owns the past?" *Quarterly Essay* 23: 1-72.
Dedukhina, E. 2010. Interview with Rose Tremain by Knizhnaya Vitrina. http://wisdom-and-sense.blogspot.com/2006/10/interview-with-rose-tremain.html. Accessed 7th January 2012.
Lebra-Chapman, J. 1986. *The Rani of Jhansi: A study in female heroism in India*. Honolulu: University of Hawaii Press.
—. 2008. *Women against the Raj: The Rani of Jhansi regiment*. Singapore: ISEAS Publishing.
Marr, D. Ed. 1994. *Patrick White: Letters*. Sydney: Random House.
MacGregor, C. 1969. *In the making*. Melbourne: Nelson.
Morrison, T. 1987. "The Site of Memory," *Inventing the Truth: The Art and Craft of Memoir*, ed. William Zinsser. Boston: Boston University Press: 186-200.
Sahgal, L. 1997. *A revolutionary life: Memoirs of an activist*. New Delhi: Kali for Women.
Schaffer, K. 1998. *In the wake of first contact.*Cambridge: Cambridge University Press.

Tremain, R. 2012. Rose Tremain on becoming a historical novelist. *The Guardian*.
http//www.theguardian.com/books/2012/sep/28/rose-tremain-restoration-book-club. Accessed October 2nd 2012.
Ungari, E. 2010. "Patrick White's sense of history in *A Fringe of Leaves*," *Australian Studies* 2: 1-10.
vanden Driesen, C. 2009. *Writing the nation: Patrick White and the Indigene*. Amsterdam-New York: Rodopi
White, P. 1975. *The Aunt's Story*. New York: Avon Books.
—. 1977. *A Fringe of Leaves*. London: Penguin.

Chapter Fifteen

The Spirit of the Creative Word in Patrick White's *Voss*

Antonella Riem
University of Udine

Preamble: This paper originates from an interdisciplinary non-binary critical approach, which applies Riane Eisler's (1987) partnership model to World literary texts. By analysing the works of authors writing in the varieties of English, including those of Indigenous populations where the dynamics at work are caring and sharing rather than exploiting and dominating, the coloniser's word is explored in its creative potential to transform the dominator values of colonisation and globalisation into cooperative and partnership codes. More specifically, as Raimon Panikkar points out, the modern degeneration of 'the word', stripped of its dialogical power and reduced to a mere term, has a devastating effect, for it becomes a simple transferring of notions, devoid of a deeper meaning. (Panikkar 2007)

The creative word operates within a co-operative system of values that differs from the dominator model, which is tied to the Westernised scientific and technical term. In this discussion, Eisler's partnership/dominator continuum along with Panikkar's theory of the spirit of the word will be applied in order to focus on the power of the mythical and archetypal word of the Aboriginal guides Dugald and Jackie in *Voss*. Here 'the word' is seen giving expression to a multitude of Aboriginal oral traditions, narratives and myths operating within analogical frameworks, rather than logical ones, and including silence as a form of creativity and communication, thus manifesting its full symbolic and poetic power as expression of a partnership approach to life.

Although White's engagement with Indigenous issues was necessarily embedded in political and historical implications, his "historical imagination," as Walsh defines it (1977, 41), is at the same time beyond history, a place where he searched within himself and his fellow beings for "a new sense of self and of reality which would contest "the triumph of radical evil." (Brady 2010, 127) In this paper, I intend to explore further White's journey towards this new sense of self and focus on his concern with Aboriginal lore and spirituality in relation to white settler society by applying the theoretical paradigms espoused by both Riane Eisler and Raimon Panikkar in the study of world literatures, languages and education since 1998. (Riem et al., 2003, 2007, 2010; Dolce et al, 2009)

In particular, the paper will focus on the power of the creative, analogical, mythical and archetypal word of the Aboriginal guides Dugald and Jackie in Patrick White's *Voss* (1981) to show how they give voice to a partnership cultural paradigm as an alternative mode of living and a different form of dialogue from that of white settler society which is characterised by a dominator cultural paradigm. White's portrayal of Dugald and Jackie's use of the word indicates that Aboriginal oral traditions, narratives and myths work predominantly within analogical frameworks, typical of partnership social systems, rather than logical ones, upon which dominator social systems are based. In this sense, vanden Driesen's idea of "the possibility of white indigeneity" in her study on Patrick White is of particular significance as it highlights "the potential for the white settler to belong within the land as does the indigene." (2009, xxvi) Her new and interesting approach provides us with a significant bridge that holds and joins together 'difference' as in the "concept of zeugma, which allows for an absence of complete grammatical fit between two elements but nevertheless admits of an overlap that brings them into a close relationship. "These concepts point toward "a negotiation between contending influences" (vanden Driesen 2009, xxvii) – white settler society and the Australian "Indigene" in her study – and Eisler's *dominator* and *partnership* cultural paradigm along with Panikkar's concept of *word* and *term* in this paper.

According to Eisler's Cultural Transformation Theory, two fundamental models of society operate dynamically within the great surface diversity of human culture:

> the first, which I call *dominator* model, is what is popularly termed either patriarchy or matriarchy – the ranking of one half of humanity over the other. The second, in which social relations are primarily based on the principle of linking rather than ranking, may best be described as differences in our species, between male and female – diversity is not equated with either inferiority or superiority." (Eisler 1987, xvi, my italics)

The dominator model primarily refers to social systems generally characterised by hierarchic and authoritarian structures, in which power and the central roles of political leadership and moral authority are accorded to only one half of humanity, either female or male. From an 'equalitarian' perspective, both patriarchy and matriarchy are undesirable as they correspond to two sides of the same coin based on relations of control – the *ranking* of one half of humanity over the other, and therefore characterised by a high degree of institutionalised violence. The word 'equalitarian' is deliberately used to denote relationships in a society where men and women are accorded equal importance. (Eisler 1987, 216) Conversely, in the partnership model social systems are structured on the principle of *linking*, thus valuing diversity and honouring equal recognition and inclusion of any difference through mutually caring relationships.

In the same vein, Eisler's partnership and dominator configurations are reflected in Panikkar's theory of the spirit of the word, (2007, 96-125) particularly the distinction between *word* and *term*, where the creative, analogical and mythological function of the word is juxtaposed with what he defines as the scientistic term. Kary Mullis (1998) has shown how scientism is a kind of fundamentalism hindering the progress of both knowledge and science. Scientism is an exaggerated form of scientific thought that becomes unscientific in its exclusion *a priori* of all that cannot be (yet) demonstrated. Whilst for Eisler, dominator societies are founded on hierarchy and encoded violence (the *blade*) and partnership ones are based on systems of cooperation among equals (the *chalice*), for Panikkar, one of the most significant features of the word is that it begins and ends in an inner silence that is at the foundation of true dialogue and the creative word, whereas 'term' denotes a technical means to communicate 'objective' data, typical of our globalised society.

The Aboriginal creative word, which also includes silence as a form of dialogue, creativity and communication, can be read as still manifesting and retaining its full symbolic and poetic power and expressing a partnership, co-operative and 'equalitarian' approach to life. I do not intend to mythologise Aboriginality according to a westernised perspective, but on the contrary, to show how the language of the dominator world often overlooks the analogic and creative power of the word, which is still found in Indigenous storytelling, lore and traditional approaches to life. Panikkar indeed criticises the imperialistic mode of dominant languages, with their globalising all-inclusive perspective, and reasserts the importance of native and local languages as an immense treasure for the world. (2007, 80-94) In Voss's journey across the desert, White portrays the fundamental dismantling of the white explorer's belief that he possesses the power to logically define, circumscribe and understand a place and a culture he does not know. In crossing the Australian desert Voss will have to progressively acknowledge that the Aboriginal world presents an important and different approach to life that is essential in truly interpreting and 'mapping' not only Australia but also human territory in all its complexities and sacredness.

As Ashcroft points out, the two significant features of White's apprehension of the sacred are "its presence in the simple proximate reality of material things, and the persistent inability of language to fully apprehend it." (2010, 96) In this sense, the use of analogy, symbol and myth are central instruments in White's fiction, in which his search for a meaning can often be elusive, sometimes misleading or obscure, but, as Uhlmann points out: "while meaning is … uncertain, it is … certain that there is meaning." (2010, 75) White's European cultural background greatly influenced his writing, often creating a sense of dismay in the 'common' reader, because of the complexity and intercultural, philosophical, spiritual and sacred dimensions of his texts. (Ashcroft, 2010) For this reason

Panikkar's approach and definition of the *dialogic word*, contrasting with the *scientistic term*, offers a new and important critical tool with which to analyse White's work.

According to Panikkar, (2007, 96-125) the modern degeneration of the *word*, stripped it of its dialogical power and reduced it to a mere *term*. This has had a devastating effect, for it becomes a simple transferring of notions, devoid of a deeper meaning. With the Galilean and Cartesian fracture between material world and spirit, the western scientific approach to reality rejected analogy as instrumental for scientific research. After his experience of World War II, Patrick White must have felt this fracture at the core of his being and his contact with G.E. Moore's philosophy, in Veronica Brady's view, set him further on a quest for a philosophy or spirituality where good is not so much a rational knowledge but "a matter of intuitive experience, to be perceived in personal experiences or in response to beautiful objects." (2010: 130) This capacity to experience something at the level of intuition and analogy, rather than mere logical thinking, is a fundamental tool for most important human discoveries – scientific or otherwise. (Panikkar 2007,106)

Indeed, logical thinking always needs the power of imagination and creativity to open horizons beyond what is temporarily accepted and acknowledged as *true* and *real*, until the next scientific *discovery* has been achieved. In archetypal, mythical and analogical thinking the word has a true creative power, which is transformed and renewed every time we utter, sing, act or write a word. In the process, we renew both the word and ourselves. Nowadays, in the globalised world, language is becoming increasingly a tool for materialistic ends, which results in the nominalism of our contemporary technocratic society. On the creative power of the word, it is worth quoting in full the often quoted famous phrase re White's struggle with the "rocks and sticks of words"

> Possibly all art flowers more readily in silence. Certainly the state of simplicity and humility is the only desirable one for artist or for man. [...]. Writing, which had meant the practice of an art by a polished mind in civilised surroundings, became a struggle to

create completely fresh forms out of the rocks and sticks of words. I began to see things for the first time. (Brennan and Flynn 1989, 16)

In *Voss*, White uses the same parallel between sticks, and words, describing Dugald like "a thinking stick, on which the ash had cooled after purification by fire." (170) Both in "The Prodigal Son" and *Voss*, White highlights a different quality that language has, depending on the cultural background from which it springs: one is the language of possession expressed by colonisation, the other is a type of symbolic and highly sacred way of expressing humanity that can *happen* simply through physical presence, myth and silence and the creative and dialogic *word*.

In both texts White stresses the difference between a language shaped by a "polished [European] mind," that is refined and accomplished, ready for use but often worn out and devoid of creative power, and the freshness of words that originate from the "refreshed landscape" of Australia, with its long horizons, its sand, rocks, sticks. Therefore, while crossing the Aboriginal land, Voss has to progressively abandon his pride as a white explorer in order to reach a different understanding of reality that reads like archetype, myth, symbol, analogy, poetry and silence, because "language, the mode through which the white man has exercised control, is bereft of its power in the world of the black man." (vanden Driesen 2009, 38)

White's approach, in this sense, is, interestingly, connected to both Eisler and Panikkar's views on the function of the scientific *term* (language from a polished mind) as instruments of colonialism, connected to a *dominator* cultural paradigm. Globalisation and world economic exploitation use language and scientific *terms* as an encoded apparatus to impose power, which led our contemporary world to the greatest world financial crisis since the Depression. The same imposition of a dominator, colonising power is found in *Voss*, where White criticises the colonial enterprise of Australian settler society, dismantling and diminishing its impact in the progressive peeling off of Voss's egotistical and superhuman stance and his slow progress along the "three stages of mysticism." (Beatson 1970)

Aboriginal lore and mythology offer to White an important counterpoint to a world-view where one must possess the land rather than be its humble 'custodian.' (Limpert 2011, 10-11) According to Ashcroft "if White's orientation seems pantheistic at times, it is because the energy of his work is to locate the sacred in a place in which, to European eyes, *it does not belong*" (2010, 102). What the West – or Europe or a dominator culture – defines as pantheism is indeed a different form of spirituality that can be found in many Indigenous traditions wrongly accused of adoring idols or Nature by Western theologians and scholars. Indeed, in Aboriginal mythology and spirituality the sacred can and must be located in the land; every single detail of reality is sacred and the notion of the profane is absent. (Berndt and Berndt 1994, 5)

In *Voss*, White makes his protagonist cross the desert in order to grasp the land's elusive meaning and give it expression in the truest essence of language as spiritual communion: this can only happen through the use of the creative *word* of silent empathy with the Australian landscape, its prime inhabitants and their lore and spirituality. This is further expressed in the form of the telepathy Voss establishes with Laura Trevelyan. This very same search for an intuitive experience of the sacred is at the foundation of Aboriginal spirituality. (Cowan 1994, 3-4) The land Voss is trying to possess, understand and map is under the safe protection of Dugald and Jackie, Voss's two Aboriginal guides, who represent and embody this mythological and archetypal world, where myth is in itself an inner network guiding one along the *Songlines*, a more accurate and exact form of mapping the Aboriginal landscape (with its inner cartography) than the one used by white settlers.

Jackie, who becomes an Aboriginal spiritual man, embodies the fullness of a type of humanity still in tune with Mother Earth, speaking poetical words of truth and sacred wisdom, living in partnership, sharing cooperative and mutual values both with the land and his fellows. Since their first meeting at Jildra, his Aboriginal guides emerge as two quite extraordinary and mysterious beings in spite of his initial attempts at patronising them. These attempts are always futile. Voss is only able to grasp their truest essence, imaginatively and intuitively, only just before his own death – after having left behind all his cultural expectations and colonial projections as a white explorer. Voss will also understand that the Land the Aborigines inhabit and of which they are custodians, is not only an important part of their lore and mythology, but also part of himself as a human being. This was perhaps one of White's aims at the time, when he was trying to come to terms and rise above what he called "The Great Australian Emptiness." (Brennan and Flynn 1989, 13)

Voss's first meeting with Dugald and Jackie takes place at the second 'station' of his journey, Jildra, a hellish place, brutally ruled by Boyle, epitome of the debased white coloniser ruthlessly exploiting both land and Aboriginal peoples. With that dramatic irony often found in White's work, Voss's destiny of sacrifice and death is anticipated by Boyle, who becomes a kind of unintentional prophet:

> 'To peel down to the last layer,' he yawned. 'There is always another, and yet another of more exquisite subtlety. Of course every man has his own obsession. Yours would be, it seems, to overcome distance, but in much the same way, of deeper layers of irresistible disaster. I can guarantee', … 'that you will be given every opportunity of indulging yourself to the west of here. In stones and thorns. Why, anyone who is disposed can celebrate a high old Mass … with the skull of a blackfeller and his own blood, in Central Australia. (V. 167-68)

Boyle, despite himself, is also a knower of the Aboriginal ways of life, which he describes with scorn: "I cannot recommend these blacks as infallible guides and reliable companions, … Like all aboriginals they will *blow with the wind*, or *turn into lizards* when they are bored with their existing shapes." (169, my italics) Behind the *terms* Boyle uses, though, we can perceive a deeper truth, another more profound meaning present in the *words* themselves, which, once uttered, surface to acquire a life of their own. In an analogical form, Boyle unconsciously describes the capacity for inner metamorphoses that Aboriginal culture has, and, at the same time, briefly and unexpectedly, conjures up the whole world of the Dreamtime. Shape-shifting, a common form of shamanic power acknowledged by numberless traditional peoples, including Australian Aboriginals (Pattel 1996a). In Aboriginal lore, both wind and lizards have a great significance, as they testify to the power of the land and their connection to it. In this passage White, is unveiling and dismantling the patronising attitude of both Boyle and Voss, and also, at the same time, indicating a different form of understanding and interpreting reality that the Europeans have lost in their own culture and lore.

Voss replies in a rather presumptious and purely rational way to Boyle's statements : "In general … it is necessary to communicate without the knowledge of language." (169) Voss will have to explore in the depths of himself the intuitive quality and premonition of his own words. His journey will be the unfolding of this sacred mystery of language (and silence), with its final revelation of truth. For their part both Dugald, the elder, mentor and interpreter, and Jackie, the young boy, already live this revelation exuding it through their own skins. When they silently and unexpectedly arrive on the scene, the strength of their presence is immediately asserted: "Their bare feet made upon the earth only a slight, but very particular sound, which, to the German's ears, *at once established their ownership.*" (169; my italics) This light sound, this soft touching of the soil represents the deep relationship of love, reverence and connection the Aborigines have with their land. vanden Driesen clearly underlines the "irrelevance to the black world of the white man's urgencies" (2009, 35) as in the departure scene at Sydney harbour, where the narrator observes two Aboriginal women intent on preparing some food, totally indifferent to what is happening around them but fully present in their "most distinguished silence." (99) Here, White clearly wants to stress the strong and powerful presence of the two Aboriginal women, characterised by their communicative silence (the *word*) as juxtaposed to the white settlers' empty sense of superiority (the *term*).

In Voss's meeting with Dugald and Jackie, Voss expresses the same sense of superiority and defines them as 'creatures.' However, Voss is attracted, if only intellectually, by the perfection of a possible silent, intuitive communication with Dugald and Jackie:

> Voss would have liked to talk to these creatures. Alone, he and the blacks would have communicated with one another by skin and

silence just as dust is not impenetrable and the message of sticks can be interpreted after hours of intimacy. But in the presence of Brendan Boyle, the German was victim of his European, or even his human inheritance. (170)

In spite of the fact that he is "victim of his European inheritance" where the stress of communication is mostly upon the *term,* rather than the poetic *word*, Voss realises that to use *terms* with the Aborigines is inadequate, for only the creative *word*, spoken or silent, delicate and intuitive, working at skin-level can open a truthful communication: "Jackie was really quite young. He stood about with the delicacy of a young girl, while absorbing all details, *listening with his skin*, and *quivering his reactions*" (170) - my italics. Since in "many Aboriginal languages the word for *listen* and the word for *understand* are the same." (Lambert 1993, 12) Italics are mine. Jackie's capacity for listening at skin level is a sign of his ability to understand that goes beyond the limits of a plain encounter between a white man (the explorer) and an Aborigine (his native guide).

White's aim here also seems to be that of juxtaposing two different ways of communicating: the logical-linear way of the white man that reaches its extreme in the vulgarity and brutality of Boyle, and the poetic and symbolic way of the Aborigines that has its highest expression in a poetic silence, in a capacity for listening that goes far beyond the limits of conventional and standard communication. With this I do not mean so much that White wants to limit the Aboriginal world to a pre-logic and 'primitive' type of communication, but rather to indicate that scientism and a blind belief in a horizontal unlimited progress has deprived our modern society, predominantly structured upon a dominator paradigm and the use of the *term*, of the creative and poetic *word* as a harmonising and complementary form of knowledge in order to read and interpret our world and life

In the episode, Voss's unease and embarrassment in a situation he cannot control with his mental structures impels him to give a brass button to Dugald. This apparently simple action implies a sense of superiority, but, in truth, it reveals Voss's impotence and fear in front of the mystery he is about to face, in the desert, in the

Aborigines and in himself. Dugald is aware of Voss's mysticism, he indistinctly perceives what even Voss does not know yet: that his desire to 'map' Australia responds to a spiritual yearning – that of knowing himself as a part of the Whole. Dugald, purified by the fire of myth and smoke, has already accomplished this ancestral goal. Then, in tragic anticipation, Voss hands Jackie a pocket knife, which Jackie, at the end of the novel, will use to kill Voss in a sort of sacrificial rite:

> The youth ... had been brought to animal life. Lights shone in his skin, and his throat was rippling with language. He was giggling and gulping. He could have eaten the brass button. ...
>
> Jackie, however, would not receive, except by the hand of his mentor, and then, was shivering with awful joy as he stood staring at the knife on his own palm. (170-71).

Imaginatively eating the brass button corresponds to a kind of communion, similar to the one Voss will experience, just before his death, when he is given a "whole wichetty grub" by the tribe elder, and "the solemnity of the act was immense." (388) Jackie's language is highly symbolic here; he is embracing whole inner worlds in the "rippling" sounds made in his throat: a laughter that remains engulfed inside, an emotion needing to be swallowed down again and again, for it surfaces too powerfully and needs to be contained. Only a shiver can truly express it. This language for a moment has Voss translated, deciphered, transformed, decoded, made and read out: "Voss, too, was *translated*. The numerous creases in his black trousers appeared to have been sculptured for eternity" (171, my italics). Only a brief instant, though, for he will have to journey across Australia in order to fully embody this revelation. At the same time, in this scene, Voss epitomises what white settler society will make of him after his death: a bronze statue, a myth to commemorate, with solid bronze trousers that are actually sculptured for eternity. (440)

Another highly symbolic moment, connected to the function and power of the *word*, is when Voss gives some letters for Laura to Dugald, for him to bring back to Jildra. This happens when Voss has almost completed his quest and most of his men have left him or are dead. Linear time and the use of *terms* instead of *word*s is connected to a scientistic and dominator world view, therefore Dugald, the old man of the Dreamtime and the poetic word, can only laugh at the white man's naïveté and lack of understanding, at his attachment to a system of values and beliefs that is totally out of place in the desert. Dugald can only laugh, not so much to deride the white man's worldly preoccupations, but out of the sheer joy of going back. He will not go to Jildra but will return to the Aboriginal world, to his own tribe, to his ancestral traditional habits, to his people and his Dreamtime (219).

Dreaming, or the Dreamtime, is a state, not a time or a place, and one who is aware of this inner reality can enter it at any moment, or rather is always cocooned in it. Voss's letters to Laura, though, still tie Dugald to the world of the whites. To get free from this last bond, he strips both the coat and "the conscience he had worn in the days of the whites," (219) for they are useless now. Then, ritually, he tears open the seals of the letters, to shed light on the white man's obscure black signs:

> The old man folded the papers. *With the solemnity of one who has interpreted a mystery, he tore them into little pieces.*
>
> How they fluttered. The women were screaming, and escaping from the white man's bad thoughts.
>
> Some of the men were laughing.
>
> Only Dugald was sad and still, as the pieces of paper fluttered round him and settled on the grass, like a mob of cockatoos. (220, my italics)

This passage has been criticised as an example of white settler's ideology that saw the Aborigine as 'illiterate,' disinterested in books and writing (Van Toorn 2006, 1). I believe however, that White's aim in this novel is that of unveiling the white man's arrogance and stressing the capacity of the Aborigine to survive and thrive in what is, for the white man, an alien and dangerous environment.

Moreover, White is aware of Aboriginal lore and spirituality and he also wants to show how the Aborigines always connect the natural/spiritual world they know with different realities: the black marks on the white paper become fern roots, and the fluttering pieces of torn paper are a mob of cockatoos. This could be regarded as a clear example of analogical thinking; giving voice to a world where material and spiritual are always symbolically united, where ritual actions and words still have a profound, simple and straightforward power: "They went walking through the good grass, and the present absorbed them utterly." (220) The group is pictured as moving together as a community living in partnership, without needing to say aloud what is clear to all and comes naturally; it is an intensely mythological and archetypal moment. These people live within the cyclical rhythms of Nature; they move together towards the right and plentiful season of being, which is the source, the goal and meaning of our human life. There is no linear time in this, only an eternal present that wholly and perfectly absorbs them.

This profound connection with the Dreaming is also manifested in Jackie's role, at the end of the novel. If Boyle and the white community call him "mad" he has certainly acquired a life and power of his own, detached from his black mentor Dugald and his white leader Voss. Alone now, he can face his visions, the Spirit world of the Ancestors and the desert, with all their voices that breathe into his soul. We observe Jackie's connection with his ancestral world when, during a flood blocking the expedition for some days, he and Voss visit a sacred cave full of Aboriginal graffiti. Jackie does not translate the rock-paintings, but *interprets* them, in the literal sense: he performs and acts out their meaning for Voss. The German is "doubly locked in language," (274) he asks for a translation that Jackie cannot really give, for he can only *be* his Ancestors, *embody* them in the moment, a reflection of the Dreamtime:

"Snake," Jackie explained. "Father my father, all blackfeller."

"Gut," added the boy, for the special benefit of the German, and *the word lit the whole place.*

The man was yielding himself up to the simplicity of the drawings. Henceforth all words must be deceitful, except those sanctioned by necessity, the handrail of language.

"Kangaroo," said the boy. "Old man," he smiled … (274, italics mine)

Jackie, who is describing the sacred ties the Aborigines have with their Ancestors, can only use names as creative words in all their full potency, still uncorrupted by use, in order to create "completely fresh forms out of the rocks and sticks of words" (White 1989, 16). These names symbolically correspond and perfectly adhere to the Aboriginal drawings and these in turn coincide with the sacred and spiritual reality they evoke, personify and make ever present.

Even the German word *gut* is uttered by Jackie to build an imaginative link with the white man, to bridge the cultural differences between them. This is why a simple everyday German word totally illuminates the place with the inner light Jackie infuses in it through the brilliant intensity of his own feelings. Voss starts to yield to the symbolic power of the place, beginning to understand that *words*, if used outside a sacred and spiritual context, can easily lose their simplicity and become mere *terms*. These are deceitful and deluding; they can only shadow truth, but never give it real body and form. Jackie then performs more of the Dreamtime paintings:

"Men gone away all dead," the boy explained. "All over," he waved his arm. "By rock. By tree. No more men … *They come out. Usfeller no see. They everywhere.*"

"Now I understand," said Voss gravely.

He did. To his fingertips. He felt immensely happy. (275, my italics)

In the Aboriginal world, death is not a tragic event; it simply is a passage of continuity into a different but ever-present dimension

The immensity of Voss's happiness relates to an understanding of this truth that is not of the mind but of the body – he understands to his fingertips, and soul – he feels immensely happy. It is a physical sensation and an intuitive feeling. It is a deep connection he feels inside, evoked by Jackie's simple and profound storytelling of the Aboriginal paintings. This immediately calls to Voss's mind his love for Laura: "the woman who was locked inside him permanently." (275) He would like to "contribute to the rock drawings," marking in the same warm ochre colour present in the ancestral caves the "L of happiness" (275); the L suggests this: L for Laura, L for Love. When Jackie ritually kills his white 'master', there is some kind of love in the act: "The boy stood for a moment beneath the morning star. The whole air was trembling on his skin." (394) The same trembling of Jackie's skin characterises their first and last moments together, as a sign, an omen of a different reality vibrating in the air.

Jackie subsequently becomes the visionary man walking the desert, seeing ghosts, hearing voices, making silent prophecies to sand, rocks and lizards; Jackie's solitude is another kind of initiation, where desert, sun, and elements are co-protagonists and mirrors of his inner being. This strong relationship with the land is the reason behind Jackie's spiritual power that finds expression in the creative poetic word shouted aloud, but also murmured in silence: "For it is not possible to communicate lucidly with men after the communion of souls, ... He was slowly becoming possessed of the secrets of the country, even of the spirits of distant tribal grounds." (420) Once one has touched, like Jackie, the deep essence of things, as White himself seems to have done in his personal experienceas described in his essay "A Prodigal Son" it is impossible to communicate lucidly, that is, through reason only, through the scientistic term, and within an understanding of reality that is merely linear. Once visited by the creative word, Jackie's soul opens totally to the communion of being with being, of grain of sand with grain of sand; he is able to *translate* the spiritual dimension into a dialect, into a more human and more understandable language; and he is ready to let himself be engulfed into the Dreamtime with a smile:

> Death had just apprehended Jackie, crossing a swamp, during a thunderstorm, at dusk. The boy had not attempted to resist. He lay down, and was persuaded to melt at last into the accommodating earth. (427)

Like dawn, dusk is the time of the day when material and spiritual worlds get closer and whisper truths in the soft breeze, opening thresholds towards different dimensions. So Jackie does not die, but stays in the land, with all the other ancestral spirits, ready to tell his truth to those who are ready to listen

In death, Voss shares the same destiny and becomes part of the country like the Aboriginal Ancestors of the Dreamtime: "the blacks talk about him to this day. He is still there – that is the honest opinion of many of them – he is there in the country, and will always be." (V. 443) Echoing Judd's testimony, at the end of the novel, Laura says: "Voss did not die, ... he is there still, it is said, in the country, and will always be." (V. 448) As Limpert states, the Australian Aborigines' connection to the land "embodies the spirit of the place they are born from and they will go back to. The spirit of each person is in the land, comes from it and returns to it." (2011, 11) In being finally one with the land, Voss has thus become a "white indigene." (vanden Driesen 2009) The country of which Jackie and Voss have become Ancestors cannot be limited to what the scientific mind calls 'inert matter'; it actually manifests the creative force that formed stones and seas, stars and flowers, comets and corals, crystals and ants in the millions of years before humanity evolved.

White poetically shows his readers how death is a powerful dramatic mystery equal to birth; in ancient traditions death is not an end but a transformation within the tripartite spiralling and labyrinthine structure of life, death and regeneration. The pathways between worlds are trodden by humans in magic song, word, dance and ritual – within a circle, or labyrinth, a desert place,-in the web of Aboriginal *Songlines* allowing entry only to the initiated. Voss and Jackie walked this ancestral path of the creative word and song. They tapped the terrestrial currents and cosmic energy fields, danced this ritual winding and unwinding within the spiralling movement of the stars, repeating the rhythmical pulsation of molecules, reaching back to the still centre of the heart and the cosmos providing a source of inspiration to all those who witness this enactment.

Works Cited

Ashcroft, Bill. 2010. "The Presence of the Sacred in Patrick White," *Remembering Patrick White: Contemporary Critical Essays*, ed.Elizabeth McMahon and Brigitta Olubas Amsterdam: Rodopi: 95-108.
—. 2005. "The Horizontal Sublime," *Antipodes* 9.2: 141-51.
Barua, Krishna. 2010. "The Cosmic and Acosmic – a re-definition of Being and Time in Patrick White's *Voss*," *The Indian Review of World Literature in English*, 6.2. http://worldlitonline.net/the-cosmic-and-the.pdf. Accessed 1 September 2011.
Beatson, P. 1970. "The Three Stages: Mysticism in Patrick White's *Voss*," *Southerly* 2.1:11-21.
Berndt, R. M. and C.H. Berndt. 1992. *The World of the First Australians. Aboriginal Traditional Life: Past and Present.* London: Angus & Robertson.
Berndt, R.M. and C.H. Berndt. 1994. *The Speaking Land. Myth and Story in Aboriginal Australia.* Rochester, VT: Inner Traditions International.
Beston, John B. and Rose Marie. 1974. "The Theme of Spiritual Progression in *Voss*," *Ariel* 5 (July): 99-114.
Bjorksten, I. 1976. *Patrick White. A General Introduction.* St. Lucia: University of Queensland Press.
Black, C. F. 2011. *The Land is the Source of the Law. A Dialogic Encounter with Indigenous Jurisprudence.* London: Routledge.
Brady,Veronica. 1981. *A Crucible of Prophets: The Australians and the Question of God.* Sydney: Australian and New Zealand Studies in Theology and Religion.
—. 1981 "Patrick White and the Difficult God," Veronica Brady, *A Crucible of Prophets.* Sydney: Australian and New Zealand Studies in Theology and Religion: 69-88.
—. 2010 "The Dragon Slayer. Patrick White and the Contestation of History," *Remembering Patrick White: Contemporary Critical Essays*, Elizabeth McMahon and Brigitta Olubas eds. Amsterdam: Rodopi: 125-135.
Brennan, Paul and Christine Flynn. Ed. 1989. *Patrick White Speaks*: Sydney: Primavera Press: 13-17.

Collier, G. 1992. *The Rocks and Sticks of Words: Style, Discourse and Narrative Structure in the Fiction of Patrick White*. Amsterdam-Atlanta: Rodopi.

Cowan, James. 1994. *Myths of the Dreaming*. Roseville: Unity Press.

Dolce, Maria Renata and Antonella Riem. Ed. *Bernard Hickey, A Roving Cultural Ambassador. Essays in His Memory*. Udine: Forum.

Eisler, Riane. 1987. *The Chalice and the Blade: Our History, Our Future*. San Francisco: Harper & Row.

Eliade, Mircea. 1964. *Shamanism: Archaic Techniques of Ecstasy*. Trans. Willard R. Trask. Princeton NJ: Princeton University Press.

Lambert, Johanna. Ed. 1993. *Wise Women of the Dreamtime. Aboriginal Tales of the Ancestral Powers*. Rochester: VE: Inner Traditions.

Limpert, D. G. 2011. *The Politics of Space in Contemporary Australian Aboriginal Art*. Norderstedt, Germany: Grin Verlag. Druck und Bindung Books on demand.

Mullis, K. 1998. *Dancing Naked in the Mind Field*. New York: Pantheon.

Odier, C. 1947. *L'Angoisse et la Pensée Magique*. Neuchatel: Delachaux et Niestle.

Panikkar, Raimon. 2007. *Lo spirito della parola* Milano: Bollati Boringhieri.

Pattel Gray, A. 1991. *Through Aboriginal Eyes: The Cry from the Wilderness*. Geneva: WCC Publications.

—. 1998. *The Great White Flood: Racism in Australia* American Academy of Religion, Cultural Criticism Series 2. Atlanta: Scholars Press.

—. Ed. 1996 a. *Aboriginal Spirituality: Past, Present, Future* Melbourne: Harper Collins.

—. Ed.1996 b. *Martung Upah: Black and White Australians Seeking Partnership*. Melbourne: Harper Collins Religious.

Riem, A. 1986. *L'universo Terra in* Voss *di Patrick White*. Verona: Il Segno.

—. 1988. *The Labyrinths of the Self*. Leichhardt, NSW: FILEF Italo-Australian Publications.

—. 2009. "The Goddess Slid into the Australian Desert: *Voss* a Revisitation," *Bernard Hickey, A Roving Cultural Ambassador. Essays in His Memory,* ed. M.R Dolce and Antonella Riem Udine: Forum: 251-63.

Uhlmann, Anthony. 2010. *The Symbol in Patrick White*, *Remembering Patrick White: Contemporary Critical Essays,* ed.Elizabeth McMahon and Brigitta Olubas. Amsterdam: Rodopi: 65-75.

vanden Driesen, Cynthia. 2009. *Writing the Nation: Patrick White and the Indigene.* New York-Amsterdam: Rodopi.

Van Toorn, Penny. 2006. *Writing Never Arrives Naked: Early Aboriginal Cultures of Writing in Australia.* Canberra: Aboriginal Press.

Walsh, W. 1977. *Patrick White's Fiction.* Sydney: Allen & Unwin.

White,Patrick.1981. *Voss.* Harmondsworth: Penguin.

Chapter Sixteen

"Violent" Aboriginals and "Benign" White Men: White's Alternative Representation of the Encounter in *Voss*

Harish Mehta
McMaster College Canada

White published his fifth novel, *Voss,* in 1957, a time when the 'White Australia Policy' was being gradually relaxed, ahead of its eventual abolition in 1966. It was a significant historical moment for the appearance of the novel because it historicised the encounter between whites and Aborigines. It has never been sufficiently noted that in this work White's portrayal runs counter to the conventional rendition of the clash between Europeans and Aborigine as one in which the superior might of the European culture and the degeneracy of the Aboriginal meant an unequivocal conquest and domination which left no possibility of resistance or struggle on the part of those peoples whose lands fell so easily under the domination of Imperial powers.

The clash between European explorers and the Aboriginal people of Australia as presented in this novel can be viewed as a form of early exploratory diplomacy between colonialists who aimed to 'discover' an imagined homeland, on the one hand, and the pre-existing nation of the Indigenous people, on the other. As Johann Ulrich Voss, the protagonist in the novel *Voss,* sets out to 'explore' the continent in 1845, his contact with Aboriginal communities could be regarded as constituting a form of informal diplomacy, or unofficial amateur diplomacy – i.e. the diplomacy conducted by ordinary people. By contrast, formal diplomacy is conducted by the formally appointed representatives of countries, as understood in Diplomatic History and International Relations History.

There is a rich historical literature on informal diplomacy and early contacts between white settlers and Aborigines, both in North America and Australia, many of which resulted in the signing of treaties and informal pacts (Ford 2010, Berman and Johnson 1977, Forslund 2002, and Beisner 1975). The literature on exploration is an integral part of Australian consciousness, as generations of Australians through the 1970s have imagined a homeland formed through the exploits of 19th century explorers. (Beston 2010, 240)

In *Voss,* White carefully constructs diplomatic interaction between the two parties: he catalogues conversations, both verbal and non-verbal sign language, between Europeans and Aborigines, as they talk, negotiate, and compromise. It is far from being the conventional account of the clash between European and Aboriginal cultures which ends in establishing the unquestioned hegemony of the European order. White's account dramatises the presence of a range of viewpoints and reactions that come into play and removes the narrative from being the conventional dramatisation of the clash between cultures in which the victory of white supremacy is virtually a foregone conclusion.

The diplomatic aspects of the encounter (contained in dialogue, in Voss' letters, in journal entries, and in the cultural myths of both sides) generate several discourses: Aboriginal collaboration with explorers alongside of others who view the whites with suspicion; Voss' own complex attitude of respect for the Aborigines along with a desire to rule over them; the other white explorers' denunciation of natives in racialised language, and the response of the Aborigines with violence and theft of settlers' livestock; Aboriginal peoples' understandings of explorers' language and letters as carriers of "bad" thoughts; fleeting expressions of shared friendship and sympathy; efforts to understand the cultural myths of the other; and only at the end the use of violence by Aborigines when diplomatic encounters end in disaster. The encounters are not dominated by white explorers. The Aborigines exhibit powerful political and social agency when they accept, resist, or rebuff Voss's proposals, and when they signal an end to cordial diplomacy by resorting to violence.

The narrative of sympathy that runs through White's writing alongside his colonial discourse has attracted critical comment from scholars. Simon During, for instance, argues that the theme of the failure of European domination in *Voss* signposts the fact that White was a precursor to postcolonialism. (During 1996, 27) White's move out of colonialism took a circuitous route: he had to first historically re-create colonialism, and the early encounters between Europeans and Aborigines, which he found fascinating because of the resistance that the latter offered. White also seems to Orientalise Aborigines by conflating their human identity with nature and suggesting that they belong more to nature than to humanity, thereby discounting their prior claims to the land. This is debatable, but what can be demonstrated is that White presents the black/white encounter in this text as no simple encounter leading to white conquest, as so many canonical historical records tend to do.

White himself did not care about historical novels. He argued in 1989: "Personally, I tend to dislike historical novels, and have avoided writing them because of the strictures they impose on the imagination. Instead, on a couple of occasions, I have taken a historical character or moment, as the starting point." (Brennan and Flynn 1989, 84) White however, did consult the journals of German explorer Ludwig Leichhardt, a 19th century adventurer who died while exploring the Australian outback. Scholars have located White as a "historical novelist" in his novels *Voss,* and *A Fringe of Leaves.* (Beston 2010, 17) Nonetheless, in *Voss* White does not let the heavy hand of history mar his art. The novel is a triumph of the imagination. For all his dislike of the historical novel, White was enmeshed in Australian history, especially the history of its Aboriginal people. There is much evidence to be found, within the ideologies espoused by White himself, of White's personal sympathy for the Indigenous peoples of Australia. Indeed there is much of White within his protagonist, Johann Ulrich Voss. In 1984, White spoke about his "personal duty" toward the Indigenous people, in words that sounded both like those of an enlightened colonialist, and of a sympathiser with the plight of the Aborigine.

... like a white colonist's duty to the Australian Aborigines – my duty to the so-called ethnics in these days of rage from certain quarters against Asians – the rage in past decades against dagoes, Jewish reffos, Balts – and the rest of those we see when we come to our senses have contributed immeasurably to our culture. (Brennan and Flynn 1989, 171)

White based his principal character, Voss, on Ludwig Leichhardt the German who had explored central and northern Australia from 1842-1848. After securing the financial backing of wealthy sponsors, Voss, begins a journey to 'explore' the Australian continent in 1845. None of the characters in the novel concern themselves with the reality that the continent had already been 'explored' thoroughly by the Indigenous people to whom it had belonged. (Stevens 1981, 1-56) vanden Driesen has argued that the role of the explorer in the history of imperialism is significant and paradoxical because the explorer was always a tool of European imperialism; his heroic endeavours earned him admiration and he acquired the aspect of a hero but masked the fact that he was the tool of an expansive colonial empire. (vanden Driesen 2009, 29) While Voss was, indeed, an instrument of European colonialists who desired to map and settle the new country, Voss's goodwill and empathy towards Aborigines sets him apart from the other Europeans who only desired to occupy Aboriginal lands.

In *Voss,* White has clearly avoided exploring the most troubling aspects of European conquest: that the settlers used violence in their effort to destroy an entire race. Australian scholars have pointed out that violence between Europeans and Aborigines had been endemic since 1788. (Reynolds 1991, 17) The historian Geoffrey Blainey has demonstrated that by 1830 disease had killed most Aborigines in Tasmania, but warfare and violence by ordinary settlers had also been devastating. (Blainey 1980, 75) Despite the historical record, there is an absence of white-initiated violence in *Voss,* which is set more than two decades after the documented episodes of violence. The fact is that when Voss begins exploring the continent, massacres of Aboriginals by European settlers were already a regular occurrence. These uncomfortable facts, do not appear in the novel. It was as if White deliberately avoided repeating documented history. As a work of the imagination, White creates an alternate history of Australia, a world in which whites and Aborigines might have co-existed, if there had been more sympathetic Europeans like Voss. Alas, Voss was in the minority. Most settlers wanted to get on directly with the brutal business of driving out the Aborigines and occupying their lands.

The scholar Colin Tatz argues that there were three parties in the extermination of Australian Aborigines: perpetrators, victims, and bystanders. Without implicit support of bystanders, perpetrators could not have committed their crimes. (Tatz 1999, 317) Tatz explains that the genocide against the Aboriginal population caused their numbers to plunge from 750,000 at the time of British arrival in 1788 to just 31,000 in 1911 (320). On a visit to Australia more than 130 years ago, British writer Anthony Trollope described the varied atrocities perpetrated against the Australian Aborigines: "We have taken away their land, destroyed their food, made them subject to our laws ... have massacred them when they defended themselves, in addition to forcibly separating children from parents, and exposing them to deadly new diseases." (qtd. inTatz 1999, 320)

In *Voss*, the encounter between whites and Aborigines shows the violence is initiated by the latter. The historical record of the arrival of European settlers is replete with violence. Several Australian scholars have described how settlers dehumanised Aborigines by treating Aboriginal land as wasteland peopled by "troublesome wild animals to be shot and hunted down," categorising them variously as "vermin," "creatures scarcely human," and "hideous scandals to humanity." They were a "nuisance" regarded as fair game for white "sportsmen." (Evans, Saunders, and Cronin 1988, 75-78) The killings, conducted by ordinary European settlers, were astounding even to a visiting British diplomat. In a letter, written in 1883, Arthur Hamilton-Gordon, the British High Commissioner to New Zealand, wrote to British Prime Minister William Gladstone: "The habit of regarding the natives as vermin, to be cleared off the face of the earth, has given the average Queenslander a tone of brutality and cruelty." He added that Queenslanders speak about "the individual murder of natives exactly as they would talk of a day's sport, or having to kill some troublesome animal." Violence also permeated life in New South Wales, where massacres of Aborigines began after this colony introduced a police force.

The world of *Voss* is one where Europeans do not initiate violence. Instead, although at the start they exercise hegemony over the Aborigines, they employ, the European explorers quickly realise that their principal instrument of establishing control – language – has no power in the unfamiliar terrain of Indigenous people. (vanden Driesen 2009, 38) Many members of Voss's expedition worry that they would not able to communicate with Aborigines because they did not know their language; but Voss responds pragmatically: "In general, it is necessary to communicate without knowledge of the language." (162-163). Voss was entirely correct: the explorers did not really need to know the language of the Aborigine in order to communicate. They managed to make themselves understood through signifiers such as signs, and some words. White writes about Aborigines with deep respect, as the possessors of an unique voice: "The [Aboriginal] youth [Jackie], on the other hand, had been brought to animal life. Lights shone in his skin, and his throat was rippling with language." (164)

White is concerned with maintaining lines of communication, and repairing ruptures. The explorers struggle to find the right voice to communicate with the Indigenes, and White recognises the Aborigines' right to express themselves. Yet, the white explorers miss the nuances of their speech because they do not know the language. They are, however, able to grasp the meaning of their words through non-verbal communication. White depicts Aborigines speaking out loud, laughing out loud, and demonstrating that they are at ease in the consciousness that they are the masters of their land. They do not see themselves as belonging in the margins and when they speak, they are not speaking from the margins to the 'Centre.' They are at the centre of their world, which is now being rudely invaded by white explorers.

In *Voss,* White shows forth Orientalist attitudes of white Australians yet also seems to stand outside of these as sympathiser and fellow traveller with the Aborigines. He presents the Orientalist gaze, through the denunciatory voices, racialised language which are an integral part of the white settlers' dealings with the Aborigines. The plot of the novel is woven around an Orientalist adventure: wealthy white Australians provide funds and logistical support to the explorer Voss to lead an expedition into the undiscovered parts of Australia, to bring back maps and journals for the benefit of the sponsors who are now planning to take over the entire continent.

Both Michel Foucault and Edward Said saw the creation of knowledge – novels, travelogues, art – as forms of domination. (Sharp 2008, 110) But then, White the writer himself does not align himself with the Orientalist stance. His language is finely attuned to the sensitivities of the Aborigines. There is so much of White in Voss that one might be the *doppelganger* of the other. Scholars have found close resemblances between White and the Voss character. John Beston argues that both White and Voss were born in Europe, and that White felt a commitment to advance Australian culture, much in the manner in which Voss was determined to construct a map of Australia. (Beston 2010, 7) While Voss remarked that he would make the map of Australia, Beston argues that White had a grander personal mission to "create" Australian literature by absorbing European and Australian culture.

White frequently uses the racialised signifier, "blacks," to describe Aborigines, repeatedly emphasising colour as a marker of race. Such characterisation was not inappropriate in a strictly historical sense because that was the common way of addressing the other in the Australian society that White inhabited in the 1950s. One of Voss's sponsors, Brendan Boyle even, denounces the traditional knowledge of Aborigines about their own environment: "I cannot recommend these blacks as infallible guides and reliable companions they will blow with the wind, or turn into lizards when they are bored with their existing shapes." (V. 162)

While Voss's mission is to establish good relations with the Indigenous people, at times his politics are ambiguous. On seeing an Aboriginal settlement in the frontier town of Jildra, with its shacks and tents, where an Aboriginal woman "of spreading breasts, sat giving suck to a puppy," Boyle comments: "Dirty beggars, but a man could not do without them." (165) Voss does not rebuke or prevent Boyle from making such comments. A subsequent white-Aboriginal encounter is marred by mistrust when one of Voss's expedition members, the former convict Judd, "loses" a compass.

Judd remarks: "These blacks would thieve any mortal thing, I would not be surprised." (175) Judd soon enough realises that the lost compass was kept safely inside his own saddle-bag but "Voss had turned and walked away" from the incident, leaving his personal views on the "theft" unclear (176): his silence towards Judd's patently unfair allegation cannot be justified.

As the expedition moves forward into the vast Australian continent, Voss makes a much greater effort to reach out to the Indigenous guides but while not aligned with the whites in general he indicates a wish to impose himself as master – a third position as, it were, in this hitherto purely colonialist relationship between whites and blacks. The difference between his attitude and that of the other whites is that he respects their value and dignity and cherishes what he thinks he enjoys as a special relationship. Riding on horseback alongside the two "black" guides, Dugald and Jackie, he "was happiest with his loyal subjects." Voss begins chatting with Dugald, telling him: "You were foolish to bring along that fine coat. Now, if you lose your life, you will lose your coat too." Voss laughs, and the old native laughs too because "no one had ever spoken to him like this." And then, "Dugald smiled. He was shy. But they were happy together." (V. 182-183) It soon becomes obvious that the only white member who is actually treating the "black" guides with dignity is Voss, and as the journey progresses Voss's empathy with the Indigenous guides becomes apparent to the white members of his expedition. By the time the expedition has its first sighting of an Indigenous settlement, there is no further doubt that Voss views them with respect, and that he eagerly wishes to make closer contact, but the local inhabitants avoid them.

> The strange natives looked at the white man, through the flies, and the whisks of grey leaves, with which they brushed them away. The explorer would have liked to talk to these individuals, to have shown them suitable kindness, and to have received their homage. But they disappeared. (184-185)

White endows the Aborigines with social and political agency, making them powerful actors in their own history. The Voss expedition is, in fact, often powerless when confronted with the more numerous Indigenous people it encounters. When cattle belonging to the expedition disappear, Dugald, who serves Voss loyally, comments: "Blackfeller no good this place," implying that cattle had been stolen by Aborigines living in that particular area. Voss himself concludes: "It is probable that blacks have driven off the cattle. There is nothing we can do for the present." (195) The other members of the expedition's members exhibit uninhibited prejudice towards the Indigenous people: Did you ever see such a filthy race?" asked Ralph Angus ... whose strength and looks prevented him from recognizing anything except in his own admirable image. (197)

Voss's efforts to assure the Aborigines of his sympathy and support face frequent challenges from his team of explorers, some of whom, on seeing the naked bodies of the Aboriginal women, allude to them lewdly:

> Turner, naturally, was provoked to immoderate laughter, and was shouting:
>
> "What will you bid for the molls, Mr Le Mesurier?"
>
> And when Le Mesurier was silent:
>
> "Or are they not to your taste?"
>
> Finally, he took the handle of the iron frying-pan, which he still had about him from the previous night, and presented it to one of the more impressive blacks.
>
> "You sell wife," he demanded. "I buy. But the pretty one. The one that has not been singed right off."
>
> Everyone was by this time repelled by Turner ... (198-199)

Voss warns: "Turner, your behaviour will always live down to what I would expect. You will please me by not molesting these people who are my guests." He then begins conducting his form of informal diplomacy. He approaches the Aborigine who had rejected Turner's offer, and holds out his hand: "Here is my hand in friendship." The "blackfellow" is reluctant at first, and then takes the hand "as if it had been some inanimate object of barter, and was turning it over, examining its grain, the pattern of veins, and, on its palm, the lines of fate. It was obvious he could not estimate its value." White writes that "each of the white men" in the expeditionary team "was transfixed by the strangeness of this ceremony," and that "it would seem that all human relationships hung in the balance, subject to fresh evaluation by Voss and the black." When the Aborigine "dropped his hand," Voss is disappointed, but then, offers flour to the natives in the hope of getting a response from them about the "stolen cattle." It is evident by now that both the Aborigines and the explorers consider Dugald and Jackie as persons who had left their own people to serve white explorers and are in fact collaborators with the whites Dugald raises the issue with the Indigenous people, but receives no answer.

It begins to be apparent shortly after that the explorers are losing their hegemonic authority over these collaborators as well and cannot count always on their willingness to serve them. The aging Dugald informs Voss that he wishes to return to his home, in Jildra, to die in a familiar place. Voss gives letters to Dugald to carry back to Boyle, who would forward them on to Laura. The Indigenous person carrying the letter is a trope for an accord, a bridge, and from the perspective of the white explorers, a desirable collaboration between their two worlds. On his way back to Jildra, Dugald arrives at a community of blacks living by a lake. In their company Dugald breaks open the seals of Voss's letters.

> These papers contained the thoughts of which the whites wished to be rid, explained the traveller, by inspiration: the sad thoughts, the bad, the thoughts that were too heavy, or in any way hurtful … the crowd began to menace and call.
>
> The old man folded the papers. With the solemnity of one who has interpreted a mystery, he tore them into little pieces.
>
> How they fluttered.
>
> The women were screaming, and escaping from the white man's bad thoughts.
>
> Some of the men were laughing.

Only Dugald was sad and still, as the pieces of paper fluttered round him and settled on the grass, like a mob of cockatoos. (213-214)

The destruction of the letters is a ritualised performance of collective resistance. The letter is first speared by a young warrior before being torn to bits by Dugald. They are united in opposing the arrival of white explorers and would-be settlers. They consider the letters to contain the "bad" and "sad thoughts" of which the whites had wished to be rid of. Here, the Indigenes are resisting the written tradition, which was alien to their culture of an oral tradition, of telling stories (Attwood and Magowan 2001, xiii).

It is apparent that Voss's soul-mate and love, Laura, would share his attitudes toward the Aborigines: she states that Australia is a country which the settlers "have been presumptuous enough to call ours," and that "a country does not develop through the prosperity of a few landowners and merchants, but out of the suffering of the humble." (233) There are moments of collaboration between the larger group and the Aborigines as when Jackie explains that his people laid the bodies of their dead on leafy platforms for their souls to ascend skyward, by joining together the palms of his hands and opening them up. This has a palpable effect on some members of the expedition, one of whom (Palfreyman) sees a white bird rising out of Jackie's hands. (237-238) A second moment of collaboration occurs when Voss asks Jackie to explain the meaning of the drawings on the walls of a cave that they have discovered. Jackie begins explaining, in his own language, which Voss does not understand. But Voss's response, *"Verfluchte Sprachen!"* implies his double dilemma: failure to understand the language and failure to understand the meaning of the drawings. Voss was so "doubly locked in language," and he described their language as "cursed" and "damned." (267) This episode carries great significance because, here, Voss fails to comprehend the written histories of the Aborigines, and the stories they contained. For their part, the latter were not contained within the language of the settler: they were beyond it, and did not need knowledge of a European language to understand the mind of the settler.

There is another collaborative episode when the expedition loses some of its cattle, and Jackie disappears. At this time, one member of the group complains that "these blacks are all alike" and are not to be "relied upon." But Voss expresses confidence in the boy, who returns later with the lost cattle. (279) Voss announces the principles underlying his diplomatic encounter with the Aborigines when the expedition comes upon a group of Indigenous people, one of whom is singing. Voss describes him as a "poet," and approaches the group:

> Voss rode across, sustained by the belief that he must communicate intuitively with these black subjects, and finally rule them with a sympathy that was above words. In his limpid state of mind, he had no doubt that the meaning of the song would be revealed, and provide the key to all further negotiations. (327)

Even though the Aborigines have, in this instance, run away from the presence of Voss, he generously comments: "It is curious that primitive man cannot sense the sympathy emanating from relaxed muscles and a loving heart."

Voss had hoped to use his Aboriginal guides as interpreters, to at least learn something of their language, their myths, their poems, their life and death rituals, so that he could "negotiate" with them. White depicts Voss as an informal diplomat who would conduct the diplomacy of peace and sympathy with the Aboriginal people of the land, yet, it is never clear what Voss wishes to negotiate. Perhaps, the terms of negotiation are best left unclear because once these terms are formally spelled out, they could only threaten the Aboriginal idyll with intimations of the onrush of colonial civilisation with its ideologies of modernisation. Within the parameters of the novel, Voss' Orientalist mission was sponsored by white colonialists who coveted the land of the Aborigines but the terms of Voss's own negotiations are spiritual: to spread peace and love, to act Christ-like if that was at all possible.

In the following days, columns of Aborigines begin accompanying the expedition, although keeping a distance and hiding themselves amongst the tall grass and trees. Voss, again, employs Jackie's local knowledge to ascertain what their intentions are, and why the group is singing. All that Jackie reveals is that they are "glad." Voss's initial diplomacy had succeeded admirably in its icebreaking phase: the offering of flour and the shaking of hands should have clarified the intentions of the white explorers. But Voss's aid diplomacy goes off the rails: the Aborigine's view his outstretched hand as an object of curiosity, and the white floury powder is understood by them as something to cover their faces and hair with. The standard tools of diplomacy and aid have little meaning within the self-sufficient Aboriginal ecosystem that has its own sources of food and sustenance.

Soon, both sides begin to fear each other. A group of Aborigines, surprised by the sudden arrival of the whites, runs away in fear, an emotion that now seizes the expedition members. These now undergo an escalation of mistrust that the expedition members, barring Voss, harbour towards the locals. When a compass is believed to have been "stolen" – again – many members denounce the locals as "dirty blacks" and one of them blames Voss for demonstrating sympathy and goodwill for them: "A lot will come of your hob-nobbin' with the blacks … [I] cannot dream dreams no longer. Do you not see our deluded skeletons, Mr Voss?" Voss retorts: "As my friend Judd is jealous of my attempts to establish understanding and sympathy between the native mind and ourselves, I will ask Mr Palfreyman to go amongst them, and investigate this matter of our stolen property. He, at least, is unprejudiced, and will act politic." (333) As Palfreyman, an ornithologist, advances towards the Aborigines, showing them his empty palms in a display of peace and faith, they appear "fascinated" by the white palms, and the "curiously lidded eyes of the intruder." Then violence erupts: an Aborigine flings a spear at Palfreyman which enters his side, another thrusts a short spear between his ribs. A member of the expedition fires at one of the assailants, killing him. Voss shouts: "I forbid any man to fire, to make matters worse by shooting at this people." (335-336)

The expedition is followed thereafter by two columns of Indigenous people. Jackie has now decided to assert his Aboriginal identity: "These blackfeller want Jackie. I go. Blackfeller no good among white men. This my people," and adding: "Jackie belong here." Voss requests him: "Tell your people we are necessary to one another. Blackfellow white man friend together," but Jackie is not convinced, and argues that white men had recently killed a "blackfeller." Efforts by Voss to offer the hand of friendship and forge accommodation between the two sides collapse. (357) The Aborigines begin killing the white man's horses, and eating their flesh raw, but they are not satisfied. The expedition ends with the boy Jackie stabbing Voss with his knife "between the windpipe and the muscular part of the throat." (356-357)

> The boy was stabbing, and sawing, and cutting, and breaking, with all of his increasing, but confused manhood, above all, breaking. He must break the terrible magic that bound him remorselessly, endlessly, to the white men.
>
> When Jackie had got the head off, he ran outside followed by the witnesses, and flung the thing at the feet of the elders, who had been clever enough to see to it that they should not do the deed themselves. (386)

The encounter is both catastrophic and liberating. The Voss expedition ends in disaster. By killing Voss, Jackie breaks the "terrible magic" that had yoked him to the white explorers. It is, then, a liberating moment for Jackie, who seeks and finds his true identity within his community of the Indigenous people, severing his connections with white explorers that represent the colonial world. Voss's explorations, nonetheless, would be remembered by the white comunity.They would "write about him in the history books," and he would be adored with "garlands of rarest newspaper prose." (431) The Orientalist-explorer would die a gruesome death, but his effort to map a continent for the benefit of white settlers would be always acknowledged in the colonial world. The love of his life, Laura, mythologises him in these words: "Voss did not die. He is still there, it is said, in the country, and always will be. His legend will be written down, eventually, by those who have been troubled by it." (439)

Many white men were, indeed, "troubled" by Voss's achievements. They never saw him as one their own: he stood apart from them, he did not share their desire to displace the Aborigines, and he irritated them with his constant admonitions to befriend them, to empathise with them, and win their trust. Voss was a dedicated practitioner of collaborative diplomacy, which was based on respect for the Aborigine. But the members of }exploration team preferred to attempt to stamp their authority over the Aborigines instead of engaging with them in patient diplomacy. They pulled in the opposite direction: constantly accusing Aborigines of theft, attempting to purchase their women for sexual purposes, denouncing them in racialised language. In the end, they caused irreparable harm to Voss's attempts at diplomacy, and antagonised the Aborigines.

The novel departs from the colonial representation that presents the Indigene as being innately inferior to the Europeans and unable to assert themselves against the powerful whites. In the end, it is the whites who are defeated by those who actually owned the land they had lived on for centuries prior to the arrival of the Europeans. This account of the black/white encounter registers the several nuances in the interplay of relationships: variations in the attitudes of the whites to the Aborigines and vice-versa. What is constructed for the reader here are what could have been an alternative version of Australian history; a variation of the colonialist encounter which offers more insight into possibilities that were simply obliterated by the majority of colonialist narratives

Works Cited

Attwood Bain, and Fiona Magowan. Ed. 2000. *Telling Stories: Indigenous History and Memory in Australia and New Zealan*d. Crows Nest, NSW: Allen & Unwin.

Beisner, Robert. 1975. *From the Old Diplomacy to the New, 1865-1900.* Arlington Heights IL: AHM Publishing.

Berman, Maureen and Joseph Johnson. 1977. "The Growing Role of Informal Diplomacy," *Unofficial Diplomats.* New York: Columbia University Press.

Beston, John. 2010. *Patrick White Within the Western Literary Tradition.* Sydney: Sydney University Press.

Blainey, Geoffrey. 1980. *A Land Half- Won.* Victoria: Macmillan.

Brennan, Paul and Christine Flynn 1989. Ed. *Patrick White Speaks.* Sydney: Primavera Press.

Chakravorty-Spivak, Gayatri. 1999. *A Critique of Postcolonial Reason: Toward a History of the Vanishing Present*. Calcutta: Seagull.
During, Simon. 1996. *Patrick White* Melbourne: Oxford University Press.
Evans, Raymond, Kay Saunders, and Kathryn Cronin.1988. *Race Relations in Colonial Queensland: A History of Exclusion, Exploitation and Extermination.* St. Lucia, Qld.: University of Queensland Press.
Ford, Lisa. 2010. *Settler Sovereignty: Jurisdiction and Indigenous People in North America and Australia, 1788-1836.* Harvard Historical Studies. Cambridge MA.: Harvard University Press.
Forslund, Catherine. 2001. *Anna Chennault: Informal Diplomacy and Asian Relations*. Wilmington, DE: Scholarly Resources.
McCredden, Lyn. 2010. "*Voss*: Earthed and Transformative Sacredness," *Remembering Patrick White: Contemporary Critical Essays*, ed. Elizabeth McMahon and Brigitta Olubas. New York - Amsterdam : Rodopi.
Reynolds, Henry. 1991. "Violence in Australian History," *Australian Violence: Contemporary Perspectives,* ed. Duncan Chappell et al. Canberra: Australian Institute of Criminology.
Sharp, Joanne. 2008. *Geographies of Postcolonialism.* London: Sage.
Stevens, Frank. 1981. *Black Australia*. Sydney: Aura.
vanden Driesen, Cynthia. 2009. *Writing the Nation: Patrick White and the Indigene*. Amsterdam - New York: Rodopi.
White, Patrick. 1957. *Voss.* New York: Penguin.

CHAPTER SEVENTEEN

WHITE'S TRIBE:
PATRICK WHITE'S REPRESENTATION
OF THE AUSTRALIAN ABORIGINE
IN *A FRINGE OF LEAVES*

JEANINE LEANE
AUSTRALIAN NATIONAL UNIVERSITY

This paper traces the construction of a nameless tribe of Aborigines in Patrick White's novel *A Fringe of Leaves* (1976) and asks the following questions: How are the representations constructed through language that perpetuate the civilized/savage binary and familiar British colonial tropes of savagery? And, is this text a 'reconciliation text' as some settler critics suggest (e.g. Brady 1977; vanden Driesen 2009) or does it 're-settle the settler' (Leane 2010, 93) who can undertake a journey beyond the colonial zone with Ellen, experience 'the tribe' mediated through Ellen's eyes and return to civilisation, enlightened by the Blacks. The aim of this paper is to provide a reading of this novel from an Aboriginal cultural stance in response to the questions posed above.

Patrick White in his post-Nobel Prize years carried a certain authority in his publicly expressed thoughts on the Australian (un) consciousness of his time and, arguably, his reputation as an insightful provocateur influences the way his authorial voice is analysed and interpreted. His status as an iconic Australian writer has also ensured that he has been the subject of a detailed biography (Marr 1991) and his works well reviewed and analysed; for example Beatson (1976), Brady, (1977) Bliss (1976), Heltay (1983), Ben-Bassat (1990), Collier (1992, 1999), Goldie (1993),

Schaffer (1995), During (1996), Giffin (1999), Concilo (1999) and vanden Driesen (2009). Aboriginal scholars, Lynette Russell (1998) and Larissa Behrendt (2000) critique the Eliza Fraser narrative in colonial discourse but the focus and purpose of this paper is to look specifically at the language of savagery and otherness in this novel.

In his seminal work, *Fear and Temptation: The Image of the Indigene in Canadian, Australian and New Zealand Literature* (1989) Terry Goldie establishes similar semiotic codes in Canadian, Australian and New Zealand white literatures for representing the Indigene. Goldie's discussion of the Indigene in Canadian, Australian and New Zealand literature is framed by Edward Said's (1978) notion of representation and Michael Foucault's (1972) notion of discourse. Goldie argued that images of the Indigene in white literatures may not be the reality of Indigenous peoples and cultures but they have become self-perpetuating representations. Over time, these images and texts produce not only impressions, but also, the reality of the Indigene they appear to describe: and a discourse emerges that is responsible for the production and continued reproduction of the Indigene as 'the Other.' The central concern of Goldie's argument is that these images of the Indigene are worth analysing for their ability to reflect back onto the white culture in which they have been produced.

The purpose of this discussion is to ask whether these representations of and discourses on 'the Aborigine' within *A Fringe of Leaves* disrupt or disturb the noble savage trope in Australian settler society in the later part of the twentieth century and, to argue that White's representations of 'the tribe' do not, in fact, disturb or disrupt familiar images of and discourses on the Aborigine as the 'Other' in the Australian settler imagination; these being identified essentially by the basic commodities of sex, violence, morality, mysticism and the prehistoric. Rather, it reinforces and reinstates familiar images and discourses through a reworking of familiar colonial tropes mentioned by Goldie.

A number of issues drive my interest here. One is the historical event to which White himself acknowledged it owes much, namely, the survival of the English woman Eliza Fraser who was rescued by Aborigines following the shipwreck of the *Sterling Castle* on the shores of what is now Fraser Island, Queensland in 1836. By constructing a fictional narrative containing some parallels to the Eliza Fraser story, White writes retrospectively almost a century and a half after the time in which these events occurred. This provides opportunities for considering the positioning of the Aboriginal subject in a narrative of the frontier written from the vantage point of historical distance. White makes use of an historical event that has been the subject of much documentation and creative development, and which continues to capture the Australian imagination. Not only did Eliza Fraser write her own accounts of her ordeal, there is some official reporting in archives that have been utilised to detail the historical record (Russell 1888).

There have also been a number of artistic and fictional representations over time that revisit, re-invent, or re-present the assumed facts of the event for artistic purposes. These include Sydney Nolan's series of paintings; films, most notably the 1976 film, *The Rollicking Adventures of Eliza Fraser*; artwork by Badtjala artist Fiona Foley called *Eliza's Rat Trap* (Healy 1997). More recently, analytical contributions by Aboriginal academics and others, including the descendants of the Aboriginal people who rescued Eliza Fraser have put forward various versions of events which have been passed down and augmented or contested the non-Aboriginal interpretation of the same events such as those by Russell (1888), Foley (1997), Behrendt (2000). In these ways, the story of Eliza Fraser, with its archive of documented, fabricated, and creative iterations provides rich grounds for rediscovering the blurred lines between actual events, what becomes established as historical fact, and what is regarded as fiction.

In this novel White explores psychic dislocation by narrating his protagonist's journey through a series of physical and social dislocations, each moving her closer to her most extreme experience of physical and mental dislocation - her encounter with Aboriginal society. Through the engagement between Ellen Roxburgh and the Aboriginal 'tribe,' he positions his readers to consider how immigrant 'settlement' in the Australian landscape requires reflection of more than their imported heritages but must also consider what might need to be re-viewed, discarded, or transformed when imposing themselves on the land of the now dispossessed original inhabitants. He suggests, in effect, that non-

Aboriginal Australia, as an immigrant society, is not just about adjustment to a physical relocation but requires a mental journey also to understand the relocation of the self in relation to place, which includes relations to the original inhabitants of this place.

White writes this from the context of the 1960s and 1970s when issues regarding the massacres of Aboriginal people, the theft of lands were beginning to be openly discussed in the wake of events such as the Freedom Rides of 1965, the Referendum of 1967 and the Tent Embassy of 1972. The social context that produced the narrative shapes White's use of 'the Aborigine' to explain the changing values and consciousness of non-Aboriginal society.

At the beginning of this journey into the Aboriginal world we witness Ellen's symbolic severance from white society at the hands of Aboriginal women. While the reader knows she is captive, when the women strip her naked "she [is] also finally unhooked ... and [with the removal of her last shift] she was entirely liberated." (244) This is an early unsettling of oppositions, in this case captivity and freedom, symbolising perhaps, the importance of location and standpoint to consciousness.

The concept of time also shifts to represent this severance. Aboriginal timelessness provides a distinct contrast to the progression, pace, organisation and structure that characterises the society that Ellen has left behind. Up to this point Ellen marks time very specifically in days, dates and years through the entries she makes in her journal. As readers, we are never sure of exactly how long Ellen spends with the tribe as days, weeks, months meld together. This disconnect with Western time is one of many severances that Ellen is forced to make with her past and her culture.

As an element of romantic/anthropological discourse, timelessness naturalises the concept of Aboriginal society as undeveloped and innocent, content to just 'be' as they always have been, rather than act in any purposeful way in response to change in their world. In this way, Ellen is severed from her own European world and gets to take a journey back to where time stands still and less developed humans live a more natural state devoid of the human-made trappings of 'civilisation.' But the tribe seemingly has nothing to learn from this interaction and there can be no parallel mental journey for people who lead unchanging lives.

White uses 'the Aborigine' as a literary subject to locate non-Aboriginal consciousness in a not so familiar terrain. His construction of the 'tribe of Aborigines' serves to illuminate a space of possibility, in this case, of the psychosocial transformation of a British woman immersed into Aboriginal land and society and disconnected from her own. White emphasised, in a letter to Peter Sculthorpe in 1974, that "… all other characters are only there for her [Ellen's] sake." (Marr 1994, 252) The representation of Aboriginal society is secondary to his purposes. They are, for him, a vehicle through which Ellen gains new awareness and knowledge of her own social origins, values and practices.

The representations of 'the tribe' are subject to the influence of a range of historical, contemporary, and popular or commonsense discourses and observations of Aboriginal people, including the anthropological, the romantic and the racist (Muecke 1992). For example, White declared in an interview with David Marr; 'I have read accounts of aboriginals (sic) in their *normal state* (emphasis mine) in the last century eating maggots and lice on one another's heads' (1994, 196). White did indeed include a grooming scene in the novel and since his Aboriginal 'tribe' has not yet been in contact with 'civilisation,' he draws romantic and anthropological discourses to represent them, 'essentially' savage, albeit sometimes noble.

David Marr (1994) Kay Schaffer (1995) and Cynthia vanden Driesen (2009) point out that in the course of his research, White met with Wilf Reeves, a descendant of the Badtjala people who rescued Eliza Fraser.Reeves advised him to be sceptical of non-Aboriginal versions of the event. White also knew that the Badtjala people's version had been handed down orally as well as recorded. vanden Driesen claims that White was not concerned with either side's version of historical events but rather constructed the predicament of his central protagonist for his own purposes. Nevertheless, not buying into either side is not to assume a position of neutrality when White's textual production is firmly embedded in the wider contests of the historical truth of the Eliza Fraser story.

And what are White's 'own purposes' that vanden Driesen refers to in relation to the central protagonist, Ellen?

I propose that White grappled with the problem of being Australian in the context of an imposed European heritage over a landscape which has provided the conditions that shaped the older culture of the original inhabitants who have been summarily dispossessed. White grapples with this aspect of being Australian in the twentieth century by drawing attention to and attempting to highlight the nature-society duality. As he grapples with his own position of being an immigrant Australian he poses the idea that Australia as a settler society is not just about physical adjustment and relocation, it requires a psychological journey to understand the relocation of self and the dispossession of the original inhabitants. The Aboriginal subject is positioned for the intellectual consumption of the non-Aboriginal reader in an attempt to create a sense of belonging in contemporary Australia. By taking readers back a century and a half and drawing stark contrasts between British and Australian physical and social landscapes, White extends the possibilities for non-Aboriginal Australians to consider, what vanden Driesen now interprets in the 21st century as "the possibilities of a myth of indigenisation for the erstwhile white invader." (2009, 35) She contends that like other creative writing by settler societies, White's imaginative reworking of the Eliza Fraser story works to "rewrite the nation" (2009, 35) by increasing the sense of belonging of those not Indigenous to this land. But what of those who are Indigenous to the land? Where does this position Aboriginal people in the rewritten, re-imagined nation?

The reader of the novel comes into contact with Aboriginal society via the gaze and thoughts of Ellen Roxburgh. The representations of Aboriginal society and characters are hers alone. The mental journey of Ellen, expressed via descriptions of the Aboriginal society and their treatment of her, her responses, adjustments, and her reflections on all she has experienced in her varied life, leads the reader to journey with her amongst 'the tribe', seeing, experiencing and learning from them as she does. This journey is an allegory that symbolises the mental journey non-Aboriginal Australians need to undertake to transform consciousness about their place and relations to the Australian environment, including its original inhabitants. On this journey, Ellen is detached from her social and psychological moorings and placed in a state of psychological and temporal suspension. The physical location, actions and demands of the 'savages' force her across the boundaries that distinguish her world from the Aboriginal world.

From this vantage point, she eventually comes to a consciousness of the savagery within her own society. It is through her relationships and shared experiences with members of 'the tribe' that she also recognises her shared humanity with Aboriginal society. The relativity of meanings to their own social and cultural contexts is revealed to highlight the assumptions that inform judgments of 'others' shaped by different contexts and sets of circumstances and social relations. Through Ellen, the author hints at cultural relativism – quite different social practices serving recognisable social functions. But it is the differences that are most pronounced as White writes of 'the tribe' in the discourse of the savage.

White's first task in taking readers on this journey into Aboriginal society is to draw the Aboriginal character through Ellen's eyes as a recognisable *bone fide* savage. Without this there is no contrast through which to force her reflections, prepare her to reconsider the assumptions on which her notions of what is civilised and savage are based, and to illuminate her consciousness of her own society. Aboriginal subjects in these ways are framed through familiar colonial discourses. In positioning Aboriginal characters and society in this manner, Patrick White moves within these available discourses. While not having first-hand knowledge of Aboriginal people and having determined not to be swayed by any historical re-telling of the Eliza Fraser story, White can only imagine his Aboriginal subjects by drawing on the historical, colonial, and anthropological archive for language, context and imagery for description.

For example the descriptors of Aboriginal characters are familiar colonial ones. Aboriginal subjects are unnamed. Individuals within 'the tribe' are distinguished from each other through physical characteristics, for example "the old woman with heavy jowls", "the beefier woman", or the "wrinkled old man" (236). The reader comes to know 'the tribe' through the narrator's repeated and largely negative descriptions such as "hostile" (238) "savages" (239) who are "starving and ignorant" (272), "all sinew, stench" (242), "runtish" (278), "hags" and "nubile girls" (243) who move around arbitrarily to escape their fleas (257), which set them "scratching themselves with the vigor of their similarly afflicted dogs" (262). Aboriginal actions are those of the uncivilised and brutal men who "lounged about the camp ... scratching themselves" or "gorging themselves" (247); "scornful blacks", "vindictive" enough to "thrust a firestick into her buttocks" (263). The children "pinch" and "jab with vicious sticks" (245). "Wretched" women "grovelled" (248), "slouched, grown slummocky ..." and "the monkey-women snatched" (243). They are "tormentors" (243) and "depressed", "plodders, or innately dejected souls" (278), inclined to "pinch or pull" (278). None of these characters speak for themselves. The men utter "gibberish" (238, 279), "emitted horrid shrieks" and "howls" (239). The women are prone to wailing (248, 249), they "glowered and cowered" (243) on hearing Ellen's voice. At night Ellen is surrounded by "grunts and cries of animal pleasure" (254).

Interspersed are glimpses of the noble male savage of romantic discourse who is described in clear contrast to degraded women to whom "occasional morsels were thrown ... in keeping with their humble station" (248). These men "with the solemnity of the superior sex ... did look superior" (250). Ellen, as narrated by the author, recognised them as "exultant in their mastery" (242), as "superior beings" of "physical splendour" and "solemnity" (247) who were "worthy of celebration" (248). Through this gaze "evening light coaxed nobler forms out of black innocent savages and introduced a visual design into what had been a dusty hugger-mugger camp." (247)

In the above descriptions the colonial black savage is contrasted with and measured in terms of distance from the civilised white European. The 'blacks' are rendered as Other to 'whites' in the broader descriptions of the activities, which in the eyes of Ellen and her narrator preoccupy them. In these ways, Aboriginal characters are positioned towards the more familiar 'animal-like' rather than the 'fully human' end of the savage-civilised continuum. The women's minds do not produce thoughts but "flitter on in search of further stimulus" (244) like Pavlov's dogs. Their capacity for human feeling and grief is brought into question as the animal instinct to feed takes over. The burial scene captures this: "At once their grief evaporated, except in the mother's case, who was prepared to keep up her snivels, but only a while, for they were returning to the fish feast." (261).

No colonial discourse is more representative of barbarity than cannibalism (see Dixon 2001). Certainly, it is the most powerful discourse at the author's disposal to establish a baseline of savagery against which both civilised behavior and the relative contingency of morality upon cultural and contextual circumstances is measured and wielded. White's use of cannibalism draws the clearest line of contrast between the civilised and the savage and deploys the most powerful trope of colonial literature.

In the many contrasts White constructs between civilised and savage society, and in her many transgressions, Ellen begins to apply the language of savagery to herself, describing her soul as ' dull and brutish' (262) and when eating vermin from the children's heads she 'reflected on the level of bestiality at which she had arrived' (276). However, nowhere does she transgress settler morality and engage in savagery more clearly than with her own act of cannibalism. As she flings away a thighbone (but, only after she had finished devouring it) Ellen attempts to separate "fear from amazement, disgust from a certain pity she felt for these starving and ignorant savages, her masters." (272) Detached from her social moorings, her movement into the world of savagery is clearly articulated and completed through her participation in it.

Ellen crosses the established civilised-savage divide. The conditions of mental dislocation that produced her transgression are highlighted, as she becomes a singular embodiment of both the Christian and savage- the settler. She blurs the boundaries as she attempts to rationalise her action as the partaking of "a sacrament" in Aboriginal society and elevates Aboriginal practices as "rites" (273). Ellen understands in her subsequent reflections that her eating of human flesh has been a spiritual experience that has represented an adjustment to her circumstances accompanied by deeper insight into herself. But where does this leave 'the savage'?

Scholars such as Schaffer (1995, 169) and vanden Driesen (2009) claim that White uses cannibalism as a vehicle to unsettle non-Aboriginal consciousness of what constitutes readers' notions of the savage and the civilised. vanden Driesen, for example, claims that "cannibalism in the Aboriginal world has a spiritual motivation that dictates the indigenes' (sic) practice" (2009, 97) and that the narrative by White shows quite clearly that cannibalism, which Europeans regard as the ultimate signifier of savagery, is sometimes practised by whites themselves and is in such circumstances bestial compared to the mystical purpose prompting Indigene behavior.

While Ellen and the reader can move on to 'resettle' a transformed consciousness of themselves and where they belong, the Aboriginal subject is left out in the symbolic wilderness, the savage in perpetuity. That is, to achieve his protagonist's transformation, White moves Ellen into the space of the primitive-savage-Aborigine rather than moving his Aboriginal subjects into the fuller humanity that colonial literature inscribes as the domain of the 'civilised' and white European. In this way, the language, discourse, and imagery of Aboriginal savagery is reinforced and re-circulated, even when re-framed by the discourse of cultural relativism. In such ways, the work offers different reasons for reader consideration for why 'the tribe' is savage, rather than disrupting the familiar settler images of the savage, primitive Aboriginal existence.

Literary texts by nationally and internationally acclaimed authors such as White are manifestations of 'cultural territories' in that they map the cultural terrain in which the author writes. This novel is the product of a new direction in urban consciousness of Aboriginal people and of a new consciousness on the part of non-Aboriginal people of themselves in relation to Australia's Aboriginal past. As a literary artist, White attempts to change the consciousness of his time but his narrative is fundamentally aligned with the more familiar colonial discourse about Aboriginal Australians. As Kay Schaffer argues, White's text is a

> new version of an old, increasingly vulnerable, 'white man's ... mythology' where the identity of Aborigines is absorbed and their concerns appropriated by a cultural elite in a quest to re-establish a

founding myth in the socio-political context of the 1970s (1995, 175).

For me, Patrick White's novel serves as a powerful reminder that to increase the sense of belonging of those not Indigenous to the land through writing and rewriting the nation the author assumes creative license to overwrite and 'other' the Aborigine in the cultural territory of the settler text.

Works Cited

Beatson. P. 1976. *The Eye in the Mandala.* London: Paul Elek.
Ben-Bassat. H. 1990. "To gather sparks: Kabbalistic and Hasidic elements in Patrick White's *Riders in the Chariot,*" *Literature and Theory: An international journal of Theory, Criticism and Culture* 4.3: 327-345.
Behrendt. L. 2000. "The Eliza Fraser Captivity Narrative: A Tale of the Frontier, Femininity & the Legitimization of Colonial Law," *The Saskatchewan Law Review* 65: 45-84.
Bliss. C. 1986. *Patrick White's Fiction: the Paradox of Fortunate Failure.* New York: St. Martin's.
Brady. V. 1977. "A Fringe of Leaves: Civilization by the Skin of Our Own Teeth," Southerly 37.2: 123-140.
Collier, G. 1992. *The Rocks and Sticks of Words, Style, Discourse and Narrative Structure in the Fiction of Patrick White.* New York - Amsterdam: Rodopi.
Concil, C. 1999. "The magic of language in the novels of Patrick White and David Malouf," *Coterminous Worlds: Magic realism and contemporary post-colonial literature in English,* ed. E. Linguanti, F. Casotti and C. Concilo New York - Amsterdam: Rodopi: 29-45.
During. S. 1996. *Patrick White* Oxford: Oxford University Press.
Foley. F. 1997. "A Blast from the Past," *Periphery* 31 (May): 165-168.
Foucault, M.1972. *The Archaelogy of Knowledge.* London: Tavistock.

Goldie, T. 1989. *Fear and Temptation: The Image of the Indigene in Canadian, Australian and New Zealand Literatures*. Montreal: McGill-Queen's University Press.

Leane. J. 2010. *The Whiteman's Aborigine*. PhD Thesis, University of Technology, Sydney. Unpublished.

Marr, D. Ed. 1994. *Patrick White Letters*. Chicago: University of Chicago Press.

Muecke, S. 1992. *Textual Spaces Aboriginality and Cultural Studies*. Kensington: University of New South Wales Press.

Russell. L. 1998. "Mere Trifles and Faint Representations: The Representations of Savage Life Offered Eliza Fraser," *Constructions of Colonialism: Perspectives on Eliza Fraser's Shipwreck,* ed. Ian McNiven, Lynette Russell and Kay Schaffer. London: Leicester University Press: 56-57.

Russell, H. 1989. [1888]. The *Genesis of Queensland.* Ed. Turner and Hendersen. Sydney: Vintage Books.

Said, E.1978. *Orientalism,* New York: Random House.

Schaffer, K.1995. *In the Wake of First Contact: The Eliza Fraser Stories.* Melbourne: Cambridge University Press.

vanden Driesen. C. 2009. *Writing the Nation: Patrick White and the Indigene*. New York - Amsterdam: Rodopi.

White, P.1976. *A Fringe of Leaves.* London: Jonathan Cape.

Chapter Eighteen

Patrick White's Children: Juvenile Portraits in *Happy Valley* and *The Hanging Garden*

Elizabeth Webby and Margaret Harris
University of Sydney

Although himself never a parent biologically, Patrick White has sketched a number of remarkable portraits of children and adolescents throughout his works – novels, plays and short stories. There is, for example, Joyleen, better known as Pippy Pogson, whose curiosity is one of the drivers of the action in *The Season at Sarsaparilla* (1963). Stories collected in *The Burnt Ones* (1964) give us both the persecuted namesake and the persecutors of "Being Kind to Titina" as well as the adolescents from "Down at the Dump" whose encounter there exudes so many significant possibilities, such as, an Australia without class barriers, as well as one with a recognised place for artists. The novels include numerous child characters, most memorably the artist-in-the-making, Hurtle Duffield who, at the beginning of *The Vivesector* (1970), is literally sold from one class to another. This essay, however, will concentrate on the juvenile portraits in White's first published novel, *Happy Valley* (1939) and the most recent addition to his oeuvre, *The Hanging Garden* (2012).

The centenary of White's birth in 2012 was marked not only by conferences, exhibitions and other events held to celebrate his life and writing, but by the re-publication of *Happy Valley* and publication of *The Hanging Garden*. During his lifetime White did not allow the first to be reprinted. Initially it was assumed because he regarded it as 'prentice work,' a novel where the influence of modernist writers like Joyce and Lawrence is very obvious. In his biography of White, however, David Marr revealed that the real reason was White's fear that the Yen family of Adaminaby, on whom he had based the Quongs in the novel, might sue for libel if it was republished in Australia. (Marr 1991, 546) The announcement that *Happy Valley* was finally to be republished, however, produced not a libel suit but a wonderful letter from Laurann Yen, granddaughter of Minnie and Frank: "None of the Yens of Adaminaby took much notice of Patrick White's *Happy Valley* until David Marr's biography," she wrote, concluding: "White starts to sound like White in *Happy Valley* …. The revenge of the Yens is that hardly anyone knows that it is a really good read." (Yen 2012, 8)

A much later work, *The Hanging Garden,* was begun in 1981, immediately after White had sent the typescript of his controversial autobiography *Flaws in the Glass* (1981) to his publishers. If it had been completed over the next year or two it, rather than the quirky *Memoirs of Many in One* (1986), would have been his twelfth novel. But it appears that, soon after commencing the novel, he became busy writing a new play, *Signal Driver*, commissioned by Jim Sharman for the 1982 Adelaide Festival. Then came the media furore over the harsh portraits of Sidney Nolan, Joan Sutherland and other notables in *Flaws in the Glass*. After writing the 45,000 words intended to form the first part of a three-part novel, White put the manuscript of *The Hanging Garden* aside. It remained among his papers at his death in 1990 and eventually became part of the White manuscripts acquired by the National Library of Australia from his literary executor Barbara Mobbs in 2006.

Having read the manuscript, David Marr declared it "a masterpiece in the making." (2008, 30) Discussion ensued about possible publication, and as part of our ARC-funded project, 'Patrick White in the Twentieth Century', we (Margaret Harris and I) prepared a transcript for Barbara Mobbs to read. She took the decision to publish: "I'm extremely nervous of posthumous publishing, which I usually don't admire. But this is up to a very high standard and even though it is only part one, it is complete in itself … I have no doubt it deserves to see the light of day." (Marr 2012, 224)

Happy Valley and *The Hanging Garden* therefore come at the beginning and the end of a chronological list of White's novels. There are obvious differences between them and not just because the later book was left unfinished and the work of a much more mature writer. *Happy Valley*, unlike most of White's later novels, is strongly focussed on one particular place, the small town of the title and its surrounding countryside, in the Snowy Mountains of New South Wales White had worked in this region, as a jackeroo, early in the 1930s. It also covers a fairly restricted time-span of one year, allowing for some set-piece descriptions of the changing seasons as well as of the highlight of the town's year, the annual races and ball.

Within these limits, however, we are introduced to a wide range of characters who interact with each other in complicated ways, mostly involving various aspects of love or desire. While White's later novels also include a large range of characters, their focus is usually on one or two central figures in particular. This is not the case in *Happy Valley*, where White shifts between the consciousness of eight main characters, two of them children. Significantly, the novel begins with the birth of a dead baby, suggesting, in the words of the epigraph from Mahatma Gandhi, the impossibility of doing away "with the law of suffering, which is the one indispensable condition of our being." It ends with a number of other deaths, both literal and symbolic, when the discovery of Ernest Moriarty's dead body thwarts Oliver Halliday's plans for escaping from Happy Valley with Alys Brown and ends any chance of a happy future for the lovers. Besides the Moriartys and Oliver and Alys, the two other main adult characters are Sidney Furlow, daughter of a local station owner, and Clem Hagan, her father's overseer. These two marry, but there is little sense of a happy future for them, since Clem too has, like Oliver earlier, been trapped into marriage.

In addition, we are also privy to the thoughts and feelings of two juvenile figures, Rodney Halliday and Margaret Quong. A chapter outline for *Happy Valley*, included in one of White's literary notebooks now in the National Library of Australia, shows the careful way in which he introduces his eight main characters in the first eight chapters of the novel. Chapter 6, where we meet the children, as well as their schoolteacher Moriarty, is summarised as

"The persecution of Rodney and Margaret by the other children. They walk home together." (White Notebook p.2: 142) Rodney, who shares with the younger White a love of reading, a paleness of skin colour and a tendency to illness, and also has a fat, younger sibling, is a recent arrival in the town, where his father is the doctor. Margaret, though a local, is set apart from her peers by being part Chinese. In a scene where White obviously draws on his own feelings of difference as a child, we are introduced to Rodney in the school playground, standing with some other boys "in a little aimless group behind the urinal." (HV. 54) Although Rodney knows what is going to happen to him he seems unable to stay away, and so has to endure some classic schoolyard bullying and violence. White skilfully captures the words and actions of the local boys, though his main interest is in the reactions of the victim, whose feelings about life as being a nasty business that must be endured also seems to have been shared by White as a child:

> It was over, Rodney Halliday said. He would go inside and do arithmetic. But it was over for the day. He tried to brush the mud from his coat. He was aching. He was bleeding. He was also free. And he would go home for lunch and read that book on Columbus till it was time for afternoon school. There was no break in the afternoon. He used to run home as fast as he could. Sometimes they chased him and threw stones. But he could really run very fast. And now there was a feeling of exhaustion and of triumph … (57).

Bored with his arithmetic problems, Rodney thinks that he would prefer to spend the break with Margaret Quong but she is thirteen to his nine, and, of course, a girl. When the lunch bell sounds, the focus shifts to Margaret and we see that gender is not the only boundary being rigidly policed by the school children. As they walk home, Margaret asks one of the other girls if she would come to her house in the evening, but her invitation is met with a refusal followed by teasing. Again White provides a sensitive portrait of a child reacting to discrimination and persecution with an accepting stoicism:

> Margaret walked on quickly bending her head. She did not listen. She tried to avoid unpleasantness. She did not ask for reasons,

because reasons were unpleasant, and she knew already, vaguely underneath, that it was Father that made Emily giggle and compress her lips. (62-3)

Like many of the fathers in White's work, Margaret's has a roving eye, and she, like Rodney, is the child of an unhappy marriage. Her mother 'had been a housemaid at Government House' and feels she has been trapped into marrying beneath her (63). In the Halliday household, in contrast, it is Oliver who feels he has been trapped into marrying the older Hilda when he was just 24, obliging him to give up his earlier dreams of becoming a writer (19).

When Rodney has run far enough to feel safe, he stops to watch "a bull serving a cow," (64) no doubt also an experience shared by the young White, and is ashamed of his interest when he sees Margaret coming towards him. She is trying to hide her tears and not knowing what else to do, Rodney offers her a shell he has in his pocket. As always in White's work, the natural world can provide some solace for the torments of the human one. In return, she invites him to come to her house to look at some new pups.

Margaret's strongest relationships, however, are not with Rodney but with her aunt Amy, who runs the local store, and her music teacher, Alys Browne. Mary appears to accept her inevitable future as one of White's spinsters: "I shall help Aunt Amy, two old maids, because that is what I shall become." (95) Margaret also represents White's first attempt at sketching same-sex attraction, through her crush on Alys but Alys is preoccupied with Oliver Halliday: "It is beautiful, felt Margaret Quong, she is beautiful, if only my hair was not quite so straight. I am nothing at all, sighed Alys Browne, he made me feel I am nothing at all." (99) When Oliver arrives to visit, the lesson is abandoned, and Margaret once again feels rejected. By Chapter 12, to quote White's outline again, we discover "Margaret's growing jealousy of Oliver." While Alys does feel some responsibility for Margaret's obvious unhappiness, her attention is totally on Oliver: "she was fond of Margaret who could not see that this was different, when he came to the house and she played him Schumann, as she and Margaret played, only the whole tempo was different then." (135)

Margaret's problems multiply in Chapter 16, a *tour de force* set in the schoolroom during a hot afternoon. As the children drone through a chapter on English history, typical of Australian school lessons at the time, we are privy to Rodney's thoughts about the future, to Margaret's unhappiness over the affair between Alys and Oliver, to Ernest Moriarty's worries about the relationship between his wife Vic and Clem Hagan. When Moriarty falls asleep the children begin throwing oranges at each other, with Rodney scoring a hit onto the face of his main persecutor. But it is Margaret who suffers when Moriarty wakes up and takes out his frustrations on her with a ruler. (175) While Margaret's mother wants to complain to the school authorities, Amy Quong plans her own revenge: "'what will it do, she said, 'writing, or telling the Inspector, not very much, no, Ethel, we'll see, we'll wait a little,' she said." (189)

As rumours begin to circulate around the small community about both Alys and Oliver and Clem and Vic, Amy sees a chance to get even with Moriarty: "she seized on the significance of adultery and Hagan and Moriarty's wife with a kind of inner exultation" (205), and sends him an anonymous letter. This in turn leads to Moriarty's murder of Vic and his own death which, as mentioned earlier, results in the end of the planned escape by Alys and Oliver, as well as Sidney's marriage to Clem.

Although Rodney had earlier thought that he and Margaret might eventually marry, the fact that he and his family are leaving Happy Valley now fills his mind at the expense of both his friendship with Margaret and his earlier fatalism:

> Rodney Halliday's preoccupation with the idea of death was no more than spasmodic because – well, they were going away. This was a release from the immanent shadow on the wall, the group behind the urinal, all those fears that Happy Valley implied. These would not exist in the vague but soothing state the future, somewhere behind the hills, to which the telephone wires were mentally attached. (308)

When he goes to say goodbye to Margaret he finds that she has also changed, displaying a new maturity: "I like Rodney, but really what can you say, Rodney is very young. She had all the composure of one who had just put up her hair, only she had no hair to put up."

(309). She has moved out of home to live at the store with Amy and knows she will soon leave school for good. She has also decided not to have any more music lessons with Alys. As the Hallidays drive away in the final chapter they pass the Quongs standing on the store verandah: "Sometimes you thought that the Quongs were exotic, foreign to Happy Valley, but not as they stood outside the store, the first and last evidence of life." (326)

Life, at least as perceived by Patrick White in the late 1930s, aware of being set apart by his sexuality as well as his vocation, but not yet having found success as a writer or his life partner, was something to be endured. Celibacy seemed the only sure way to avoid misery and violence. By the time he came to write *The Hanging Garden*, he had won the Nobel Prize for Literature and been involved in a tumultuous but always stabilising relationship with Manoly Lascaris for forty years. Some thirty years earlier he had also come to believe in something other than the material world, to see life as more than the stoic endurance represented as essential in *Happy Valley*. Although now decades away from his own unhappy childhood, he was still able to present the thoughts and feelings of two displaced adolescents with sensitivity and insight. Of course, he had recently been revisiting that childhood, in writing *Flaws in the Glass* which, interestingly, begins with White as a fourteen-year-old boy in a house in Sussex, which "meant solitude in which wounds were healed, until country voices reminded me I was a foreigner." (White 1981, 1) As a note on the manuscript reveals, the two protagonists of *The Hanging Garden* are fourteen by the time their story ends. Like White at the same age, they find themselves in a foreign country, where wounds inflicted by adults and other children can be healed through solitude and nature.

The Hanging Garden lacks the more complicated plotting of *Happy Valley*, centering on a Greek girl and an English boy, who both end up in Sydney during World War 2. Gilbert Horsfall's mother is dead, his father is serving in India, so he has been evacuated from London to Sydney where he is staying with Mrs Bulpit, the widow of another English soldier. Also sharing the house on the edge of Sydney Harbour is Eirene Sklavos, evacuated from Greece, where she had been born to a Greek father, now dead, and an Australian mother. Like Rodney and Margaret, as well as the young White, the children are outsiders, though not so obviously the subject of persecution by their peers. Gil, as he soon becomes known, does have to endure one session of playground violence but unlike Rodney Halliday is prepared to stand up for himself:

> He talked like a girl, the oldest Lockhart jeered. He hit out at the Lockhart face, which began to jigger and blink as if standing on a fixed spring. Then the lot of them went into action. They rubbed his face in the asphalt where the tree roots had lifted it up. (HV 17)

Although Eirene's name is also soon Australianised to Irene or Reenie, she is not as adept as Gilbert at adapting to Australian ways of speaking and behaving. Like Margaret Quong, in pre-multicultural Australia she is stamped as foreign by her appearance and is never allowed to forget that she is Greek. At her first school, she is befriended by Viva Jenkins, a girl without any other friends, though someone still prepared to assert her superiority when two other girls ask Eirene if she is Jewish:

> 'Piss off, Eva – Lily, she's not,' Viva hisses through a spray of chocolate.Eva and Lily are not put out. As they walk away they are wreathed in disbelieving smiles and pity for one who is Viva Jenkins' friend.'Bloody reffoes!' Viva grumbles. (100)

White's ability to recreate juvenile embarrassments and crudities, as well as the attitudes of the time, is also well demonstrated in the way he traces the slow development of a friendship between Eirene and Gilbert. Initially, both are resentful and fearful, seeing the other as an unwelcome intruder on the solitude they have found in Mrs Bulpit's overgrown garden, much as White remembers feeling about anyone, "even cherished friends," who wanted to share "surroundings associated with my own private mysteries" (White 1981, 16). But the shared loneliness of their situation soon leads to moments of connection in laughter and later a shared bed. Eventually the two homeless children construct a cubby, a house of their own, built of odds and ends, high up in a Moreton Bay fig tree. For Eirene and Gilbert, as for the young White, nature, as represented by this garden on the edge of the bay, is a place where they can escape from the demands of adults, from loneliness and unhappiness. But their idyll is short-lived; Mrs Bulpit dies and they are separated. Eirene is sent to live with her aunt and cousins, the Lockharts; Gilbert to live with another guardian at Vaucluse. After the move the focus is very much on Eirene, with Gilbert appearing only via a letter he sends her that emphasises their common link as 'reffoes' (182), and a later report by a school friend who finds him very attractive. (203-4)

Apart from the letter, there is little to tell us exactly what Gilbert feels for Eirene. White stresses his material hungers, initially for food, later for sex, rather than his spiritual ones, though there are hints that there is more to Gil than the masculine persona that, like Eddie Twyborn, he has had to adopt to survive in Australia. He is, in particular, frustrated by Eirene's unwillingness or inability to explain the meaning of the *pneuma*, something she knows but is unable to put into words. Towards the end of the story, she wonders:

> Transcendence is something I am never sure about in Australia. It is a word I keep looking up in the dictionary while knowing about it from experience almost in my cradle, anyway from stubbing my toes on Greek stones, from my face whipped by pine branches, from the smell of drying wax candles in old mouldy hill-side chapels. (197)

Certainly, in *Happy Valley*, there is nothing in the way of transcendence, with even the music proving only a brief respite from the material and human realities and the love shared by Oliver and Alys who remains the least convincing of all the characters. In *The Hanging Garden*, Eirene, thanks to her Greek background and especially her time with Great Aunt Cleone reading Shakespeare, Racine and Goethe and discussing religion (92-3), is aware that transcendence is possible. She begins to keep a diary and it seems from several passing hints that she is a writer in the making. Like the young White, Eirene is no innocent, however, having been aware of sexual desire and its effects on behaviour from a young age through her mother's lovers and her reading. Yet, Eirene does believe in love, even though she has known little of it in her life so far. She and a school friend, the wealthy Trish Fermor-Jones, discuss their interests: Trish, like her father – and it is implied, most

Australians – is interested in 'money and success.' But when she throws the question back at Eirene:

> I feel my black skin turning dark red as she continues looking at me and expecting a definite answer.
>
> She caught me out well and truly. I didn't know what to answer but did. I was so nervous I let off a bomb equal to hers. 'Well' I said '*love* I think is what I'm most interested in.' Trish shrieked 'that's not very ambitious Ireen you can have it any night of the week.' 'That's different' I said 'surely that's sex isn't it?' I could have killed myself. (196)

The final chapter of *Flaws in the Glass*, entitled "What is Left?," begins: "Memories – friendship – love, however thin its ice – food, if teeth allow – sleep – the dark … Would it have been any different had I begotten actual children? I doubt it. I'd have been a rotten irritable parent." (251) A little later, like Eirene, White declares his belief in love, distinguishing between it and sexual desire: "When I say love redeems I mean the love shared with an individual, not necessarily sexual, seductive though sexuality may be." (252) Since *The Hanging Garden* was never finished, we will never know where the love Eirene feels for Gilbert was to lead or whether it was to be reciprocated. We also do not know whether she, unlike Oliver Halliday, was to succeed as a writer. We only know that White originally planned to end the novel in 1981 when Eirene and Gilbert would have been fifty. While this incompleteness is frustrating in terms of the narrative, Eirene, Gilbert and all their peers, the last of White's imagined children, are as fully realised as any of his earlier juvenile portraits.

As the last chapter on *Flaws in the Glass* goes on to show, his insights into the way young people feel, think, talk and behave, were not just based on memories of his own childhood. They seem to derive also from his own continuing observations and knowledge of children. For instance, after recalling a fruitless attempt at speaking with a local 'young god' of a teenage boy, he declares that the 'smaller children are still a joy' and recounts conversations with three of them, all girls. One, for example, "is standing in the thin shade of the mulberry tree, naked except for her long pale hair and her briefs – and the shade and her ruthless innocence. Sara R. is a born back-fence gossip, a gift for any novelist, perhaps a novelist herself." (White 1981,25)

Works Cited

Marr, David. 1991. *Patrick White A Life*. Sydney: Random House.
—. 2008. "Patrick White: The Final Chapter." *The Monthly*, April: 28-42.
—. 2012. "A Note on *The Hanging Garden.*" in *The Hanging Garden* Sydney: Random House: 217-224.
White, Patrick. c.1935. 'Notebook 2', NLA MS9982, box 4, folder 2.
—. 1939. *Happy Valley*. London: George G Harrap & Co.
—. 1981. *Flaws in the Glass*. London: Jonathan Cape.
—. 2012. *The Hanging Garden*. Sydney: Random House.
Yen, Lauran. 2012. Letter to the Editor, *Sydney Morning Herald.* 30 May.

Note

Research for this essay has been carried out with the support of an Australian Research Council Discovery Grant to Margaret Harris and Elizabeth Webby for the project "Patrick White in the Twenty-first Century." They thank Barbara Mobbs, literary agent for Patrick White's estate, for permission to quote unpublished material.

Chapter Nineteen

The Hanging Garden

Alastair Niven
Harris Manchester College, Oxford

Sanditon by Jane Austen, *The Mystery of Edwin Drood* by Charles Dickens, *Arctic Summer* by E.M.Forster, *The Good Soldier Švejk* by Jaroslav Hašek, *The Ivory Tower* by Henry James, *Mr Noon* by D.H.Lawrence, *Billy Budd, Sailor* by Herman Melville, *Titus Awakes* by Mervyn Peake, *The Weir* of Hermiston by R.L.Stevenson, and *The Pale King* by David Foster Wallace are all examples of uncompleted novels. They probably have little in common except to reveal tantalising glimpses of the might-have-been. Because their author's intentions were never made clear, their incompleteness seems to act less as a spur to the critic's imagination rather than as a source of frustration. These books are rarely scrutinised with the rigour that is applied to finished fiction by the same writers, though each suggests new, though necessarily opaque, twists and turns in their author's literary odyssey. Patrick White's *The Hanging Garden* joined their number in 1992 when it was first published eight years after the writer's death.

The story of the book's genesis and near still-birth is well documented. White began the novel on 27th January 1981, within hours of despatching his autobiography, *Flaws in the Glass,* to his London publishers. Though not in good health, he went hammer and tongs at the new novel throughout February of that year. It is reasonable to suppose that the confessional passion which impelled him to write about his own life in his Autobiography carried over into his new fiction. He made excellent progress and appears to have been happy with what he was producing. However, the theatre director Jim Sharman was keen to extract a new play from him for the Adelaide Festival of that year. "With all this, the novel I had begun is hanging fire, but I shall come back to it as soon as I can; it is all in my head." (Marr 2012, 220)

Correspondence with his translator Jean Lambert and his publishers at Cape, Graham Greene and Tom Maschler, show that he was intermittently working on the book until at least August of the same year, despite "this dreadful old age business, and one's dread of blindness and senility." He may have intended to complete it, or, as he had done with other stories, re-cast it into a different entity. There is no proof of his working to accomplish either end, but this does not mean it did not happen. We cannot be certain whether the unfinished novel discovered in his desk at his death in 1990 was the same script he appeared to have laid aside nine years earlier. Although White kept a journal, he did not record every nuance of his writing life, particularly in his last years. Equally, despite small indicators that he planned a future for the book, there is the possibility that on re-reading what he had already written, White felt that he had said enough, that the novel, by the very fact of being left dangling, was in fact finished. Such a sophisticated writer did not require that his last novel must have formal closure. He may conceivably have come to see that what he at first intended to be a much bigger novel worked well at its present length.

Patrick White conceived *The Hanging Garden* in three parts. *The Aunt's Story* has the same structure. Many of his novels have partite divisions. The relic we have of his last novel amounts to approximately fifty thousand words, most likely a completed Part One and an extension into Part Two. The surviving work is, however, so finely tuned that it reads as a virtually finished work in itself. We are bound to speculate about the fate White may have planned for his main characters in the unwritten sections, with the scribbled note regarding their futures on the last page of the manuscript "14 in 1945, 50 in 1981" – seeming to indicate that his young teenagers at the end of the Second World War will reach the era in which White was writing about them. But we cannot be sure. What we can confidently assert is that White, though he was in a state of physical decline at the time he wrote it, and fending off repeated calls on his time from charitable and literary causes, was still at his best in the writing of this novel. It is an achieved, if sadly not a fully achieved, work of art, and not simply an embarrassing *coda* to a great career.

From the sixteenth-century first telling of the "Babes in the Wood" story, via Jacques-Henri Bernardin de Siant-Pierre's *Paul et Virginie* to Ian McEwan's *The Cement Garden*, (1978) fiction has made the abandoned child an archetype. Abandonment comes in many forms, sometimes, as in *The Hanging Garden*, organised and ostensibly carried out in the name of compassion and common sense. As John Boswell puts it, in his study of child abandonment in medieval and Renaissance Europe, 'abandonment' refers to the voluntary relinquishing of control over children by their natural parents or guardians, whether by leaving them somewhere, selling them, or legally consigning authority to some other person or institution," (Boswell 1988, 24) White's depiction of abandonment is the third kind, legal, respectable and well meant, but emotionally disconnected from the subject, who is the victim of a kind of rehearsed abuse. Boswell glosses his definition further thus: "This is a modern concept, both more and less precise than the rubrics employed in ancient and medieval documents, which usually referred to specific modes of abandonment rather than the general phenomenon." (Boswell 1988, 24)

In the case of Eirene Sklavos and Gilbert Horsfall, the children whose story is told in *The Hanging Garden*, the decision to send them away from war-torn Europe for their own safety appears to be sensible, but there is no evidence that the psychological condition of either child had been examined, let alone empathised with, before they were plucked from their familiar surroundings and sent to what for both of them is literally 'Down Under', an Australian Hades. If pushed to explain it, the decision makers would no doubt point out that between the two children there are only two parents still alive. Gilbert's mother has been killed by a bomb in the London blitz, while his father is somewhere in India. Eirene's father has been executed in Greece for murky political reasons which are as obscure to us as they are to the child. The children we first encounter in the novel are, traumatised as much by the bewilderment of their arrival in Australia as by the violence of their parental losses in Europe.

On Eirene, the adults' verdict is that "You'll find her a quiet, reasonable child." It made the reasonable child feel grave, important, while remaining unconvinced. (3) Of Gilbert; the verdict is: "What he wanted he didn't know. To be left alone, to be himself." (4) Lack of conviction, loss of knowledge, these are the realities of the children's self-concepts, plucked as they have been from normality into a world that has not been explained to them. They are sent to it for protection, but in the process the emotional carapaces that keep our human psyches together have been stripped from them. They have lost the familiarity of their parents, their homes, their friends, their countries and their climates. White was probably not thinking of the Stolen Generations of Aboriginal children who, with the connivance of Government and Church, were snatched from their parents and sent elsewhere in Australia for education and upbringing, or the 130,000 white British children forced by authority to be transported from the United Kingdom to Australia between the 1930s and 1960s. This novel can hardly be read, however, in ignorance of these historic horrors.

From the outset the two children are both under the control of adults yet also strangely undirected by them: "'I'm sure she won't give you any trouble,' (Mamma was saying in the saloni)." (5) – the first of many occasions in the novel when the oddity of presentation, in this case the brackets, raises the question of whether White intended a stylistic conceit or simply left an *ur* version of the text uncorrected. "'Oh dear no,' replies her interlocutor, 'I can see she is quite the grown-up little lady.'" Thus is the child Eirene defined and labelled, though all too inadequately, as we go on to discover. It is the same for Gilbert: "'Most Australian kiddies love these biscuits, and I expect you will too Gilbert.'" (6)

The children are intended to fit into a pre-ordained order of polite and conventional behaviour. But what exactly is polite for a little girl whose father has been judicially murdered and whose surviving parent is packing her off from Greece to an English-speaking extremity on the other end of the planet? What is conventional for a child whose mother and best friend have been blown apart and who is transported from bombed London via the United States to Australia, two cultures cocking a snook at the old country whilst at the same time preserving in aspic some of its most constraining manners? Some of the Americans say of him, when Gilbert passes through their country: "'Too many privileged British children, arrogant little bastards.'" (7) On arrival in Sydney, however, it is obvious that the boy is expected to conform: "'We mustn't forget our grammar, Gilbert.'" (8)

The Hanging Garden is a study in child development. The steady progress of growing up in secure surroundings is shattered by war and by adult emotional brutality, which often shows itself in the most casual and thoughtless ways. There are few things more personal than one's name. Children often play around with shortenings of their given name, or invent new ones, but they are not happy to have adaptations foisted on them by grown-ups believing they are doing the best to help them assimilate. Thus Eirene is renamed Irene when she reaches Australia as though a cleansing soap was being applied to remove the stain of her Greek ancestry. Gilbert is usually Gil, a more 'matey' soubriquet which somehow diminishes his private dignity.

What children most covet, apart from the parental love which is denied these two, is a space of their own. Eirene and Gilbert have to create this for themselves in the hanging garden, but they live constantly with the risk of it being invaded or taken away. When Gilbert first meets the olive complexioned Eirene, "Her colour worried him less than her trespass on his territory."

> As he dawdled up the path on the evening of this intruder's arrival, it was the threat of his innermost life which made him go slower still, not her foreignness, her Greekness, her blackness, but the fact that she might skip down this same path staking a claim to this or that, the sea wall with the writing on it, the little figs (which weren't figs at all) fallen from the dark old trees (the fig things were his to crush if he wanted and did crush hurtfully) any part of the garden which rejected even the midday light, she would come ferreting out the smells which he knew by heart in the undergrowth, laying claim for sure to the broken statue lying with her legs apart in fern, her tits palpitating with what looked like cut-outs of yellow rubber, her head gone, he had never found it. (9)

White's rhythms perfectly capture the thought stream of a child walking up a path in a territory he has defined as his own, but which is now threatened by a newcomer. This sense of threatened space is a recurring motif. As Eirene lies awake, for example, her reverie is interrupted by the nearby presence of her guardian Mrs Bulpit:

> The room she has got ready for you has started to become yours, not from any effort on your part, but simply by your being there. This could be something to remember, to use as a consolation for being anywhere at all ... The blue light of dawn starts to flow in through the crack in the curtain clean water shadows lapping over this stagnant swamp where you are lyin ... Bulpit snores are sighing sucking ebbing and returning. (10)

Mattering far more to a child than a sense of identification with a city or a country is a sense of belonging to a small known space which he or she can call their own. As Eirene later reflects,

> 'What happiness is, I can't find out. Silences? Being left alone? That can become loneliness. Nearest with Gil in the arms of a great tree, in the garden which hangs above the water in Cameron Street.' (11)

The children feel ownership of the hanging garden in which they spend much of their time. We the readers, however, are constantly reminded that private spaces are only part of a wider world. The war rumbles on in the distance, while on the margins of the conflict Sydney has its own pressures. *The Hanging Garden* has its place in that corpus of White's work which examines Australia's emergence as a nation and a distinctive culture, rooted in the cross fertilisation of ethnic and regional identities. There is an almost comedic recognition that, even while attending school, in order to become fully accepted in Australia, Eirene and Gilbert have to lose as much education as they gain. Eirene's interview with the head teacher Mr Harbord pinpoints this. The girl is asked what she was taught 'over in Greece'. (12) Eirene replies that she was taught in English and learned about kings and queens, whilst being introduced to the works of Shakespeare, Racine and Goethe. "'What you'd call a practical start in life,'" is her aunt's sarcastic observation, through teeth "grown brown and jagged again behind the cracks in her purple lips." (13) It is a philistine environment, seldom beautified or generous, but with its own stern propriety. Eirene feels her English growing worse as the interview proceeds. Her introduction to the school achieves precisely the opposite of what education should be about, as she endures a closing of options and a narrowing of experience.

Eirene's had been a Marxist household back in Greece, her father presumably executed as much for his political leanings as for his role as a partisan. Gilbert, by contrast, comes from a white middle-class of military pedigree and a Kensington provenance. What they now become part of is the classically prim, unself-reflective, socially narrow Australia of white middle class British origin. "'Thank God for Australia,'" says Mr Ballard, the clergyman who is charged with his wife to escort Gilbert and seven other boys through the United States to their refuge in Sydney. "'At least it is ours, Emily – home soil. They speak the same language.'" (14)

Food looms large in the rituals of Gilbert's and Eirene's new lives. They are constantly picked up for wrong usages of English or for minor breaches of social etiquette. They constantly seem to be awaiting instructions from elders who have no interest in their inner lives or their imaginative development. They muse as to what the grown-ups really want of them and whether they really care. The answer is that the adults seek to make the children Australian clones of themselves.

The history they learn is a history of discovery and colonisation, not interference and imposition. Yet as outsiders newly arrived they are also exotic, creatures both to be homogenised and treated as rarities. They have various role models they could emulate, if inwardly they were not working out strategies just to be themselves. Miss Hammersley, for example, the principal of Ambleside school, has managed to preserve an air of 'Pom' superiority, showing that even the most assured Australian Anglo-Saxon can be made to feel a little bit cowed by the real deal from Home. There are Eirene's judgemental relatives, the Lockharts, and Mrs Bulpit, who smokes and drinks through her responsibilities as chief carer of the children.

No wonder Eirene and Gilbert fall back on themselves and their hanging garden.

The garden is a primeval place of escape, somewhere to observe the teeming natural world, with its multifarious insect life and its rich foliage. The garden is so different from the cold order of life in the house, with its set meal times and stiff proprieties. The very title of the novel is an echo of the alternative civilisation of Babylon. This is the secret garden of Frances Hodgson Burnett, the mythic garden of Eden, an Arden in which disputes can be sorted and love inspired. It is also the 'little patch of land' over which wars are fought, a threat to stability as well as a consolation for loneliness.

> Soon there will be the garden alone. If only you could take the form of this red thread of a centipede or beetle that might have crawled out of the dregs of an inkwell to claw and scratch and burrow … You could no longer want either house or garden for your own. Only to burrow. Only this other enemy would come, and crush the beetle out of you.
>
> Crush you as a girl too, if you did not resist. … The gate squeals – it is Gilbert Horsfall, socks around his ankles, the battered case with very little joggling round inside it, returning to dispute your ownership? (15)

Patrick White had a great understanding of spaces that lie on the edge, or even beyond, human cultivation. In one of his earliest poems, 'Requiem', written while he was still at school, he evokes the privacy and sense of escape that a secret place can engender:

> I built me a garden small
> Wherein to hide myself,
> And round it built a hedge so tall
> That only birds could spy me. (Qtd. Marr 1991, 85)

The wilderness in which Stan Parker lives before his marriage in *The Tree of Man*, 'Voss's sufferings in the desert, the garden of Xanadu in *Riders in the Chariot*, are three examples from White's mature novels, of found private spaces, each of a different scale. In *The Vivisector*, just as in *The Hanging Garden*, he had placed a young boy and girl, Hurtle Duffield and Rhoda, in a primordial garden setting.

> It was like old times, in which they were brother and sister, down by the liquid manure at the bottom of the garden; till an elderly custodian restored them to their present ages, their formal relationship, by severely frowning at them. (VIV:19)

White and his partner Manoly Lascaris bought a six acre plot of land in 1948, perhaps, as Ruth Brown puts it, "a way of self-consciously acting out a fable in a 'barely inhabited country', as if both land and language were devoid of prior meaning." (1991: 21) Their modest success as gardeners, born from their struggles here with wildness and fecundity, are described in White's autobiography, *Flaws in the Glass* (1981, 22). White was a writer who described what he saw. His hours in a real garden are as much behind the hanging garden of his last story as all the myths and allusions of his wide reading.

Surrounding the house and garden in which much of the action takes place is the graded life of the city of Sydney. It cannot be described as bustling, even though for the most part the 'world war' being fought elsewhere is received news rather than enacted experience. White's Sydney of the early 1940s is stratified and class conscious. There is hardly a conversation in the book which does not reflect this. Snobbery thrives in the ruling class almost as much as it can be presumed to do back in England Mrs Bulpit, even though she sets strict rules for her young charges, is decidedly not of the best stock, with her drinking, her body odours and her penchant for sentimental popular music, which we imagine to be sung by English stars such as Gracie Fields or Vera Lynn. Skin colour plays a major part in how a person is judged. Even though the novel barely mentions Aborigines, it is difficult for a reader now not to see in Eirene's sense of her self an elliptical comment on their marginalisation.

> From being a black reffo Greek, I am told I have something exotic about me, an olive complexion, classic features. The mirror won't let me accept these honours. I am never more than a dark blur …' (23).

In such a situation she is drawn not only to Gilbert but to her part Brazilian friend Viva, who displays greater self confidence and who is not scared of slugs.

Viva seems first to dominate Eirene and encourage her sexual questioning. So does blonde Trish. At the same time Gilbert is turning into a man without really understanding what is happening to himself: a passer-by glimpsed exposing himself, a wet dream, the memory of his only London friend Nigel killed in the blitz. We are given pieces of a jigsaw, but too few of them to know what the final picture would have been had White continued Gil's and Eirene's story into late teenage or adulthood. Would the two young people, drawn together by fate, have fallen in love, parted bitterly, or established very different sexual identities? Perhaps White, conscious that he was writing late in life at the same time as he was also absorbed by memoir, would have made Gilbert Horsfall a recreation of his own young homosexual self. After all, as David Marr points out , 'White's urgent purpose in writing *Flaws in the Glass* was to make a public, dignified declarationof his homosexuality.'(1991, 595) It is not improbable that his next fictional creation of a male could therefore have been moulded by this confession.

The Hanging Garden is a novel in which fate plays a specific part. Eirene's modern Greekness links her to classical legends of 'Delphi, Olympia, Dordona, the Parthenon' (25). Greek tragedy is evoked several times. The children are both playthings of the gods, maliciously abandoned by them in Australia, and independent beings learning through their necessary bonding to overcome the loneliness and despair to which they might otherwise be sacrificed. When the novel ends, the children's future, now that the war is over, is unsure. There may be a return to London for Gilbert and to Greece for Eirene. Does it matter?

Most critics have written warmly of this novel as though it is an interesting *coda* to White's career. Despite the snippets of forecasting which David Marr refers to in his postscriptum Note at the end of the book, I raise the possibility that the novel is in fact not unfinished, that White, whilst realising that it needed major editorial attention, had achieved what he wanted to do with his story. What happens next is a speculation that every novel ever written poses the imaginative reader. With *The Hanging Garden* we do not need to know about the future of these characters - partly because, save for the finding of new evidence, we simply never will know what it might have been, but also because Gilbert and Eirene are complete as they are. We will never know what Maisie knew next, but we know what she has learned already in Henry James's account of her. Similarly we have witnessed in White's novel an attempt by grown-ups to re-condition two sensitive and traumatised children, and their counter strategies to make of themselves something they want to be rather than what they have been told they must become. In this respect *The Hanging Garden* is not a prologue to a novel that never was, but a work of art in itself, a just completion, in its simplicity and insights, to a great novelist's journey.

Works Cited

Brown, Ruth. 1991. "Patrick White and Australia as *Terra Nullius*," *Patrick White, Life and Writings: Five Essays*, ed. Martin Gray. Stirling: University of Stirling Centre of Commonwealth Studies, Occasional Papers No. 2.

Boswell, John. 1988. *The Kindness of Strangers: The Abandonment of Children in Western Europe from Late Antiquity to the Renaissance.* Chicago: University of Chicago Press.

Marr, David. 1991. *Patrick White: A Life.* London: Jonathan Cape.

White, Patrick. 1957. *Voss.* New York: Penguin.

—. 1955. *The Tree of Man.* London: Eyre and Spottiswoode.

—. 1961. *Riders in the Chariot.* London: Eyre and Spottiswoode.

—. 1970. *The Vivisector.* London: Jonathan Cape.

—. 1981. *Flaws in the Glass.* London: Jonathan Cape.

—. 2012. *The Hanging Garden.* Sydney: Random House.

Chapter Twenty

Patrick White: Twyborn Moments of Grace

Brian Kiernan
University of Sydney

By the end of the 1970s it was clear that critics were deeply divided over the nature of Patrick White's work and his achievement. At that time, I attempted to identify their fundamental differences by asking whether White was to be seen as a traditional novelist with a religious or theosophical view of life, or as a sophisticated, ironical modern mistrustful of language and sceptical of ever being able to express what might lie beyond words? (Kiernan 1980).

Since then, literary criticism has registered some changes, and shocks. Indeed that term, 'literary criticism', has come to suggest the kind, or kinds, of exegesis and evaluation that prevailed in the ages that preceded our own brave new theoretical world. (I speak in general terms but have contemporary Australian academia specifically in mind.) How, I wonder, would a new reader, one coming to White for the first time through his most recent novel, *The Twybom Affair* (1979) perceive him? (the 'Twyborn moment of grace' is the concludmg phrase of the White autobiography, *Flaws in the Glass*, 1981).

In imagining this 'new' reader I have in mind a younger generation, particularly of students, who need not have encountered White's earlier novels and criticisms of them, and for whom the terms and concerns of Anglo-American New Criticism which affected the academic reception of White's work from at least the 1960s on are likely to be less immediate than those of Continental and North American theorists who have been influential during the last decade or more. Knowing such readers, especially among graduate students, I begin to speculate on how White's most recent novel might answer to their interests.

My imagined new readers would be suspicious of such enshrined concepts as 'the novel', or even 'literature'. They would see these as 'privileging' and 'valorising' assumptions which should be subjected to sceptical reappraisal. Their interests would be in 'writing': in 'texts', their 'discourses', their 'strategies', and their 'intertextual' relationships with other writings. Their reading of 'Theory' would encourage them not to attempt to construct a single, stable interpretation of a text but to 'deconstruct' it: to search for the paradoxes embedded in its discourses and concealed gaps or 'absences', and to celebrate the 'play' of diverse meanings these reveal. Such readers coming to *The Twybom Affair* innocently – that is, approaching it as a contemporary fiction and not as the latest (and a very late) step in White's long and much discussed development – would, I conjecture, discover a text that demands 'decoding,' in that it explicitly plays with contradictory possibilities of significance, and deconstructs itself in its unfolding.

The opening of the novel invites us to recognise its mode as that of comedy of manners *a La* Edith Wharton, whom Mrs E. Boyd ('Joanie') Golson is reading. It invites us to read it as a study of repressed sexual attraction between wealthy married women holidaying on the French Riviera before the first World War, as a period comedy in which New World naivety and insecurity encounter Old World sophistication, and decadence. This mode is sustained through Joanie's voyeuristic point of view while at the same time being ironised by the reader's 'modern' awareness that the object of Joanie's infatuation, Madame Eudoxia Vatatzes, is 'male'. This drag-show comedy culminates in the Vatatzes 'entertaining' the Golsons with a Chabrier piano duet (or duel) and M. Vatatzes's appalling display of bad manners – a scene exquisitely embarrassing for the Golsons, and farcical for the reader because a disruption of the social and literary conventions lovingly evoked in the establishment scenes.

Clearly, linguistic as well as literary play is being indulged in. The comedian as the letter 'E' confuses signifiers and signifieds, names and genders, and relationships within the Twyborn family. Admittedly, these confusions may pose only initial difficulties for readers, who either struggle to sort them out for themselves or wait for the narrative to clarify them (unless they have already lost their innocence through reading reviews). However, that readers cannot be sure, initially at least, which 'E.' is being referred to (and desired) nor of his or her gender signals a deliberate playing against the conventions that the opening has lead them to expect. And even though the innocent reader discovers in Part Two that Eudoxia is 'really' Eddie Twyborn, who becomes Edith Trist in Part Three, the radical indeterminacy of signifiers, linguistic and sexual, and the indeterminacy of gender itself, continue throughout as the novel passes into, and mixes, other modes. Other discordant elements, other kinds of writing, also enter early to upset the readers' expectations.

Angelo Vatatzes's obsession with Byzantine history seems calculated to perplex in that it introduces, through his confused consciousness, highly specific but, for most of us, unfamiliar references. Helpfully, in a traditional humanist reading of the novel, A. P. Riemer has elaborated the arcane textuality and etymological play ('bugger' is derived from 'Bulgar', OED*)* behind these lengthy passages. (1980, 29)

I'd like to suggest further that the 'subversive strategy' behind them is that they 'defamiliarise' our, admittedly stereotyped, literary expectations of how European culture will be presented, *a la* Edith Wharton or the early Henry James, in a novel opening in the Edwardian period and presenting the comedy of New World manners encountering those of the Old. White's Australian variation on this by now time-honoured 'international theme' intercuts Vatatzes's Levantine memories and Byzantine fantasies with Joanie's equally 'untypical' reveries over her personal, and homoerotic, past in the New World.

Another early example of discordance is that odd, seemingly excrescent interlude with M. Pelletier, the sour keeper of the beach kiosk who masturbates over the distant, androgynous, Hellenic figure of Eudoxia in the sea. Is this a disgusted parody of Romantic afflatus, with the *petit bourgeois* voyeur presuming to imagine that be has glimpsed the transcendent. Or is it, having in mind another voyeur masturbating on the strand, a blurring of Joycean epiphanies, high and low? (In *Ulysses,* Cissy, object of Mr Bloom's desire, herself ejaculates, 'Oh, will you ever forget the evening she dressed up in her father's suit and hat and the burned cork moustache and walked down Tritonsville Road, smoking a cigarette?' (Joyce 1937, 333) – which is not unlike Joanie's obsessive memory of Eadith ('E.') Twybom's cross-dressing prank.

M. Pelletier's moment of 'tremulous abstraction' may seem no more than the result of a 'sordid ejaculation', as inconsequential as those other 'expostulatory ejaculations' of the coffee pot as it boils over on the rickety little spirit lamp. But for him, as he returns to this world and the damp newspapers presaging the coming war, it remains "a triumphant leap into the world of light and colour" which he craves, into the poetry he has never written and the love he has never expressed for (and note the gender mix) 'Simone or Violette-or Mireille, Fernandel Zizi Jacques Louise Jeanne Jacques Jaccques ...' (76)

This incident, we might say, oozes semiosis. Yet its counterpoising of Romantic and anti-Romantic attitudes and styles is so diffused with ironies that it seems pointless to ask whether M. Pelletier has truly glimpsed transcendence or only, laughably, presumed he has. Assuming readers 'know' by this stage that Eudoxia is 'male', they might feel they are joining with the author in relishing the dramatic irony at Pelletier's expense. But any sense of shared superiority is then undercut by the play on 'ejaculation' (Pelletier's and the coffee pot's), which insists that any 'significance' is merely coincidental, an etymological accident, an empty effect of writing.

This brings us directly, if uncertainly, to what seemed the issue in White criticism throughout the 1970s. What was it precisely that *his* characters' perceptions of 'pure being' signified? Discussions then focused on such epiphanic moments as M. Pelletier feels he has experienced. Whether or not the majority of commentators saw White as successful while those that didn't found something like 'tremulous abstraction' – they agreed on seeing him as attempting to 'realise' in language what new readers would now recognise, and knowingly dismiss, as the 'transcendental signified'. If, however, M. Pelletier seems too peripheral a character and this episode excrescent, we might consider a moment of transcendence for Eddie himself in the central section of *The Twyborn Affair.*

This section rings satiric changes on the conventions of the Australian novel rural life-conventions which White has returned to intermittently since his first published novel *Happy Valley.* (1939) *The Twyborn Affair* also returns to the London of *The Living and the Dead* (1941) and the southern France of *The Aunt's Story* (1948). The moment occurs when his feeble-minded workmate Denny invites Eddie home for a beer and to meet his wife Dot and their baby. Once there, within a setting that is one of White's familiar moral landscape, where rocks suggest an irreducible core of reality and life is stripped to its essentials, Denny dandles the infant that, unsuspected by him, is the issue of Dot and her father, Dick the rabbiter.

As she contemplates her husband blissfully salivating over the baby, the frazzled, feral Dot is momentarily touched, we are told, by a 'revelation.' But then there occurs a 'violation of grace' when Dick, father both of Dot and her daughter (and, as a rabbit-skinner, another kind of *pelletier*?), approaches on horseback. Denny drives 'Dadda' away with oaths and gunshots. As Eddie rides away he wonders 'whether he wasn't leaving the best of all possible worlds'. (276-78)

This scene is so encoded lexically and conventionally that it can be read as both low satiric, but not unsentimental, rustic farce and as an ostensibly blasphemous allegory of the Holy Family and the Incarnation. Again, it is parodic and portentous at the same time; and for White's 'old' readers, what it is parodying would have to include all those much discussed 'epiphanies' in his own earlier novels. A frequent criticism of those earlier 'revelations'was that they were granted only to an elite and denied to the caricatured 'normal' members of a society from which these visionaries were alienated. Here, Eddie's Panglossian but provisional epiphany is bodied forth by the caricatures, as though White were revisiting ironically not only his own earlier texts but that wider text that by this time constituted 'Patrick White'.

Yet another example occurs towards the end of Part Three, in which other modes and conventions are operating. Eadith recalls an Australian captain having told her/him during the first World War of his furtive coupling with a 'Frog' woman in her farm-house, and how he felt they had been enfolded by giant wings. While the captain, a caricature of crude Australian maleness, insists he believes in 'nothun', what he recounts could be interpreted as an experience of the Holy Spirit, despite the lowness of his diction and the iconographically incongruous imagery (cockatoos rather than doves). Remembering this towards the end of her life, Madame Eadith Trist reflects that "In certain circumstances, lust can become an epiphany." (TA 417-19) While yet again an 'old' reader might ask whether this is a portentous gesturing towards a deeper, religious significance, or a parody (and self-parody?) of literary pretensions to incarnate the transcendent through language, 'new' readers, rather than agonising over White's precise 'tone' or 'stance' might less problematically see him as his maximising the play, and clash of disparate signifying codes.

The Christian lexicon, so often the stabilising element for 'old' readers of White's previous novels, continues to pervade *The Twyborn Affair*. It enters in Part One with Eudoxia seeing Joanie Golson's appearance as a 'Visitation' and dreading her 'Second Coming' (TA 33), and becomes most pronounced in Part Three. Like the play with the letter 'E' in the first section, the play on the brothel-as-nunnery/nunnery-as-brothel in the final section foregrounds a radical ambiguity. Is it elevating prostitution by equating it with the religious vocation, or degrading that vocation to an institutionalisation, and therefore a profanation, of divine love (as prostitution is of human love)? Or is it freely, 'irresponsibly' indulging in the elaboration of a given trope which turns the conventional world upside down?

The latter would be my answer: the brothel/nunnery is a classic catachresis in the pornographic tradition (Diderot and Sade readily come to mind) invoked here to play with, and against, readers' expectations of decorum, of clear and proper distinctions, fictional, social, and sexual. Another level of literary style (but problematically 'literary 'for 'old' readers?), that of pornography, is being added to the predominant mode of international comedy of manners in Part One and, in Part Two White's return to Australian *topoi* and his own local moral landscapes. Behind White's texts there have always been (inescapably the Barthesian would mutter) other texts; here they include his own, and fictional parallels with his now widely known life-history, the extended text that is 'Patrick White', in an act of flamboyant auto-intertextuality.

Now, of course, one does not have to be a 'new' reader at all to discern such diverse discourses running through this text. With *The Twyborn Affair,* the process of 'deconstruction' is inverted. Instead of disparate literary conventions, dissonant lexical codes, and radical ambiguities lying beneath its surface, they obtrusively are the surface. Structurally foregrounded (shades of *The Aunt's Story*) are the narrative jumps from Eudoxia to Eddie to Eadith and to Eddie again (and back and forth within these), and jumps in the fictional modes and literary styles that mirror his/her search for a life-style.

Pervasively there are the linguistic play with, and clash of, religious and psychoanalytic codes (all those oneiric passages in which the characters indulge their polymorphous perverse propensities), farcical disruptions, as when Reg and Nora Quick 'cooeee' around the country house garden in Part Three; the shifting, partial perspectives-through windows, reflections in mirrors, peepholes on the brothel of life, which turn the reader into a voyeur. All of these would frustrate any 'old' reader's attempt to reconstruct the narrative in accordance with traditional expectations of a consistent central character and situation, a single authorial point of view, and a single, stable 'meaning'.

Such an attempt would fail not because there is insufficient characterisation, situation, motif, etc. to be interpreted along conventional psychological-realist, and liberal or Christian humanist lines but because there is an excess of, and conflict among, such interpretative possibilities. This novel could be read one-dimensionally, as White's earlier novels have (variously) been read, only at the cost of repressing its often outrageous play with its readers and its transgressions of linguistic, literary and social codes.

Responding to these transgressions, my 'new' reader would almost certainly be reminded of Bakhtin's carnivalesque-grotesque tradition in fiction (Bakhtin 1969, 14). The carnivalesque masquerade, in which the normal world is turned upside down or inside out, and the 'other' (the rogue, the fool, the clown or the *hetaera*) becomes, in the case of *The Twyborn Affair,* queen for a day, has an obvious appropriateness, not only for the brothel scenes but also the cross-dressing masquerades that run throughout the novel and subvert notions of a 'natural order'.

In this light, *The Twyborn Affair* could be seen as in a venerable, if subversive, tradition and its author's playfulness on so many levels simultaneously in accord with Bakhtin's summary of this mode's functions:

> to concentrate inventive freedom, to permit the combination of a variety of different elements and their rapprochement, to liberate from the prevailing view of the world, from conventions and established truths, from cliches, from all that is humdrum and universally accepted. And so, to offer instead, 'a new outlook on the world, to realise the relative nature of all that exists, and to enter a completely new order of things. (1969, 5)

We seem so to have entered a completely new order of things also for the interpretative and evaluative exercises we used to call 'literary criticism'. If *The Twyborn Affair* seems calculatedly to answer to those interests that characterise my 'new' readers, how will they read (or re- read) the earlier novels? Will they find that White changed course with this latest novel, or that, at least since *The Aunt's Story,* he has been both the 'readerly' novelist explicated and evaluated by earlier commentators and a self-consciously literary, ironically playful, 'writerly' postmodernist writer in the most literal sense that he has absorbed earlier twentieth-century experiments with fiction, and also a postmodernist in our current sense of scepticism towards any of the absolutes postulated in even the recent past?

If you want (as many have wanted) to seize on White's statement that he sees himself as essentially an old-fashioned writer, and to present him as adopting such modes as the historical novel, the comedy of manners, or the *Bildungsroman* for traditional ends, then the protean nature of his work will allow this. You will focus on *The Tree of Man*, *Voss*, *The Vivisector*, *A Fringe of Leaves*, possibly *The Eye of the Storm*. If, however, you wish to present him as a proto-postmodernist, then you will stress *The Aunt's story*, possibly *Riders in the Chariot*, *The Solid Mandala*, and – the winning card in your pack – *The Twyborn Affair*. But really, of course, he is and always has been both; and my unsurprising conclusion is that, as critical interests and emphases continue to shift, White's work will continue to answer to them, as it has answered to different, and even opposed, interests in the past.

Works Cited

Bakhtin, Mikhail. 1969. *Rabelais and His World.* trans. Helene lswalsky. Cambridge.MA: MIT Press.
Joyce, James. 1937. *Ulysses.* London: Bodley Head.
Kiernan, Brian. 1980. *Patrick White*. London: Macmillan.
Riemer A. P. 1980. "Some Observations on *The Twyborn Affair,*" *Southerly* 40: 12-29.
White, Patrick. 1979. *The Twyborn Affair.* London: Jonathan Cape.
—. 1981. *Flaws in the Glass.* New York: Viking.

Note

This chapter is reprinted from: Brian Kiernan, *Studies in Australian literary history* (1997).Sydney Studies in Society and Culture 17. Sydney: Shoestring Press.

Part IV

Comparative Studies

Chapter Twenty-One

The Shift from Commonwealth to Postcolonial Literatures: Patrick White's "The Twitching Colonel" and Manuka Wijesinghe's *Theravada Man*

Isabel Alonso-Breto
University of Barcelona

Commenting on the Post Cold War situation of literary theory one critic states:

> the axes of comparison have become very complex and are no longer based primarily on national or linguistic differences to adopt a conceptual apparatus that presumes to speak for the totality of the world literary space is untenable What is possible however is to 'read the world' through an optic that traces difference and connectivity – between genres, themes, styles, chronologies – across discrete translocal sites." (Ganguly 2012, 16)

It is thus possible to carry out a comparative analysis based on perceived thematic and political similarities between two works which share a linguistic continuum but which are widely apart in time and place. The validity of such work is confirmed also by Frank Schulze-Engler:

> The task of the comparative study of English-language literatures is not to celebrate the emergence of a worldwide 'Engl.Lit.', but to critically analyse the worldwide communicative framework formed

by these English language literatures, and to explore the complex articulations between this framework and the specific local and regional modernities negotiated in individual literary texts." (2012, 12-13)

This kind of analysis, aware of the complex political articulations and the specific modernities that each of the works presents, is what I propose to carry out in the present article.

Bearing in mind the plurality of comparative approaches, this study adopts two: first to draw a comparison between the main characters in Patrick White's short story "The Twitching Colonel" (1937) and in Manuka Wijesinghe's novel *Theravada Man* (2009). Each of these characters, two mature men, holds a peculiar relationship to his (post)colonial environment, both are engrossed by what we could call "the lures of religious bliss," to the extent that both decide at a point in their lives to renounce material comforts and give themselves over to religion, each in his particular way. I intend through this analysis to illustrate the fundamental idea that Commonwealth or Postcolonial Literatures cannot be dissociated from progressive politics. It is my contention that although separated by a time span of seven decades, both stories and characters have the common purpose of unsettling, in Homi Bhabha's terms, "the epic intention of the civilizing mission" (Bhabha 1984:156);that is,.they can be read as symptoms of a pervasive wish, frequently latent and therefore not necessarily explicit in (post)colonial literary artefacts, to destabilise the hegemonic vocation of colonial discourse.

Colonial discourse was characterised by the attempt to make systematic practices of dispossession and exploitation appear as negligible and, at best, as necessary to carry on with a very convenient civilising mission. Colonial Secretary Joseph Chamberlain stated in 1897, "You cannot have omelettes without breaking eggs," thus justifying and minimising the wrongs of colonialism. In other words, against the discomforts and hypothetical *bad press* of colonialist practices, colonial discourse had to be made to appear as flawless as possible. However, the analysis of literary works produced in different periods reveals significant fissures in this pretended homogeneity -we need think no further than Joseph Conrad's *oeuvre*. Homi Bhabha's theoretical intervention has been crucial in this disclosure, showing how colonial discourse always carried within itself its own latent undermining. Thus, using tools developed by Bhabha to detect the fallacies of colonial discourse, it is my intention to show that the two works compared here lend themselves to explorations of these dissensions, albeit in significantly different ways.

Interestingly, the two works lend themselves as well to a comparison of another kind. While they are separated by many aspects, among which count authorship, date and place of publication and literary genre, these two stories can also be seen as connected to each other. In fact, they represent two extremes in the evolution of what in the past was called Commonwealth Literature and later on, "Postcolonial Literatures" or "New" or "World Literatures in English." Published in 1937, "The Twitching Colonel" stands at the beginning of this sequence and shows many features inherent in this early period of Postcolonial Literatures. By contrast, *Theravada Man*, (2009) can be seen to integrate some major innovations which have taken place in one century of existence, and which both attest to its present healthy state. Thus an ancillary yet integral aim of the paper is to trace this chronological connection, highlighting commonalities as well as differences so as to spur reflection upon the past and the present of the area of Postcolonial Literatures.

Connected stories

"The Twitching Colonel" was the first fictional work published by Patrick White. Appearing in the *London Mercury* in 1937, it is a modernist story where the highly suggestive set of impressionistic descriptions, the sense of unreality and the strongly sensorial images collaborate to construct a deeply ironical comment on the effects of the colonial enterprise on the psyche of a member of the British Army.

Colonel Trevellick is a retired military officer living in London who spends his days in idleness, haunted by memories of his time in India. A widower, whose wife had died in India, Trevellick is now imbued by a nostalgia for the "dark faces" of Indian people he used to live surrounded by and, especially, for Hinduism. As a symbol of his alienation from the world where he presently lives, in the very heart of imperial London (White significantly chooses the setting of Albion Street), Trevellick suffers from a face twitch and the children from the area have taken to following him around and mocking this twitching, a practice that emphasises the Colonel's out-of-placedness. Yet, absent-minded Trevellick does not really care about this. He is often lost in daydreams, and his charitable landlady, Mrs. Whale, keeps trying to bring him back to reality by asking him to tell stories about his past. But when he attempts to do so, the colonel soon gets lost in his memories of colonial missions, and the story suggests that he revives intuitions he had as a young soldier in India. Indeed it is suggested that back then, although immersed in his colonial duties, he had begun to perceive imperial values and the principles of alleged colonialist heroism to be a fake.

To his neighbours Trevellick seems to have gone mad, yet in his mind the colonel seems to be gaining a new clarity of insight, gradually leaving aside everything which to him is unimportant, in particular the material and mundane aspects of life. The story, closes when one evening, apparently inspired by his past contact with Hindu mysticism, Trevellick surprises the neighborhood by setting himself on fire on the roof of the building, an action full of metaphorical and political significance.

Colonel Trevellick can be linked to Piyatissa Weerasinghe, the main character in Wijesinghe's novel *Theravada Man*, published in 2009, seventy-two years later. Weerasinghe is an *Iskolemahaththaya*, a retired schoolmaster, a few years younger than Trevellick and like him, portrayed as living out his old age at the onset of World War Two. He is a Sri Lankan, and thus one of those "brown faces" (5) that both trouble and comfort the Twitching Colonel. The schoolmaster is a product of British colonial education and an admirer of the Empire; at the same time, he is a convinced *Theravada* Buddhist. As with Trevellick and the influences on him of Hindu values, the *Iskolemahathathaya* lives by Buddhist values. His religious commitment dominates his entire life. This strong allegiance to Buddhism alienates this character from the world that surrounds him.

The position of authority he occupies as venerable *Iskolemahaththaya* draws a distance between him and the others around him, his wife included. Buddhism estranges him from others because of his desire to transcend his everyday world and by the end of the novel, the *Iskolemahaththaya* gives up his family life to devote himself completely to a life of contemplation. This flight from reality is analogous to Trevellick's. His end may seem less radical, as he does not put an end to his life in the literal sense, as Trevellick does,but it is as drastic and as far-reaching a decision. Trevellick had no family or relatives whom he would leave unattended; the schoolmaster leaves several small children to be raised by his wife on her own.

The similarity between these two characters is again noticeable. in that they are both alienated in different ways by what reality has to offer each of them. Both men yearn to attain another existential dimension, and both give themselves over to the pursuit of the metaphysical. The similarity of this pattern is remarkable, in that it is due to the fact of both being immersed in a colonial situation. Interestingly, each of them occupies a different extreme of the colonial spectrum. Colonel Trevellick belongs with the colonisers, and the schoolmaster, a native Sri Lankan, belongs to the colonised. Yet both of them are, in different ways, victims of the colonial entrapment; both are affected by their sociopolitical circumstances and are hybrid subjects in different ways.

Attesting to the evolution of the Postcolonial

These two fictions invite comparison at different levels and can be read in contrast to each other and interpreted as symptomatic of the different periods in which they were written. More than seven decades span the publication of "The Twitching Colonel" in 1937 and *Theravada Man* in 2009, and not surprisingly, these stories are testimony to the evolution of postcolonial literatures, from their early stirrings to the contemporary moment. Textual and para-textual aspects can be explored that account for a sense of progression, beginning with the fact that in the early short story the main character belongs in the colonial faction, while in the more recent novel the central role is accorded to the once-colonised.

Together with this important political shift, matters of genre, authorship and location can be usefully revised with the aim of reflecting on some gains and losses to our discipline.

The genres of the two works illustrates a change and an evolution. White's choice is the short story, a genre cherished by writers in the early stages of their career, and which here also corroborates the idea that Commonwealth or postcolonial literatures were just in their infancy when he began writing. White would publish his first novel, *Happy Valley*, two years after the publication of "The Twitching Colonel," in 1939. By contrast, seven decades later, Sri Lankan Manuka Wijesinghe chooses the novel, a major literary genre, and sets out to write a complete trilogy, of which *Theravada Man* is the second volume. Dense and full of humour, *Theravada Man* is the prequel to the already published and very successful *Monsoon and Potholes* (2006) and also to *Sinhala Only*, recently completed but still unpublished. This contrast shows again the progression in the strength and impact of the 'New Literatures.' In her ambitious trilogy, Wijesinghe attempts to document from a witty and mordant perspective nothing less than the political history of her country, beginning in the 1920s, when *Theravada Man* begins. There is thus an epic and mythopeic dimension in her endeavour which was lacking at the early stage, when Trevellick was created.

The epic intent of the new literatures would gain significance in the 1950s, with the works of Chinua Achebe, and reached a climax with the advent. in 1981, of Salman Rushdie's *Midnight's Children*. In these works, as in others published in the central decades of the century, the epic/mythopoeic intention was often connected to anti-colonial movements and the creation of postcolonial nations. More recently, novels like Earl Lovelace's *Salt* (1996), Amitav Ghosh's *Ibis Trilogy* – of which only *Sea of Poppies* (2008), and *Rivers of Smoke* (2011) have been published so far – or Aziz Hassim's *The Lotus People* (2003), have continued this postcolonial tradition. Like *Theravada Man*, many of these contemporary works, expose the cracks and fissures of the postcolonial nation(s), and construct appealing and compelling visions of their worlds underscoring their complexities.

Regarding authorship, there is a shift in our samples from a male to a female author. Patrick White is representative of an early generation of writers from the Commonwealth where male names were the norm – without disregarding the pioneering work of a few exceptional women like Katharine Mansfield or Jean Rhys. Against this, the number of women writers has increased steadily through the 20th century yet at present the situation is not as felicitous as one might hope. Since its inception in 1901, only 12 out of 108 women have been awarded the Nobel Prize for Literature. More significantly for us in our area, in its twenty-five years of existence only five women have been awarded the Commonwealth Writers' Prize for Best Book, an award instituted in 1987: Olive Senior, Janet Frame, Andrea Levy, Kate Grenville and Aminatta Forna. The imbalance of these figures is surprising, and it opens up a whole field of speculation. Certainly it can have different readings. It can, on the one hand, give away a certain neglect of women's works in the publishing industry which reaches into the global cultural fabric and also affects the politics in the distribution of literary prizes awarded women and men. It also suggests that there is a long way to go in terms of women's rights worldwide also that progress needs to be made in terms of women's access to cultural and publishing circuits, particularly in the Anglophone areas.

Authorship is also relevant in connection with location. Patrick White is but one of the many budding writers of the period who chose to stay in London after obtaining a university degree in order to launch a literary career. London, or alternatively wider Europe (often Paris), was the place to be if a young writer wanted to gain a reputation in the 1930s. However, throughout the decades, the leading, virtually exclusive role, of the Metropolis in granting literary recognition has changed and nowadays many successful Commonwealth writers choose to remain in their countries of origin and only, at most, spend occasional stints in Europe.

Still, a distinction can be made: whereas Australian, Canadian and New Zealand writers tend to live in their countries of origin, writers from the former non-settler colonies, such as Pakistan, India or Nigeria, often leave their places of origin and settle in either the UK, US, Australia or Canada, to return only temporarily to their countries of birth. Manuka Wijesinghe is a good illustration of this reality. She lives in Germany, but she travels frequently to Sri Lanka, which, she admits, remains the centre of her intellectual and creative activity. We can speak of her, as of many others as a transnational and transcultural writer, that is, one of those writers who, "by choice or by life circumstances, experience cultural dislocation ... [and] expose themselves to diversity and nurture plural, flexible identities" (Dagnino 2012, 1). Thus these writers' choices are not restricted by their socio-political reality:

> While moving physically across the globe and across different cultures, [transcultural writers] find themselves less and less trapped in the traditional migrant/exile syndrome and become more apt instead to embrace the opportunities and the freedom that diversity and mobility bestow upon them. (Dagnino 2012, 2)

Diversity and mobility have always existed when it comes to literary production, all the more so in the area of postcolonial literatures in English. Therefore the ultimate difference between White and Wijesinghe in this sense would be a sense of celebration of de-centredness present in the contemporary writer apparently lacking in the former, for whom, if we follow Dagnino, "decentredness" should have been a Modernist source of gloom or, at least, uneasiness:

> Unlike in the past ... contemporary transcultural authors are not at odds with their destabilized, decentred selves. On the contrary, they aim at being culturally and/or geographically dislocated, or 'dispatriated', in order to gain a new perspective: on the world, on different cultures, on humanity and, ultimately, on themselves. (Dagnino 2012, 3)

"The Twitching Colonel" is representative of the early period of Commonwealth literature also in its being authored by an Australian. In the 1930s, after the Statute of Westminster was passed in 1931, the British Commonwealth was formed by Britain and the former white colonies, now politically labelled as 'dominions.' With notable exceptions of Rabindranath Tagore, Mulk Raj Anand, Raja Rao, Narayan or Jean Rhys, not so many writers from the extant "coloured" colonies were published in the metropolis and those published were not widely known by British audiences. Commonwealth literature did not exist as a category; it would only become a recognised area of production and research in the 1960s (McLeod 2000, 12).

Finally, the places of publication of the works are also illustrative of progression. *The London Mercury* was in existence between the years 1919 and 1939. It was a major journal and published many works by major authors, such as W.B. Yeats and interestingly, Rabindranath Tagore. In the database 'Making Britain,' from the Open University, we read that

> After Rolfe Arnold Scott-James took over as editor in 1934, the magazine increasingly featured short stories and poetry by Indian writers. It also included survey articles and reviews by Indian writers on topics such as Indian art and Indian literature. Reviews of books on India were also increasingly published by the journal. http://www8.open.ac.uk/research.projects/makingbritain/content/london-mercury.

Given its thematic connection to Indian philosophy, it is significant that Patrick White should have published this first short story in this particular journal. It is remarkable that this significant interest in South Asian authors and themes should subsist in such a journal as, well-established and prestigious as *The London Mercury* which was a premier *British* literary journal.

In contrast, *Monsoons and Potholes* was published in the former margins of the Empire: in Colombo. Sri Lanka. Perera & Hussein is a young and very successful publishing house. Founded in 2003, its website explains that, "it was formed ... to enable and encourage talented South Asian writers to gain exposure and recognition by publishing their work." This is a self-managed enterprise, which so far falls beyond the reach of transnational publishing companies. With the facilities brought about by the internet, marketing and especially distribution is not a problem anymore, and this has resulted in Perera & Hussein's success in publishing emergent as well as more established Sri Lankan authors, based on the island or abroad, authors such as Karen Roberts or Neluka Silva. It would appear that the former distinction between the metropolis and colonies, traditionally designated in our discipline through the metaphor of centre and margin can now be regarded as outdated. Nowadays Sri Lankan authors, like all world authors for that matter, have the freedom to publish at home if they wish. We can once more read this shift as a progressive development in relation to the new literatures.

One would be tempted to think that, so as to become established, writers do not need to be 'discovered' by the West anymore but we know, this is an utopian hope, as transnational Western publishing houses, have an undeniable advantage over local publishers in terms of distribution and marketing (Narayanan 2012). All in all, however, comparing different para-textual aspects of these two works allows us to conclude that the times have changed for good, from the early stirrings of Commonwealth writing to the present times of postcolonial literatures.

The representation of mimicry as a strategy against totalising narratives

Despite these differences, and however different and displaced in time and context, it is my contention that comparing the characters of Colonel Trevellick and the *Iskolemahaththaya* can be useful to illustrate some complexities of the colonial scene, and to trace a commonality in the political agenda of two characters separated by so many factors. Trevellick went to India as part of the military force of occupation. The story does not specify the campaigns he was involved in, but there is reference to the fact that "he kept those niggers in order." (4) The allusions to the English colonialist endeavor "the twiddle-de-dee of England across the sea," (4) particularly in India, are recurrent: there is reference to Lucknow, to Rudyard Kipling, to "the voices of England keeping her End Up, Doing her Bit." (4) The Colonel remembers "the ponies, the band at dusk, the fluid brass," images which seem to suggest that he was part of the regiment's band, or which perhaps just connote the orderly luster of the Imperial Military. Back in time, Trevellick seems to have been a convinced colonialist, "with his appropriate ration of sentiment, of fervor, but well in hand and fastened by uniform buttons." (4) He had even won some medals.

However, Trevellick's imperial commitment soon dwindled as the worm of doubt broke through his convictions. Increasingly attracted to Indian cultures, he began to wonder about "the hub of Western importance" (5) and to question it. After his wife's death, Trevellick experienced "a gradual recession of sympathy with bands and public occasions, as if … on closing her parasol his wife had torn the muslin veil that is protection or illusion of greatness that lies in patriotic songs, British supremacy, and the Stiff Upper Lip." (5)

Finally, influenced by Hindu beliefs variously embodied in the image of Siva's eternal dance, of Maithuna's completeness, or of "the Buddha's blossoming from his lotus throne" (6) and of "Vishnu's opening the door to renewal," (8) he started seeing material reality as futile, as *maya* or illusion. He ended up forsaking his identity as Western colonialist and set out, "to strip himself of, the onion-folds of prejudice …" (7) After his return to London, the seat of the Empire, and after the years, a peculiar colonial nostalgia still critically alienates the colonel from the imperial pomp surrounding him.

In this process of disavowal of colonial values, Trevellick becomes a vivid illustration of mimicry, as he mimics the native to the extent of imitating, and distorting, the Hindu funeral rites in his fiery self-immolation. As Homi Bhabha writes, "the ambivalence of mimicry does not merely 'rupture' the [colonial] discourse, but becomes transformed into an uncertainty which fixes the colonial subject as a 'partial presence.' (1984, 127) This is a fitting description for Trevellick, who, through his former acknowledgment of the other's culture and his later nostalgic remembrances was a partial presence in the past as he is in the present, never fully and unquestioningly embracing his own society's values.

In creating this character, White manages to undermine the colonialist discourse hegemonic and worldwide during the time he was writing this story in 1936. Against totalitarian discourses of history and of cultural encounters, Colonel Trevellick tests what Bhabha (paraphrasing Edward Said) describes as "the conflictual economy of colonial discourse," which consists of "the tension between the synchronic panoptical vision of domination – the demand for identity, stasis and the counter-pressure of the diachrony of history -change, difference" (1984, 126). The story set as it is in London, manages to inscribe historical dissension precisely at the site of production of traditional history and where Trevellick meets his end. His vital experience succeeds in unsettling the totalising narrative of colonialism and locates "a threat to both 'normalised' knowledges and disciplinary powers" (Bhabha 1984, 126) within the very cradle of the colonialist project.

The *Iskolemahaththaya*, is another unique illustration of mimicry. Ironically, while Trevellick disavows his own class and empathises with the colonised's *weltanschauung*, this character, without explicitly disavowing his culture quasi pathologically embraces it through the *Theravada* Buddhism which is a marker of Sinhalese culture, yet he is also a keen advocate of colonialism and of his own status as colonial subject. It is easy to see a mimic subject in somebody who proudly describes himself as "a living, eating, British educated *Theravada* man born from the womb of woman" (39) and who is described by a fellow Sri Lankan as somebody who "venerates the English." (189)

The schoolmaster is an upholder of British rule over his country and throughout the story he unwaveringly embraces the values of British rationalism. There is an explanation for this: he was born in 1883, which means that he grew up in years when intense Buddhist revivalism coexisted on the island with the solidification of English rule after decades of British occupation of the island. His loyalty to the Empire is understandable inasmuch as he is one of those Sinhalese government employees who, in the late 19th century, "came to enjoy higher salaries (and earnings) and greater prestige" (2005, 418) than the majority of the population, including those of his own class and caste.

A leading Sri Lankan historian, K.M. de Silva recalls that, from 1870 on "government resources were devoted largely to the spread of vernacular education, English education being left almost entirely to the missionaries." (2005, 416) The English government thus favored the education of the peasant masses in Sinhalese – and this provided people like the schoolteacher with comfortable jobs. However, in those areas where there were no missionary schools open in the vicinity (schools which would teach in English), the government maintained English schools. The fact is that although hundreds of Sinhalese schools were opened in the last decades of the 19th century by the colonial government, the local educational system, and society at large, continued to be deeply elitist, valuing English above an education in the vernacular.

In an animated argument with his son Tissa who, as shall be discussed later on, is conspicuously less convinced than his father of the benefits of colonialism to Sri Lanka, the schoolmaster is proud to commend the profitable harvest he has reaped. Ananda College, the institution selected to cater for the son's education in English, was founded in 1886, during the above- mentioned period of Buddhist revivalism. It was founded by Rev. Henry Steel Olcott, also founder of the productive Theosophical Society. The prejudice-ridden schoolmaster is therefore a product of his time and place.

Yet, as with "The Twitching Colonel," the complexities of the colonial scene – the already referred to "conflictual economy of colonial discourse" – manifest in our anglophile *Theravada Man*. Mockery, menace and eventually disavowal and disestablishment of colonial power are always (already) lurching lurking somewhere behind in the colonial picture. Bhabha writes that "from the very moment of a colonial encounter between the white presence and its black semblance, there emerges the question of the ambivalence of mimicry as a problematic of colonial subjection." (1984, 131) It is precisely because of his double affiliation, Buddhism and Englishness, that the character of the *Iskolemahaththaya* is textually in-scribed at an unstable point where "*mimicry* – a difference that is almost nothing but not quite" (271) dangerously runs the risk of becoming "*menace* – a difference that is almost total but not quite." (Bhabha 1984, 132)

According to the text's premises, it was British rationality injected into the society through the medium of education which allowed Buddhism to regain the status it had lost with colonialism. Paradoxically, Buddhism itself soon became associated with the anti-colonial movement. This shift is illustrated in the novel through generational replacement. The risk of mimicry becoming menace, apparently absent but latent in the *Iskolemahaththaya's* youth emerges when he is in his mature years, in the person of his son Tissa. Whereas the mimic *Iskolemahaththaya* is vocal in his support of the British control of Ceylon, Tissa, precisely because of his being educated at Ananda College becomes, to his father's annoyance, a staunch supporter of the anti-colonial cause and a Marxist. Ironically, then, via the Buddhist revival in the Sri Lanka of the turn of the 20th century, repetition and mimicry – commitment to British rationality and Buddhist values – are seen to contain the seed of difference and dissent – anti-colonialism and secularisation.

Through this subtle twist, the agency which in colonialist narratives was denied to the colonised peoples through what Bhabha has called "the metonymy of presence," is restored in *Theravada Man* more than one century after the recounted events. The coexistence of the apparently contradictory pulsions of mimicry and difference or, in other words, of repetition and dissent, is thus unmasked in a narrative that turns out to contain, as in the story of the Colonel, a strategy of resistance.

Further, this cohabitation of contradictory impulses is seen to fully inform a particular historical moment and a key one in the history of modern Sri Lanka – the politically dense turn of the 20th century. This cohabitation of contradictory tendencies, then, reads as a means to underscore the flaws in the pretended homogeneity of totalising colonialist narratives, and manages, in the same vein as "The Twitching Colonel" and in spite of the huge differences in terms of textual production and re-production, to unsettle and disrupt the totalitarian project of colonialism.

A close analysis of White's "The Twitching Colonel" and of Wijesinghe's *Theravada Man* shows that, in spite of the differences of the explored subjectivities, through their explorations of mimicry the two stories read as refutations of too simplistic, binary readings of the colonial enterprise in terms of coloniser vs. colonised. Both stories illuminate the colonial scene from different angles, but both manage to steer clear of what Abdul JanMohamed had denounced as a recurrent *topos* of colonialist literature: the Manichean Allegory. Rather, in different, but subtle ways, both fictions succeed in offering sophisticated depictions of the colonial scene, throwing light on the manifold affiliations of those involved in the quicksands of colonialism, no matter at what end of the spectrum they are placed.

Conclusion

The usefulness of the comparative approach is multiple. In our particular analysis, it has helped us pinpoint a tangible evolution in the shift from "Commonwealth Literature" to "Postcolonial Literatures in English." However, this discussion has shown that while the distinction between these two tags may illuminate aspects of history, it is not unproblematic. John McLeod comments on this shift as follows:

> The imperious tones of 'Commonwealth literature' made this term fall increasingly out of favour from the 1980s. In stark contrast to liberal humanist readings by critics of Commonwealth literature, the (newly re-christened) 'postcolonial literatures' were at a stroke regarded as politically radical and locally situated, rather than universally relevant. They were deemed to pose direct challenges to the colonial centre from the colonized margins, negotiating new ways of seeing that both contested the dominant mode and gave voice and expression to colonised and once-colonised peoples. Postcolonial literatures were actively engaged in the act of decolonizing the mind. (2000, 25)

This is an impeccable explanation of a distinction that has preoccupied a good number of critics (Ako 2004). Yet through our comparative analysis we have seen that "challenges to the colonial centre" are already traceable even in so-called Commonwealth Literature. Through strategies perhaps more subtle than the ones developed later on, "Commonwealth writers" such as Patrick White were already engaged in the attempt to challenge "the dominant mode."

It is difficult not to acknowledge that the label "Postcolonial Literatures" encompasses a more political outlook than the previous title conferred on the literatures produced in ex-British colonies, because they are irredeemably linked to anti-colonialist movements as well as, subsequently, to the heavily political critical practice of postcolonial criticism – which, *pace* the seminal works *Orientalism* (1978) and *The Empire Writes Back* (1989), became an increasingly burgeoning archive. Yet, using tools devised by postcolonial criticism, particularly the concept of mimicry as developed by

Homi Bhabha, our analysis has shown that two writers apparently situated in the extremes of the progression from "Commonwealth" to "Postcolonial" literatures can have analogous concerns and, eventually, a corresponding political purpose a purpose none other than unsettling "the epic intention of the civilizing mission."As Bill Ashcroft has pointed out, the shift from the category of Commonwealth Literatures to that of Postcolonial Studies reflected the need to "evolve a way of *reading* the continuing cultural engagements of colonial societies" (2012, xv). Whatever the newer labels and the ways of reading these liteatures, it appears that writers like Patrick White had been telling us about these cultural engagements all along.

Works Cited

Ako, Edward O. 2004. "From Commonwealth to Postcolonial Literature." *CLCWeb: Comparative Literature and Culture* 6.2. http://docs.lib.purdue.edu/clcweb/vol6/iss2/1. Accessed 27 January 2013.

Ashcroft, Bill. 2012. "Introduction: A Convivial Critical Democracy – Postcolonial Studies in the Twenty-First Century," *Literature for Our Times: Postcolonial Studies in the Twenty-First Century,* ed. Bill Ashcroft, Ranjini Mendis, Julie McGonnegal, Arun Mukherjee. Amsterdam: Rodopi: xv-xxxv.

Bhabha, Homi. 1984. "Of Mimicry and Man: The Ambivalence of Colonial Discourse," *Discipleship: A Special Issue on Psychoanalysis.* 28: 125-133.
http://www.jstor.org/stable/778467. Accessed 27 January 2013.

Dagnino, Arianna. 2012. "Transcultural Writers and Transcultural Literature in the Age of Global Modernity," *Transnational Literature* 4.2.
http://fhrc.flinders.edu.au/transnational/home.html Accessed 2 November 2012.

De Silva, K. 2005. A History of Sri Lanka. Colombo: Vijitha Yapa.

Casanova, Pascale. 2004. *The World Republic of Letters.* Cambridge MA: Harvard University Press.

Ganguly, Debjani. 2012. "Global Literary Refractions: Reading Pascale Casanova's The World Republic of Letters in the Post-

Cold War Era," *Literature for Our Times: Postcolonial Studies in the Twenty-First Century*, ed. Bill Ashcroft *et al.* Amsterdam: Rodopi: 15-35.
Ghosh, Amitav. 2008. *Sea of Poppies*. London: John Murray.
—. 2011. *Rivers of Smoke*. Harmondsworth: Penguin.
Hassam, Aziz. 2003. *The Lotus People*. Braamfontein: STE Publications.
Jan Mohamed, Abdul R. 1985. "The Economy of the Manichean Allegory: The Function of Racial Difference in Colonialist Literature," *Critical Inquiry* 12: 59-87.
McLeod, John. 2000. *Beginning Postcolonialism*. Cambridge: Cambridge University Press.
Rushdie, Salman. 1981. *Midnight's Children*. London: Jonathan Cape.
Shepherd, Ron. 1978. "The Twitching Colonel," *Patrick White:a Critical Symposium*, ed. Ron Shepherd and Kirpal Singh. Adelaide: Centre for Research into New Literatures in English: 28-33.
Schulze-Engler, Frank. 2012. "The Commonwealth Legacy: Towards a Decentred Reading of World Literature," *Literature for Our Times: Postcolonial Studies in the Twenty-First Century*, ed. Bill Ashcroft *et al.* Amsterdam: Rodopi: 3-14.
UK Research Projects. http://www8.open.ac.uk/researchprojects/making britain/content/london-mercury). Accessed 15 October 2012.
White, Patrick. 1937. "The Twitching Colonel," *The London Mercury* 35.210: 602–609.
—. 1939. *Happy Valley*. London: George C. Harrap.
Wijesinghe, Manuka. 2006. *Monsoons and Potholes*. Colombo: Perera & Hussein.
—. 2009. *Theravada Man*. Colombo: Bay Owl Press: Perera & Hussein.

Chapter Twenty-Two

The Unity of Being-Synergies Between White's Mystic Vision and the Indian Religio-Spiritual Tradition

Gursharan Aurora
Independent Scholar

The man who sees the world in the self,
And the self in the world, sees
The world as it is and is not perplexed.

Sorrow and delusion do not touch him,
The world is one with his self
He has attained Unity of Being.
(*Isa Upanishad*.Trans.Lal. 1971)

White's religious vision, particularly its Judeo-Christian aspect; has been broadly investigated by critics. This discussion attempts an innovative task in attempting to trace parallels between the philosophy within the novels and aspects of Indian religious belief. 'Indian' religion here will mainly signify Hinduism, though there will be some allusions to Buddhism and also to Sikhism. Obviously there can be no possibility, given the limitations of time and space, to embark on an in-depth comparison between these enormously complex systems of religious belief and the novels, which are multi-layered and complex systems of signification. Nevertheless, the similarity of certain motifs that dominate these religious systems and appear also as dominant in White's works can be meaningfully discussed. Some degree of necessary compression will be gained by allowing generally widely recognised features of White's works to be only broadly referred to through alluding to acknowledged critical works which have, in a sense, established these points beforehand. This discussion will attempt to emphasise the relevant points of comparison as these may be broadly discerned in the body of Indian religious thought.

The attainment of the 'Unity of Being' that this passage from the *Isa Upanishad* (Verse 6,7) celebrates as the ultimate state of realisation and transcendence finds an echo in almost all the works of Patrick White. The 1973 Nobel Prize citation recognised and celebrated his "epic and psychological narrative art which ... introduced a new continent into literature." (Lundquist 1973) However, this contribution also meant the introduction of a mystic vision which appeared to reflect the amalgamation of various religious traditions from around the world. Many critics like Peter Beatson, Carolyn Bliss, Michael Giffin, Krishna Barua and David Coad, among others, have asserted that religious and theological concerns form a major part of White's creative vision. Coad observes:

> White's greatness lies in his ability to invent and give expression to mythopoesis ... his sources are classical and biblical myth, Plato and the Kabbala, Eastern religions and Jung, as well as Aboriginal mythology. (Coad 1993, 510).

In a similar vein, Ingmar Bjorksten has commented:

> The world he (White) moves in is that of Judeo-Christian attitudes and of mysticism. Greek mythology has influenced him and his interest in Eastern philosophy, in Hinduism, and Buddhism, is apparent. Carl Jung's depth psychology and archetypology have served as literary guides. (Bjorksten 1976, 1).

White's own words also demonstrate his vision and intent:

> Religion. Yes, that's behind all my books. What I am interested in is the relationship between the blundering human being and God ... In my books I have lifted bits from various religions in order to come to a better understanding ... (McGregor 1969, 216, 218).

White's vision is reflective of a core of spiritual and mystic yearning not confined to any particular region or time. Many of its aspects are reflected in scriptures, myths, art and literature of all lands and all ages, and is relevant to such concepts as that of the term 'perennial philosophy' invoked by Huxley. It holds that all religious traditions share the same fundamental universal truth, and that there is a common essence or core to all mystic traditions; that philosophical and spiritual insights recur universally, and are not time, region or religion specific. (Huxley 2013).

This assumption of a transcendent universal core of all religions is the starting point for this paper. The paper focuses on the spiritual quest of three of White's protagonists: Theodora Goodman, the Aunt with a hairy upper lip and manly shoes, "some bloke in skirts" (AS, 67) of *The Aunt's Story*; the reticent Stan Parker, the ordinary man of *The Tree of Man,* who "had in him great words of love and beauty, below the surface, if they could be found" (TM. 39); and Voss, "a shabby stranger" (V. 12), who was "a bit of a scarecrow" (V. 16), are all restless seekers yearning, always for that elusive radiant horizon from where their yearning souls can take a flight into infinity.

Each blunders towards spiritual insight in his or her own way: Theodora, through rejection of reason; Voss, through renunciation of ego and arrogance and Stan, through immersion in the workaday life that proffers insights into the nature of the divine. The specific intent of this discussion is to identify a few points of correspondence between Patrick White's mystic vision as reflected in his protagonists' quests and some important Indian religio-spiritual concepts namely: *'Shunyata* (emptiness, void); *'Tapasaya'* (spiritual struggle for transcendence)*, 'Tayag'* (renunciation), *'Maya'* (worldly illusions) and *'grihasth mein udasi'*(spiritual quest in the midst of an ordinary householder's life). With White's works I shall confine myself mostly to *The Aunt's Story* (1948) *The Tree of Man* (1956) and *Voss* (1957).

Whether White used Indian religio-spiritual motifs or themes intentionally can only be a matter for conjecture and indirect inference. Nevertheless, his words and speeches amply demonstrate that he was no stranger to these tenets and these ancient traditions. One has only to recall his first short story "The Twitching Colonel" published so early in his career: the story of the English colonel who has been spiritually transformed by his experience in India, and also the quotation from Gandhi which is the epigraph to his first published novel, *Happy Valley* (1939). He has so many allied themes in his novels such as the solitariness of human beings, the impossibility of building a bridge from one life to another; human alienation from God that stems from the ego which is constantly at war with those urges which would impel recognition of the divine. Underlying all these is the theme of spiritual quest and the realisation that suffering is an indispensable condition of human life which finds parallels in the Indian religio-spiritual tradition and mystical vision of life.

The English translation of *Shunya or Shunyata* is emptiness, nothingness or void. However in the Indian religio-spiritual tradition, the word does not denote only emptiness. It denotes, paradoxically, both emptiness and fullness and is seen as the source from which all beings and all the phenomena of the created world emanate. It stands for an infinite space in which nothingness can manifest itself into a dynamic universe animated by various entities and living beings. It also denotes the inherent, but not always visible interdependence and connections that exist between human beings and the created world.

In Buddhism, *shunnayata* is not seen as emptiness only, but as "transcending and embracing both emptiness and fullness ... Emptiness is seen as a mark or characteristic of every phenomenon, and as the ground of all phenomena." (Randrup and Bagchi 2006)In the *Advaita* Hindu philosophical and mystical tradition *shunya* denotes Brahma, the divine Hindu Trinity of 'Creator, Preserver and Destroyer.' *Shunyata* also stands for the state of the human mind and soul characterised by freedom from all worldly shackles of ego and material ties – a state of absolute emptiness ready to be filled by divine light. It also symbolises the true consciousness, which lies latent and which must be realised in order to attain enlightenment.

However, external forces cannot illuminate the soul, though they can act as catalysts for realisation to dawn on a receptive soul. Thus the quest for comprehending the truth must necessarily be directed inwards before moving outwards. Experience of *Shunyata* symbolises the epiphanic state of *Samadhi* (state of deep meditation), a state wherein the mind is at absolute rest and in tune with the pulse of the created world. The state is characterised by absolute stillness of mind and a complete absence of stream of thought. Such a state is ready to be bathed in blissfulness and illumination. If the divine grace fills this *'shunya'*, the mind and soul become one with the Creator and His creation and the "opaque world becomes transparent." (AS 63).

In such a state, there is no 'I' or self because 'I' is not separate from the Creator or everyone or everything contained in the created world. The following *'doha'* (couplet) of the great Indian *Bhakti* (devotional) poet, Kabir aptly reflects this very thought:

Jab main tha tab Hari nahin, Ab Hari hai main nahin
Sab Andhiyara Mit Gaya, Jab Deepak Dekhya Mahin.
(Kabir 2010, 56)

(When "I" was then Hari (God) was not, Now Hari "is" and "I" am not all the darkness (illusions) mitigated, when I saw the light (illumination) within (trans. Krishan, 2002).

The quest of White's blundering seekers is to achieve just such a state of *shunyata* that can be realised only through going beyond the phenomenal world to attain a state of spiritual emptiness through humility, annihilation of ego and unquestioning acceptance of one's place in the pattern of existence. White asserted that, "the state of simplicity and humility is the only desirable one for artist or man." (1958, 39) Most of his protagonists experience such moments and states of *shunyata* wherein their inner selves appear to throb in tune with the eternal pulse of the universe. Even Voss, White's supreme egoist who starts from a position of arrogance and defiance, in the end experiences this bliss, but only after he accepts his human self and cleanses his soul through humility:

Humility is my brigalow ... As I grow weaker, so I shall become strong
Now that I am nothing, I am, and love is the simplest of all tongues
...
Then I am not God, but man
O God, my God, I pray that you will take my spirit out of
this body's remains, and after you have scattered it, grant

that it shall be everywhere, and in the rocks and in the empty water holes, and in true love of all men, and in you, O God, at last. (V 296-297)

The quest of Voss is monumental. Out of all White's seekers, his travails are most arduous, maybe because he has, within him, the most powerful demon to conquer. His supreme egotism makes him a compelling, awe-inspiring figure. He does not mind undergoing the most excruciating physical suffering but even the idea of submission to any force beyond his own self is abhorrent to him. Arrogance is a habit with him. Humility does not come naturally to him. He is a man driven by the will to be God himself. The priest at Moreton Bay tells him, "Mr. Voss, you have contempt for God, because he is not in your image." (V 50) He seeks to be complete within himself and does not admit or allow any closeness to any other being lest it render him weak and vulnerable. So strong is his obsession with his own self-sufficiency that when he thinks he might be getting too fond even of his own dog, he executes it. Laura's love cannot pierce easily through his hard armour: "He was forced to many measures of brutality in defence of himself." (V 14)

He appears to be an unlikely spiritual pilgrim yet the beauty of the created world can, and does, stir something inside him and he is entranced and, for a little while, transported out of his confined self and made to feel part of God's creation. The beauty of the valley at Rhine Towers appears to penetrate his egoistic veneer and, for a fleeting moment, frees him of all the shackles that hold his soul prisoner. He succumbs to its almost intolerable beauty of the valley:

> It was the valley itself which drew Voss. Its mineral splendours were increased in that light. As bronze repeated, vein of silver loomed in the gullies, knobs of amethyst and sapphire glowed on the hills, until the horseman rounded that bastion which fortified from sight the ultimate strong-hold of beauty.
>
> "Achhh!" cried Voss, upon seeing. ...
>
> This was for the moment pure gold. The purple stream of evening flowing at its base almost drowned Voss. (128)

Thus, Voss, the megalomaniac explorer explores not only the vast, harsh Australian desert but also the aridity inside his own soul and towards the end, experiences *shunyata* through the eclipse of the self and submission to God's will: "I have no plan," said Voss, "but will trust to God." (V 379) His words prefigure Laura's summation at the end: "' When a man is truly humbled, when he has learned that he is not God, then he is nearest to becoming so. In the end he may ascend.'"(V 387) Krishna Barua has noted: "Transcendence resides not beyond but within, where the basic psyche merges with the soul and consciousness in celebration of what can be appropriately called 'the mystery of Unity." (2010, 5)

Theodora, another of White's seekers, who is destined to be "This thing a spinster which, at best, becomes that institution, an aunt," (AS 12) is almost bereft of meaningful human contact, also experiences *shunyata* when the true meaning of existence shines through the opacity of the world. One such moment is the suspension of her consciousness when she merges with the spirit of the created world while watching the hawk tear at a carcass:

> He was a little hawk, with a reddish golden eye, that looked at her as he stood on the sheep's carcass and coldly tore through the dead wool. The little hawk tore and paused, tore and paused ... Theodora looked at the hawk. She could not judge his act, because her eye had contracted, it was reddish-gold, and her curved face cut the wind. Death, said father, lasts for a long time. Like the bones of the sheep that would lie, and dry, and whiten, and clatter under horses. But the act of the hawk that she watched, hawk like, was a moment of shrill beauty that rose above the endlessness of bones. (AS 33)

Such moments intersperse her barren life but these are, in the words of her headmistress, epiphanic moments "of passing affection, through which the opaque world will become transparent ..." (63)

For Stan Parker, who is "torn between the images of gold and ebony and his own calm life of flesh," (39) one such heraldic moment comes when he experiences a gradual eclipse of his own identity in the tempestuous storm:

> The man who was watching the storm and who seemed to be sitting right at the centre of it, was at first exultant. Like his own dry

paddock, his skin drank the rain. He folded his wet arms, and his attitude added to his complacency. ... But as the storm increased, his flesh had doubts, and he began to experience humility. The lightning which could have struck open basalt, had it seemed, the power to open souls. (TM 151)

Overcome by the moment "full of wonder," Stan is bathed in humility and is grateful for the support of "the wooden post that he had put there himself years before ... (TM 151).

Such moments of fleeting illumination are precursors of the ultimate enlightenment sought by these seekers but these moments of clarity in an opaque world are elusive and rare because the subjugation of true consciousness to worldly forces obscures them. The world and all its material phenomena are considered impermanent and illusory in Indian religio-philosophical thought. The Hindi word for this illusory world is *'Maya'* (worldly illusions). The concept of *Maya* is central to almost all Indian philosophies. Thoughts and the word carry a host of connotations but at the simplest level it stands for the veil of illusory perception of the world that blurs an individual's ability to perceive and experience true reality.

> *Maya* as a power of God is indistinguishable from Him, just as the burning power of fire is from the fire itself. It is by this that God, the Great Magician, conjures up the world-show with all its wonderful objects. The appearance of this world is taken as real by the ignorant, but the wise who can see through it find nothing but God, the only reality behind this illusory show. (Chatterjee and Datta 2011, 337).

A spiritual pilgrim seeks to pierce this veil and look beyond. White, as a writer, is himself embarked on just such a quest in his works – to go beyond the illusion and see reality:

> "I have the same idea with all my books: an attempt to come close to the core of reality, the structure of reality, as opposed to the merely superficial." (McGregor 1969, 219)

His pilgrims, too, are embarked on a similar quest – to look beyond the superficial play of the illusory physical world to find the real purpose and meaning of God and His creation. Theodora, whether she is at Meroe, the *jardin exotique* or the "blank house." (.AS 274) in America, is waiting for life to "forsake its queer opaque manner and come out into the open." (140)

For Voss, reality is obscured by his own unwillingness to see beyond the *maya* of his ego and arrogance. He looks at the world and the people around him through his own warped perceptions and therefore fails to understand reality. It is only towards the end before he is beheaded by the Aboriginal boy, Jackie, with the knife that he had himself given him, that Voss attains humility, humanity and transcendence through the dissolution of the self and through a sense of identification with the created world. Laura aptly sums up his experience; "True knowledge only comes of death by torture in the country of the mind." (V 446)

Stan perhaps is the only one who, despite his ordinariness, starts from a position of strength. His simplicity and acceptance of life, as it is lived, shields him, from the web of *'maya'* though final understanding and perception, in all its totality, comes to him only moments before his death when he is sitting at the centre of his *mandalic* garden: "It was perfectly obvious that the man was seated at the heart of it, and from his heart the trees radiated, with grave movements of life … All was circumference to the centre and beyond that the worlds of other circles … " (TM 474).

The evangelist who comes to save his soul appears an ignorant intruder rather than a saviour. Smug in his shallow knowledge he asks, "Don't you believe in God, perhaps?" Stan's reply reflects his new awareness: "Then the old man, who had been cornered long enough, saw, through perversity perhaps, but with his own eyes. He was illuminated. He pointed with his stick at the gob of spittle. 'That is God,' he said." (TM 476) The simple yet powerful words are as profound as Blake's 'heaven in a grain of sand' and echo a salient tenet of *'Advaita Vedanta'* 3 that only the innermost core, the *Atman* (soul) of all living creatures and the essence of all inanimate objects, is real because it emanates from the Brahma and as such is the sole underlying absolute reality of the whole universe. *Advaita* refers to the non- dualistic school of Hinduism. Its basic premise is that *Brahma* is the only reality and everything else is mere appearance or illusion. (Hinduism, 2013) *'Kan kan mein Bhagwan'*

(God in each and every particle) is an oft repeated phrase in the Hindi-speaking belt of India. Thus, in the Indian religio-philosophy the Creator abides in all His creations and is the Absolute energy animating the universe:

> All existence – earth, heavens, planets, gods, living and non-living objects are part of one great person, who pervades the world, but also remains beyond it. In Him all that is, has been and will be, are united. (Chatterjee and Datta 2011, 323)

The Supreme Reality is thus both immanent and transcendent. The *Atman* flows from this Supreme Reality, the Brahma and seeks to merge back into Him. The way to achieve this union is through *Tapasay* (spiritual suffering) *and Tayaag* (renunciation) which are considered complementary in Indian thought. Each is inherent in the other. Spiritual 'suffering' does not imply any form of self-infliction or torture. Rather, it denotes the restlessness, suffering and pangs caused by *Bairaag,* the separation of the spirit from its source. The human being's quest is to reunite with the eternal life force through a journey within to find the inner self, come to terms with the evil within, annihilate it, and then move out again on a journey towards transcendence, a journey from humanity to divinity.

Tayaag is renunciation of all that impedes the *Atman's* ascent towards fulfilment and ultimate reunion with Brahma. Both these features of spiritual quest in the Indian mystic tradition find an echo in Patrick White's novels, albeit in a different context. White believes that spiritual suffering is an essential means of spiritual salvation and he quotes Mahatma Gandhi, in the epigraph to his first novel, *Happy Valley* (1939): "the law of suffering is the one indispensable condition of human existence." Progress is to be measured by the amount of suffering undergone: "the purer the suffering, the greater is the progress." (7).

White's vision and the Indian spiritual tradition seem to converge on the belief that suffering is a necessary route to spiritual progress. Both are based on the concept of the movement into the world and back to faith." The quest of Voss spans three stages "of God into man. Man. And man returning to God" (V 386); Stan

Parker's yearns for moments when he would begin "to know every corner of the darkness as if it were daylight" (TM 151) even while engaged with the sheer ordinariness of life; Theodora Goodman's fleeting experiences of clarity lead to the ultimate realisation that worldly illusions cloud reality and one must pierce through the haze to reach it; these seekers are all directed towards finding the union between man and God, between *Atman* (soul) and *paramataman* (the supreme soul) or *Brahma*. Theodora's glimpses of lucidity come paradoxically, at a time when she is descending into what rational observers would decide was madness: "... the process of disintegration that was taking place at the foot of the mountains should have been tragic, but was not. The shapes of disintegrating light protested less than the illusions of solidity with which men surround themselves." (`AS 275)

Teetering on the edge of sanity and insanity; opaqueness and clarity, she is filled with anxiety: "She doubted whether flesh was humble enough" (AS 275) and is finally led into clarity by Holstius, an imaginary amalgam, a figment of her latent consciousness, of all the men who had impacted on her life. He tells her: "You cannot reconcile joy and sorrow ... there is sometimes little to choose between reality and the illusion of reality." (AS 278). She does ultimately succeed in choosing reality rather than its mere illusion: "She looked at the world with eyes blurred by water, but a world curiously pure, expectant, undistorted." (AS 279)

This distinction between reason and intuition as modes of spiritual realisation is also a central concern of Indian religio-spiritual tradition. All schools of Hindu philosophy believe that *Atman* is distinct and independent from mind and matter. Therefore logic and reason are not considered to be a conclusive means of spiritual realisation. White too, envisions the soul as wholly distinct from the reasoning mind. He insists on the inadequacy of reason to solve the ultimate problems that beset man. His protagonists explore the hidden path that would make them realise like Stan Parker that "One and no other figure is the answer to all sums." (TM 477) The words are an echo of the assertion in the *Rig Veda*: *Ekam Sat; Viprah bahudha vadanti*. That which Is, is one. Wise men speak of it in many ways." (*Rig Veda* 1.164.46)

Just as Theodora renounces her sanity in order to understand the divine truth, Voss sheds his arrogance to find ultimate realisation. Renunciation, in Indian thought, does not imply giving up one's worldly possessions, though simplicity in life is advocated. Rather, it implies the abnegation of the five sins, *kaam* (lust), *krodh* (anger), *lobh* (greed), *moh* (attachment) and *ahankaar* (pride). In some schools of thought, it also implies a movement away from the routine of life to lead an ascetic and celibate life in order to pray and meditate. In Hinduism also, *'Sanyas'* (ascetic and celibate living), a deliberate withdrawal and detachment from life is considered an integral part of the spiritual quest, but is advocated as the fourth and last phase of human life

Assuming that the average human life spans 100 years, *Manu Smriti* and other Classic Sanskrit texts divide it into four *Ashrama(s)* (stages) of 25 years each: *Brahmacharya* (student life); *Grihastha Ashram* (Householder's life); *Vanaprastha* (forest dwelling as a hermit to lead a life of partial renunciation so as to prepare. oneself for the next stage) and *Sanyasa* (complete renunciation of material and worldly life in order to pray and meditate to attain *Moksha* (salvation). (Hinduism, *ashramas* 2013) Glimpses of movements away from life, reason, being or self can be discerned also in White's works. Most of his major characters renounce their given existence to embark on journeys, whether physical or spiritual in order to find ways to make the incoherent, imperfect world cohere into one whole. This deliberate movement away from their normal way of life is symbolic of *tayag* (renunciation): Theodora's journey to the United States, Voss's ill-fated but spiritually fulfilling exploration of the Australian desert as well as his own self are symbolic of movements away from the superficiality of daily existence.

When a man, becomes troubled by some inexplicable restlessness of the soul, he must retreat into the natural world, away from human contact, and there, must try to find the answers that would dissolve the restlessness of his soul. The experiences of Theodora and Voss are based on such withdrawals from life but Stan Parker's quest is different. It stands out in contrast because he does not reject or move away from life. However, his journey is all the more pertinent because he seeks the sublime through immersion in all that an ordinary life can throw up: birth and death; joy and sorrow; flood and fire; acceptance and rejection; trust and betrayal; marriage and adultery; a sick daughter and wastrel son; in fact, the whole gamut of human experiences. His movement away takes the form of periods of detachment from the surface of life around him. The reticent man is unable to really be part of the buzzing township. A part of him is closed even to his wife, Amy. His yearning is for something beyond the ordinary: "There were veins in him of wisdom and poetry, but deep, much of which would never be dug." (TM 29).

Stan's spiritual journey is in tune with the concept of *'grihasth mein udasi'* (spiritual quest in the midst of an ordinary householder's life) advocated in Sikhism. Unlike many other schools of Hinduism, Sikhism does not recommend abnegation of one's duties as a householder. Detachment, according to Guru Nanak, the founder of Sikhism, does not imply abdication of one's duties as a.human being. In fact, the concept of seeking realisation while being actively engaged in the day-to-day life of the householder is considered an ideal:

> *Nanak satguru bhetiye poori hove jugat*
> *Hasandeyan, khelandeyan, painandeyan, khavandeyan, which he hove mukat.*
> (SGGS, 522)
> By realizing the True God, one's life becomes worthwhile.
> One can find salvation even while laughing, playing, dressing and eating.

The tenet of *'grihastha mein udasi'* looks askance at the concept of withdrawal and escape from the demands of life. The ideal life recommended by the holy gurus is that of the householder engaged in beneficent activity, keeping his mind absorbed in contemplation and devotion. Sikhism enjoins its followers to adopt *Parvirti Maarag* (way of active activity by a householder). It recommends that one should try to realise one's spiritual yearnings while being actively engaged in the life of a householder. Arvinder Singh has noted that:

According to Sikhism, the suppression of desires and self-torture do not control mind as mind can be disciplined only by purging one's ego. In Sikh thought spiritual pursuits and temporal living are not viewed separately and independent of one another … Spiritual pursuits have to be accomplished even as one is engaged in mundane responsibilities inherent in life as a householder with all its challenges, constraints and entanglements (Singh 2012, 43).

Stan Parker, White's quintessential ordinary man – a husband, a father, a tiller of the soil – is an epitome of just such a householder. From the moment he lights his first fire in the bush as a young man when "Life had not yet operated on his face," (TM 9) he seeks to find the meaning of reality even while he is immersed in everyday life, in the cracks in the ground, a lizard, and even in a gob of spittle: "He went about ploughing, chopping, milking, reaping, emptying buckets and filling them. All these acts were good in themselves, but none of them explained his dream life, as some word might, like lightning out of his brain." (TM 297)

Thus, he goes through life which inflicts all that an ordinary life can inflict upon an ordinary man but all the time, somewhere deep within him, he has a sense of unacknowledged detachment and a longing for transcendence: "His Gold Coast still glittered in a haze of promise" (42) The moment of his epiphany is, like his life, simple yet profound. Illumination does not come to him with fanfare. The mandalic revelation dawns on him in the form of the concentric circles of trees, clouds he observes as he sits in his garden and is concentrated and finally reflected in a gob of spittle, a very unlikely and mundane object to be the vehicle of such a momentous and sacred experience. Yet, that almost sickening gob becomes the mirror that satiates his yearning to find a unifying thread between man, nature and God, and the theme central to this, as indeed to all White's novels, is realised.

White uses a consistent pattern of images and symbols to depict the different stages of the spiritual quest of his protagonists, the most important and recurring of them being the image of a Mandala, which is the ultimate symbol of the integrated consciousness. The word 'Mandala' derives from a Sanskrit word which first appeared in the *Rig Veda*5. In the Buddhist and Hindu religious traditions their sacred art often takes a Mandala form. The literal meaning of the word is 'a circle'. The basic form of a Hindu or Buddhist Mandala is a square with four gates (one on each side), containing concentric circles with a centre point, which is the seat of the Creator. These Mandalas play a significant spiritual and ritual role in both these religions. In various spiritual traditions, Mandalas may be employed for focusing the attention of aspirants as well as of adepts, as spiritual teaching tools, for establishing a sacred space, and as an aid to meditation and trance induction.

White has used the Mandala as a symbol in many of his novels and has even used it in the title of his novel *The Solid Mandala*. He has described the Mandala as "a symbol of totality. It is believed to be the dwelling place of the Gods. Its protective circle is the pattern of order superimposed on psychic chaos. Sometimes, its geometric form is seen in a vision." (SM 229) His words are an echo of what Carl Jung states in *Mysterium Coniunctionis*: "The Mandala is symbolic of the unity of all archetypes as well as of the multiplicity of the phenomenal world." (Jung 1956, 463) The symbol of the Mandala appears in White's works in varied ways most strikingly perhaps when Stan Parker, just before his death is seated "at the centre of concentric circles of shrubs and trees and "the cold and golden bowl of winter" (TM 474) and also reflected in the "gob of spittle" (TM 476) which becomes the medium for his ultimate realisation that God is in all things. Another more unusual manifestation perhaps is when Judd kills the goat for the Christmas feast surrounded by the other members of the rag tag team of Voss's explorers. Watching him, Voss is struck by the perfection of the scene, "As he saw it now, perfection is always circular, enclosed. So that Judd's circle was enviable." (V 198) Critics like Peter Beatson, A.P Riemer and others have explored the occurrences and significations of this image with admirable clarity yet with due attention to its complexities; the further expansion of their insights here would be simply redundant.

Two other striking similarities between White's vision and the Indian religio-spiritual tradition are the archetypes of the non-conformist seeker and the cyclic pattern of the human quest for spiritual transcendence. The protagonists of his novels embark on purely mystical quests but they repudiate formal religious institutions. They stand out as 'different,' even odd and eccentric beings amidst a sea of conformists because they break free from what they are supposed to be and are embarked on a quest for what they want to be. They all suffer greatly and most of them die during the passage of the narrative but even though they find it difficult to express themselves and bond with other human beings, they have the gift of communion with the created world. Isolated by the strength of the impulses which drive them in their quest for transcendental insights, they become outcasts and are regarded by most of their acquaintances as odd, stupid or mad.

Indian mythology is also filled with such characters who, like Prince Siddhartha Gautama (the revered founder of Buddhism), renounced his royal heritage and embarked on a quest which ultimately led to his attaining Enlightenment and his becoming a *Mahatma* (Great Soul). Others pursue the path to redemption after rising from a fallen state: the sage Valmiki author of the Hindu scripture *The Ramayana* was a highway robber before his conversion. That is why the theme of the outsider's quest and transcendence through suffering in Patrick White's novels are familiar to Indian readers who are no strangers to these concepts. The most striking example in White's fiction is Voss, the tragic superman who is perhaps his most powerful character, not physically, but spiritually. His other seekers have their weaknesses and inadequacies but none has the monumental, demonic arrogance that Voss has. Through him, White affirms that, even the damned can be saved if they seek redemption long enough and hard enough. Voss's quest is the longest and the most tortuous because he has, within his own arrogant self, a more powerful demon to overpower.

The cyclic pattern of the spiritual quest of White's characters symbolises the universal human yearning for realisation. Often the quest of the seeker is taken over by a child – Theodora's niece Lou, Stan's grandson and Laura's adopted daughter, Mercy are all symbols of the endless quest for spiritual enlightenment on which humanity is eternally embarked. These children are the inheritors who will also traverse the hinterlands that their predecessors walked before them. At a time when the protagonist is ending his quest, this archetypal child is starting his. At a time when the former is emerging from the dark night of the soul after a relentless grappling with the demon within, the inheritor child is preparing to journey into the arena a summary comment of the process is reflected in the last line of *The Tree of Man*: "So that, in the end, there was no end." (480)

The passing on of the spiritual quest from one generation to the next is echoed in the words of Aurobindo Ghose, the great Indian poet and philosopher:

> Our yearning for the human Godward climb
> Till all is done for which the stars were made
> Till the heart discovers God
> And the soul knows itself. And even then
> There is no end. (1991, 100)

White's central theme – man's eternal and cyclic quest for meaning and value, is universal and timeless and is enriched by the hues and colours of various religious, spiritual and mystic traditions of the world. He has expressed this universal theme through his own land and time – twentieth century Australia and Australian suburbs like Sarsaparilla, the imaginary territory that provides the setting for his works. It could be claimed that White manages to condense the whole universe into his little suburb and succeeds in conjoining the events of an Australian present with eternity. The Australian protagonists are inextricably linked to, and conditioned by the vastness of the never-never land yet their narrative breaks out of the boundaries of Australia and symbolises human beings living out their common destiny.

Each of White's novels depicts this contrast between existence and essence; between what one is supposed to be and what one wants to be. In novel after novel, White explores these dualities and seeks to harmonise them. His works are not, as some critics have implied, pessimistic statements. A.P Reimer has pointedly asked: "Must one agree that only through absolute alienation from social existence can man have a possibility of visionary achievement?" (Riemer 1967, 17) Leonie Kramer has dubbed White's vision a "pessimistic view of man's spiritual potential." (Kramer 1971, 135) However, in the light of the Indian religio-spiritual tradition, such comments would lack relevance because *'tapasaya'* is considered a prerequisite of spiritual enlightenment. In that light, White's works are affirmative assertions that after a journey through the cleansing fires of suffering, the soul rises again, renewed and regenerated. His characters seek to see the benign face of God in every animate and inanimate object of the world. White himself has been troubled by the question of divinity and he has felt the divine presence everywhere: "God is everywhere they told me. Is he in the Bunya-bunya tree? Yes, everywhere" (White 1981, 70).

White's mystic vision confirms that the spiritual quest is not confined to any region, age, religion or culture. It is eternal and universal. The core of most religio-spiritual traditions converge at some point or the other and any writer delving into these questions, depicts traces of various traditions and, in the process, enriches his work and his worldview. His works, his mystic vision, his creative genius and his multi faceted worldview are evocative examples of this convergence of various religio-spiritual traditions. He sees the created world as a manifestation of divinity. In his autobiographical work *Flaws in the Glass* White has himself described the potent and purifying magic of the natural world:

> And yet even the most exasperated and temporarily scornful pilgrim can be raised from the slough of his cynicism by the silence of the pine trees ... the blue and gold crag of the mountain itself, an icon in its details of jagged rock, tufts of grass, the florets of a stubborn plant rendered with Byzantine formality. (1983, 161)

The writer's poetic, mystic vision visualises a unity between man, God and the natural world and manages to span the seemingly unbridgeable chasm between the finite and the infinite. His characters seek to see the benign face of God reflected in every animate or inanimate object of the world. To sum up, I quote a poem from Rabindranath Tagore's *Gitanjali* India's own first Nobel Laureate in literature who also showed a deep and continuing affinity with religious themes in his work, explaining the perennial quest of the religious seeker:

> I thought that my voyage had come to its end at the last limit of power, that the path before me was closed, that provisions were exhausted and the time come to take shelter in a silent obscurity.

But I find that thy will knows no end in me. And when old words die out on the tongue, new melodies break forth from the heart; where the old tracks are lost, new country is revealed with its wonders. (1967, 29)

Works Cited

Arora, Prakash Udai and Singh, Abhay Kumar. 2007. *Udayana: New Horizons in History, Classics and Inter-Cultural Studies.* New Delhi: Anamika Publishers.

Beatson, Peter. 1976. *The Eye in the Mandala. Patrick White: A Vision of Man and God.* Sydney: A.H. & A.W. Reed.

Bjorksten, Ingmar. 1976. *Patrick White: A General Introduction.* St. Lucia: University of Queensland Press.

Bliss, Carolyn. 1986. *Patrick White's Fiction: The Paradox of Fortunate Failure.* London: Macmillan.

Chatterjee, Satischandra and Datta, Dhirendramohan. 2011. *An Introduction to Indian Philosophy*, Kolkatta: University of Calcutta.

Coad, David. 1993. "Patrick White, Prophet in the Wilderness," *World Literature Today,* 67. 3, Contemporary Australian Literature: 510-514.

Ghose, Aurobindo. 1991. "Is This the End?," *Literary Petals,* ed. D.V. Jindal. Mohali: PSEB.

Hansson, Karin. "Patrick White: Existential Explorer," *Nobel Laureates in Search of Identity and Integrity: Voices of Different Cultures*, ed Anders Hallergrenm. Singapore: World Scientific Publishing: 103-116.

Huxley Aldous, http://parvati.tripod.com/perennial.html. Accessed 16.june 2013.

http://www. hinduism/concepts/advaita: Accessed 16 June 2013.

http://www.hinduwebsite.com/hinduism/concepts/ashramas. Accessed 16 June 2013.

Jung, Carl. 1977. *Mysterium Coniuntionis*, *Collected Works of C.G. Jung.* Vol. 14 Princeton: Princeton University Press.

Kabir, Sant. 2010. *Kabir Dohavali.* Ed. S. Nilotpat. New Delhi: Granth Academy.

Krishan, Rajender, 2013. "Kabir,"

http://www.boloji.com/index.cfm?md=Content&sd=DohaDetails&DohaID=33. Accessed 27 May 2013.

Lal, P. 1971. "Search for Values in Literature," *Studies in Australian and Indian Literature*, ed. C.D. Narasimhaiah and S. Nagarajan. New Delhi: Indraprastha Press: 87-111.

Lundkvist, Artur. 1973. Nobel Prize Award Ceremony Speech. http://www.nobelprize.org/nobel_prizes/literature/laureates/1973/presentation-speech.html?print=1. Accessed 3 August 2012.

Mc Gregor, Craig. 1969. *In the Making.* Melbourne: Nelson.

McDougall, Robert. 1966. *"Australia Felix: Joseph Furphy and Patrick White" Commonwealth Literary Fund Lecture.* Canberra: Australian National University Press.

Moffit, Ian. 1957. "Talk with Patrick White," *New York Times Book Review*, (18th August): 18.

Morley, Patricia A. 1972. *The Mystery of Unity*. Montreal: Mc-Gill Queen's University Press.

Randrup, Axel and Bagchi, Tista. 2006.*Correspondence between Jewish Mysticism and Indian Philosophies* (CIRIP), http://cogprints.org/4796/ 1/indianjewish.html. Accessed June 11 2012.

Riemer, A P. 1967. "Visions of the Mandala in *The Tree of Man,"* Southerly 27: 3-19.

Singh, Arvinder. "Sikhism: A Householder's Religion," International Journal of Humanities and Religion (IJHR). www.humanitiesjournal.info Online ISSN: 2319-5630. December, 2012 IJHR, 2(8): 43-49. Accessed 6 May, 2013.

Tagore, Rabindranath. 1967. *Gitanjali.* London: Macmillan.

—. 1968. *Lovers' Gifts and* Crossings: London Macmillan.

White, Patrick *Happy Valley*. 1939. London: George G.Harrap.

—. 1948. *The Aunt's Story.* Harmondsworth: Penguin.

—. 1956. *The Tree of Man*. London: Eyre & Spottiswoode.

—. 1957. *Voss*. London: Eyre & Spottiswoode.

—. 1958. *"The Prodigal Son,"* Australian Letters 1.3: 37 - 40.

—. 1961. *Riders in the Chariot.* London: Eyre & Spottiswoode.

—. 1981.*Flaws in the Glass: A Self Portrait*. London: Jonathan Cape.

CHAPTER TWENTY-THREE

ESTABLISHING A CONNECTION: RESONANCES IN *GURUGRANTH SAHIB* AND WORKS OF PATRICK WHITE

ISHMEET KAUR
CENTRAL UNIVERSITY OF GUJARAT, GANDHINAGAR, INDIA

Comparative Literature, as a discipline, opens up possibilities of establishing connections between what might seem to be apparently diverse and far-fetched. These connections make sense if they are understood in context of the contemporary concern with plurality and diversity, both cultural and linguistic, yet also remain conscious of certain similarities encountered at several points of contact. The present paper is an attempt to underline certain similarities on which comparison is made possible between two different genres in different centuries and across different continents. The main focus here is on establishing a comparison between Patrick White's *The Tree of Man* and the scriptural text *Guru Granth Sahib*.

Henry Remak, in his seminal essay "Comparative Literature, Its Definition and Function," has provided a useful definition of Comparative Literature

> Comparative Literature is the study of literature beyond the confines of one particular country, and the study of the relationships between literature on one hand and other areas of knowledge and belief, such as the arts (e.g. painting, sculpture, architecture, music), philosophy, history, the social sciences, (e.g. politics, economics, sociology), the sciences, religion, etc., on the other. In brief it is the comparison of one literature with another or others, and the comparison of literature with other spheres of human expression. (Remak 1961, 2)

As quoted above, the comparison of literature with "other spheres of human expression" legitimises the claim for the present comparison between *Guru Granth Sahib*, a scripture and Patrick White's novels, works of literature. Remak explains that the prerequisite for any study be "systematic and if a definitely separable, coherent discipline outside of literature is studied as such." (Remak 1961, 8) Therefore the emphasis is on following a more inclusive model of Comparative Literature by being more *"functional"* than theoretical. He explains that despite the "disagreements on the theoretical aspects ... there is agreement on the task" and suggests that:

> It can do best by not only relating several literatures to each other but by relating literature to other fields of human knowledge and activity, especially artistic and ideological fields; that is by extending the investigation of literature both geographically and generically. (1961, 9)

These principles outline the bases of the present comparison. The next section traces the connection between literature and religion and will be followed by an introduction to *Guru Granth Sahib* and works by White.

The art of storytelling has been amongst the precursors, not only of literature but of religion as well. Literary in form and religious in content, the ancient art of storytelling suggests an inseparable connection between literature and religion. Literature seems to have always facilitated religion from earliest times and in many cultures. Similarly, the texts that supported religion also suggested the persistence of a literary activity. In this connection, the purpose of religion and literature seems to complement each other particularly through their concern for human beings universally. Later literature and religion developed in such ways as to establish separate disciplines independent of each other.

The very notion of dealing with scriptures in academic discussions calls for an understanding of scriptures as texts and their scope. However, "Scriptures cannot be considered as merely texts," states Wilfred Smith, "they have to be understood as entities which participate actively in the life of human beings subjectively."

(Qtd. in Singh 2000, 5) The scriptures influence and impact on the lives of human beings by being an integral part of their lives especially through providing guidelines to how a life should be lived by dictating the moral and ethical values to a particular community.

In the case of *Guru Granth Sahib,* the scripture has to be discussed in terms of the traditions it evolves from and also, in connection with the philosophy rendered by it. Since the scripture evolves out of the *Bhakti* and the *Sufi* traditions, it challenges the established religions of its time, questioning the social factors that divided human beings from each other, such as religious dogmas, rituals and caste system. *Guru Granth Sahib* does not stay attached to a particular community but addresses several communities including the lower classes and different castes. At the same time, it includes the voices of all communities equally by recording their creative writings in the form of poems and songs. Thus, the scripture extends itself beyond the boundaries of scripture and spreads into other areas of human expression such as music, and literature.

The premise of this comparison is that the scripture may be studied as literature, and fiction may be regarded as having scriptural values. *Guru Granth Sahib*, the Sikh scripture challenges the traditional order established by the instituted religions and voices resistance against the discriminating caste system. The scripture qualifies as a literary anthology as it is a collaboration of songs, poems and verses by seven *Gurus,* fifteen *bhagats* (devotees) and eleven *Bhattas* (bards) who belonged to different castes, sects, religions and regions. Compiled in 1604 by Guru Arjun Dev, and completed in 1706, the text is an embodiment of spiritual, religious, cultural and social values. It is a volume of wisdom and spiritual philosophy full of secular, social and democratic values. The following observation describes *Guru Granth Sahib* as literature and its association with different languages, texts, scriptures and religions, thereby highlighting its permeability:

> The Sikh *Gurus* preached their principles in the language of the masses. They adopted popular forms of poetry such as *salok chhant, Bara Mahan, Thhittin Bawan Akhari, Var* (heroic ballad).

> The *Var* is also a song of praise. The Guru praised the Name and at the same time denounced egoistic pursuits.

The Sikh *Gurus* enriched Panjabi literature. The crude and poor language became in their hands a treasury of thoughts. They absorbed the diction of saint-language and current philosophies. In *Sri Guru Granth Sahib* are found words associated with the *Vedas, Vedanta, Vaishnavism, Shaivism, Shaktism,* Buddhism, Jainism and Islam. Panjabi was also enriched by words of saint-language, which owed its origin to Sanskrit. Persian and Arabic words [which] came through Islam (Mansukhani 2004, 1).

> The scripture stands for moral and social justice for the entire human race. The text claims the oneness of God with all human beings. Discarding all dividing factors, the focus remains on equality.

In the same context, literature too performs a scriptural function, as it offers a critique of social, political and cultural norms. It is interesting to observe how reverberations of a similar philosophy can be seen in Patrick White's novel *The Tree of Man* (1956). David Coad explains how White had given up all inclination towards institutionalised religion before he began writing *The Tree of Man* but his experience of falling in the mud became a 'turning point' in his life:

> White underwent a religious conversion in the early 1950s. He had thrown away religion, especially institutionalised Anglicanism, in his teens. After falling on his back in the mud and rain on his way to feed the dogs one day, White cursed a God in whom he started to believe. The farce of his "fall," and its subsequent humbling led White to have inklings of the divine Presence in this world. (Coad 1993: 512)

White's denial of institutionalised religion becomes the central point of this comparison since, *Guru Granth Sahib* too evolved out of a tradition where institutional religion is questioned. This point shall be evaluated in detail when the comparative analysis is attempted. Though similar themes run across his oeuvre his treatment of them varies from novel to novel. For White, religion is not viewed through typical symbols or deities; rather he perceives it through actions and experiences of speculative beings that are in search of divinity. Coad continues to explain that, "White's novels, plays, and stories of the next forty years are the testimony of a private-made-public search for the sacred and the transcendental, for the imprint of God's intervention in human affairs …" (Coad 1993, 512)

For White, as quoted by David Marr, religion is at the back of all his books: "What I am interested in is the relationship between the blundering human being and God. I think there is a Divine Power, a Creator who has an influence on human beings if they are willing to be open to him." (Qtd. in Marr 1991, 282) Thus, the only Australian to have won the Nobel Prize in literature is unmistakably inspired by life and the deeper issues of existence. Often his protagonists have a universal appeal in that they are representative of ordinary humanity and they seem to search for a greater reality beyond the realm of institutional religions.

In *The Tree of Man* White addresses questions not only related to physical existence alone, but also to the metaphysical. Most of his novels cover almost all aspects of life, beginning from birth and continuing to death. This particular novel about Stan and Amy Parker's lives, based on the biblical myth of Adam and Eve, begins with a man who seems to have concluded a journey and now stops and decides to settle at a place in between "two stringy barks" in a part in the bush where these were the "dominant trees … rising above the involved scrub with the simplicity of true grandeur." (9) He begins by cutting the trees and making a fire for himself amidst the cold of the bush. The "man" is the 'first man' (comparable to Adam) who comes in contact with this part of the bush. He is introduced only after the first experience of the man and land are narrated in great detail, as "The name of this man was Stan Parker." (TM 11)

Stan's introduction to his mother's God "a pale- blue gentleness" built as a result of her biblical reading was different to that of his father's conception of a "fiery God." Stan did not seem to be completely influenced by these notions, neither by his mother nor his father, as he remained "somehow a separate being" (13); a being who developed his own understanding of a God that was very personal based on life-time experiences and a continuous struggle for enlightenment. As William Walsh suggests the novel is White's "version of Genesis and Redemption" (1974, 203) the conception of Stan and Amy based on the biblical analogy of Adam and Eve, seems to develop a sense of beginning in order to provide a justification for all aspects of life.

Similarly with *Guru Granth Sahib,* it is difficult to reach a historical explanation as to how the world was created but the text establishes a notion of pre-existence and moves beyond these dimensions. It declares God as 'self-existent.' *Brahma,* the Creator was followed by the rest of creation. The word is considered to be the primary source of creation: "The whole excellent creation is created through the word of Brahma [God]. [This creation is] true, beautiful and keeps the mind in perennial joy." (Singh 2000, 10).

> First of all, the lotuses bloomed in the woods; from them, all the swan-souls came into being ... First of all, there was only the Primal Being. From that Primal Being, Maya was produced.
>
> All that is, is His. In this Garden of the Lord, we all dance, Women and men both dance. ... The [God] says, "This creation and I are one and the same." || 2 || Like the pots on the Persian wheel, the world sways high and low ... I have come at last to Your Door. (Singh, 2000: 693-694)

According to this philosophy, God and His creation are identical. In the novels of Patrick White a similar sense of the oneness of God with nature prevails. In *The Tree of Man,* the revelations of the Divine come to Stan Parker's through experiences of oneness with nature, not only in times of peace and tranquillity, but also when nature is experienced in its most furious form. During the storm, he chooses to stay outdoors, Nature even in its most destructive form, takes on another meaning for him, it becomes a source of "ecstasy":

> But as the man Stan Parker sat in the flickering darkness waiting for the storm, the form of his wife faded into insignificance. A great fork of blue lightening gashed the flat sky ... That torment of darkness of lashing, twisted trees, became rather, an ecstasy of fulfillment." (151)

Stan seeks help from God: "... in his confusion he prayed to God, not in specific petition, wordlessly almost, for the sake of company." (152). Beatson contrasts Stan's relationship to God and nature with Amy's pursuit of human love: "Stan Parker loves God through nature, while Amy must find her love personalised in those around her. ... Her need to express love through the body is frustrated by Stan's ability to fulfil himself in nature ..." (Beatson 1977, 42)

Robert McDougall comments that in White's novels "Human and phenomenal natures are no longer separated, they are one, welded together in a juncture that shows no cracks." (1966, 8) Revelation comes to him through experiencing oneness with nature. At the end, Stan is seen walking around the landscape, an experience that enables him to communicate with nature. It is a "communion of soul and scene":

> the landscape moving in on him with increased passion and intensity ... with tenderness ... For this scene which was his, and which was not too poignant. So he stooped to watch some ants dragging a butterfly's wing through a desert of stones. (397)

Suddenly, Stan slips and falls in the garden and while still lying on the ground, sights a comet in the sky. This incident is a fulfilling experience in Stan's life: "It was not natural that emptiness shall prevail, it will fill eventually, whether with water, or children, or dust, or spirit." (407) Stan, thereafter, is in unison with surrounding nature realising the invisible dimensions of the Creator as well as the creation.

Like Stan Parker, Voss also opens up to the wonder of nature and attains a state of harmony with the world: while sitting under the tree he "became familiar with each blade of withered grass at which he stared, even the joints in the body of the ant" (V 27). It seems that he becomes one with nature, feeling himself placed at the centre of land and sky: "He was drawn closer to the landscape, the seldom motionless sea of grass, the twisted trees in grey and black, the sky ever increasing in its rage of blue; and of that landscape, always he would become the centre. (V. 169)

Stan Parker's God is a very personal entity, conceived only through personal experience and refuting all other perceptions even of his mother's or father's perceptions. They had each introduced Stan to their respective notions of God – the one a benevolent, "blue gentleness" and the other, appropriate to the strong blacksmith, "a fiery God." Stan Parker refuses to define his notion of God in any form.

God has been described as formless in *Guru Granth Sahib*. God, being formless, takes the shape perceived by his worshipper, therefore, there is no specific form or shape of God. In *Guru Granth Sahib* God is perceived in varied forms by various Bhagats and Gurus. Bhagat Kabir perceived God in a dog and Bhagat Namdev in a stone figure, even Shaikh Farid experienced God in various forms which could be perceived through His creation. In *Guru Granth Sahib,* God is described as follows:

> One (God) is formless, dynamic. True is (His) name. (He is the) creator. (He is) beyond fear and animosity (all love). (He is) eternal Being. (He is) not subject to birth and death. (He is) self-existent. (He is) realized by the grace of Guru.

The entire philosophy of Sikhism is based on the idea that 'There is but one God'. *Guru Granth Sahib* declares that God is one, who is the sole deliverer of the soul; the only one who provides consolation to beings in their sufferings:

> Only one being has the knowledge of all other beings, only He is the protector. My mind has placed hope on one He is the sustainer of life ... The One is my brother, friend. He is mother and father. Only He is the hope of my mind, who gave me life and body. (Singh 2000, 91)

In *The Tree of Man* White's protagonist Stan, finds at the end of his life that God is indeed the answer to all problems:" As he stood waiting ... he prayed for great clarity, and it became obvious as a hand. It was clear that One, and no other figure, is the Answer to all sums." (TM 447) Since, the scripture evolved as a reaction against the inequities of the caste system, the essence of the human being is considered to have originated from the one source; therefore, there can be no artificial distinctions between human beings: "He made all other beings. From the one light has welled up the entire universe. Then who is good and who is bad?" (Singh 2000, 693)In this connection, another of White's novels, *Riders in the Chariot*, seems to explain this concept of Hindu teaching:

> Men are the same before they are born. They are the same at birth, perhaps you will agree. It is only the coat they are told to put on that makes them all different. There are some, of course, who feel they are not suited: They think they will change their coat. But remain the same, in themselves. (RC 445)

In the *Tree of Man* White has explained that he tried to suggest every possible aspect of life in his portrayal of the lives of "an ordinary man and woman," but at the same time he affirms, he wished "to discover the extraordinary behind the ordinary." (Marr 1991, 282) In *The Tree of Man*, he constructs Stan Parker as a normal, even a commonplace man: "He was nothing much ... Certainly, he had seen the sea, and the hurly-burly of it did hollow out of him a cave of wonderment and discontent." (13) In this connection, Alan Lawson comments that "The novels evolve through the *developing* perception of a *fallible* central character in which much of the novelist's viewpoint is only apparently invested." (1979, 287)

By way of comparison, it should be noted that Guru *Granth Sahib* aimed at *addressing* all people from all castes and classes equally, thereby going against the traditional hegemony of the upper castes and higher classes. Even as White does not construct his characters as superheroes or perfect human beings, so also does the *Guru Granth Sahib* render equal treatment to people belonging to different social, political and economic contexts. There are other synergies which may be observed between works of this Australian writer and *Guru Granth Sahib*. Both texts affirm a religious faith free from any link with institutional or organised religion. *Guru Granth Sahib* was composed by *Guru*s and *Bhagat*s of different sects and places of origin. Similarly, White declares: "I belong to no church, but I have a religious faith ... In my books I have lifted bits from various religions in trying to come to a better understanding ..." (Qtd. in McGregor 1969, 219).

In relation to modes of writing, strategies of style, further parallels suggest themselves on the basis of figurative language and the mode in which images and symbols are deployed. For example, the recurring image of the *mandala* in the novels echoes the concept in *Guru Granth Sahib*, that God is the centre of the rest of the world, conceived as circle. In *Guru Granth Sahib*, worldly beings are constantly striving to merge with the centre. Interestingly, the *mandala* image that recurs in White's novels has echoes in *Guru Granth Sahib* as well. The psychoanalyst Jung explains that *Mandala* is a Sanskrit word for circle and it is interesting to note that the mandala image appeared in White's work long before he acknowledged his awareness of Jung's work in his writing of the novel *The Solid Mandala* where there are direct quotations from Jung's teaching on the mandala. The *mandalas* taken together form a blueprint for entirety and the spiritual wholeness that integrates mind, body, and spirit.

In *The Tree of Man*, the *mandalic* image overshadows the entire novel in the form of trees. Therefore, the tree represents the *Mandala* in the novel, symbolically depicting Stan's spiritual progression and growth. Moments before his death as he sits in his garden, everything that surrounds him seems to have a circular form and he himself is the centre of this natural mandala:

> Out there at the back, the grass, you could hardly call it a lawn, had formed a circle in the shrubs and trees ... It was perfectly obvious that the man was seated at the heart of it, and from this heart the trees radiated, with grave movements of life ... All was circumference to the centre, and beyond that the worlds of other circles ... The large, triumphal scheme of which he was becoming mysteriously aware ... (474)

Symbolically, the garden signifies the life of a human being and the fact that there was "little of design in the garden originally, though one had formed out of the wilderness" suggests the random-ness of the pattern of life. Man is governed by the mysterious super-natural forces and seems to have little choice in the midst of deterministic forces. Stan Parker has limited choice in the events of his life yet his position at the centre of the garden suggests that perhaps he was the *mandala* himself. Stan, at this moment of revelation, is absorbed in the mystery of God whose presence he has felt in the shabby paddocks of the farm as he moved about his humble work.

Another recurring image in White's works and perhaps most dominant in *The Tree of Man* is that of the tree. The tree "denotes the life of the cosmos: its consistence, growth, proliferation generative and regenerative processes. It stands for inexhaustible life ..." (Cirlot 1962, 328). Correspondingly, the tree symbol has been extensively used in *Guru Granth Sahib* as well. Sher Singh explains the concept of God, annotated in *Guru Granth Sahib,* in the word '*Tarowar*' or '*Ped*' meaning Tree. In White the analogy is between man and tree as the title of the work underlines. Singh describes that "God is Tree, not like a tree but His nature is to be understood after the structure of a tree (Singh 1998, 123) but in *Guru Granth Sahib* God has also been called a tree:"You are a tree; Your branches are flowering ..." (Trans. Khalsa 102)

In *The Tree of Man*, the tree becomes also a symbol of the Creator. This novel is the canvas where White draws the detailed image of the tree making it the central image which remains dominant throughout the novel. Its overwhelming influence is visible from the very beginning till the end. The novel begins with the image of two stringybarks, strong and dominant. "... the two big stringybarks ... were the dominant trees ..." (9) These "dominant trees" influence the life of the Parkers to the end. Every significant event in the lives of Amy and Stan is marked by the presence of the trees. The trees remain as an ever-present setting during the natural catastrophes and the cycle of the seasons. Later, in the novel, in Stan's life, the trees begin to have a comforting influence as they provide solace to his disturbed mind after the discovery of Amy's adultery:

> Trees turning up silver in a wind, or just the dead trees, to which he had always been mysteriously attracted, consoled as he rode amongst their silences through a silence of grass, drifted this side of glass and concrete. (323)

Towards the end, after Stan's death, his grandson is presented considering how he could "write a poem of life." (479) "So that in the end there were the trees. The boy walking. So that in the end, there was no end." (480)

Another point of synergy is that the theme of conflict between materialism and spiritualism is central in White's work; it is also foregrounded in *Guru Granth Sahib* where human beings are expected to forsake the pursuit of the mundane and to probe deeper into consciousness, to seek spiritual illumination of the highest realities of existence. White's protagonists in almost all his novels are engaged in a similar quest for understanding of ultimate truth while trying to define the self, reality, permanence and impermanence. The relationship between Stan and his wife Amy is instructive. Amy Parker is preoccupied with the mundane, with things, such as the silver nutmeg grater, and the yearning for human love and attachments, whereas it is the metaphysical that fascinates Stan. This difference signifies a contrast between a materialistic view of life and a spiritual.

Mackenzie terms this disjointing as a "qualitative separation." (1966, 405) He sees Amy: "… as a study in the neurotic self-destruction. In brief, Amy continues to long for a permanence which Stan senses to be illusory." (Amy remains yearningly possessive of her husband and of her son: Stan remains detached. Amy is never able to come to terms with this detachment and her numerous attempts to possess Stan result in disillusionment. Both Stan and Amy experience the temptation to infidelity. Madeleine, with whom Stan sins in the mind, signifies temptation, as does Leo for Amy. There is a remarkable difference between these temptations. Amy surrenders herself repeatedly to her lustful feelings for Leo. In contrast to this, Stan's short-lived temptation is destroyed in the fire and Stan succeeds in coming out of that state of sin. He obliterates the incident from his memory: "… he did not return to the woman with whom he had been standing at the head of the stairs. He put this away and did not think about it." (182)

Stan dies in the end, but the continuity of life is suggested through his grandson who proposes to write a "poem of life." In *Guru Granth Sahib* too, continuity of generation is suggested as one generation replaces the other. It is quoted that "… no one's life is permanent in this world. That seat, upon which we now sit – many others sat on it before us and have since departed." (Khalsa, 488). It is explained that one should love God as one's mortal body will perish and the graveyard where one will be buried will be neglected and forgotten.

This study allows only space to explore a few of the commonalities that appear to link *Guru Granth Sahib* and White's work. There is no possibility of tracing these through the whole gamut of his considerable oeuvre, and perhaps the novel *The Tree of Man* offers the best scope for such a comparison. While the work of fiction has necessarily to be much more tentative in the way its 'lessons' are proffered, the basic similarities of the works can be summarised as follows: both works show a preoccupation with questions relating to the meaning of human existence; and probing the appropriate place of the human being in the phenomenal world Both appear to insist that for the human being, the basic truth of life is to be sought working out a relationship with God. They need to forge a relationship with the immortal, curtailing all other relationships. Both indicate that acknowledgement of this dominating reality, leads to the liberation of the spirit from fear, doubt and uncertainty.

Guru Granth Sahib condemns institutional religions and addresses the entire human race irrespective of class and caste, in order to lay emphasis on truth. In White's philosophy in so far as I have been able to illustrate it with reference only to the one novel, *The Tree of Man* is that, the resolution to all conflicts is to be sought in the everlasting union with God who is eternal, infinite. My hope is that despite the narrow scope of this discussion, it has demonstrated that a comparative study of this nature can still work to link diversities and cultural pluralities and contribute towards establishing a broader appreciation of issues related to humanity in general.

Works Cited

Beatson, Peter. 1977. *The Eye in the Mandala-Patrick White: A Vision of Man and God*. Sydney: A.H. & A. W. Reed.
Cirlot, J.E. 1962. *A Dictionary of Symbols*. Trans. J. Sage. London: Routledge and Kegan Paul.
Coad, David. 1993. "Patrick White in the Wilderness," *World Literature Today* 67,. 3, "Contemporary Australian Literature" (Summer):510-514
http://www.jstor.org/stable/40149345. Accessed: June 29, 2012
Hansson, Karin. 1984. *The Warped Universe: A Study of Imagery and Structure in Seven Novels by Patrick White*. Lund: CWK Gleerup.
—. 2001. Patrick White - Existential Explorer". Nobel prize.org. Accessed: 14 Nov, 2012 n.p.
http://www.nobelprize.org/nobel_prizes/literature/laureates/1973/white-article.html.
Heltay, Hilary. 1973. "The Novels of Patrick White," *Southerly* 33. 2: 92-104.
Khalsa, Sant Singh. English Translation of Sri Guru Granth Sahib U.S.Hand Made Books. nd. (digitised version).
Lawson, Alan. 1979. "Meaning and Experience: A Review-Essay on Some Recurrent Problems in Patrick White Criticism," *Texas Studies in Literature and Language*. 21: 80-95.
Mackenzie, Manfred. 1966. "Apocalypse in Patrick White's *The Tree of Man*," *Meanjin* 25 Accessed: June 26, 2012. 147-168
http://www. jstor.org/stable/40654564.
Mansukhani, Gobind Singh. "The Quintessence of Sikhism." http://www.sgpc.net/sikhism/guru-granth-sahib.html.
Accessed15 Feb. 2013
Marr, David. 1991. *Patrick White: A Life*. Sydney: Random House.
McDougall, Robert L. 1966. "Australia Felix: Joseph Furphy and Patrick White" Commonwealth Literary Fund Lecture. Canberra: Australia National University Press, 1966.
McGregor, Craig. Ed. 1969. *In the Making*. Melbourne: Nelson.
Morley, Patricia A. 1972. *The Mystery of Unity: Theme and Technique in the Novels of Patrick White*. Montreal: McGill-Queen's University Press.

Reimer, A.P. 1970. "Visions of the Mandala in The Tree of Man," *Ten Essays on Patrick White*, ed. G.A. Wilkes, (Selected from *Southerly* 1964-1967). Sydney: Angus & Robertson: 109-26.

Remak, Henry. 1961. *Comparative Literature: Method and Perspective*. Ed. Newton P. Stallknecht and Horst Frenz. Carbondale: Southern Illinois University Press.

Singh, Darshan. Guru Granth Sahib: Sentence by sentence (Gurmukhi Script, Roman Transliteration and English Translation) Belgium: International Publishing House: nd.

Singh, Pashaura. 2000. *The Guru Granth Sahib: Canon, Meaning and Authority*. New Delhi: Oxford University Press.

Singh, Sher. 1998. *Philosophy of Sikhism*. Amritsar: Golden Off set Press.

Walsh, William. "Fiction as Metaphor: The Novels of Patrick White," *The Sewanee Review*. 82.2 (Spring 1974). John Hopkins University Press. Accessed June 29, 2012. 197-211 http://www.jstor.org/stable/27542824.

White, Patrick. 1976. *Riders in the Chariot*. London: Penguin.

—. 1985. *Voss*. London: Penguin Modern Classics

—. 1989. "The Prodigal Son," *Patrick White Speaks*, ed. Paul Brennan and Christine Flynn. Sydney: Primavera Press: 13-17.

—. 1994. *The Tree of Man*. London: Vintage Books.

Wilde, William H; Joy Hooton, Barry Andrews. 2000. *The Oxford Companion to Australian Literature*. Melbourne: Oxford University Press.

CHAPTER TWENTY-FOUR

PATRICK WHITE AND JAMES K. BAXTER: PUBLIC INTELLECTUALS OR SUBURBAN JEREMIAHS?

MARK WILLIAMS
VICTORIA UNIVERSITY OF CANTERBURY

In 1968 New Zealand novelist and cultural critic, Bill Pearson, published a book, *Henry Lawson Among Maoris*, on Lawson's time in New Zealand especially his period teaching at a Native School near Kaikoura in the South Island. The book is deeply critical of Lawson's understanding and representation of Maori in the story "A Daughter of Maoriland," the only work of any substance to emerge from his plan to write a major fictional study of "quaint and queer" Maori life. (1897, in Roderick 1970, 71) Among the book's most negative Australian reviewers was Lawson's editor, the critic, Colin Roderick. Writing in *The Age*, Roderick charged Pearson with "reducing the story to propaganda." (1968, 23). Pearson's attack not only on an iconic Australian literary figure but also on the code of mateship and the racial attitudes that informed Australian literary nationalism clearly rankled with Roderick, but Pearson did have some Australian support: Nancy Keesing, for example, in 'Lawson as a Racist' welcomed the New Zealander's debunking of 'the Lawson myth.' (1968, 83)

In this forgotten contention about a little-read book we find a point of contact between the difficulties encountered in Australia and New Zealand from the 1960s on as both countries have sought to reconfigure national identities derived from common sources in Victorian imperial racial attitudes, attitudes which, especially in Australia, were often incorporated into rather than expelled from settler cultural nationalism. This process of national 'rebranding' has been conducted at state level as a managerial response to an urgent need to differentiate contemporary national imageries from colonial ones so as to attract migrants and capital, and in both countries this elite-driven managerialism has been in conflict with the populist politics of settler recidivism. Yet in both countries also, ethically charged advocacy of a more just national order and fierce condemnation of the inherited order led by artists and intellectuals has been crucial in articulating the terms of change and broadening its appeal to the majority white populations. Among these 'public intellectuals' was Patrick White. But we need to be careful how we use this term in respect of his idiosyncratic engagement both with his country and with other intellectuals.

It is more than thirty years since Brian Kiernan observed that "the range of engagement with society" in White's work needs to be addressed. (1980, 136) Certainly, since the 1990s critical attention has shifted to White's status as an Australian public intellectual and cultural critics dismissively by Simon During and enthusiastically by Bridget Rooney (During 1996, 37; Rooney 2010, 3-18). This is a welcome shift from the 1970s and 80s when White criticism was primarily preoccupied with his religious vision. Yet I wish to return to that religious dimension in considering what kind of role it had in White's ethical engagement with Australia, referring by way of comparison to the New Zealand poet, James K. Baxter, a writer both deeply religious and vehemently critical of his nation's moral life and political history.

What, does it mean to call White a public intellectual? White's criticism of contemporary Australian life is dispersed through a variety of causes that he publicly endorsed – the anti-nuclear movement, opposition to urban development, protest against political allegiance to the United States, republicanism, the rights of Indigenous Australians. His fiction is less inclined than Baxter's poetry to take up direct political positions. Yet in White's fiction we encounter a reflection of an emerging Australian multi-culturalism, in large part through his own associations with Jewish and Greek communities, where he found relief from the monocultural blankness of Menzies-era Australia. White's fiction from the early 1960s increasingly addresses Australian urbanism, and moves tentatively towards a recognition of Aborigines within the contemporary cultural pattern of the nation. Most daringly, in *Riders in the Chariot*, White acts out the terrible drama of the Nazi persecution of the Jews in contemporary suburbia. Australia here is not an escape from European political extremism and persecution but an extension of it. This is a critique so uncompromising as to be beyond the scale of reproach of even as severe a public intellectual as Pearson, who detected an incipient fascism in New Zealand's suspicion of the outsider. (1952, 201-30)

It is, however, also found in other literary artists of the time, notably Janet Frame, whose *Faces in the Water* (1961) evokes the concentration camps in the psychiatric hospitals of pastoral New Zealand and, more famously and excessively, in Sylvia Plath's 'Daddy', written one year later (See Williams 2011 and Evans 2011). The crucifixion of Mordecai Himmelfarb in a Sydney factory – 'melodramatic' according to Roderick – is crucial to White's moral critique of his country because it identifies the nationalist values of mateship, democracy and humour not with Australian difference from the larger evils of the world, but as their local instantiation. (Roderick 1962, 74)

Bill Pearson was a very minor player in White's life. He dined at Centennial Park and corresponded with the great man. His scholarly study of Henry Lawson's time among the Maori people of Maungamaunu made no discernible impression on White. But both writers produced influential complaints against the cultural attitudes of their respective countries, Pearson's "Fretful Sleepers" of 1952 echoes White's 1947 essay, "The Prodigal Son," as an attack on the thinness of local intellectual life. Both found themselves at odds with the dominant forms of nationalism, dissatisfied with the limitations of political culture, and both diagnosed a fatal torpor induced by materialism and the fetishisation of white-mateship and the ordinary bloke. Both made strenuous efforts to understand cultural knowledge outside their own backgrounds: White in respect of the Jewish mystical tradition, Pearson in respect of the protocols of Maoritanga. Both, moreover, reflected on the place of the Indigenous communities in nations with colonial legacies, Pearson much more painstakingly and comprehensively than White.

Pearson was an early mover in a bicultural movement which transformed New Zealand in the period after 1983 as the Maori presence in New Zealand became worked into its evolving identity and *Pākehā* discovered an enthusiasm for Maori culture that was not merely patronising or appropriative as in the late-colonial 'Maoriland' period (see Stafford and Williams 2006). White's Aboriginal characters are limited at times by ethnographic and romantic assumptions, as has been the case in both countries in the colonial, modern, and even the postcolonial periods. More significantly, White lacked the close personal contact with Indigenous people that both Baxter and Pearson enjoyed. There is a significant difference between the *presence* of Maori and that of Aborigines in the two countries and their literatures; Indigenous Australians have not permeated so extensively the conscience, the consciousness or the everyday normalities of modern white Australia, far less become involved in the shaping of a bicultural nationalism.

Pearson is of note here not because he is the crucial figure in the collective self-invention of *Pākehā* New Zealand in postcolonial terms – Baxter is that figure – but because of his links to White and because he demonstrates commonalities and points of difference in post-war intellectual life in the sibling nations. Pearson's chief point of difference from White and Baxter is that he speaks from the position of the secular academic, spurned with different degrees of vehemence by both White and Baxter. An aversion to the intellectual Australian – dismissed in "The Prodigal Son" as "the teacher and journalist" – has implications for White's status as a public intellectual and for his engagement with the Australian reading public. (White 1989, 15) Brigid Rooney locates White among those literary intellectuals whose power to goad the national conscience has abated since the 1960s, as the cultural power of educated baby-boomers has progressively dissipated. (2009, ix-xvii) But writers can engage the national conscience without identifying specifically or exclusively as intellectuals. Indeed, the moral force of White's condemnation of Australian political and public life cannot fully be accounted for within the category of the public intellectual.

White's criticism of Australia, like the young Katherine Mansfield's of New Zealand is initially aesthetic; for both, an aesthete's style serves to establish the author's superior distance from the vulgarity of national life. But White declined the exile's luxury of distance, famously returning after the war in a spirit both of complaint and determination to make permanent art out of his unfinished country, richness out of its 'rocks and sticks'. Being present throughout the material expansion of the post-war years produced that literary art but it also exacerbated the irritation. Moreover, White's aesthetic distancing progressively gave way to a direct and morally charged cultural engagement, chiefly by way of his satirical portraits of suburban materialism and inanition. In his fiction of the 1960s, White's indignant address to his errant nation recalls that of Baxter at the same time, who provoked in a generation of middle-class New Zealanders the stirrings of what Stephen Daedalus in *A Portrait of the Artist as a Young Man* calls the "uncreated conscience" of the race. (Joyce 1991, 253)

Baxter's critique of racism and materialism was expressed by way of a theatrically mediaeval Christianity and ready recourse to the prophetic voice. Yet his religious idealisation of poverty and communalism met a need among young middle-class, apparently non-religious *Pākehā* for a sense of possession not only of an authentic culture – like that possessed by Maori – but also of a spirituality that seemed to have departed from the available modes of First World living. White's religious convictions were not conducted publicly, like Baxter's. Nevertheless, they had a role in fixing the ethical, critical and public aspects of his fiction in the white Australian imaginary. Religious thought in White's work, as in Baxter's, allows the author to touch on an ethical afterlife in Christianity that is still worked into middle Australasian life, in spite of the decline of belief or practice. The passage from Kirk or convent to Labour hall, to the anti-nuclear and anti-racist movements and, latterly, ecology and anti-consumption continues to shape the enthusiasms of the morally alert and culture-consuming middle class in both countries.

Theory – whether Marxist, Freudian, or postmodern – has no ready access to a language with which to connect to the ethical receptivity of that broad class of readers who have responded, often eagerly, to the defining moral texts of their modern national literatures: *Riders in the Chariot* and Thomas Keneally's *The Chant of Jimmie Blacksmith* (1972) and Keri Hulme's *the bone people* (1983). My purpose here is not to argue for or against the presence of religious conviction in literature – it seems to me no more to be admired or condemned than the presence of, say, socialism or animal ethics. I wish, rather, to situate the religious element in White's fiction in the social and the cultural; that is, the ethical rather than the mystical and esoteric – in particular, an ethics involving affective attachment and moral aversion rather than intellectual decision.

The focus in White studies in the 1970s on the abstruse mythopoetics of his late-modernist Australian fiction, translated its religious content into something curious, interesting even, but not requiring to be engaged with in the way his representations of suburbia, migrants or Aboriginals must be – as that which knits the text to the world it figures. The metaphysical systems – Kabbalah, Gnosticism, nature mysticism and (surely parodying the whole enterprise) Bogomilism – that have distracted critical commentators, including Roderick, have no relation to White's ethical positions on modern Australia. They are wholly disengaged from his querulous but passionate engagement with society. Yet, in White's dramatisation of cultural difference from the white norm as transformative, of social relations in terms of 'lovingkindness', in his use of parable and his forcing the reader to make moral choices between extreme examples of good and evil, we find a mode of engagement very like that of Baxter.

Curiously, Baxter's grandfather, Archibald, was actually 'crucified' as a conscientious objector under military discipline on the Western Front in World War I (See Archibald Baxter 1968). It is necessary, then, if we are to understand what kind of public intellectual White was, that we disentangle religious views in his fiction from the metaphysical or mystical systems that exist at a distance from the judgements that his writing offers on nation, history and race, while recognising their place within his commitment to the cultivation of 'conscience' as both consciousness and sympathy, and as the basis of a nation-making that confronts the nation's moral failings.

White's interest in mystical systems appears during his most intense engagement with the nation, which he both seeks to bring into moral being yet also despairs of. The analogy to W.B. Yeats here is obvious but only partially useful. White is not simply, like Yeats, or the New Zealand poet, Allen Curnow, enacting the modernist paradigm of writing high art in a provincial context. The context itself is more mobile than that of Yeats' Ireland and less provincial than Curnow's New Zealand. While post-revolutionary Ireland retreated into an enclosed and conservative cultural separatism, Australia in the decades after World War II, willingly or unwillingly, was transformed by its expanding relations to the larger world, especially Europe and Asia. In adopting his symbolic systems White keeps his superior distance from the public he seeks to change and make worthy of his writing; in rooting those systems in the familiar trope of the social outsider and in channelling a moral criticism of Australian life through his ethnically diverse outsider figures, White connects his fiction to a public negotiating its own distance from an increasingly embarrassing past. Similarly, his belated and idiosyncratic modernist style which seemed at the time provocatively *un*-Australian, while it also distances the author from a traditional national reading public, also connects White to a new one very like that which in New Zealand two decades later would respond with semi-religious enthusiasm to the mixture of modernism and revisionary nationalism in Kerri Hulme's novel, *The bone people* (1984).

Roderick praises *Riders in the Ch*ariot but focuses on its ethical dimension in wholly abstract terms: "Mr White is not interested, except incidentally, in mundane ethics: they are past redemption anyway. His view is the larger one of metaphysical conflict." (1958) Here Whitean ethics placed at one end of a polarity between those of ordinary behaviour and the Manichean struggle between spirit and matter. This is to overlook the relative fragility of those metaphysical systems in the book. They arise out of and compensate for the human failings of the separate characters; they give them no privileged interpretative power over experience; and they are not wholly endorsed by the narrator or the narrative. This is not to say that there is no authorial investment in Himmelfarb's Jewish mysticism or Mary Hare's nature mysticism, but those belief systems do not constitute a coherent collective religious structure external to the partial viewpoints of the characters who embrace them. They are, moreover, continually tested against the disappointments of actual experience and as explanatory systems they fail the characters at crucial moments.

It is failure rather than transcendence that White responds to as a novelist, and without this strategic mixture of longing and doubt the fiction, at time, would evaporate into metaphysics. (Graham-Smith, 177) The emphasis on the failure of his religious visionaries does not discredit their beliefs: rather it shifts the religious instinct in White's fiction towards the everyday and informs his moral critique of the dominant forms of social thought. And it connects ethical discussion in Australia to modes of political evil difficult to accommodate in national terms.

In this respect *Riders in the Chariot*, more than *The Tree of Man* (1955) or *Voss* (1957), is White's exemplary text. In the two earlier novels White dramatises an Australian past – Stan Parker's rural-suburbia being an extension of that past into a broken present – that breaks with literary nationalism in its high baroque style, but which lacks the moral force of *Riders*. Colonial settlement and the treatment of Aborigines are not attached, as is the persecution of an immigrant Jew, to the international issue of genocide. The workers in *Riders* do not set about exterminating Jews systematically but in crucifying a representative Jew they demonstrate their complicity with all those Germans who allowed the Holocaust to unfold. This is a fundamental criticism of the values of normative Australia and it reverses the assumption that mateship, democracy and a subversive attitude towards authority are fundamentally positive markers of national character.

Just so, Baxter challenged the moral self-regard of cultural nationalism, addressing the situation of poverty in New Zealand by reference to his transformative visit to India in 1958-59, and calling on white New Zealanders to confront the massive wrong of their history and abandon the myth of their exceptional benevolence towards Maori in offering to raise them towards their own superior condition of civilisation. In *Riders*, the Indigenous Australian, Alf Dubbo, does not provide an alternative ethical centre for White, as Maori do for Baxter. He suffers for his vision as an artist as much as his status as an Aboriginal Australian. Baxter, however, places an Indigenous person at the centre of his most extreme criticism of white New Zealand's conviction of its exemption from the larger evils of world history.

In 'The Maori Jesus' (1966) Baxter shows his Maori Christ figure persecuted by a State claiming to be not only advanced but also beneficent, inducting the story of the Passion into his lobotomising:

> I saw the Maori Jesus
> Walking on Wellington Harbour,
> He wore blue dungarees.
> His beard and hair were long.
> His breath smelt of mussels and paraoa.
> When he smiled it looked like the dawn.
> When he broke wind the little fishes trembled.
> When he frowned the ground shook.
> When he laughed everybody got drunk.
>
> The Maori Jesus came on shore
> and picked out his twelve disciples.
> One cleaned toilets in the Railway Station;
> His hands were scrubbed red to get the shit out of the pores.
> One was a call-girl who turned it up for nothing.
> One was a housewife who'd forgotten the Pill
> And stuck her TV set in the rubbish can.
> One was a little office clerk
> Who'd tried to set fire to the Government Buildings.
> Yes, and there were several others;
> One was an old sad quean;
> One was an alcoholic priest
> Going slowly mad in a respectable parish.
>
> The Maori Jesus said, 'Man,
> From now on the sun will shine.'
>
> He did no miracles;
> He played the guitar sitting on the ground.
>
> The first day he was arrested
> For having no lawful means of support.

The second day he was beaten up by the cops
For telling a dee his house was not in order.
The third day he was charged with being a Maori
And given a month in Mount Crawford.
The fourth day he was sent to Porirua
For telling a screw the sun would stop rising.
The fifth day lasted seven years
While he worked in the asylum laundry
Never out of the steam.
The sixth day he told the head doctor,
'I am the Light in the Void;
I am who I am.'
The seventh day he was lobotomised;
The brain of God was cut in half.

On the eighth day the sun did not rise.
It didn't rise the day after.
God was neither alive nor dead.
The darkness of the Void,
Mountainous, mile-deep, civilised darkness
Sat on the earth from then till now
(Baxter 1988, 347-348)

In colonial literature Aborigines do not figure as extensively as do Maori in 'Maoriland' (the colonial name for New Zealand) where they were both archaised and idealised. In spite of romantic figurings of Aboriginals, they were not caught up in settler nationalism or employed to advertise a positive difference from other British colonies, as were Maori. Embedded in *Pākehā* New Zealand's colonial narrative was the myth of exceptional racial harmony: the joining together by heroic journeying of two peoples destined to realise empire's elevating purpose.

This view was challenged subsequently not only by the Maori sovereignty movement, especially from the 1970s, but also by the Pākehā literary nationalist movement of the 1930s and '40s, eager to expel colonial complacencies. Baxter in the late 1960s articulates a radical critique that connects the treatment Maori have received from the Pākehā state, colonial and modern, to Christ's Passion and death. How do we account for the public receptivity to such extreme modes of national critique – Baxter's poem is actually inscribed in the Wellington cityscape as part of the Wellington Writers' Walk – in countries where neither intellectuals nor citizens have traditionally identified as religious yet where religious values have a resilient 'afterlife'. Perhaps in rejecting the cultural assumptions of their Victorian-colonial pasts, including a Christianity soaked in empire, the postcolonial citizens revive unconsciously residues of that Christianity that also at times resisted empire and its racism.

Cultural nationalism in Australia and New Zealand has been of a sceptical and secular character, but with different inflections in the literature of each country. Allen Curnow, the son of an Anglican minister, trained for the clergy but abandoned his faith for poetry and his work rests on a stern rejoinder against hankering after the lost metaphysical world or the lost colonial home. Maturity is acceptance of the world to hand as it is, and there must be no recourse to visionary experiences except those focused on the quotidian. A 1938 essay puts this view in terms that might be a specific rejoinder to the visionary aesthetics of *Riders in the Chariot*:

> By visions it is meant, of course, things actually seen and faithfully reported: not Ezekiel wheels but real wheels, not turnip spooks but turnips at market prices. It is out of such things that vision is required of a poet here and now. (Curnow 1987, 10)

Yet religious imagery, including Christ's Passion, is worked into his major poetry, often in relation to the bloody history of colonisation. In 'Landfall in Unknown Seas' (1943) it is "the stain of blood that writes an island story." (Curnow 1974, 136) What we do not find in his poetry is the mixing of the transcendent with worldly particulars that we find, at times outrageously, in Baxter's poetry. Both White and Baxter exhibit a stylistic, and perhaps temperamental, liking for combining the scabrous with the religious language they employ. Baxter enacts a debased Christianity in 'Ballad of Calvary Street' (1960), where imagery of Christ's passion must co-exist in suburban amnesia with 'grunt grotto out the back'. The 'blowfly on its bed of offal' that is also 'a variation on the rainbow' in *Voss* that is often read in terms of the mystical doctrine of immanence, but it also similarly mixes transcendence and banality (White 1957, 441; Morley 1972, 233; Beatson 1974, 10).

Curiously Baxter, in whom belief is more absolute, does not generally seek to figure transcendent visions in his poetry. In 'Ballad of Calvary Street' various religious myths including the Christian one collide in the world of the ordinary couple. Yet for both writers, Christian sacramentalism is a crucial means of figuring cross-cultural discovery or exchange. In *A Fringe of Leaves* (1976) Ellen Roxburgh experiences a sense of the sacramental participating in a cannibal meal; Baxter figures his most radical assimilation into the Maori world in one of the 'Jerusalem Sonnets', where his own body becomes a Eucharistic feast ('Tribe of the wind/You can have my flesh for kai, my blood to drink,' *Jerusalem* Sonnets, no 34, in Baxter 1988, 471).

In this willingness to introduce religious language, concepts and values into their work, including that which critiques the national life, White and Baxter are at odds with the dominant secular and sceptical line in the literary nationalism and public intellectual discourse of each country. Yet this does not seem to have alienated them from their reading publics or dissipated the force of their social criticism. Curiously the more extravagantly and publicly religious of the two writers, Baxter, managed to carry more of the citizens with him in his heroic rejection of contemporary life, contributing to the bicultural activism that transformed the education system, the churches and much of the public service in the 1980s.

Simon During somewhat intemperately, charges that White's writing by the 1970s had reached an end-point in respect of the deep changes occurring in Australian cultural realities (1996, 100). The new interest in his status as public intellectual is a necessary corrective to this stringent view. But neither does White serve as the Australian equivalent of Baxter, a 'hero' of biculturalism, as During has described those New Zealand writers and artists of the 1960s who led Pākehā towards a new engagement with Indigenous people (1994, 1–53). I see each writer as a figure who articulates a critical consciousness of the dominant white nationalism and, more importantly, as a public intellectual not so much by way of the limited appeal of intellectual argument to the sluggish public but by way of a morally charged and vividly symbolist art in which the remains of the Christian *mythos* has a more than symbolic presence. Both at their most socially engaged, especially when lambasting suburban life, are Jeremiahs more than public intellectuals.

Works Cited

Baxter, Archibald. 1968. *We Will Not Cease.* Christchurch: Caxton.
Baxter, James K. 1988. *Collected Poems of James K. Baxter.* Ed. J.E. Weir. Auckland: Oxford University Press.
Beatson, Peter. 1976. *The Eye in the Mandala: Patrick White: A Vision of Man and God.* London: Elek.
Curnow, Allen. 1974. "Landfall in Unknown Seas," *Collected Poems 1933-1973.* Auckland: A.H and A.W Reed.
—————. 1987. "Rata Blossom or Reality: New Zealand and a Significant Contribution," *Look Back Harder: Critical Writings 1935-1984*, ed. Peter Simpson. Auckland: Auckland University Press.
During, Simon. 1996. *Patrick White.* Melbourne: Oxford University Press.
—. 1994 "Here's Trouble: Tony Fomison's Life and Work," *Fomison: What Shall We Tell Them?,* ed. Ian Wedde, Wellington: City Gallery: 41–53.
Evans, Patrick. 2011. "They Kill on Wednesdays": Janet Frame, Modernity and the Holocaust," *Journal of Commonwealth Literature* 46.1: 83-101.
Graham-Smith, Gregory. 2010. "Against the Androgyne as Humanist He(te)ro," *Remembering Patrick White: Contemporary Critical Essays*, ed.Elizabeth McMahon and Brigitta Olubas. New York - Amsterdam: Rodopi: 163-81.
Joyce, James. 1991. *A Portrait of the Artist as a Young Man.* New York: Signet.
Keesing, Nancy. 1968. "Lawson as a Racist," *The Bulletin*, 30 November: 83-4.
Kiernan, Brian. 1968. *Patrick White.* London: Macmillan.

Lawson, Henry. 1897. Letter to Hugh Maccallum, 25 June, *Henry Lawson: Letters 1890-1922*, ed. Colin Roderick. Sydney: Angus and Robertson. 1970: 71.

Morley, Patricia. 1972. *The Mystery of Unity: Theme and Technique in the Novels of Patrick White*. Montreal: McGill-Queen's University Press.

Pearson, Bill. 1952. "Fretful Sleepers: A Sketch of New Zealand Behaviour and its Implications for the Artist," *Landfall* 6, 23 (September): 201–230.

Roderick, Colin. 1962. "Riders in the Chariot," *Southerly* 22, 2: 62-77.

—. 1968. "Lawson's Maori Friends." Review of W.H. Pearson, *Henry Lawson Among Maoris*. Canberra: Australian National University Press. [Bill Pearson Collection. MS – Papers 433–130, Alexander Turnbull Library, Wellington.]

Rooney, Brigid. 2009. *Literary Activists: Writer-Intellectuals and Australian Public Life*. St Lucia: University of Queensland Press.

—. 2010. "Public Recluse: Patrick White's Literary-political Returns." *Remembering Patrick White: Contemporary Critical Essays*. ed. Elizabeth McMahon and Brigitta Olubas. Amsterdam: Rodopi: 3-16

Stafford, Jane and Mark Williams. 2006. *Maoriland: New Zealand Literature 1872-1914*. Wellington: Victoria University Press.

White, Patrick. 1989 [1958] "The Prodigal Son," *Patrick White Speaks*.ed Paul Brennan and Christine Flynn. Sydney: Primavera Press:13-17.

—. 1957. *Voss*. New York: Viking.

Williams, Mark. 1993. *Patrick White*. Houndmills, Basingstoke: Macmillan.

—. 2011. "Tending the Ovens": Janet Frame's Politics of Language." *Commonwealth Essays and Studies*. 33,2 (Spring): 66-77.

CHAPTER TWENTY-FIVE

SMELLY MARTYRS: PATRICK WHITE'S DUBBO USHERS IN ROY'S VELUTHA AND MALOUF'S GEMMY

JULIE MEHTA
UNIVERSITY OF TORONTO

Patrick White has been considered an "outsider," and his characters are often outcasts – marginal beings, savaged by the mainstream, subjects of brutal alterity. Frequently marked because of their bodies, Alf Dubbo, the Aborigine in White's *Riders in the Chariot*, Gemmy the hybrid, in David Malouf's *Remembering Babylon,* and Velutha the untouchable, in Arundhati *Roy's The God of Small Things,* become repositories for social differentiation, representing the raw and disturbing physicality of the abject corporeal body that is a threat to Power. I argue that the palpable discomfort that White, Malouf and Roy create in the reader's mind through these encounters with the filth, defilement and ultimate horror of the marginalised body, are transformed into a new episteme for postcolonial writers who use the "strange" body to simultaneously reveal the savagery of power, to subvert its reach and, perhaps most subtly, to make a scathing comment on our moral ineptitude for acceptance of difference even as we politicise our success in constructing a more accepting "global" world.

Drawing on Julia Kristeva's theories of abjection, Sara Ahmed's exploration of bodily encounters, and Judith Butler's analysis of the "unlivable" zones where these bodies must reside, I hope to raise questions about how White's Dubbo is an iconic "somebody" who could, quite conceivably, have inspired a whole generation of writers such as Malouf and Roy. In the process, I will attempt to examine why Power uses violence, social injustice, and degradation to annihilate the outcast body.

Perhaps Malouf's narrative best unveils the ugly face of the racial ideology of the extermination of the outcast:

> From the beginning there were those among them, Ned Corcoran was the most vehement, for whom the only way of dealing with blacks was the one that had been given scope elsewhere. 'We ought to go out,' he insisted, controlling the spit that flooded his mouth, 'and get rid of 'em once and for all. If I catch one of those buggers round my place, I'll fuckin' pot him.' (Malouf 1993, 62)

Gemmy Fairley is literally an outcast, cast ashore after being cast out to sea, Velutha is a *Dalit* and therefore an outcaste and Dubbo is a black native in need of saving, in a cruel white, world.

White's vision of the divine as straddling both worlds – the sacred and the profane – is mirrored in the postcolonial vision of two novelists from Australia and one from India, who also draw inspiration from this contested, controversial and "cusping" space of binaries that White had so deftly created. The central and reiterative symbol within the book is the Chariot, as described in the Book of Ezekiel, with its Four Horsemen of the Apocalypse, and the Seven Seals, along with biblical warnings about blood, fire, and destruction from the Book of Revelation. The chariot as a symbol is the vehicle of choice in several cultures and religions as the divine transport of God's elect or chosen ones. What is most alluring for this project is White's tongue-in-cheek derision of the idea of purity that is institutionally promoted by all religions. Thus in White's Chariot, the Riders are not angelic beings but four ordinary humans – who are welcomed into the Heavenly vehicle.

Read against the backdrop of one of Rabindranath Tagore's poems in the *Gitanjali,* which is about this very Chariot and the potential riders that might inhabit it, the reader witnesses the far-reaching universal value of the symbol:

> See on the chariot that drives through the air-
> Out on the way, flag flying. He is there.

You inside, in a corner installed-
come out running, the rope's to be hauled,
fall to it, join in, dive in the crowd-
somehow, anyhow, grab your rope's share. (1998, 39)

Though in this chapter I will focus mainly on White's re-writing of the body as represented in Alf Dubbo the "Abo," "blackfellow, or "half-caste" to create a conflation between spirit and nature, I will also draw on Gemmy's and Velutha's bodyscapes, to connect these three subjects of brutal alterity to the dichotomous, ambiguous and the borderless idea of the divine.

At the outset, Cynthia vanden Driesen's claim is useful to contextualise this suture:

> White was acutely aware of the difficulties inherent in the exploration of religious themes in the context of the time but was convinced of the possibilities of negotiating the challenge: 'Now as the world grows more pagan one has to lead people in the same direction in a different way.' (McGregor 1969, 218) In the context of a world which continues to be obsessed with scientific and technological advancement and material progress it is precisely the religious experience which lacks this sense of human relevance. (2008, 2)

Dubbo is first introduced to us by Himmelfarb, the Jew, who ironically is also an outsider and a martyr. In fact, the four riders in the chariot are all outcasts: Miss Hare the heiress of Xanadu, Mrs Godbold the washerwoman, Mr. Himmelfarb the Jew, and Alf Dubbo the Aborigine/half-caste artist. It is the very undeniable corporeality of the outcast: that he or she is there, in our face, and will not go away, that is the issue in Riders. The threat to the larger community, represented by Rosetree and his wife, just "regular folk," is the very presence, the existence, the excess of the real body of the outcast. Thus, for the "regular folk" the outcast as abject must be expelled from the community and she or he must be expelled because she or he is such an integral part of the community. These outcasts are White's visionaries, and though treated as aliens, their bodies are all- encompassing of the secular and the sacred.

White's interest in the sacred is well attested as vanden Driesen indicates. To Clement Semmler, White said: "What I am increasingly intent on trying to do in my books is to give professed unbelievers glimpses of their own unprofessed factor. I think most people have a religious factor but are afraid that by admitting it, they will forfeit their right to be considered intellectual." (Qtd in vanden Driesen 2009, 185) Rosemary Dinnage's observation that White himself is an outsider, and that his characters are almost all "outsiders, outlaws, afflicted and linked by their affliction," (Dinnage 2002, back cover book blurb) finds exquisite and horrible representation in *Riders*. What the reader is surprised by, as Dinnage so perceptively points out is: "The visionary element in his novels is inseparable from a tough irony and a microscopically close, sometimes savage attention to physical minutiae. The coarser the texture of the physical – bodies especially – the more likely to be illuminated by flashes of meaning and power."

White's confronting mixture of horror and beauty finds an interesting theoretical corollary in the connection Mircea Eliade makes between the religious and the profane. Eliade states that by its very hierophanic nature, the sacred can at any given moment catapult itself into the secular. "All nature is capable of revealing itself ... the cosmos in its entirety can become a hierophany." (Eliade 1971, 12) And in the hands of gifted writers, the sacred can appear most naturally in the mundane. That is what makes the spiritual sutured to reality – like a jack-in-the-box the spiritual manifests itself to provide a continuum, allowing for the best to be salvaged from the hopeless, hapless profanity of our jaded humanity.

The concept of hierophany (manifestation of the sacred in the secular) and Julia Kristeva's concept of the "powers of horror" along with the idea of the "abject," something that is excreted (such as bodily fluids and blood), as an inherent part of the subject, both elaborate White's vision. The ultimate martyrdom of Christ and his transformation from flesh to spirit cannot be divorced from the palpability of his corporeal body with open, weeping wounds. Thus, in the course of *Riders in the Chariot*, Alf Dubbo's body is continuously a point of reference and his moment of epiphany holds in its space the image of a martyred Christ whose body is being received: "So, in his mind, he [Dubbo] loaded with panegyric blue the tree from which the women, and the young man, His disciples, were lowering their Lord. And the flowers of the tree lay at its roots in pools of deepening blue."(RC 569) In the context of Christ and martyrdom, the image of the Jew Himmelfarb being ministered to by Mrs. Godbold in his state of sickness and pain is evocative of the two Marys who minister to the body of a wounded Christ: "As Dubbo watched his picture nagged at him, increasing in miraculous detail, as he had always hoped, and known it must."

The metaphor of the body as chiasmic crucible for binaries: pain and pleasure, life and death, is employed with remarkable power in *Riders in the Chariot*. White's ultimate edict is that the transformative power of martyrdom of not just the soul but the body, too, is possible in the meekest of humans. Alf Dubbo, who is introduced to us as "a dark-skinned individual," a "blackfellow," whose stoop made his "vertebrae protrude in knobs," when straightened up "composed of bones and veins, thin strips of elastic muscle," and "dark face" (260) – is also a gifted artist who is able to imagine and "see" Christ after he is taken down from the cross. Again, it is a powerful disrobement and disempowering of Dubbo that causes a disturbance in the reader as it does in Dubbo, when he is berated at the "whorehouse" by Hannah's friends: When Hannah's colleague Reen called, "What can you do, Dubbo? Tear your clothes off and show your bottom like everybody else?" ... Dubbo himself had been overtaken by a sudden sadness." (464).

The hierophanic also appears in the intersection between Dubbo's endemic alcoholism at Abercrombie House, while Hannah and the "whores" put on drag performances, and his visions of "The Chariot" and hearing of the voices of the prophets while he read the ragpicker's frayed Bible. These "intoxicated him as much as the alcohol that burned him." (460-461) Alf Dubbo is significant to this project and stands out amongst the group of four main characters not merely because he is Aboriginal, but because he is the crucible in which the sacred meets the profane. In Dubbo's geography, White relates a struggle with homosexuality when the young boy is molested by his homosexual guardian.

As he remembered the voice, so Dubbo was still able to see the drawing of the "Chariot-thing". He would have known how to draw it, detail by detail, inch by inch, for he never forgot the places where he had been. There was simply the question of physical strength ... All that night he was haunted by the wings of the Four Living creatures. The tips of their wings stroked his eyelids. He would reach up and touch their feathers ... And began at once to restate his conception of the Chariot." (596-7).

Also present in this complex arena where the sacred and profane play out the dance of Life and Death are the other outcasts like Mrs Godbold who brings "the milk of human kindness" and "light" into the abject existence of the disempowered Dubbo: "Then Dubbo looked inside, and saw as well as remembered that this was the shed in which lived Mrs. Godbold, whom he had first encountered at Mrs Khalil's. And who had bent down and wiped his mouth as no body had ever done." (568).

In *The Powers of Horror*, Kristeva argues that the emergence of the "self" depends on the constitution of the "not-self." (Kristeva 1982, 3) In addition to excluding that which is ostensibly the "object," ... the "subject" also needs to separate itself from what she terms "the abject". To illustrate, she cites the example of "refuse" or waste. "Dung" signifies for Kristeva, "the other side of the border, the place where I am not, and which permits me to be." In this the abject is understood as the part of ourselves that we wilfully discard. "I expel myself, I abject myself," states Kristeva, "within the same motion through which I claim to establish myself." (3) Addressing the question of "embodiment" and "identification" within the "heterosexual hegemony," Judith Butler argues that the abject not only designates the "unlivable" and the "uninhabitable", but also "constitute[s] the defining limit of the subject's domain." (Butler 1993: 3) Iris Young describes abjection as a unique form of contemporary oppression that is executed not as a brutal state tyranny but as an underground, unconscious, yet structural immobilisation and reduction of a group. (Young 1991, 4-42)

Dubbo dies alone, and the landlady declares that there is an awful "smell" from under his door and later "smell" is replaced by "stench." (RC 600) "There was a good deal of blood on his pillow and on his hands" and he lay on his bed "twisted round." (461) After the doctor carried on "a distasteful examination" of the dead body, with Dubbo's landlady Mrs Noonan, he declared that Dubbo had probably died of a "tubercular haemorrhage," (601) when, in fact, the reader knows from several accounts that Dubbo died primarily of neglect, homelessness, loneliness and being an outcast. Blood, sweat, tears and bodily fluids like semen and urine are natural excretions of the corporeal body and punctuate Dubbo's death.

In the context of the outcast, there are several parallels between Dubbo and Arundhati Roy's outcaste Velutha, the untouchable or *Paravan*. The brutal murder of Velutha, the father that the single mother Ammu resurrects for her children, also mirrors the overriding theme of death being a necessary presence in giving voice to, and for the retrieval of, subaltern or outcast identity. Victor Li demonstrates that the subaltern Velutha's sacrificial death, like Dubbo's, is necessary "in order to serve as an irreducible idea." He argues that "the subaltern is perfected as a concept so pure, no living referent can contradict or contemplate it." (Li 2009, 276). In this respect, Dubbo in *Riders in the Chariot* Gemmy in David Malouf's *Remembering Babylon* and Velutha in *The God of Small Things* share the glory of afterlife, a kind of martyrdom that is Christ-like. Li further suggests: "the ideal subaltern other must be seen as a figure that is inaccessible to and inappropriable by statist, hegemonic, and academic knowledge" (2009, 277). Though death is foreshadowed in these three novels, these deaths glorify the subversive acts by those at the margins, and "express [the] utopian possibility of love and transcending social differences." (Li 2009, 285)

The martyrdom of Velutha and Ammu is similar to that of two of White's outcasts – Alf Dubbo and Mordecai Himmelfarb. Furthermore, L. Chris Fox finds the intersection of trauma and the abject contained in Velutha's and Dubbo's dying bodies. Fox explains that "the abject is everything the human body excretes in order to live, all that might endanger our lives if we touch or ingest it," gesturing towards the outcaste status of Velutha, who is a personification of abjection. The violence he is subject to creates a trauma of formidable proportions. Velutha's excrement, urine, blood, and bodily fluids that flood the floor of the police station emit a "sickly sweet" odour and take up residence in Estha's skull, rendering him a witness and a kind of participant in the trauma of Velutha's death. Fox invokes Cathy Caruth's contention that there is no definable external determinant for trauma. (Caruth 1995, 3-12) So, abjection and trauma are strangely similar. They are elusive to any solid definition, "each is oddly fluid, slippery, in motion." (Fox 2002, 35-60) Fox maintains that the novel "does unveil the abject for readers; however, in the spirit of testimony the novel also implicitly calls for resistance to a social institution that it presents as unjust." (Fox 2006, 36) Dubbo's untimely death and corporeality with all the trappings of blood and stench are mirrored in Velutha's tragic murder by a corrupt police force at Ayemenem:

> He was semi-conscious but he wasn't moving.
>
> His skull was fractured in three places. His nose and both his cheekbones were smashed, leaving his face pulpy, undefined. The blow to his mouth had split open his upper lip and had broken six teeth, three of which were embedded in his lower, hideously inverting his beautiful smile ... The blood on his breath bright red. Fresh. Frothy. His lower intestine was ruptured and haemorrhaged the blood collected in his abdominal cavity. His spine was damaged in two places, the concussion had paralysed his right arm and resulted in a loss of control over his bladder and rectum. (Roy 1997, 310)

In the case of Gemmy, Lachlan finds his remains:

> There were bones – not so many. Eight parcels of bark, two of child size, resting a little above eye-level. He looked at one dried bundle, then another – they were not distinguishable – and felt nothing more for one than for any of them ... one of these parcels, which could not be disturbed, contained the bones of a man with a jawbone different from the rest, enlarged joints, the mark of an old break on the left leg, whose wandering at last had come to an end, and this was it. (Malouf 1993, 310)

Just as White's narrative, embedded in the dichotomous geobody of Dubbo, echoes the Eliadean sense of the "hierophanic" dialectic, so also do Malouf's and Roy's construction of the sacred in the corporeal remains of Gemmy and Velutha. Mircea Eliades's idea of the need for humanity to live in the continual present, and "myth" being synonymous with "eternal return," coupled with the desire to be at one with a cosmic beginning in "a continual present," is the strongest theoretical anchor for my argument. In his luminous chapter "Chaos," in Myth (2009) Laurence Coupe draws attention to Eliade's celebration of hierophany, treating antique narrative paradigms as if active in the present:

> Any form whatever, by the mere fact that it exists as such and endures, necessarily loses vigour and becomes worn; to recover vigour, it must be reabsorbed into the formless if only for an instant; it must be restored to the primordial unity from which it issued; in other words, it must return to the chaos (on the cosmic plane) to 'orgy' (on the social plane), to 'darkness' (for seed), to 'water' (baptism on the human plane, Atlantis on the plane of history, and so on). (Eliade 1971, 88)

This idea of resurrecting an ancient myth as an act of muddying a monolithic space, and subversion, resonates with Owen Barfield's idea of how literature awakens "an almost universal consciousness" and characterises the "golden age" of poetry as "premetaphoric and alive," (Barfield 1928, 64). The constant re-launching of an ancient myth into the experiential cacophony of the present is also addressed in James Hillman's work on metaphor, where he urges readers to stay within the "permanent ambiguity of metaphor," (Hillman 1975, 154) and by Viktor Shklovsky who claims that through defamiliarisation the literary text, provides the reader with an "amazing childhood." (Shklovsky 1977, 20)

Foucault's concept of "heterotopia" may also be applied to the novels where sites such as the bodies of Dubbo, Gemmy and Velutha may be seen to be "destabilising spaces" inhabited by cultural and religious practices, and mythologies that exist in opposition to each other (Higgins and Leps 2009, 201-212). The idea of heterotopia pervades all three narratives where often the body of the outcast is at once a location for life, nourishment and nurture, as well as a danger zone where the outcast must die. The outcast's body is also a space where corporeal desires and the divine world collide, as in the case of Dubbo's Gemmy's and Velutha's flesh. Such examples are properly linked to Foucault's remarks about the heterotopic concept of space that contains within it an idea of oppositional forces, a unique kind of hybridity and heterogeneity:

> I believe that the anxiety of our era has to do fundamentally with space, no doubt a great deal more than with time … And perhaps our life is still governed by a certain number of oppositions that remain inviolable, that our institutions and practices have not yet dared to break down. These are oppositions that we regard as simple givens: for example between private space and public space, between family space and social space … All these are still nurtured by the hidden presence of the sacred (1967, 23).

Foucault further claims that Gaston Bachelard's "monumental work" and the "descriptions of phenomenologists" have shown that the body does not live in a homogeneous and empty space, but on the contrary in a space thoroughly imbued with heterogeneities and perhaps thoroughly fantasmatic as well. The space of our "primary perception," the space of our dreams, and that of our passions hold within themselves qualities that seem intrinsic:

> There is a light, ethereal, transparent space, or again a dark, rough, encumbered space; a space from above, of summits, or on the contrary a space from below of mud; or again a space that can be flowing like sparkling water, or space that is fixed, congealed, like stone or crystal. Yet these analyses, while fundamental for reflection in our time, primarily concern internal space. (1967, 23)

In these representations of alterity the marginalised males are often seen as the "polluters" and the "unchaste," and the marginalised male is often represented as a martyr in postcolonial fiction. The martyrdom of the lower caste male is a subversion of the patriarchy because in their martyrdom the lower castes are able to continue the struggle on behalf of their caste. The martyrs successfully expose the patriarchy's anxiety about being challenged by those at the margins (Agamben 2005 and Ganguly 2008). Debjani Ganguly suggests that because most Indian nationalist leaders and nationalist historians were predominantly upper-caste

Hindus, "the image of subcontinental unity was configured in Aryan-Hindu terms with disastrous consequences for Hinduism's 'Others' – the Dalits and Muslims." (Ganguly 2008, 80) As explained earlier, Victor Li (2009) and L. Chris Fox (2002) have shown that there is a dialectical relationship between the concept of martyrdom and the death, dispossession, and disempowerment of the subaltern individual. As Li says, "In death, the subaltern is perfected as a concept so pure no living referent can contradict or complicate it." (276)

The social abyss revealed in Dubbo the outcast – "blackfellow," "abo," is pried open by Roy with remarkable audacity in her creation of Velutha. The success of her craft is largely due to the way she is able to universalise Velutha's death as a martyr who attains salvation and self-hood for not just himself but for his community. Chelva Kanaganayakam further explores this idea of martyrdom in the framework of Christianity and provides an insightful and provocative reading. He connects religious myth to subversion and argues that as it reconfigures Christian myth, *The God of Small Things* forms a "radical critique of religious practice," and unveils the "collective ideology of an [elite] group that refuses to accommodate the margins except in very limited terms." Kanaganayakam notes that Roy has appropriated Christian tropes of the abandoned Garden and the symbolism of mythical return, as well as the image of Christ as the gifted carpenter.

Like Dubbo, Velutha is also a creative artist. This collusion of Christian and Hindu myth is not oppositional but related in that it suggests that traditional religions work in unison to preserve the status quo (Kanaganayakam 2000, 141-149). The omnipresent images of death (a total of fifty-two in the novel) which are mostly connected with images of water or rain or the River Meenachi, and the metaphors that embellish these images, are the literary devices Roy uses to present a convincing argument against an oppressive, monolithic caste structure that continues to beleaguer India. Consequently, the questioning of an oppressive authority that directly causes the negation of life suggests an unexpected and novel, albeit tenuous, bond in the narrative: a link between the death of innocent victims Velutha and Dubbo at the hand of political and social authority, and the death of colonialism (and empire) itself.

In January 1999, two years after she had won the Booker Prize for *The God of Small Things*, Arundhati Roy attended a reception in her home state of Kerala organised by the Dalit Sahitya Akademi. There, she spoke out in support of the cause of untouchables in India in much the same way Patrick White had about Aborigines, through his speeches and writings.There are synergies between them: Roy is an activist as much as a great writer; White is a nuanced and powerful craftsman a global soul and a visionary. Both have strong opinions about the outcast and the Indigene. Though their work might stem from different continents and from different times, it is the theme of the transformative power of encountering hardship, alterity and pain and the endurance that comes from desiring equity and dignity for the outcast that brings the sense of a shared vision into the works of writers like White, Malouf and Roy.

I suggest that the palpable discomfort that White, Malouf and Roy create in the reader's mind through encounters with the filth, defilement and ultimate horror of the marginalised body, are transformed into a new episteme for Postcolonial writers who use the "outcast" body to simultaneously reveal the savagery of Power, to subvert its reach and, perhaps most subtly, to make a scathing comment on our moral ineptitude for acceptance of difference even as we politicise our success in constructing a more accepting "global" world. It is fitting that centenary celebrations for White are being held in India. With all its contestations of identity and diversity, India, more than any other place can do with a mega dose of White's persistent questions about how we should treat our sisters and brothers who still live on the fringes – sixty-five years after Independence.

Works Cited

Agamben, Giorgio. 2005. *State of Exception*. Chicago, Illinois: University of Chicago Press.

Bachelard, Gaston. 1958. *The Poetics of Space*. Paris: Presses Universite de France.

Barfield, Owen. 1928. *Poetic Diction: A Study in Meaning*. London: Faber.
Butler, Judith. 1993. *Bodies that Matter: On the Discursive Limits of "Sex."* New York: Routledge.
Caruth, Cathy. 1995. "Introduction," *Trauma: Explorations in Memory*, ed. Cathy Caruth. Baltimore, Maryland: Johns Hopkins University Press.
Coupe. Laurence. 2009. *Myth*. London & New York: Routledge.
Dinnage, Rosemary. 2002. Book Blurb, New York Review Books.
Eliade, Mircea. 1971. *The Myth of Eternal Return; Or, Cosmos and History*. Princeton, New Jersey: Princeton University Press.
Foucault, Michel. 1967. "Of Other Spaces," *Diacritics* 16 (Spring 1986): 22-27.
Fox, Chris L. 2002. "A Martyrology of the Abject: Witnessing and Trauma in Arundhati Roy's *The God of Small Things*," *Ariel* 33:3.4: 35-60.
Ganguly, Debjani. 2008. *Caste and Dalit Lifeworlds: Postcolonial Perspectives*. New Delhi: Orient Longman.
Hillman, James. 1975. *Re-Visioning Psychology*. New York: Harper & Row.
Kanaganayakam, Chelva. 2000."Religious Myth and Subversion in *The God of Small Things*," *Literary Canons and Religious Identity* ed. Erik Borgman, Bart Philipsen, and Lea Verstricht.Aldershot, UK: Ashgate: 141-49.
Kristeva, Julia. 1982. *The Powers of Horror: An Essay on Abjection*. New York: Columbia University Press.
Li, Victor. 2009. "Necroidealism, or the Subaltern's Sacrificial Death," *Interventions: International Journal of Postcolonial Studies* 11:3: 275-292.
McGregor, Craig. 1969. *In the Making*. Melbourne: Nelson.
Malouf, David. 1993. *Remembering Babylon*. New York: Alfred Knopf.
Roy, Arundhati. 1997. *The God of Small Things*. London: Harper Collins.
Shklovsky, Viktor Borisovich. 1977. *Third Factory*. Ann Arbor, Michigan: Ardis.
Tagore, Rabindranath. 1998. *Gitanjali*, Kolkata: Writer's Workshop.

vanden Driesen, Cynthia. 2008. "Heaven in a grain of sand – Patrick White's Contemporary Vision," Forum on Public Policy. http:///.forum on publicpolicy.com/papershtm. Accessed January 15, 2014.
White,Patrick.1961.*Riders in the Chariot*.New York:Viking.
Young, Marion. 1990. *Justice and the Politics of Difference*. Princeton: Princeton University Press.

Part V

Socio-Political Issues

Chapter Twenty-Six

Australia and its First Peoples

Fred Chaney AO

[Plenary Speech presented at the Patrick White Centenary Conference, India Dec. 5-7, 2012]

It is an honour and a privilege to participate in a conference held in India to celebrate the work of Australian Nobel prizewinning writer, Patrick White. My lack of literary scholarship makes me an odd participant in this conference. I was invited I gather, to contribute because I have an expertise in dealing with a particular public issue that White saw as central to Australian life: Australia's treatment of its Indigenous people. Despite my disclaimer, I have a value for White's writings. In fact, I read *Voss* from cover to cover as I sat with my wife during the long labour which produced our first son. "Gloomy reading for a birth" was the verdict of the obstetrician but perhaps the gloom (and perhaps some of the subtleties of that great novel) were blown away by the joy of a new life. In any event I thank the Association for the Study of Australia in Asia for the opportunity to participate in the conference and to present an address leading to new understanding I hope, of an important aspect of our national life.

The year 2012 was designated 'The year of Australia' in India. The Australian Prime Minister visited India and the commercial and cultural links between India and Australia were strengthened. Perhaps the most important link we have between us is that our countries are democracies. As democracies we share the privilege of freedom to dissent. What distinguishes our two countries also from some other areas of the world is that citizens of our countries have the right to be contentious and express views on public issues without fear of persecution by government. In his later years Patrick White, for instance could publicly rail against the Government of the day, knowing he would remain secure from any form of retaliation. It is something we need to rejoice in, and celebrate – our possession of that freedom.

As well as shared ideals of freedom and democracy Australia and India share a history of colonisation by Great Britain; yet these are very different histories. In our case a vast part of Australia with a relatively small population of Indigenous people spread across it was taken possession of as a colony in 1788. In subsequent years the whole island continent was brought under British colonial rule. In 1788 the gradual usurpation of the land, the dispossession and often dispersal of the estimated three quarters of a million Aboriginal people who had occupied the land for tens of thousands of years before the arrival of the British began. Unlike India, where the politics in place when the British arrived were dealt with as polities, the colonisation of Australia in its various stages was an absolute takeover from the existing inhabitants; the land was regarded as *terra nullius*, simply there to be taken

In a short time the Indigenous inhabitants were swamped by the British conquerors except in remote areas, bypassed because they were unsuitable for the settlers' crops animals or health. Post-colonial history in Australia is completely different from post-colonial history in India. In India on the departure of the colonial power the colonised peoples were left to govern their country. In Australia the original inhabitants, the colonised people, were a minority and the colonisers remained and were the majority group at the time of independence. At the time Australia achieved nationhood, Aborigines were seen as 'a dying race'; they had lost all control over their own lives and lands, and their numbers seemed to have settled into a steady decline.

I shall attempt to trace only the more recent path 'White' Australia has followed in its relationship with Indigenous Australia. (The early stage of this relationship has been recounted many times from many perspectives, and is too well known to be rehearsed yet again within the limitations of this context. Australia was recognised as a nation in 1900. I will outline how we have moved from legal and constitutional exclusion of Aborigines in those early years to their achievement in *de jure* terms, of full citizenship. We are now pursuing explicit constitutional recognition, as well as working towards a closing of the gap in economic and health outcomes. In the field of civil and political rights I have a story of positive achievements to tell. In the social and economic areas I can describe considerable effort, particularly over the last forty years, but a more mixed record of achievement. We recognise that we have a long way to go still.

How will I relate this to Patrick White? I do so only in passing. It could appear, to some that White's direct contact with Aboriginal Australians was limited and his interest it seems was primarily intellectual. Others might argue with conviction of "the significance of the Aboriginal presence" in his texts and the fact that in those texts Aborigines are afforded dignity and due recognition of their humanity. (vanden Driesen, 2009) I respectfully agree with that view and allow that it places him ahead of many in his generation. But it would be foolish of me to try to repeat or build on such comments on his writings. Instead, I see in White's recorded life a similar trajectory to that of Australia itself – a move from ignorance and indifference, to consciousness and concern, through to a determination to support recognition and change. In that sense White's journey is reflective of our national journey with respect to Aboriginal people, an unsteady, irregular, as yet incomplete, but clearly discernible, move towards a more enlightened position

A paragraph from David Marr's splendid biography referring to White's early life is the one limited reference to Aborigines in that substantial book:

> Walgett was not much of a town, a grid of weatherboard houses on stumps, a courthouse and seven or eight pubs built by the river. Walgett was white. Aborigines of many tribes lived on the mission and in humpies along the river bed, but they were not allowed into town, unless they were going on an errand. The rule was: straight in and straight out with no loitering. Blacks were not allowed to drink, though not much notice was paid to the colour of a man's hand in the trapdoor at the back of the Royal, and whites took bottles of wine down to the camp to trade for 10 shillings or a root. In the months at Walgett White did not meet an Aborigine, they were everywhere but did not cross his path. Clem, alone of his

neighbours, didn't take a black boy on the back of his sulky to open the gates. (Marr 1992, 108)

What is clear is that his expressed sympathy towards the circumstances of Aboriginal Australians, particularly in his later more politically active years, seems real enough, even if, in my view, it cannot be compared with the intensity of his concerns about environmental issues, the risk of nuclear war and the need for nuclear disarmament. For example in 1981 he addressed a nuclear disarmament meeting and suggested that beside the issue of nuclear warfare "nothing else matters." (Brennan and Flynn 1989, 99) This is not meant as a criticism but rather that, given his well-known connections with such personalities as Gough Whitlam, Judith Wright, and Nugget Coombs, it would have been odd if Aboriginal concerns had not surfaced in his political interventions.

In 1973 Patrick White was Australian of the Year. In his address in January 1974 he said, "... we still have that apparently insoluble problem of what to do about the Aborigines we dispossessed." (Brennan and Flynn 1989, 47) In 1974 speaking in support of the re-election of the Whitlam Government he justified that support in part on "... its attempts to come to grips with that most complex of all our problems, the Aborigines, both tribal and urban. (Brennan, 52) In 1988, our bi-centenary year, he explained why he would not have any new work published or presented during that year: "More than anything else, it was the need for justice for the Aborigine which put me against the Bi. Very little has been done to give them a sense of security in the country we invaded. Aborigines may not be shot and poisoned as they were ... but there are subtler ways of poisoning them." (Brennan and Flynn, 1989, 183) Over a fifteen-year period, he showed undoubted sympathy growing over time for the plight of Aboriginal people.

Let me enter two caveats about any analyses I offer today. First, in 1969 Patrick White said of himself "I am not a philosopher or an intellectual. Practically anything I have done of any worth I feel I have done through my intuition, not my mind ..." (Brennan and Flynn, 1989, 21) The first sentence of that quotation I feel I could apply to myself; the second I would alter slightly and say that practically anything of any worth I feel I have done because of my intuition has been aided and informed by greater minds and hearts than my own. Second, I have given priority to action over academic analysis. I have acted on my sense of what needed to be done to alleviate the injustices done to Aboriginal people rather than write about it. When, after my political career, I spent a brief time in a university as a Research Fellow my Professor sensibly posed the question – "Do you want to do things or study things?" I left the University to resume the former course.

What I say today therefore should not be regarded as an academic treatise. These are the observations of a participant or practitioner: a player of many roles as a lawyer, politician, Minister, public servant, and citizen. I cannot claim to be a disinterested observer. My general observations about the circumstances of Aboriginal people would be little different from those recorded in the public political utterances quoted above, of Patrick White in his later years. My observations have, in the main, led me to direct personal engagements rather than verbal articulation of views and opinions, of pronouncements and detached study.

I must record that I have been aided in my work by the intellectual leadership of others, Aboriginal and non-Aboriginal, whose more systematic and intellectual analyses have allowed me to check my intuitive responses to necessarily episodic observation of complex intercultural and inter-racial issues. There is no space to expand on these here and I will limit myself to describing briefly my own personal perspective. That perspective is of a person proud of his country's progress, seeing it as being on a journey from a past rooted in an age of racial discrimination and injustice towards a time devoted to evolving a proper relationship with its first peoples.

The modern Australian nation came into being when six separate colonies of Australia established by Great Britain sought to become one federal nation. The Australian constitution, enacted by the United Kingdom Parliament at Westminster, was written at conventions held by the six colonies in the 1890s. It reflected the thought patterns and ideologies of the times in which it was created. Its references to Aboriginals were, in simplest terms, exclusionist. The language of those conventions was also of those times The Constitution permitted disqualification from voting on the basis of race, it excluded counting Aboriginals in the census, and gave power to the new Commonwealth Parliament to make laws for the people of any race for whom it was deemed necessary to make special laws, except Aboriginals who were to be the legislative preserve of the States. This particular power to make laws, commonly referred to as the' race power', was designed to ensure the Commonwealth could control and exclude coloured races from access to power

The attitude to Aboriginal people then was part of a wider canvas. Attitudes to race were clear and distinctly part of the legacy of imperialist policy which had led to the founding of Australia. This audience would be aware that for the first half-century of the existence of the Australian nation there was a rigid White Australia policy in place which was only gradually dismantled over the period 1949- 1973. In the first Parliament in its first year, 1901, the second Prime Minister of Australia, Alfred Deakin, regarded as the father of Australian liberalism, stated:

> Little more than 100 years ago Australia was a dark continent in every sense of the term. There was not a white man within its borders. In another century the probability is that Australia will be a white continent with not a black or even dark skin among its inhabitants. The aboriginal race has died out in the South and is dying fast in the North and West even where most gently treated. Other races are to be excluded by legislation if they are tinted to any degree. (Hansard Report 1901)

The first Prime Minister of Australia, Edmund Barton, speaking in the same debate on the Immigration Restriction Act 1901 said:

> I do not think either that the doctrine of the equality of man was really ever intended to include racial equality. There is no racial equality. There is basic inequality. These races are, in comparison with white races – I think no one wants convincing of this fact – unequal and inferior. The doctrine of the equality of man was never intended to apply to the equality of the Englishman and the Chinaman. There is deep-set difference, and we see no prospect and no promise of its ever being effaced. Nothing in this world can put these two races upon an equality. Nothing we can do by cultivation, by refinement, or by anything else will make some races equal to others. (Hansard Report 1901)

These attitudes took a long time to die. but dead they are, as a walk around any Australian city today, will tell you. In 1949 the policy wall was breached when Japanese war brides and mixed-race refugees were admitted. I can still remember seeing newspaper photographs of nervous looking young Japanese women, clad in kimonos. They were in the papers because it was so out of the ordinary that such people should be admitted into Australia. These initial changes were made by the first Minister for Immigration in the Menzies government Harold Holt who later became became Prime Minister of Australia. Changes were gradual thereafter with the substantial shift to a non-racial immigration policy in the mid-1960s, again under a Liberal government. The final technical steps however were taken under the Labour government of Gough Whitlam in 1973.

Over the same period attitudes towards Aboriginal people also began to change. Australia was not of course immune to world events. The process of de-colonisation around the globe, in Asia, in Africa, in South America, across the colonised world, and the demands for self-government culminating in the achievement of Independence by so many of the erstwhile colonies, and later the civil rights movement in the United States, the greater emphasis on human rights internationally were all part of the process of re-shaping how Australians saw such matters. The winds of change were blowing also through other countries which had been settled by a White majority like Canada, New Zealand and Australia. There have been too many detailed and wide-ranging studies of the complex influences which worked these changes and brought about the transition from Empire to Commonwealth and beyond to necessitate further rehearsing here.

My account will focus mostly on the changes here in Australia to the gradual changes in the legal status and rights of the Indigenous people, the area in which I may claim a degree of participation that stretches over a long period. In 1961 the limited access of Aborigines to voting was addressed by the Commonwealth Parliament following an enquiry by a Parliamentary Committee. On a personal note this was my first contact with changing public policy in this area as the University Liberal Club, to which I belonged, drafted the submission to the Parliamentary Committee which was put forward by the State Liberal Party and submitted to the Commonwealth Government.

The next step forward was the 1967 referendum, which removed the constitutional exclusion of Aborigines from Australian citizenship and extended Commonwealth legislative power to enable the Commonwealth to legislate for them. This was seen at the time as a positive measure. It was not till much later that the reality became apparent – that the power to legislate for their benefit was also a power to legislate to their detriment. Nevertheless, the 1967 referendum is significant in many ways. The long campaign for the referendum was led by an effective coalition of Aboriginal and Islander interests. It was a campaign based on a demand for equality. And it was the most successful referendum campaign in Australia's history with more than 90% of voters voting 'yes.' The 1967 referendum holds a special place in the hearts of many Aboriginal people. They see it as marking their admission to citizenship and indeed to voting rights. In my view the overwhelming support for that referendum reflected a deep-seated Australian belief that all Australians be regarded as equal in the eyes of the law.

It is that belief in equal treatment which made the next stage of the Aboriginal struggle for justice much more complicated. Since 1788, Aboriginal rights to land had not been legally recognised. The legal position was that land was held by the Crown and only the Crown could create titles in land. Aboriginal people challenged this. The Yolnu people of Arnhem Land brought a case in the Supreme Court of the Northern Territory seeking recognition of their traditional rights to land. This 1971 case, *Milirrpum v Nabalco and the Commonwealth*, commonly known as the *Gove land case*, heard detailed evidence of the Aboriginal connection to country. In the final outcome the case failed not because the connection was not found to exist but rather that precedent determined that communal native title did not form any part of the law of Australia. The judgement of J Blackburn. is however a splendid exposition of how Aboriginal people are connected to country by their law and culture. In a critical passage the judge acknowledged that the evidence put before him was of a system which he described as "a government of laws and not of men."

At that time it was not thought that the superior courts in Australia would overturn such a decision and so the battle was moved to the political arena. The newly- elected Whitlam government commissioned the man who had been counsel for the Aboriginal plaintiffs in the Gove land case to advise on how native title could be recognised in the Northern Territory. It is important to note that the enquiry was not about *whether* native title should be recognised but rather on *how* it should be recognised.

The two Woodward reports resulted in an all-party agreement that Land Rights should be recognised in the Northern Territory. Legislation had been introduced by the Whitlam Government but the Government was dismissed before the legislation was passed. The incoming Fraser Government reintroduced the legislation which was finally passed in 1976. The outcome has been that about half of the Northern Territory is now held communally, by traditional owners under perpetual inalienable freehold. Another critically important step was the passage through the Parliament in 1975 of the Racial Discrimination Act. This Act also received all-party support and has been an important factor in subsequent gains made by traditional owners with respect to securing legal rights to traditional lands. It is also an important marker of the fact that both *de facto* and *de jure* Australia had moved away from the discriminatory attitudes of the past.

Over subsequent years a number of the States passed Land Rights legislation related to their jurisdictions. There was however virulent opposition to recognition of Land Rights in some parts of the country, particularly in the States of Queensland and Western Australia, and in sections of the mining industry. Eventually, in the 1980s, the governing Labour Party adopted a policy for national Land Rights, which would involve overruling those States which would not take action at state level. The opposition of State governments and the mining industry was enough to force a Government back down and the struggle for Land Rights appeared to lose its political impetus.

However further Land Rights cases were raised in a number of jurisdictions. The critical case was in Queensland where Torres Strait Islanders claimed traditional title to their islands. The importance of the Racial Discrimination Act became apparent when the Queensland government tried to ensure the lead case in Queensland, the *Mabo* case, would be rendered ineffective. In the case known as *Mabo No 1*, that legislation was struck down by the High Court as being in breach of the Racial Discrimination Act.

Subsequently, in the second *Mabo* decision, the High Court overturned the law denying recognition, which it said had come out of an age of racial discrimination. It held that there could be common law recognition of native title where it had not been extinguished by a prior grant of title from the Crown. In 1993 the Commonwealth Parliament passed the *Native Title Act* which confirmed existing government created titles, provided mechanisms for obtaining new titles from government where native title existed and provided for a process for obtaining determinations of native title which would recognise and confirm native title interests which been found to exist.

In my view the *Mabo* case effected the greatest change in the balance of power between the majority of Australians, and the Aboriginal people since the latter had lost all power in 1788. Its outcomes were geographically uneven because, of course, the best well-watered land on the dry continent had long been settled and alienated. However, across Australia it is now possible for Aboriginal people to come to the table of negotiation as stakeholders with an interest rather than as mendicants. The initial opposition by the mining industry was quickly replaced by a publicly expressed determination to work with Aboriginal people as stakeholders. In mineral rich areas there are substantial economic outcomes for Aboriginal people with native title rights.

The current most positive sign of our progress on the civil and political front is the present preparedness of all political parties in our national Parliament, and the independent members, to work towards constitutional recognition of the rights of Aboriginal and Torres Strait Islander people. As a distinguished Aboriginal leader put it, we started with exclusion in 1900, we moved to neutrality in 1967, and now we are moving toward recognition. A panel appointed to consult the Australian people and report on this issue delivered its report in January of 2013. (That report is available on the website www.youmeunity.org.au). The report is an important step in the journey towards constitutional recognition and the

Government has funded a two- year education campaign through Reconciliation Australia to increase public understanding of the issues. Given the record of constitutional referenda in Australia, only 8 referenda have succeeded over our 112 year history as a nation, success in achieving constitutional recognition will not be easy. Nevertheless, the important point is that, at a time of great political division in Australia, on this subject there is some sense of shared purpose among the parties on this topic.

My objective has been to explain my sense that the shifts which have occurred in my lifetime have moved Australia in the direction of becoming a better, more moral, more united country. It would however, be a lopsided version of the journey if I were to skate past the continuing disadvantage of many Indigenous Australians. All of the measurable social indicators show a gap between Indigenous Australians and the rest of the population. Those who wish to examine the detail of this disadvantage will have no difficulty in finding the facts on the official public record. I will select only three of the hundreds of reports available, to access information on the broad historical and present circumstances.

The first of these is the Report of the Expert Panel on Recognising Aboriginal and Torres Strait Islander Peoples previously referred to and which was handed to the Prime Minister in January 2012. In addition to addressing the legal and constitutional journey I have described, it deals with colonisation and Aboriginal resistance, the periods of so called protection and assimilation, and the notion of closing the gap between Indigenous and other Australians in a range of areas relating to health and education:

As the report records: The gap in life expectancy is estimated at 11.5 years for men and 9.7 years for women. Infant mortality for Indigenous infants is 1.8 to 3.8 times higher than for non-Indigenous infants. 25.8% of indigenous young people receive a year 12 school certificate as against 56.1% for non-indigenous. Employment rates for the non-Indigenous Australians of 53.8% contrast sadly with that of the 76% figure recorded for Indigenous Australians. These current realities are the outcome of dispossession and dispersal, past racial social and economic policies including, at times, separation of mixed race children from their families. This last matter has been extensively documented in the Bringing Them Home Report, which is the 1997 report of the National Inquiry into the Separation of Aboriginal and Torres Strait Islander Children from their families. (www.humanrights.gov.au/ social_justice/bth_report/index.html).

The Report illustrates the complexity of issues and motives which are part of our history in this area. Removing children from their families was seen, by its exponents, as a way of providing an opportunity for mixed-race children to become part of the wider society and adopt the way of life of the majority community. In just the same way, a generation ago in Australia, the children of unwed mothers were widely seen as better off adopted by a married couple. Views and standards change with time. In 2008, the then Prime Minister, Kevin Rudd, delivered in the national Parliament an historic apology for the pain, suffering, and hurt of these stolen generations as they are now generally known. (The text of the apology can be found at many websites including, www.dfat.gov. au.)

In the same vein, apologies have been made by various governments to child migrants and to mothers deprived of their children by Government policies of the past. Many would agree, justifiably, that our nation still carries the psychological scars of those past actions. Time does not permit me to do justice to the many different approaches which have been adopted by governments over the last 200 years. Those of you, with an interest, will have no difficulty finding material on public record which documents our failings. The Report on Aboriginal Deaths in Custody released in 1987 is one and details can be checked online. (www.human

rights.gov.au/social_justice/publications/deaths_custody). In fact, there is now a statutory framework in place for the regular disclosure of a large range of economic and social statistics relating to the welfare of Aboriginal peoples to the Parliament and to the general public.

Since 2002 the heads of all Australian governments have required the principal advisory body to the Commonwealth on economic matters, the Productivity Commission, to provide a public account of progress against six headline targets set by the

Council of Australian governments together with other significant indicators. These reports help governments monitor and address the disadvantage that limits the opportunities and choices of many Indigenous people. The targets set by the Council of Australian governments to close the gap between Indigenous disadvantage and the majority of Australians are as follows:

i) Closing the life expectancy gap within a generation;
ii) Halving the gap in the mortality rate for Indigenous children under five within a decade;
iii) Ensuring all Indigenous four-year olds in remote communities have access to quality early childhood programs within five years
iv) Halving the gap in reading, writing and numeracy achievements for children within a decade;
v) Halving the gap for Indigenous students in year 12 attainment rates or equivalent attainment by 2020;
vi) Halving the gap in employment outcomes within a decade.

The steering committee reported in August 2011 on the advances made:

Nine years after this series was commissioned, there is still a considerable way to go if we are to fulfil COAG's commitment to close the gap in Indigenous disadvantage. Wide gaps in average outcomes remain across most indicators. Of the 45 quantitative indicators in the report, for example, available data show improvement in outcomes for only 13 indicators including in employment educational attainment and home ownership. For 10 there has been no real improvement, while for another seven, including social indicators such as criminal justice, outcomes have actually deteriorated.

Importantly, the Commission has also advised on identified success factors in programs that appear to be making a difference. These have been set out in successive reports as follows:

i) Cooperative approaches between Indigenous people and the government – often with the non-profit and private sectors as well;

ii) Community involvement in program design and decision-making – a 'bottom-up' rather than 'top-down' approach;
iii) Good governance – at organisation, community and government levels
iv) Ongoing government support – including human, financial and physical resources.

My own experience can confirm evidence of these success factors. The Commission points out that the lack of any of these factors can result in program failure. The real difficulty we have is in delivering centralised policy decisions through top-down bureaucracies in a way that can work to ensure these success factors. In addition to the detailed reporting on expenditure on Indigenous Australians and the public reporting through the steering committee headed by the Productivity Commission the Prime Minister reports annually to Parliament. The most recent report tabled in Parliament on 15 February 2012 is available on the website of the relevant Department (www.fahcsia.gov.au.). It is a comprehensive overview of how the Government is attempting to deal with our first peoples.

Of course Government action is only part of the story. In 1991 with all-party support in Parliament, the Council for Aboriginal Reconciliation was established by statute. Between then and the year 2000 the Council promoted dialogue between Indigenous people and the wider community and promoted an agenda for Reconciliation. When the council completed its statutory term in 2000 it left behind to a non-government organisation called Reconciliation Australia the task of carrying on its work. By the end of the year 2000 there had been many declarations of good intentions. Since then we have seen many of those declarations of good intention turned into plans for action. There are now well over 300 Reconciliation Action Plans involving major Australian corporations, government departments, non-government organisations including universities and hospitals setting out how they are developing respectful relationships and effecting change.

This is one of the major changes for the better, this broadening acceptance that reconciliation is not only just a matter for government and Indigenous Australians, but also a matter for all of us. This part of our progress can be explored on the Reconciliation Australia website, www.reconciliation.org.au. My own experience is an almost daily stream of contacts with people anxious to do their bit. It was not like that in the past.

How can I try sum up where we stand with regard to caring for the well-being of our First Peoples? From my perspective, after years of working in the field it is 'a work in progress' but the direction of travel is more positive than it has ever been before, certainly in my lifetime. There is still much to lament about the material circumstances of too many of our Indigenous people. Incarceration rates and other social statistics so regularly reported on show we have still a long way to go. Nevertheless, 2012 also saw Aborigines and Torres Strait Islanders making huge contributions in every aspect of Australian life. Their contributions to creative writing, to the visual and performing arts, and to sport are disproportionate to their numbers. Their engagement in academic and business life is steadily increasing. The first Aboriginal Rhodes Scholar currently is, with six other Aboriginal postgraduate students, at Oxford University. My *alma mater*, the University of Western Australia, takes pride in having graduated more Indigenous doctors and lawyers than any other University in Australia.

The present time is marked by unprecedented levels of engagement across the Australian community. This has provided hope and opportunity as never before. Today Aboriginal people are legally entitled to full citizenship. They have indeed a degree of recognition of communal rights which are unique to them, and are active participants in working out a shared future with the majority of Australians. They have yet to achieve the settling of the relationship between themselves and the rest of society and the full enjoyment of the bountiful lives Australia offers to most of its people.

For this observer at least the past, rooted in an age of racial discrimination, is a foreign country. The present is a time of some real progress and hope. The future must be one of true reconciliation. I cannot speak as an Aboriginal or Torres Strait Islander Australians but it seems to me that until we arrive at a reconciled future Australia will not be wholly freed of the colonial legacies of prejudice and injustice. There are big issues yet to be faced and another generation will have to deal with those challenges

Works Cited

Brennan, Paul and Christine Flynn.Ed.1989. *Patrick White Speaks.* Sydney: Primavera Press.
Marr, David. 1991. *Patrick White: A Life.* London: Random House.
vanden Driesen Cynthia. 2009. *Writing the Nation: Patrick White and the Indigene.* Amsterdam and New York: Rodopi.

Websites for Further Information

www.youmeunity.org.au
www.reconciliation.org.au
www.fahcsia.gov.au.
www.humanrights.gov.au

Chapter Twenty-Seven

Aboriginal Progress in the Native Title Era: Truth and Substantive Equality in *Terra Australis*

Anne de Soyza
Independent Scholar

Introduction

Australia's Nobel Prize winning novelist Patrick White, particularly in his later years, was profoundly concerned with Australia's treatment of its Aboriginal peoples as the numerous impassioned speeches he made over a 15 year period during his activist involvement with Aboriginal causes attest. (Brennan and Flynn, 1989) Besides the overt declaration of his views, at least three of his novels, *Voss, Riders in the Chariot*, and *A Fringe of Leaves*, have these concerns embedded as central thematic issues. (vanden Driesen 2009) Other contemporary writers like Grenville (2005) and Malouf (1993) have explored these themes particularly the relationship to the land and its impact on issues of belonging and settler identity. It is a matter for ongoing soul-searching and regrets that it was not till very recently that Indigenous people were formally recognised in the law as having been present on the continent prior to its colonisation by the Europeans. This discussion will focus on little-known aspects of that long delayed recognition and indicate that in itself, these well-intentioned reforms cannot offset the negative outcomes of dispossession and marginalisation that has been the Australian Aboriginal inheritance for so many years after the European arrival in the land.

Colonising societies have modes of representing those whom they colonise, modes that rationalise and justify the colonial project of subjugation and expropriation. Where the receding tide of colonial rule leaves a settler society in political control and in dominant numbers, as was the case with Australia, a series of problems arise. For the settler-society there is the problem of establishing legitimacy and of creating a native identity, rather than one that refers back to the country of origin and the link with the colonising power. For the colonised the challenge is initially to survive the onslaught of colonisation and then to find their own method of engagement with, and participation in, the wider postcolonised community that has emerged. For Indigenous Australians any claim to the land arising out of their occupation of the continent prior to colonisation was accorded no legal significance on the basis of two interconnected legal expedients: the enlarged doctrine of *terra nullius* under international law and the denial of a doctrine of native title as forming any part of the common law of Australia. Australia's foundation story was based on the idea of *discovery* rather than conquest and the law supported it.

In relatively recent times the High Court, the highest judicial institution in the land, driven by the pressure of events and ideas, particularly in the post World War II era, reversed the foundation story in its judgement in *Mabo v Queensland* i.e. *Mabo* (No 2). This has had consequences (and caused tensions) particularly among Australians of European descent as to the re-telling of their own history of presence and endeavour on the continent. Twenty years after having remedied the discursive and legal omissions in the foundation story, the outstanding questions for both Indigenous and non-Indigenous Australians relate to the removal of the continuing barriers to the substantive inclusion of Indigenous people in Australian society In other words, the symbolic acknowledgement of prior occupation and the recognition of native title in many parts of Australia which has brought some economic benefits has not caused any widespread alleviation in the general marginalisation of Indigenous people in Australian society. There is continuing evidence of the general disadvantage of the Indigenous community on social and economic indicia of well-being relative to other Australians.

One issue is that far too much expectation has been placed on native title to remedy social and economic disparity between Indigenous and non-Indigenous Australians. The fact that Aboriginal communities in the Northern Territory with long-established interests in land held under the *Aboriginal Land Rights (Northern Territory) Act 1976* (Commonwealth) continue to live in poverty and dysfunction, should have tempered the expectations placed on native title. Nevertheless native title, especially through the operation of the *Native Title Act* 1993, does present expanded opportunities for economic advancement. (Langton 2013)

A proposition to be considered is that the problem may lie in the incompatibility of traditional culture with participation in a modern society. This is the central proposition advanced by anthropologist Peter Sutton in his work *The Politics of Suffering* (2009). If the problem (or a major part of it) lies here, then native title presents a paradox: It provides both the leverage for Indigenous groups in improving the circumstances of their lives, but it also encourages (and requires) an orientation towards a traditional pre-modern past that may be a barrier to this improvement. I discuss this paradox further below.

It may at this stage be prudent to state unequivocally that the conclusion to this essay is not a call for abandonment of culture but an acknowledgement of the complexity of the situation at hand. What is at stake is Indigenous uniqueness and the question to be faced is how this can be retained while reaching simultaneously for the indispensable need for economic and social parity. Sutton calls for a cultural redevelopment, which he says can only be generated by Indigenous people themselves.

The foundation story

The Anglo-Australian story was constructed as a narrative of discovery, exploration and achievement. If Africa was 'the dark continent' then Australia was the empty one and therefore it had to be populated and made productive. The presence of Aborigines was known of course, but not accorded any significance in the sense that their prior occupation of the land did not yield any interests recognisable by the received common law. If they could not show any recognisable interest in the land then they could not be dispossessed of it, so in that sense, they were invisible or irrelevant to colonial expansion.

The principle of *terra nullius* was a means of acquisition of sovereignty over unoccupied territories and in its enlarged form, it enabled the State's acquisition of occupied places where the inhabitants were considered backward and/or the land uncultivated (Brennan, *Mabo (No2)* 1992). The consequence of an acquisition under this principle was that the sovereign became the absolute beneficial owner in possession of all land in the colony. The 1971 decision of *Milirrpum v Nabalco Pty Ltd* (i.e Milirrpum) confirmed previous case law that rights and interests in land springing from pre-colonial laws and customs of Indigenous people were not recognised by the common law of Australia. While *Milirrpum v Nabalco* was a decision of a single judge of the Supreme Court of the Northern Territory it was never appealed, so that the legal principles confirmed in the case stood until the High Court's decision in *Mabo (No 2)* in 1992.

The cross-currents

However, there were cross-currents in this foundation story primarily because the colonial project was never completed in Australia. Much of the continent is harsh desert untouched by European settlement where Aboriginal people have continued to live in traditional ways. Elsewhere European settlement was loosely established through the device of 'pastoral leases' a statutory form of title that enabled sometimes vast tracts of land to be held for the grazing of livestock. Aboriginal people were vital to the operation of the pastoral industry and in turn, until developments in the late 1960s, which I don't propose to delve into here, they were able to maintain their traditional way of life despite the demands made upon them as labourers in this industry. In fact, the statutory provisions creating pastoral leases often reserved a right for Aboriginal entry and use of the land for traditional purposes.

The Milirrpum decision confirmed that the Crown acquired absolute beneficial title to the lands of the colony upon the acquisition of sovereignty and that no doctrine of native title existed in the received common law in the colony through which Aboriginal interests could be recognised. It is noteworthy however that the judge, while finding that the Aboriginal claims could not be described as proprietary in nature, also observed that the evidence had displayed "a subtle and elaborate system ... which provided a stable order of society and was remarkably free from the vagaries of whim or personal influence. If ever a system could be called 'a government of laws and not of men' it is that shown in the evidence before me." (Blackburn *Milurrpum* 1971).

Following the Milirrpum decision the Commonwealth Government established a Royal Commission – the Aboriginal Land Rights Commission - to enquire into how Aboriginal interests in land could be appropriately recognised under a legislative scheme. The ultimate result was the bipartisan *Aboriginal Land Rights (Northern Territory) Act* 1976 (i.e. the ALR Act) drawn up during the term of a Labour Government and passed by an incoming Coalition Government. It is noteworthy however that this action was confined to the Northern Territory a place regarded in the national imagination as isolated and exotic. In the 1980s a Commonwealth Government proposal for a national legislative scheme that would provide for inalienable freehold title, control over mining and mining royalty equivalents to Aboriginal groups – all of these elements based on the ALR Act approach was abandoned under political pressure and the implications of this is discussed further below (Jennett 1990).

The point is that these cross currents driving against the foundation story gathered power in the post – war period for a range of reasons. These reasons included the ideas behind de-colonisation based on liberal ideas such as the idea of equality, and in Australia the undeniable reality that not only had Aborigines survived colonisation but in many parts of the continent non-Indigenous Australians had barely established a presence. In the 1980s, pushed by these currents Australia tried but failed to provide a national land rights regime that would enable Indigenous interests in the land to be recognised and accommodated across the nation under a statutory scheme. The original proposal for a national uniform land rights scheme had been part of the 1983 election commitments of the new Commonwealth Labour Government. The election commitments repeated in the first year of government and based on the ALR Act approach related to:

Recognition of inalienable freehold title;
Protection of Aboriginal sacred Control over mining on Aboriginal land;
Access to mining royalty equivalents;
Compensation for lost land to be negotiated.

By 1985 when the Commonwealth Government's "preferred national land rights model" was released for discussion the proposal had been significantly watered down in response to pressure from the Western Australian Government in particular. The final 1985 proposal did not include control over mining, access to mining royalty equivalents and compensation for lost land. By 1989 the Government had abandoned its proposal for national land rights legislation altogether (Jennett 1990).

The new foundation story

Responding to the pressures of the time, Australia's High Court stepped in where political will had ultimately failed, overturning previous case law on the subject to establish in *Mabo (No 2)* that a doctrine of native title was part of the common law of Australia. Indigenous people did have rights to the land under their laws and customs prior to the acquisition of sovereignty by Britain and those rights (or some part of them) could be recognised by the common law of Australia. The High Court's project was to bring the common law into line with the reality of Indigenous presence and with the values of the times. Justice Brennan delivering the lead judgment in the *Mabo* case had this to say:

It must be acknowledged that, to state the common law in this way [i.e. to acknowledge that traditional title can survive the acquisition of sovereignty] involves the overruling of cases which have held to the contrary. To maintain the authority of these cases would destroy the equality of all Australian citizens before the law. The common law of this country would perpetuate injustice if it were to continue to embrace the enlarged notion of terra nullius and to persist in characterizing the indigenous inhabitants of the Australian colonies as people too low in the scale of social organisation to be acknowledged as possessing any rights and interests in land. Moreover, to reject the theory that the Crown acquired absolute beneficial ownership of land is to bring the law into conformity with Australian history.

It followed that if Indigenous people had rights to the land they could be dispossessed of it. Importantly the court acknowledged that Indigenous dispossession underwrote the formation of the Australian nation. This then was the formal end of the old foundation story. Ever since, a battle has ensued among European Australians over reinterpretations of their own history on the continent in what has come to be called 'The Culture Wars.' The Culture Wars underscore that the flip side of recognising Indigenous pre-colonial sovereignty and dispossession has meant a struggle to redefine the settler story. At the heart of that struggle are the questions: what can be made of the endeavour and achievement of European settlers and their descendants in Australia, built as these were based on the forcible dispossession of others? Can a settler history under such circumstances be a noble one?

Native title and opportunities for participation in the real economy

Native title under the common law is inherently fragile and capable of extinguishment without compensation at common law (although the Australian Constitution's 'just terms' compensation provision in section 51(xxxi) does provide protection). "Sovereignty carries the power to create and to extinguish private rights and interests in land within the Sovereign's territory. The sovereign power may or may not be exercised with solicitude for the welfare of the indigenous inhabitants" (Brennan, *Mabo (No 2)* 1992). Further, establishing native title or in other words, becoming a native title holder under the law would be a complex process in large measure because of the way the High Court formulated what would constitute a sufficient continuing connection to land in *Mabo (No2)* and the 2002 decision of *Yorta Yorta v Victoria.*

Thus the court's decision in *Mabo (No 2)* may have been little more that a symbolic gesture in correcting the foundation story and rescuing the reputation of the common law, had the Commonwealth Government of the day not risen to the occasion by vowing a principled legislative response to the decision. Importantly the Government promised to honour the non-entrenched protections that the *Racial Discrimination Act 1975* would provide to native title holders as a result of the High Court's decision in *Mabo v Queensland (No 1)*.

It was that legislative response in the form of the *Native Title Act* enacted in December 1993 that has given native title more robust implications. Importantly for the points I want to make here, the Native Title Act gives both groups- those who have established their native title and those who are *claiming* to hold native title a set of statutory rights in relation to proposed third party dealings in land. In particular the Native Title Act gives a *right to negotiate* in respect of, amongst other things, activities that involve mining, which is the key economic activity in many parts of rural and remote Australia. This means that anyone seeking a title to mine must negotiate with native titleholders and groups.

While many have argued that this is a weak procedural right, particularly relative to the right of veto under the *ALR Act*, it has resulted in many resource businesses negotiating with Indigenous groups. Some of these agreements have delivered very significant monetary and non-monetary benefits. For example, the agreements between Rio Tinto and native title groups in the Pilbara region of Western Australia delivers monetary benefits as well as a range of measures designed to increase the participation of Aboriginal people in Rio Tinto's extensive Pilbara iron ore operations. The point is that native title, through the agency of the *Native Title Act*, has given Indigenous groups considerable leverage to win a stake in economic activity.

However the experience in the Northern Territory would tend to suggest that land and leverage in relation to economic activity do not inevitably result in the sort of improvement that is being sought. In the Northern Territory under the *ALR Act*, this became operational in 1976. Aboriginal communities have regained control of significant tracts of land including and through the coveted "right of veto," a level of control over access that is not available under the *Native Title Act*. Notwithstanding this level of control over third party access to their lands for economic and other activity some of the worst examples of dysfunction and poverty are to be found in these very communities. This is not to say that the right to land is not part of the solution but rather it is not in itself sufficient to secure improvement in the living standards of Aboriginal communities.

Tradition v modernity

If remedying disadvantage is the goal, one matter to consider is whether or not traditional systems and values (and not solely effects of colonisation) could be involved in perpetuating disadvantage, and in fact to consider whether cultural traditionalism is in fact incompatible with entry into modern life. This is a question that has been asked by others but most notably by anthropologist Peter Sutton in his work *The Politics of Suffering* (2009). Sutton was concerned not merely with statistics of social wellbeing but with what he called *suffering* – the violence and dysfunction in many Aboriginal communities most of which, as he notes, have been in those least affected by European settlement.

The issue of Indigenous inclusion is not just about changing the bases of the foundation story but about understanding and addressing why the very real and often dire circumstances of Indigenous people in a 'first world' region like Australia persists. The disenchantment of some Indigenous leaders with the fixation among elites on symbols of recognition and reconciliation is precisely because engagement in the symbolic arena has led away from an honest appraisal of what it would take to alleviate the very real conditions of many, which in some communities rates poorly even by' third world' standards.

In his work Sutton tries to deliver this honest appraisal. His central proposition is that there is a "profound incompatibility between modernisation and cultural traditionalism in a situation where tradition was, originally at least, as far from modernism as it was possible to be." (2009, 40) A key issue in attempts to understand and address the situation is the contradiction that lies in the view that "Aboriginal people would find it feasible to maintain major cultural and social structural patterns from their traditional past while at the same time pursuing economic and other forms of modernisation." (41) Sutton's call is not for abandonment of culture but rather for "a cultural redevelopment" which is a "precondition of radical improvement in people's chances of ending the suffering that is currently going on" and importantly that this cultural redevelopment "is something that, in the final analysis, only Indigenous people themselves can make effective"

Aboriginal lawyer Noel Pearson in his essay *Radical Hope: Education and Equality in Australia* asks, "Surely, assimilation is not the only road to success?" (2009, 53) The challenge is to maintain and transmit a coherent minority culture and identity while also promoting achievement in the mainstream. His proposals entail perhaps the sort of cultural redevelopment that Sutton refers to. The response to the impact of colonisation on traditional Aboriginal societies requires embarking on a reorientation of culture and identity "with radical hope," a term Pearson borrows from Jonathan Lear a hope directed at a future goodness that transcends our current capacity to understand just what that might be.

Lear's book *Radical Hope: Ethics in the Face of Cultural Devastation* (2006), using the North American Crow nation as its subject, is a study of how, following the catastrophic collapse of their former way of life, a society can transform itself in order to survive. This cultural redevelopment that is, the kind of change necessary may not be compatible with native title, which requires the maintenance of collective kin-based traditional systems. It is important to remember that native title is not Indigenous traditional title in itself, rather it is a device of the common law through which elements of traditional entitlements arising out of pre-sovereignty Indigenous legal systems, can be recognised by the (post-sovereignty) common law.

The High Court found that whatever rights and interests were derived from pre-sovereignty Indigenous laws and customs had crystallised upon the acquisition of sovereignty and could not be expanded nor could a different system of traditional law and custom supplant that in existence at the relevant date. What this means is that in order to establish native title Indigenous groups must show that, from the date upon which British sovereignty was acquired, they have retained a continuous connection with the land according to the system of traditional laws and customs in existence at that date. In some parts of Australia that date is 1788 and in others it is more recent; in Western Australia for example it is 1829.

On the face of it this "connection test" is onerous and initially it was thought that Indigenous people in the more settled parts of the continent would not be able to satisfy it. The test has been mitigated by subsequent decisions in that substantial change in both the society and the system of traditional law and custom have, in some cases at least, enabled groups to obtain a native title decision in their favour. For example and very notably the Noongars of south Western Australia obtained a finding of native title in their favour of the area surrounding the city of Perth in *Bennell v Western Australia*. The southwest is one of the most intensively settled parts of Australia. Notwithstanding this development however, a continuous connection to the land by way of the traditional law and custom in existence at the date of the acquisition of sovereignty is still the test and this inevitably orients people back to traditionalism in order to jump the bar.

Native title has come to be the iconic symbol of survival for Indigenous people themselves and the importance of establishing it has become for many not just a question of rights but of identity. In the years since the beginning of their conjoined history European Australians have moved from the horse and cart to jet propelled flight but Indigenous people must remain much as they were on those fateful dates in order to be recognised and recognisable. Sutton proposes that a high emphasis on kin relationships in the political economy of Aboriginal groups may be central to some of the multitude of factors blocking serious gains for Aboriginal people and that any real shift in addressing the present problems will require "much greater social integration with non-kin as than occurs at present." (Sutton 2009) However these kin-based links and the obligations they entail are important in establishing the continuance of a group's connection to land under pre-sovereignty laws and customs.

As a result, at the same time that Indigenous Australians were given a solid means of winning a place in the economic life of the nation through the Native Title Act, they were also pointed towards antique traditional systems in order to establish that native title. It is important to remember that even after having established native title, groups may yet lose it if they cease to follow the system of traditional law and custom from which their rights and interests are derived. It could be surmised perhaps that it may have been better if the nation had been able to rise to the challenge in the 1980s and provided a legislative framework through which Indigenous interests in land could have been given effect. A contemporary connection to land could have provided the touchstone rather than systems derived from a classical traditional past.

Conclusion

It needs to be emphasised again that none of the foregoing is an argument against the recognition of Indigenous rights to land, rather, it is important to recognise that those rights will not, of themselves, address disadvantage; a more fundamental transformation is necessary, which need not (and ideally will not) result in cultural abandonment and assimilation. While the gravitational pull of modernity in a globalised world is culturally and linguistically homogenising, other peoples while being transformed by it, have succeeded in retaining language and cultural identity. Pearson argues passionately for bi-culturalism, education and a radical hope: surely his plea deserves to be heard if there is to be fundamental change in the conditions in which so many Aboriginal Australians continue to live.

Works Cited

Grenville, Kate. 2005. *The Secret River*. Sydney: Text Publishing.
Jennett, Christine. 1990. "Aboriginal Affairs Policy," *Hawke and Australian Public Policy : Consensus and Restructuring,* ed. C. Jennett. and R. Stewart. South Melbourne: McMillan Press.
Langton, Marcia. 2012. *The Quiet Revolution: Indigenous People and the Resources Boom.* Sydney: Australian Broadcasting

Corporation. www.abc.net.au/radionational/programs/boyerlectures.Accessed July 25 2013.

Lear. Jonathan. 2006. *Radical Hope: Ethics in the Face of Cultural Devastation*. Cambridge MA.: Harvard University Press.

Malouf, David. 1993. *Remembering Babylon*. Sydney: Random House Australia.

Pearson. Noel. 2009. *Radical Hope - Education and Equality in Australia, Quarterly Essay*, 35.

Sutton. Peter. 2009. *The Politics of Suffering*. Melbourne: Melbourne University Press.

vanden Driesen, Cynthia. 2009. *Writing the Nation – Patrick White and the Indigene*. Amsterdam - New York: Rodopi.

Legal Judgements Cited

Bennell v Western Australia. 2006. FCA 1243.

Mabo v Queensland 1992 (Mabo No.2) 175 CLR 1; 107 ALR 1 per Justice Brennan.

Milirrpum v Nabalco Pty Ltd. 1971. 17 FLR 141 per Justice Blackburn.

Yorta Yorta v Victoria. 2002.2.214 CLR 422; 194 ALR 538; 77 ALJR 356.

CHAPTER TWENTY-EIGHT

REWRITING AUSTRALIA'S FOUNDATION NARRATIVE: WHITE, SCOTT AND THE *MABO CASE*

KIERAN DOLIN
UNIVERSITY OF WESTERN AUSTRALIA

The centenary of the birth of Patrick White coincided in Australia with other celebrations: the bicentenary of the birth of Dickens; the centenary of the death of Joseph Furphy; and the twentieth anniversary of the historic decision of the High Court of Australia in the case of *Mabo v. Queensland*, which for the first time recognised 'native title' as part of the common law of the nation. This paper uses the conjunction of the White centenary and the *Mabo* celebration as the occasion to reflect on the connections between literary and legal narrative, and the emergence of cross-cultural understandings within Anglo-Australian law and literature.

In my home city of Perth, WA, there is a mural near the Town Hall that shows an event that nominally marks the foundation of the Swan River Colony, namely the chopping down of a tree by a Mrs Dance, an event that all school children of my generation were taught about in primary school. This 'ceremony of possession' is echoed on the opening page of Patrick White's novel, *The Tree of Man*, when Stan Parker strikes an axe into the side of a stringybark tree. (Seed 1995) However White's imagining of this act includes the alienating silence of the land, the bleeding of the trees, the warfare of the scrub that flings itself onto Stan's back. White, as we know, resists complacent public symbols and nationalist myths, inflecting them with the mythopoeic art of international modernism. For example, he revisits 'the pastoral saga in *The Tree of Man*' and 'the explorer narrative in *Voss*,' deepening and de-romanticising those cultural narratives. (Dixon 2009, 251)

Among its many insights, *The Tree of Man* explores what we might call the phenomenology of possession, the complex and shifting experience of setting up a home and a farm in the bush. Although Stan owns the land and although it answers a deep need for stability in him, White represents the relationship between person and place as a fragile, developing one: "The house looked quite frail. They were themselves strangers to their own place. Until the lamp was lit, it would not be theirs." (37) The early episode involving their first guest, the Bible salesman, opens up the experience of ownership to question. The impoverished salesman raises desires for life beyond their wire fences, but he also allows the Parkers to feel expansive amid their meagre possessions, the food, the rum and the silver nutmeg grater. Once again it is only the reassuring light of the domestic fire that leads Stan and Amy to feel that they belong on their land. What is presented here is a familiar theme in white Australian writing, the quest to feel at home in the land. As Amy drives to visit Mrs O'Dowd the land appears "quite desolate": "Nobody would ever want it. They threw things into it." (TM 139) Yet this devaluation follows her recognition that "They were possessed by the land, and the land was theirs." Property and possession consequently appear as ambivalent experiences, inseparable from struggle and alienation.

In this passage White reprises the opening motif of the axe:

'Voices could be heard where once the sound of the axe barely cut the silence ... Man had come, if it was not the Irish.' White presents the 'myth of settlement' 'from the inside,' including the ethnic tensions imported from home (McLaren 1995, vii)

But his drive to universalise the drama has led him to overlook the historical dispossession of the Aborigines, as Kerryn Goldsworthy and others have pointed out (Goldsworthy 2000, 111). Humans were present in this landscape long before Stan Parker's axe broke the silence. The possession White explores with such subtlety is an implicitly white possession. *The Tree of Man* was produced within the period of the 'great Australian silence,' that W.

E. H. Stanner identified in his 1968 Boyer Lectures on ABC Radio. Perhaps the only trace of the dispossessed culture in the novel lies in the official name given to the district, Durilgai, which ironically is said to mean 'fruitful.' (99) The name is resented by the new owners, who prefer possessive place names. In discussing the erasure of Aboriginal presence from White's myth of Australian foundation, Russell West-Pavlov has argued the Durilgai name is a "resurfacing of a repressed Aboriginal name," and more importantly for my purposes, that "any Australian post-*Mabo* reader cannot but hear in this passage an echo-in-advance of later Indigenous claims for compensation after two centuries of dispossession." (West-Pavlov 2005, 67-8) West-Pavlov's point that after the 1992 *Mabo* case Australian readers inhabit a context in which Indigenous rights and representation figure far more prominently than that of White's original readers, and that the discourse of land rights and native title inform our response to this scene, is a good one. However, I think the argument that White foreshadowed this subsequent development in Australian politics and culture applies more strongly in relation to his next novel, *Voss*.

The earlier historical setting of *Voss* required a direct representation of Aboriginal people. Cynthia vanden Driesen has drawn attention to ways in which White's historical sources, especially his reading of the journals of Ludwig Leichhardt and Edward Eyre, informed his account of racial interactions during the exploration journey. (2009, chapter 2) As Voss's exploration party approaches the outlying station of Jildra, it is met by the proprietor, Boyle, whose manner of riding signifies "the arrogance of ownership." (165) The tart construction of this display of masculine power is typical of White. More surprising is a passage shortly afterwards: after Boyle disparages the Aboriginals as guides, "two blacks came round the corner of the house. Their bare feet made upon the earth only a slight, but very particular sound, which, to the German's ears, at once established their ownership." This insight, that Aborigines were "primary owners of the land," was remarkable for 1957 (vanden Driesen 2009, 45).

Though couched in the demanding syntax that White developed to register the multiple nuances of feeling and judgment, it is an unqualified and direct statement. Voss is sensitive to the implications of a fluid and unselfconscious bodily movement. This image of the sound of bare feet upon their native ground may be interpreted as a metonym of the intimate and assured Aboriginal relationship with the land. While this perception is allied to a European consciousness, not an internal presentation of Aboriginal experience of possession, White's complex prose registers both Voss's perception of this Aboriginal reality and his judgment of the white owner Boyle's obtuseness.

This episode is a key stage in the German explorer's gradual transformation. I wish to follow the lead of Russell West-Pavlov and read this scene from *Voss* in a post-*Mabo* way. I would like to approach this by way of Nancy Williams's account of the meaning of the word for 'foot' in the language of the Yolngu people of northeast Arnhem Land, *djalkiri*. According to Williams, this word also means 'footprint' or 'foundation,' and carries with it the enlarged sense of an individual's relationship to the world. (qtd. Isaacs 2002, 5) It is interesting that the figurative dimensions of White's imaginative word-choice carry with them the same cultural symbolism as this Indigenous language. It is probable that this was an accident, a coincidence, but it may be that White had read of this in anthropological writings of the 1950s. He would certainly have found cogent arguments for Aboriginal property in land in the writings of one of his sources, Edward Eyre.

White's novel predates the Yolngu campaigns of the 1960s to secure recognition of their proprietary rights to their traditional lands. Nancy Williams's work is an example of what A. L. Becker calls "a modern philology": "The task of the philologist," Becker says, "has always been to make communication easier across cultures, or across time within one culture: to help us understand texts distant in time and space" (Becker 1996, 370). Translation and philology require an awareness of the silences in both cultures' languages, and how they bear on what statements can be made in a language. Williams's research provides a context that is available to readers of *Voss* in a post-*Mabo* Australia, one that supplements White's intuitive imaging of Aboriginal ownership.

As is well known, Patrick White's Nobel Prize citation praised his 'epic and psychological narrative art.' *The Tree of Man* and *Voss* are counted among modern Australian Literature's epics of national foundation. The world of narrative and the world of law are connected, as Robert Cover argues: "no set of legal institutions or prescriptions exists apart from the narratives that locate it and give it meaning. For every constitution there is an epic, for every decalogue a scripture." (Cover 1983-4, 4) The decision of the High Court of Australia in *Mabo v. Queensland [No. 2]* can be understood in Cover's terms. It overturned the legal fiction of *terra nullius*, the assumption that the land was either unoccupied or occupied by people without a recognisable system of law or government, upon which the British colonisation of Australia was founded.

In rejecting that assumption, the court recognised that traditional Indigenous property in land was part of Australian law. These declarations of legal principle drew on modern understandings of Australian history and Indigenous society, and therefore entailed a narrative intervention in the national culture. Although it circumscribed the operation of native title, the *Mabo* case offered a judicial acknowledgment of Aboriginal dispossession, as the majority judgments included ethically explicit historical narratives alongside legal reasoning. For example, the leading opinion written by Justice Brennan included the following reflections on earlier cases:

> According to the cases, the common law itself took from indigenous inhabitants any right to occupy their traditional land, exposed them to deprivation of the religious, cultural and economic sustenance which the land provides, vested the land effectively in the control of the Imperial authorities without any right to compensation, and made the indigenous inhabitants intruders in their own homes and mendicants for a place to live. Judged by any civilised standard, such a law is unjust and its claim to be part of the common law to be applied in contemporary Australia must be questioned. (para 28)

While announcing a change to the law, concern was expressed that the overturning of precedent should not "fracture ... the skeleton of principle" of the common law (para 29), thereby recognising a need to balance the demands of justice with preserving the integrity of the legal system. In a joint judgment

Justices Deane and Gaudron referred to the history of violent dispossession of the Aboriginal peoples as the practical corollary of the jurisprudential erasure of the rights of the Indigenous peoples:

> The acts and events by which that dispossession in legal theory was carried into practical effect constitute the darkest aspect of the history of this nation. The nation as a whole must remain diminished unless and until there is an acknowledgement of, and retreat from, those past injustices. (para 56)

These excerpts reveal the narrative dimensions of the law as Cover expounded them:

> The codes that relate our normative system to our social construction of reality and to our visions of what the world might be are narrative. The very imposition of a normative force upon a state of affairs, real or imagined, is the act of creating a narrative. (Cover, 1983)

The past and the future of Australian law, and of the nation, were placed in question in the *Mabo* case: the court sought to align the inherited law with other normative systems, and to re-imagine the ethical community of the nation. Thus, through their language and their decision the judges attempted "to reconstitute the national narrative," as Judith Pryor has put it. (2009, 134)

American jurist Mark Osiel has argued, on the basis of *Mabo* and older international examples, that such "legally induced transformations of collective identity ... can and do contribute to the kind of social solidarity that is enhanced by shared historical memory." (Osiel 1995, 463) A political backlash against the *Mabo* decision indicated that "social solidarity" had yet to coalesce around the narrative that it proposed. The overturning of precedent and of the inherited myth of settlement had a "seismic" effect on the dominant understanding of the national story. (Mead 2007, 529 fn 4) Given the fragile experience of possession and home among Anglo-Celtic settlers, that White so memorably distilled in *The Tree of Man*, the *Mabo* case functioned not only as a call to a new beginning, but as a catalyst for further unsettlement.

Critical legal scholars since Cover have taken a more materialist view of the workings of courts and stories. Penelope Pether, in a recent reflection on narrative jurisprudence, emphasises that 'instability' is an element in any act of redemptive constitutionalism (2009, 109). Tim Murphy has argued forcefully that claims for the socially constitutive power of legal categories need to be tested, that laws do not implement themselves but require the support of other institutions in society. He proposes that law is "limited in its fabricatory possibilities," that its greatest capacity is that of "recognising" identities and properties produced elsewhere in the culture, rather than making them itself. (2004, 123, 128)

Murphy's work offers an implicit corrective to some influential arguments of Pierre Bourdieu, which analysed the law as a "form of the symbolic power of naming." Law, politics and art, Bourdieu argued, all use the creative power of representation. All exhibit "the will to transform the world by transforming the words for naming it, by producing new categories of perception and judgment." (Bourdieu 1986-7, 839) Bourdieu observed realistically that such new visions "can only succeed if [they] ... announce what is in the process of developing." Bourdieu identified the 'special efficacy' of law as being the ratifying and institutionalising of such developments, a point with which Murphy agreed. Applying this debate to *Mabo*, we may propose that the High Court legislation "recognised" native title, rather than "constituted" it, thereby enabling claims of traditional ownership to be adjudicated in the public sphere.

One of the most comprehensive cultural analyses of the *Mabo* case is *No Ordinary Judgment*, by Nonie Sharp, an anthropologist who was involved in the early stages of the case. Sharp presented a cross-cultural account of the case, placing the claim in the context of traditional Islander beliefs and Western legal concepts. Noting the hopes invested in the case and the various reactions to it, she concluded that national re-foundation was a process just begun: "The High Court decision is itself a step in the reshaping of identity, albeit minimal, conservative and qualified." (1996, 223) Communal native title to traditional lands had been recognised, but it had also been declared capable of being extinguished, and subject to strict standards of proof.

It would be wrong to discuss this narrative reconstitution only in terms of the official legal system. As instigators of the claim, Edward Koiki Mabo and his co-plaintiffs in the case engaged in a form of modern philology: in having their narrative accepted, they overcame what has been called "the immense difficulty of translation." Of these difficulties, it has been said, that "translation is a matter of saying in a language precisely what that language tends to pass over in silence." (Ortega y Gasset, qtd. Becker 1996, 6) Mabo and his fellow litigants found a way of saying in English what English language and law had formerly failed to accept: Indigenous peoples' property rights in their traditional lands. In his life story of Mabo, Noel Loos recounts a discussion that took place in Henry Reynolds's office at James Cook University in the early 1970s:

> Mabo told us of his land holdings on Murray Island, and Reynolds and I had the unpleasant responsibility of pointing out to him that the outer Torres Strait Islands were Crown Land; indeed they were designated on a map ... as "Aboriginal Reserve". We remember how shocked Koiki was, and how determined that no-one would take *his* land away from him. (1996, 11)

Here the lived experience of ancestral property rights came up against the official reality of Australian law. Mabo's determination and mastery of two cultures enabled him and his fellow workers eventually to translate the Meriam tradition of ownership into terms recognisable to English law.

The High Court responded respectfully, but circumspectly to this work of translation in its recognition of native title. As a final court of appeal the High Court ruled on the principle, the legality of the claim that traditional Indigenous ownership land could survive the proclamation of British sovereignty. It left judgments about the evidence in support of the case to the lower court. Interestingly, it also left the nature and content of native title to be decided on a case-by-case basis:

> Native title has its *origin* in and is given its content by the traditional laws acknowledged by and the traditional customs observed by the indigenous inhabitants of a territory. The nature

and incidents of native title must be ascertained as a matter of fact by reference to those laws and customs. (Brennan J para 64)

Though 'native title' is a category created by High Court using the law's "symbolic power of naming," it remains a distinctive and culturally specific form of title, an aspect of Indigenous law that is "recognised" by the state apparatus of law and government. This acknowledgment of traditional custom and law, of rights and responsibilities to land that have continued to be exercised and performed since before colonisation had profound implications for the nation as an imagined community. It involved an official acceptance of past injustice, though without conceding grounds for compensation. It imagined black and white Australians sharing the land to a much greater extent than previously. And as mentioned above, its measured idealism held out the possibility of founding a new vision of national identity.

Despite its limitations, and its contested reception, the *Mabo* case has gained a place in "the history of the transformation of Australia's political and legal systems," as Ali Gumillya Baker and Gus Worby have stated. (2007, 20) They raise the question whether its implications will continue to shape ethical, legal and political action in Australia. While there is no doubt that a "psychological terra nullius persists in many sections of Australian society (Behrendt 2003, 3), the popularity of Indigenous film narratives such as *Bran Nue Day* and *The Sapphires* and other cultural forms offers a sign of hope for ongoing transformation.

One noteworthy change in recent years has been the use of native title agreements to resolve claims, rather than litigation. While some analysts have questioned the relative power of the white and Indigenous parties to these negotiations, others have welcomed the underlying acceptance of native title by governments and corporations (Ritter 2009; De Soyza 2012). In the public cultural space sponsored by the national broadcaster, the twentieth anniversary of the *Mabo* judgment was acknowledged prominently in a telemovie about the life of Eddie Mabo, and in the selection of Indigenous scholar Marcia Langton AM to deliver the Boyer Lectures on ABC Radio National.

Worby and Baker look to Indigenous writing and art as vehicles of hope for "responsibility and reconciliation." (37) One of the most considered literary contributions to the imagining of Australia's ongoing "dialogue about land justice" (Strelein) is that of Kim Scott. In *Kayang and Me*, a family history co-written by Scott and his aunt, Noongar elder Hazel Brown, Scott reflects on the rivalry and conflict generated between claimants in a native title claim: "So even Native Title becomes just another way of dividing people, providing an opportunity to dispute one another's Indigenous identity while prioritising white law and racism." (2005, 193) Despite these difficulties, the family acts to "get some land in traditional country," and the book records their deep understanding that "language and culture and place went together." (248) He is an equally clear-eyed reader of Australian literature, noting that the *Mabo* decision has not reshaped the understandings of all Australian novelists: he cites two examples of novels by David Foster and Anson Cameron in which the representation of native title and of Aboriginal identity remains tied to past stereotypes. Scott critiques the persistence of colonialist representations of Aboriginality in the fabric of national identity. Playing with this metaphor, he concludes,"there's something missing in the pattern, the texture ... We all need some other yarn." (256)

Taking up the task of a new narrative, like White and Mabo, Scott views his role as citizen, not as a bard: regarding writing is a form of "action and struggle",a gradual one-at-a-time bringing together of hearts and minds as a way "to contribute to a Noongar and increasingly wider community." (208) One of the threads that runs through *Kayang and Me* is Indigenous language: the belief that readers would get a deeper relationship with land and place by learning the words that were spoken there over millennia, in his phrase, "the sounds of Noongar country." Such knowledge might also be foundational: "We might be part of a nation-state fused to its continent by Indigenous roots and blossoming arrivals." (257)

Scott's 2010 novel, *That Deadman Dance*, represents the beginnings of such a community through an example drawn from Australia's past. Set in the colonial outpost of King George Town, later known as Albany, from its first settlement as a military outpost in 1826 to the consolidation of British rule in Western Australia in the 1840s, it details contrasting approaches to colonisation, one based in reciprocity and friendship, and the other in domination. The former is embodied by Dr Cross and the latter by the entrepreneurial Geordie Chaine. However, the main protagonist is Bobby Wabalanginy, who grows up in the contact zone between their traditional Noongar society and that of the new arrivals.

In *Voss* Patrick White represented Aborigines' first contact with writing as an experience of utter incomprehension and fear, but *That Deadman Dance* opens with Bobby mastering the art of writing. The joy of invention is matched by the labours of translation and spelling:"'*Kaya!* ... Nobody ever writ *hello* or *yes* that way.'" Indigenous hospitality is here shown as a form of cultural agency, as an opportunity for exchange. With the death of Dr Cross and the ascendancy of Chaine, relations between Indigene and white begin to assume the patterns of the theory of *terra nullius*, and deteriorate into violence and exclusion. Bobby joins Chaine's whaling team, and blends his traditional whale song with shanty-like verses of his own composition, which the whole crew joins in singing. When the whales disappear, however, apparently fished out, the logic of private property overcomes the image of a community of workers, despite the Aborigines' protest: "We share the whales, you camp on our land and kill our kangaroos and tear up our trees and dirty our water and we forgive, but now you will not share your sheep and my people wait here because of you ..." (342-3) Bobby's presence as translator and the self-evident truth of this statement are unavailing; a new order is born.

In the wake of the *Mabo* case, many Australian novelists have turned to historical fiction to try and emplot a new national foundation narrative. From David Malouf's *Remembering Babylon* to Kate Grenville's *The Secret River*, the trope of the white native, or 'wild white man' as the convict Judd is described in *Voss* after he has lived with an Aboriginal tribe when the Voss expedition has become hopelessly lost (436), has recurred with varying degrees of dramatic centrality and imaginative intensity. Scott observes history from both sides of the frontier, and represents two cultural worlds, with particular focus on their forms of interaction and the possibilities for identity formation in that space. As such, the story he tells is as much an imagining for the future as a new perspective on the past. As he told Toni Whitmont in an interview:

> *That Deadman Dance* is a work of fiction, but one that is inspired by, and that draws on, specifics of the early history of a region ... I see the novel as a sort of 'analogue', drawing upon a reasonably specific history in order to tease out the possibilities still latent today. Crucial to that inspiration is the Noongars' confidence, innovation and inclusiveness, as well as their willingness to appropriate and use European cultural forms and transform them within their own traditions. (Whitmont 2010, 39)

True to that inspiration, Scott's novel enacts its own transformation, mingling Indigenous song and understandings of nature with Western narrative forms, and affording contemporary Australian readers a bi-lingual representation of place, action and ethics.

Patrick White's poetic discernment of Aboriginal ownership of country emerged from his attempt to forge in Australia what Franco Moretti has described in his concept of what constitutes a 'modern epic' (Moretti, 1996). The *Mabo* judgment gave legal sanction to that cultural reality, and in doing so prompted the development of a new national narrative. As Drucilla Cornell remarked of the aesthetic element in law, "the moment of [ethical] commitment is aesthetic in its orientation. It demands not only the capacity for judgment but also the ability to dream of what-is-not-yet." (Cornell 1985, 380) *That Deadman Dance* offers a compelling realisation of such a dream in the Australian context, tempered with an astute understanding of the limits of the aesthetic when opposed by economic imperatives and racial ideologies. Dr Cross articulates the problem as he lies dying of tuberculosis, shivering in his kangaroo skin blanket:

> What had possessed him? Now men bragged of the land they'd been granted, and never thought that it was seized, was stolen. Why must it matter so much to him that the lives of the natives would be altered forever, and their generosity and friendliness be betrayed? He could not change that; what made him think he could do anything, or show another way to go about it when he would not even be able to make an independent life for himself and provide for his own loved ones? (62)

In his judgment in *Mabo* Justice Brennan attempted to minimise cultural and legal instability by invoking the need not to 'fracture the skeleton of principle which gives the body of our law its shape and internal consistency' (para 29). In her novel *Home*, Indigenous lawyer and writer Larissa Behrendt engages with this metaphor, seeing it as an 'excuse' for circumscribing the scope and effect of native title, but also as an insight into how legal language works: lawyers, her heroine argues, can promote justice "if [they] can find a way to put flesh on while keeping the skeleton intact." (2004, 14)

What is also apparent from this paper's admittedly selective study of the interrelations of literary and literary narrative is that in the domain of literature, the forms may be changed as well as the external details, the skeleton as well as the flesh that clothes it, allowing new structures of thought and feeling to compete with inherited "schematic narrative templates." (Wertsch 2004, 57) That is one of the legacies of modernism taken up by Patrick White, the quest for "new forms" that reveal the altered perceptions of modernity (Reichman 2003, 398).

For an avowedly postcolonial writer such as Kim Scott, that literary heritage is but one source of story, technique and understanding. *That Deadman Dance* places Indigenous knowledge and culture at the centre of a novel of colonial foundation, showing the Noongar peoples' 'traditional connexion with the land' and the injustice of their violent dispossession (*Mabo* para 66). Where the old myth of Australian settlement took the felling of a tree as its inaugurating gesture, its replacement is likely to offer a different image of place and community. In *Voss* Patrick White ends by declaring the death of the explorer material for a legend of presence 'in the country' (448). Kim Scott's image of the shared grave of Dr Cross and Bobby's uncle Wunyeran, repressed by Geordie Chaine, might introduce a new narrative of joint possession.

Works Cited

Baker, Ali Gumillya and Gus Worby. 2007. "Aboriginality after Mabo: Writing, Politics and Art," in *A Companion to Australian Literature since 1900*, ed. Nicholas Birns and Rebecca McNeer, Rochester: Camden House.

Becker, A. L. 1996. *Beyond Translation: Essays toward a New Philology.* Ann Arbor: University of Michigan Press.
Behrendt, Larissa. 2003. *Achieving Social Justice: Indigenous Rights and Australia's Future.* Annandale: Federation Press.
—. 2004. *Home.* St Lucia: University of Queensland Press.
Bourdieu, Pierre. 1986. "The Force of Law: Towards a Sociology of the Juridical Field," *Hastings Law Journal* 38: 814-53.
Cornell, Drucilla. 1985. "Toward a Modern/Postmodern Reconstruction of Ethics," *University of Pennsylvania Law Review* 113: 291-380.
Cover, M. Robert. 1983-4. "Foreword: *Nomos* and Narrative," *Harvard Law Review* 97: 4-68.
De Soyza, Anne. 2012. "Aboriginal Process in a New Era: Indigenous Self-Determination and Disadvantage." [paper presented at Hyderabad conference].
Dixon, Robert. 2009. "Australian Fiction and the World Republic of Letters, 1890-1950," *The Cambridge History of Australian Literature*, ed. Peter Pierce, Melbourne: Cambridge University Press.
Eyre, Edward J. 1845. *Journals of Expeditions of Discovery into Central Australia, and Overland from Adelaide to King George's Sound, in the Years 1840 to 1841; including an Account of the Manners and Customs of the Aborigines and the State of their Relations with the Europeans.* London: T & W Boone.
Goldsworthy, Kerryn. 2002. " Fiction from 1900 to 1970," *The Cambridge Companion to Australian Literature*, ed. Elizabeth Webby, Melbourne: Cambridge University Press.
Grenville, Kate. 2005. *The Secret River.* Sydney: Text Publishing.
Isaacs, Jennifer. 2002. *Spirit Country: Contemporary Australian Aboriginal Art.* South Yarra: Hardie Grant.
Langton, Marcia. 2012. *The Quiet Revolution: Indigenous People and the Resources Boom.* Sydney: Australian Broadcasting Corporation. www.abc.net.au/radionational/programs/boyerlectures/.
Loos, Noel and Koiki Mabo. 1996. *Edward Koiki Mabo: His Life and Struggle for Land Rights.* St Lucia: University of Queensland Press.

Malouf, David. 1993. *Remembering Babylon*. Sydney: Random House Australia.

Moretti, Franco. 1996. *Modern Epic: The World System from Goethe to Garcia Marquez*. London: Verso.

Murphy, Tim 2004. "Legal Fabrications and the Case of Property," *Law, Anthropology and the Constitution of the Social*, ed. Alain Pottage and Martha Mundy, Cambridge: Cambridge University Press: 115-41.

Osiel, Mark. 1995. "Ever again: Legal remembrance of administrative massacre," *University of Pennsylvania Law Review* 144: 463-704.

Pether, Penelope. 2009. "Comparative Constitutional Epics." *Law and Literature.* 21: 106-128.

Pryor, Judith 2009. *Constitutions: Writing Nations, Reading Difference*. London: Routledge.

Reichman, Ravit. 2003. "'New Forms for our New Sensations': Woolf and the Lesson of Torts," *Novel: A Forum on Fiction.* 36: 398-422.

Ritter, David. 2009. *The Native Title Market*. Crawley: University of Western Australia Press.

Scott, Kim and Hazel Brown. 2005. *Kayang and Me*. Fremantle: Fremantle Arts Centre Press.

Scott, Kim. 2010; 2012. *That Deadman Dance*.Sydney: Picador.

Seed, Patricia. 1995. *Ceremonies of Possession in Europe's Conquest of the New World, 1492-1640*. Cambridge: Cambridge University Press.

Sharp, Nonie. 1996. *No Ordinary Judgment: Mabo, the Murray Islanders' Land Case*. Canberra: Aboriginal Studies Press.

Stanner, W. E. H. 1969. *After the Dreaming*. Sydney: Australian Broadcasting Commission.

Strelein, Lisa. Ed. 2010. *Dialogue about Land Justice*. Canberra: Aboriginal Studies Press.

vanden Driesen, Cynthia. 2009. *Writing the Nation: Patrick White and the Indigene*. Amsterdam - New York: Rodopi.

Wertsch, James V. 2004. "Specific Narratives and Narrative Templates," *Theorising Historical Consciousness*, ed. Peter Seixas, Toronto: University of Toronto Press: 49-62.

West-Pavlov, Russell. 2005. *Transcultural Graffiti: Diasporic Writing and the Teaching of Literary Studies*. New York: Rodopi.
White, Patrick. 1981 [1956]. *The Tree of Man*. Ringwood: Penguin.
—. 1957. *Voss*. Ringwood: Penguin.
Whitmont, Toni. 2010. "First Contact," *Australian Bookseller Publisher Magazine* 90.3 (October 20): 39.

Cases Cited

Mabo v. Queensland [No. 2] (1992) 175 CLR 1.
http://www.austlii.edu.au/ au/cases/cth/high_ct/175clr1.html.

Note

The research for this chapter was conducted with the aid of an Australia Research Council.Grant awarded to the author for research into the impact of the *Mabo* decision on Australian Literature.

Chapter Twenty-Nine

Patrick White, "Belltrees" and the 'Station Complex': Some Reflections

Vicki Grieves
University of New South Wales

In this centenary year of Patrick White's birth I have found myself reflecting on his relationship to Australian history and indeed the nature of history itself. While seeking to reflect Australia's social, intellectual and cultural life back on itself as a novelist and playwright, he was deeply engaged with issues in Australian history as they existed in his time. He understood the difficulty of coming to terms with the most unsavoury aspects of our past. In this regard, he has advised Australians that, "The flow of history is what we have to face and adapt ourselves to. The adjustments we may have to make may be pretty agonising. But they will have to be made (Brennan and Flynn 1989, 85).

Through his knowledge of Australia's history White became a champion of the rights of Aboriginal people particularly in the latter part of his life. He had deep suspicions about the nature of Australian history

> ... when accepted or shrugged off, the lies and chicanery, the moral crimes committed by important members of society are passed on like contagious diseases through every level of the community. ... When the moral standards of so many of us are rotted, how can we renew ourselves and join humankind in facing the greatest test of all? We must search our hearts (Brennan and Flynn, 143).

It is interesting to imagine what White might have made of what has become a watershed turn in the understanding of Australian history that has recently emerged. My particular interest in this discussion is to explore what seems to be White's ambivalent relationship to aspects of the cultural life of the station *Belltrees*. I seek to juxtapose this with my knowledge of pastoral stations as the site of illicit sex between European men and Aboriginal women and the subsequent births of mixed race children. I see this as the crux of "the lies and chicanery" and the "moral crimes" that Patrick White knew existed, along with the original massacres and poisonings of Aboriginal people in nineteenth century in NSW. However, the subsequent use of Aboriginal survivors as slave labour on pastoral stations, the sexual abuse issue that interests me in this is a theoretical position to do with the changing nature of history. History as we know it is always a fabrication, how can we truly know about the past? In fact there are some things that occurred in the past that are truly lost in the vagaries of time. And, history changes with the nature of the people writing it. What is chosen to be written about, how it is written, tells us more about the person writing it than it does of the "truth" of the past. In fact, history as we know it is shifting and slippery, it changes over time.

How much of the history and practice of illicit sexual relationships did White actually know of in his lifetime? This is a question that interests me. I write this on the eve of the publication of Fiona Probyn-Rapsey's book *Made to Matter: White Fathers, Stolen Generations* (2013) in which for the first time the activity of the men, the white fathers of Aboriginal children, is documented systematically. In this book the author chronicles the overwhelming disregard of the mothers and the children born of these liaisons. The children were dealt with in various ways by the white men who fathered them or those who had allowed this activity to happen, or by the state on behalf of these powerful interests. They were mostly dealt with in such a way as to take them out of the public eye, out of the immediate district, and so remove the living evidence of the sexual abuse of Aboriginal women. The station *Belltrees*, the seat of the White dynasty in Australia, is one likely site of this activity over the 150 years or so of its history.

How can I say this with conviction? My research preoccupations are in the history of the Aboriginal family and increasingly about the interplay between race and gender that have produced so many people of mixed race in contemporary Aboriginal communities. Quantitative research carried out as a part of the Australian Research Council funded project I am currently managing ("More than family history: race, gender and the Aboriginal family in Australia"), besides the Probyn-Rapsey publication mentioned above, demonstrate that the pastoral stations, the mining camps and the fringe dwelling communities, in that order, have been the most common sites of the birth of children due to illicit interracial sex. In fact the nature of station life was such that this type of sexual interaction was an important and accepted part of the operations of the station. Amongst other evidence is the fact that some station owners were exploiting their own workforce, in much the same way as the plantation owners of the slavery states of the south of the USA (Grieves 2011, 142; Henningham 2000, 257-8; Willey 1971, 54).

The stories of interracial sex on stations have been there for decades as indeed they have been in the histories of most colonised races. They are in the autobiographies of Aboriginal people. Importantly, Aboriginal people themselves have not always shared the same reserve and considerations of respectability of white people, when it comes to revealing who their kin relations are. What is interesting is that Patrick White did not seem to be cognisant of this area of Australian history; perhaps there was an idea that this activity was confined to the north and west of the country, rather than the southeast. By the twentieth century the society of the Hunter Valley of NSW had developed notions of respectability and perhaps more formal and rigid ideas of segregation than existed in the frontier period. This does not mean that illicit interracial sex did not occur in the southeast Australia of the twentieth century. Even 'legitimate' love relationships were frowned upon by the white families of the men involved, as occurred with Darryl Tonkin and his wife Euphie of Jackson's Track. (Tonkin and Landon 2012)

There are many stories of interracial sex now documented in the approximately 400 Aboriginal biographies and autobiographies that have been published since the 1970s. These Aboriginal authors of their own life stories have nothing to lose by breaking the silence. And they have much to gain in establishing their identity and exploring their own history. This includes the autobiography from just north of the Hunter in the Taree district. The life of Ella Simon, herself a mixed-race child of a (mixed-race) Aboriginal mother and the white man head of the household in which her mother had worked as a maid. Simon also tells of her family being descended from station men in the Gloucester district (Simon 1978, 14). Her book was published ten years before the Bicentenary in 1988, in which Patrick White demonstrated his views on the exploitation of Aboriginal people through his refusal to take any part in the celebration or to have any of his works published in that year. White's actions made him a prominent figure, through his absence from the celebrations as a form of protest.

Many more stories from the history of stations tell of biological relatedness and descent from the squattocracy. For example, in the book *Proud Heritage* (1980), Clara Jakamarra (nee Roe) places herself as the granddaughter of the first surveyor general of Western Australia, John Septimus Roe. Her father George Harriot Roe had children with at least four Aboriginal women: all the children were subsequently removed from their mothers. At least Clara found her mother again. (Kelly 1980) The consequence of being of mixed-race and the uncertainty over parentage is that a sense of shame exists amongst those who carry the "black bastard" tag as explained by Charles Perkins in his landmark book: *A bastard like me.* (Perkins 1975) It is hard to imagine that White had not read this book and others like it, given his interests and sympathies during the lead up to the Bicentennial.

My research focus is driven by concern for the lives of children born as a consequence of illicit interracial sex and I seek to know about the trajectory of their lives and indeed the extent to which they were 'owned' and cared for by their white fathers. There is evidence of a history of a range of contacts, relationships and intimacies that the elite, the 'squattocracy' in Australia have long had silenced. Thus it is that the true parentage of many of the children born on stations such as *Belltrees* in all probability will never be known. And this is more especially the case when the full force of the power of the squattocracy was brought to bear on the situation; there would not be even a birth certificate; if there was one, would leave out the paternity of the child or the mother may be forced to relinquish the child. All of these conditions are entirely conceivable in the context of pastoral stations.

It is only within the last two decades that a scholarship has begun to emerge within the Australian history academy that recognises the widespread nature of these activities and the offspring of interracial sex as a fact. (Grieves 2007, Grieves 2011, Probyn-Rapsey 2011, 2012) White did not incorporate any of this kind of information into the creative process of his writing but this does not mean that he did not know about it. Australian cultural life promises to showcase more of these histories as they become incorporated into the national consciousness. More than this, I wonder is it possible that the Aboriginal community in the vicinity of "Belltrees" might contain people who are related to the White family?

Only at this stage of Australia's historical development are we coming to terms with the close relationships, intimacies and sexual relationships, both coercive and consensual that developed in a society marked by an extreme self-consciousness about race. In fact this is such that the defining characteristic of Australian society is the racial binary between Aboriginal people and settler colonials evident in the society which also exists alongside of a secret and covert sexual engagement across racial lines. Our understanding of the past changes with contemporary intellectual engagement, that is in turn influenced by many factors in cultural development including popular culture. In Australia the facts and details of intimacies crossing the boundaries of race, boundaries that became more fixed and segregationist in the first decade of the twentieth century, were emerging within Patrick White's lifetime but have been becoming more public since. Indeed the threads of these hidden histories are still being explored and disentangled and the cultural imaginary has begun to incorporate this history and process into new work.

Australian women historians such as Pat Grimshaw, Marilyn Lake, Mary-Ann Jebb, Ann McGrath, Ros Kidd and Anna Haebich have recently recognised the impact of the colonial power balance in sexual relationships that have often produced children and led to the large mixed-race populations of the whole of Australia by the early decades of the twentieth century. In fact, in relation to the early colonial period there was an overriding violence in colonial relationships, thus "consent was rarely an issue: if Aborigines resisted the Europeans' sexual demands, white men stole and raped the women anyway." (Grimshaw et al. 1994, 138) Later, when women were brought into servitude in pastoral and domestic contexts there is no doubt that the compliance that comes with the expectation of severe consequences, including violence, was the automatic response of the slave woman to sexual overtures. (Bailey 2003, 243)

However, it was within White's lifetime that the political arm of the state moved to institutionalise Aboriginal children, remove them from their mothers and control Aboriginal populations. The NSW Aboriginal Protection Act of 1908 legalised and formalised the social segregation of Aboriginal people and arranged the training of fair-skinned children to be assimilated into white society. Any Aboriginal 'orphan' child was likely to come under the operations of this board. Before the time of White's birth, Aboriginal babies began to be sent to the Cootamundra Hospital from 1897, and children to the Singleton Home not far from "Belltrees" from 1910. Later, girls were sent to the Cootamundra Domestic Training Home for Aboriginal Girls from 1911 and the Singleton Home housed only boys, and was closed when the Kinchela Training Home for Aboriginal Boys opened in 1924. Aboriginal children became indentured servants under the provisions of the Aboriginal Protection Act that provided for the "training" of young Aboriginal men and women in private homes. The concept of indentured servants came from the time of the abolition of slavery in the British Empire when former slaves were indentured to their masters for a period before full manumission. This is a curious but telling concept to be used in relation to Aboriginal people in the Australian context.

What has become apparent is that the primary site for these hidden histories of interracial sex is the pastoral station. For example, Howden Drake-Brockman, owner of "Corunna Downs" station was first identified by Sally Morgan as her great-grandfather in her landmark book *My Place* which was published in the bicentennial year, 1988. Howden's non-Aboriginal descendants have fiercely defended him from this charge for reasons including that he had a very strict policy against fraternisation between the races on his property. Probyn-Rapsey argues that the pursuit of illicit sex from Aboriginal women in the face of segregation was part of a "station complex" whereby the patriarch's power made the "rules" and it was also the patriarch's power that had the "rules" remain as the truth, even in the breach of these rules by the patriarch himself. In fact, she argues, "[white men's] mobility across both (racial) spheres afforded them an unequalled structural advantage to enforce and breach segregation simultaneously." (Probyn-Rapsey 2011, 70-71).

This is what can be called hegemony, it was complete rule over Aboriginal people, as tight as a drum. This was how secrecy was maintained - no victim had the freedom to talk about it. Important in this too is that such a powerful patriarchy allowed only an ongoing matriarchal family formation in Aboriginal contexts. This was such that the children followed the mother, and the power of the Aboriginal father as husband and father was non-existent. This development in Australia has mirrored the gender relationships of slavery societies in all areas of the colonial world whereby white men constructed social relations so as to have unfettered access to black women for sexual purposes. (Grieves 2009)

So what of "Belltrees", this stellar landholding of a famous Australian family, the White dynasty? Why would it be an exception to the "station complex"? The station itself was formidable in its reputation under the White family stewardship, having employed as many as 350 people in its heyday and also raised its own Light Horse regiment to fight with the British in the Boer War (White 1981). It is a given that this station would have employed Aboriginal workers in this period and perhaps organised labour from the St Clair Aboriginal mission on the fringes of Singleton. "Belltrees" was referred to by White as "our family station "and the evidence that it remained alive and active in his imagination is evident in, for example, in his creative work such as in *The Eye of the Storm*. In that book, the station remained in the family members' psyche "in flashes and in dreams" and while beautiful it was also sterile. (Marr 1993, 461) As White saw it, it was a social and emotional environment that was destructive of originality and creativity.

For White, the Australian squattocracy were insufferable: a group without intellectual reflection and a spiritual *raison d'être*. While he could have become the grazier master of "Belltrees" he was not so inclined. He was capable of pastoral work but his passion lay elsewhere. The Whites accused him "of not loving the land," that is, the life they led of "working as labourers and living as grandees, spending their days in the paddock and their nights talking sheep and politics, polo and weather" (Marr 1993, 104). Marr cites a mutual dislike between Patrick and his cousin and joint heir to "Belltrees", Alf White, whom Patrick found "bombastic and disagreeable." Alf's "enmity was cast in iron" when he learned of Patrick's homosexuality, and he prided himself on being "one hundred percent man." This is the same aggressively heterosexual bush tradition that produced the men who traded alcohol for sex in the blacks' camp at Walgett, which was part of White's earliest contact with Aborigines. We now understand that in fact there were a range of possible mixed-race intimacies in the past, including consensual and loving relationships. One can only speculate whether, if had White known of the 'station complex,' he would have been interested in exposing it.

It can be argued that while a fiercely intellectual and passionate critic of Australian mores, White could also have been restricted in his critique. There is some extent to which he was confined by aspects of the settler-colonial beliefs, secrets and lies that were perhaps too deeply buried for his consciousness or sharp intelligence to recognise. It is a truism that we are the products of our childhoods and the cultures that have raised us and while we can do battle with the things we recognise, those influences that are subliminal and subconscious are the most difficult to interrogate.

In this connection, there is only the one reference to Aboriginal people he viewed from a distance during a boyhood visit to his uncle in the country (in Walgett) in Marr's biography of White. This is not meant as a criticism but as an observation of the sensibility of the time. White only began to make associations with Aboriginal people and to understand their issues from dispossession later in life and even then we know very little of what exactly he may have known. Australia was, and in many ways still is, essentially a segregationist society. In spite of a range of attempts to move away from this it is not easy to shake such an inheritance. During White's lifetime and at the time of the writing of the autobiography, the gendered history of conquest was only beginning to be recognised and he may not have had an opportunity to learn much of this aspect of Australian history.

Interestingly, White betrays his own sense of the settler becoming (or supplanting) the Aborigine in his description of his position as a writer from within the Australian settler ethos. Marr reports how White was bitterly despondent about the nature of the society of the country of his fate, he felt himself to be an Australian but as some kind of an anachronism "something left over from the period when people were no longer English and not yet *indigenous*' (my emphasis). At first glance this can be read as a nihilist position - as if it is possible for the settler Australian to ever be Indigenous without supplanting the Aboriginal people. However, the more generous reading and the one that I prefer, is that White hoped to be at one with the landscape in the same spiritual sense that is open to Aboriginal people. He was not interested in the defence of the settler-colonial and had little time for nationalism: "I feel what I am, I don't feel particularly Australian. I live here and work here. A Londoner is what I think I am at heart, but my blood is Australian and that's what gets me going." (Marr 1993, 498) The idea of being "Australian" is to be settler colonial and he rejects that. He would prefer to be back in the metropolis rather than to be a settler colonial and is referred to as being "of London" in his father's death notice. (SMH 1937, 7).

Patrick White, essentially an unusual but in many ways representative English settler colonial found his true home, his comfort, in the metropolis where he was born. This is essentially the home of settler colonials, so many of his family and others referred to it as "home" and dutifully returned. A more strident Australian nationalism has emerged in more recent times and, from its inception, White rejected it He suffered the deeply unsettled life of the intellectual settler colonial, caught in the love-hate relationship with the society produced by settler colonialism and that produced him. Inside his own mind he yearned for a true meaning for living in this country. It seems the closest he came to this was at "Belltrees."

White's grandfather Francis White and his brothers had first leased the property "Belltrees." from William Charles Wentworth in 1848 and then bought it in 1853. Francis had six sons, of which Victor Martindale White was Patrick's father. He spent most of his life in the vicinity of "Belltrees" in the Hunter Valley until his marriage at forty-two years of age when he and his wife Ruth travelled to England where Patrick was born. When the Whites returned to "Belltrees" at the request of his cousin's son Michael in the late 1970s the initials "V. M. W" were still on the tag on his father's former room key. His father, he remembered as the "gentlest of human beings." (Marr 1993, 475) During this visit to "Belltrees" the son Patrick, who had enjoyed a vibrant and vigorous sexual awakening in his early adolescence, wondered what the father had done for sex before his marriage late in life. One can assume that he was not celibate. This of course had been Dick's secret life, not discussed or revealed and not likely to be in the absence of any legally sanctioned union. The son thought of the possibilities in terms of homosexual or heterosexual, a provocative, brave and unusual observation for the time it is true. (Marr 1993, 550) He did not mention the possibility that Dick's sexual activity, or indeed, that of any white Australian male, may have crossed a race-line. This is the most unmentionable, deepest, secret side of Australian country and even urban life at the time.

From an early age White seemed conscious of the inbuilt injustice in Australian society and he reveals in his autobiography *Flaws in the Glass* his difficult position and inability to fit into Australian society. He speaks of his early discomfort with his family's affluence and his take on "truth" that he gleaned from this experience. It also reveals his empathy with the "other" that outside group constructed by the rich and powerful of Australia. For this empathy and his refusal to toe a line of allegiance to some colonial ideal of "high culture" he was severely criticised and ostracised by his own class.

As a child I felt embarrassed at my parent's affluence. I was aware of a formless misery as well as material distress the other side of the palisade protecting the lives of the favoured few. For that reason I have never been able to enjoy what any "normal" member of my parent's class considers his right. What is seen as success, my own included, has often filled me with disgust. No doubt the "normal" members of the affluent class will pounce on this confession as explanation of what they think a distorted viewpoint in all I have written; while to me, the refractions from that many-sided crystal, truth, are more diverse than they would have been had I remained blinkered by the values of the Australian rich. (1981, 151)

Given this position it is unsurprising that White came to defend "Aboriginal sites and rights" (Lawson 1994, 207; White 1990, 81, 98, 182). He lamented that "we still have that apparently insoluble problem of what to do about the Aborigines we dispossessed." (White 1990, 46) He flew the Aboriginal flag in his garden on the occasion of the Bicentenary of British settlement of Australia in 1988 (White 1990, 129). In that year White refused to allow any of his plays to be performed or his books published (Webby, 2012). He left generous bequests to the NSW Aboriginal Education Council and the National Aboriginal and Islander Skills and Dance Association (NAISA) in his will.

We have no way of knowing exactly why he became so moved by the plight of the Aboriginal people. We know that he had personal friendships and associations, for example he met Shirley C. Smith and the journalist John Newfong, travelled with Kath Walker later known as Oodgeroo Noonuccal, the Aboriginal poet. We can only assume he became more informed about Australian history and its impact on contemporary Aboriginal disadvantage. He had a shyness and a reluctance to appear to be prying; it is hard to imagine him asking many questions. It seems he had an affinity with Aboriginal spirituality but not surprisingly felt locked out of it. Having said this, it can also be argued that he held some of the values and attitudes of his class who had won great material success from the takeover of Aboriginal lands. Even though he may not have agreed with the circumstances surrounding his family's wealth and privilege, he did develop as a child within a certain social and cultural milieu. And, for the class he belonged to, mostly Aboriginal people simply did not exist; they are seen as an unfortunate inconvenience. It was important to keep them out of sight.

The settler colonial relationship to Aboriginal people was essentially genocidal. The conquest of the original owners and custodians of the country had been a gendered conquest; huge liberty had been taken in the sexual exploitation of Aboriginal men, women and children. This can be explained through a relatively new approach to understanding the conquest of Australia and the continuing dispossession of Aboriginal people, the interplays of race, gender and sexuality. As it happened when White was born in 1912, racism in Australia had peaked following the introduction of the White Australia policy in 1901. This policy set the stage for the segregationist Aboriginal Protection Acts of the first two decades of the twentieth century, developing regimes that reflected the prevailing caste-like social system.

The Australian settler colonial society has been characterised by sexual double standards, whereby continuing white male access to Aboriginal women demeaned and degraded the women. The impact on Aboriginal men was a huge decline in authority and status such that their position was equivalent to the "free black" of post slavery in the southern states of the USA. (Grieves 2009) It is maintained that this "racialised gender regime" has been so widespread as to form the complex cultural basis of Australian racism. This gendered and racialised history is "a central but hidden basis of the ambivalent stand white Australians take toward lighter-skinned Aboriginals today." (Williams, Thorpe & Chapman 2003, 25, 28)

In the course of researching the background to this chapter I asked David Marr whether Patrick may have been aware of any family connection with Aboriginal people. David's response was, as follows: "Having an Aboriginal cousin would have delighted Patrick White but there is no sign he believed it to be true. He wrote nothing about it in his memoir *Flaws in the Glass* and never mentioned the possibility to me." I do think White would have been delighted and it is interesting to think what he might have made of it, indeed how his life may have changed with this knowledge. Would this have led him to a close engagement with this relative, a sense of greater relatedness, and would he have felt more at home in Australia?

While there is a danger in constructing Patrick White outside of his own contexts and lifetime, was his forthrightness such that, if he had known of this hypocrisy and injustice affecting Aboriginal people would he have named it for what it is? If he had known of the close genetic connectedness of settler colonials to those people known as "Aboriginal," would he have embraced that? And is it fair to say that if he knew this well, this interplay of race and gender, would the close relatedness of settler and Aboriginal in Australian society have emerged in his literary work? By asking these questions I am also honouring the legacy of the man that was Patrick White, a person who knew much about the true nature of human behaviours and who was prepared to stand up for what he knew was fair dealing.

History reveals many tantalising opportunities for research about past phenomena that we may never know the full truth about. Any mixed-race descendants of the station owners and their families are arguably those with a close, personal association with the doctrine of *terra nullius*. They know what it means to have uncertainty about identity and meaning; they have the legacy of parents and grandparents who were denied any birthright in terms of access to land as an Aboriginal person and as a descendant of white landowners. In these ways they may see themselves as disadvantaged but this is not always the case because they still have access to a special relationship to the natural world, what they call their spirituality.

In my reflection on the life of Patrick White and his relationship to this history, I like to imagine a different past: one in which the children born of "the station complex" and one where children like Patrick born outside of it, in remarkably uncomplicated and untroubled circumstances, enjoyed similar nurturing and care. What if they had shared meals, schools and teachers, and growing experiences, contact with each other's family members, as equals? In the absence of the removal of the troubling aspects of their birth, these children deserved every opportunity to take their place in the nation as equals. More than this, in the absence of this shared experience, not only are the Aboriginal children born of *terra nullius* deprived; the sterile hand of settler colonialism seared and soured all it touched, including the Australian settler descendant like White. They also were denied the opportunity to truly and meaningfully connect with this land and its people.

Works Cited

Bailey, J. 2003. *The Lost German Slave Girl: the extraordinary true story of the slave Sally Miller and her Fight for Freedom.* Sydney: Pan Macmillan.

Brennan, P. and C. Flynn, Ed.1989. *Patrick White Speaks.* Sydney: Primavera Press.

Grieves, V. 2009. "Aboriginal Spirituality: Aboriginal Philosophy, The Basis of Aboriginal Social and Emotional Wellbeing." Discussion Paper 9, Darwin: Cooperative Research Centre for Aboriginal Health (CRCAH).

—. 2011. "The McClymonts of Nabiac: Interracial Marriage, Inheritance and Dispossession in Nineteenth Century New South Wales Society," *Rethinking the Racial Moment: Essays on the Colonial Encounter,* ed.Alison Holland and Barbara Brookes.Cambridge: Cambridge Scholars Publishing: 125-156.

Grimshaw, M P. et.al. 1994. *Creating a Nation: 1788 – 1990.* Melbourne: McPhee Gribble.

Henningham, N. 2000. 'Perhaps if there had been more white women in the north the story would have been different': Gender and the history of white settlement in North Queensland 1840 – 1930." Ph.D dissertation. University of Melbourne, Vic.

Lawson, A. 1994. *Patrick White: Selected Writings.* St Lucia: University of Queensland Press.

Marr, D. 1991. *Patrick White. A life.* Sydney: Random House.

Nicoll, F. J. 2001. *From Diggers to Drag Queens: configurations of Australian national identity,* Annandale, NSW: Pluto Press.

Perkins, R. 1993. *Freedom Riders.* Sydney: SBS Independent.

Probyn-Rapsey, Fiona. (2013). *Made to Matter:White Fathers,Stolen Generations.*Sydney: Sydney University Press.

CHAPTER THIRTY

MABO – TWENTY YEARS ON: AN INDIGENOUS PERSPECTIVE

KEITH TRUSCOTT
CURTIN UNIVERSITY OF WESTERN AUSTRALIA

Introduction

I need to explain first how I come to be contributing a Paper to a collection of studies on the work of the Australian literary giant Patrick White; although I am no specialist in the field of literature. A few years ago, while I was still teaching at Kurongkurl Katitjin at Edith Cowan University, a colleague working in the field of literature launched her book on White's construction of the Indigenous characters in his works, a portrayal which respected their human dignity. This was a radical departure from earlier Orientalist representations which had dominated Australian writing for decades. (vanden Driesen 2009) The book presented White's work as making a contribution to white Australians' perception of the importance of dealing rightly with the nation's Indigenous peoples.

Subsequently, I have become aware also of the passion that White displayed in the later stages of his life as a dedicated activist for the promotion of empathy with and understanding of Indigenous causes. Statements he has made on public platforms within Australia, and through his writing to international audiences the world over must surely work towards redressing the years of neglect. Certainly, *Mabo* would have been regarded by him as an occasion for rejoicing. It is highly appropriate that this memorial conference in his honour should also provide a platform for highlighting contemporary developments in the field of Aboriginal rights of which perhaps the most important has been the historic event of the *Mabo* decision.

The great historic event of *Mabo* (1992) twenty years ago has been celebrated in various ways by Indigenous peoples. For instance, it was part of the annual Indigenous Reconciliation Week Calendar which was started in 1998.The event was marked first in 26 May 1997 when *The Stolen Generation Report* was tabled in Parliament; secondly, 27 May when the 1967 Referendum passed the two 'power' clauses i.e. those which gave the Commonwealth power to make laws including Aboriginal peoples who had been an excluded race before, and to count them in the census from which they had been excluded before; third, 3 June 1992 when the High Court of Australia acknowledged the existence of *native title* on Mer Island and that it could exist also on the Australian mainland.

Videos, lectures songs and plays have also been created to celebrate it. I would like to commemorate *Mabo* twenty years on by suggesting a new definition of Indigenous identity and applying it to three areas. In this chapter I interchange the term 'Indigenous' freely with 'Aboriginal' or 'Torres Strait Islander people.' Over the last decade there has been a preference to use 'Indigenous' to fit in with international terminology. (The East Coast of Australia appears to have warmed to the use of 'Indigenous,' but in Western Australia there is still a preference for 'Aboriginal.') In this discussion I move from a general Australian and United Nations definition to a new one, one which includes four elements of *earth, fire, wind* and *water*.

First, I identify myself and two other Australian Indigenous people and indicate our diverse Australian Indigenous identities. Second, I identify a famous Indigenous Australian by the name of Eddie Koiki Mabo in terms of the four elements and the impact he made upon the Australian Indigenous and non-Indigenous community since 1992. Third, I conclude by showing how the *Mabo* legislation strengthened the *earth, fire, wind* and *water* of the Indigenous community in not only its historical, political and social aspects but also in symbolic and metaphorical ways such as standpoint, self-determination, sovereignty and security.

A New Definition of Indigenous

Before the new definition is outlined, the two current definitions will be explained. First, the general Indigenous community definition of Aboriginal, as defined by the *Aboriginal Land Rights Act 1983* is "a person who; is of Aboriginal descent; who identifies as an Aboriginal person; is accepted by the Aboriginal community in which they live." (Queensland Studies Authority 2010, 10) The key points are that the person has biological links, community connections and community validation. From personal experience, I recall that in the 1970s, in order to apply for an Aboriginal scholarship or service it was imperative that the applicant had a written statement of proof of Aboriginality from a local Aboriginal organisation before being able to receive the scholarship or service. In those days a claim to Aboriginality was fairly simple, straightforward and dependent upon one's "living" link to the Aboriginal community in which one lived. Today all this still applies.

Second, the United Nations left it to the local Indigenous peoples to define the term, 'Indigenous.' The long research on Indigenous peoples done by Special *Rapporteur* Jose R. Martinez Cobo (1986) has become the base of the working definition, consisting of four key points identifying an Aboriginal community as one which: acknowledges a historical continuity with pre-invasion and pre-settler societies that developed on their territories; claims a distinct self-identify with other societies presently living on their own land areas or part thereof; forms a non-dominant sector of society; has a commitment to maintain and reproduce their historical, cultural, community continuities in a accordance with their distinct cultural, social, economic, political patterns and systems. (2004, 2) The United Nations definition emphasises self-identity, historical continuity, specific land territory and self-preservation.

The third definition is the suggested new one, which I have decided to explore in this paper; it seeks to combine the general Australian definition of Indigenous with that of the United Nations definition. Four common themes emerge, that of 'country', 'culture', 'community' and 'continuity'. These can be transposed into the four elements of *earth, fire, wind* and *water* respectively. Hence, an Indigenous person is one who lives on a specifically inherited place or 'country' (represented by *earth*), shares a common 'culture' (represented by *fire*), lives in a specific 'community' (represented by *wind*) with a desire to maintain cultural, social and political 'continuity' (represented by *water*). So the new definition of "Indigenous identity" is couched in terms of the four elements. The benefit of the application of *earth, fire, wind* and *water* is that it allows room to combine the historic, cultural and political patterns and continuities with various symbolic and metaphorical terms like resilience, life, spirit, sovereignty, strength, diversity, standpoint, security and self-determination. This will be applied to some examples of living Indigenous people across Australia and also that of the now deceased Eddie Koiki Mabo. The legacy that the Mabo case has left for both Indigenous and non-Indigenous peoples will then become more apparent.

Applying a New Definition of Indigenous identity

From this new suggested definition of 'Indigenous' according to the four elements *earth, fire, wind* and *water*, I will offer three examples so as to underscore the strength, life and diversity of Indigenous identity. I will begin with myself as an example, then pass on to consider two other contemporaries and finally consider the case of Eddie Koiki Mabo.

The first element of *earth* indicates my own 'country' origins I am from Antakarinyin country in the middle of South Australia. My mother was removed from her traditional country as part of the stolen generation events of the time. I was born in Darwin further northwards and my first eight years was spent in a Mission. I am a second-generation stolen generation person having been removed to the Central Coast of NSW at 8 years of age. At 24 years of age I re-connected with my traditional country by learning its language and keeping in touch with extended family members there. I have now settled in Perth Western Australia where I have spent the last 37 years. The element of *fire* in relation to myself lies in respecting and promoting the Indigenous 'culture' in sensitive and enthusiastic ways wherever I live. This is done primarily in my dual role as a

University lecturer and pastor of a small Indigenous Christian congregation in the shire where I live. *Wind* is my contribution to the Indigenous 'community' which has always been strong since the mid-1970s. This derives from my working in the context of both profit (via University teaching) and non-profit organisations (via community development programs). Then there is my pastoral work for the past 30 years such as supporting birth, death and marriage events in the Aboriginal community. The final element is *water*, which signifies 'life commitment' and 'well-being' which goes hand in hand with formal and informal ways of reconciling generations contributing to the 'continuity' of the Indigenous community within and alongside mainstream society.

The second example is a Pilbara group of Indigenous dancers and a local Nyungar university academic. The *earth* for the Pilbara group is the Nyangumarta language group in North-West Western Australia "(Nyangumarta: the people and their traditional country." Online) where their traditional land of 33,843 square kilometres takes in Eighty-Mile Beach extending into the Great Sandy Desert area (see "Nyungmarta celebrate recognition of country and culture." (See website). The *fire* of their culture is still strong as they still practice their language and law ceremonies. The *wind* of their contribution to community is shown by respecting an ongoing close co-existence with pastoral stations and themselves as Native Title holders through Indigenous Land Use Agreements. To the local Nyangumarta people their continuity is maintained by the *water* of empowerment through the legal recognition of their *Native Title* rights and interests on June 11, 2009.

With the third example, Kim Scott, his 'earth' is between Gairdner River and Cape Arid in the Wudjari/Koreng dialect area of the Nyungar language group of the South-West Western Australia. Kim's 'fire' is represented by his enthusiasm to acknowledge his Wirlomin clan as part of the Nyungar cultural area. His 'wind' is to contribute to his Indigenous community via his profession as a teacher, lecturer and author of three novels, poetry and several short stories. Kim's 'water' of sustaining the continuity of his culture and community is through remaining in his local country as a university lecturer and Professor of Writing, researcher and renowned author and his involvement with numerous projects, such as the Wirlomin

Nyungar Language and Stories Project (2012) which is an excellent example of ensuring cultural and linguistic continuity. This project has produced two books, *Noongar Mambara Bakitj* (2012) and *Mamang: An Old Story* (2012).His influence in the non-Indigenous community is also important. He was Western Australian of the Year in 2012 and has won over a dozen literary awards across Australia and overseas. A summary of these 'four elements' of diversity of Indigenous identity for the three previously mentioned Indigenous persons is given below.

Table 1. Four Elements of Australian Aboriginal Identity

dkm	Four Elements of Australian Indigenous Identity			
Example/s	Country (Earth)	Culture (Fire)	Community (Wind)	Continuity (Water)
1. Keith Truscott	Antakarinyin language SA; Mission NT; 2nd generation *Stolen Generation* NT; now city-based	Promotional mixed role as academic and pastor,o	Profit and non-profit organisation involvement	Reconciling generations in Indigenous within and alongside mainstream society
2. Pilbara Group	33,843 sq. kms remote-based area; Traditional setting south of Broome, WA;	Nyangumarta language; dancers; Pilbara in North-west WA;	Traditionally focussed: male and female elder recognition	'Empowered' *as Native Title* holders 2009; celebrate by dance; *Indigenous Land Use Agreements* with pastoralists
3. Kim Scott	South-east part of South-West WA; Wudjari/Koreng dialect	Wirlomin clan as part of Nyungar language group;	Professional teacher; academic; author.	'Professor of Writing'; internationally renowned author; many lit. awards; Western Australian of the Year 2012

Eddie Koiki Mabo Identity

In defining his Indigenous identity, the 'earth' for Eddie Koiki Mabo was Mer (Murray Island) in the Torres Strait, where he was born Eddie Koiki Sambo on 29 June1936 (approximately). He changed his name later in life. His mother died early in his life and he was brought up by his mother's uncle, Benny Mabo. At age 23 he married Bonita Neehow and they raised ten children between them. Eddie died on 21 January 1992. The roots to his *earth*, country, and island of the Torres Straits for Eddie were strong and continuous.

The actual Torres Strait stretches 200 kms from the top part of Queensland to the southwest coast of Papua New Guinea. It covers an area of more than 35,000 square kms and there are more than 100 islands (Environmental management in the Torres Strait 2013 Online). Murray Island itself, consists of three islands, Mer, Dauar and Waier situated at eastern end of Torres Strait Islands and at the top end of the Great Barrier Reef. It is a basaltic island formed from an extinct volcano and has a plateau about 80 metres above sea level that rises at the western end to 230 metres. The island has red fertile soil and is covered in dense vegetation with a tropical climate and a wet and dry season. Today on the small island there is also a small airport.

The 'fire' for Eddie Koiki Mabo was his island's culture based on management of its rich land and sea environment by fishing, hunting and agricultural gardening. There are eight Meriam tribes who were fearless warriors of their *earth*, bounded territories and skilled mariners. Mer Island utilised the good soil for gardening worked and owned by an inheritance system. The people are of Melanesian origin. Their god, Malo is powerful and is celebrated for having travelled from New Guinea and protecting the island. Malo also provided the laws and ceremonies to govern the Murray Islands.

The 'wind' of traditional community on the Torres Strait was organised by senior men through totemic clan membership. Social interaction was based on kinship and reciprocal obligations. Song and dance was part of seasonal celebrations. But this regular pattern was changed by three historic events (Shnukal 2001). First was the discovery of commercial deposits of pearl in 1870, which meant an influx of arrivals via many steam ships and seamen from Indonesia, Pacific Islands and Europe. The unfortunate results were sexual abuse and intrusive use of land resources. Second was the arrival of Christianity on 1 July 1871, the date when the first Christian service was held [and is commemorated annually as *The Coming of the Light*. A school was opened two years later. Christianity profoundly influenced the Torres Strait Islands as whole and the general feeling is that it fulfilled traditional beliefs. Third there was the controversy of the Asian pearlers, many of whom had been brought across as indentured labourers; this was sufficient reason for the annexation of the Torres Strait Islands by the colony of Queensland in 1879. This move gave the community some protection from abuses but it also introduced new evils like colonialism, alienation of land and more outside control.

There was then the 'Protection era' from 1904-1932. During this time a curfew was introduced and a pass system was put in place, which restricted travel, and wages were under control of the Protector. Many superintendent-teachers were agents of the Protectors. Pearling centres Broome, Darwin and in the Torres Strait e.g. Thursday Island can claim to be among the first multi-cultural communities. On 12 October 1939 the *Torres Strait Act* recognised the Torres Strait people as a separate people and they were to be governed by the Department of Native Affairs, sub-department of Queensland Health and Home Affairs. In 1965 the restrictions of the 1939 *Torres Strait Act* was replaced by the fairer Department of Aboriginal and Islander Affairs (DAIA) under *The Aboriginal and Torres Strait Islander Affairs Act*. In 1976 the Torres United Party was formed seeking independence from the Queensland government. This was a precursor to *Mabo* legislation of 1992. So throughout these historical developments, the winds of traditional cultural practices continued to blow on Mer, despite varying non-Indigenous incursions.

Table 2. Eddie Koiki Mabo Identity

Example	Four Elements of Australian Indigenous Identity			
	Country (Earth)	Culture (Fire)	Community (Wind)	Continuity (Water)
Eddie Koiki Mabo	Eastern end of TSI; top of Great Barrier reef; an extinct volcano; red soil; tropical climate	Malo god beginnings; song, dance, stories; skilled mariners; 1871 Coming of the Light; pearling trade; annexed by QLD 1879	Governance by inheritance, councils; Fishing, agriculturalist, hunters; more a multi-cultural community	Creole language; Meriam; English; Native Title starting point; now seeking self-government for TSI

The 'water' of continuity to sustain and adjust Mer culture and community is symbolised with the introduction of a new lingua franca, the Torres Strait Creole in the 1890s besides the already Meriam language. It was not till the 1990s that the use of Australian Standard English began to increase with children educated on the mainland. The greatest contemporary 'water' event that sustains life and continuity at Mer Island was the *Mabo* legislation of 1992.

Prelude to the *Mabo* Case 1992

The Mer land inheritance system was tested in the High Court of Australia. Eddie Mabo, as a member of the plaintiff group, challenged the Queensland Government on the grounds that their Island had never been ceded to the Queensland Government and that the Murray Islanders' land inheritance system had remained unbroken despite the arrival of the British settlers, especially into the northern parts of Australia. This High Court challenge took ten years to be processed but ended with the conclusion that the new term of "native title" had existed before and still existed on Mer. This decision is often called 'Mabo.' So the name 'Mabo' is not only that of an Indigenous person whose first name was Eddie from

Mer in the Torres Straits, but a symbol of the Indigenous struggle for identity and overcoming the colonialist theory which depicted Indigenous peoples as having no laws or settled social organisation.

One of the interesting anecdotes regarding the significance of the name Mabo was recited by Mabo's daughter. When the High Court ruling was brought down for the existence of *Native Title* on Mer, Gail Mabo was a teenager. Her father, a proud Torres Strait Islander, had once in the past sat her down and promised her: "One day, my girl, all Australia is going to know my name." That was in 1985 and in 1992 when the High Court made its decision Gail Mabo added, 'I cried and said, "Dad you were right."' (*The Australian*. 2012)

Mabo – 1992

The findings of the High Court in acknowledging Native Title in *the Mabo Case* were amazingly and logically consistent. Native Title is a proprietary right, i.e. a legal right in relation to property or land. It recognised the existing land rights of Aboriginal people. So when an Aboriginal group have native title recognised it does not create any new rights. This process to recognise or not to recognise native title is called 'a native title determination.' The High Court established that the inhabitants of Mer (Meriam) were entitled to the possession, occupation, use and enjoyment of Mer Islands; the common law recognised 'native land title' which could be applied to mainland Australia, not just Mer; 'native land title' exists where Indigenous people have maintained connection with the land and the title has not been extinguished by the Government (e.g. Freehold land). The High Court ruling rejected the tradition of *terra nullius* (land belonging to no-one and therefore assumed by the [British] Crown). It found that native land title rights survived colonisation even though Indigenous people were subject to the sovereignty of the Crown.

Reasons for the native title decision were threefold: High Court Judges Brennan, J, Mason, C.J. and J. McHugh, ruled that the Court could not perpetuate a view of the common law that was unjust, did not respect all Australians as equal before the law and was out of step with the norms of international human rights. Justices

Gaudron, J. and Toohey, also rejected the doctrine of *terra nullius* as repugnant and inconsistent with historical reality; the conclusion of the Court was expressly subject to the *Racial Discrimination Act 1975* (Cwth) and S.51 (xxxi) of the Australian Constitution that states the acquisition of property by the Commonwealth and the States can occur for any purpose according to payment of 'just terms.' So 'Native Title' was added to other forms of 'land ownership' such as freehold, leasehold and mining tenements in The *Native Title Act 1993*. It took the longest parliamentary sitting in Australian political history to pass the *Native Title Act 1993* (J.Hughes, R. Frankland, et al. 1997) such was the division and the anxiety of the non-Indigenous farming and mining lobby groups who needed constant clarification that something workable and acceptable to all parties could be worked out with present and future Indigenous *Native Title* holders.

Since Mabo: The *Native Title Act* 1993

The Australian Government has sought to make 'Native Title' workable for pastoral, business interests. So 'Native Title' was added to other forms of 'land ownership' such as freehold, leasehold and mining tenements in *The Native Title Act 1993* Some basic principles were established in relation to "Native Title" in Australia. It provided for the validation of past acts which may be invalid because of the existence of 'native title'; the National Native Title Tribunal was set up, through which native title rights were protected and some conditions were imposed on past acts affecting native title land and waters; the determination of native title rights could be made and if not, then compensation negotiated as well as other matters e.g. setting up the Aboriginal and Torres Strait Islander Land Fund.

The 1990s was indeed the decade of Reconciliation with *Mabo* legislation being the high point of acknowledging the existence of Aboriginal rights. Other high points were the push for Aboriginal equity and justice through the re-writing of Australia's Foundation history though the conflicts engendered resulted also in the 'culture wars'; recording the stories of the *Bringing them home: the 'Stolen Children' report* (1997) and fulfilling the recommendations of the report into the *Royal Commission into Aboriginal Deaths in Custody* (1998).

Since *Mabo*: 2006 and the 2008 Single Noongar Claim

Since 1992 numerous Aboriginal groups have been determining their arguments for the existence of their "Native Title" and the entitlements that follow. One of these has been the Single Noongar Claim of 2006, in the area of Australia where I now live and work. It seemed unthinkable that a non-dominant Indigenous group could claim that *Native Title* exists over Perth Metropolitan city area (Host, J. and C. Owens 2009) but this did in fact happen.

Conclusion

This article has been written to commemorate the work of Eddie Koiki Mabo in the landmark decision of the High Court of Australia in 1992 acknowledging the existence of "native title" on Mer Island and the possibility of its existence occurring on the Australian mainland. To do so I have moved away from the two usual recognised Australian and United Nations definitions of Indigenous identity and suggested a *four elements* formula of *earth* (country), *fire* (culture), *wind* (community) and *water* (continuity). The new formula has been applied initially to three Indigenous people groups and finally to Eddie Koiki Mabo.

Four effects are recognisable and salutary.

(i) The effects of *native title* continue across a diverse number of Australian Indigenous peoples living at present in Western Australia. More research may find similar results for other Indigenous peoples in other States and Territories.
(ii) The four elements highlight the interdependence of the holistic dimension of *tangibles* or *macro elements* e.g. geography, humanity with the *intangibles* or *micro elements* e.g. the mental and spiritual.
(iii) There appears to be a priority in Indigenous identity beginning with *earth* which then is validated and completed

by *fire* of culture, *wind* of community and *water* of continuity.

(iv) Values also may be prioritised using the four elements as symbols and metaphors. For instance the *earth* is the standpoint, *fire* is self-determination, *wind* is sovereignty and *water* is security. Other symbols like resilience, life, strength, weakness, restriction, liberty, justice, empowerment and freedom can also be identified as one of the four elements.

The overall effect of Mabo the person and the political legislation is a perennial reminder of the empowerment of the Indigenous individual and community right across Australia. The post-*Mabo* years have been the "beginning of justice" (French 1996, 2-11). Furthermore, the four elements that Indigenous people walk on (earth), gather round (fire), breathe (wind) and drink (water) are all around us to remind us to be thankful for Mabo the person and the political legislation to which the term is also applied.

Works Cited

Cobo Jose R. Martinez. 1986. "The Martinez-Cobo study" in UN document E/CN.4/Sub.2/1986/7.

Eddie Mabo Biography http://www.biographybase.com/biography/Mabo_Eddie.html Accessed 29/1/2013.

Environmental management in the Torres Strait. Accessed 29/1/2013 from
http://www.tsra.gov.au/the-tsra/programs-and-output/env-mgt-program/environmental-management-ts#Theregion.

French, R. 1996. "The Wentworth Lecture, Native Title: the beginning or the end of justice". Accessed 29/1/2013.
https://www.google.com.au/#q=R.+French+The+Wentworth+Lecture%2C%22+the+beginning+or+the+end+of+justice.

Host, J. and C. Owens 2009. *It's still in my heart, this is my country': the single Noongar claim history.* Crawley, W.A.: University of Western Australia Press.

http://www.humanrights.gov.au/publications/bringing-them-home-stolen-children-report-1997. Accessed 28/1/2013.

Kildea, J. 1998. "Native Title: A simple guide - A paper for those who wish to understand *Mabo*, the *Native Title Act*, *Wik* and the Ten Point Plan." Human Rights Council of Australia: 1-22.

Scott, K. and Woods, I. 2012. "Mamang: An Old Story." Wirlomin Noongar Language and Stories Project Crawley. W.A.: University of Western Australia Press.

Scott, K. and Roberts, L. Noongar Mambara Bakitj Wirlomin Noongar Language and Stories Project. Crawley, W. A.: University of Western Australia Press.

Moreton-Robinson, A. 2006. "Towards a new research agenda: Foucault, Whiteness and Indigenous sovereignty," *Journal of Sociology* 42.4: 383-395.

Nyangumarta celebrate recognition of country and culture www.yamatji.org.au/download.cfm?DownloadFile=D3C60955. Retrieved 28/1/2013.

Nyangumarta: the people and their traditional country. http://www.wangkamaya.org.au/index.php?option=com_content&view=article&id=179&Itemid=341. Accessed 28/01/2013.

Queensland Studies Authority. 2010. *Aboriginal and Torres Strait Islander Studies Handbook 2010* Brisbane QLD: 10.

Reynolds, H. 1996. "After Mabo, What about Aboriginal Sovereignty?" Australian Humanities Review http://www.australianhumanitiesreview.org/archive/Issue-April-1996/Reynolds.html. 1-6. Accessed 28/01/2013.

Rigney, L. 2001. "A first perspective of Indigenous Australian participation in Science: Framing Indigenous research towards Indigenous Australian intellectual sovereignty." http://www.flinders.edu.au/yunggorendi-files/documents/Paper%20no2%20lirfirst.pdf. 1-13.

Royal Commission into Aboriginal Deaths in Custody 1998. http://www.austlii.edu.au/au/other/IndigLRes/rciadic/. Accessed 28/1/2013.

Shnukal, A. 2001. "Torres Strait Islanders," *Multicultural Queensland: 100 years, 100 communities, A century of contributions*, Brisbane QLD:Department of Premier and Cabinet.

The concept of Indigenous peoples 2004 Workshop on date collection and disaggregation for Indigenous peoples (New

York, 19-21 January) United Nations PFII/2004/WS.1/3 Original: English.
Watson, I. 2004. "From a hard place: Negotiating a softer terrain," *Flinders Journal of Law Reform* 7.2: 205-223.
Weir, M. 2002. "The Story of Native Title," *The National Legal Eagle* 8,4: 8-10.
Winner, Kim Scott. 2011.
http://www.milesfranklin.com.au/bio_kims. Accessed 28/1/2013.

CHAPTER THIRTY-ONE

"THIS POEM IS A SEA ANCHOR":
ROBERT SULLIVAN'S ANCHOR

JANE STAFFORD
VICTORIA UNIVERSITY OF WELLINGTON, NEW ZEALAND

> Point this poem to Kopua.
> Please memorise it.
> *Waka 65 Venus*

The 1890 poem 'The March of Te Rauparaha' by Thomas Bracken is work, in the words of Bridget Orr, of 'fictive ethnography' (Orr 1996, 74); that is, it presents itself as fiction but as having an ethnographical or documentary accuracy or truth. The Māori warrior Te Rauparaha speaks in a poetic rendition of the primitive voice, noble, war-like, at one with the natural and the spiritual world. However, the poem has a fundamental invalidity: the author is Pākehā – it is a mimicked assumed voice, and the poem itself acknowledges that when it begins:

> Rauparaha's war chant
> Rauparaha's fame song
> Rauparaha's story
> Told on the harp strings
> Pakeha harp cords
> Tuned by the stranger. (Bracken 1890, 42)

The source material for Bracken's poem was one of the many works of Māori ethnography produced during the colonial period George Grey's *Polynesian Mythology* (1855) or Elsdon Best's *Māori Religion and Mythology* (1924) written by Pākehā [European] scholars and antiquarians, amateurs but erudite and knowledgeable about mythology and anthropology generally, not just that of New Zealand and working with Māori society. Elsdon Best lived in the Uruwera district for years; Grey was a fluent Māori speaker. But they were not Māori, and contemporary critics have pointed out that, almost inevitably, they tended to present their Māori material in terms of the forms and conventions of European culture. So Maui is seen in terms of a Prometheus, the Hinemoa story becomes a parallel to Hero and Lysander, Te Rauparaha becomes like a hero of Old English or Celtic mythology. The material they collected was not presented without unconscious and conscious refashioning. Their co-option of that mimicked voice was based on a dubious myth of the Māori being a dying race, that the material would otherwise be lost, and that there was, or would soon be, no valid owners of it.

While the dying race myth seems to have been historically inaccurate, it is none the less true that the authentic voice of Māori writers was almost completely absent from the mainstream of New Zealand literature throughout the first half of the twentieth century. Māori literature had traditionally been an oral literature, and continued in that mode. There were a number of Māori language publications – newspapers and journals – from the 1840s, but as the century progressed, native speakers dwindled, confronted with a dominant English speaking culture, and Māori writers in English were few. The nation's story, the idea of 'New Zealand literature', was very much *a Pākehā,* settler narrative – of heroism and distance meeting sensitive appreciation of local surroundings, and of a topos of landscape conceived of as entirely empty.

The reinvention of Māori writers as writers in English, but an English inflected in terms of Māori culture, began in the 1960s, encouraged by the journal *Te Ao Hou*, a Māori Affairs Dept publication. The 1970s was a period of political protest, and of a radicalisation of Māori society over such issues as land, sporting contacts with South Africa and social justice, manifested in the Land March of 1975, the occupation of Bastion Point 1977-78, the Springbok Tour of 1981. The accommodating nostalgia of the *Te Ao Hou* made way for a more politicised voice, known as the 'Māori Renaissance', an upsurge in creative activity and cultural assertion. Along with this was the postcolonial writer's paradigm – that while writing in English and in English literary forms one should reflect or convey not just the material but the values and forms of one's original language and culture.

Robert Sullivan's poetic sequence *Star Waka* was published in 1999 and is one of the most significant works of the second generation of Māori Renaissance writers. It demonstrates the postcolonial writer's paradigm – that while writing in English using English literary forms one should none the less express not just the subject matter but the world view of one's original language and culture. The collision of modes may be painful – the Irish poet Seamus Heaney said that he aimed to "make the English lyric eat stuff it's never eaten before" (Heaney 1973, 8) – but it will be at the same time rewarding and renewing.

Star Waka is a work of ambitious scope. It consists of 101 poems and 2001 lines, the latter being a nod towards the millennium date of its publication. The work as a whole is divided into three sections, indicated by roman, Arabic and finally '*Waka*' numbering. Every poem contains a reference to either a star, a *waka*, or the ocean. In his introductory note, Sullivan describes these as 'threads', as follows: "This sequence is like a *waka*, members of the crew change, the rhythm and the view changes – it is subject to the laws of nature." (Sullivan 1999)

'*Waka*' is the Māori word for canoe. Traditional Polynesian canoes came in different forms – from the simple dugout or raft to elaborate outriggers with decking, sails and steering paddles. In *Star Waka* Sullivan imagines the great canoes of New Zealand Aotearoa's first fleet, the migration from the mythical homeland of Hawaiiki in Polynesia. These *waka* were sail and oar- powered, and used celestial navigation – a central theme of Sullivan's poem – as well as a sophisticated knowledge of winds, currents, and bird and fish migrations to journey across vast distances.

Although there is no overarching narrative in *Star Waka*, this voyage of Māori from their place of origin to New Zealand – which historians date to the eleventh century – is a central theme. As the poem says, "Star Waka is a knife through time." (3) The poet celebrates the heroic past, and speculates about a future in which the *waka* becomes a space ship: "it is feasible we will enter// space/ colonise planets call our spacecraft *waka*/" (50); he imagines such a *waka* as a container for Māori society as a whole, "a great living library of people, trillions of brain cells indexed// from the heart, cross-referenced/ through usefulness to life, powered// by the stuff of life itself." (74) But linear historical time is only one of the threads that hold the sequence together and Sullivan's use of the *waka* as metaphor is fluid and malleable: in the poem "*Honda Waka*" the *waka* is not the canoe of tradition and legend, or a spaceship of the future, but the poet's rusted old Honda car, now surrendered to the wreckers, which has carried his family to births, funerals, celebrations and holidays, part of the everyday.

The *waka*, then, "waka, ark, high altar/ above the sea," (93) is a container – of historic and legendary voyagers; of indigenous culture and its future manifestations; of family present but also past: the image of the *waka* is used, in *Star Waka* but reflective of Māori culture generally, to convey *whakapapa* or ancestry. Each Māori iwi or tribe claims descent from a specific *waka* which arrived in Aotearoa/New Zealand in a particular place which then became ancestral land – *turangawaewae*, the standing place for the feet. For Sullivan of the Nga Puhi tribe, *turangawaewae* is Karetu, a small settlement in the north of the North Island: he makes the link between family history, place and his tribal *waka* when he talks of going back with "my ancestors/ buried in the cemetery and the cave nearby/ whose *waka* navigated to the soil there." (57) And the image of the *waka huia*, a traditional small carved box shaped like a *waka* designed originally to contain *huia* feathers – the *huia* being a bird, now extinct, whose feathers were highly prized and worn on ceremonial occasions by men and women of high rank – is also evoked. The poet points to the term's reappearance as the title of a television Māori language show (63) – language is the thing of value that must be treasured. In both these cases – *waka* as ancestry, *waka* as treasure chest – are traditional metaphors. As the poem asserts, "Waka spring from our unconsciousness// the deep structures of Polynesia/ to reappear in the modern world".

I suggest that one of the ways in which postcolonial writers work is by integrating their Indigenous traditions with English literary forms. In New Zealand this has been to a certain extent contaminated by nineteenth-century colonial literature's appropriation of Māori material. Nevertheless Sullivan's work engages with

Māori culture's modes of expression and address. *Star Waka* begins with "*He karakia timatanga*" or a beginning prayer, a formal part of Māori ceremonial protocol. The prayer marks both the start of the *waka's* voyage and the start of the poem, "to guide our waka out the throat between Hawaiiki's teeth." The image of the *waka* setting out across the Pacific Ocean from Hawaiiki is overlaid with another image, of words being spoken – out of the throat and between the teeth. The canoe fleet is described as the 'mother of tales,' (2) a narrative container as well as a vessel of transportation. Voyage and poem coalesce. Both are made objects, crafted sometimes with difficulty: "I have tried to draw a waka with words" Sullivan complains, "but it is becalmed by its own weight,/ and the grunting of its maker." (88) In poem 65 he directs: "Point this poem to Kopua./ Please memorise it." Kopua is the Māori name for Venus, the evening star, so vital to navigation. The poem thus, like a *waka*, is being sent out on a journey.

Star Waka's opening prayer finishes with "the chanted rhythms/ *hoera hoera ra*' of *tuki waka* or canoe chant" that traditionally regulated and encouraged the oar strokes of the sailors. *Waka 61* is, similarly, a fragment of a canoe chant which Sullivan tells us is "adapted from Hetaraka Tautahi," a kaumatua or elder of the Ngati Rauru tribe and a direct descendant of one of the legendary captains of the first fleet. In this poem, the paddle speaks as it cuts through the sea, which is figured as the sea god Tangaroa:

> This is the paddle of Te Roku-o-whiti
> who stays close to the side
> encircles the side
> stands forward flies ahead
> springs onwards
> slaps Tangaroa's back
> (who sometimes slaps back) (69)

This form is used again at the end of the sequence in *Waka 100* where the chant conveys the *waka* and their passengers traversing time, past the age of European discovery, past the time of colonisation, into the present:

Stroke past line 1642
into European time.
Stroke past 1769
and the introduction of the West.

Stroke in the approach to 1835 and formal Northern Maori sovereignty.

Stroke into the New World and Stop.

Crews alight, consign waka
to memory, family trees ... (110)

Yet despite this use of traditional Māori forms, *Star Waka* is a work which is deeply conscious of the restricted and necessarily mediated fashion in which contemporary Indigenous writers access their past. 'Who interprets history?' the poem asks. 'Who stores the manuscripts and books/ of the lost?' (54) Sullivan has trained and worked as a librarian and *Star Waka* repeatedly references printed texts, research, collation, translation and transmission. The work of other, generally European writers is signalled in the poem as one of the available routes back to a pre-contact past. Hetaraka Tautahi's fragment is a good example of this process. It was recounted to the ethnologist S. Percy Smith in 1900, recorded at the time in *The Journal of the Polynesian Society* (Tautahi 1900, 221-3) and republished in 1997 in *Nga Waka O Nehera: the First Voyaging Canoes* by Jeff Evans.

Thus it is both distant from its Indigenous source and possesses an impeccable provenance back to its pre-contact owners. *Star Waka* uses these scholarly lines of transmission quite overtly. The poem references colonial collections such as the Alexander Turnbull Library and *The Journal of the Polynesian Society*, colonial collectors and ethnographers such as Smith, Best and Harold Gatty (1943), modern scholars like Margaret Orbell (1985), Anne Nelson (1991), and Jeff Evans. Unlike many Indigenous writers who figure colonial and European record-making as an appropriation or despoliation of Indigenous knowledge, Sullivan the librarian sees books and reading as acceptable tools. In one poem he puts his work on top of a book by Anne Nelson, and the result is not a diminution but a more sharply envisioned sense of the past:

> I rest *Star Waka* on *Nga Waka Maori*
> by Anne Nelson, white tipped
> paddles raised to catch
> the setting sun
> which sets them
> yellow, red bodies
> the colour of waka,
> men hongi'ing the nose
> of the waka,
> faces touching before
> their launch
> into the mind
> of Tangaroa. (30)

Star Waka's innovation is to see such lines of transmission as inevitable and not wholly negative – although, as we are directed to these various textual approximations of the past, the poet wonders "or should one concentrate on the beauty of the waka slicing though/ concentration." (9) Sullivan writes, "oh to be that generation/to write in freefall picking up the tools/ our culture has given us" (50) but is aware that such freedom is difficult while the poem exists within what he describes as a "Western Paradise true/ to its own logic, boulders parked like stops/ across the text." (61) So while the poem acknowledges this textual and research-based access to Indigenous knowledge, the limitations of such transmitted material are made clear. In the poem "Some definitions and a note on orthography" Sullivan points out that even the word '*waka*' is inadequately translated as 'canoe': "the ancestral waka" he tells us, "were as large/ as the European barks/ of eighteenth century explorers." (21) In the same way, he observes, the word processor that he is writing the poem on cannot deal with Māori stylistics. In the transition from oral to written, meaning dissolves:

> To understand one's culture one must speak
> the language of its poetry, world
> philosophy, reach untranslated
> ambiguities. For language deals out

meaning. Meaning is the star above our
species. Specifically our waka
follows this. Meaning is food for chiefs. (63)

Writing then becomes a means of control – or at least partial control. In *Waka 74 Sea Anchor* we are told:

In storms the waka would lower
a sea anchor halfway to help control

the vessel. In a way this poem
is a sea anchor. We are waiting

for a storm to pass, one preventing
control of the narrative. (83)

'Control of the narrative' in the future will depend on lines back to the past, but also the deployment of the technology of the modern. The poem titled *'Formats (1)'* lists all the ways in which *waka* have been represented in the past and in the digital present:

sepia
paint
text
video
dat
email
html
doc files
water
cd rom
cd photo
waka

The sly insertion of the words 'water' and 'waka' inserts the real in among the mimetic categories of reproduction. But *Star Waka* acknowledges the modern world of the Foodtown supermaket (65), of Macdonalds (68), of *'waka* wallpaper' and *'waka* duvet covers' (98) where Indigenous knowledge is transmitted by the NativeNet email discussion list (43). Sometimes these new structures are problematic: in a thread concerned with *whakapapa* or genealogy,

Sullivan describes 'a database/ containing information about *whakapapa*. Some *tapu*/ information, not for publication./ A dilemma for the library culture/ of access to all, no matter who or why.' (59) In an almost apocalyptic poem, '*Kua wheturangitia koe*' ('you appear above the horizon'), he despairs of 'mechanical culture', 'this culture of menace,' 'the congress of scars.' (20)

While Sullivan as a contemporary Indigenous author works with traditional material tempered by a sense of the effect of colonial and later transmissions and re-presented in terms of modernity, he is also aware of other literatures and other postcolonial literatures. Māori writers do not work in a vacuum. Any epic writer who bases his work on a sea journey has to be haunted by Homer's *Odyssey*; any postcolonial writer who does so has to see Homer's work through the lens of Derek Walcott's *Omeros* (1990). Sullivan seems at first to acknowledge this source by rejecting it. In '*Waka 62 A narrator's note*' he writes, "There is no Odysseus to lead this fleet" stressing the oral archive as a counter-narrative to the European canonical:

> I have only waka floating beneath the stars
> at night and in the day, directed by swells,
> whose crews are sustained not by seabirds
> or fish, but by memory – some in conflict
> with the written record. (70)

But later in the sequence this postcolonial confidence seems in doubt. In *Waka 88* the canonical reasserts itself and Odysseus reappears, as he puts it 'summoned to these pages by the extraordinary claims of the narrator', as a representative of a kind of ur-text. 'I run through all narratives' Odysseus claims,

> Look closely at the narration. Who
> is holding sails taut, commanding the paddles,
> seeing that the carvings follow the patterns
> of waka that follow the patterns of the sea?
> I. Odysseus. I have put myself here
> because this is a text. A very Western text.
> The navigators sail with me now.
> I sail as a member of the crew,

and can speak for them. (98)

Odysseus is reminding us that Sullivan is limited by – even compromised by the European forms he is employing.

This is a salutary but rather reduced note for an Indigenous writer to conclude with. So Sullivan, while not contradicting Odysseus, sets his assertion of authority alongside other powerful voices. The last section of *Star Waka* has competing narrators – Odysseus is matched by the god of the sea Tangaroa, Tane god of the forest; Kupe the traditional captain of the exploratory fleet; and Maui the trickster hero Prometheus figure. Maui's complaint is textual:

> Yo, I'm Maui …
> and I am expressing ANGER ANGER
> at being denied a significant portion of the text
> of the Star Waka. The copyrights are mine …

In legend Maui fished up the North Island of New Zealand, 'a matrix to tie/ their culture to'. In the poem he wants credit. 'And' he adds, 'no more anthropologists./ I belong to cosmology. Dig, Odysseus?' (99). *Star Waka's* careful accommodation of systems of scholarship and classification is rejected.If the question at the beginning of *Star Waka*, as the fleet sets sail, was 'Will our high magic work here?' the competing voices at the end suggest that it will to an extent. Perhaps finally that extent is measured not by separations of culture but by collectivity. Sullivan has been looking for "ways of narrating a story of waves." (15) He has found it both in Indigenous and in European forms, direct and mediated in both cases. In the poem which despairs of the West's "boulders parked like stops/ across the text," (61) he recognises the physicality of human existence as being both reductive and releasing:

> Everything
> a collection of tiny connections.
> For beauty has delightful components
> The molecule of water sliding by
> molecules of waka, powered by breeze
> molecules in muscles, on sails – its scales
> notes on the firmament, melodious

oration, song, rhythm of pahu, flute
feet braced on boards swinging torso, elbow,
thought. This thought passed down lengths of men
through earth –
we came by waka, we leave by waka,
pass it on. (62)

Works Cited

Beatty, Warner. Durham: Duke University Press.

Best, Elston. 1924. *Maori Religion and Mythology: being an Account of the Cosmogony, Anthropogeny, Religious Beliefs and Rites, Magic and Folk Lore of the Maori Folk of New Zealand.* Wellington: Government Printer. (Dominion Museum Bulletins 10-11).

Bracken, Thomas. 1890. *The March of Te Rauparaha. Musings in Maoriland.* Dunedin: Arthur T Keirle.

Evans, Jeff. 1997. *Nga Waka O Nehera: the First Voyaging Canoes.* Auckland: Reed.

Gatty, Harold. 1943. *The Raft Book: Lore of Sea and Sky.* New York: George Grady Press.

Grey, George. 1855. *Polynesian Mythology and Ancient Traditional History of the New Zealand Race as furnished by their Priests and Chiefs.* London: John Murray.

Heaney, Seamus. 1973. "Interview with Harriet Cooke," *Irish Times*, 28 (December): np.

Orbell, Margaret. 1985. *The Natural World of the Maori.* Auckland: Collins, David Bateman.

Nelson, Anne. 1991. *Maori Canoes: Nga Waka Maori.* Auckland: Macmillan.

Sullivan, Robert. 1999. *Star Waka.* Auckland: Auckland University Press.

Tautahi, Hetaraka. 1900. *The "Aotea" Canoe: the Migration of Turi to Aotea-roa (New Zealand), dictated by Hetaraka Tautahi, assisted by Werahiko Taipei, of Taranga-a-ilka near Waitotara, Nov.* Translated and annotated by S. Percy Smith, *Journal of the Polynesian Society*, 9.4 (December 1900): 221-3.

Te Ao Hou, 1952-76, http://teaohou.natlib.govt.nz/journals/teaohou/index.html. Accessed 26.2.2013.

Walcott, Derek. 1990. *Omeros*. New York: Farrar, Straus and Giroux.

Note

(From the author). I have used macrons – for example, Māori, Pākehā – in my discussion as is now normal practice but have followed my sources' usage in quotations.

CHAPTER THIRTY-TWO

FLAWS IN THE GLASS: WHY AUSTRALIA DID NOT BECOME A REPUBLIC ... AFTER PATRICK WHITE

STEPHEN ALOMES
ROYAL MELBOURNE INSTITUTE OF TECHNOLOGY

In thinking about Patrick White's concerns re the need for an Australian Republic and why Australia did not become a Republic in 1999 (the date of the last referendum of the issue) my mind first turned to the relationship between everyday experience and larger worldly aspirations in two very different novels. One was set in, still technically, monarchical Australia and the other in republican India. While some purists differentiate between literary and popular fiction, these books, one literary, the other popular, raise Patrick White-related questions about colonial mentalities, social class and the power of materialism.

Madeleine St John's semi-autobiographical literary gem, *The Women in Black* (2007), portrays a young girl in Sydney in the 1950s. Her projected dreams take her from the suburban Lesley' to cultivated 'Lisa' when working in the rarefied atmosphere of 'model gowns' imported from Paris and London in a grand department store, based on the image of the large Australian department store, David Jones. A very different, contemporary novel by Chetan Bhagat is a serious if picaresque work, popular amongst University of Hyderabad students. In *One Night at the Call Centre* (2005, 2007) the metropolitan dreams of a young graduate woman, her mother, and an ambitious and ruthless, but not very bright, Indian call centre boss with an MBA are of American metropolises, Seattle and Boston, respectively. The lesser people in the pecking order of the call centre have different dreams of elevation: through writing, in the media and politics and in modelling.

That fantasy relationship between the humdrum everyday workplace and dreams of overseas success is an Australian and an Indian story. In Australia, my corpus of artistic expatriates responded to *When London Calls* in the 1950s-60s (Alomes, 1999). Today, many Indians desire to make money in the global system while some academics wish to become gurus in the US. These novels and patterns also answer the question of why Australia has not 'cut the painter' and become a republic – it is about the 'flaws' in Australian society and politics, including social class. Indians might also think about the Faustian bargains, materialist trades or compromises, ones that we all make with global economics and culture, as well as with more local origins, including class and caste.

A Portrait of Patrick White:
From Elitist and Artist to Man of the People

Patrick White came from a different world to that of the department store staff of *The Women in Black* and the call centre workers in Chetan Bhagat's novel. Like them, however, he acquired a comparable sense of the realities of class and culture. The imperial to colonial context shaped the young Patrick White as an Australian boy. In this elite landed family, the Whites of Belltrees in New South Wales, his mother assumed that an English private school was somehow superior, "a seed sown in an ambitious mother's mind by an English headmaster" in Australia (White 1981, 12). Those English private schoolboys daily tortured the 'colonial' boy who never forgot those "bitter days when I [he] was a despised Colonial attempting to pass himself off as an English schoolboy." (White 1981, 33) Scorned, Patrick the victim would also learn to scorn.

Patrick was the scion of an elite grazier family. In the provincial days of the interwar period – which I term 'Dominion Culture' – they sought status in the British cultural sphere. Consciously, and unconsciously, they were Anglo-Australians. Of course he was, as he acknowledges, someone different, although despite being 'born with a silver spoon' in his mouth he was regarded by his own mother as being a 'freak' (White 1981, 34, 46-7). English schooling, the White family background, his predilections as writer, artist, intellectual and gay man, made him an outsider, even when released from the 'prison' of his English school. An imperially anglicised 'colonial', despite his resistance, he then found himself 'a stranger in my own country'. Harry England, who trained horses for his father at Belltrees, and respected wealth and status, unwittingly cut him deeply by describing him as 'the real gentleman' (White 1981, 46-7).

Given his elite and outsider aspects, and perforce a childhood exile who partly grew up in another culture, Patrick White could have been an alienated individual, separating himself entirely from the 'common people' and their aspirations. However, this 'prodigal son,' in White's essay of that name, returned, seeking to contribute something deeper to what he saw as a material culture lacking in respect for ideas. That national condition had been engendered by admixed imperial-colonial structures: the practical demands of pioneering, the off-shoring of much professional Australian cultural life to metropolitan London (Alomes 1999), and the materialism of a new world immigrant society. However, White the international modernist schooled in German romanticism also sought to explore social experience and its meanings.

Was White entirely the difficult character graphically portrayed in David Marr's biography? Was he just the sacred monster, who entertained generously, but then fell out with old friends? He dismissed both the prolific and popular writer Geoffrey Dutton and the lyrical expressionist painter Sid Nolan, later Sir Sidney Nolan from his inner circle without compunction. In White's assessment, (which I share) the esteemed Australian artist based in London personified the artist in search of imperial status, the tram-driver's son as a social climber in search of an English knighthood (Marr 1991, 602, 606-7, 612-15). Marr was partly wrong in emphasising Patrick's curmudgeonly side. The weakness of his analysis stems from the third of his several hats, serious writer, thorough researcher and tabloid journalist. The latter shaped the chapters which offered a kind of revolving salon tale of whom Patrick White had fallen out with. As English singer Billy Bragg observed in one of his performances, the famous, eventually fall victims to academics, and other researchers, who are like possums going through their garbage bins. Gossip interests us all, whether our tipple is fine literature such as Jane Austen or daytime television's *The Bold and the Beautiful*.

White's relationship with Australia and its peoples was more complex than such clichés allow. In 1958, in his 'The Prodigal Son' essay in Australian *Letters*, he had condemned the materialism which he saw as dominating Australian life: "in all directions stretched the Great Australian Emptiness, in which the mind is the least of possessions." (White 1958) However, in his work he could transcend this dismissive view of Australian society. His capacity for understanding was also apparent in his relationship with the everyday people whom he met when shopping for meat, vegetables and other cooking ingredients when living near Castle Hill.

Colonial to Neo-colonial Inheritance:
Consumption and Empire in an affluent island

In two significant plays, Patrick White turned his literary scalpel to dissecting the body of materialism and social pretension, in different settings, across, time, place and class. In *Season at Sarsaparilla* (1962), he exposed suburban ordinariness in outer Sydney that he discovered upon his return – the Australia of backyards, lawns and Hills Hoist clotheslines. In contrast, *Big Toys* (1978) is set in the *nouveau riche* society of Eastern Suburbs Sydney, said to be the Australian city most characterised by conspicuous consumption, in which the 'toys' include jewellery and flash cars.

White was aware both of materialism in its different forms and of Australia's vestigial appendix – the connection to the former British Empire and continuing monarchy, although its popular appeal was usually expressed only in Royal tours by the English Queen and by younger princes and over Ashes cricket matches. Otherwise, British (empire) and monarchical connections remain only as a vestigial appendix. In a global era, despite the popular appeal of nationalism (in sport and Anzac war memory), the dances with the post-imperial or 'global' devil, usually clothed in the media garments of popular culture, are more important.

Broadening the frame from Patrick White at Dogwoods and in Martin Road, Centennial Park, to Australian society then and now, we can understand both writer and country better. Consider the social-cultural context that explains why today only 45% of Australians support a republic, and why the proposal was defeated at the 1999 referendum. Like Patrick White's other major 1980s political commitment, to nuclear disarmament, it has not been realised, and seems even further away (Marr 1991, 601-2, 611-12).

Earlier, White had railed against materialism, provincial insularity and Australia's lack of respect for intellect. Today, change and continuity are apparent. Despite the vestigial appendix, the old traditions of imperial loyalty, British Empire patriotism and a primary metropolitan orientation to London have weakened (Alomes 1988, 1999, 2004, 2010). Although London remains a global English language media centre and airline hub, Australians' international orientations are now more multi-polar, including the many different Asias. Today, the nearest to London's traditional role in *The Women in Black* is the global cult of New York, as reflected in David Jones' 2012 fashion marketing of model/ ambassador Miranda Kerr in Manhattan and Melbourne's new high rise apartment developments which are strangely marketed as 'Midtown' and 'Upper West Side'.

However, the transition from the colonial to national past to the global present has been more complex than that inadequate word 'post-colonial'. The neo-colonial reality is central rather than some fantasy of a hyphenated 'post-modern' world, however cool it may seem to affluent, mobile and knowledgeable cosmopolitan intellectuals able to enjoy the global world of play.

Every Australian's Right to Consume: The Rise of a Consumocracy

In Australia, we now have a new form of democracy, which the flood of festive shopping advertising in urban and affluent India, the 'celebrate shopping' theme of *Divali* in 2012, seems to resemble. In Australia, these social-cultural values are encapsulated in the mission statement of Target, the Australian version of the middle market department store. Target, which aims for quality and economy, has its 'democratic' version of the rights of every Australian as a consumer rather than a citizen – their 'right to look good and feel good about themselves and what they wear.'

Australia is a 'consumocracy' (my term) in which the title of the consumers' association magazine is *Choice*. Appropriately, that noun sounds like a neo-liberal concept of democracy as only a 'marketplace' of ideas. Australians today may have chosen consumption over citizenship, screen culture over democracy, and individualised consumption over past egalitarian ideals. Considering the mails (during the time of my recent visit to India) responding to *Divali* advertising in the Hyderabad and other newspapers, and in the need, that is desire, for money of the principal characters in *One Night at the Call Centre*, I reflected that this may also be the emerging reality of global, urban India.

Why the 1999 Republic Referendum Failed

In the 1990s, why was the republic proposal defeated at a referendum? That question can be answered by macro analyses of social-cultural values as well as by micro reasons, specific causes. Arguably, a popular preference for materialism and consumption has displaced politics, as well as thought, as White might have observed, from the top of most people's priorities. Other specific reasons are more distinctive, and even technical.

One reason, as Fred Chaney suggested in his presentation at the ASAA conference Hyderabad, (Dec. 2012) is that only eight referenda have passed in 112 years. Simply, no referendum passes in Australia without the support of both parties, allowing it to win the necessary majority of votes coupled with four of the six states. Prime Minister Howard and the governing Liberal Party's opposition ensured its inevitable defeat. Why did Australians choose the status quo, leaving them in the eyes of many peoples, as being no more than mere British colonials? A large part of the reason was to be attributed to Howard's tactical mastery, the slow process from constitutional convention to referendum and a second confusing part of the proposal voted on - that the parliament, that is the politicians, would choose the president. The more questions asked in a referendum the more likely they are to fail! As the last of the Queen's men, Howard was not quite on the sidelines, and phrased the questions in a way guaranteed to create uncertainty. In the British tradition, he had confounded the 'knavish tricks' of the enemies of Britannia. (Alomes 1988; 1997; 2000; Alomes & Jones 1991; McKenna; 1996; McKenna and Hudson; 2003).

Populist Presidentialism:
A Contraceptive against the Birth of a Republic

Paradoxically, the defeat stemmed from neither the minority of monarchists, nor the other minority of people with an "if it ain't broke, don't fix it" conservative argument for stability over change (Alomes 2000). My argument is that, shaped by vague awareness of the American presidential model, Australians succumbed to a foolish version of populism. They hoped that an elected president – rather than one more sensibly chosen by the joint houses of parliament – would provide a people's leader expressing the will of the people. Not being constitutionally savvy, they did not understand that in the party adversary politics of Australia (Westminster in origin, but with greater party solidarity) even more than in the French 'co-habitation,' a President from one party and a parliamentary government from another, could not work effectively together.

In Australia, populism offers both reasonable and unreasonable scepticism about elites and a class society – although the latter is rarely acknowledged in public discourse. Populism is also a variant of the Australian tradition of 'knocking' which includes 'anti-Canberra' when the city name becomes a metonym for taxes and political corruption, although corruption, beyond an odd fraudulent Cabcharge voucher, is rare in Australian federal politics. Tabloid media, from the Murdoch press to radio shock jocks, reinforce populist scepticism, as media elites pretend that they are a voice for the dispossessed. Such views grow with distance. The referendum 'No' vote was strongest in regional Queensland and Tasmania, two states in which conservative politicians have dabbled in regional patriotism/populism, in the form of a Queensland Day and a Tasmania Day (Alomes 2007, 2010; Patience 1985).

Populism does not offer solutions or policies. It is an *expressive* politics often embodied in a prospective leader, as in the 'Joh for Canberra' (Queensland Premier, Johannes Bjelke-Petersen) campaign of 1988 and the Pauline Hanson 'One Nation 'movement of 1996, which soon disappeared (Patience 1985; Grant 1997; Alomes 2012). Expressive populist fantasies, or dreams, of the will of the people embodied in a leader, or in the abstract 'our President', appeal emotionally. They can seduce people who only have vague images of the American presidential model.

The 1990s referendum campaign for a republic with an Australian head of state emerged after several decades of globalising change endorsed by both major political parties. Often illogical distrust in politicians is one all-pervasive result. Their 'Trust us. Change will be good for you in the long run' formulation, also used by 1990s Labour Prime Minister Paul Keating, brings to mind J.M. Keynes' conclusion that 'in the long run we're all dead'. Perhaps subconsciously, one more restructuring proposal reminded many voters of the instability that had become the norm. As a result, then and now, many preferred unthinking stability (Alomes 2000, 2007).

Populism today appeals to those who feel dispossessed or have been hurt by the structural changes. The 'No' vote was strongest in working class and rural areas. Many 'Yes' voters had greater international experience: those of European, Asian and other immigrant extraction (the more 'ethnic' Labour seats), the educated and travelled who felt embarrassed at the visible vestige of colonialism of an English monarch as formal head of state. Australians overseas, with some rare exceptions amongst older conservatives, also feel strongly about the symbolic need for Australia to choose autonomy over the British monarchical connection. The largest branch of the Australian Republican Movement was in London.

Negative Populist Politics vs. New Celebrity 'Elites'

The republic debate anticipated today's destructive negative politics, modelled on American politics. The constitutional monarchists outgeneralled the republicans. Preferring tactical skill to the courage of their convictions, their ruthless fear campaign stressed negativism, the rejection of 'a politicians' republic.' They appealed to more general popular anxieties even though support for the monarchy had been as low as 10-20%. Even celebrities, normally dominant in the media in an era of the 'dumbing down' of public life, were a negative. A century before, popular and populist opinion in the radical press mocked the pretensions of Government House and polite 'society'. Now, due to the monarchists' cleverness in not mentioning the 'M' word, the pompous rejected 'silvertails' and 'snobs' became the Sydney 'chardonnay republicans' - a dramatic inversion in the land of colonial paradox.

Patrick White was always aware of the venality that went with social status, and with the short-term character of many politicians' visions. For many voters, even 'worse' than celebrities were politicians and the prospect of 'a politicians' republic' – a 'President' chosen by parliament. The Australian Republican Movement's invocation of politicians guaranteed the referendum's defeat. Once it would have mattered, at least to the politically interested, that Gough Whitlam and Malcolm Fraser could finally agree that 'It's Time'. To an alienated electorate, two politicians added up to two politicians. Cynicism has grown as ideas and ideologies have retreated. Populism's powerful emotional logic was felt by those who had experienced Australia becoming a more divided society.

The Fading of the Republican Cause

After the Whitlam Labour era's 'New Nationalism' of the 1970s, which influenced White, and even the Bicentenary, nationalism focused on the 200 years since 1788 of the 1980s, the republican cause might have gathered strength, despite John Howard's conservative government. However, arguably, a transition from colony to dependent and 'loyal' Dominion towards an independent republic, with full nationhood had been supplanted by another transition. My major argument is that fundamentally Australian society had transitioned from a persistent colonial consciousness, even in the era of nation from 1901, to becoming a dependent consumocracy, both under the umbrella of an imagined alliance with a great power. In the era of the shopping mall, the materialism that Patrick White had discerned in suburbia and in aspirational bourgeois Sydney was ramifying, in different ways; national aspirations were marginalised. That macro analysis is fundamental as a context for the retreat of republicanism as a political cause since 1999, but several specific factors also engendered its decline as I, and my former Deakin colleague David Lowe, have noted. (Personal communication 2012). Reasons include, as well as John Winston Howard's success in looking backwards:

- the inevitable valley or trough after the peak of the referendum campaign;

- the republican, who could also appeal to some Liberal Party supporters;

- the failure of civic concepts of republicanism to engage with old and new nationalist traditions, and with Aboriginal nationalism, and to engage the emotions of most citizens;

- Labour's tactical retreat, aiming to win the next election rather than lose a crucial 3-5% of votes on the republic issue;

- political leaders' inability to explain to the public the negative consequences for stable government of the populist and romantic impulse towards a directly elected president. Young voters particularly, engrossed in screen lives of new and old media, brand culture and cultural tribes, the 'global' successor to the suburban materialism which Patrick White lamented, are often indifferent to politics.

The republic hardly rated a mention in the 2012 Asia White Paper, even though such a symbolic change would reduce erroneous clichés (based only on cultural lag) about a British, 'white Australia' which persists in much of Asia. Such clichés are as valid as ideas of kangaroos in the city streets of Sydney and Melbourne. Over the last decade, republicanism has faded, even as clichéd and idealist Anzac and sports nationalisms have thrived. Opinion polls in recent years demonstrate that support for the republic has fallen from the 1990s highs of over 50% to as low as 41%, with 20% 'don't knows' (*Australian* 25 April 2011). Perhaps, even more than the English queen's jubilee year or the beauty of Kate Middleton, now dubbed, in that bizarre rhetoric 'royal', or her sister's stunning dresses, the real reason has been years of political and economic instability. Despite their having the best performing economy in the developed world, Australians view their glass as only half-full.

Wearing a futurologist's hat, I predict that a republic will only be achieved when the initiative is taken by a Liberal (that is, conservative) Party leader, ensuring bi-partisan party support. When that will be, we do not know. How have forms of sovereignty – political, economic, social and cultural - changed? In the still colonial worldview of the 'society' ladies buying gowns in *The Women in Black*, the imperial European centres were in the *haute couture milieu* of Paris and in London, the metropolitan centres for Sydney social elites. In *One Night at the Call Centre* the new centres of the world are Boston, where the American contracting company is based, and Seattle, headquarters of Microsoft. The book is weak in its treatment of the American callers, who rarely appear, but stronger in its awareness of the contradictions facing the overnight white-collar factory workers. Central are the cutting remarks of Vroom, the nationalist and critic of America, who declares that "an air-conditioned sweatshop is still a sweatshop" and that "we're sacrificing an entire generation to service their call centres." (Bhagat 2007, 190-1)

The Faustian Bargain:
Selling National Sovereignty for a Global Mess of Pottage

These imperial-colonial (and metropolitan-provincial status) relationships relate to other contemporary contexts in the global, that is post- or neo-imperial, world system. Chetan Bhagat's prologue in *One Night at the Call Centre* asks the reader to consider three things: one, what you fear; two, what makes you angry; and, three, what you don't like about yourself. In *Flaws in the Glass*, Patrick White was brave in assessing his own weaknesses. Today, in the globalising era many of us, if pressed to consider 'unto thine own self be true,' would recognise something we don't like about ourselves – too often we also take the easier choice. We accept unacceptable work, which allows us income to indulge, sharing some of Vroom's consumer tastes. We might compare individuals' and countries' compromises with the Devil of materialism and with the homogenising tendencies of globalisation and the individuals' choices in the workplace. The Bhagat questions are about fears, angers, and self-criticism. What individuals often fear is loss of employment, while countries fear the costs of exclusion from the dominant world system, economically and militarily-politically. What makes many people angry is to see fraud, pretension and corrupt networks ruling workplaces and beyond. Many citizens feel angry about our sell-out to materialism and inequality, with little concern for higher social ideals or the consequences of global warming.

Similarly, our countries have sold their countries and their cultural souls, for economic membership of the global world system. To use a word I first encountered in the *Deccan Chronicle* (2nd November 2012, 11) our governments have become more and more 'Globitarian', that is a government in which decisions are determined by global market forces. It is a scary concept, which Patrick White, as a republican, an opponent of uranium mining and a critic of materialism and colonial deference, might appreciate. In the global era, like the imperial-colonial eras, ordinary people's psychology, as well as that of artists and writers, reflects the fears, angers and frustrations of our individual and national Faustian bargains.

Patrick White was aware of the 'flaws in the glass' of the domestic social fabric. We should also reflect on the complex relations of elites and people to the dominant world system. Some of the settler colonial, commercial and even industrial elites of Australia worked as agents of empire for their presumed mutual benefit. Indians may also enter into compromised arrangements, supping with the god and the Devil of the old and new world systems. In globalisation, the costs are usually borne by those below them. We are all being globalised now – even if in different ways, and with different compromises with our local institutions and mores. In Patrick White's words, 'the poisoning influence of money' makes greed central in these processes (Marr 1991, 6).

Conclusion:
'Flaws in the Glass' in Politics, Society and Culture

Patrick White was acutely, even painfully, aware of the implications of a society shaped by provincial elites, an omnipresent if often forgotten class system (forgotten because it was less explicit than Indian caste systems and English class systems marked by accent), and by the power of materialism over thought. In the 21st century, we might find that as the idea of symbolic independence retreats everywhere as globalism erodes all national sovereignties, even as it brings greater affluence to some, that there are echoes from the past. This is not the same as nationalist reaction or symbolic national boosterism over flag-waving, or in sporting chants. Capitalist neo-liberal conceptions underlie globalisation. These imperatives privilege markets over governments, companies over people and cultural 'product' over cultural traditions. This turns a world of nation-states into a global market.

Nationalist and ethno nationalist independence movements notwithstanding, from Scotland to Catalonia to Andhra Pradesh, the juggernaut of globalisation is as powerful as the 2011 *tsunami* that struck Japan. It seems unstoppable. In fact, it echoes an earlier world system in the period of the new imperialism. Then, idealist and romantic ideas of empire, underpinned by guns, money and missionaries as well as mercenaries, ignored Indigenous sovereignties and even gave short shrift to settler colonials' ideas of independence. In the late 19th century, in the 1880s-1890s, an Australian nationalism seemed possible. Australia and New Zealand were building progressive societies free of foreign evils, except, in that era of racial ideology, for the invaded Indigenous peoples. Soon, the New Imperialism contest between the powers, the rise of British imperial rhetoric (or ideology) and the capitalists' revenge against social reform and Labour and trade union progress stopped all that.

Now, over 120 years later, we might look at the defeat of the republic referendum and the languishing of the republican cause, and make comparisons. Yet I must note other more sanguine views of how Australia negotiated its national interests within the context of the British Empire, particularly Stuart Ward (Schreuder and Ward 2008). The US-Australia free trade agreement (2005) threatens to erode the freedom to control pharmaceutical prices in the public interest (in contrast to the Indian Supreme Court's April 2013 judgment against Novartis' proposed patent extensions) and government support of Australian film and other cultural forms. Australian novels are often out of print. Some traditional and some 'pomo' elites share many young people's lack of interest in a republic and in Australian culture. In 2011, the University of Melbourne English Department offered no course in Australian literature, although some writers' popped up' in other courses. In part this was a globitarian reality - market forces, student demand, also had a role in the decision. A concerned Australian undergraduate, who had discovered Argentinean awareness of their literary traditions, organised an informal Australian literature course on Friday afternoons, with prominent visiting writers (Guest 2012; Brady 2011).

Contemporary realities involve global neo-colonialism in the digital age, globalisation, the temporarily fading republican cause and the everyday realities of a brand-driven 'consumocracy'. Therefore, we might reflect on writers and national aspiration today. Indian scholars might also reflect on globalising materialism in India at this time of 'Designer *Divali*' and the festive imperative 'Celebrate Shopping'. India's internal contradictions, including caste, old and new elites and poverty, politics and corruption, and work and consumption, including call centres and India's consumocracy, as also expressed in Hyderabad's Orbit Mall, might also be analysed in their local and global contexts. Compare the transitions of Hyderabad from the 'princely city' and India's crossroads to 'Cyberabad'. Significantly, imperial/global hierarchies over lesser 'colonials' are in fact the peak of the domestic class system.

Today, Patrick White, scion of an elite class but an outsider as a creator, would have been disappointed by the flaws in the glass of contemporary Australia. He would be disappointed by John Howard's return to symbolic monarchism, and saddened by Prime Minister Julia Gillard's fawning 2011 address to the US Congress. He would regret governments' and universities' limited support for

Australian culture, despite authors receiving copyright agency and library lending rights payments. An artist in temperament, as well as a writer, he would want to paint pictures or write plays depicting a general infatuation with a digital new world of 'big toys'. Would he ask whether Australians lack faith in their own culture and their own people? Or, do they, just prefer the philosophy of 'she'll be right', with or without 'mate' added? If he were alive today, White might well exclaim "Shame Australia Shame!"

Works Cited

Alomes, Stephen. 1988. *A Nation At Last? The Changing Character of Australian Nationalism1880–1988.* Sydney: Angus and Robertson.

Alomes, Stephen and Catherine Jones. 1991. Ed. *Australian Nationalism: A Documentary History.* Sydney: Angus and Robertson.

Alomes, Stephen. 1997. "The Australian Republican Paradox," in Cultures of the Commonwealth 3: 19-38.

—. 1999. *When London Calls: The Expatriation of Australian Creative Artists to Britain.* Cambridge: Cambridge University Press.

—. 2000. "Populism, Disillusionment and Fantasy: Australia Votes," *Overland* 158 :92-94.

—. 2007. "Past Caring: Political Alienation and Populism in Australia and Beyond," *Past Caring,*ed. David Callahan. Perth: API Network: 287-301, 354-8.

—. 2010. "Postcolonial Legacies and the 'Small Country Syndrome,'" *Change – Conflict and Convergence: Austral–Asian Scenarios,* ed Cynthia vanden Driesen and Ian vanden Driesen. New Delhi: Orient Black Swan.

Bhagat, Chetan. 2007. *One Night at The Call Centre.* London: BBC/Windsor/Paragon edition.

Brady, Nicole. 2011. "Uni brought to book for snub to local literature." *The Age.* 21 August.

Davidson, Jim. 2004. "The De-dominionisation of Australia." *Meanjin.* 63.3. (September): 139-153.

Guest, Stephanie. 2012. "Finding Australian Literature at the University of Melbourne," *Australian Book Review*, February.
Grant, Bligh. 1997. ed. *Pauline Hanson: One Nation and Australian Politics*. Armidale, New England: University of New England Press.
Holloway, Peter. Ed 1987. *Contemporary Australian Drama* Sydney: Currency Press.
McKenna, Mark. 1996. *The Captive Republic: A History of Republicanism in Australia 1788-1996*. Cambridge, UK: Cambridge University Press.
McKenna, Mark and Wayne Hudson. Ed. 2003. *Australian Republicanism: A Reader*. Melbourne: Melbourne University Publishing.
Marr, David. 1991. *Patrick White: A Life*. Sydney: Random House.
Nixon, Rob. 1992. *London Calling: V. S. Naipaul, Post-Colonial Mandarin*. New York: Oxford University Press.
Packham, Ben and Matthew Franklin. 2011. "Republic support lowest in 17 years, " *The Australian* 25 April.np.
Patience, Allan. Ed. 1985. *The Bjelke-Petersen Premiership 1968-1983*. Melbourne: Longman Cheshire.
Phillips, A. A. 1958. "The Cultural Cringe, " *The Australian Tradition: Studies in a Colonial Culture*. Melbourne: Cheshire.
Schreuder, Deryck M. and Stuart Ward. Ed. 2008. *Australia's Empire*. Oxford: Oxford University Press.
St John, Madeleine. 2009. *The Women in Black*. Melbourne: Text.
White, Patrick. 1981. *Flaws in the Glass: A Self-Portrait*. London: Jonathan Cape.
—. 1958. "The Prodigal Son,". *Australian Letters* 1, 3: 37-40.

CHAPTER THIRTY-THREE

NEGOTIATING "OTHERNESS": THE MUSLIM COMMUNITY IN AUSTRALIA

AMEER ALI
MURDOCH UNIVERSITY, WESTERN AUSTRALIA

Patrick White has stated unequivocally that

> All races – all faiths – can, I feel, be brought together if we try ... We are certainly up against it in stiff-necked Australia. When I returned to live in my native land after World War II, we were raging against the Jewish 'reffos' of Central Europe. Later it became the Balts. There are still side swipes at the 'dagoes' ... and now of course there is perhaps the greatest rage against the new wave of Asians. (Brennan and Flynn 1989, 136).

Unfortunately he did not live to witness the current animosity against the Muslims in Australia. The difficulties the Australian Anglo-Celtic mainstream community experiences in understanding the Muslims and their culture, and the slowness in accepting the Muslims as equal partners in nation-building and development, is the tragic consequence of an inherited Anti-Islamic European legacy. Islamophobia, which can be defined as an instinctive and unthinking dread and hatred of Islam leading to the fear and dislike of all Muslims has a long history in Europe. It has subsisted from the time of the birth of Islam in the seventh century right through to the Crusades in the eleventh to the thirteenth centuries and down to the Ottoman rule over parts of Europe between the fifteenth and eighteenth centuries. Europeans have been continuously fed, by their temporal and spiritual leaders, on a *smorgasbord* of anti-Islamic ideas. In the Christian-manufactured image, as has been traced in the work of Daniel (1960) Muhammad was presented as the Antichrist and his message was heresy. In the words of Edward Said: "Islam was a lasting trauma" for Europe (1991, 59). Islam and Muslims became the permanent 'Other' in the European mind-set. Given that mind-set European colonisation of Muslim countries in the 19th century was deemed a sacred business and a civilising mission.

Australia, one of the 'Western Offshoots' as described by Angus Maddison (2002, 27), inherited this fear of Islam and Muslims from the beginning of its establishment as a British settlement. To colonial Australians, Islam was not simply of "faint interest" as Blainey notes (1994, 191) but also as Stevens describes a "bizarre and foreign religion." (1989, 167) The editor of the *Inquirer* Frederick Vosper had this to say about the Muslims in one of his editorials on 3 May 1895:

> We object to servile labour of all kinds, and my reason for giving special prominence to the believers in Islam, is that they are at present the most unpleasantly conspicuous and obnoxious of the servile races. At the same time I admit that I should regard the establishment of Islamism in this country as being nothing short of a national calamity. (Deen 2011, 8)

Beginning with the Chinese, then the Albanians and Jews, shifting later to the Italians and Greeks, and Turks, and finally to Muslims of all varieties, the identity of the 'Other' has had a nomadic existence in Australian history and appears to have permanently affected the Australian psyche. However, while the otherness of the previous groups tended to melt away in the face of economic development and the politics of multiculturalism the Muslim otherness on the contrary remains stubbornly unchanging and therefore hard to be eliminated, partly possibly because of the strength of the anti-Islamic European legacy. A decentralised Islam with a resurgent *asabiyya*-consciousness or "hyper-*asabiyya*" which, as will be elaborated later, simply means group solidarity (Ahmad 2003, 15) amongst diasporic Muslims, a robust social media, and the synchronisation of Australian security policies with those of her Western allies have all combined to make negotiation of otherness problematic and harder for Muslims.Incidentally, this paper was written in the immediate aftermath of the Sydney' riots 'in September 2012, which was part of an orchestrated and almost worldwide Muslim protest against an amateurish video documentary produced by an obscure American with the deliberate intension of insulting the Prophet Muhammad and Islam. This single incident, as many others in the past, has once again widened the 'us/them' gap between Australian Muslims and their co-citizens despite years of attempts to narrow it.

There are basic facts that one should bear in mind when referring to the Muslim community in Australia. Firstly, the Muslim presence in the country is older than the British arrival toward the end of the eighteenth century: Muslim fishermen from Macassar in Indonesia's Sulawesi region were frequenting the shores of Australia from the beginning of the 18th century, in search of trepan or sea cucumber, which they traded with China. It was commerce and not conquest that brought the Macassar Muslims to Australia, and on that account their relationship with the Aborigines of Arnhem Land in the Australian Northern Territory was cordial and not confrontational as was to happen later under the British. For a period the Macassan language even became the *lingua franca* in that part of the country (Cleland 2002, 6-8). Secondly, unlike in the case of Europe, the largest Muslim country in the world, Indonesia, with 203 million Muslims (that is, 12.7 percent of the world Muslim population) is the closest neighbour to Australia.

There are two other nations, Malaysia with 20 million Muslims and oil-rich Brunei with another 400,000, which also lie relatively close to Australian shores. Thus, Australia's proximity to nearly 224 million Muslims strategically places its own local Muslim community of 476,000 (2011 census), at the centre of Australasian regional relations. And thirdly, contrary to what mainstream Australians, their leaders, and the Australian media believe, the Muslim community is not a monolithic entity. Apart from its multi-ethnicity, multi-linguistics and multi-traditions, even in matters of religious belief and practices there are variations within the community. The failure to recognise this fundamental fact is the cause of several undifferentiated value judgements that makes social inclusion a harder-to-achieve objective for Muslims.

The so-called War on Terror unleashed after the September 11, 2001 terrorist attack in New York and Washington, by the Bush Administration in the United States (2001-2009) and the invasions on Iraq and Afghanistan (in which Australia has participated willingly), the influx of Muslim immigrants from the invaded countries; the extraordinary security measures adopted by the Australian government under its 2005 Anti-Terrorism Bill have all, resulted in the negative portrayal of Muslims and Islam in the Australian media. The media here almost inevitably, "tend to take their lead from British media" (Bouma 1994, 86) and this has, as inevitably, promoted the growth of an Australian 'Islamophobia.' (Aslan 2009) One should also note that in Europe as well as in Australia, in times of economic adversity and rising unemployment Islamophobia grows as a subset of xenophobia against foreign workers. (Dabashi 2012, 11, 193) As Jeremy Northcote and Suzy Casimiro (one an academic sociologist and the other an academic psychologist) have observed, Muslims in Australia "are seen as fanatical, violent, deceitful, irrational, uncivilised, despotic and socially oppressive." (Qtd.in Yasmeen 2010, 147)

To mainstream Australians therefore, Muslims are the distant 'Other.' "Either assimilate or get out" was the message that came out loud and clear from the most vocal section of this group, whose representative voice at one time was the One Nation Party led by Pauline Hanson. The predicament that this community faces in this country, especially after September11, was succinctly described by Anne Aly when she wrote: "Australian Muslims were … placed in a paradoxical bind – as Australians they were expected to respond as the victims of terror; (and) as Muslims they were positioned as the objects of terror." (Qtd. Yasmeen 2010, 83) The first half of the bind forces them to demonstrate uncritical support of state actions of counter-terrorism and anti-immigration policies, while the second half subjects them to all sorts of prejudices, innuendos and discrimination, driving them ultimately to social exclusion.

In attempting to loosen this bind and negotiate its way to achieve social integration and inclusion the community also has to find a solution to what An-Naim calls "a permanent paradox" (An-Na'im, 2008, 43-44). It is a paradox where, Muslims as a religious community need the co-operation of the state in order to fulfil its religious mission while the state has to seek some measure of control or influence over this mission in order to limit the ways in which the community or its social and religious institutions can influence or shape the public behaviour of its members. As he argues, "even when the state is not required or allowed to provide material and administrative support for … well-organised religious communities, it cannot afford to grant them complete freedom to propagate whatever values or engage in whatever activities they wish to pursue independently in the name of freedom of religion and belief." (An-Na'im 2008, 44) The extraordinary restrictions and difficulties placed upon the Muslim community by government authorities when Muslim organisations apply for permission to construct mosques or schools is sad evidence of An-Naim's permanent paradox.

The 'us–them' dichotomy in Australia should be viewed concurrently from the perspective of Muslims as well as from that of mainstream Australians. From within the former, the otherness of mainstream Australia emanates from a socio-economic rather than a religious platform. After all, Islam belongs to the Abrahamic family of which the elder sibling is Christianity, with 61.14 per cent of the population in the 2011 census, dominates the Australian spiritual landscape and on that basis Muslims should find an affinity with Christian Australia. In terms of religion therefore there is no otherness and they are all 'People of the book,' even though the post-World-War II innovation of Judaeo-Christian values would appear to segregate the Muslims. However, it is the socio-economic marginalisation experienced by Muslims that acts as the fundamental cause of discontent and a source of social exclusion. The vast majority of first- generation Muslims migrated to Australia not to preach Islam and convert 'non-believers' but in search of a 'better life' (Bouma 1994, 11) for themselves and their progeny. Naturally, therefore, when those hopes are shattered by social exclusion they become despondent frustrated and, eventually alienated from mainstream society.

Professor Riaz Hassan of Flinders University in his wide-ranging survey of the social and economic conditions of Australian Muslims (2008) found that the unemployment rate of young Muslims of the age group 19-24 was twice as high as the national average of 8 per cent, notwithstanding the fact that Muslims are more likely to have tertiary qualifications than non-Muslims. As the age cohort increases the gap widens: 12:5 for 25-44 and 11:4 for 45-64. More shockingly, he found that 40 per cent of Muslim children were living in poverty which, again, was double the rate compared to non-Muslim children. These are alarming figures especially when one finds that nearly 60 per cent of Muslims in Australia are below 29 years of age compared to only 40 per cent nationally. Economic disempowerment creates social instability. The Cronulla riots in Sydney on 11 December 2005 which was sparked off by a violent incident a week earlier when a group of young men of 'Middle Eastern appearance' (a journalistic euphemism for Muslims) attacked the volunteer surf life-savers at the Cronulla Beach were essentially a reflection of this socio-economic disempowerment and discontent.

Marylyn Parker, an award-winning education columnist and a former teacher, in an article in the *Daily Telegraph* (2009), attributed the reasons for these high rates of youth unemployment and child poverty to the proliferation of Islamic Schools and discrimination by non-Muslim Australia. Just as there are Christian and Jewish faith-based schools in Australia so also there are over thirty Islamic schools but unlike the other faith-based schools the Muslim schools have become another ethnic and religious identifier like the female *hijab* and *halal* food. This identity is further strengthened by the fact that while Muslim children are admitted to Christian schools non-Muslim children do not normally find a place in Islamic schools. One unfortunate consequence of this religious identity of Muslim Schools and Muslim families' preference to send their children to these schools is that "they may be excluding ... [Muslim children] ... from the usual job networks found amongst public schools and other private school communities." (Parker 2009, np) Be that as it may, the point to note here is that the Muslim sense of alienation from the mainstream Australian community arises from a socio-economic reality. The greater the degree of socio-economic exclusion of a particular group, the greater the distance between the groups.

To mainstream Australians on the other hand, Muslims are regarded as other not simply because of their religion, dress, food, and lifestyle, all of which is perceived as alien to the Anglo-Celtic culture, but more importantly because of the strong *asabiya*-consciousness of the community which is demonstrated openly and perhaps sometimes even violently in response to perceived anti-Islamic events that originate from outside Australia. *Asabiyya*, a pre-Islamic concept, which literally means 'making common cause with one's agnates' was utilised by the fourteenth century Arab historian and sociologist, Ibn Khaldun, to explain 'group solidarity' or a kind of e*spirit de corps* which existed within the ruling Arab dynasties (Ibn Khaldun 1967, lxxviii). This concept, over a period of more than fourteen centuries and due to the Quranic injunctions on Muslim unity and brotherhood, has transcended its original meaning and has metamorphosed into the *umma*-consciousness which, in the eyes of many non-Muslims, appears to be a phenomenon of Muslim transnationalism. This extraordinary Muslim sensitivity to remote incidents and the *umma*- solidarity founded on religion is a phenomenon that baffles mainstream Australians and makes them question the Australianness of the Muslim community.

The Sydney riots of September 2012 provoked by an obscure documentary film, produced by an even more obscure American citizen are a classic example of Muslim demonstration of hyper-*asabiya*. These riots led to an equally hyper anti-Muslim reaction by far-right Australia, which, thanks to prompt action by the state security forces was prevented from exploding into an open confrontation between the two groups. On a broader perspective, it is an irony that at a time when the Westphalian consensus over nation-states, national sovereignty and citizenship is being progressively eroded due to shared global governance and economic and financial globalisation, Muslim transnational solidarity is being treated by the Westphalian conservatives as a sign of anti-patriotism and extra-territorial allegiance. While this dilemma raises important political issues to be resolved in all countries where Muslims live as minorities, in Australia it has rigidified the otherness of Muslims in the Australian Anglo-Celtic consciousness. In the light of the incidents cited above whose root causes actually lie in the socio-economic exclusion of Muslims. The

Australian Anglo-Celtic mindset considers the community to be a threat to law and order and security of Australia.

Thus, while Muslim attitude towards the Australian 'Other' solidifies on account of socio-economic deficits, Australian attitude towards the Muslim other is grounded partly on the inherited European legacy and partly on a suspected Muslim deficiency in patriotism. It is this contradiction between an experienced Muslim reality and a wider Australian perception or rather a misperception that makes it difficult to negotiate the issue of otherness. The policies of Australian governments towards Muslims have varied from a law and order and security approach under John Howard to a socio-economic and welfare approach under Kevin Rudd and Julia Gillard.

The Muslim Summit held by the Howard Government on 23 August 2005, soon after the Prime Minister returned from London after witnessing the London transport terrorist attacks in July, the creation of a Muslim Advisory Group following that summit which had a one year term, a government sponsored a first ever conference of imams held in Sydney in 2006, and an eight million dollar investment by the same government to establish a Centre of Islamic Higher Learning at Melbourne University with the specific purpose of producing and training Australian qualified *imams*, were all measures intended to prevent home grown Islamic terrorism in Australia.

It was with the same counter-terrorism and security agenda that the Australian government under John Howard inaugurated and financed generously the first International Inter-faith Dialogue in Jakarta, which continued thereafter every year for the next five years. Such inter-faith dialogues and colloquiums were also undertaken privately by local religious groups in Australia. The Abrahamic Forum in Sydney is one among several such inter-faith non-government organizations that are actively involved in dispelling some of the prejudices that exist between mainstream Australians and Muslims. However, on the issue of socio-economic empowerment of young Muslims the Howard Liberal-National Coalition Government had little to offer.

The Rudd Labour Government, to its credit, focused specifically on issues of social inclusion and in December 2007 established a

Social Inclusion unit under the Office of the Prime Minister and Cabinet. In January 2009, it set up the Community Response Task Force, which encouraged the private sector to interact directly with the government on issues relating to 'vulnerable Australians'. The Government's social inclusion agenda envisions a society "in which all Australians feel valued and have the opportunity to participate fully in the life of our society." (http://www.socialinclusion.gov.au/)

This vision and the focus on social inclusion is what the Muslim community desires and hopefully it will help to bring them closer to mainstream Australia. Attacking social exclusion is the best strategy against counter terrorism. However, from the point of view of the Muslim community, for this vision to materialise there needs to be a protracted campaign through a comprehensive program of public education to eradicate the lingering prejudices that still prevail in mainstream Australia. The Muslims on their part also need to participate in this campaign through their mosques, societies and schools. This educational campaign which was one of the recommendations of Garry Bouma's 1994 study will be a fitting tribute also to the memory of Patrick White a writer who fits the mould of the 'public intellectual' as outlined by Said, one whose loyalty was owed not only to a particular group or even to a country but also to the whole of humanity. (Said, 2001)

Works Cited

Aslan, A. 2009. *Is lslamophobia in Australia?* Sydney: Agora Press.
An-Na'im, Abdullah Ahmad. 2008. *Islam and the Secular State.* Cambridge MA and London: Harvard University Press.
Blainey, G. 2000. *A Shorter History of Australia.* Sydney: Vintage.
Bouma, D. Gary. 1994. *Mosques and Muslim Settlement in Australia.* Canberra: Australian Government Publishing Service.
Dabashi, Hamid. 2012. *The Arab Spring.* London, New York: Zed Books.
Daniel, N. 1960. *Islam and the West: The Making of an Image.* Edinburgh: Edinburgh University Press.
Deen, H. 2011. *Ali Abdul V King* CrawleyWA: University of Western Australia Press.

Hassan Riaz. 2008. "Social and Economic Conditions of Australian Muslims: Implications for Social Inclusion." Paper presented at the NCEIS International Conference: *Challenges to Social Inclusion in Australia: The Muslim Experience*, Melbourne University. Unpublished.

Ibn Khaldun, 1967. *The Muqaddimah*: A*n Introduction to History.* Vol. 1. trans. Franz Rosenthal. Princeton NJ: Princeton University Press.

Maddison, Angus. 2002. *The World Economy: A Millennial Perspective*. OECD.

Parker, Marylyn. 2009. "The Trouble with being Muslim Australian," *Daily Telegraph*, 17 February.

Said. Edward. 2001. "The Public Role of Writers and Intellectuals," 17 September http://www.thenation.com/doc/20010917/essay. Accessed 20 January 2014.

Steven C. 1989. *Tin Mosques & Ghantowns: A History of Afghan Cameldrivers in Australia.* Melbourne: Oxford University Press.

Westrip, J. and P. Holroyde. 2010. *Colonial Cousins: A surprising History of connections between India and Australia.* South Australia: Wakefield Press.

White, Patrick. 1989. "In This World of Hypocrisy and Cynicism," *Patrick White Spea*ks ed.Paul Brennan and Christine Flynn. Sydney: Primavera Press: 151-158.

Yasmeen, Samina. Ed. 2010. *Muslims in Australia: The Dynamics of Exclusion and Inclusion*. Islamic Studies Series. Melbourne: Melbourne University Press.

CONTRIBUTORS

Isabel Alonso-Breto teaches literatures in English at the University of Barcelona (Barcelona, Spain). She has published critical articles on the works of writers of Caribbean, Canadian, Indian and Sri Lankan origin and is herself a creative writer. She is a member of the Centre for Australian Studies of the University of Barcelona, and of *Ratnakara*, a research group devoted to the study of literatures and cultures from the Indian Ocean.

Bill Ashcroft is a renowned critic and theorist, founding exponent of post-colonial theory, co-author of *The Empire Writes Back* (1989) the first text to examine systematically the field of post-colonial studies. He is author and co-author or co-editor of sixteen books and over 160 articles and chapters, variously translated into six languages, including *Post-Colonial Transformations* (2001), *On Post-Colonial Futures:Transformation of Colonial Culture* (2001) and *Caliban's Voice*. (2008). He holds an Australian Professorial Fellowship at the University of NSW and is currently working on a project entitled, "Future Thinking: Utopianism in Postcolonial Literatures."

May-Brit Akerholt has tutored at Macquarie University and Lectured in Drama at the National Institute of Dramatic Art (NIDA); worked as Resident Dramaturg at the Sydney Theatre Company and as Artistic Director of the Australian National Playwrights' Conference. She is a freelance translator and dramaturg, and recently completed a PhD (*The Dramaturgy of Translation*) in Performance Studies at the University of Sydney. May-Brit has translated a large number of plays from several languages and worked as dramaturg in more than 20 of her translated plays. She has published three volumes of translations of plays by Ibsen, Strindberg and Jon Fosse with a fourth in press. Her book, *Patrick White* (Australian Playwrights Monograph Series), was published by Rodopi, Amsterdam in 1988.

Ameer Ali was educated at the University of Ceylon and completed postgraduate studies at the London School of Economics, and the University of Western Australia. He has taught at several overseas universities and is now a senior academic at Murdoch University, Western Australia. His research focuses mainly on the socio-economic development of Muslim minorities and he has published widely in this field. He is the author of *From Penury to Plenty: Development of Brunei Darussalam from 1906 to Present*. Ameer has been vice president and president of the Australian Federation of Islamic Councils and was appointed by the Howard Government as the Chairman of the Muslim Community Reference Group. Currently, he is the vice-President of the Regional Da'wa Council of South East Asia and the Pacific (RISEAP).

Stephen Alomes has explored Australian society and culture, as a contemporary historian. He has also written about expatriates, nationalism and republicanism, and popular culture and now pursues understanding society through paint. His latest book *Australian Football The People's Game 1958-2058* was published in August 2012. Earlier publications include: *Islands in the Stream: Australia and Japan face Globalisation* (2005); *French Worlds, Pacific Worlds* (1999); *When London Calls: The Expatriation of Australian Creative Artists to Britain* (1999).

Gursharan Aurora joined Sikkim Manipal Institute of Technology, Majhitar, East Sikkim, India as Assistant Professor in January, 2011. She decided to return, after several years in secondary education (resigning from the Principalship of a reputed school in Punjab), to research and tertiary teaching. In 1984, she wrote a dissertation on 'Patrick White's Characters as Seekers' for her M. Phil and has now registered for a doctoral thesis on 'The Spiritual Quest of Patrick White's Non-conformist Characters and Parallelisms to the Indian Religio-Spiritual tradition.'

John Barnes is Emeritus Professor of English at La Trobe University. He had previously taught at the Universities of Melbourne and Western Australia; and also the University of Barcelona. His publications in the field of Australian literature include: *World Unknown: An Anthology of Australian Prose* (co-edited with Hume Dow); Works on Joseph Furphy as well as on Henry Kingsley in the series Australian Writers and their Work; *The Writer in Australia: A Collection of Literary Documents 1856-1964; An Australian Selection: Short Stories by Lawson, Palmer, Porter, White and Cowan; Cross-Country: A Book of Australian Verse* (co-ed. with Brian McFarlane).He has been a co-editor of *Westerly* and served on the editorial board of *Meanjin* before founding *Meridian: The La Trobe University English Review*, and serving as its editor for 15 years. He has recently completed a biography of Charles Joseph La Trobe, the first Governor of Victoria.

Greg Battye is Professor and Associate Dean of Education in the Faculty of Design and Creative Practice at the University of Canberra. Besides publications on culture and security, his research includes photography, narrative theory and new writing technologies, and new media forms. He teaches an online Master's Unit in interactive writing and currently supervises postgraduate projects in fiction, non-fiction and script-writing. Greg is also a skilled photographer and his works are held by the National Gallery of Australia, the National Library of Australia, the University of Woollongong and the Australian Defence Force Academy.

Fred Chaney AO graduated in law from the University of Western Australia in 1962 and worked as a lawyer in New Guinea and Western Australia until he entered the Senate in 1974. He has held a large number of responsible positions relating to Aboriginal Affairs: co-founder of the Graham (Polly) Farmer Foundation for the advancement of Aboriginal youth (1994); a Member of the National Native Title Tribunal, and its Deputy President from 2000 to 2007. He served as Co-Chair of Reconciliation Australia (2000 to 2005) and appointed a member of the Panel on Constitutional Recognition of Indigenous Australians. (2012). He was Leader of the Opposition in the Senate (1983 -1990) and a member of the House of Representatives (1990-1993) in the Fraser Government and held the portfolios of Aboriginal Affairs, Social Security. He was later Chancellor of Murdoch University (1995-2003) and was appointed an Officer of the Order of Australia in 1997. He was recently selected Senior Australian Citizen of the Year. (2014).

Meira Chand is of Indian-Swiss parentage and was born and educated in London. She lived mostly in Japan after her marriage, and five of her early novels are set in Japan. She spent time in India in the 1970s, and since 1997 she has lived in Singapore. Her novels, explore issues of identity and cultural dislocation. Her latest novel, *A Different Sky* (2010) is set in pre-Independence Singapore and was long-listed for the Impac Dublin literary award 2012 and the Commonwealth Writers Prize .She has been Chairperson for the Commonwealth Writers Prize for the region of South East Asia and South Pacific and a Visiting Fellow at Mansfield College, Oxford. Meira has a doctorate in English (Writing) from the University of Western Australia and is an Associate Member of the Centre for the Arts, National University of Singapore

Anne De Soyza has degrees in law and history from the University of Western Australia and is widely published in both discipline areas. She has wide experience in native title law in particular - an emerging area of legal practice and public administration and has held senior positions both in the State and Commonwealth Public Service. Anne worked with the Australian Federal Government before returning to Western Australia in 2002 to take up the inaugural role of Executive Director of the Office of Native Title. She has acted as consultant legal adviser to the West Australian Governmen in negotiations pertaining to Aboriginal groups before joining Rio Tinto Iron Ore in 2010. She is responsible for negotiating agreements with Aboriginal groups over land use and development in the Pilbara region.

Kieran Dolin is chair of the English and Cultural Studies discipline group at the University of Western Australia and director of the *Westerly* Centre. His main teaching and research interests are in

Australian Literature and Nineteenth-Century English Literature. His publications include: *Fiction and the Law: Legal Discourse in Victorian and Modernist Literature* (Cambridge University Press, 1999), and *A Critical Introduction to Law and Literature* (Cambridge University Press, 2007). His current research project, for which he has received an Australian Research Council (ARC) Grant, is related to the *Mabo* case and its impact on Australian Writing.

Victoria (Vicki) Grieves is an ARC Indigenous Research Fellow at the University of Sydney is Warraimay from the midnorth coast of NSW. The first Aboriginal graduate with BA Honours and with a double major in history, her book *Aboriginal Spirituality: Aboriginal Philosophy and the Social and Emotional Wellbeing of Aboriginal people* is widely accessed and much cited. She is currently developing the ARC funded research project *More than family history: Race, Gender and the Aboriginal family in Australian history*. Vicki works to progress Indigenous Knowledge within Australia; her approach to research is cross-disciplinary and deliberately from within a Warraimay epistemology.

Bridget Grogan is a post-doctoral research fellow in the University of Johannesburg's Department of English. She has lectured on postcolonial and contemporary world literature, researches literary depictions of affect and the body, and has recently completed a PhD on the topic of corporeality in the fiction of Patrick White.

Margaret Harris FAHA is Director of Research Development, Faculty of Arts and Social Sciences, University of Sydney, having formerly held the Challis Chair of English Literature there. With the aid of an Australian Research Discovery Grant she has, (with Elizabeth Webby), been exploring the rich archive of Patrick White documents held at the National Library of Australia and is currently preparing an electronic edition of White's literary notebooks.

Sissy Helff is a guest professor at the Technische Universiät Darmstadt teaching literary and cultural studies with a special focus on digital narratives, literature, film and photography. Helff has published widely in the fields of media studies, diasporic literature and postcolonial literary and cultural studies, with a special focus on Australia. Her most recent publications include: *Die Kunst der Migration Aktuelle Positionen zum europäisch-afrikanischen Diskurs. Material – Gestaltung – Kritik* (2011); *Facing the East in the West: Images of Eastern Europe in British Literature, Film and Culture* (2010); *Transcultural Modernities: Narrating Africa in Europe* (2009) and *Transcultural English Studies* (2008). She is currently working on a book on the image of the refugee in the British writing and a collection of essays on adaptations of *Alice in Wonderland.*

Ishmeet Kaur is an Assistant Professor in the School of Language, Literature and Culture Studies at the Central University of Gujarat, Gandhinagar. She teaches courses in English literature, language and communication studies and has also worked on translations of texts from Punjabi into English Her specialist interests in research lie in Australian Literature, Post-colonial Studies and Sikh Studies She also works on Indigenous writing from Australia and India. Her doctoral thesis was a comparative study of Patrick White's novels and *Guru Granth Sahib*. She has recently published (2014) a work entitled, *Patrick White: Critical Issues.*

Brian Kiernan is the author or editor of a dozen books on Australian writers, including *Patrick White* (London and New York. 1980).Perhaps one of the best-known of his works, *Images of Society and Nature, Essays on Seven Australian Novels* (OUP, 1971) still remains an important work of Australian literary criticism. Formerly an Associate Professor at the University of Sydney, he has served as president of the Association for the Study of Australian Literature and was a founding member of the American Association of Australian Literary Studies.

Jeanine Leane is a Wiradjuri woman from South-west New south Wales. A Doctorate in the literature of Aboriginal representation followed a long teaching career at secondary and tertiary levels. Formerly a Research Fellow at the Australian Institute of Aboriginal and Torres Strait islander Studies, she currently holds a post-doctoral fellowship in the Australian Centre for Indigenous History at the Australian National University. In 2010, Jeanine's first volume of poetry, *Dark Secrets After Dreaming*: AD 1887-1961 won the Scanlon Prize for Indigenous Poetry from the Australian Poets' Union and her manuscript, *Purple Threads* won the David Unaipon Award at the Queensland Premier's Literary Awards and was shortlisted for the 2012 Commonwealth Book Prize. Jeanine is the recipient of an Australian Research Council grant for a proposal entitled, "Reading the Nation: A critical study of Aboriginal/Settler representations in the contemporary Australian Literary Landscape."

Lyn Mc Credden is a professor, teacher and researcher in Literary Studies at Deakin University, Melbourne, Australia. Her publications include monographs on James McAuley, Australian women's poetry, feminism and the sacred, and most recently, two volumes which focus on the sacred: *Intimate Horizons: the Post-colonial Sacred in Australian Literature* (with Bill Ashcroft and Frances Devlin-Glass, 2009), and *Luminous Moments: The Contemporary Sacred* (2010). Lyn was recently awarded an Australian Research Council Grant to work on the writing of Tim Winton.

John McLaren AM, is Emeritus Professor in the College of Arts, Victoria University, Melbourne. His books include *Journey without Arrival: the life and writing of Vincent Buckley*, (2009) which shared the Walter McRae Russell prize for literary criticism. He has edited a book of essays on Patrick White, and has been editor of *Australian Book Review* and *Overland*.

Harish C. Mehta has taught history at McMaster University, Trent University, and University of Toronto. He has written three books on Cambodian politics and media, and his articles on U.S.-North Vietnamese diplomacy have appeared in *Peace and Change, Diplomatic History,* and *The Historian.* A new and expanded edition of his 1999 book, *The Strongman: Rise of Hun Sen from Pagoda Boy to Prime Minister of Cambodia, An Oral History* (co-author Julie Mehta) is being published in 2013 by Marshall Cavendish. He is preparing his latest book, *People's Diplomacy of North Vietnam* for publication.

Julie Mehta is the author of *Dance of Life: Mythology, History and Politics of Cambodian Culture* (2001) and co-author with Dr. Harish C. Mehta of *Hun Sen: Strongman of Cambodia* (1999). Her translation of Tagore's *Dak Ghar* (The Post Office) was performed in Toronto in 2011.She teaches Canadian Diasporic Literature and Asian Cultures in Canada at University College and holds several Fellowships at the University of Toronto. Her doctoral dissertation was on Postcolonial representations of the 'Divine Feminine' in South Asian fiction. Her research focus is on Postcolonial literatures, globalisation of foodways, and Asian diasporic writers. Julie worked as a newspaper correspondent in several Asian countries, before commencing her academic career.

Satendra Nandan was born in Nadi, Fiji.He was elected to Parliament in Fiji in 1982 and 1987 but later migrated to Australia as a result of political unrest in the island. Satendra studied at the universities of Delhi, Leeds, and London and completed his doctoral studies at the Australian National University on Patrick White's Fiction. Satendra is an Emeritus Professor at the University of Canberra. He is also widely known for his creative work as a biographer and as a poet. In March 2012 he was awarded the prestigious Harold White Fellowship at the National Library of Australia to write his autobiography. He has lately been appointed a member of the Fiji Constitutional Commission (July 2, 2012) and has been assisting with the re-writing of the Constitution of Fiji.

Pavithra Narayanan is Associate Professor of English and faculty affiliate of the Centre for Social and Environmental Justice at Washington State University Vancouver and has completed a doctoral dissertation on the work of Patrick White. She is the author of *What are you reading?: The world market and Indian Literary production* (Routledge 2012). Pavithra is also a documentary filmmaker.

Alastair Niven is a Fellow of Harris Manchester College, Oxford. He graduated from the University of Cambridge, and completed further degrees at the Universities of Ghana and Leeds. He has published books on D.H.Lawrence as well as on Indian fiction in

English and over a hundred articles and essays on aspects of post colonial literature. He was editor of *The Journal of Commonwealth Literature* for thirteen years and president of English PEN (2003 to 2007). Alastair held office for ten years as Director of Literature at the Arts Council of Great Britain and also served as Director General of the Africa Centre in London. He was Principal of Cumberland Lodge Windsor (2001to 2013) and a panellist for the award of the Booker Prize (1994) as well as for for the Man Booker Prize (2014). Awarded an OBE in 2001; he was recently personally appointed Lieutenant of the Royal Victorian Order by the Queen. (2013).

Nathanael O'Reilly teaches Australian, British, Irish and Postcoloni.al literature at Texas Christian University in Fort Worth. He is editor of *Postcolonial Issues in Australian Literature*; and has co-edited special issues of *Antipodes* (June 2009); *Millennial Postcolonial Australia*, *The Journal of Commonwealth and Postcolonial Studies* (December 2011) He is the author of *Exploring Suburbia: The Suburbs in the Contemporary Australian Novel* (2012) and of several journal articles, and book chapters. He has also published two poetry chapbooks: *Symptoms of Homesickness* (2010) and *Suburban Exile: American Poems* (2011) and is the recipient of an Emerging Writers Grant from the Australia Council for the Arts (2010-2011).He is currently the President of the American Association of Australasian Literary Studies (AAALS).

Glen Phillips is patron, founder life-member and first chairperson of the Katharine Susannah Prichard Writers Centre, Perth. Glen writes poetry and fiction and has presented readings of his work internationally. He graduated with first class honours in Education from the University of Western Australia and obtained his Ph.D in Writing from Edith Cowan University where he is now an Honorary Professor and Director of the Landscape and Language Centre He co-edited *Lines in the Sand* (2008) and John Kinsella's landscape lectures in *Contrary Rhetoric* (2008). To date Glen has published twenty collections of poetry and is represented in a large number of/Australian and international anthologies.

Antonella Riem is full Professor of the Literatures in English; Dean of the Faculty of Foreign and Modern Languages, University of Udine, Italy; President of the Italian Permanent Conference of the Deans of the *Faculty* of Foreign Languages; Founder of the Partnership Studies Research Group (PSG); former member of the EASA committee, member of EACLAS Her publications include: *The Art of Partnership. Essays on Literature, Culture, Language and Education Towards a Co-operative Paradigm (2003); The One Life: Coleridge and Hinduism* (2005); *The Goddess Awakened. Partnership Studies in Literatures, Language and Education* (2007) and *Partnership Id-Entities: Cultural and Literary Re-inscription/s of the Feminine (2010).* She was recently appointed a vice-president of the University of Udine.

Jane Stafford is Associate Professor in the School of English Film and Media Studies at Victoria University of Wellington. She has published widely in the areas of English and New Zealand literature including Maori work as in her book (with Mark Williams): *Maoriland: New Zealand Literature 1872–1914.* (2006) With Ralph Crane and Mark Williams she is currently editing volume nine of the Oxford History of the Novel in English.

Keith Truscott was born in Darwin, Northern Territory of Western Australia, Keith's first eight years were spent in an Aboriginal Church Mission. He was later fostered out to a family in Sydney, a fostering which worked out well. Keith has lived in Western Australia for the past thirty-five years. He is a second-generation child of the 'stolen generation,' but has survived to be restored to his people, place and parables. His research interests are life-histories, world-views, theology and cultural studies. He has taught for several years at Edith Cowan University while also being engaged in doctoral studies at Murdoch University. He has submitted his doctoral thesis and is now working as Head of the Indigenous Studies Programme at Curtin University.

Elizabeth Webby AM. FAHA is Professor Emerita of Australian Literature at the University of Sydney. She was Chair of Australian Literature at the University of Sydney until 2007. She is an expert in nineteenth-century Australian literature with particular interests in theatre, popular culture, short fiction, and the work of Patrick White, Henry Handel Richardson, and Katherine Mansfield. She has written and edited numerous books, including *The Cambridge Companion to Australian Literature* (2000), collections of essays on nineteenth-century Australia and feminism. She was editor of *Southerly* for twelve years. Currently she is collaborating with Margaret Harris on a project which entails working on the archive of Patrick White papers at the National Library.

Jessica White is a novelist and a researcher. Her first novel, *A Curious Intimacy*, (2007) won a *Sydney Morning Herald* Best Young Novelist award in 2008 and was also shortlisted for the Dobbie and Western Australia Premier's Awards, and long listed for the international IMPAC award. Her second novel, *Entitlement* was published in 2012.With the assistance of the Sir Arthurs Sims Travelling Scholarship Jessica completed her PhD, at the University of London. She is currently working in Australia on her third novel and on a book of creative nonfiction on 19th century novelist and spiritualist Rosa Praed. Jessica also has a familial connection to Patrick White: her great-grandfather F.G. White, and Patrick White's father Victor White, were cousins.

Mark Williams is Professor of English at Victoria University in Wellington New Zealand. His most recent books are : *Maoriland: New Zealand Literature 1872-1914* (2006), written with Jane Stafford, and *The Auckland University Press Anthology of New Zealand Literature (2012),* which he edited with Jane Stafford. With Ralph Crane and Jane Stafford he is currently editing volume nine of *The Oxford History of the Novel in English.* An earlier publication of note is his book, *Patrick White* (St. Martin's Press, 1993) which discusses all of White's novels, the connections between his life and the works and assesses his achievement in the context of the contemporary novel.

INDEX

abjection 46, 49, 52, 63, 64, 65, 67, 68, 69, 77, 78, 79, 80 81, 108, 368, 373, 374, 375 380
Aboriginal Land Rights 384-457, *passim.*
Aborigine 87, 88, 90, 117, 134, 135, 136, 137.146, 147, 214, 229, 230, 231, 232, 233, 235, 237, 241, 242, 243, 244, 245, 246, 247, 248, 249, 250, 251, 252, 253, 254, 255, 257, 258, 260, 261, 266, 268, 288, 356, 357, 361, 363, 368, 370, 371.379, 385, 386, 387, 390, 391, 398, 402, 404, 414, 415, 423, 426, 434, 436, 437, 439, 488
"A Cheery Soul" 152, 153, 154
Adams, Phillip 131, 139
A Fringe of Leaves xviii, 42, 52, 53, 62, 65, 81, 88, 97, 142, 210, 212, 213, 214, 215, 217, 221, 243, 257, 258, 267, 268, 298, 365, 400
Agamben, Giorgio 377, 379
Akerholt, May-Brit 152, 152
Ako, Edward 317, 318
Alomes, Stephen 470, 471, 477
Altman, Rick 193
Appadurai, Arjun 193
ASAA (Assn.for the Study of Australasia in Asia) xiii
Ashcroft, Bill 22, 64, 107, 317, 318, 496, 502
Attwood and Bain 255
Aurobindo, Sri 335, 337

Australian Literature 3, 5 18 20, 22, 98, 107, 108, 109, 126, 206, 247, 337, 352, 353, 415
Bachelard, Gaston 377, 379
Barfield, Owen 376, 380
Bhagat, Chetan 470, 471, 484
Brady, Veronica 67, 99, 146, 147, 226, 238
Brennan and Flynn 4, 8, 12, 14, 127, 129, 132, 133, 134, 135, 136 137, 222, 229, 243, 244, 387, 400, 429, 486
Brissenden, R. F. 18, 159, 162

Cabaud, Jacques 123, 124
Chand, Meira 210. 221
Chomsky, Noam 132, 138
Chong, W. A. 164, 179
Classen, Constance 142, 150
Clendinnen, I. 218, 221
Concil, C 267
Coad, David 63, 320, 342
Coates, John 68, 81
Collier, Gordon 239, 267
Colmer, John 80
colonialism 102, 217, 227, 243, 268, 303, 313, 314, 315, 379, 437, 441, 450, 477, 483
Craven, Peter 138
Curnow, A.36, 369

Dinnage Rosemary 128, 139, 371, 380
Dovey, Lindiwe 189, 194
Drysdale, Russell 15
Dutton, Geoffrey 16, 17, 20, 81, 128, 131, 472

508 Index

Eisler, Rian 223, 224. 227, 239
Ekman, Paul 176, 177, 179, 180
Eliade, Mircea 239, 371, 378
Emig, Rainer 192, 193, 194
Engledow, Sarah 172, 179
Foucault, Michel 25, 26, 42, 157, 163, 247, 258, 267, 376, 377, 380, 456
Fox, Chris 374, 375, 37
Flaws in the Glass 11, 21, 23, 24, 42, 47, 48, 60, 62, 108, 140, 148, 150, 172, 179, 198, 201, 207, 270, 275, 278, 279, 280, 288, 289, 290, 291, 299, 336, 338, 438, 440, 470, 480, 481, 482, 483, 485
Fosse, Jon 152, 163
Fraser, Eliza 210, 213, 214, 217, 219, 258, 259, 261, 262, 263, 268

Gadamer, Hans 38, 42
Gandhi, Mahatma xiii, 135, 271, 322, 328, 339
Ganguly, Debjani 302, 317.
Garebian, Keith 67, 81
Giffin, Michael 184, 194
Goldie, Terry 257, 258, 268
Goldsworthy, Kerryn 107
Green, Dorothy 129, 139
Green, H.M 20
Grenville, Kate 306, 308, 423, 426
Grieves, Vicki 429, 442
Grogan, Bridget 63, 85, 91
Grosz, Elizabeth 64, 81

Hancock, Matthew 187, 194
Happy Valley xiii, xix, 5, 7, 83, 92, 93, 97, 124, 269, 270, 271, 277, 279

Heseltine, H. 207
hierophany 371, 372, 375, 376
Hope, A.D. 16, 17, 18, 19, 20, 21
Hulme, Kerry 359, 360
Hutcheton, Linda 194
Huxley, Aldous 320, 337
Hyderabad xiii

Ibsen, Henrik 152, 154, 155, 156
India, Indian vii, xii, xiv, xv, xx, 81, 98, 136, 139, 211, 213, 215, 276, 277, 220, 238, 275, 282, 304, 305, 308, 310, 311, 312, 319-337, *passim.* 338, 360, 361 369, 377, 378, 379, 384, 385, 470, 471, 475, 482, 483, 495, 496, 497, 501, 503
Indigenous viii, ix, xix, xxii, xxiii, 28, 7, 83, 132. 136, 137, 143, 144, 214, 217, 223, 225, 228, 238, 241, 243, 246, 248, 249, 250, 253, 254, 255, 258, 262, 267, 355, 356, 361, 362, 365, 385, 390, 394, 396, 397, 398, 400-424 p*assim,* 443-457 *passim*, 461, 463, 464, 465, 466, 467, 482, 498, 500, 501, 502, 505

Japan xviii
Jung, Carl 320, 333, 334
Jones, Gail 148

Kant, Immanuel 66, 81
Kanaganayakam, C 378, 380
Karalis, Vrasidas 9, 10, 11, 21
Kiernan, Brian 63, 131, 291, 299, 355, 501
Kippax, H.G. 207

Kristeva, Julia 50, 54, 59, 61, 64, 67, 75, 79, 81, 368, 371, 380
Kramer, Lucia 184, 185, 193
Kramer, Leonie 335

landscape 15, 24, 28, 29, 30, 77, 94, 141, 173, 181, 183, 187, 199, 227, 228, 259, 262, 295, 296, 345, 414, 437, 459, 490, 501, 504
Lascaris, Manoly 8, 9, 10, 12, 15
Lawson, Alan 348, 352,
Lawson, Henry 355. 356, 367

Mabo xxii, 384-457, *passim.*
Mabo, Eddie 'Koiki' 445, 446, 449, 451, 452, 454, 455
McGregor, Craig 326, 338, 380
Magaroni, Mara 51, 53, 54, 61
Malouf, David xxi, 104, 267, 368, 374, 423
Maleuvre, Didier 167, 168, 164, 165, 167, 175, 178, 179, 180
Maori 354, 356, 357, 358, 361, 367, 459, 460, 461, 462, 463, 464, 466, 468, 469, 505, 506
Marr, David 2, 8, 10, 99, 128, 131, 139, 141, 197, 261, 270, 289, 343, 386, 440, 472
McCredden, Lyn 43, 64, 108
McKenzie, Seaforth 21
McLeod, John 317, 318
McMahon and Olubas 80, 81, 97, 238, 240, 256, 366, 367
Memoirs of the Many in One 90, 97, 480
Merleau-Ponty, Maurice 42 52, 57, 58, 61
Moran and Vieth 188, 195
Morley, Patricia 124, 367

Morrison, Toni 218, 220
Muslim ix, 486-495 *passim.*
Nancy, Jean Luc 33, 42
national 5, 7, 19, 20, 22, 43, 61, 82, 83, 98, 129, 131, 133, 137, 150, 164, 171, 172, 186, 193, 213, 266, 270, 271, 302, 354, 357, 358, 359, 360, 361, 363, 365, 377, 384, 386, 392, 393, 395, 404, 405, 416, 417, 418, 419, 421, 422, 423, 424, 433, 442, 472, 474, 479, 481, 482, 483, 487, 490, 492
Native Title 384-457, *passim.*
Nevin, Robyn 152, 153
New Zealand xx, xxi, xxiii
"Night on Bald Mountain" 155
Nolan, Sidney 270, 472

Oliver, H.J. 16, 21
O'Reilly, Nathanael 98, 108
Osmania University xiii
outsider vi, 10, 22, 24, 50, 52, 56, 93, 94, 106, 124, 127, 128, 130, 131, 133, 135, 137, 139, 148, 201, 276, 286, 334, 356, 360, 365, 370, 377, 482, 473

Pakeha 357, 358, 363, 365, 458, 459, 468, 469
Panikkar, Raimon 222, 223, 225, 226, 239
Pascale, C. 317, 318
postcolonial 22, 23, 26, 28, 34, 39, 192, 219, 303, 304, 306, 307, 309, 311, 316, 318, 357, 364, 368, 369, 377, 379, 425, 459, 460, 461, 466, 500
Prichard, Katharine Susannah 196-209, *passim.*

Probyn-Rapsey, Fiona 430, 431, 433, 435, 442
prodigal son xv, xxiii, 1, 2, 4, 13, 20, 99, 101, 109, 124, 127, 147, 227, 353, 356, 357
public intellectual xxi, xxiii, 129, 130, 131, 132, 135, 354, 355, 356, 357, 359, 365, 366, 494
Punday, Daniel 70, 81

religion 15, 47, 51, 52, 54, 70, 83, 102, 103, 121, 149, 164, 217, 238, 239, 277, 303, 319, 321, 333, 336, 339, 338, 340, 342, 343, 347, 369, 378, 487, 490, 491
republicanism xxiii, 355, 479, 497, 485
Reynolds, H. 255
Richardson, Henry Handel 5, 31, 82, 506
Riders in the Chariot xvii, 18, 19, 28, 35, 46, 52, 53, 54, 55, 59, 61, 81, 98, 99, 102, 106, 107, 108, 109, 112, 116, 117, 124, 128, 145, 150, 267, 287, 290, 298, 338, 347, 353, 356, 359, 360, 361, 364, 367, 368, 370. 371, 372, 374, 381, 400
Riem, Antonella 222, 227 240, 505
Riemer, A.P 62, 81, 293, 299, 338
Rooney, Brigid 357, 367
Roy, Arundhati xxi, 368, 374, 379, 380
Sahgal, L. 221
Singapore xiv
Said, Edward xvii, 130, 247, 258, 312, 487

Schaffer, Kay 220, 258, 261, 266, 268
Schepisi, Fred 181, 182, 183, 184, 189, 192, 193, 194
Schechner, Richard 152, 163
Scott, Kim 422, 423, 424, 427, 447, 448, 457, 441, 449, 451, 451
Semmler, Clement 371
Sharman, Jim 152, 153
Shepherd and Singh xiv, 80, 81, 318
Singh, Kirpal xiv
Singapore xiv
Shklovsky, Victor 376, 380
South Africa xvi
spirituality 14, 24, 80, 86, 102, 103, 215, 223, 233, 358, 439, 441, 499
Stead, Christina 5
suburbia xvi, 47, 49, 83, 98, 99, 100, 101, 102, 103, 104, 105, 106, 107, 356, 359, 361, 479, 504
Sullivan, Robert 458-469, *passim.*
Sutton, Peter 408, 412

Tacey, David 20, 76, 131
Tagore, Rabindranath 309, 310, 336, 369, 380
Terra nullius 85, 290, 385, 401, 403, 406, 417, 421, 423, 441, 452
The Aunt's Story 7, 8, 12, 15, 21, 28, 42, 84, 97, 110, 124, 210, 211, 212, 213, 221, 281, 295, 298, 321, 338
The Eye of the Storm xviii, 42, 55, 65, 81, 181, 183, 189, 192, 193, 194, 195, 298, 435

The Gossamer Fly, 220, 221
'The Great Australian Emptiness' 13, 100, 113, 127, 147, 229, 473
'The Great Australian Novel' 13, 15, 16, 17, 127
"The Ham Funeral" 155, 157, 159
The Hanging Garden xix, 26, 42, 126, 130, 140, 269, 270, 271, 275, 277, 278, 279, 280, 281, 282, 284, 285, 287, 288, 289, 290
The Living and the Dead 7, 12, 84, 97, 295
"The Night the Prowler" 47, 62
The Ploughman and otherPoems 196, 198, 199, 200, 201, 203, 206
"The Season at Sarsaparilla" 159
The Solid Mandala 12, 41, 42, 48, 50, 52, 58, 62, 98, 99, 109, 298, 333, 348
The Tree of Man 11, 13, 14, 15, 16, 17, 18, 19, 21, 27, 42, 55, 65, 81, 84, 85, 86, 97, 101, 110, 124, 287, 290, 298, 321, 335, 338, 339, 342, 343, 344, 346, 347, 348, 349, 351, 352, 353, 361, 413, 414, 416, 418, 428
"The Twitching Colonel" xx, 302-317, *passim*
The Twyborn Affair 24, 42, 55, 62, 81, 90, 92, 97, 128, 295, 296, 297, 298
The Vivisector xvii, 41, 42, 53, 55, 62, 110, 112, 119, 120, 122, 123, 124, 287, 290, 298

Thirteen Poems 196, 207
Tremain, Rose 217, 221
Turner, Ian 18, 21

vanden Driesen, Cynthia 63, 83, 144, 227, 223, 240, 243, 256, 258, 260, 266, 2, 68, 261, 370, 381
van Toorn, Penny 229, 240
Voss xvii, 3, 4, 17, 18, 19, 20, 24, 27, 29, 30, 2, 46, 53, 55, 56, 57, 61-82 *passim*, 82, 86, 87, 97, 110, 112. 113, 114, 115, 116 124, 126, 127, 128, 139, 140, 141, 144, 145, 146, 147, 150, 163, 218, 221-240, 241-246 *passim*, 287, 290, 298, 321, 323, 324, 325, 327, 328, 330. 333, 334, 338, 345, 362, 384, 400, 415, 416, 423, 428

Walsh, William 240
Webby, Elizabeth 99, 108, 269, 279, 426, 500, 505
Weil, Simone 111, 124
white indigene 77, 217, 223, 237
Whitely, Brett xvii, 166, 170 175, 177, 179, 180
Wijesinghe, Manuka 302, 307, 309
Wilkes and Herring 111, 124
Williams, Mark 354, 367

Yang, William xvii, 165, 166, 174, 177

Zunshine, Lisa 176, 180